THE PSYCHOL
OF HUMAN SOCIAL
DEVELOPMENT

The Psychology of Human Social Development provides a comprehensive introduction to the essential core topics and exciting new findings in this thriving field of developmental psychology. Following a thematic approach, the book looks at key topics in social development in childhood and adolescence, including personality development and research methods, taking the reader from first principles to an advanced understanding. The book explores socioemotional development and social learning, as well as the history of thinking, and the evolutionary roots of social development, whilst also providing a clear balance between nature and nurture approaches. Taylor and Workman's user-friendly writing style accommodates readers with no previous knowledge of the subject area whilst exploring the most up-to-date theories and research from various areas of psychology which have gained relevance to developmental psychology.

Featuring student-friendly pedagogy throughout, including end-of-chapter summaries, further reading recommendations and questions for discussion, *The Psychology of Human Social Development* is essential reading for undergraduates on social development or developmental psychology courses and relevant for related fields such as education, gender studies and nursing.

Dr Sandie Taylor is a visiting Lecturer at the University of South Wales, UK, and has 20 years' experience teaching criminological and developmental psychology. She has previously published: *Forensic Psychology: The Basics* and *Crime and Criminality: A Multidisciplinary Approach*.

Professor Lance Workman is a visiting Professor at the University of South Wales, UK, and has published widely on biological and evolutionary psychology. His previous books include: *Evolutionary Psychology* and *Evolution and Behavior* (both with co-author Will Reader).

THE PSYCHOLOGY OF
Human Social Development

From Infancy to Adolescence

Sandie Taylor and Lance Workman

Routledge
Taylor & Francis Group

LONDON AND NEW YORK

First published 2018
by Routledge
2 Park Square, Milton Park, Abingdon, Oxon OX14 4RN

and by Routledge
711 Third Avenue, New York, NY 10017

Routledge is an imprint of the Taylor & Francis Group, an informa business

British Library Cataloguing in Publication Data
A catalogue record for this book is available from the British Library

Library of Congress Cataloging in Publication Data
Names: Taylor, Sandie, author. | Workman, Lance, author.
Title: The psychology of human social development : from infancy to
    adolescence / Sandie Taylor and Lance Workman.
Description: Abingdon, Oxon ; New York, NY : Routledge, 2018. | Includes
    bibliographical references.
Identifiers: LCCN 2017035343 (print) | LCCN 2017044345 (ebook) | ISBN
    9781315441320 (Ebook) | ISBN 9781138217164 (hardback : alk. paper)
    | ISBN 9781138217171 (pbk. : alk. paper)
Subjects: LCSH: Social psychology. | Developmental psychology.
Classification: LCC HM1033 (ebook) | LCC HM1033 .T388 2018 (print) |
    DDC 302—dc23
LC record available at https://lccn.loc.gov/2017035343

ISBN: 978-1-138-21716-4 (hbk)
ISBN: 978-1-138-21717-1 (pbk)
ISBN: 978-1-315-44132-0 (ebk)

Typeset in Times New Roman
by Swales & Willis Ltd, Exeter, Devon, UK

Printed and bound in Great Britain
by Bell and Bain Ltd, Glasgow

We would like to dedicate this text to our mothers:
Erika Taylor and Margaret Workman.

Contents

Acknowledgements   *viii*

1. Introduction to themes and theories of development   1

2. Research methods in social development   39

3. Emotional development and attachment   73

4. Cognition and communication   109

5. Development of social cognition: theory of mind   143

6. Influence of the family   177

7. Influence of peers and friends   211

8. Development of self-concept   245

9. Social development through play   269

10. Moral development and prosocial behaviour   299

11. Antisocial behaviour   343

12. Individual differences: temperament and personality   389

13. The role of the media   415

14. The future for our understanding of social development   449

References   *474*
Glossary   *540*
Index   *563*

Acknowledgements

We would like to thank Lucy Kennedy and Hannah Kingerlee for their continued support throughout this project. We would also like to thank the reviewers for their helpful comments and in particular Professor Peter K. Smith.

Contents

Introduction   1

Themes of development   4

Theories considered in developmental psychology   7

Summary   34

Chapter 1

Introduction to themes and theories of development

What this chapter will teach you

- The subject matter of social development.
- The main themes and debates surrounding social development including: biological–environmental explanation; continuity–discontinuity and individual–cultural influences.
- An understanding of the main perspectives that have been developed in order to examine social development including: biological and behavioural genetics; structural–organismic; learning; contextual; dynamic systems and finally ethological and evolutionary.

INTRODUCTION

The development of social behaviour is a continuous process occurring through-out the lifespan: from infancy to senescence. It is, however, during the earlier phases of lifespan development that the roots of social behaviour are established through both biological and environmental factors. Biological and environmental factors are often pitted against one another using a nature (innate biology) versus nurture (learned environment) framework. Over the years of research, however, a two-camp approach to understanding social development has proven to be sim-plistic and misleading. There is a bi-directional interaction between the effects of nature and nurture – hence nature and nurture influence each in a profound way. This will be explored in future chapters. In this chapter the importance of having a multi-varied theoretical approach to understanding social development will be considered. First, however, we need to consider what is meant by the term 'social development'?

What do we mean by social development?

Social development encapsulates a host of behaviours and skills considered to enhance interpersonal interaction – these behaviours are considered to be socially related. The following areas come under the remit of social development (all of which will be considered in future chapters):

- Emotional development
- Attachment behaviour
- Cognition
- Social cognition
- Communication
- Behaviour within the family
- Relationships with peers and friends
- Play behaviour
- Self-concept
- Morally influenced behaviour
- Impact of temperament and personality
- Antisocial and prosocial behaviour

Social development has been studied within the context of the individual and how she or he interacts with others. The impact of the social, situational and cultural context on the individual and how the individual, in turn, further influences these is complex, often requiring more than one type of explanation. Despite these difficulties, developmental psychologists are in broad agreement about **normative** timescales for the development of different social behaviours based on age. What we mean by normative in this context is behaviours expected to occur at different ages based on the statistical frequency with which they present (see Figure 1.1). When children deviate long-term from these age-dependent expected

Plate 1.1 Children playing. (Shutterstock 59018779.)

behaviours, their behaviour becomes concerning and is assessed as being 'different' from most other children. Psychologists studying social development are therefore not only interested in normative behaviour but also in that which deviates from the norm.

Below, in Figure 1.1, we present a flowchart of behaviours that are considered as antisocial or 'challenging' at various ages but that are not unexpected for each age range. Although these behaviours are frequently displayed by children, they are often unwelcoming and challenging to parents. Most children eventually learn through parental guidance that these behaviours are inappropriate and adopt behaviours considered as acceptable by society. For a few children, however, early challenging responses such as temper tantrums continue to be displayed through adolescence and into early adulthood. In cases where environmental factors can largely be ruled out as the main contributors to such behaviour, then a biological explanation might be more appropriate for the child in question. Hence, when considering social development, it is important to stress the heterogeneity of causes of behaviours (including antisocial behaviours). Children are, of course, all different despite some similarities in the way they express antisocial behaviour. They might exhibit similar **trait** clusters of antisocial behaviour, but that does not necessarily mean the same underlying causes are responsible for their expression. Normative behaviour and timescales will be an issue returned to in future chapters.

The content of Figure 1.1 suggests that most children are likely to portray challenging behaviours at different points during their childhood and adolescence. This is perfectly normal and will eventually disappear, provided they receive appropriate socialisation and nurturance from their parents. There are, however, some children who continue to exhibit challenging behaviours into late adolescence and beyond. These challenging behaviours in many cases are regarded as antisocial and can even develop into criminal behaviour. In some cases, however, the behaviours exhibited involve problems of social and verbal communication. The following case example of Tommy demonstrates this challenging problem.

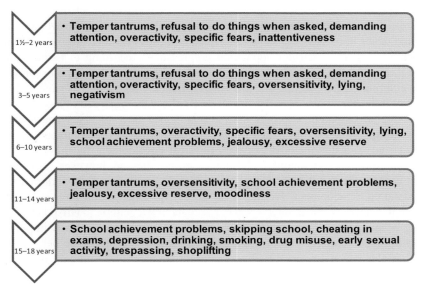

Figure 1.1 Flowchart of normative age-related challenging behaviour.

Tommy, a five-year-old child, is assessed by a psychologist after concerns expressed by a teacher. Observations of the child over a couple of weeks suggest a communication problem. This is highlighted by Tommy's refusal to do what he is told and seemingly to ignore the teacher by failure to form any kind of rapport – including no eye contact, no speech response to others except for the continuous repetition of specific words, fidgeting with pencils and being aggressive. In the playground Tommy stands alone shaking a wire fence and sometimes spinning. There is no attempt to interact with the other children who are busy playing games with each other.

In Tommy's case we can see that some of the behaviours might be seen as normal, if challenging, but collectively the pattern of behaviour deviates from the norm. So how can this child's behaviour be explained? Indeed, might there be more than one explanation? As highlighted earlier, there are many different developmental theories that can be used to account for social development (and problems with social development). In the case of Tommy, however, the behaviours exhibited are consistent with symptoms on the autism spectrum, which will be returned to in Chapters 3 and 4. The different developmental theories vary in the extent to which they err on a biological or environmental explanation; whether social development is a continuous process (building upon earlier experiences) or discontinuous (discrete steps or stages); and the extent to which individual factors such as temperament or contextual factors such as cultural influences impact on social development. These three themes are prevalent to varying degrees in the theories that will be considered below. While the biological–environmental theme is concerned with aspects of the origin of social behaviour, the continuous–discontinuous theme addresses patterns of developmental change throughout the lifespan. The individual–contextual theme considers how various individuals behave across similar situations. This allows us to unravel the extent to which a person's specific characteristics or those inherent within the situation impact on the behaviour exhibited.

THEMES OF DEVELOPMENT

Biological–environmental

As stated before, nature and nurture interact in complex ways (see Figure 1.2). Biological factors influence the development of an individual to progress in an orderly fashion. In other words, if the members of a cohort are compared, their pattern of growth and development would occur in broadly the same orderly pattern provided there are no environmental adversities causing abnormal developmental progression. According to Lewis (2007) this occurs as a consequence of having an evolutionary and **genetic karyotype** or blueprint that ensures a common developmental and growth experience. Some theorists have included this notion in their theories, such as Swiss developmental psychologist Jean Piaget who considered cognitive development as progressing in a universal stage-like way courtesy of years of evolved **adaptation**. Plomin et al. (2007) consider human development as being genetically influenced, and this includes not only physical development but how some aspects of our **socioemotional** and cognitive abilities progress. They do, however, also include the important contribution of nurture. Hence this has been labelled an **interactionist** approach to understanding development. Plomin et al. (2001) for example, in their examination of maltreatment, demonstrated an interaction between having a **genetic predisposition** towards exhibiting behaviour problems and living in abusive environments. This is important as it shows the cumulative effect of biological traits expressed as problematic behaviour by the child, and an abusive environment such as inappropriate parenting – all contriving to put the child at risk of expressing future problems such as delinquency.

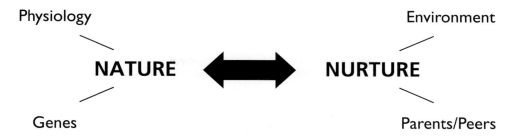

Figure 1.2 Bi-directional interaction between **nature–nurture**.

The importance of the environment in social development cannot be ignored. In conjunction with biological factors, the social environment contributes to how an individual will learn and respond towards others such as family members and peers. There has been a preponderance of research findings suggesting that if children and adolescents are appropriately socialised and supervised by their parents then they are less likely to engage in **deviant behaviour** in the way of delinquency or drug abuse (Maccoby 2007). Furthermore, research by Dodge et al. (2006) showed how children who are rejected by their peers can develop behavioural problems. A large body of research by developmentalist John Bowlby (1989) established the importance of parental engagement for the development of a secure attachment between carer and child. This was expanded by Ainsworth's 'strange situation' where different types of attachment behaviours between carer and child were observed (Ainsworth 1979, see Chapter 3). An intergenerational effect occurred whereby the caregiver's own attachment experience was later repeated by the grown-up child with his or her own children. This demonstrated a robust effect of repeating the attachment experiences in childhood later in adulthood.

Although studies have been designed to estimate the contributions biological and environmental factors make to development, it is important to realise that the two interact in complex ways. Nature can be driven by nurture and nurture can be driven by nature. This will be explored in future chapters.

A continuous–discontinuous process

Developmental psychologists have questioned whether our development occurs gradually but continuously or in distinct stages. A continuous process implies that previous experiences inform new events. These new events effectively build upon previous experiences stored in memory and transition in a gradual and cumulative way, therefore increasing our developmental abilities with time. This therefore assumes that developmental changes are constructed, developed, extended and remoulded from earlier abilities achieved through our experiences. This type of developmental change is often synonymous with a skill developing slowly, and often unobserved, but which nevertheless improves quantitatively. Children's problem-solving abilities often improve with practice, for example. Alternatively, a discontinuous model assumes that progress is made in a stage-like manner where there is a sudden change in the acquisition of a skill – hence a qualitative change. Piaget's theory of **cognitive development** is one such example, where he postulated four universal stages of cognitive development that all children must progress through. According to Piaget the order in which children progress through these stages is fixed.

In order to consolidate the fourth stage, children have to have progressed from stage one through stages two and three.

Most experts today consider that children demonstrate both continuous and discontinuous pathways of skill acquisition. This, of course, includes social skills. Developmental psychologists investigate how continuity is maintained but also how individual environmental experiences can disrupt this process. It has been noted by Rutter et al. (2001) that positive experiences such as adoption into a loving family can reverse the effects of years of an aversive upbringing. This will also be explored in future chapters.

Impact of individual and contextual factors

Russian-born American developmentalist Urie Bronfenbrenner introduced the **Ecological Theory**, which combines the influence of the child's individual traits with aspects of its environment. Not only does Bronfenbrenner stress the important individual characteristics that a child contributes to the immediate environment but also how these characteristics impact on others by way of their response to the child. Bronfenbrenner (1979) advocated an infrastructure describing a series of concentric layers surrounding the child, which impact on the child's development directly or indirectly. These layers describe environmental factors – the first being the family and friends (the closest to the child) followed by more distant environmental influences such as education, the law and media, and finally the culture to which the child is subjected. One important point concerning Bronfenbrenner's model is that it acknowledges the contribution of individual factors (i.e., the child's traits) and both contextual and cultural influences (i.e., the values and attitudes of society) to the development of the child (see Figure 1.6 and Contextual theories).

Some developmental psychologists, however, focus primarily on the individual. Much of this derives from studies addressing risk resilience where the child experiences either biological or psychological risk (e.g., having health problems or having a parent who has a personality disorder), or environmental risk (e.g., being bullied at school or living in poverty). Developmental psychologists interested in this area consider how these children respond to these risks during development and whether they succumb to **'sleeper' effects**. Sleeper effects refer to the fact that, in many cases, there may be delayed developmental reactions to early problems. In contrast to developmentalists who focus on the individual, others emphasise the contribution of contextual and cultural factors to lifespan development. In the case of contextual factors, the family home and the school setting are just two examples of how the context can influence the social development of the child. If a child experiences bullying in the school it is likely to have a profound effect on self-esteem and the ability to develop socially. Culture also influences development. This can be demonstrated through different styles of family upbringing. In some cultures the aim is to encourage the child to walk early whereas in other cultures the use of a cradleboard or swaddling delays motor development (Chisholm 1980).

An understanding of the three themes above is important as different theories address these to varying degrees. We turn our attention now to the different theories used by developmental psychologists in explaining developmental phenomena throughout the lifespan. Theories can be classified under the following banners: biological and behavioural genetics; structural–organismic; learning; contextual; dynamic systems and ethological and evolutionary. Theories under biological and behavioural genetics will be considered next.

Plate 1.2 Negative experiences at school (such as bullying) can have a long-lasting effect on resilience. (Shutterstock 284501792.)

THEORIES CONSIDERED IN DEVELOPMENTAL PSYCHOLOGY

Biological and behavioural genetics perspective

The contribution of biological and behavioural genetics provides a context in which the child develops socially. In order to understand the contribution of biology (and more specifically genes) to the developing child, it is necessary to describe prenatal development and the consequences of genetic abnormalities for behaviour (see Boxes 1.1, 1.2. and 1.3).

Biological

Biological (also referred to as physiological to distinguish from genetics, although the two are related) approaches to understanding social development consider the involvement of brain maturation and both the nervous and **endocrine** systems. The development of the brain, nervous and endocrine systems are strongly linked with what happens during gestation, not only in terms of inherited genes but also the prenatal environment per se.

Box 1.1   Prenatal development

In humans the period of gestation is nine months or 38 weeks and this is divided into three stages: germinal, embryonic and foetal. The germinal stage (the first trimester) refers to conception and the division of cells. The zygote is the fertilised cell and after a week it already implants

(continued)

(continued)

onto the wall of the uterus. After two weeks this process is complete and the zygote is now referred to as an embryo. The embryonic stage (the second trimester) lasts from the third to the eighth week after conception. The embryo is only one inch long but already has everything intact that makes it human. It is connected to the placenta via the umbilical cord. The foetal stage (the third trimester) is when the foetus begins to grow and develop the already existing structures. By the seventh month the foetus is able to breathe, cry, swallow, digest and excrete. Physical growth follows orderly patterns known as cephalocaudal and proximodistal development. The cephalocaudal pattern of development refers to the fact that growth occurs in a head-to-toe direction. At two months the head is very large in contrast to its total height. Within the head itself the eyes and the brain grow faster than the jaw. The proximodistal pattern of development refers to the fact that development occurs outwards from the centre of the body – neck and trunk before fingers and toes.

Box 1.2   The genes and chromosomes of development

We have trillions of cells and inside every cell is a nucleus that contains rod-like structures called **chromosomes**. Chromosomes store and transmit genetic information and there are 23 matching pairs with the exception of the sex chromosomes, XX in females and XY in males. Chromosomes are made of **DNA** (deoxyribonucleic acid) and a gene is a segment of DNA along the length of the chromosome. The DNA can duplicate itself through a process of mitosis, resulting in new cells each containing the same number of chromosomes and identical genetic information. Sex cells, or gametes as they are referred to, such as sperm and ovum, contain 23 chromosomes – half the number to that of other bodily cells. Gametes are formed through cellular division called meiosis, which ensures that the same number of chromosomes is transmitted. Thus, during fertilisation, the sperm and ovum unite forming a **zygote** consisting of 46 chromosomes. This means that half of the genetic material comes from the mother and the other half from the father. In meiosis the chromosomes pair up and exchange segments, so that genes from one are replaced by genes from another. Mistakes in genetic transmission at the gene level, however, can result in genetic abnormalities at the chromosome level.

To have a better understanding of the importance of patterns of development during gestation (pregnancy) – in other words the crucial windows of development – we need to first consider basic **Mendelian genetics**. Genes operate in pairs (one from each parent) and can be either dominant or recessive. In the case of a dominant gene, only one copy is needed for a characteristic to appear in the phenotype, whereas for recessive genes you need two copies for the characteristic to become apparent. An example of the action of dominant and recessive genes can be illustrated by considering the genes that code for eye colour. The genotype of someone with brown eyes can be: BB, Bb or bB. In other words, to show brown eyes in one's physical make-up (the **phenotype**) the genotype has to have the dominant gene 'B'. The 'b' for blue eyes is recessive and is therefore masked by the dominant 'B' gene. Because one form of the gene, i.e., 'b', comes from one parent the other gene or **allele** comes from the other parent, i.e., 'B'. (Note 'allele' refers to the various forms of the gene that can exist at a particular **locus** (location) on a chromosome). In order to have the phenotype blue eyes, one would have to inherit both recessive genes: bb. Those with the Bb or bB genotypes will have brown eyes but carry the recessive gene for blue eyes: they are known as heterozygous – because they have two different genes for eye colour, but the dominant gene will show. Those who have genotypes BB or bb are **homozygous** – because they have two of the same gene for eye colour. It is also possible for **co-dominance** to occur. This occurs when heterozygous genes both express their traits with equal force. For example, in the case of blood grouping both 'A' and 'B' are dominant. Thus the person who inherits the A from one parent and the B from the other will have AB.

As discussed in Boxes 1.1 and 1.2, the impact of cellular division during prenatal development has repercussions for post-natal development, especially in terms of continued brain maturation. Conditions arising from abnormal cellular (technically nuclear) division – **mitosis** and **meiosis** – can result in a multitude of syndromes affecting brain development and therefore how the individual comes to behave socially (see Box 1.3). Therefore knowledge of the typical time-line of brain development inside and outside of the womb is important to understanding why an individual behaves in the way they do. Of course contemporary developmental psychologists advocating a biological approach also consider the important influence of environmental factors. This stance is encapsulated in the **epigenetic view** of development. The epigenetic view (or 'epigenetics') emphasises a bi-directional interaction occurring between nature (i.e., genetic inheritance) and nurture (i.e., environment) – demonstrating a **biosocial interaction**. We will return to the concept of epigenetics later in this chapter and in future chapters.

Box 1.3 The genes and chromosomes of development – when things go wrong

A number of diseases are caused by 'faulty' genes that people inherit. There are two broad types of genetic diseases: autosomal (Cystic fibrosis, PKU, Sickle cell anaemia) and sex-linked (haemophilia, muscular dystrophy). **Autosomal chromosomes** are all chromosome pairs 1–22 excluding the 23rd pair responsible for sex differentiation. Some inherited characteristics, however, are affected by genes found on only the X or Y chromosome, so they are sex-linked characteristics. Most of these are carried on the X chromosome, and because females receive two X chromosomes they receive one of these from their father. Normal males receive only one X chromosome from the mother and thus have only one copy of each faulty gene that is on the X chromosome. This difference makes males more susceptible to genetic defects that do not normally affect females. If a daughter has a harmful recessive gene on one X chromosome, she will often have a normal dominant gene on the other X chromosome to override it. A son, however, will not have the dominant gene to override this faulty gene. For example, Lesch-Nyhan is a genetically determined X-linked disorder affecting uric acid metabolism and central nervous system function. Subsequent research has shown it to be due to an almost complete lack of the enzyme hypoxanthine phosphoribosyltransferase (HPRT). This is due to a mutation or deletion of the HPRT gene on the X chromosome (Stout and Caskey 1989). The physical and behavioural symptoms appear early on in life, with the development of involuntary movements and evidence of developmental delay. Severe self-harming behaviour develops between 2–3 years of age (Anderson and Ernst 1994).

There are autosomal conditions (chromosome pairs 1–22) known as trisomy because an individual has three copies of a specific chromosome instead of two. Edward's syndrome or Trisomy E18 and Patau's syndrome or Trisomy P13 tends to result in early death or miscarriage.

(continued)

(continued)

Generally this is the fate of autosomal abnormalities. Down syndrome or Trisomy 21 occurs in about 1 in 800 live births: 1 in 9,000 for mothers 20–24 years of age and 1 in 30 for mothers over 45. In 95 per cent of cases it results from a failure of the 21st pair to separate during meiosis, so that the individual inherits three of these chromosomes rather than two. It could also happen by an extra broken piece of the 21st chromosome being **translocated** (moved) on the upper arm of the chromosome (or p arm). People with Down syndrome tend to have a flat appearance to the face, low bridge to the nose and high cheekbones, upward and outward slanting eyes with upper eye-lid folds, stocky build, protruding tongue, a simian crease across the palm of the hand and floppy muscles. They also experience mental retardation, slow reaction times, poor memory and speech, and a limited vocabulary (Chapman and Hesketh 2000).

In the case of sex determination the inheritance pattern is XX or XY (although this can go awry and possible combinations are XO, XXY and XYY). Individuals with **sex-linked** abnormalities tend to survive but problems are not expressed until adolescence and adulthood. In the case of Klinefelter's syndrome (XXY) a boy is born with an extra X or Y and has the genotype XXY: the XX comes from the mother – due to failure in meiotic division. This occurs in 1 in 900 males born in the USA. They appear to develop normally until adolescence when they fail to show signs of male maturity. They do not acquire facial hair, sex organs do not mature, voices do not change, low levels of testosterone persist through the lifespan and they are sterile. Most have speech and language problems and are usually tall. They can be given testosterone at 11–12 years of age which will help these individuals develop more masculine characteristics.

In the case of Turner syndrome (XO) individuals have only one X chromosome: in most cases this comes from the mother, which means that the cause of the XO lies with a defective sperm (Knebelmann et al. 1991). Because a Y chromosome is not present, testes do not develop and because an X is missing the ovaries do not develop either. Even though they do not have gonads they still develop as females with normal female internal sex organs and external genitalia. They are unable to have children as they cannot produce ova.

In the case of XYY syndrome, the YY comes from the father as there is a failure in meiotic division. Individuals tend to be tall and disproportionately represented in prisons (but this could be because they are more likely to be caught due to their low intelligence than the average man). They are supposed to be more aggressive but this does not necessarily hold true.

The brain is composed of a series of structures consisting of nerve cells known as neurons. The brain is divided into the left and right hemispheres. The outer covering of the brain, the cortex, is divided into four major areas (for each hemisphere) referred to as lobes. The brain works holistically by making connections to process information both within and between these lobes. In addition to sending information between the lobes each has its own specificity of function. The frontal lobes, for example, process much of our thinking and planning behaviour and contribute to our personality. The temporal lobes process aspects of hearing, language and memory, while the parietal lobes register attention, motor control and spatial location. The occipital lobes play a central role in our vision. Beneath the cortex further ('sub-cortical') structures are sited, such as the amygdala, hippocampus, pituitary gland and hypothalamus. The former two play major roles in the processing of emotions and memory, while the latter two control the endocrine system.

In the brain the neurons form neural circuits that process specific types of information. There are many neural circuits in the brain, such as those processing information about spatial location or aspects of memory. For these circuits to function efficiently, various chemicals known as **neurotransmitters** are released by neurons to allow neurons to communicate.

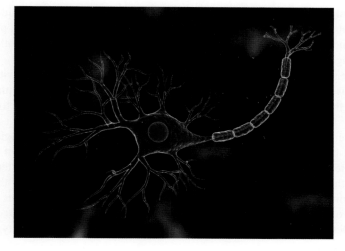

Plate 1.3 A neuron, the basic unit of communication and processing in the brain. (Shutterstock 13643509.)

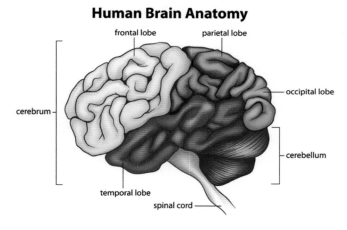

Plate 1.4 Human brain anatomy showing main lobes of the forebrain, spinal cord and cerebellum. (Shutterstock 139691548.)

Impulses (action potentials) travel down the length of a neuron (or its axon) and, on reaching the **terminal end**, communicate with other neurons via the release of a neurotransmitter such as dopamine, which crosses the minute gap between neurons called the synaptic cleft. On reaching the receptor sites of another nerve cell (the post-synaptic neurone) such neurotransmitters can then either cause an increase or a decrease in the firing rate of that neuron. In short, the way that neurons communicate with each other is by either increasing or decreasing the firing rates of each other to form neural circuits. Hence neural circuits involved with information concerning planning and decision-making are particularly active in the (pre) frontal lobe when such activity is required. Furthermore, each hemisphere of the brain is particularly associated with specialist processing. As a general rule the left hemisphere is associated with the processing of language and the right with spatial awareness; hence the brain is **lateralised** for function. Despite this broad lateralisation of function many tasks involve a great deal of **interhemispheric transfer** of information. Reading, playing instruments and complex thought are all considered possible as a consequence of both hemispheres communicating with each other (Peru et al. 2006).

The endocrine system consists of a series of glands that are involved with the process of **homeostasis** (the maintenance of body regulation to create equilibrium within its internal environment) through the release of hormones (some of which affect the activity of neurotransmitters).

The endocrine system is involved in a very wide range of physiological processes from moment-by-moment body temperature regulation to the development of secondary sexual characteristics during adolescence. Biological psychologists interested in development suggest that during adolescence, in addition to changes in morphology that accentuate male–female differences, neural circuits involved in gender-typical responses are activated. Hormones involved in sex and gender development are divided into the **oestrogens** and the **androgens**. Oestrogens are 'female hormones' secreted to promote female-typical physical

HUMAN ENDOCRINE SYSTEM

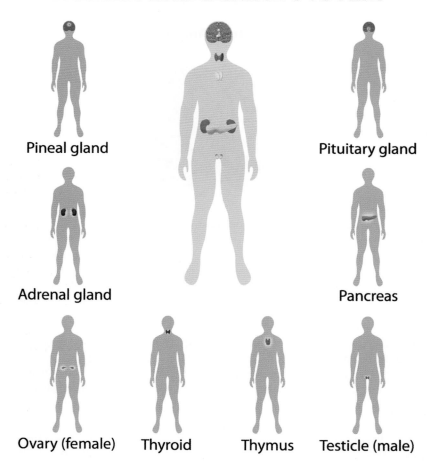

Pineal gland   Pituitary gland

Adrenal gland   Pancreas

Ovary (female)   Thyroid   Thymus   Testicle (male)

Plate 1.5 Location of the organs associated with the endocrine system. (Shutterstock 226804177.)

sex characteristics such as development of the ovaries and breasts. They are also involved in controlling the menstrual cycle. In the case of male sexual development, androgens such as **testosterone** develop the physical sex characteristics such as activating the testes. There is some evidence that high levels of circulating testosterone are related to aggressive behaviour in men (Archer 1991, 2006). Some biological developmentalists have suggested that the rise in aggressive behaviour associated with males during adolescence is related to this rise in testosterone (Archer, 1991, 2006). Once again, however, this relationship is not clear cut and we should bear in mind that levels of aggression also increase in females during adolescence (Campbell in press).

It is of interest to note that evolutionary psychologists relate this time of sex hormone increase (and increases in aggressive response) to the period when adolescents, of both sexes, are competing for potential mates through **intra-sexual selection** (within sex competition, Campbell in press 2018). This implies that increases in aggressive behaviour at this point in development may be functionally related to competition for mates (see Box 1.4 later in this chapter).

Behavioural genetics

Behavioural genetics is the field that attempts to estimate the relative contributions of genes and environment to internal states and behavioural responses (Plomin et al. 2008). People often assume that the contributions to behaviour that genes and environment make are independent. This, however, is a simplification. Genes themselves influence the environment in which a child grows up.

Scarr (1996) described three ways in which genes can influence a child's environment:

- passive effects
- active effects
- evocative effects

In the case of passive effects a child passively 'inherits' the environment that the parents have provided. Think of reading. A home that contains a large number of books will mean a child is more likely to examine these and therefore may be more likely to read at an earlier age than a child growing up in a home with few books.

Active effects mean that the child actively seeks environments that are compatible with her genotype – often referred to as **niche picking**. In relation to reading again, it is not inconceivable that the genes she has inherited increase the chances of her seeking out books to read (in a sense the child is actively seeking stimuli due to the genes she has inherited). Finally, in relation to evocative effects, a trait possessed by the child can influence the way others will react to him or her which then reinforces the trait. Once again, if a child is observed reading a lot, adults are more likely to buy her books (she has evoked this response in them). In fact, evocative effects can be observed pretty much from birth. A baby who smiles a lot is considered to be a friendly easy-going infant. Such babies are regarded as temperamentally easy and evoke positive reactions from others – hence the baby smiles and others smile back, which then reinforces the genetic predisposition to be 'easy-going'.

Interestingly, in recent years behavioural geneticists have made claims that specific genes can affect the development of an infant's temperament and, in so doing, influences the ease with which they form attachments to their caregivers. Some experts have claimed that one such gene, labelled DRD4, which can occur in various forms, plays an important role in the development of an infant's temperament and influences the ease with which infants will form attachments to their caregivers. This gene has been studied in relation to disorganised

Plate 1.6 A star is born who finds a piano in the house. (Shutterstock 94676254.)

Plate 1.7 Irresistible smiling baby-faced boy. (Shutterstock 2375239.)

patterns of attachment, leading to the label of 'D-infants' (Lakatos et al. 2000; Gervai et al. 2005). We will return to this debate in Chapter 3 when we consider different attachment types. For now it is sufficient to note that DRD4 may be worthy of examination in relation to the concept of the evocative effects of genes on the development of social behaviour.

As each parent shares 50 per cent of their genes by common descent with each of their offspring they clearly exert a genetic influence. The difficulty that behavioural geneticists have, however, is differentiating this from the social influence parents exert over their children. Genetic and social influences generally impact on the child simultaneously since, as we saw above, they generally co-occur. This means that any similarities in behaviour between parents and child are difficult to attribute to a genetic or social causality – and for most of the time it is a combination of the two. One way of researching the extent of genetic or environmental causality in children's behaviour is to consider offspring of varying levels of genetic and environmental relatedness. Identical twins, also known as **monozygotic twins**, share 100 per cent of their genes as they develop from a single fertilised egg. Unlike identical twins, fraternal twins (or **dizygotic twins**) are non-identical and can be same-sex or opposite-sex siblings, developing from two separate fertilised eggs. This means they share the same proportion of their genes by common descent as normal siblings do, but happen to share their prenatal environment by virtue of developing in the womb at the same time. It is possible to examine gene and environmental influences by considering the differences in relatedness across identical and non-identical twins and other siblings in the family in relation to their similarities (or differences) on a variety of measures. If genes are of particular importance to the development of a trait then we would predict that monozygotic twins will be more similar for this trait than dizygotic twins. Additionally, identical twins reared together or apart can be studied for behavioural similarities. If there are considerable differences in behaviour across twins reared apart, then, given their identical **genotype** profile, these differences can be attributed to an environmental influence. It is the environment that differs between the two identical twins and must therefore be responsible for dissimilarities in behaviour and performance on various tests of cognitive and social ability. Research findings based on these kinds of study estimate an environmental contribution of between 50 and 60 per cent to differences between children; conversely, it therefore follows that a genetic contribution to differences between individuals must be on a scale of 40–50 per cent (Plomin et al. 2008). This estimation, however, fails to partial out the direct and indirect effects of our genes. For example, being treated differently as a consequence of physical attractiveness might impact on a person's level of assertiveness. Hence, while physical attractiveness may be largely the outcome of having a 'good combination' of genes, assertiveness arises, in part, out of the way other people react positively to a good-looking person – hence an evocative effect of our genes.

A study by Turkheimer et al. (2003) demonstrated the extent to which the environment accounted for variations in intelligence among identical and non-identical twins from poor backgrounds. From a sample of 320 twin pairs who had taken IQ tests aged seven years at the time, Turkheimer was able to perform correlations on their data. The correlations showed that IQ results for identical twins varied just as much as they did for fraternal twins. This was interpreted by Turkheimer to suggest that the heritability of IQ played a very small role in these children from poor backgrounds. In the case of identical and non-identical twins from comfortably well-off backgrounds, Turkheimer found that the heritability of IQ was very high, especially for identical twins (hence genes played a larger role). This appears to be rather a strange finding. Why should it be that for different socioeconomic groups we find quite different levels of heritability? A possible explanation is that the environment will help improve a child's intelligence from a poor family if books and parental input towards educating their child is implemented. A rich child already has these things hence the environment

Plate 1.8 Identical teenagers. (Shutterstock 43716982.)

will have less of an impact. These findings suggest that at some point improvements to the environment will cease to enhance further development of a child. Any observable differences will be due to differences in genetic profile.

> *If you have a chaotic environment, kids' genetic potential doesn't have a chance to be expressed. . . . Well-off families can provide the mental stimulation needed for genes to build the brain circuitry for intelligence.*
>
> (Turkheimer quoted in New York Times, *23 July 2006*)

Nevertheless, behavioural geneticists continue to investigate twins by introducing the concept of the '**shared environment**' and the '**non-shared environment**'. In the case of the shared environment, factors common to all siblings, such as the same parents and attending the same local school, are considered in the mix. For the non-shared (or unique) environment, factors specific to one sibling and not the others are considered. Such factors might include, for example, a childhood illness causing one child to be tutored in the home. The contribution of the shared environment can be calculated by looking at differences between:

- identical twins reared together, hence sharing both genes and the same environment;
- identical twins reared apart, hence sharing their genes only.

Any differences arising can be attributed to the effects of a non-shared environment. The contribution of a shared environment can also be calculated through the consideration of similarity across unrelated adopted siblings who have very different genes but share the same environment. In this case it is assumed that any similarities are a consequence of having a shared environment. Plomin et al. (1994) found there to be very little difference in terms of heritability of cognitive ability and personality between identical twins reared apart; suggesting a robust genetic contribution to their behaviour. Plomin and Daniels' (1987) findings indicate very little similarity between unrelated adoptees nurtured within the same family environment for cognition and personality. Turkheimer (2000) concluded that there was a 10 per cent variation among individuals in shared environments. This suggests that variation among individuals is 50 per cent attributable to our genes and 10 per cent attributable to a shared environment. This means that 40 per cent of variation can be attributed to non-shared environmental factors. This will be considered further throughout the text in relation to the nature–nurture debate. We now turn our attention to the **structural–organismic approach**.

Structural–organismic perspective

The two main proponents of the structural–organismic perspective are Sigmund Freud and Jean Piaget. Although they have very different approaches, in common they offered descriptions of how psychological systems work. In relation to psychological development Freud used **structuralism** to explain how emotions and personality develop whereas Piaget adopted a structural approach to understanding cognition. Structuralism, an approach to explaining behaviour, was popular in the early 19th century, and was used to describe psychological structures and processes that change as development progresses through the early stages of the lifespan. Please note that the term structuralism[1], as understood in the 20th century, is quite different from the term's original use in the 19th century. French philosopher Michel Foucault[2] is often associated with what has become known as post-structuralism, a philosophical stance that denounces some of the concepts held by the 19th century structuralists (and many of the concepts held by natural scientists).

The incorporation of a biological stance is clearly observed in both Freud and Piaget's theories. Their approach to development is a discontinuous one where developmental changes occur distinctly as the individual progresses from one stage to another – hence a structural–organismic perspective. In relation to social development, in addition to Piaget and Freud, it is also necessary to consider Erik Erikson.

Sigmund Freud (1856–1939)

The Viennese father of psychoanalysis, Sigmund Freud argued that early childhood experiences impacted on the development of personality in adulthood. His approach became

Table 1.1 Freud's five stages of psychosexual development.

Age (in years)	Stage	Focus of pleasure zones
0–1½	Oral	The mouth is the focus point where the infant finds pleasure (sucking on a teat).
1½ –3	Anal	The anus is the focus point where the infant finds pleasure (retaining or expulsing faeces at will).
3–6	Phallic	The genitals are the focus point where the toddler finds pleasure. This coincides with the Oedipus complex where boys want to be in a physical relationship with their mother and girls with their father. This can lead to the castration complex in boys where they fear their father's wrath on discovering the Oedipus complex. In girls this can lead to penis envy as she wants to have a penis like her father.
8 to puberty	Latency	During this period children repress sexual interest in others. Instead they concentrate on developing their cognitive and social skills.
puberty onwards	Genital	During this period adolescents develop sexual interest in others and obtain sexual pleasure from relationships outside of the family.

known as psychodynamic theory and his methods as psychoanalysis. The three facets of personality development introduced by Freud are the **id**, **ego** and **superego**. The id encapsulates our basic or instinctual drives that dominate the infant who is in constant need of immediate gratification. Through experience with the family and immediate environment, the ego gradually takes control and introduces the id to rationality. The rational element of the ego, also known as the reality principle, satiates the id's gratification using socially appropriate behaviour. As the child develops further the superego emerges and becomes fine-tuned to the parental socialisation of appropriate and morally acceptable behaviour. This becomes internalised to form the conscience. Changes to the id, ego and superego occur as a consequence of five psychosexual stages: oral, anal, phallic, latency and genital (see Table 1.1). These different psychosexual stages will impact on future development, especially if the individual becomes fixed at any of the stages. For example, an adult fixated at the oral stage of psychosexual development might be considered greedy for the breast according to Freud.

Erik Erikson (1902–1994)

German-born American developmentalist Erik Erikson was influenced by Freud but, rather than focusing on psychosexual development, his scheme involved a series of psychosocial stages. Comprising of eight stages throughout the lifespan, Erikson's theory describes developmental tasks that individuals should acquire at each stage. Also included are the possible risks encountered at each stage if these developmental tasks are unsuccessfully solved. Each of Erikson's stages involves conflict between a positive (engaging successfully in a 'task') and a negative outcome (succumbing to a 'risk'). Erikson's proposed stages are outlined in Table 1.2.

Table 1.2 Erikson's eight stages of psychosocial development.

Age (in years)	Task vs risk	Stage
0–1	Trust vs mistrust	Infancy: task is to develop basic trust in the self and other selves. Risk occurs when there is a failure to trust others coinciding with low self-confidence.
1–3	Autonomy vs shame/doubt	Toddlerhood: task is to learn some self-control and begin autonomy. Risk occurs when the presence of shame and self-doubt arise.
3–6	Initiative vs guilt	Early childhood (preschool): task is to demonstrate an inclination to master the immediate environment. Risk occurs when guilt is experienced over aggressiveness.
6–12	Industry vs inferiority	Middle and late childhood (school): task is to expand imagination, use knowledge and be industrious. Risk occurs when the inability to master tasks causes an inferiority complex and perceived unproductivity.
12–20	Identity vs identity confusion	Adolescence: task is to attain self-identity. Risk occurs when there is a lack of role clarity defining self-identity.
20–30	Intimacy vs isolation	Early adulthood: task is to be able to initiate and maintain intimacy with others. Risk occurs when there is confusion of self-identity resulting in avoidance of others and isolation.
30–65	Generativity vs stagnation	Middle adulthood: task is to be able to express and show concern for others, including the nurturance of younger others (generativity). Risk occurs when there is a lack of ability to create ideas, products and children hence leading to stagnation.
65+	Integrity vs despair	Late adulthood: task is to achieve integrity and self-fulfilment. Risk occurs when desires have been unfulfilled leading to self-doubts and despair.

Jean Piaget (1896–1980)

In a different vein, Piaget used the structural–organismic perspective to understand intellectual development or cognition. From biology he used the concepts of organisation and adaptation. In the case of organisation, cognitive development is conceived of as a biologically organised process. This means that an individual's perceptions of their environment alter in an organised way during progressive development. Adaptation refers to the process enabling changes to intellectual development. The environment is of particular importance here as intellectual change is a consequence of adapting to the environment. Piaget developed a universal four-stage theory of cognitive development: sensorimotor, preoperational, concrete operational and formal operational. The qualitative differences and nature of these stages will be considered in more detail in Chapter 4. Table 1.3 provides a brief description of each stage.

Table 1.3 Piaget's four stages of cognitive development.

Age (in years)	Stage	Expected abilities
0–2	Sensorimotor	Learns to organise and interpret sensory information and to co-ordinate motor activity as a way of understanding the world. There is a focus on motor and sensory experiences – reflex activity such as sucking, repetitive reactions and kicking.
2–7	Preoperational	Thought is unsystematic in nature and self-centred (egocentric thought). Can use symbols to represent objects, classify objects, use simple logic and learn new words at a rapid pace. Failure to understand that quantity does not change even if the shape changes (a facet of conservation).
7–11	Concrete operations	Reasoning ability is now more logical. Classification and ordering objects is mastered but not using abstract ideas. These new skills are applied to concrete objects (those they have experienced). This means that imagined or abstract objects or the hypothetical continues to be a mystery. Understanding of conservation has been achieved. An increased ability to focus on more than one aspect of a stimulus develops.
11 onwards	Formal operations	Deductive and inductive thought and hypothetical thinking is achieved. An abstract view of the world is entertained. Conservation of the concrete and abstract and imagined is achieved. In-depth understanding of cause and effect is comprehensible.

Learning perspectives

Learning is an activity that humans appear to do instinctively. Learning is most expansive during the early phases of the lifespan, where the appetite for experiencing new events and gaining knowledge in infants and children appears limitless. The acquisition of language and the rules of social engagement appear early in the lifespan. The question of how this learning occurs and how the brain processes and makes connections between different bytes of information has been of immense interest to psychologists over the years. In this section we consider the approaches of behaviourism, cognitive social learning and information processing – beginning with the movement known as behaviourism.

The psychological field of 'behaviorism' can be traced back to the work of American psychologist John B. Watson. Unlike previous psychologists, Watson was interested purely in the behaviour of organisms rather than what is happening in the mind/brain. In fact, Watson bypassed studying, and referring to, processes occurring in the mind (brain) by referring to these as the 'black box'. To Watson the aim of psychology should be:

> *To predict, given the stimulus, what reaction will take place; or given the reaction, state what the situation or stimulus is that has caused the reaction.*
>
> *(Watson 1930, p.11)*

Watson incorporated the **classical conditioning** studies conducted by Ivan Pavlov into the behaviourist ideology. Russian physiologist Pavlov, in 1927, demonstrated in a series of experiments that dogs would innately salivate to the presentation of food, calling this an **unconditioned response** (UCR) to an **unconditioned stimulus** (UCS) (i.e., the food). Unnaturally, however, Pavlov showed that dogs could learn to salivate to a stimulus, such as the sounding of a bell, as long as the bell is associated with the presentation of food. Pavlov attached a tube to the dog's throat so that the extent of saliva secreted could be measured when food was presented. After a few trials, when food was presented at the same time as the sounding of the bell an association was made between food and bell. The dogs continued to salivate when no food was presented but the bell sounded – known as the **conditioned response** and **conditioned stimulus** respectively (see Figure 1.3).

Although classical conditioning was originally used to explain how animals learn, Watson began to apply the classical conditioning approach to help explain how children learn new skills. One famous study of his involved an infant known as 'Little Albert'. An association was made between patting a white rabbit and a loud noise (created above Albert's head). The response was crying, which later extrapolated to seeing the white rabbit in the absence of the loud noise (Watson and Rayner 1920). This demonstrated how classical conditioning could play a role in the acquisition of phobias. Burrhus Frederic Skinner introduced an alternative learning to classical conditioning known as **operant conditioning**. The underlying assumption here is that behaviours that produce rewarding consequences are more likely to be repeated, whereas those resulting in a negative outcome (such as punishment) are less likely to be repeated and instead avoided in the future. It is through the combination of reward and punishment that an individual's behaviour is shaped and directed by his or her experiences with their environment. If, for example, a child receives praise for sharing toys with another child then he is likely to continue being a cooperative game-player. A child chastised for hitting a younger sibling is less likely to repeat the behaviour. Skinner's operant conditioning has been widely adopted as a successful approach to modifying behavioural repertoires via **shaping behaviour** in educational settings – especially in children who exhibit inappropriate social behaviour in the classroom. Behaviourism has had a profound influence in the understanding of how social behaviours in children are developed. It is, however, when combined with cognitive approaches to explaining the acquisition of appropriate social behaviour that it excels as an empirically formidable theoretical perspective. One such approach that has combined behaviourism with cognitive psychology is Bandura's **Cognitive Social Learning Theory**, which will be considered next.

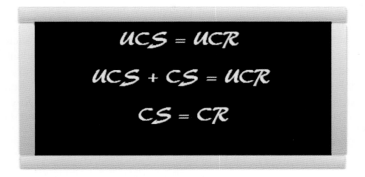

Figure 1.3 On the board – classical conditioning formula.

Albert Bandura (1925–present)

Albert Bandura is an American developmentalist who is renowned for triangulating cognition, the environment and behaviour. In a similar vein to behaviourist approaches he emphasises the importance of observing behaviour, which evolved into his Social Learning Theory. Bandura introduced observational learning, which became widely known as **modelling** – a form of imitation enabling the child to learn from others by merely watching and then copying what they did. A child could therefore acquire a specific behaviour through direct experience of an event and indirect (or vicarious) observation. Vicarious observation entails a second-hand experience of the event – hence observing someone else's experience. Both direct and vicarious experiences of the event can be equally influential on future behaviour. Modelling can even be applied to the acquisition of phobias. For example, a girl who sees her mother scream on seeing a spider is more likely to enact her mother's fear on encountering a spider at a later date. In other words, the girl has cognitively represented her mother's behaviour and, in this case, adopted her behaviour.

Bandura examined how children learn aggressive responses through imitation via a series of experiments whereby children observed adults punching and kicking a **Bobo doll**. Before children observed this violent display towards the Bobo doll they played non-aggressively. After observing adults play aggressively with the Bobo doll, children began to punch and kick the doll, unlike the control group who had not witnessed such adult aggressiveness (see Chapter 2 for a critique of the methodology). Bandura claimed that children choose specific behaviours to imitate and that this depends on four cognitive processes:

1 Attention towards the exhibited behaviour.
2 Retention of observed behaviours in memory.
3 Competency to reproduce the behaviour.
4 Motivation to reproduce the behaviour.

In 1986 Bandura changed the name of his Social Learning Theory to Cognitive Social Learning Theory to reflect an added cognitive element to the way that behaviour can be learned. While Bandura remains renowned for his Social Learning Theory and, in particular, the Bobo doll study, he has continued to publish beyond 2011. His theory evolved over the years to highlight the importance of cognition, hence the name change of his theory. More recently, Bandura (2007) emphasised the important three-way interaction between behaviour, the environment and person or cognitive factors (see Figure 1.4). He also considers in this model how we are producers as well as products of our social environment – something he refers to in his **agentic perspective** of social cognitive theory in 2008.

The behaviourist approach has been criticised for ignoring person factors such as cognition. However, Bandura's Cognitive Social Learning Theory has provided an important link between environmental factors and how connections are forged between stimulus and response – the mystical 'black box' can now be examined using a cognitive intermediary. Another learning approach that seeks to look inside the black box is information processing theory.

Information processing theory

Information processing theory can be defined as a perspective that 'views the mind as a symbol-manipulating system through which information flows, that often uses flowcharts to map the precise series of steps individuals use to solve problems and complete tasks, and

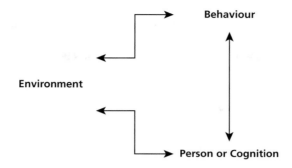

Figure 1.4 Multi-interactions in Bandura's Cognitive Social Learning Theory.

that regards cognitive development as a continuous process' (Klahr and MacWhinney 1998). This means that, from presentation to the senses at input to behavioural responses at output, information is actively coded, transformed and organised. It is not uncommon for researchers in this area to make use of flowcharts to map the precise series of steps children use to solve problems. Thornton (1999), for example, introduced a task called 'building a bridge across the river'. Children of school-age are presented with blocks of varying size, shape and weight. On the floor is a pretend river that is painted to the breadth where only two of the blocks in combination could possibly cross it. Older children can complete this task successfully but in Thornton's study only one five year old managed to do so. It was concluded that the five year old successfully completed the task through a trial and error approach until hitting on the idea of using the blocks as counterweights. The observation that older children can do this task easily prompts questions such as, 'Does a child's ability to solve problems become increasingly organised with age?'

Plate 1.9 The making of a bridge using building blocks. (Shutterstock 186414830.)

In a similar vein to Piaget, the **information processing approach** considers individuals to be active in their pursuit of making sense of their environment. Unlike Piaget, however, there are no discrete stages to development. The information processing approach considers facets of thought processes such as attention, perception, memory, planning and comprehension to be similar across the lifespan, but to be present to a lesser or greater degree depending on age. This means that development is in continuous flux as the brain matures with age. Siegler (1994) proposed that children acquire new strategies through **trial and error** and experimentation. His research suggests that children do not acquire solutions to problems immediately but instead progress using a series of rules. When one rule is no longer helpful they apply the next level of rule and so on. Siegler (2006) stated that, 'thinking is information processing'. The information processing approach can also be applied to the learning or acquisition of social behaviours. Kupersmidt and Dodge (2004) applied information processing as a medium for understanding social problem-solving and aggression in children. They found differences in the way children deal with solving socially related problems – those who were aggressive tended to have negative interpretations of other children's behaviour and intentions. They often believed that other children were deliberately being negative towards them (which was based on hostile attributions about others' behaviours) and as a result they responded by behaving aggressively.

Another theoretical approach to explaining social development comes under the umbrella of contextual perspectives, discussed next.

Contextual perspectives

According to a **contextual perspective** individuals encounter a diversity of contexts during their lifespan. These encounters influence individual development in different ways but certainly have a profound effect on social development during the early years of the lifespan. There are three main forms of contextual perspective: ecological, sociocultural and lifespan.

1. Bronfenbrenner's ecological model (1917–2005)

Urie Bronfenbrenner (1979) argued that there is an important interaction between the developing child and layers of environmental systems – some of these layers having more direct impact on the child than others. He considers that,

> understanding of human development demands going beyond the direct observation of behaviour on the part of one or two persons in the same place; . . . multi-person systems of interaction not limited to a single setting and must take into account aspects of the environment beyond the immediate situation containing the subject.
>
> *(Bronfenbrenner 1977, p. 514)*

Bronfenbrenner's **ecosystem model** consists of different environmental layers that influence the development of the child: **microsystem**, **mesosystem**, **exosystem** and **macrosystem** (see Figure 1.5). The child is at the centre of all the external factors influencing her development and **socialisation**. The socialisation process is complex. It involves the teaching of rules, attitudes, values and mores representative of the society in which she is nurtured. Socialisation occurs as a consequence of both direct and indirect contact with various informal (i.e., parents and family) and formal (i.e., branches of the law and media) socialising agents. The socialisation of children helps to perpetuate the mentality of their society. Through the socialisation process, parents teach their children how to behave appropriately and, in so doing, develop the moral behaviour that enables them to become a part of society and behave as a model citizen. The interaction of informal and formal socialising agents traverses the microsystem, mesosystem, exosystem and macrosystem. The child is central to Bronfenbrenner's model because the child is born with inherited factors that will influence the way in which he or she engages with the environment. The microsystem is the first environmental layer to envelop the child. It is the home setting by which the child is surrounded. In this home setting the child encounters informal socialising agents such as the parents and family and close peers. This also includes the community and local school establishments. In the case of the parents or carers, bonding enables survival and is imperative for social development (see Chapter 3). The mesosystem provides a space for connections between the different microsystems to occur. It is here where experiences at home can be compared with experiences at school. These can be very different, such that in the home the child behaves submissively and fears an abusing parent whereas at school he or she becomes an aggressor and bullies other children. Here we have two very different social behaviours by the same child as a consequence of two contrasting microsystem experiences. The exosystem has a general influence over the child. For example, there are laws of the land to follow that will impact on the child directly once he or she fails to obey them. Hence individuals come into contact with branches of the legal system such as the police only when they have contravened the law. For the most part, however, the child is only affected by the exosystem when changes to the immediate environment occur as a consequence of work commitments (for example, the father having to work away for long periods will impact on the nature of quality time spent with the child). The macrosystem refers to the cultural context the child experiences. Markus and Kitayama (1991) construed two types of culture: individualistic and collectivist. Whereas individualistic societies focus on autonomy and personal responsibility, collectivist societies emphasise the importance of interdependence between citizens in the formation of social ties to expanded social groups. Bronfenbrenner considers a further environmental layer (not shown in Figure 1.5) called the chronosystem. The chronosystem factors in the influence of sociohistorical circumstances that occur during the life course of the individual. Such sociohistorical events cause transitions in the developmental pathway. We might, for example, ask what effect does civil war have on the developing child? Or what are the effects of a less aversive event such as divorce on the child's future behaviour? Bronfenbrenner and Morris (2006) now refer to the ecological model as a bioecological model as a result of addressing the importance of biological factors in the mix.

2. Sociocultural

When developmental psychologists concentrate on **sociocultural contexts** they tend to emphasise the impact of factors such as gender, ethnicity and culture. Culture arises from long-term interaction between a group of individuals – large or small in size. The key determinate is how long the group has been together. Things that members of a culture have in common include shared values, mores and attitudes, all of which take time to emerge. The group's culture, however, will influence the behaviours of the following generations and creates an overarching footprint of what is socially acceptable behaviour. According to Cole (2006) **cross-cultural studies** provide indices of behaviours that are shared across cultures and those considered to be **culture-specific**. Given that cross-cultural studies consider people from different countries, issues of race and ethnicity often arise. The definitions of race and ethnicity are often distinguished by references to biological and cultural variables. In the case of race it is described using biological traits (i.e., skin and hair colour and facial contours). The physical attributes are embedded in factual details; however, often the psychological

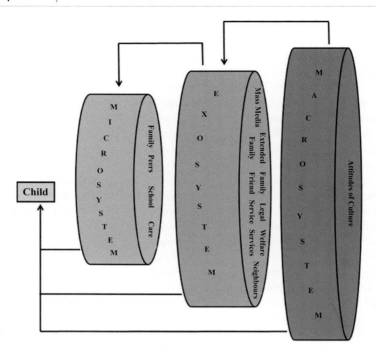

Figure 1.5 Bronfenbrenner's Ecosystem Model. (From Taylor 2016, *Crime and Criminality: A Multidisciplinary Approach*.)

descriptors are masked by inaccurate speculation. These inaccurate speculations can often be used to fuel discrimination and prejudice against specific individuals. The term 'race' therefore receives criticism for not being politically correct, especially when used inappropriately to describe unfounded psychological attributes. Hence, ethnicity is more acceptable because it does not cause offence (Grammarist accessed 30/05/16). Although race and ethnicity are not perfect synonyms, ethnicity is often used instead of race. Whereas ethnicity refers to individuals belonging to a social group, race has often been used to distinguish people on the basis of them having common physical or genetic traits. Currently there is an on-going debate amongst biologists as to the scientific validity of the concept of race. For our purposes here, ethnicity will be used. Ethnicity has its roots in cultural heritage, often describing a range of characteristics originating from a cultural identity such as religion, nationality and language. The term 'ethnic group' has sometimes been used to denote people who share a nationality (even though 'nationality' is a separate social construct from ethnicity) such as Irish Americans – immigrants who travelled initially from Ireland and were then brought up as a family in America. The descendants from such families are American but maintain their Irish roots, and for this reason generally consider themselves as Irish Americans. **Gender** is another important factor studied. Gender prevails in all aspects of our development – our behaviours, identity and how we interact socially with others. Its influence on society is profound and has taken many transitions over the past 50 years. During this period we have seen great changes in the way women in particular are perceived in society. This involves changes in attitude to female competency in the workplace, in the school classroom and in the activities normally associated with men. Attitudes held of women have changed in a largely positive way so that women are seen today, at least in western societies, as equal to their male counterparts.

One of the most important proponents of a sociocultural approach is Russian-born Lev Vygotsky. Vygotsky's sociocultural approach involves the interaction between three factors: the influence of culture, language and the **zone of proximal development**. For Vygotsky biology played an important role in the child's development but it was only a piece of the jig-saw. While biological maturity enables development, it is the child's surrounding environment that helps promote intellectual acumen. As the child is subjected to constant social interaction in the form of verbal and nonverbal communication, the ability to understand potentially complex concepts and acquire new problem-solving skills becomes less daunting. Moreover, according to Vygotsky, it is this social interaction that enables the child to develop cognitively beyond the confines of their biology. Hence, it is the combination of the social culture and language that help to increase a child's cognitive potential. Also, it is the 'zone of proximal development' that increases the cognitive potential of the child. Put simply, the zone of proximal development distinguishes the difference in cognitive ability achieved without social interaction and that acquired when help is at hand. This help or support provided through social interaction is often referred to as **scaffolding**. The notion of scaffolding is often used synonymously with the zone of proximal development. However, it is a concept introduced by American psychologist and educationalist Jerome Bruner first described in a paper by Wood et al. (1976).

Vygotsky highlighted the importance of how people relate to one another and to their cultural environment. In particular he was interested in how language is manipulated within our respective culture and the ways in which children use it. In Table 1.4 the three types of speech used by children is highlighted as a means of communicating thought. Vygotsky viewed thought and language very much as co-existing processes. We will revisit Vygotsky in Chapter 4.

3. Lifespan

The **lifespan perspective** considers development from birth until senescence (and ultimately death). It addresses a host of historical factors that are likely to impact on psychological development, in particular social behaviour, throughout the human lifespan. Baltes (1987) is very much a supporter of this approach to understanding social development and describes how age cohort effects can influence the behaviours of individuals, more so than differential experiences that they might encounter. For example, a group of individuals born in the same year during wartime Britain will experience similar wartime events marking this historical period. Children living in London at this time were under constant threat of airstrikes so many were evacuated to rural areas in England and Wales, and became known as evacuees.

Table 1.4 Vygotsky's stages of language.

Age of child	Stage of speech	Function of speech
0–3 years	Social	Controls how others behave; expresses simple thoughts and emotions.
3–7 years	Egocentric	Controls own behaviour through overt spoken language – considered to be a bridge between social and inner speech.
7+	Inner	A form of self-talk that directs both actions and thought; considered to be a 'stream of consciousness' that is involved in all higher mental functioning.

Some of the evacuees enjoyed their experiences away from London but many felt homesick and misplaced. These childhood experiences were the consequence of an historic event that had repercussions for future social development. As adults, many of these evacuees recounted broadly similar socioemotional experiences resulting from a childhood in wartime Britain.

Another area of lifespan events researched is what makes children resilient to adversity. Masten and her colleagues (2001, 2004, 2006 and 2007) considered aspects of childhood **resilience** and divided the factors promoting resilience into three categories: individual, family and extra-familial context. In the case of individual factors, having self-confidence and high self-esteem as well as intellectual competency will help to cushion the effects of adversity. Additionally, having a talent such as being good at sport will increase popularity and this, in turn, may boost resilience. In addition to sporting prowess, having an easy-going sociable personality will also appeal to others. For some children having a religious faith helps them to overcome negativities in their life. In the case of family, factors such as having a good bond with at least one caring parent helps stave off the negative effects of adversity. The manner in which parents nurture their children can have a big impact on how the child will overcome adversity. This includes authoritative parenting (that which shows warmth and structure) and high expectations (which boosts self-confidence and self-esteem). **Extra-familial factors** involve relationships with those outside of the family – hence caring bonds with non-family adults and social ties with organisations such as the scouts or girl guides can all aid resilience. Having a multitude of these factors is a good thing as the beneficial effects are cumulative.

Dynamic systems perspectives

The **dynamic systems** approach to understanding how the child develops through change over time focuses on how the individual elements of a system work together as part of an integrated system. Advocates of this approach Ross Parke and Mary Gauvain (2009) state that, 'individuals and their achievements can be understood and interpreted within the framework

Plate 1.10 The support of a caring family can help stave off the effects of adversity. (Shutterstock 433319491.)

of the interacting components of the system' (p. 11). Thelen and Smith (1994) generalise the notion of biological organisation to child development. **Biological organisation** is defined by Solomon et al. in 2002 as, 'the hierarchy of complex biological structures and systems that define life using a reductionistic approach' (pp. 9–10). Biological organisation occurs through the process of **self-organisation**. Self-organisation describes the emergence of pattern and order that occurs when components within a complex system interact. A concrete example, such as reaching behaviour shown in infants of 3–4 months of age, might help to put this into context. Reaching out to objects and attempting to grasp them is a motor skill relying on perceptual coordination that all infants appear to develop. Reaching and grasping behaviour is poorly coordinated at first where there are more misses than there are hits, but with practice infants become skilled at grabbing objects.

First examined by Halverson (1933) and later expanded by von Hofsten (1991), over time the reaching behaviour of infants improves in accuracy and smoothness of execution. According to the dynamic systems approach, reaching behaviour involves the interaction of a multitude of component structures and processes. This includes a host of physiological mechanisms relating to skeletal and muscular control, and neural-brain activity enabling visual acuity. These components are in constant change as the infant ages – but not all components change at the same rate. Thelen et al. (1996) addressed the question of what controls the differences in rate of change of the different components by using a design that measured reaching behaviour. Four infants' reaching as well as non-reaching movements were observed on a weekly basis over a period of three to thirty weeks. A multitude of measurements relating to reaching behaviour was considered – including the coordination of the arms, patterns of muscular activity, force used to move joints, posturing and the infant's motor ability. The infants were presented with objects to reach each week and their transitional movement from non-reaching to reaching was recorded. Thelen and co-workers concluded that the action of reaching is a product of a dynamic system. They suggest the pattern recognition of objects occurs as a consequence of how our brain acquires motor control. This means that pattern recognition is a slave to motor coordination. The dynamic systems approach also incorporates the notion of the **epigenetic landscape**.

Plate 1.11 Baby demonstrating motor coordination involved in reaching for an apple. (Shutterstock 21969766.)

4. Epigenetic landscape

Reference to the epigenetic landscape was first introduced by Conrad Waddington (1957) as a symbolic representation of how our genes and the environment conspire to determine the structure and function of brain cells and ultimately our behaviour. In Figure 1.6 a landscape is depicted consisting of a valley that subdivides a number of times – hence creating a multitude of valley pathways. Waddington makes the case that if a ball is placed at the top of the valley and is allowed to roll there is a number of possible pathways it might take. The pathway taken is synonymous with the developmental trajectory adopted by the developing child. He argued that different pathways represent diverse environmental conditions. These diverse environmental conditions ultimately influence the nature of development experienced by the child. Waddington, however, alluded to the self-stabilising nature of development whereby the different pathways travelling down the landscape will eventually converge to the original path. This means that development will proceed in a universal fashion despite the initial perturbations experienced by the child.

Waddington (1977) referred to the epigenetic landscape as an 'attractor landscape'. This has important ramifications for what happens under adverse environmental conditions. He claimed that if we tried to change the epigenetic landscape, the system will resist and bounce back to restore itself to its former structure. Furthermore, 'the system resists some types of changes more than others, or restores itself more quickly after changes in some directions than others' (Waddington, 1977, p. 113). This means that, although environmental conditions can influence the ball's trajectory, the trajectory taken is constrained by the epigenetic landscape. Hence, from infancy onwards, the structure of the epigenetic landscape is partially influenced by learning but this learning is constrained by the parameters of the (genetically influenced) epigenetic topography present at the time. Such constraints direct development towards a universal blueprint despite differential learning experiences and extreme forms of environmental conditions.

Ethological and evolutionary perspective

Charles Darwin introduced the world to his evolutionary theory in *On the Origin of Species* in 1859. In the *Origin of Species* Darwin considered behaviour to change over time as a

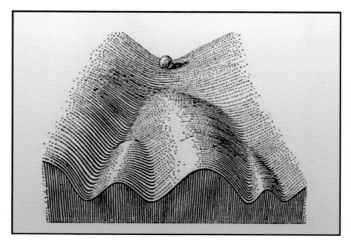

Figure 1.6 Epigenetic landscape. (Reproduced with permission.)

consequence of the adaptive or survival and reproductive value the behaviour performed has for the **organism**; a process that he called **natural selection**. In this book and in later publications Darwin made it clear that he also saw natural selection as operating on our own species to alter internal states and overt behaviour (Darwin 1859, 1871, 1872). Hence one approach to understanding social behaviour in children is to view responses as Darwinian adaptations to the ecosystem. In more concrete terms the ecosystem might include the playground where the child operates. The social behaviours exhibited in the playground are a consequence of an interaction between the child's biological temperament and the needs posited by the playground environment. During the 20th century a number of approaches were developed that related development to evolutionary pressures. These include the ethological approach and evolutionary psychology. We now examine each in turn.

Ethological perspective

The **ethological perspective** 'holds that behavior must be viewed and understood as occurring in a particular context and as having adaptive or survival value' (Parke and Gauvain 2009, p. 16). Ethology is commonly associated with the observation of animals in their natural habitats; this, however, has now extended to observing infants and children and making sense of their behaviour in the context of an adaptive value (**human ethology**). One major contribution of ethology to the understanding of infant behaviour is imprinting. It was Konrad Lorenz (e.g., 1965) who developed the concept of imprinting, which he considered to be an early attachment process. Lorenz noted that many animals were **precocial**, meaning they were born in a relatively mature state, and that they would enter a critical (or sensitive) period after birth during which they rapidly learned the visual characteristics of their mother. These animals became imprinted on their mother as an adaptive process enabling them to survive. Lorenz even managed to have greylag geese imprint on him – they would follow him everywhere as he was the 'maternal figure' who would ensure their survival.

Ethologists argue that a similar innate process occurs in human infants. By imprinting on the mother (or caregiver) the infant is boosting its chances of survival as recognising her

Plate 1.12 Young boy with baby chick. (Shutterstock 135994952.)

helps to establish a bond or attachment (see Chapter 3). The process of imprinting in infants is manifested in the guise of face recognition, which can be conceived of as a species-specific behaviour; a behaviour that is typically performed by humans as a means of forming attachments with others. We, as humans, are extremely good at recognising faces, which is believed to be possible through an innate ability arising from two face recognition mechanisms: **conspec** and **conlern** (Johnson and Morton 1991). Conspec is a (arguably innate) rudimentary form of face identification and recognition that is important to the infant. This mechanism enables the infant to identify what a human face looks like, and is embellished further through conlern (which fine-tunes the primitive representation of the face developed by conspec). Imprinting therefore has been influential in developing a theory of attachment between caregiver and infant (discussed in more detail in Chapter 3). Species-specific behaviour is important in other ways to the development of the child such as the expression and understanding of emotions. Following Darwin's (1872) original suggestion, Ekman and Friesen (1975) identified six universal emotions that are expressed in the same way cross-culturally: happiness, sadness, fear, anger, surprise and disgust (see Figure 1.7 for posed examples). New-borns arguably show two emotional states designed to aid survival: approach and avoid. As their brain matures and through interacting with the environment these states expand and develop into the six universal emotions (and later into **secondary emotions** that develop out of combinations of these six). Smiling and crying have biological origins that are initiated to act as 'elicitors' of parental behaviour. Parents will respond to a crying baby as the crying causes a state of distress – something intended (albeit not consciously) on the baby's part – resulting in the parents attending to their baby's needs.

Evolutionary perspective

Due, in part, to developments in human ethology, during the late 1980s and early 1990s a new field began to emerge – **evolutionary psychology**. Evolutionary psychology is a relatively new sub-discipline that relates modern-day internal states and behaviour patterns to the pressures our ancient ancestors faced during our evolutionary history. Evolutionary psychologists derive and test hypotheses based around the Darwinian concepts of natural selection ('survival of the fittest') and **sexual selection** ('survival of the sexiest' – see Box 1.4).

Importantly, such hypotheses include developmental ones that, via **life history theory** (LHT), allow evolutionary psychologists to consider each stage of life as a part of a bundle of adaptations. Life history theory concerns the way that organisms allocate time and resources to different activities (such as feeding, learning and reproduction) throughout the lifespan in an adaptive manner (Workman and Reader 2014). An example of the adaptive nature of development is the time course for various childhood fear responses (see Chapter 3). Some experts relate specific fear responses to children's abilities to defend themselves at various ages during our evolutionary past (Field and Workman 2008). Toddlers, who are totally dependent on their parents to protect them, tend to fear changes in the environment and their parents being away. This form of anxiety makes perfect evolutionary sense because there is very little they can do about it. Between the ages of three to six animal fears become more prominent. Again this makes sense since they are becoming more mobile and more autonomous. At this age they are able to wander a little from their parents and might (in our evolutionary past and occasionally today) have come into contact with dangerous animals. But since they are unable to defend themselves at this age against a range of predators it makes sense for them to be anxious about contact with animals. When they are a little older still and physically bigger, the argument goes, they will become less worried about things like animals as they are better able to fend for themselves. At this

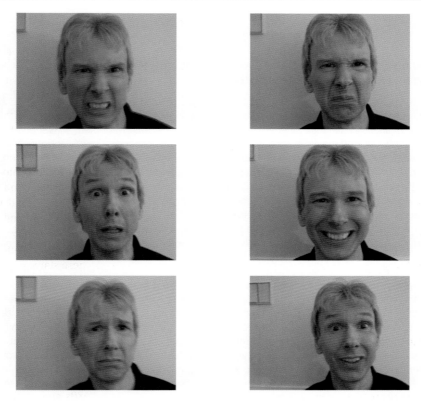

Figure 1.7 Portrayal of the six universal facial expressions of emotion. (From Workman and Reader 2015.)

point things like social cues, such as being outcast from their group, begin to take over since these become more important as they find their role in society. Hence, evolutionary psychologists argue that children have different **hot spots** for fear-provoking stimuli at different stages in their life histories because natural selection has selected these during the evolutionary history of our species.

Most experts trace the development of evolutionary psychology back to the publication of *The Adapted Mind* by Jerome Barkow, Leda Cosmides and John Tooby in 1992. The field of developmental evolutionary psychology, however, had to wait until the 21st century, when David Geary and David Bjorklund wrote an article simply called 'Evolutionary developmental psychology' for the journal *Child Development* in 2000. They suggested that 'A complete understanding of human social and cognitive development . . . requires an understanding of human evolution . . . To argue otherwise is to ignore the vast empirical literature supporting Darwin's (1959) theory of evolution and to deny the core theoretical foundation of the biological sciences' (Geary and Bjorklund 2000, p. 63).

In addition to childhood fear responses (and many other behaviours), evolutionary psychologists have also examined the ability of children to develop an understanding of the internal states and intentions of others. This is known as 'mind reading' or, more scientifically, developing a theory of mind (ToM) (Wimmer and Perner 1983; see Chapter 5).

Box 1.4   Natural and sexual selection

Darwin's two prime movers of evolutionary change – natural selection and sexual selection

Most people have heard of natural selection and have a broad idea of what the term means – broadly speaking 'survival of the fittest'. More technically, it is the differential survival of individuals due to differences in their inherited characteristics in a given environment. Fewer people are aware, however, of Darwin's second principle of evolutionary change – sexual selection. Sexual selection is the concept of characteristics being passed on to future generations because they are attractive to the opposite sex or because they help an individual to compete for access to the opposite sex. In a sense sexual selection is like natural selection but instead of 'nature' the opposite sex does the selecting. Whereas natural selection drives the two sexes in the same direction (because things like anti-predator adaptations and the ability to locate and gather appropriate nutrition work as well for both males and females) sexual selection drives the sexes apart.

This is because reproduction generally involves different abilities in the sexes. Think about it. Females, in the case of birds, lay eggs and, in the case of mammals, have internal gestation followed by lactation. Males, in contrast, need to impress females that they are worthy of fertilising their eggs by various means (such as looking striking or showing aggression to other males). So females produce signs of fertility whereas males show signs that they can compete for female attention. In some species sexual selection has led to huge differences between the sexes (think of deer and elephant seals) whereas in other species differences are very small (think of robins). Darwin called the degree of difference due to sexual selection **sexual dimorphism**. One question that has vexed evolutionary psychologists is to what extent are men and women different (and to a lesser extent boys and girls)? To put it another way, how much of a role did sexual selection play in human evolution, and just how sexually dimorphic are we? These are questions we will return to in Chapters 8, 11 and 12.

In typically developing children, a theory of mind begins to emerge around four years of age when they begin to attribute mental states to others – states that they realise might involve others holding different beliefs, intentions and desires to themselves. Developing a theory of mind means that the child is then able to predict (and manipulate) the social behaviour of others. Without this ability complex human social interaction would be impossible. As we will see in later chapters, deficits in the development of ToM have been linked to a number of disorders related to social development such as autism spectrum disorder and attention deficit hyperactivity disorder.

Summary

- Theories differ in the emphasis of themes such as biological or environmental explanations; continuous or discontinuous processes and individual or contextual factors. Biological or environmental themes address the nature–nurture divide. Development arises as a consequence of our evolution and our genotype (a product of evolutionary forces), which ensure an orderly and universal growth and development. Such biologically orientated developmentalists consider nature–nurture as a bi-directional interaction.

- Developmentalists are interested in brain development and consider electrochemical connections and hormonal activity – activity that is, however, often contingent on early experience. Neurotransmitters influence brain activity ultimately affecting our behaviour. Hormones play an important role in social behaviour. Our genes can have three different types of influence: passive, active and evocative effects. Behavioural geneticists focus on the relationship between our genes and the environment by considering identical and fraternal twins and adoptees living in shared and non-shared environments.
- Continuity versus discontinuity has been reflected in different theoretical approaches. Piaget theorised that children progress through stages in an ordered fashion. When a child progresses from one stage to the next there is a major developmental surge suggesting a discontinuous progression. For those supporting an information-processing approach progression is continuous.
- Individual and contextual themes are encapsulated in Bronfenbrenner's Ecological Theory. The contribution of the child's individual traits to an essentially social environment is of importance. Other theorists take a primarily individual stance such as the effect of the child's biological or psychological make-up on coping with high risk situations – in other words their resilience. Contextual or cultural factors include, for example, the influence of the family home and the school environment on the child's social development.
- The structural–organismic approach has been used by very different theorists: Sigmund Freud, Erik Erikson and Jean Piaget. While Freud focused on emotions and personality through notions of the id, ego and superego, Piaget considered the different stages of cognitive development: both embracing a biological stance in their theorising.
- The learning perspectives recognise the importance of stimulus–response associations. Classical conditioning explains how associative learning takes place via simple connections between a stimulus and a biological response. Operant conditioning explains how rewarding consequences increase the likelihood of behaviour repetition whereas punishment results in avoidance. In observational learning or modelling behaviour the child observes and copies the behaviours performed by others. Information processing theory considers different components of a system processing and passing information on to other components.
- Contextual perspectives contain at least three approaches: ecological, sociocultural and lifespan. Bronfenbrenner is the forerunner of the ecological model. He introduced this model as a multi-layered series of environmental factors surrounding the developing child. The child contributes to development via the genotype, which interacts with the multitude of environmental factors such as the family, school and the media. The more distant macrosystem impacts on the child's values, attitudes and mores learnt through the process of socialisation.
- Sociocultural approaches emphasise the impact of gender, ethnicity and culture on the way we perceive and classify ourselves. This, in turn, influences our behavioural development. There are biological trait dimensions such as hair colour that are definitive; however, psychological descriptors can be misleading if based on stereotypes (i.e., false race and gender stereotypes).

(continued)

(continued)

- Lifespan perspectives include historical factors that are likely to affect a group of people who share a common timeline. Evacuees, for example, who were brought up in the countryside during the Second World War share this historical experience. Such shared experiences are likely to have influenced their development in broadly similar ways.
- Dynamic systems perspectives have a biological emphasis. These approach development as a consequence of different systems interacting as an integrated whole. Change occurs over time as these systems mature. Biological organisation occurs through the process of self-organisation where patterns and order emerge as the various components of the system interact. Epigenetic landscapes describe how development can take different pathways but will ultimately rectify its trajectory to a universal one.
- The ethological approach considers behaviour as having a survival factor. Imprinting behaviour for humans occurs in face recognition ability through processes of conspec and conlern. Face recognition of the caregiver is essential for survival as it helps to ensure an attachment bond, which helps to ensure that all provisions necessary to thrive are likely to be provided.
- Evolutionary psychology derived from Darwinian concepts of natural selection and sexual selection explain the ultimate reasons for why we behave the way we do. Developments in evolutionary theory have allowed evolutionary psychologists to propose functional explanations for patterns of human social development. Evolutionary psychologists see the development of ToM as an adaptation that aided survival during our ancestral past.

Questions for discussion

1. In what way can classical and operant conditioning be used to understand how we develop social skills?
2. The theoretical approaches of Freud and Piaget are vastly different and yet they are considered under the structural–organismic perspective. In what ways are these theoretical approaches similar? In what ways do these theoretical approaches differ?
3. Behavioural geneticists suggest that the genetic contribution to personality differences between individuals is between 40 and 50 per cent. What does this mean? Can you perceive any problems with the methods outlined for estimating the genetic contribution to differences between individuals?
4. Bronfenbrenner's ecosystem model describes how the child's genes interact with the environment. Critically evaluate how Bronfenbrenner's model provides us with a nature–nurture account of development.
5. Evolutionary psychology introduces Darwinian terms such as sexual selection. Critically examine how sexual selection can be used to describe the social behaviours of teenagers.
6. Critically examine how the different theoretical approaches can be effectively integrated.

Further reading

If you are interested in exploring how the development of social skills is influenced by an integrated system of direct and indirect socialising agents in more detail, look at:

- Bronfenbrenner, U. (1979). *The Ecology of Human Development.* Cambridge, MA: Harvard University Press.

If you are interested in understanding a modern account of how the epigenetic landscape is formed in more detail, look at:

- Goldberg, A.D., Allis, C.D. and Bernstein, E. (2007). Epigenetics: a landscape takes shape. *Cell,* 128, 635–8.

If you are interested in exploring the concepts and theories as well as their historical roots and philosophical stances in more detail, look at:

- Lerner, R. (2015). *Concepts and Theories of Human Development.* Abingdon: Routledge.

If you are interested in an evaluation of the strengths and weaknesses of the different developmental theories in more detail, look at:

- Miller, P.T. (2016). *Theories of Developmental Psychology* (6th Edn). New York: Worth Publishers.

NOTES

1 Structuralism, as first described by German-born Wilhelm Wundt in his book *Principles of Physiological Psychology* in 1873–4, helped establish psychology as a science. Wundt established the first psychological laboratory where he designed experiments to identify the basic elements residing within the structures of the conscious mind. He believed that these basic elements could be accessed through subjective reporting and self-awareness (i.e., introspection).

2 Unlike Wundt, Michel Foucault believed that there are no underlying structures to explain human behaviour, and nor can introspection be used as an objective science method – it simply is not possible to divorce oneself from the situation of which one's narrative is a part. Instead, the method of studying human discourse should be undertaken using the process of deconstruction. Put simply, deconstruction demonstrates that words can only refer to other words and that statements made undermine their true meanings.

Contents

Introduction   39

Representative sampling   41

Methods of collecting data   44

Research designs   59

Studying change over a time span   65

Ethical research in developmental psychology   66

Summary   68

Chapter 2

Research methods in social development

What this chapter will teach you

- The importance of studying a representative sample.
- Methods of collecting data including: longitudinal studies, surveys, observational and self-report studies, research designs including correlational methods and experiments.
- The relative merits of lab verses field experiments.
- The importance of ethical considerations in developmental studies.

INTRODUCTION

Social developmentalists are interested in development throughout the lifespan, which means that the young as well as the old are studied. While research methods are generic in that they can be used by psychologists per se, developmental psychologists often have to devise specialised techniques enabling, for example, babies and infants to be observed and tested. It is important to realise that developmentalists make use of both quantitative (number crunching and analysis of the significance of such data) and qualitative (gaining insight into aspects of behaviour via observation, interview and focus groups) research methods in order to progress our understanding of child development. In this way the research methods and designs used by developmental psychologists are modified to accommodate the needs of their participants. Observation techniques using simple testing conditions were developed by researchers such as Jean Piaget. Piaget (1960), a master at observing infants and young children, made use of quite simple experiments to explore social and cognitive development. An example of this was hiding a watch while an infant observed him doing this and then waiting to see if the infant looked in the direction of where the watch was hidden or simply looked away – leading him to claim that, for children of this age, 'out of sight means out of mind'. Later developmentalists such as Rene Baillargeon (1987) provided a more systematic method of observing babies using the habituation–dishabituation paradigm (see Box 2.1).

Depending on the research methodology adopted, findings could vary enough to influence their interpretation as was found in the case of Piaget versus Baillargeon in Box 2.1. It is therefore important to be familiar with the diversity of methodological approaches available to developmental psychologists. There are many facets to research methodology that will be explained in this chapter but, as we are interested in the early stages of lifespan development such as infancy, childhood and adolescence, it makes sense to begin by increasing our awareness of the importance of sampling used by developmental psychologists.

Box 2.1   Baillargeon found that infants understand how objects 'behave' earlier than Piaget suggested

Habituation–dishabituation is sometimes referred to as the looking paradigm, whereby infants only look at objects for as long as they are interested in them. When they disengage from looking at an object then this suggests that they are bored (habituated) with it. When, however, it is altered in a way that makes them re-look at it then they are said to be disinhibited. Baillargeon adapted this habituation–dishabituation paradigm to examine what it is that infants understand and know about the way objects behave physically. She asked, for example, if an object fails to fall to the floor given it is in mid-air adjacent to a surface top, then will infants look longer at the incongruent physical behaviour of the object? Baillargeon found that they did, and not just for this example but for many others. One example was the 'short and tall rabbit' scenario where infants were shown a familiarisation trial of a short and tall rabbit 'walking' behind a wall. They were hidden by the wall until they re-appeared past the wall. In the test condition, there was a block taken out of the wall. In this case the short rabbit was too short to be seen passing behind the wall unlike the tall rabbit that was tall enough to be seen walking behind the wall (where the missing block created a window). In the possible event the short rabbit remained unseen until re-appearing past the wall. In the impossible event the tall rabbit remained unseen until re-appearing past the wall, despite there now being a 'window' (see Figure 2.1). Infants (five to six months and one day old) looked longer at the impossible event, suggesting that what they observed was unexpected. This new approach to studying infant understanding of the physical attributes of objects produced different results to Piaget's earlier studies. Baillargeon's findings suggest that infants can understand the physical attributes of objects at a much earlier age than Piaget had predicted. Through adopting the habituation–dishabituation method, Baillargeon was able to demonstrate that infants were more capable of understanding the relationship between objects and how they react in the physical world. Developmentalists have used Piaget's theory of cognitive development as a framework for researching the age at which infants understand facets of their environment but, in doing so, many have modified his methodology leading to modifications in our understanding of infant competencies. Hence researching old or new phenomenon stimulates further developments in the field and can initiate a paradigm shift in the way lifespan psychology is considered.

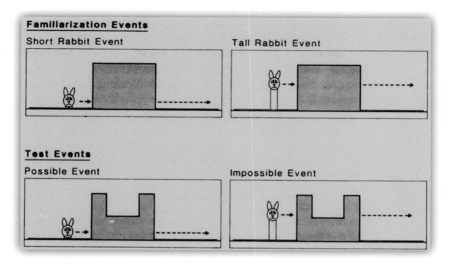

Figure 2.1 Schematic representation of the familiarisation and test events of the short and tall rabbit scenarios. (Used with permission: Baillargeon and Graber 1987.)

REPRESENTATIVE SAMPLING

In order to further our knowledge of social development it is important that researchers in the field conduct reliable and valid research. This involves studying participants who are of interest and relevance to the developmental phenomenon under investigation. So, for example, if developmental psychologists want to know how young toddlers learn new words, then it is important to study word acquisition in toddlers and not children who have started school. With the introduction of the school environment new variables influencing word acquisition have been introduced into the equation and the impact of age becomes attenuated. Therefore, the sample of participants used is of importance, especially in developmental research. The sample has to be representative of the participants being studied and this is closely associated with what is being investigated. Furthermore, a **representative sample** is a population that resembles the larger population about which data are being gathered. In developmental psychology participants of all ages are studied at any point during the lifespan. There are, however, specific developmental periods during the lifespan that might be of interest to researchers in the field, and as these are age-dependent, studying a representative sample of participants will improve the validity of the findings.

Striano (2016) provides an example of one way of sampling infants for social monitoring behaviour (i.e., paying joint attention with another person). Striano begins by outlining an aim of the study: 'to establish the development and function of joint attention/social monitoring skills in the child's first year' (2016, p. 27). In the case of the hypothesis she provides the following, 'By as early as 3–4 months of age, infants will show sensitivity to joint attention skills and use these cues to learn' (2016, p. 27). The aim and hypothesis determine who should be tested and at what age range. It is obvious that the youngest infant has to be at least three months old but, to ensure that there is no social monitoring occurring prior to this age, including two-month-old infants makes for a superior sampling approach. Furthermore, to test that these infants will use the acquired cues for learning, the timeframe needs to be

Table 2.1 Different types of sampling method.

Random sampling	Anyone in the target population has an equal chance of selection. Selection can be through pulling a name out of a hat or by computer generation. This method eliminates sampling bias.
Stratified sampling	In this case the researcher identifies different 'types of individual' comprising the target population (e.g., age, gender and ethnicity). To be fully representative the correct proportion of each type of individual comprising the target population needs to be calculated. This ensures that each type of individual has fair proportionate representation. This method is time-consuming and difficult to implement but will ensure a representative sample.
Opportunistic sampling	This method enables individuals from the target population to volunteer as participants. This can be achieved through asking individuals to participate and they can decide if it is convenient to do so. Although a quick and easy method, it cannot always be guaranteed that the sample is bias free.
Systematic sampling	In this case participants are selected in an orderly or logical way from a target population. This can be achieved by selecting the nth participant from a list of names. If the sample is to consist of 100 participants from a sports club of 1,000 children, then every 10th name would be selected. Although difficult to achieve due to time and effort, this method should ensure a fully representative sample.

extended beyond the acquisition of social monitoring. Striano suggests the sample should include infants of two months old and to study them for two years. Note that studying infants of this age raises a whole series of ethical issues that we will return to later in this chapter. Developmental psychologists use a range of sampling methods to obtain a representative sample (see Table 2.1).

Given that researchers strive to obtain representative sampling, there are different ways in which to approach this. One method of gathering data is to make use of **surveys**. Surveys are often conducted at national level to gain a representative sample of the population of interest. A UK-based example of this is The Avon Longitudinal Study of Parents and Children (ALSPAC, used to be Pregnancy and Childhood) (Golding et al. 2001; see Box 2.2). National surveys can also help to provide information about issues concerning development. In the US the National Longitudinal Survey of Youth (NLSY) was initiated in 1979 to examine the impact of family factors (e.g., working mothers), the school environment (e.g., standards) and the quality of the community on children and their family. Participants ranging in age from 14 to 22 years were drawn from 235 geographical areas spreading across the US. This sampling method enabled conclusions to be generalised to this age range across different states of the US. Some of the developmental factors assessed included memory, maths and reading; temperament and self-confidence; behaviour problems and risk taking; and physical health measurements. Findings were based on reports made by the mother using, for example, the Behaviour Problems Index (BPI). A host of findings arise from the NLSY that have been used by developmental psychologists to evaluate the wellbeing of the children born as of 31 December 1978.

Box 2.2   The Avon Longitudinal Study of Parents and Children

In this survey 14,500 families in the Avon area have been studied since 1991/1992. Mothers who were pregnant at the time were key to the study as the main aim was to find ways of improving the health of future generations. Improving the health of future generations was based on discoveries made about the developing foetus and the journey throughout its lifespan (currently in early adulthood). The collection of data started before the children were even born. This longitudinal study has been extended and continues to follow the individuals who are now in their twenties. Some of these children (now adults) are even parents themselves. This survey is based in Bristol, hosted by the University of Bristol, and called locally 'Children of the 90s'. It has resulted in many publications and important recommendations and research findings concerning child development and parenting. The study per se has adopted multiple methods but the major approach involves the administration of surveys at particular time points (usually twice a year). Section A of the survey questionnaire focuses on aspects of school (e.g., questions concerning their experiences and opinions of schooling) that children aged eight years answered using a tick-box exercise from a choice of four possible answers (see Figure 2.2). Various surveys (i.e., questionnaires) in the study were completed by multiple respondents including parents, teachers and the children themselves. Questionnaires were also completed by partners of the main caregiver. This provided researchers with multiple viewpoints on particular issues, and enabled them to look at both child and parental factors involved in specific aspects of child development (e.g., impact of maternal anxiety in pregnancy and the child's likelihood of developing asthma).

A representative sample of participants from the general population for inclusion in the ALSPAC study meant that there was a range of individuals from birth until their mid-twenties. This enabled researchers at Bristol University to discover possible factors influencing the wellbeing of the participants. As researchers were interested in every aspect of development concerning these children born in 1991/2, it meant that the mothers and details concerning their pregnancy were important. As children do not develop in an insular world, researchers rightly decided to include proximate factors such as the immediate environment impacting on development – hence the inclusion of parents/family and school teachers in their sampling. As the children became adults and had jobs, this extended to include experiences in the workplace. Numerous findings suggest that mothers have an impact on the child's development. For example, a link was found between mothers eating seafood when pregnant and higher intelligence and reduced problematic behaviour in their offspring. Children develop over many years, which is why the study is known as 'longitudinal'. We will return to longitudinal studies later when discussing methods used to explore changes in development over time (i.e., cross-sectional, sequential and longitudinal methods).

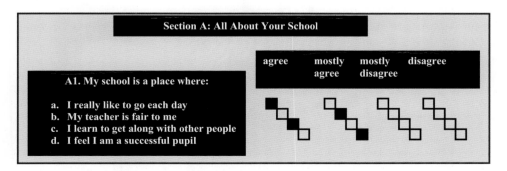

Figure 2.2 Example of the question format used in the ALSPAC.

Most countries will have various national-survey-based studies that can inform us about worldwide patterns in development and cultural differences, especially if these studies are compared using **meta-analysis**. Furthermore, collaborative research with other nations (i.e., international studies) can also provide such information. As long as the factors studied across the different surveys are consistent (i.e., looking at the same age group, studying effects of schooling on development or investigating the impact of siblings on development), then reliable and valid comparisons can be made. This is essentially what studies using a meta-analysis approach do – they compare studies that have been conducted separately but which focus on similar variables such as age or gender or level of communication. When using a meta-analysis approach, valid sampling techniques used in the different studies compared become very important. As we can see, the correct use of sampling technique in developmental psychology is very important. The survey method illustrates this quite clearly. In the next section we will explore the different ways of collecting data as used by developmental psychologists, continuing with the survey approach.

METHODS OF COLLECTING DATA

The survey

The survey approach to collecting data often involves the use of **questionnaires**, **self-reporting** and **reports by others** about the individual concerned, and highly **structured interviews** that follow a questionnaire format but are read out loud to the participant. The **focus group** is often considered to be a type of in-depth interview conducted within a group setting. It is worth noting that the survey method can be used to gather both quantitative and qualitative information (see earlier). The survey method relies predominantly on the distribution of questionnaires, simply because this is an easy way of attaining an abundance of data about the same issue(s). Under these circumstances the questions are uniformly presented to a representative sample of individuals. In developmental psychology, this is likely to be administered to parents and teachers when the children are very young.

Plate 2.1 Child filling in a questionnaire while being supervised by his dad. (Shutterstock 157279385.)

Questionnaires can be used in clinical assessment geared towards a more individual level to assess functioning of a particular child or adolescent. They can also be used with specific groups of children and adolescents (e.g., those with high levels of depression, maladaptive behaviour or poor physical functioning). Such questionnaires are often scored and compared with 'normative' samples. These are samples of 'healthy' children who have completed the same questionnaires and provided with a score to give an idea of what 'normal' functioning is.

Questionnaires are typically more focused on a particular topic than surveys and contain **subscales**. These are smaller sub-sections of the questionnaire that focus on separate yet related aspects of the phenomenon under study. The Spence Children's Anxiety Scale (SCAS) is an example of an Australian questionnaire designed to examine different types of anxiety experienced by children and adolescents (Spence et al. 2003; see Box 2.3).

Box 2.3   The Spence Children's Anxiety Scale (SCAS)

The questionnaire provides an overall anxiety score but also includes six smaller subscales looking at specific types of anxiety such as separation anxiety. As a means of providing normative scores on the SCAS, the questionnaire was administered to healthy girls and boys – this provides an index of how children considered as 'normal' might score. Normative scores help developmental psychologists evaluate individual children by comparing their scores with the norm and to assess the degree to which they differ from this.

Questionnaires are often used within a clinical context to identify the following behaviours:

- adaptive and maladaptive;
- generalised anxiety – anxiety about everything;
- separation anxiety – anxiety induced by the possibility of separation usually from the caregiver;
- physical injury fears – concerns about possible injury due to risk taking or over the possible longevity of the effects of long-term injury;
- social phobia – anxiety induced by the possibility of having to network with others;
- panic and agoraphobia – anxiety of having a panic attack outside of the home;
- obsessive compulsive – anxiety and distress caused by having repetitive thoughts that can be believed to cause harm to others; anxiety caused by the failure to carry out (repetitive) behaviours such as hand-washing or checking.

Self-reports and reports by others

Self-reports are an effective way of obtaining information from the person in question, but fall short when the child of interest is preverbal. This method can be used effectively even when the child has just started developing language – in fact it is useful in studying how language is used in play. The narrative provided in play can be considered a form of self-reporting about the play object. The child might, for example, refer to teddy in play as a person who is preparing dinner. Although in play, this provides researchers with an index of how the child is interpreting the play situation – a self-documentation of the current play event. Generally, however, self-reporting is reserved for children who are confident at using language to communicate. The objective of self-reporting is to enable individuals to provide information about themselves by answering set questions. Cummings et al. (2000) used the self-report method to attain information about how a child feels about another person and a specific negative family experience encountered. By asking children questions about their

Plate 2.2 Separation anxiety (clinging to mother). (Shutterstock 125389001.)

feelings and how they cope during episodes of parental conflict, Cummings et al. found that these children were at risk of developing poor interpersonal skills and low social competence. They argued that obtaining detailed information of this nature would be difficult using other methods of investigation.

Encouraging family members, friends and teachers (see Box 2.4) to communicate what they know about a child can provide useful information. This information is usually based on observations about the child in question across many different situations and over a period of time. The problem with this approach, however, is the fallibility of the memory retrieval process and interfering biases of the observers. Parents, for example, can overestimate the abilities of their children because of their own expectations, which is why researchers, such as Patterson (1996), create interview techniques encouraging more accuracy of event recollection. Asking parents to recall recent events; contacting parents daily at the end of the day; a tick-list exercise of specific behaviours (e.g., tantrum) shown by their child in the last 24 hours; and keeping an ongoing structured diary of their child's behavioural repertoire (Hetherington 1991) are accurate measures for reporting observations of their child.

Box 2.4   Teachers' perceptions of the child

Rubin et al. (2006) asked teachers to rate children in their classroom by applying specific dimensions such as the sociability of the child in the classroom and playground, and how dependable and popular the child is. These dimensions are also distributed to all class members as an exercise to see how peers are rated by other peers. The questions are simple but help to provide a socio-metric profile of all the children. For example, one question might be 'who I like to play with the most' or 'who my best friend is'. All the ratings from the teacher and children are combined to formulate each child's social status within the class.

Interviews

While surveys generally involve the administration of questionnaires, conducting **interviews** can also be a part of the survey approach. The difference between the two methods is that a questionnaire is structured by having a set of questions geared towards obtaining peoples' self-reported attitudes. This has its problems given that what people say and do can be incongruent. People like to be seen as behaving in a socially acceptable manner and so portray this by espousing attitudes and opinions in keeping with social expectations (Best and Kahn 2006). In the case of interviews, with face-to-face interaction and direct requests for information, it is more difficult for interviewees to provide false information. Interviews can be unstructured so that questions require extended responses or they can be structured and address specific issues. We will return to interview techniques as a method in its own right later in this chapter. The use of interviews in attaining information from children about their understanding of specific issues overlaps with the self-report approach. Box 2.5 provides an example of how asking children about their understanding of transgressive behaviour can provide enlightening and positive findings.

Plate 2.3 Girl being interviewed with mum present. (Shutterstock 376087585.)

Box 2.5   Children understand wrongness

Researchers like Smetana (1981) showed children of 3–4 years of age to be morally quite astute. She found that they were sensitive to the differences between what constitutes a conventional transgression and a moral transgression. Conventional transgressions involve violations of the rules, some of which are arbitrary such as a household rule that there is no speaking when the news is on television. More common household rules might include keeping one's bedroom tidy by putting toys away into the cupboard. Moral transgressions, however, have serious consequences for others and break the moral code. This often involves causing harm to others as is the case in behaving aggressively. Smetana found that the 3–4 year olds described hitting another child as very bad because it involves hurting them. In the case of a conventional transgression they described putting toys in the wrong place as 'a little bad'. In another study, Davidson et al. (1983) asked children to justify what makes a moral rule. The children were good at judging the seriousness of another's actions. They mentioned harm and distress caused to others when a moral transgression occurs but failed to do so when dealing with conventional rules. Therefore, asking for information from young children can produce valuable insight into their level of understanding of what are, potentially, complex concepts.

The focus group is an example of an in-depth interview conducted using a group of individuals who meet to discuss a specified topic. The focus of attention is the interactive quality between the participants themselves and how their responses, expressed ideas and comments impact on the counter-responses made. This method typically generates qualitative data in the form of discourse transcription. Hill et al. (1996) had 12 focus groups with six children in each where some groups were mixed and some were single-sex groups. This was to ensure that certain issues were more likely to be raised in a mixed-sex group whereas others were more likely to be raised in a single-sex group. The age range was 5 to 12 years. The topic considered revolved around emotional needs and well-being. Using the focus-group method allowed children to discuss openly what they felt was important to them, such as the emotional impact of losing friends, having nightmares and anxiety concerning parental separation. Most of the children in this study expressed how happy they felt but many wished that adults would listen to them more often.

Observation

Observational methods play a large part in developmental research and are often referred to as direct observation. Jean Piaget, for example, observed his own children's behaviours, which he used to inform his theory of cognitive development. When using observational methods it is important to know what to observe in advance so that preparation can be made concerning which recording technique is most appropriate. Decisions concerning the level of observational detail required and the frequency of recording necessary need to be made before the study begins (Bakeman and Gottman 1997). As pointed out by Graziano and Raulin (2007), the process of scientific observation requires specific skills such as attending to the behaviours observed so as not to miss anything relevant, to know what is important to consider and to follow the behaviours that are constantly changing within a dynamic situation. This is one reason why it is important to be systematic in the way observations are made (McBurney and White 2007). Questions such as 'who', 'where', 'when' and 'how' need to be considered as part of the preparation process. According to Best and Kahn (2006), when we observe in a scientific way, extraneous factors influencing behaviour need to be controlled so that attention is focused on factors at the centre of the study. This type of observation is normally conducted in a laboratory where complex real-life interfering factors can be removed. Even laboratory-based observation, however, has drawbacks. It can be unnatural, causing contrived behaviour; can create an unrepresentative sample as individuals are drawn from volunteers; can induce stress among participants, hence questioning whether the situation created is an ethical one and participants unfamiliar with a university environment can feel intimidated.

Observational methods have thus been criticised for causing participants to behave unnaturally and perhaps distort aspects of their behaviour. Parents have even been accused of inhibiting their own negative behaviour when they know they are being observed (Russell et al. 1991). According to Boyum and Parke (1995), however, participants become accustomed to being observed and will eventually show their true colours. Children, alternatively, are more likely to exhibit positive behaviour when they are being observed in an unfamiliar setting (Lamb et al. 1979). It appears that observation of individuals can be considered as obtrusive, which is why researchers have resorted to observational methods that are less obvious such as the use of cameras and sound recordings. Feiring and Lewis in 1987 pointed out that paying regular visits at the home, perhaps arranging to be there during dinner hours over an agreed period of weeks, is less obtrusive than being there all the time.

Due to their differing strengths, the two main settings in which infants, children and adolescents can be observed are **naturalistic settings** (see Box 2.6) and **laboratory settings** (see Box 2.7). Naturalistic or field settings, where children are observed in an environment they would naturally be found in such as at home or in the playground at school, do not require any effort to manipulate the situation being observed nor to control for extraneous factors. Observations are made in places either where the individual lives or commonly frequents. A study conducted by Crowley et al. (2001) showed that insightful conclusions can be made by observing children's conversations in a science museum. They found that parents were more likely to engage boys than girls in explanatory talks about the exhibits – up to three times more. Through naturalistic observation, they concluded that the parents helped to create a gender bias towards an interest in science, such that boys were more drawn towards science-related subjects than girls.

With naturalistic settings, as pointed out earlier, there is the problem of how to observe unobtrusively. If the observer is obvious, it can affect the child's behaviour; after all we all behave differently when we know someone is observing us. There is also the issue of how long do we observe the child's behaviour in the playground? What constitutes an 'adequate sample of behaviour?' Does five minutes of observation provide enough time to capture a representative time-log of the child's usual behaviour in the playground? Coding of behaviour can also be an issue. Which types of behaviours should we record in the specified timeframe and what are the appropriate ways to record them? Should we adopt a record of everything or focus on a specific types of behaviours approach? If the approach taken is to record specific types of behaviour, then a structured observation strategy is required such that a specific situation to observe the behaviours is created.

Box 2.6   Dale Hay's naturalistic observation study

In 2006 a paper published by Hay concluded that the 'ability to think about what is "mine" and "yours" marks a very early step in the development of constructive approaches to inevitable conflicts that occur between peers' (p. 50). This study was about the connection between toddlers using possessive pronouns and positive relations with their peers. The 66 toddlers were

(continued)

(continued)

observed in their home in the presence of their mothers, peers and the mothers of their peers. A longitudinal design was used because the focal toddlers (i.e., those being observed and not their peers) were also observed six months later. The focal toddlers were 18, 24 or 30 months of age and the peers were no more than 6 months older. The procedure involved the observation of social behaviour and speech utterances used by the dyadic pairing of the focal toddler and peer. These episodes were recorded on video for 45 minutes and the focal toddlers were followed wherever they went (e.g., into the garden). Dyadic interaction between the toddlers was transcribed from video using the Peer Interaction Coding System (PICS). There were two independent transcribers to increase inter-rater reliability (i.e., a means of ascertaining the accuracy of the resulting transcriptions). Findings during the first observation session showed an association between toddlers using words of possession such as 'mine' or 'yours' and how they interacted with their peers. Possessive pronouns usage was associated with physical aggression (e.g., 'that's mine' and grabbing the toy). By the second observation session those who used possessive pronouns were more likely to share with their peers. Hence the earlier usage of the possessive predicted the toddlers' prosocial behaviour. They asked politely for things – 'can I play with your toy'.

Bakeman and Gottman (1997) labelled three ways in which behaviours can be recorded when studying children's behaviour: specimen record, event sampling and time sampling. In the case of **specimen record**, the researcher is interested in recording everything a child does within a fixed period of time (although the behaviours are commonly specified before the recording begins). Using this method enables the researcher to consider a spectrum of behaviours occurring during a specific situation. For example, when observing the strategies children use to modulate their emotions whilst engaged in a challenging task, the researcher might consider recording all the behaviours relating to this.

Event sampling is different because here the researcher is interested in how children respond to particular events. Hence all behaviours are recorded after the occurrence of the specific event in question. For example, the way maltreated children respond to aggressive acts from their peers would be recorded following the aggressive behaviours. The response would be of interest to the researcher and other behaviours occurring during non-aggressive periods would not be recorded. The third method is **time sampling**, which is useful for studying more than one participant simultaneously. Incidents of aggressive interactions between siblings could be recorded in sections of 10-minute periods amounting to 180 minutes of observational time. During these 10-minute periods, behaviour could be recorded for one minute (hence one minute in every 10 minutes) for any signs of aggressive interaction between siblings. This would amount to repeated recording at set intervals regardless of the type of behaviours being exhibited – hence observing aggressive acts only if they occurred during the recorded periods of time. The disadvantage of this method relates to there being no way of predicting how siblings will react to each other. One of the advantages of using time sampling is that it allows for the study of many individuals concurrently.

Depending on what developmental psychologists are studying, a laboratory setting might be the most appropriate. Laboratory-based observations also have their disadvantages. There are obvious problems about situational demands. Children 'know' they are being studied (depending on age) and this can, in turn, influence their behaviour. They may feel that they are expected to behave in a certain way to please the researcher and, as a consequence, behave atypically. Clearly placed recording equipment can influence behaviour and so covert methods of observing can be used to help reduce the possibility of unnatural behaviour. As with naturalistic observation, the method of coding can also have an impact on behaviour recorded in laboratory-based settings.

Let us take a moment to consider observational methods in laboratory settings. What are the advantages of laboratory settings? One advantage of laboratory over naturalistic observation is the ability to standardise conditions so that all children observed undergo the same conditions. An example of this is the strange situation paradigm introduced by Mary Ainsworth (1979, see Box 2.7), who followed in the steps of British developmental psychologist, John Bowlby. Bowlby was interested in caregiver–child attachments, which Ainsworth developed further by devising a method of observing these attachment patterns – the **strange situation**. A laboratory setting enabled Ainsworth to control environmental variables (e.g., temperature, noise and the presence of others) that was not possible in a field setting. By eliminating these potentially confounding (i.e., interfering) variables the researchers were able to concentrate on the effect that the selected variable, such as separation from the caregiver, has on the infant.

It is also possible in a laboratory setting to conceal cameras and to use one-way mirrors to observe behaviour. It is therefore possible to design the study so that the caregiver and child are unaware they are being observed and their reactions recorded – hence controlling for the

Plate 2.4 Girl toddler playing but looking at her mum for reassurance. (Shutterstock 168357302.)

effect of observation on behaviour. Furthermore, within a laboratory environment physiological measures of observation, such as EEG to measure brain activity (discussed later in
this chapter), are possible.

Another example of a laboratory-based observation study was the Bandura modelling
experiment. Albert Bandura argued that observational learning or modelling was widely
used by children. He believed that children would learn new behaviours simply by watching others and then imitating what they did. Specific behaviours could therefore be acquired
through both experiencing and observing an event. In his modelling experiment children
were allowed to play with toys in a room on their own.

Children played on their own in a corner for 10 minutes. In one condition they saw an
adult behaving aggressively towards a five-foot tall inflated Bobo doll that stood upright but
bobbed up and down when hit – hence an aggressive role model. In the other condition an
adult played in a subdued and quiet manner. In the control group there was no adult present.
To make the children feel annoyed they were prevented from playing with the toys and
instead taken to a different room containing a Bobo doll and other toys. Their behaviour was
then observed through a one-way mirror (the researchers could see the child but the child
could not see their observers). The results of the observation showed that the adult's behaviour towards the Bobo doll earlier had influenced the way in which the children interacted
with the doll. In other words they exhibited aggressive behaviour towards the doll – mimicking the adult's aggressive behaviour. On the other hand, the children who observed the adult
playing quietly and in a subdued manner modelled on that behaviour. Children subjected to
non-aggressive behaviour were less likely to behave aggressively towards the Bobo doll.
This study provided information concerning how children can learn through imitating the
behaviour of others. The Bobo doll experiment has not been without criticism. Various criticisms have been made in response to the methodology such as the unrepresentative sample
of children selected to take part and experimenter bias causing the children to behave according to researcher expectations. A further criticism from ethologist Nicholas Blurton-Jones
(1972) was directed at the children's facial expressions while punching the Bobo doll. In
re-analysing film footage of Bandura's Bobo doll experiments, Blurton-Jones was able to
show that the children were using a 'play-face' (i.e., open-mouthed, grinning and laughing)
whilst striking the doll. This suggests that in many cases the children were engaged in rough
and tumble play rather than showing aggression.

Box 2.7   The strange situation

Mary Ainsworth (1979) created a method called the strange situation. This method enabled
Ainsworth to study the bond between caregiver and child. The child was observed playing for
about 20 minutes while the caregiver enters and leaves the room – hence creating a familiar and
unfamiliar situation for the child. The study follows a set method:

    The caregiver and child enter the room
    They are by themselves in the room
    The child is allowed to explore the area alone
    An unknown person enters the room
    This person communicates with the caregiver then the child
    The caregiver leaves the room

SEPARATION EPISODE ONE

The person attends to the child

The caregiver reunites with the child and provides comfort

Both the caregiver and person exit the room

The child is alone.

SEPARATION EPISODE TWO

The person returns to the room and tries to provide comfort

The caregiver reunites with the child and provides comfort

The person leaves the room quickly and quietly.

Two types of child behaviours were observed: the child's first reaction to the room and engagement with the toys and the child's behaviour towards their caregiver leaving and returning to the room. Most children were distressed when the caregiver left the room but happy when they were reunited. They also showed signs of distress when left alone with the stranger and were very wary of the stranger's presence even when the caregiver was present. Most children were reassured by the return of the caregiver. Some, however, responded less positively to the return of the caregiver. On the basis of such responses Ainsworth concluded that there were three types of attachment interaction between the caregiver and child. The A-dyad was called insecure avoidant; the B-dyad securely attached and the C-dyad insecure resistant. At a later stage a fourth group, the D-dyad, showed a disorganised pattern of attachment relationship. Only the B-dyad were securely attached to their caregiver and showed anxiety when left alone and alone with the stranger but emotions of delight when reunited with the caregiver.

Interviews

Interviews are normally conducted as part of a survey. However, there are specific situations demanding only an interview approach to obtaining information about the child. Once more the use of interviews allows for the gathering of both quantitative and qualitative data. There are three types of interview method commonly used by developmental psychologists: clinical, structured and semi-structured interviews, which will be considered in turn. Firstly, **clinical interviews** are a good method of obtaining in-depth information about the child. When Piaget used clinical interviews he obtained information that illuminated a child's perspective of the world. Not only did he have information relating to their behaviour but also how they feel and think about their surrounding environment. Advantages of using the clinical interview revolve around the breadth and depth of information obtained in a short period of time and the flexibility of adapting the interview for individual children. **Structured interviews** are less flexible than clinical ones as the same questions are asked of all children individually in the same sequential order. While this can be a disadvantage, as there is a loss in depth and breadth of information obtained, it does mean more agreement in the responses given across the sample of children interviewed; this enables researchers to generalise findings to other children with similar attributes to those in the sample.

Semi-structured interviews are a combination of the clinical and structured interview format and tend to be used as a tool in research rather than for clinical purposes. Unlike the structured interview, questions can be asked in a non-sequential manner. This is because the objective is to explore topics in the questions asked and, depending on the response given at the time, they

Plate 2.5 Teenager being interviewed. (Shutterstock 1295912.)

might need to be reordered accordingly. This also provides a space for children to elaborate on their answers and for researchers to prompt them to expand more. An example of how the semi-structured interview can be used in developmental research is described in Box 2.8.

Regardless of the type of interview technique adopted, there are disadvantages concerning the accuracy of recalling memories, being honest, inflation of information by exaggerating events or opinions and the need to conform to consensus attitudes. In the case of children this might be reflected in the need to be accepted by other group members. Of course it is difficult to interview very young infants who have not yet developed verbal language proficiency in order to communicate their feelings and thoughts. In these circumstances researchers need to think outside the box and adopt other methods. One such method is to use physiological measures that provide indirect evidence of how an infant might be feeling or thinking about what they are seeing – as considered next.

Box 2.8   Children and TV alcohol advertising

In 2009, Nash et al. carried out a UK-based study using a semi-structured interview approach. Seventeen children (nine boys and eight girls) from a school in Hertfordshire (years 3, 4 and 5), whose mean age was eight years and nine months, were asked to respond to a series of advertisements about alcohol and non-alcohol products. The procedure involved children in groups of two or three who were of the same sex and from the same year watching two alcohol and two non-alcohol related television advertisements on a computer screen. After these advertisements were viewed the children took part in a group discussion. They were provided with a series of questions using a semi-structured interview format. The questions examined their perceptions and interpretation of alcohol advertising on British television. For example, questions asked were centred around their opinions about the advertisements such as 'what did you think about that advert?' or 'what does this advert say about the product?' The alcohol and non-alcohol products were matched in their style of representation such as using humour or emphasising the quality of the product. Other matched features included, for example, a male or female agent, a cartoon or an animal.

Nash et al. found that children in years 3 and 4 unanimously liked all the alcohol adverts and expressed a particular liking for the humorous adverts as they made them laugh. Children in year 5 were more likely to express negative views towards the alcohol adverts. Interestingly, one boy in year 5, when prompted further, suggested that he did not like the Bacardi Breezer advert but revealed on further questioning that he found the football and cat clip in the advert likeable. As these clips were shown before any reference to the drink, Nash et al. concluded that he liked the advert in its own right but not the reference to the product being advertised. Other examples revealed that the children in year 5 were more likely to draw upon information they knew about alcohol rather than the sentiments expressed in the advert. When asked what message one of the alcohol-related adverts was disseminating, a year 5 girl responded, 'it makes you drunk' (p. 91). When an alcohol advert was portrayed in cartoon format (e.g., Boddington's beer), one girl from year 5 responded, 'we like cartoons more because, cos . . . it's like boring if it's grown up' (p. 91). Nash et al. suggest that alcohol adverts in cartoon format might be considered by children as advertising aimed at them. Children in years 3 and 4 generally regarded the alcohol adverts as effective in that people would buy these products. Those in year 5 thought this was not the case with the exception of the Boddington's beer advert broadcast in cartoon format.

Physiological measurements

Physiological measurements are particularly useful when studying infants and young children as they can be used to examine how biological processes underlie emotional states. One way that physiological measurements can be used is to explore the influence of our biology at different points in the lifespan. The hormonal changes that occur during the period of puberty in adolescence, for example, can be examined through samples of blood taken from willing participants. Analysing blood samples for fluctuations of the male hormone testosterone can help to understand sexual interest behaviours in teenaged boys.

There are many different physiological measurements that can be used but we will only describe four here. The first measurement known as **electroencephalogram**, or EEG for short, is used to record electrical activity in the brain. Small passive sensors or electrodes, which are adhered to the surface of the scalp using a gel that helps conduct the electrical activity occurring in the brain, are wired-up to a computer. The EEG amplifies any electrical activity detected by the electrodes and the computer analyses these recordings. EEG measurements are often taken at the same time as the participant views a series of stimuli such as

Plate 2.6 Curved sensor net used to record electrical signals. (Used with permission: courtesy of Science Museum, London, Wellcome Images.)

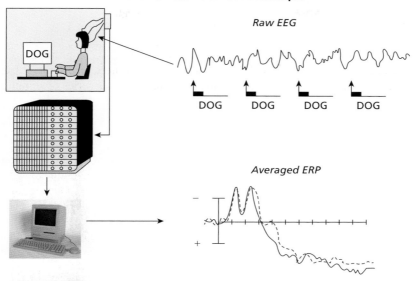

Figure 2.3 The EEG set-up and ERP.

faces (see Box 2.9). Infants' brains can also be recorded using this method by applying a net full of electrodes that is worn like a shower-cap, known as a geodesic sensor net.

The brain's response to a specific sensory, cognitive or motor stimulus, such as seeing a face, is called the **Event-Related Potential** (ERP). The ERPs can be detected using an EEG and appear as a waveform with component spikes (see Figure 2.3).

Box 2.9 The geodesic sensor net and face processing

Johnson (2000) adopted the technique of Event-Related Potentials as a means of 'reading' what goes on in a baby's brain. It's a revolutionary technique as it enables us to study the baby's brain in action. The method involves putting a 'geodesic net' composed of a large number of electrodes gently on to the baby's head.

When the baby is presented with a stimulus, such as a picture of a face, groups of neurons become activated in the brain. The electrodes detect any electrical changes in the scalp due to the firing of these brain neurons. The combined output from all the electrodes generates a map of the active areas across the baby's head. This information is analysed by a computer, which calculates where in the brain these electrical activities (i.e., voltages) originated from. Most neurons in the brain are in situ around birth but the dendrites and axons (i.e., the conducting fibres that extend from neurons) and the number of synapses (i.e., junctions between neurons that pass on signals) increase dramatically postnatally.

Looking at faces provides the new-born with the input necessary for training areas of the cerebral cortex of the brain that is still developing (Johnson 2000). Furthermore, Johnson and

(continued)

(continued)

de Haan (2001) observed more widespread brain activity in infants than in adults when shown faces. As the infant's brain developed with age and encounters with faces, their brain responses became increasingly selective such that the areas active when shown faces corresponded to the same patterns of brain activity in adults. This can be taken as evidence that, while the brain of a very young infant is less finely tuned than that of an adult for observing faces, by 12 months of age a similar pattern to adults is already emerging.

The EEG methods have been used to enhance our knowledge of children's perception of language. For example, Molfese and Molfese (1979) used the ERP technique to demonstrate that the left hemisphere of the brain elicits a faster response to speech sounds in infants than the right hemisphere. Their findings were consistent with the notion of there being a left hemisphere bias for processing linguistic stimuli. Researchers Kraus et al. (1996) used ERPs in their study when considering the auditory discrimination deficits in children with learning problems such as dyslexia. By adopting this technique they found that children with dyslexia were having problems associated with differentiating similar but different sounding phonemes. The ERPs technique demonstrated that the brain was not processing the difference between the two sounds.

Functional magnetic resonance imaging (fMRI) is our second physiological measurement. This non-invasive technique provides an abundance of information about how the brain functions. It operates by detecting changes in the blood flow to the brain using magnetic fields to provide images of active areas in the brain. This is potentially useful when researching the areas of the brain active during the performance of specific cognitive tasks (e.g., saying words out loud or naming pictures). Baron-Cohen et al. (1994) used fMRI to demonstrate the involvement of the frontal lobes of the brain in performing tasks requiring the interpretation and reasoning about the mental states of others.

The third physiological measurement used by developmental psychologists is referred to as **vagal tone**. This is a biological process affecting the activity of the vagus nerve that regulates heart rate. Vagal tone cannot be measured directly, but the influence of the vagus nerve on heart rate can. Signals from the vagus nerve act to relax heart rate, which has a calming effect on the person – it slows the heart beat down. By measuring heart rate, vagal tone can be indirectly observed. The conditions under which heart rate varies, in particular the situations provoking heart-rate variability, can be informative to developmental psychologists. In particular, it could be a good indicator of the emotional state of an infant and how well the infant is able to self-regulate under stressful situations (see Box 2.10).

Box 2.10   What does vagal tone say about new-borns and children?

In infants of five to six months vagal tone relates positively with expressing emotional states but negatively to repressing them. Porges et al. (1994) examined the literature on vagal tone and temperament in infants. They found that new-born vagal tone is linked to irritability whereby the higher the vagal tone the more irritable they were. After 5–6 months of age high vagal tone becomes associated both with positive emotional adjustment and with irritability. This would suggest that by responding in an irritable way to stressful situations, new-borns are expressing how they feel and by doing so are behaving appropriately. In three-year-olds, Fox and Field (1989) reported that a higher vagal tone is positively related to preschool adjustment.

Our final physiological measurement is **galvanic skin response** (GSR), which is used to measure changes in electrical conductance of the skin. Different ways of interpreting skin conductance have been introduced such as **electrodermal reactivity** (EDR). The underlying assumption for both GSR and EDR is the same – under stressful situations the skin sweats and suggests the individual is anxious (see Box 2.11).

Box 2.11   Skin conductance as a predictor of empathy

Liew et al. (2003) demonstrated how skin conductance was related to empathy and sympathy in children whose mean age was nine years and five months. The researchers examined 154 children for their socioemotional functioning. Both heart rate and skin conductance were used as measures for empathy and sympathy responses to slides depicting negative emotions such as distress and fear. Boys exhibiting higher skin conductance to the negative slides were better adjusted to regulating their own emotions – they were less intense and more emotionally balanced. In a similar vein, Fabes et al. (1994) studied skin conductance responses in kindergarten and children in the second grade to film footage depicting children being hurt in an accident. Both groups of children with high skin conductance responses to the footage also showed facial expressions of distress. Negative emotions in these children reflected a prosocial disposition.

Physiological measures have contributed towards understanding the underlying physiology of many of our behaviours and emotions. These are commonly used in a laboratory setting and make use of an experimental design. Experimental designs are used quite widely in developmental psychology. In the next section we will consider the different research designs used in developmental research as a method of establishing patterns and causes.

RESEARCH DESIGNS

So far we have considered the different methods of collecting data. While these methods can be very useful in exploring behaviour shown by infants, children and adolescents, it does not enable researchers to examine what causes the behaviour. It only allows us to speculate that a specific factor might be related somehow to the behaviour exhibited. This is why research designs such as the experiment have been devised so that empirical links between cause and effect can be established. The three research designs that will be explored in this section are: descriptive, correlational and experimental. **Descriptive research designs** will only have a brief mention here because the different data collection methods discussed previously can be incorporated in to this type of design. For example, by using naturalistic observation it might be established that boys' play is more physical than that of girls. This difference can be described and is interesting in its own right but any explanations of why they are different cannot be established. In the case of correlational research designs, the data obtained provides more than descriptive information, as discussed next.

Correlational research design

The idea behind using **correlational designs** is to examine whether an increase or decrease in one variable corresponds to an increase or decrease in another variable.

According to Jackson (2006), it should be possible to predict one event from the other if they are strongly correlated (associated or related). If, for example, we wanted to see if parental punishment is more likely to make a child rebellious then we would need to observe the parents punishing the child and the child's response to it (e.g., being rebellious). All observations are recorded and analysed by adopting a statistical test (either the Spearman or Pearson test) to provide a numerical measure. Such a test will yield a correlation coefficient ranging between $+1$ to -1, giving a degree of association between the two factors – parental punishment and rebellious behaviour. A perfect positive correlation is $+1$ whereas -1 is a perfect inverse correlation (meaning that as punishment increases rebellious behaviour decreases). McMillan (2007) alerts us to the fact that correlations do not imply causation. Correlational designs have their uses if researchers just want to know that two factors (or variables) are related to each other and whether they are strongly or weakly associated. Given that correlational designs fail to provide information about why the factors are related or what is causing the relationship, questions have been asked regarding their usefulness. Some research might be difficult to study in any other way. For example, how do researchers study the influence of viewing television and learning over a period of two years (see Box 2.12)? Hence sometimes researchers might want merely to document patterns of behaviour that occur in the home and not in a contrived laboratory setting.

Box 2.12   Can watching television improve cognitive development?

Wright and Huston (1995) wanted to know if there was a relationship between children watching television and their level of maths ability and word knowledge. Children at the beginning of the study were either two or four years of age reaching five or seven when the study was completed. These children were from 250 families living in low-income areas. The parents had to keep a record of the amount of television viewed and the type of content therein. In each year that the study ran, the children were tested for their cognitive development in maths and word knowledge. A positive correlation was found between increased viewing of educational programmes and performing well on these tests. Increased viewing of cartoon programmes, however, correlated negatively with test performance such that test scores were poor. While this finding is interesting, it does not mean necessarily that educational programmes on television induce improved cognitive development. Correlations can only predict an association between these two factors but nothing about the cause of relatedness. In this case it is entirely possible that another variable (e.g., a household where educational programmes are watched regularly might also have more books) might explain this finding.

In order to examine what is responsible for the relationship between two factors, a different design is required – the experimental research design, which will be considered next.

Experimental research design

The experimental research design is the archetypal quantitative research tool used by psychologists. An experiment is a 'regulated procedure in which one or more factors believed to influence the behaviour studied are manipulated while all other factors are held constant' (Santrock 2008, p. 35). **Experiments** are used by developmental psychologists to determine what causes a child to behave in a certain way when they are subjected to a particular stimulus. For example, in the 'marshmallow test' conducted by Mischel et al. (1972), children are presented with a marshmallow that they can either eat straight away or, if they are prepared to wait until the researcher returns, they can have two marshmallows. Mischel et al. were

Plate 2.7 The wait is very difficult for this girl who wants to eat the marshmallow on a stick right now. (Shutterstock 112396439.)

interested to understand the degree to which different children are able to delay gratification (Workman and Mischel 2014).

Hence questions he asked included will the child be able to wait and, if so, how long can they wait until they succumb to an overwhelming desire to eat the marshmallow? Here the child is subjected to two factors (the marshmallow and how long it is before the researcher returns) believed to have an impact on the child's behaviour (eat the marshmallow or wait and have two). Other possible factors such as seeing other preferable sweets are held constant so that there can be no other interfering factors swaying the child's behaviour (i.e., eat the sweets instead of the marshmallow therefore still being entitled to having two marshmallows). The child's behaviour can be attributed to the manipulated factors – marshmallow and the duration of time before the researcher returns. Hence conclusions of cause (i.e., the factors) and effect (i.e., the child's behaviour) can be made.

When using an experimental research design, the factors are referred to as variables and there are two important types of variable that are used in the experiment: independent and dependent variables. The **independent variable** (IV) is manipulated to see the effect it has on the individual's behaviour. Hence in Mischel et al.'s (1972) marshmallow study the IVs were the marshmallow and the length of time the child sat alone before the researcher returned. The **dependent variable** (DV) is the response generated as a consequence of the IV. In the marshmallow study the DV was the child's behaviour. Did the child eat the marshmallow before the researcher returned or wait in order to get two marshmallows? It was also possible to ascertain how much self-control children showed by the variations in the length of time they were prepared to wait before succumbing to their desires.

As the purpose of doing experiments is to show a **cause and effect**, it is important to have a group who are subjected to the IV in question (i.e., the experimental group) and a group who are not (i.e., the control group). The **control group** acts as a comparison and provides a baseline measure of behaviour. This only works effectively providing participants are randomly assigned to the experimental and control groups. This procedure ensures that the differences recorded across the two groups result from manipulating the IV and not pre-existing differences between participants.

Experimental research designs can be used in the laboratory, the field or in natural situations. Mischel et al.'s (1972) marshmallow study was conducted in a laboratory designed to look like a child-friendly room. It could be argued, however, that the setting was novel to the children and influenced their behaviour. In other words, their behaviour might not be an accurate portrayal of how they would behave under these circumstances had it been conducted in the home environment (i.e., in the field). This suggests that the findings might lack **ecological validity** (i.e., it was not an accurate representation of behaviours, events and processes occurring in natural surroundings). Researchers might want to get round the ecological validity problem by conducting their experiments in the field. Under these circumstances they introduce a change or a variable manipulation to the child's usual surroundings and observe the effect this has. Conducting an experiment in the field maintains the cause–effect aspect while also increasing ecological validity.

In the case of **natural experiments**, researchers observe the effects of events that have occurred in the real world without needing to manipulate any variables. An example of this is the effects of stress on the developing foetus of women who witnessed the attack on the twin-towers in New York in 2001 – known as 9/11. Among those exposed to 9/11 were 1,700 pregnant women, some of whom developed Post Traumatic Stress Disorder (PTSD).

Professor Rachel Yehuda investigated how the mother's PTSD might affect the unborn child in later life. She conducted a longitudinal study on 38 of the women pregnant at the time of 9/11 who developed PTSD (Yehuda et al. 2005). Samples of saliva were taken from the women and measured for the stress hormone called cortisol. Counterintuitively, women who developed PTSD had lower levels of cortisol in their saliva than the controls that had not developed PTSD (previous research has shown that PTSD is related to low, rather than high, levels of cortisol). A year later cortisol levels were measured in the children of both the women who had developed PTSD and those who had not. Children of the women with PTSD also had low levels of cortisol. These children showed increased distress response to novel stimuli. It is believed that the traumatic experiences of these pregnant women were transmitted to the unborn children by epigenetic processes whereby the genes interact with environmental factors – in this case 9/11. The study suggests that maternal PTSD can have a knock-on effect on later physiological measures in their unborn children, which, via cortisol levels, may increase their risk of later developing PTSD. This is an example of a naturally occurring event enabling researchers to examine the consequences of stress on the future development of the new-born.

The experimental design is very useful in the study of development but running experiments normally involves large numbers of participants. There are circumstances, however, where developmental psychologists are interested in studying a particular child's behaviour. This is possible using the case-study approach discussed next.

Case study research design

The case study is the archetypal qualitative research design. Linda Camras (1992) conducted an in-depth **case study** of her infant daughter. She was particularly interested in the emotional expressions exhibited by her daughter over a long period of time. Camras recorded her daughter's expressions using a video camera and acquired an extensive collection of video footage showing expressions across different situations. Camras' findings concur with Ekman and Friesen's (1971) study of the universality of emotional expressions (that is, that cross-culturally humans share a range of specific facial emotional expressions, see Chapter 3). Other case studies have contributed towards our understanding of child development and when it can go awry. One area where case studies have contributed to our understanding of abnormal development is language. Over the years there have been a few cases where children have been brought up by animals or have had to fend for themselves – they are called feral children and have extended our understanding of how language is acquired (see Box 2.13).

Case studies can be designed in such a way as to increase scientific validity by using what is known as **ABAB designs**. Most commonly adopted to test the effectiveness of specific types of intervention as a means of substituting inappropriate behaviour for appropriate behaviour, it has proven to be a valid design. The acronym ABAB stands for:

A – baseline level of behaviour normally exhibited to a specific situation

B – treatment intervention adopted

A – removal of treatment intervention

B – reinstatement of treatment intervention

Box 2.13   Case of feral children

A number of so-called 'feral' children have been studied in order to understand the extent to which a wild or highly restricted upbringing can affect social and cognitive development. Here we consider three such cases.

Oxana Malaya, who was born in 1983 in the Ukraine, became famous world-wide for her dog-imitating behaviour. She was a 'feral' child because she was left to fend for herself and taken into care by a group of dogs. The dogs were her only source of contact and social interaction, and so became her role models to be imitated. By all accounts, Oxana was born a normal child but was abandoned by her alcoholic parents. When Oxana was found at 7½ years of age she could not talk and lacked any of the social graces of a child that age. She behaved like a dog by running around on all fours, sleeping on the floor, eating like a dog, barking and cleaning herself in the manner of a canine. After years of therapy and education she learned to speak fluently and intelligently, however, there is some extent of intellectual impairment.

Isabelle born in 1932 was an illegitimate child brought up by her deaf-mute mother in extreme isolation. She spent all her time with her mother in a dark room separate from the rest of the family. They eventually escaped and Isabelle was taken by the authorities when she was 6 and a half years' old, at which point her mental age was of 19 months and she could only croak. By eight years of age, given intensive training, she developed normal intelligence and her language skills were at the level of other children her age.

Genie was discovered by a social worker when she was 13 years' old. She had been confined to a small room, often tied to a potty chair so that movement of her hands and feet were restricted and she was physically abused by her father every time she made a noise. Both parents and her brother rarely spoke to her and instead interacted by growling or barking at her. A team of psychologists tried to rehabilitate her after a series of assessments testing her cognitive and emotional abilities that were at the level of a one-year-old infant. She showed rapid progression in her social and hygiene skills. She was good at communicating nonverbally but her language skills remained poor despite learning words and being able to string a few together.

These three cases are interesting and demonstrate a difference in ability to 'catch-up' with language skills. Both Oxana and Isabelle (7 and a half and 6 and a half respectively when discovered) were able to develop language skills to a standard that was consistent with other children of the same age. However, Genie, who was 13 when found, could not. This raises the question of why this difference? Erik Lenneberg (1967) claimed that language acquisition is subject to set critical periods (now considered as sensitive periods because the timeframe is less restricted) where learning of language must occur. This means that children are most sensitive to learning specific skills during these particular periods, and therefore need to hear language spoken in their immediate environment (e.g., at home by the family). Lenneberg argued that this critical period is up to the age of 12, thus coinciding with puberty when language organisation within the brain becomes 'set' so that learning language after this is less effective. In effect, after the age of 12, the child has missed the boat. In the case of Genie, she was able to acquire some language but remained unable to use correct grammar. Genie's case, however, has been compromised by the fact that she might have sustained a level of mental disability arising from her childhood of physical abuse.

Despite this, the contribution of such case studies to our understanding of behaviour, social skills, and language skills in this case, cannot be ignored.

During the first treatment intervention time-period, researchers observe the effects it has on the behaviour of the child. For example, if a child constantly bangs the desk in a classroom

Plate 2.8 Disruption in the classroom. (Shutterstock 79775023.)

situation (i.e., A – the baseline level of behaviour), then by incorporating an intervention that ignores the child completely but encourages positive interaction with the child as soon as the desk banging stops (B – treatment intervention), it is hoped that there will be a change in the overall behaviour of the child. To be sure that the teacher's response to the child is responsible for the change in behaviour, the treatment intervention is removed (A – treatment intervention removed (back to the baseline level of behaviour)). Researchers will be looking to see if the behaviour returns to baseline levels in the second A (ABA). Researchers will also be looking to see whether behaviour increases or decreases (as predicted) with implementation of the intervention again. If the treatment intervention is working, then it is good practice to leave the child in a positive state and so the treatment intervention is reinstated (B – reinstatement of treatment intervention). Hence, if behaviour changes as a consequence of treatment intervention then we can be reasonably confident that the treatment is influencing behaviour.

Case studies provide developmental psychologists with in-depth information about the behaviour of an individual over a set period of time during which behaviour and behavioural change can be observed. Studying behavioural change during the lifespan is important to developmental psychologists as the nature of development can be age-related. For example, Piaget studied the behaviours of infants, children and adolescents and from these studies developed his stage theory of cognitive development. So how can researchers study change in behaviour over the lifespan?

STUDYING CHANGE OVER A TIME SPAN

Studying behavioural change over the lifespan is important in developmental psychology, given the very nature of the 'who', the 'when' and the 'what' that developmental psychologists are interested in. There are three main approaches to measuring behavioural change across the lifespan: cross-sectional, longitudinal and sequential. Each will be considered in turn.

Cross-sectional method

This method is commonly used as a means of comparing different individuals varying in age using the same timeframe. Children of age five could be compared with those aged seven on various tasks of social development such as their ability to share their toys during play or demonstrating empathy towards other children. The advantage of using the **cross-sectional method** is that children can be studied in the 'here-and-now' rather than having to wait until they age. One disadvantage is that cross-sectional studies fail to inform the researcher about how these changes occurred and how stable these changes in social behaviour actually are. In effect, cross-sectional methods conceal the increases and decreases of development and only provide a snapshot of the current behaviour.

Longitudinal method

This method enables researchers to observe individuals over a long period of time. An example where this approach has been adopted is the Avon Longitudinal Study of Parents and Children (ALSPAC, see Box 2.2). The **longitudinal method** provides researchers with in-depth information regarding many aspects of an individual's life. The advantage of using such an approach is the continuity of an individual's life that it preserves. Why behaviour has changed and under what circumstances can be surmised from the wealth of information collated over the duration of the study. However, such studies are expensive and it takes a long time before the data can be usefully analysed and interpreted.

Sequential method

The **sequential method** combines the cross-sectional and longitudinal approaches in order to understand lifespan development. Researchers often use the cross-sectional method first and then adopt a longitudinal approach. Thus children of different ages might be studied at the same time, focusing on one element of development such as self-esteem, which is then followed up at a later stage. Self-esteem might be assessed using, for example, the Rosenberg Self-Esteem Scale when the children are first seen and then again at a later stage. Normally a new group of children is assessed at the time of the second assessment for the original participants – this new group will include children representing each age used in the study. By incorporating the new group of children, changes in behaviour observed in the original group of children can be controlled for (e.g., by controlling for improvements in assessment scores attributed to practice effects or detriment due to boredom).

Thus far we have discussed the different methods and designs used to study various aspects of individual development. Of importance, however, is the ethics of observing behaviour and the ethical standards that need to be embraced when conducting such research. This deserves a section in its own right as it is fundamental to all psychological research and particularly so when addressing issues relating to infants, children and adolescents.

ETHICAL RESEARCH IN DEVELOPMENTAL PSYCHOLOGY

Learning how to conduct sound **ethical research** in psychology is taken very seriously, so much so that in the UK the British Psychological Society (BPS) provides psychologists (i.e., practitioners, lecturers and students) with a series of guidelines pertaining to ethics and how research should be undertaken. The American Psychological Association (APA) represents psychologists in the US. Most other countries will have their own associations designed to represent psychologists working in and conducting research within psychology. The BPS ethical guidelines make it very clear that it is the researcher's responsibility to ensure their research is respectful and the participants involved in psychological research are treated appropriately. The BPS ethical principles are outlined in Box 2.14.

While all four ethical principles are important and should be adhered to, the issue of **informed consent** is particularly relevant to developmental psychological research. Often researchers in this field are interested in individuals who might be vulnerable due to their age. It is therefore important that informed consent is obtained by the relevant caregiver and the procedure and objectives are clarified and understood.

Box 2.14   BPS principles of ethical research (adapted from the BPS Code of Ethics and Conduct 2009)

According to the BPS, researchers need to consider four ethical principles: respect, competence, responsibility and integrity

With regard to '**respect**', psychologists are expected to consider the dignity of their participants and should show a level of sensitivity regarding their perceived authority over them. Whilst conducting research they should respect any differences between them and their participants, such as cultural and individual differences. Differences can include age, education, gender, ethnicity, disability, religion, race and socioeconomic status for example. Respect is also due to the experience and knowledge that their participants might have. Research should avoid elements of prejudice or unfairness. Psychological researchers must be in a position to explain the bases of their study. The participants' right to privacy and confidentiality must be preserved and only if agreed can findings be shared. Permission from participants is required if any filming or photographic materials are involved. Informed consent should be sought before the commencement of any study. This is particularly important in developmental research where permission might need to be sought from a parent if a child is to be the participant. Participants should be made aware that they have the right to withdraw from any study they have signed up to at any time.

The second ethical principle of '**competence**' concerns both practising and research psychologists. For example, the researcher must be aware of ethics and the workings of their own research – i.e., demonstrate that they know what they are doing and why they have made the course of decisions that they have. They should also work within the boundaries of their research and not try to instruct beyond their level of competency.

The third ethical principle of '**responsibility**' means that psychological researchers should avoid subjecting their participants to any harm; both physical and emotional. They should avoid behaving in any manner that contravenes professionalism. Potential risks to the wellbeing of their participants, including their health, values and dignity, must be eliminated from any research. Researchers must be aware from the outset of any individual factors relating to the participant that might lead to risk or harm during the study so that measures can be taken to minimise or eliminate them. Requests for advice from participants about psychological issues should be ignored unless considered to be serious enough to warrant referral for assistance. Participants should be debriefed once the research has concluded. This should include information about the nature of the research undertaken and the outcomes to ensure that participants leave feeling contented and fully informed.

Finally, the fourth ethical principle of '**integrity**' means that, in the context of research, psychologists should aim to be honest, accurate, clear and fair in their interactions with their participants. Acknowledgements should be made to others involved in the research.

Summary

- When conducting research in developmental psychology it is important to ensure that the sample of participants represents those we are trying to understand in the general population. This means that the sample has to show representativeness such that researchers compare like with like.
- The survey is one method of gathering data that provides a representative sample. Surveys can be conducted at a national level or across different cultures using a meta-analysis approach. Here studies from different countries (as long as similar factors have been used) can be compared by using a multitude of national surveys.
- Surveys can be in the format of a questionnaire, self-reporting (and reports by others) and interviews. Questionnaires consist of highly structured questions requiring a response from a choice of answers. Self-reports can be an effective way of attaining information from children. For preverbal children self-reporting is difficult, so information can be attained from other people reporting about the child, such as parents or teachers. Interviews as part of the survey method are generally an extension of the questionnaire, i.e., highly structured. However, interviews can be unstructured in that set questions are asked but allow for extended answers.
- Observational methods can be conducted in a laboratory or a naturalistic setting. Naturalistic settings (also called field settings) occur in the participant's natural environment such as the home or school. The situation is not manipulated in any way unlike laboratory settings. Three methods can be used to record behaviour: specimen record (all behaviour is recorded within a fixed period of time), event sampling (behaviour in response to particular events is recorded) and time sampling (study more than one participant at a time). Observational methods in laboratory settings can be standardised so that all participants are subjected to the same conditions.
- Interviews can be of the clinical, structured or semi-structured format. Clinical interviews are a good way to obtain in-depth information about an individual. In structured interviews the same questions are asked in the same order, so that there is less flexibility than the clinical interview. Semi-structured interviews combine the clinical and structured interviews such that questions can be asked in a non-sequential order depending on the responses to questions provided. The clinical part of the semi-structured interview allows for the expansion of responses.
- Physiological measurements are likely to be used in a laboratory setting. Physiological measurements are particularly useful in examining biological influences at specific points of development in the lifespan. The EEG is used to record electrical activity in the brain. It is possible to obtain ERP readings using the EEG, which appear as a waveform with individual spikes. Use of the fMRI scan has provided information about areas of the brain that become active when doing specific cognitive tasks such as naming pictures or reading words. Vagal tone is an indirect measure of heart rate that has been used in research looking at the role of heart rate in emotional regulation. Skin conductance technology has helped to understand the role played by the skin sweating during times of anxiety.
- There are three research designs: descriptive, correlational and experimental. Descriptive designs provide descriptions of behaviour. The correlational design can help researchers to predict future behaviour by examining the relatedness of two or more events or characteristics. The correlational design fails to inform researchers about what is responsible for the relationship between two factors, unlike the

experimental design. In the experimental design the independent variable is under the control of the researcher who manipulates it and the dependent variable is the response to the IV.

- Case studies can be performed on one individual who is observed long-term on many aspects of their life. Case studies can also be of the ABAB format, enabling researchers to, for instance, directly observe the influence of a specific behavioural intervention on behaviour.
- Studying behavioural change can be done using three approaches: cross-sectional, longitudinal and sequential. Cross-sectional allows researchers to compare different participants of different ages at the same time. Longitudinal methods enable researchers to observe participants over a long period of time, providing an abundance of information and explanations of what caused any behavioural change. The sequential method is a combination of the cross-sectional and longitudinal approach. Different ages of participants can be studied consecutively at one point in the study and then at a later juncture.

Questions

1. Suggest two ways in which observational methods are superior to experimental methods. Suggest two ways in which experimental methods are superior to observational methods.
2. The experimental design enables researchers to consider cause and effect but should developmental psychologists always be looking for causal explanations of behaviour? If not, then how can other designs such as descriptive and correlational help inform researchers about child development?
3. Devise an experiment that can be used to test children's memory performance under noisy and non-noisy conditions.
4. The use of EEGs can be informative when studying brain patterns. Critically examine the reliability of EEG in understanding a young infant's brain response to visual stimuli such as faces.
5. Critically discuss the best approach to understanding social behaviour: a survey first followed by an experiment for example?
6. Critically consider the advantages of doing experiments on children over other types of research investigation.

Further reading

If you are interested in considering up-dated reviews of developments in psychological theory (including cultural–historical approaches) and current practices involving dilemmas of child protection, ethnicity and gender in more detail, look at:

(continued)

(continued)

- Burman, E. (2016). *Deconstructing Developmental Psychology.* London and New York: Routledge, Taylor and Francis Group.

If you are interested in a comprehensive guide to understanding the applications of the Event-Related Potential in neuroscience and experimental psychopathology, look at:

- Luck, S. J. (2005). *An Introduction to the Event-Related Potential Technique: The University of Michigan.* The MIT Press.

If you are interested in an overview of research methods used to investigate developmental topics across the lifespan including cross-cultural, causal modelling and peer relations, look at:

- Miller, S.A. (2013). *Developmental Research Methods* (4th Edn). Los Angeles: Sage Publications, Inc.

If you are interested in techniques used for applied research on children of different ages and the challenges each method has, look at:

- Prior, J. and Van Herwegen, J. (2016). *Practical Research with Children. Research Methods in Developmental Psychology: A Handbook Series.* Abingdon: Routledge.

Contents

Introduction 73

What can new-born babies do? 74

The development of primary and
secondary emotions 84

Attachment 95

Summary 105

Chapter 3

Emotional development and attachment

3

What this chapter will teach you

- The emotional competencies that new-borns have.
- How infants come to recognise faces.
- The nature of primary and secondary emotions.
- The time-course for the development of emotions.
- How new-borns and infants develop attachment to their primary caregiver.
- How early attachment might affect behaviour later on in life.

INTRODUCTION

New-borns appear to have an innate ability to develop a bond or an attachment with their caregiver (most commonly the mother) and a propensity to form social relationships with others (usually other family members). Developmental psychologists are interested in how they do this, which is why they study the repertoire of behaviours exhibited by the new-born. Our knowledge of emotional development and attachment behaviour stems from research undertaken by developmental psychologists. From such research a diversity of explanations for why new-borns behave the way they do has been uncovered, which provide interpretations consistent with the theories previously discussed (see Chapter 1). Although the underpinnings of developments in emotional expression/understanding and attachment behaviour occur early on in the lifespan (infancy and early childhood), further development continues into adolescence. Hence we will focus primarily on infancy and childhood, but where appropriate examples to illustrate the challenges experienced by adolescents exist they will also be included.

The ability to form a bond with the caregiver is a phenomenon that occurs cross-culturally and, what is more, it takes a similar developmental trajectory. This suggests that biological mechanisms are involved in this universal pattern. The manner in which bonding between the caregiver and new-born ensues is of particular interest to developmental psychologists and has been the focal point of much research in the past. Not only has the social interaction between caregiver and new-born been studied but also their temperament has been considered. There is evidence that the new-born already has a reasonably well-developed temperament *in situ* that influences the nature of social interactions it has with the caregiver and others. In order to understand the intricacies of caregiver and new-born bonding, it is important to appreciate the new-born's level of ability (i.e., competency) to elicit and maintain that bond. We will therefore begin in the next section by considering the competencies that a new-born is endowed with and provide an account of what functions these might serve in terms of bonding behaviour.

WHAT CAN NEW-BORN BABIES DO?

American psychologist William James in his book of 1890, *The Principles of Psychology*, encapsulated the world of the new-born in the following quote:

> *The baby, assailed by eyes, ears, nose, skin, and entrails at once, feels it all as one great blooming, buzzing confusion.*
>
> *(p. 462)*

His words are striking and provide us with a window from which to view the new-born's world of chaos. James (1890) assumed that new-born infants are born as a blank slate, a *tabula rasa*, on which new experiences are written. This empirical stance considers development as relying upon numerous interactions between our sensations and the environment and has historically been supported by philosophers such as John Locke (1693) and Aristotle who said:

Plate 3.1 Mother comforting crying baby. (Shutterstock 233134342.)

Plate 3.2 Confused baby. (Shutterstock 87949297.)

What the mind . . . thinks must be in it in the same sense as letters are on a tablet . . . which bears no actual writing . . . this is just what happens in the case of the mind.
(Aristotle 1936, 3.4.430ᵃ1)

However, not all philosophers and psychologists subscribe to this way of thinking about the developing new-born. Nativism is the opposing position, in which the new-born is considered to have innate abilities and skills that are hardwired into the brain at birth. Supporters of this approach include the philosopher Immanuel Kant (1781) who argued that the mind actively structures reality. The mind therefore must possess the ability to process incoming stimuli from the environment using *a priori knowledge* (i.e., information already known). These two approaches, nativism–empiricism, fuelled what has since become known as the nature–nurture debate. This debate has influenced psychological ideas of human development for over a century. It has particular relevance to developmental psychology and, as we shall see, continues to influence our understanding of the antecedents of social behaviour.

Returning to the sentiment of James' perspective of the new-born as a blooming buzzing confusion – this implies that the new-born has to write on to the metaphorical blank slate everything it learns, and that nothing can be assumed. But is this really the case? With advances in scientific technology it is possible to study the new-born's ability to track a schematic face only hours after birth, and to respond to aversive stimuli using a basic approach–avoidance action of head movement. In the case of tracking a schematic face this appears to be the rudimentary beginnings of face recognition, which is so important in imprinting and bonding behaviour. Approach–avoidance, as demonstrated through head movement, is considered to be a basic form of emotional state and expression. This later becomes refined into at least six emotional expressions. Both face recognition and the ability to express emotions are essential to the development of social behaviour. Hence these infant competencies will be considered, beginning first with the ability to perceive faces and its role in imprinting and bonding behaviours.

Ability to perceive facial stimuli

As adults we are very good at recognising faces. This raises the question of whether such ability is learned through interacting with our social environment or is derived from an innate predisposition to process facial stimuli. If new-borns have an inherent ability to recognise faces, then we could ask what the purpose of this competency is. Both questions have been addressed through researching infants' competency at attending, processing, identifying and recognising human faces. The brain patterns involved in the processing of faces in new-borns have been compared with those of adults using physiological measures such as EEG (see Chapter 2). As previously described in Chapter 2, infants wear a geodesic sensor net that measures the brain's response to different stimuli. The electrodes in the geodesic sensor net amplify any brain activity in response to the infant seeing a face. The brain's response is recorded as Event-Related Potentials (ERPs). This method is non-invasive and causes no discomfort to the infant (which is why this approach is widely used in neurocognitive examinations).

In infants of less than 12 months of age, developmental studies such as those of de Haan (2001) and de Haan et al. (2002) have reported widespread brain activity across the left and right hemispheres of the brain in response to facial stimuli. With increasing age, however, this activity becomes more selective to the right hemisphere – a similar pattern to that seen in adults (Neville 1995). de Haan et al. (2002) explain this move from a more generalised to a localised brain pattern as a consequence of increasing age (hence brain development) and experience of interacting with a social world full of faces. This suggests that areas of the new-born's brain are innately involved in processing faces. Despite the 'innateness' of this ability it is clear that engagement with the social world is necessary for this development.

Fantz (1961) introduced the **preferential looking technique** as a method to investigate the development of processing facial material. Many experiments have shown that infants prefer looking at fairly complex patterns and get bored very quickly if shown a simple pattern. This has been shown by use of the habituation–dishabituation paradigm (a visual preference technique – see Box 2.1, Chapter 2). One of the most well-cited studies is that of Fantz in 1961. He showed that when infants were confronted with complicated patterns they take particular interest in them and scan the object carefully. Fantz varied the stimuli in different ways; he showed a face with the features in the right place, a scrambled face and a face shape with the top half in black and the bottom half in white. In all cases infants showed a preference for stimuli resembling a human face. Fantz concluded that this means infants have an innate predisposition for sociability. His study was criticised for not maintaining consistency across the stimuli – for example, the face figure was symmetrical, the scrambled face was not.

In order to counter this criticism Fantz and Miranda (1975) looked at different patterns that infants preferred and found that infants would look longer at patterns with curves, especially if they were the outer contour. In contrast, when embedded in a square, it made no difference whether the patterns were curved or not. In other words, infants actively search for curved outer shapes. This makes sense as the outer contour of the human face is curved. In addition to this preference for curves, infants increasingly favour complex stimuli over simple ones – a trend that continues as they get older. For instance, at one month infants prefer a 2×2 stimulus checkerboard, at two months an 8×8 checkerboard and at three months a 24×24 checkerboard.

Fantz's original studies have been followed up by British developmentalists, Mark Johnson and John Morton. Johnson and Morton (1991) were interested in whether Fantz's study indicated that infants arrive with a fully functioning face identification system, or whether they are born with only sketchy knowledge of faces, the details being filled in by experience of faces in the world. Johnson and Morton (1991) suggested that there are two processes (the two-process theory of development of face processing) used by new-borns in the processing of faces – 'conspec' and 'conlern' (see Chapter 1). Conspec is the label that Johnson and Morton (1991) use to describe an innate preference for primitive face-like visual stimuli.

Conspec is considered to be an innate processing mechanism designed to enable the new-born to identify the facial configuration of its caregiver. Identifying the facial configuration of the caregiver is vital to the survival of the new-born in order to rapidly develop a bond (more will be said about this later in the chapter). In the caregiver's case the development of a bond creates a desire to provide care for the fully dependent new-born.

According to Johnson and Morton conspec is an innate but immature mechanism enabling new-borns to process facial stimuli. It provides a rudimentary representation of faces that requires further refinement. This refinement occurs through the second processing mechanism known as conlern, which is processed in the cortex of the brain. The existence of these mechanisms has been demonstrated through research on new-borns, in particular how their focus of attention is oriented towards faces (Johnson et al. 1991). Furthermore, there are studies demonstrating that new-borns are able to recognise the facial identity of people such as the caregiver (Bushnell et al. 1989; Pascalis et al. 1995). This finding led Johnson and de Haan in 2001 to revise their two-process account by adding that faces can be processed in the same way as other visual patterns prior to the development of processing specialisation in the cortex for facial stimuli. They argue that this can explain why new-borns are able to recognise specific faces. After six to eight weeks, however, this becomes reinforced with the onset of conlern when the processing of facial stimuli resembles that seen in adults.

Other studies have adopted a different approach by making use of visual tracking methods. This involves the use of stimuli that either closely resembles a face or, while containing some facial features, are only distantly related to real faces (e.g., a scrambled face pattern). Such stimuli are moved across the new-born's field of vision (see Figure 3.1).

One study conducted in 1975 demonstrated that 10-minute-old new-borns orient their heads towards and visually track a moving stimulus resembling a face. Also, they are more likely to follow such a stimulus than they do a scrambled facial stimulus (where the facial features are wrongly located within a facial contour). Johnson et al. (1991) investigated this further by adding two other facial stimuli: a facial contour containing blackened 'blobs' located where facial features normally lie and a version where the 'blobs' had the incorrect arrangement (see Figure 3.2).

In one of their experiments Johnson et al. recorded head and eye movement in 43 new-borns averaging 43 minutes old. Unlike the method of holding the baby shown in Figure 3.1, they used a specially designed head rest that nestled on the lap of the experimenter. Video recording equipment was used to record the new-born's eye and head movement while viewing one version of the facial stimuli at a time. The results show a significant difference in eye movement between the schematic face and both inverse and linear face representations in that the new-borns focused more on the schematic and 'config' faces. Schematic and 'config' face representations only just failed to differ significantly (see Figure 3.3).

In a further study, infants (one, three and five months old) were shown slides containing one of the four versions of facial stimuli at a time. Infants sat in their mother's lap who, in turn, sat in a chair that rotated once to either the left or right (depending on the direction in which the slide moved across their visual field). This method enabled Johnson et al. (1991) to

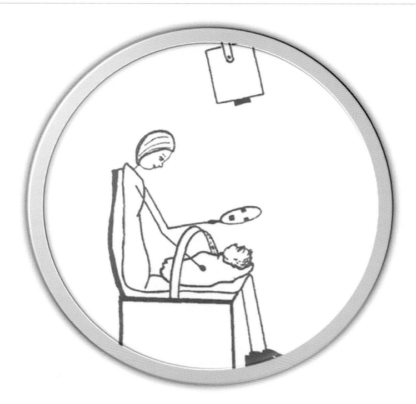

Figure 3.1 Typical arrangement of experimenter and baby during administration of the facial stimulus. (Adapted from Johnson et al. 1991, used with permission.)

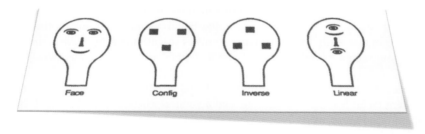

Figure 3.2 Four versions of the facial stimuli presented. (Adapted from Johnson et al. 1991, used with permission.)

record the length of time that infants attended to the facial stimuli. No difference in response was found for the schematic and 'config' face representations (see Figure 3.4).

Johnson et al.'s findings indicate that infants at one month of age clearly prefer to look at a schematic face as this was tracked for the longest. For both the three and five month olds there was no significant difference in tracking time spent on all facial stimuli types. They conclude that the decline in tracking time towards schematic face representations might be because conspec required in the initial phases of caregiver identification has served its

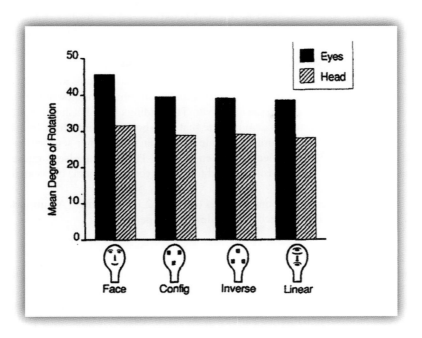

Figure 3.3 Mean eyes and head movement towards the four versions of facial stimuli. (From Johnson et al. 1991, used with permission.)

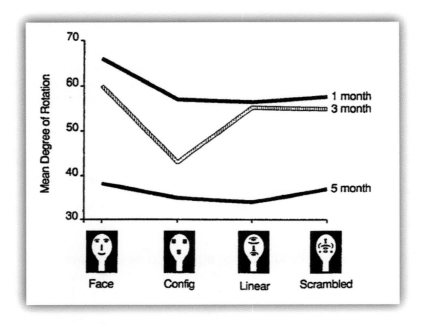

Figure 3.4 Mean rotation angle of chair at the point of disengagement from each type of facial stimuli across age group. (From Johnson et al. 1991, used with permission.)

purpose and conlern now takes over to develop facial processing further. Johnson et al.'s findings have since been replicated by numerous researchers, all of whom concluded that new-borns prefer to visually track stimuli resembling a face as long as the configuration of the features is correct (Simion et al. 1998; Valenza et al. 1996).

The fact that new-borns both orientate towards facial stimuli minutes after birth and demonstrate some ability to recognise faces suggests this is an innate competency, the function of which is to connect or bond with the caregiver. The findings from Bushnell et al.'s (1989) and Pascalis et al.'s (1995) studies demonstrate that new-borns prefer to look longer at their mother's face than that of an unfamiliar female face, even when other sensory information such as the mother's smell and voice have been masked. This finding also suggests that the processing of faces plays a pivotal role in bond formation (or attachment) between infant and caregiver.

New-borns have other innate competencies (see Box 2.1, Chapter 2). An important competency that develops as infants become mobile is depth perception.

Ability to perceive depth

Understanding of depth perception in infants was tested by Gibson and Walk (1960) using what has become known as the visual cliff. The visual cliff is best described as 'an apparent but not actual drop from one surface to another . . . created by connecting a transparent glass surface to an opaque patterned surface . . . the floor below has the same pattern as the opaque surface' (Cherry 2017). Gibson and Walk devised the visual cliff to address whether depth perception in infancy is innate or a learned behaviour. The layout of the visual cliff is entirely safe despite the perception of there being a drop. The caregiver stands at the 'deep end' of the visual cliff while the infant is placed at the 'shallow end' looking down at the fake drop. The caregiver entices the infant towards them by affectionate beckoning. An infant who has developed depth perception will remain on the shallow end and refuse to crawl to the caregiver. An infant without any understanding of depth, however, will crawl to the caregiver. Gibson and Walk found that perception of depth occurs when infants begin to crawl. Nevertheless, infants crawling at six months would move towards the caregiver, something not seen at ten months. Hence, by ten months infants have developed depth perception. Interestingly, Campos et al. (1978) found that three-month-old infants' heart rate and breathing increased when placed at the edge of the 'shallow end' but they still crawled across the visual cliff. Campos et al. reasoned that these infants fail to realise crawling across towards their caregiver will result in falling – something they later understand as they experience knocks and tumbles that come with crawling.

Another competency that new-borns are born with is the simple emotional arousal dichotomy of approach–avoidance. This emotional arousal bifurcation is simple but forms the infrastructure for the development of a profound system of at least six 'universal emotions' (Ekman and Friesen 1971). Approach–avoidance is the second infant competency, which we will consider next.

Ability to react emotionally using approach or avoidance

As adults we develop a complex set of emotional expressions and perceptual understanding of our own and others' emotional states (see Chapters 5 and 10). Infants appear to have two innate rudimentary emotional arousal responses to stimuli referred to as approach and avoidance. The infant's emotional life consists of little more than these two arousal states: an attraction to pleasant stimulation therefore eliciting approach and withdrawal or avoidance of unpleasant stimulation. Given that this is the nature of emotional arousal the new-born arrives equipped with, the approach–avoidance response makes perfect evolutionary sense. This is all the new-born needs at this juncture in their lifespan development. It might also suggest that infants are born with an innate understanding of the meaning intended in the emotional facial expressions of others. Hence if the caregiver adopts a playful posture and conveys a happy facial expression, then the infant will be in an approach arousal state and most likely respond positively by mirroring the expression portrayed. The opposite also applies, however, where parents adopting a despondent posture are likely to initiate an avoidance arousal state in the infant. Under these circumstances the infant will feel uncomfortable and will want the situation to change. In an avoidance arousal state the infant will exhibit behaviours designed to provoke a change in the parents' behaviour such as crying and 'pick-me-up' gesturing or sucking an object such as a pacifier or the edge of a blanket. A continuation of parental despondency could have serious consequences for the infant's normal socioemotional development. This could cause alterations to the infant's sleeping patterns and increase levels of irritability, anger and anxiousness. An infant's avoidance of aversive situations is limited due to their immature motor development, so they resort to simple avoidance tactics such as turning the head, gaze avoidance and crying. These types of behaviours are attempts at **modulating** their emotional arousal state. Modulation or emotional self-regulation refers to the strategies we use to adjust our emotional state to a level of intensity we feel comfortable with (see Box 3.1). In the case of infants this means reducing both the intensity and the duration of their current emotional experience. The ability of the infant to control their emotional state is also aided by the development of the capacity to shift attention, which generally occurs around four months of age. Axia et al. (1999) demonstrated that infants who modulate their emotional arousal state by turning away from unpleasant stimuli are more likely to be protected against distress. It is worth noting that infants sometimes avert their gaze when they are overwhelmed for positive reasons, such as excitement during play games with their caregiver. Hence it is not always a negative sign but a signal that they need to disengage from overstimulation and arousal (Guerra et al. 2012). Infant ability to modulate their arousal state continues as approach–avoidance develops into a range of further emotions (see Figure 3.6).

Box 3.1   Methods used to modulate (or regulate) emotions

Developmental psychologists agree that learning how to modulate emotional expression is a challenging task for infants and children (Cole et al. 2004; Thompson 2006b). Parental guidance is required in order to help children learn to control their emotions and how these are expressed appropriately in different situations and circumstances. Strategies of modulating emotions are initially limited in infants due to their need to further develop motor and sensory skills. They are, however, endowed with response reactions to pleasant and unpleasant situations. These responses are considered to be an innate survival kit designed to enable the infant to approach or avoid pleasant or unpleasant stimuli respectively.

At 6 months infants look away from strangers but by 18 months adopt behaviours that help to soothe or distract themselves when aroused or uncertain of the situation (Mangelsdorf et al. 1995). Parental and other closely associated adults' expectations of toddlers' abilities to self-regulate their emotions increase with the age of the infant. According to Malatestsa et al. (1989) unmodulated emotional expression is replaced by increasingly controlled emotional behaviour with increasing age. Emotional expressions, according to La

(continued)

(continued)

Freniere (2000) and Saarni et al. (2006), become 'conventionalised', that is, their frequency and intensity become more controlled. This can be demonstrated by differences in the portrayal of emotional expression towards discomfort caused by hunger in a baby and a child. In the case of the baby the modulating response is to cry, unlike the child whose emotional expression might be to sulk. Modulation of emotions in this way helps to promote better adjustment to future emotionally arousing situations and circumstances. Fox and Calkins (2003) argue that modulating behaviours such as these can be used to gauge how well an individual will cope with future stresses. Furthermore, Gilliom et al. (2002) claimed that the ability to show emotional modulation in infancy is a good protective factor against exhibiting externalising behaviours (such as bullying other children and being aggressive) in kindergarten. Interestingly, however, Betts et al. (2009) found that suppressing the expression of an emotion in childhood as a strategy of modulation is likely to cause mental health problems (such as depression) later in adolescence. Clearly the jury is out on the efficacy of emotional modulation in infancy.

In Box 3.2 the importance of parental socialisation in the process of teaching children how to modulate their emotional expression is alluded to. This aspect of socialisation is important as the work of Suzanne Denham (1998) demonstrates. She outlined three ways that families per se offer guidance to their children through socialisation:

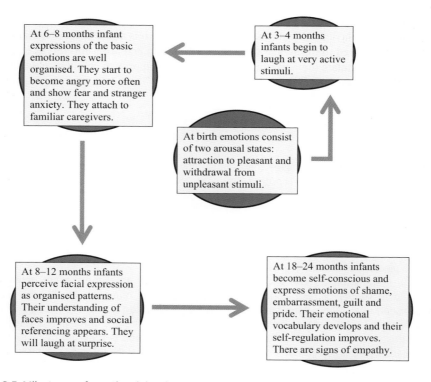

Figure 3.5 Milestones of emotional development.

1. Modelling – children use their family as models of emotional expressiveness.
2. Reactions – the way family members react to the child's emotional expressiveness in different situations and circumstances will either reinforce or discourage their future portrayal.
3. Coaching – family members, in particular the parents, will discuss emotions and the child's understanding and perception of their own and others' emotions.

Denham explains that these three socialisation functions in emotional modulation serve to induce a fuller understanding of emotions and of how they are expressed appropriately. This then combines to improve social competence (e.g., social interaction with others) and the regulation of emotions.

Box 3.2   The role of emotional display rules in the expression of emotions

As they develop, children come to learn **emotional display rules** that dictate socially acceptable exhibitions of emotional expression in a variety of situations and circumstances in a given culture. Eight to ten year olds learn, for example, that there are situations where they feel it is appropriate to mask their emotional responses. Saarni et al. (2006) argued that there are times when children should show positive emotional expression such as smiling even when covertly they feel unhappy. Sala et al. (2014) found evidence suggesting an increase in knowledge about emotions contributes towards preschoolers' ability to modulate their emotional states (Izard et al. 2008). But how do they learn emotional display rules? Social learning develops through the observation of others, in particular the parents who are responsible for the socialisation of their offspring. Socialisation is an important process where parents teach their children to adopt the attitudes, values and behaviours considered to be socially appropriate by the society they live in. This includes showing appropriate emotional expression. Of course the socialisation process conforms to societal and cultural norms – hence culture plays an important role here. The importance of culture was demonstrated in a study by Cole et al. (2002) where three matched groups of children from different cultural backgrounds were compared. Tamang (a Buddhist group) and Brahman (a Hindu group) and a group from a rural town in the US were asked for their reaction to a scenario where another child accidentally spills a drink onto their homework. The Tamang, who adhere to a philosophy of promoting harmony, responded to this scenario with shame. Children of the Brahman, who are taught to be in full self-control of their emotions, showed no emotional display of anger or shame. American children, however, consistently displayed anger. In American culture children are taught to be self-assertive and therefore are more likely to respond in an emotionally overt way. Hence, while there is clear evidence that some emotions are universal, children come to modulate the expression of such emotions as they develop in order to conform to the emotional display rules of their particular culture.

Children observe the behaviours of others and this includes the emotional states exhibited by other members of the family and their peers (see Chapter 7). It is not surprising therefore that studies by Eisenberg et al. (2001) and Halberstadt et al. (2001) found robust similarities in both the intensity of emotional expression and which emotions are typically exhibited by parents and by their children. Furthermore, the emotional environment encapsulated in the family during childhood influences the nature of emotions expressed by the child in the future. Positive emotional environments create a happy individual (Halberstadt et al. 2001) whereas a negative one promotes sadness and anger (Denham et al. 2007).

There is no doubt that parents are important to how children learn about their emotions and react to others. Denham's three ways in which families socialise their children's emotional expressions (modelling, reactions and coaching) reflect a social learning approach (see Chapters 1 and 2). In the case of modelling, children observe how their parents behave emotionally. The reactions from parents towards their child's emotional behaviours act to promote or discourage them from occurring. Coaching (that is often provided by parents who have good insight into their own emotions) encourages children to have a sound understanding and appreciation of the socioemotional world they encounter (Dunn and Hughes 1998). Parents, however, are not the only ones to influence the emotional behaviours of their children – peers can be just as influential, especially when we consider play behaviour. Play provides a safe-contained context for children to express their emotions and develop an appreciative understanding of each other's belief system and feelings (Dunn and Hughes 2001) (see Chapter 9). We will return to the influence of peers when we consider Judith Rich Harris' Group Socialisation Theory (1995; 1998) in Chapters 7, 9 and 12. Another important factor in the development of emotional responses is the temperament of the child. This is an important factor for parent–child interactions and the socialisation process (see Chapter 12).

Learning how to modulate emotional expression from the two basic arousal states of approach–avoidance helps the new-born cope with pleasant and unpleasant stimuli. As discussed earlier, however, these initial approach–avoidance arousal states develop into a range of new emotions (see Figure 3.6); the six primary universal emotions of happy, sad, fear, anger, disgust and surprise (Ekman and Friesen 1971) followed by secondary (or self-conscious) emotions of pride, shame, guilt and jealousy. The development of these primary and secondary emotions is the topic of our next section.

THE DEVELOPMENT OF PRIMARY AND SECONDARY EMOTIONS

The **primary emotions**, often referred to as the early emotions, include happiness (or joy), fear, anger, sadness, disgust and surprise. We will concentrate on happiness, fear, anger and sadness as these have been researched the most. Later emotions to develop during the second half of the first year to the second year of infancy are pride, shame, jealousy, embarrassment, empathy and guilt; these comprise the secondary emotions. These tend to be referred to as the self-conscious emotions because, as Lewis (2010) points out, they involve other people's emotional responses. According to Kagan (2010), these secondary emotions are profound and involve interpretation and much thought to be understood appropriately. Kagan therefore argues that the appearance of secondary emotions occurs later than the first year – an opinion expressed by many other developmentalists.

Obtaining data about the emergence of different primary emotions has been conducted using verbal reports from the parents of infants. These reports are based on observations of their infant's facial expressions. Based on observations from parents of their one-month-old new-born's emotional expressions, Johnson et al. (1982) obtained the following statistics in descending order:

- 99 per cent observed interest
- 95 per cent observed joy
- 85 per cent observed anger
- 74 per cent observed surprise
- 58 per cent observed fear
- 34 per cent observed sadness

These observations were based on the new-born's facial expressions, how they moved their body in response to stimuli and the type of vocalisations made – all interpreted within a situational context. Hence, in the case of joy, caregivers observe this emotional expression during a game of peek-a-boo (here the caregiver uses her hands to cover her eyes, then removes them while simultaneously smiling and saying 'peek-a-boo'). In addition to the six universal emotions outlined by Ekman and Friesen (1975), parents often identify an emotional expression depicting interest. Here the infant looks at the stimulus without showing any of the other emotional expressions but appears to be focusing its attention on what it is seeing and hearing. While parental observations and interpretations are informative, researchers have taken this further by developing empirically-based classifications of infant emotional expressions. One reliable coding system of infant emotional expression is derived from the research of Izard et al. (1995). They observed and rated changes of facial expression and body movement in infants by scoring how their facial features and body moved in response to specific stimuli. These scores were used as a means of measuring which emotion was exhibited at any point in time, and is now used as part of the Maximally Discriminative Facial Movement (MAX) coding system. It is clear that there are different emotional expressions displayed by young infants but is there an order in which these emotions develop? We will turn our attention to the development of the main primary emotions.

Primary emotions

As outlined earlier Ekman and Friesen (1971) identified six universal emotional expressions that are observed in all cultures. Interestingly, it is well established that the processing of these emotions is associated with the right cerebral hemisphere. This **lateralisation** of function appears to develop with age and can be tested through the use of **chimeric face** presentation (see Box 3.3). In this section, however, we are interested in the way primary emotions are expressed by infants and the purpose they serve. The first of the primary emotions to be considered is happiness, displayed in the guise of smiles and laughter. This is followed by fear, anger and sadness.

Happiness

Happiness is shown through smiles and laughter. Developmentalists suggest there are three basic phases of smiling: reflex smile seen immediately after birth; social smiling in response to seeing and hearing someone; and selective social smiling to familiar faces and voices beginning at three and a half months (Messenger et al. 1999, 2001). Between 6–10 weeks the human face evokes a grin called the social smile (Sroufe and Waters 1976). Smiling also occurs in response to the caregiver's voice, which is usually in the high pitch range (Campos 2005). The combination of a human face and a high-pitched voice elicits smiles from babies between two and six months old. Ellsworth et al. (1993) demonstrated how the face elicited the most smiles from three-month-olds by using an array of puppets varying in their similarity to the human face initially shown. At four weeks old the eyes of a face elicit smiles from babies, which extends to include the mouth between eight and nine weeks of age. The smile encourages caregivers to show affection, so babies smile even more as a way of reinforcing a nurturing response from those providing their care. Infants will modify their emotional expression to coordinate with their caregiver. These close interactions with the caregiver are said to be mutually regulated so that when the caregiver smiles so does the infant and vice versa. This is often described as being synchronous or reciprocal responding.

Box 3.3   Lateralisation for recognition of emotions in children aged five to eleven

The processing of facial emotional expression in adults is especially associated with the right hemisphere of the brain. We know this from studies showing deficits in the processing of emotional information among patients with brain lesions to the right hemisphere (Tucker et al. 1977). A simple experimental paradigm commonly used to ascertain the extent of right hemisphere involvement in emotional processing is known as the free vision chimeric face test. It was German psychologist Werner Wolff who in 1933 first introduced the chimeric face test. A chimeric face depicts one half of a face as being neutral and the other half showing an emotional expression (one of the six universal emotions described by Ekman and Friesen 1971). The half of the face showing one of the emotions can be on either the right or left side (see Figure 3.7). Hence when the emotional expression is on the right half of the face, it is presented to the participant's left visual field (LVF). Information presented in the LVF is processed initially by the right hemisphere of the brain and vice versa (known as the contralateral hemisphere). Levy et al. (1983) showed participants a slide presentation of chimeric faces. This was done by presenting participants with two chimeric mirror images of the same emotional expression – one above the other. Participants are required to focus at the centre of the two chimeric presentations and to note which of the two chimeric presentations appears as more intense. Levy et al. found a consistent LVF preference suggesting a right hemisphere (RH) advantage for emotional recognition.

Levine and Levy (1986) and Barth and Boles (1999) failed to find a conclusive right hemisphere advantage in young children. Workman et al. (2006) presented three different age groups of children (5/6, 7/8 and 10/11 years) with the 'Emotional Chimeric Faces Test' (Workman et al. 2000). This test, which expanded the use of chimeric faces, for the first time consisted of all six universal facial emotions. As in previous experiments each emotional half-face was combined with a neutral half-face. In total there were 48 chimeric face pairs – with the emotion expressed to the right or left side of the face and presented either in the above or below position in the booklet. Participants were asked to judge which of the pair of chimeric faces was the most emotive face. In other words, was the top or bottom face the most happy, angry, fearful, disgusted, surprised or sad. Workman et al.'s findings were consistent with previous research showing a RH bias for the perception of emotions in faces. By considering all six universal emotions, however, Workman et al. were able to demonstrate developmental differences across the age groups. A RH advantage for attending to emotional expressions develops between 5 and

Figure 3.6 A chimeric face showing the emotional expression of anger.

11 years of age. The 5 to 6 year olds showed no left or right hemisphere advantage for five of the emotions (happiness was the exception where a RH advantage was found). The 10/11 year olds showed a RH advantage for the perception of all emotional facial expressions. The fact that the perception of happiness is lateralised in the 5/6 year olds makes sense from an evolutionary perspective as happiness portrayed by smiling initiates a rapport with the caregiver thus promoting attachment. The 7/8 year olds were found to be broadly between the younger and older children on their scores which showed a shift towards a RH advantage.

Smiling is one of many **socially facilitating behaviours** infants are equipped with to ensure an emotional bond is made with the caregiver. The three-month-old baby no longer smiles at all faces it encounters, but rather selectively smiles at faces that are familiar (Saarni et al. 2006). In fact 10–12 month olds have several types of smile as identified by Dickson, Fogel and Messinger (1998). They classified smiles as the broad cheek-raised smile used for parental greeting; a reserved muted smile used to greet friendly strangers and a mouth-open smile during stimulating play. A special smile reserved for the caregiver was observed by Fox and Davidson (1988) in 10 month olds. These special smiles are often regarded as genuine smiles as they involve not only the upturning of the mouth but creasing around the eyes. This means that, as well as the features being important in smiling, the spaces between the features (known as the configurational properties) also provide cues as to the emotional state. Ekman (2003) described this as a face depicting a pleasurable emotion also known as the Duchenne smile introduced by the French anatomist, Guillaume Duchenne, in his book *Mecanisme de la Physionomie Humaine* published in 1862.

Laughter appears at three to four months (Sroufe 1996) and tends to occur in response to active stimuli such as the parent being playful. Findings by Sroufe and Wunsch (1972) suggest that infants laugh at visual, auditory, tactile and social-active (i.e., peek-a-boo game, bouncing the baby on the knee, making funny noises) stimuli. These types of facilitators of laughter change, however, as the baby ages (see Figure 3.7). All types of stimuli

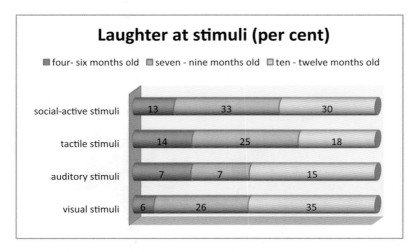

Figure 3.7 Changes in percentage of laughter displayed to different types of stimuli as a function of age.

continue to induce laughter in babies of seven to nine months old, however, while visual, tactile and social-active stimuli evoke increasing laughter, auditory stimuli continues to be constant. Visual stimuli continue to be the most laugh-inducing stimuli at 10–12 months of age. Infants smile and laugh when they achieve new skills such as walking (Sroufe 1996). Infants tend to engage in most laughter when they experience social events involving other children (Saarni et al. 2006).

Fear

If happiness can be considered as arising out of an approach arousal state, then it makes perfect sense that fear arises from an avoidance arousal state. Fear increases at the same point in the developmental timeline as happiness – unsurprising considering that the approach–avoidance arousal states are present from birth. It does, however, develop at a slower pace than happiness. As discussed previously, happiness occurs in response to pleasant stimuli and is an emotional expression designed to elicit maternal feelings towards the infant. It is just as important, however, to inform the caregiver of situations and circumstances where the infant feels uncomfortable and frightened. The way of informing the caregiver is to show emotional expressions of fear. Fear is often expressed in unfamiliar situations or when unfamiliar people present themselves and in so doing cause an arousal state in the infant known as **stranger distress**. One reason why fear takes longer than happiness to develop fully might be related to a need to form a bond with the caregiver. Showing fear to the caregiver is unlikely to facilitate bond formation. The infant needs to facilitate a bond with the caregiver to ensure she is looked after. Once this bond is formed, then developing a full fear expression under appropriate circumstances is likely to be adaptive (you may recall from Chapter 1 that evolutionary psychologists have suggested that different forms of fear are adapted to different stages of development (Workman and Reader 2014)).

The emotional expression of fear has been argued by Sroufe (1996) to emerge as two phases: wariness shown at three months and genuine fear at seven to nine months of age. Witherington et al. (2010) found that fear can occur as early as three months if the infant experiences abuse and neglect. Sroufe's two phase model is consistent with fear taking longer than happiness to fully develop and for the reasons previously discussed. Sroufe claims that babies of three months will be wary of events and people they do not understand. Between seven and nine months, however, on seeing a stranger these babies react by showing fear and anxiety – hence the term stranger distress. Wariness of

Plate 3.3 Smiling baby. (Shutterstock 379567240.)

Plate 3.4 Frightened baby expression. (Shutterstock 379567228.)

strangers provokes uncertainty even in babies of four months suggesting they are able to discriminate between familiar and unfamiliar faces. Although there is interest in novel stimuli such as a stranger, babies will look at their caregiver's face and compare this to the stranger's. Parke and Gauvain (2009) claim that this comparative gazing from stranger to caregiver is replaced at five months by a 'sober stare' and at six months is likely to be accompanied by signals of distress. According to Sroufe by seven to nine months this is then replaced by expressions of fear.

The developmental timeframe of stranger distress responses was considered to be universal, such that all infants, regardless of ethnicity, develop this at the same age. Various developmental psychologists (La Freniere 2000; Saarni et al. 2006) presented cross-cultural evidence to suggest this is not necessarily the case. Referring to research undertaken by Ainsworth (1963) in Uganda for instance, La Freniere and Saarni et al. demonstrated that stranger distress is exhibited at seven to nine months of age but not in the Efe babies of Africa (Tronick et al. 1992). Their culture is different because the caring for babies is a shared responsibility among related adults so that these babies become accustomed to seeing many different faces. Demonstrating stranger distress depends on a host of variables including the familiarity of the stranger, whether or not he or she is encountered in the home with the caregiver present and the nature of the social interaction occurring (Saarni et al. 2006). Studies show that infants are less likely to fear strangers when their mother reacts positively towards the stranger. This means that infants are continuously monitoring their caregiver's emotional facial expressions – a process known as **social referencing**.

When infants perform social referencing in this context they are trying to establish their caregiver's current emotional state by looking for facial signals indicative of how they feel. By establishing their caregiver's current emotional state, infants can gauge how they should respond to the stranger–caregiver's social encounter. Social referencing therefore involves

Plate 3.5 Infant showing distress towards a stranger. (Shutterstock 462539314.)

the interpretation of emotions in other people's faces (Cornew et al. 2012) but also serves to clarify an ambiguous situation involving an encounter with a stranger (Pelaez et al. 2012).

Stranger distress can be attenuated when the infant feels it has an element of control over the specifics of the social encounter (Mangelsdorf et al. 1991). This is related to how able they are to modulate their anxiety through behaviours that help to alter negative arousal states such avoiding the stranger's eye gaze. Infants are also more fearful of female and male adult strangers than they are of child strangers. The issue of size as a factor influencing this finding was ruled out in a study by Lewis and Brooks (1974) when infants reacted fearfully towards an adult who was height compromised. This suggests that infants can implicitly differentiate between young and older faces. Stranger distress can be further attenuated when the stranger behaves in a friendly way with a smiley face.

Another form of fear is called **separation protest** and, as the name suggests, this is a negative reaction displayed by the infant when separated from the caregiver. Separation protest consists of negative emotions such as sadness and loss and in infants this can be portrayed by behaviours like crying, following and calling out to the caregiver. The behaviour shown by the caregiver prior to the separation will influence the extent of separation protest exhibited (Field et al. 1984). Field et al. argued that preparation is key to reducing separation protest and can be achieved by the caregiver reassuring the infant of their return. Cross-cultural studies indicate that separation protest climaxes between 13–15 months of age (Kagan et al. 1978). Separation protest is one measure used in Mary Ainsworth's 'strange situation' experiment. The strange situation experiment was designed by Ainsworth to establish the nature of the attachment bond between the caregiver and infant. She found that infants who showed separation protest tended to have a secure attachment bond with the caregiver. This will be returned to in more detail when we consider attachment.

Anger

Both smiling and crying are the first two emotional expressions used by infants to communicate with their caregivers. While the motivation for smiling is less difficult to ascertain, the reasons for crying are more complex. At least three different types of crying have been identified: basic cry, angry cry and cry of pain (Bukatko and Daehler 2004; Santrock 2005). The basic cry indicates a need to be fed and sounds different to the loud wailing sound of the cry of pain. It is the cry of anger that is of particular interest here as it alludes to there being an emotional expression of anger at an early stage of infancy. Parents are particularly good at distinguishing a cry of anger from a cry of pain (Zeskind et al. 1992). Kail and Cavanaugh (2004) state that, 'by crying, babies tell their parents that they are hungry or tired, angry or hurt. By responding to these cries, parents are encouraging their new-born's efforts to communicate' (p. 88).

At 6–8 months angry expressions increase in frequency and intensity but Camras et al. (1991) argue that the identification of angry expressions is difficult to differentiate from general signals of distress. Izard (1994) has also suggested that new-borns do demonstrate negative emotional expressions such as a startle response, distress and disgust towards the taste of certain foods. It is not until infants are between two and three months that they exhibit expressions of interest, surprise, sadness and anger (Izard et al. 1995). As demonstrated in Stenberg and Campos' (1990) study, infants between four and seven months old will display expressions of anger when their arms are restricted from movement. Other studies have shown that infants of seven months old will display expressions of anger when tempted with a biscuit close to their mouth only for it to be retracted before they could suck on it (Stenberg et al. 1983).

Other situations eliciting anger include taking an object away, being left by the caregiver, being put down for a nap (Camras 1992) or receiving an inoculation causing distress, pain

Plate 3.6 Baby demonstrating anger. (Shutterstock 225089740.)

and frustration (Izard et al. 1987). Both anger and fear, although negative emotions, increase with age at a time when infants become more mobile. This makes sense as both emotions have a survival value for the infant.

Sadness

Commonly seen in infants is the anger/cry face but this negative expression often co-occurs with other underlying negative emotions. Sullivan and Lewis (2003) refer to a combination of

Plate 3.7 Toddler demonstrating sad expression. (Shutterstock 218579263.)

negative expressions as 'blends'. Blended anger and sadness commonly occur together where the upper part of the face shows anger and the lower region demonstrates sadness – usually by pouting (Sullivan and Lewis 2003). Camras (1992) suggested that the anger/cry face blend might be a reflection of distress or unhappiness rather than signalling anger. Sad pouts do not occur often but, when they do, they are commonly displayed during social interactions and at times of learning when experiencing episodes of frustration (Izard et al. 1995; Sullivan et al. 1992). Camras (1992) suggested that sad pouts could be an intermediate stage of an anger expression or a regulatory response to inhibit displays of anger. Sullivan and Lewis (2003) entertain the possibility that expressions of sadness might not be independent of anger and that the caregiver's response to a sad face effectively attenuates any angry emotions.

Infants clearly show different emotional expressions and these become refined with age. As skills at detecting what others are looking at improve, infants realise that an emotional expression is also a meaningful reaction to a specific object or event (Tomasello 1999). Infants can now engage in social referencing, in which they actively seek emotional information from a trusted person in an uncertain situation. By responding to caregivers' emotional messages they can avoid harmful situations. Parents can use social referencing to teach their infants how to react to novel events and to compare their own interpretations with others. By 18 months infants realise that the emotional reactions of others may be different to their own (Repacholi and Gopnik 1997). This improves further still with the advent of the secondary emotions, which we will consider next.

Secondary emotions (also referred to as self-conscious emotions)

Second higher-order emotions such as shame (or embarrassment), guilt, empathy, pride and jealousy are called self-conscious emotions because each involves injury to, or enhancement of, a sense of self. When ashamed or embarrassed we feel negative about our behaviour. Pride reflects delight (Saarni et al. 1998). In 18–24 month olds, shame and embarrassment are shown by the lowering of the eyes and head, and their faces are hidden using their hands. Guilt is also shown when a snatched toy is returned to a playmate by patting the friend on the shoulder in a friendly way. Jealousy is considered an emotion that is beyond the comprehension of infants under 18 months of age (Case et al. 1988) because it requires more advanced cognition (Lewis 2003). Not all developmentalists agree with this. Panksepp (2010) argues that jealousy might be a 'prepared' emotion requiring minimal cognitive processing. This means we might have a predisposition to experience jealousy very early on to ensure we get our caregivers' attention and resources necessary to survive. Adult instruction in the refinement of the self-conscious emotions is necessary as a means of teaching children when it is socially appropriate to display emotions of pride or shame for example. Emotions such as shame, guilt and empathy clearly play an important role in the development of moral behaviour (see Chapter 10). The self-conscious emotions also rely on being self-aware (Saarni et al. 2006).

Shame and pride

Shame and pride appear at about 18 months of age (Saarni et al. 2006) and involve different facial expressions – shame, for instance, leads to blushing and looking away to escape scrutiny. Emotions of shame and pride appear to be antagonistic to each other because you either feel bad about a specific behaviour or you feel good. One or other of these emotions is often expressed during the learning process where a successful outcome invokes feelings of pride unlike failure leading to shame. Lewis et al. (1992) found differences in emotional response towards the failure to solve easy and difficult problem tasks. When children fail to solve an easy problem they experience shame but when it is a difficult task and they fail then the emotion experienced is sadness. Pride is experienced when a difficult problem is successfully solved. Pride involves a complex mix of emotions. Primary emotions such as happiness at doing well but also self-awareness that others value this success means that individuals can read the current emotional state of other people (Saarni et al. 2006). Nelson et al. (2013) argue that as children get older their broad categories of emotion become more specific. This means that anger as a broad category of a negative emotion later divides into anger and disgust. Pride, they argue, becomes separated from happiness because of what initiates it (an achievement) and its consequences (recognition by others). Shame or embarrassment is one of the first self-conscious emotions to arise and plays an integral role in social interaction (Keltner and Haidt 1999). Shame helps motivate an individual to follow social norms and avoid social rejection. Shame is an emotional response to minor social transgressions that can lead to negative judgements or peer rejection. Children as young as four to five years of age show an immature comprehension of embarrassment (Colonnesi et al. 2010) but as their ability to utilise information from previous experiences to apply to present ones develops (Suddendorf and Busby 2005), their understanding of social rules protects them from making social faux-pas. This, in turn, will help them to avoid being rejected by their peers and develop a mature understanding of embarrassment (Banerjee and Watling 2005). In support of this, Chobhthaigh and Wilson (2015) found that the understanding of embarrassment that children hold changes between six and eight years of age. This can, in part, be explained by children developing social and emotional knowledge of the costs for transgressing social norms.

Empathy

Empathy refers to the ability to comprehend and share the feelings experienced by another person. Hence empathy involves cognitive processing (Hoffman 2000). It is sometimes referred to as the ability to imagine what another person is experiencing emotionally without necessarily feeling the emotions directly oneself. It is important to distinguish between **egoistic personal distress** and empathy. Egoistic personal distress differs from empathy in that there are unpleasant feelings such as being upset or perturbed. For empathy, in contrast, there is an understanding of another's emotional state without personal distress. Individuals feeling empathy are normally motivated to act in altruistic ways to reduce the other person's distress. In cases where parents show empathy in their parenting styles, their children become more likely to demonstrate empathy towards others. Mothers who show less empathy have children who mirror their level of empathy towards others. In one study children with parents suffering from Attention Deficit Hyperactivity Disorder (ADHD) were found to experience less empathy in the home. This, in turn, reduced their empathy levels to others (Psychogiou et al. 2008). Parents who are warm and encouraging, and who show sensitive sympathetic concern for their children, have children who are likely to react in a concerned way to others in distress (Eisenberg and McNally 1993). In contrast, angry punitive parenting disrupts empathy and sympathy at an early age: abused children are more likely to demonstrate fear, anger and physical attacks (Klimes-Dougan and Kistner 1990). Empathy becomes more common in early childhood and is important for pro-social behaviour – actions that benefit another person without any expectation of reward (Eisenberg and Fabes 1998). Children who are sociable, assertive and good at regulating their emotions are more likely to help, share and comfort others in distress (Eisenberg et al. 1998).

Guilt and shame

Guilt can be defined as a feeling of responsibility and anxiety at having done something wrong. A complete understanding of guilt emerges in children of nine years. Graham et al. (1994) demonstrated the difference in comprehension of guilt in children between the ages of six and nine. They found that six year olds did not fully understand the importance of being responsible for the outcome of their actions. They only concentrated on simplistic outcomes of a situation whereas the nine year olds understood the need to implicate the self as being to blame for the outcome (e.g., being too lazy to put a toy away caused someone to trip over). Shame is a more public emotion than guilt in as much as the actions of the person feeling this emotion have been made public (note guilt can be felt without others being aware of your actions). Shame and guilt are both involved in the development of a conscience and moral and prosocial behaviour (see Chapter 10). Menesini and Camodeca (2008) considered the relationship between intentional and non-intentional situations causing emotions of shame and guilt. They were interested to see how nine- to eleven-year-old children responded to ten situations of which five elicited shame only in the protagonist and five caused shame and guilt. An example of a shame-only situation was 'You did not sleep well last night and this morning you were half asleep at school. The teacher asked you a question, but you did not understand. How do you feel?' (p. 187). An example of a shame and guilt situation might involve the protagonist pushing a glass that spills juice all over the mother's letter despite being told to stop wriggling about in the chair. The children in this study were asked to imagine themselves in these situations. As a control there were a further ten situations that were ambiguous as to the intent of the protagonist's behaviour. The results showed that guilt was rated higher in situations when harm was committed intentionally. All of the children in Menesini and Camodeca's study considered situations with intentional transgressions as reasons to feel guilty. Furthermore, their findings suggest that shame and guilt are emotions that are closely linked and play important roles in avoiding future transgressions. For this reason Menesini and Camodeca (2008) concluded that emotions such as shame and guilt can be strong drivers of behaviour. Moreover, thinking and feeling are known to be closely interconnected (Lagattuta et al. 1997).

Jealousy

Jealousy is a negative emotion representing interpersonal rivalry (Aldrich et al. 2011). It also signifies a sense of loss of a close person (Smith et al. 1988). Jealousy is commonly experienced among siblings when vying for their parents' attention but can continue to be experienced throughout the lifespan – from infancy (Hart and Carrington 2002), to childhood (Bauminger et al. 2008), to adolescence (Parker et al. 2005), to adulthood (Shackelford et al. 2004). Adolescents, for example, can experience jealousy of a friend who forms a relationship with someone they also fancy. In one study children of 12 months were compared with two to six year olds in an exploration of jealousy towards a sibling who had full parental attention during a play session (Volling et al. 2002). Needless to say, the children left to play on their own experienced jealousy. The way in which jealousy was exhibited, however, varied with age. While younger children exhibited distress the older children displayed signs of anger and sadness (Volling et al. 2002). When family dynamics are positive and the relationships between child and parents are secured, the extent of jealous reactions towards siblings is considerably reduced in comparison with negative and unreliable relationships (Parke and Gauvain 2009). It is during the ages of five to eight years that children develop self-awareness and that jealousy (as well as other secondary emotions) become fully understood (Saarni 1999).

An important aspect of emotional development is forming a bond with a significant other. For neonates this generally involves an attachment to the primary caregiver (most frequently but not exclusively the mother). We now turn our attention to the nature of this attachment process.

ATTACHMENT

According to Weiss (1974) there are different types of relationship of which **attachment** is one example. These different relationships help to fulfil the various needs of individuals:

- Attachment relationships offer security.
- Social network relationships offer a shared interpretation of experience and provide companionship.
- Caregiving relationships give a sense of being needed.
- Other relationships give a sense of worth and competence.
- Kin relationships offer a reliable alliance.
- Mentor relationships provide guidance.

Some relationships such as attachments and caregiving relationships will provide an affectional bond. By **affectional bond** we mean a relatively long-enduring tie where the partner is a unique individual. There is a desire to maintain closeness to this partner. An attachment is an example of an affectional bond; hence an **attachment figure** is never wholly interchangeable with or replaceable by another. There is, however, one criterion of attachment that is not necessarily present in other affectional bonds – seeking security and comfort in the relationship.

It was John Bowlby (1958) who first described the nature of attachment relationships between caregiver and infant in his article 'The nature of the child's tie to his mother'. In this article he introduced the concept of attachment theory into developmental psychology. Bowlby showed that emotional and social ties are most apparent in new-borns and was interested in why this should be the case. From various theoretical approaches – psychoanalysis, ethology, behaviourism and evolutionary psychology – it is apparent that human new-borns are helpless, rely on others to fulfil primary drives (such as thirst and hunger) and need to be assured of non-abandonment. Thus an attachment to a **caregiver** is necessary to ensure their survival. Attachment behaviour is manifested through an emotional tie entwined with dependency, which is why the timeline for the development of emotions coincides closely with bonding between caregiver and offspring. As we have seen previously, infants are endowed with a simple dichotomous approach–avoidance arousal state where approach is preserved for the caregivers. Under normal circumstances there is no fear of parents but anxiety if separated from them. Infants are receptive to being cared for which is why they will seek out the caregiver and maintain close contact. Infants are born with the propensity to show socially facilitating behaviours such as crying when distressed, smiling and gazing at their parents when happy, and looking cute and helpless while making contact noises. These infant behaviours encourage the caregiver to respond in a positive way such as picking up and consoling a crying baby or providing attention and comfort when the infant appears helpless. Through these socially facilitating behaviours an attachment bond is made between caregiver and infant.

Bowlby made the following assumptions about the nature of attachment behaviours shown in infancy and the functions they serve:

- Caregiver provides a secure base from which the infant can explore the world and return to safely.
- Presence of proximity maintenance where the infant wants to remain close to the caregiver.
- Separation distress leads to seeking out the caregiver.
- Emotional attachment of infant to the caregiver provides a sense of safety and security.
- Caregiver provides protection from predators (in evolutionary past).
- Emotionally secure bonds lead to better long-term relationships (thereby increasing probability of reproducing successfully).

According to psychoanalytic and learning theories, the infant attaches to its mother as she fulfils primary drives such as thirst and hunger. This '**cupboard love**', as it has become known, has been looked at more closely by ethologists such as Harlow and Zimmerman's (1959) work with rhesus monkeys. They demonstrated that attachment to the caregiver is not only about cupboard love but about comfort and care. Further research by Harlow in 1962 provided evidence of a rhesus monkey's need to cling to a comforting cloth-covered wire-framed surrogate mother during all times other than feeding. In this study infant monkeys were provided with a wire-framed surrogate mother incorporating a feeding bottle and a more comfortable cloth-covered wire-framed surrogate mother. The monkeys were found to use the wire-framed 'mother' for feeding but immediately returned to the cloth-covered 'mother' for comfort. This finding suggested that attachments are easier to form with objects resembling the real mother; something that appeared to be somewhat wired into an infant's early stages of development.

Just like rhesus monkeys, human infants form attachments very early and quickly, and they do not suddenly become passive and unresponsive once all of their biological needs have been fulfilled. This suggests that attachments are more than a learned or acquired behavioural response – they occur through internal or **intraorganismic organisation**. This means that the infant is biologically organised or ready to form an attachment to the caregiver from birth (Ainsworth 1973; Bowlby 1969). Attachment to others is thought to be based on an experience–expectant neurological system, which makes sense given that contact with the caregiver is almost a certainty. Having an evolved neurological system of this nature prepares the neonate for human contact, which ultimately ensures their survival.

An intraorganismic approach like Bowlby's uses evolution to explain why infants have a biological predisposition to form attachments early on in their development. He argued that attachment is the major mode of interaction that enables infants to survive, and it is for this reason that humans evolved a neurological system that promotes interaction with the caregiver using innate socially facilitating behaviours. If these socially facilitating behaviours fail to promote a duty of care in the caregiver, then the infant may die as a result of neglect. Thus it is this need to switch on a 'maternal instinct' that influences the way infants behave socially (such as exhibiting the species-specific characteristics of smiling and crying).

Although Bowlby perceived aspects of attachment as being hard-wired he also acknowledged the views held by learning theorists that it requires both time and experience to form effectively. Specifically, infants are not born with an implicit model of whom

Plate 3.8 Mother and baby sharing a smile. (Shutterstock 113110381.)

they should become attached to. This develops as a consequence of their experiences encountered with different people to whom they might later become attached. According to Schaffer (1996), there are four phases of attachment:

1. In the first two months infants exhibit indiscriminative social responding to people.
2. By six months infants are able to identify familiar from unfamiliar people but exhibit no separation protest as yet.
3. By seven months infants form specific attachments and seek contact with their caregiver.
4. At two years infants, now considered to be toddlers, form a partnership with their caregiver and together their goals become integrated.

Schaffer's four phases suggests a developmental timeline of when attachment occurs and concurs with the learning theorists that the complexities of attachment follow a learning curve. After 18 months the attachment process becomes more profound as the infant begins to form 'internal working models' of the relationship forged with the caregiver. **Internal working models** develop from a collection of memories about the nature of the attachment relationship. These memories concern the caregiver's reactions towards the infant in a multitude of situations, and it is these reactions that enable infants to form an appraisal of the attachment relationship. These memories arise out of repeated experiences with the caregiver until eventually a profile of what to expect from the caregiver is developed. The infant begins to comprehend the nature of this relationship, and through socially facilitated behaviours will try to change the caregiver's plans to accommodate their own plans. A working model therefore encompasses the infant's internal representation of the world, the attachment figure and interrelationships between them. The working model concept plays an important role in the expression of attachment throughout the lifespan (Bowlby 1969; Bretherton 1985; Waters et al. 2000a; Waters et al. 2000b). Working models, however, can be confused and contradictory depending on the type of parental relationship experienced (see Box 3.4).

> ### Box 3.4   Rejection and inconsistent attitudes
>
> According to Bretherton (1985), children who have been rejected and abused by their parents will develop internal working models describing rejecting parents. Children who experience problems, for example, will often show incoherent attitudes concerning their attachments, which Bowlby called multiple models. Multiple models about the caregiver contain opposing attitudes existing concurrently. For example: 'I believe that mother is unfailingly loving/I believe that mother is ridiculing and rejecting' (an example of conflicting content). 'I fear that father will leave this family/I hope that father will leave this family' (an example of conflicting attitudes). Bretherton therefore saw conflict and inconsistency during early attachment as a major cause of later relationship problems.

The quality of the attachment bond between caregiver and infant has been researched by Mary Ainsworth using the 'strange situation' experiment (see Box 2.7 in Chapter 2). In the next section we will consider her findings and the implications this raises for the argument of there being an **intergenerational effect of attachment type**.

Quality of attachment and its intergenerational effect

Mary Ainsworth (1967) introduced the 'strange situation' experiment in which the infant is observed through a one-way mirror while playing with toys in a room. Contact and the nature of interaction between the caregiver and infant is observed and recorded. Further observations are made when a stranger enters the room, followed by the caregiver leaving the infant alone with the stranger and the subsequent caregiver's return. Of particular interest to Ainsworth was how the infant would react to the caregiver leaving the room and when she returned. Would the infant be distressed to see the caregiver leave but pleased to see her return? Through observing interactions between caregiver and infant throughout the 'strange situation' setup Ainsworth was able to develop three categories of infant attachment. These are based on levels of protest, despair and detachment (the **PDD model**) on separation from the caregiver:

- **Insecure avoidant** (A-dyad) infants ignore the caregiver, are indifferent towards her, show no distress on her departure and avoid her when she returns. The stranger is treated the same as the caregiver.
- **Securely attached** (B-dyad) infants play with their caregiver and accept her. They are distressed on her departure and actively seek contact when she returns to the room. The stranger is treated very differently from the caregiver.
- **Insecure resistant** (C-dyad) infants are wary whilst the caregiver is present in the room but show distress on her departure. They express anger and will actively seek contact on her return but interestingly will resist her attempts at contact when offered.

Ainsworth's categories have been subjected to an **adaptationist account** by evolutionist Jay Belsky (1997). Likewise James Chisholm (1999) has also proposed an adaptationist account but relates reproductive strategy style to the style adopted by his or her parents (see Box 3.5).

Box 3.5 Adaptationist model of attachment type

Belsky argues that research into adults classified as securely attached indicates that they tend to report higher levels of relationship security than do insecurely attached individuals. Secure men engage in more supportive relationships with their partners (Ewing and Pratt 1995); romantic relationships of secure men and women are longer lasting (Hazan and Shaver 1987); and secure partners are more likely to marry in the first place (Kirkpatrick and Hazan 1994). Furthermore, they invest and put high parenting effort into offspring (parental reproductive strategy).

Insecure-avoidant adults are more willing than others to engage in sex in the absence of an enduring relationship (Brennan et al. 1991), are more likely to have dated more than one person (Kirkpatrick and Hazan 1994) and experienced break-up of a relationship (Feeney and Noller 1992). Insecure-avoidant mothers are more likely to be ambivalent and unsupportive towards their offspring (Crowell and Feldman 1991). Insecure-resistant adults are less likely to pass on their genes but supposedly are more caring and supportive of their nephews and nieces as a strategy of increasing one's inclusive fitness. This is the most speculative part of Belsky's life history explanation for attachment. Additionally insecure-resistant females tend to mother their partner rather than romancing them (Kunce and Shaver 1994).

Confirmation of Ainsworth's attachment categories has been established by a test known as the Attachment Q Sort (AQS). This involves asking caregivers to sort cards with phrases describing their child's behaviour. These cards are sorted from the most prevalent behaviours describing their child to the least. The AQS is generally used to describe children from one to five years of age but has been used to describe children older than this (Bretherton 2005).

There has been much research examining the effects of early attachment experiences on later adult behaviour. Such studies involve questions concerning the notion of intergenerational transmission of attachment behaviour. In other words, is the way in which you nurture your children an artefact of your own childhood experiences with the main caregiver? Does the nature of attachment pattern experienced as a child continue on to your own children? Crowell et al. (2002), for example, demonstrated that Ainsworth's outline of the secure base phenomenon in childhood provides a cogent perspective on the secure base behaviour shown by adults. 'Secure base experience in childhood leads to the development of representations that in turn guide secure base behaviour later in life' (Crowell et al. 2002, p. 2). This also supports Bowlby's (1969) contention that, 'Attachment behaviour is held to characterise human beings from the cradle to the grave' (p. 129).

Main (1985) considered the question of whether there is an intergenerational effect of attachment behaviour by readdressing the work of Ainsworth. Six year olds who had previously participated in the 'strange situation' experiment at the age of one were re-examined. Main wanted to examine the nature of working models developed over the years in these children. An avoidant pattern of behaviour towards the caregiver at the age of six was compatible with avoidance behaviour seen when aged one. Hence, Main found a fixed internal working model. The next question Main addressed was whether a fixed internal working model occurred in adults also. In order to do this Main (1985) adopted the Adult Attachment Interviews approach. This approach allowed Main to probe for information about the caregiver's nature of relationships and attachments with parents by considering memories, contradictory statements and evaluations. Caregivers were asked to provide five adjectives best describing their relationship with each parent during childhood. They were asked to provide support for these adjectives by drawing upon memories of events (known as episodic memories). Once all information was analysed, Main observed four distinct maternal attachment types:

- Caregivers who had secure/autonomous attachments have secure infants.
- Caregivers who had dismissing attachments have insecure-avoidant infants.
- Caregivers who were preoccupied by past attachments have insecure-resistant infants.
- Caregivers who experienced traumatic and unresolved attachments have **disorganised/ disoriented** infants.

Note that these four attachment types focus on the caregiver's side of the equation rather than the infant's side of the equation (as in Ainsworth's model).

According to Smith and Pederson (1988), caregivers of insecure-avoidant infants respond to infant's cries and demands only when they are in the mood to do so, ignoring them at all other times. These caregivers are less sensitive to their infant's requests and needs overall. Their infants therefore entertain internal working models that prime them to expect to be rebuffed rather than comforted. These infants, in turn, avoid being rebuffed by turning away from their caregiver. Caregivers of insecure-resistant infants, however, experienced inconsistency and unreliability from their care provider. Their infants therefore react by resisting attempts at contact. Caregivers of securely attached infants had accessible, consistent and sensitive care providers who responded to their cries and signals of distress (Isabella, Belsky and von Eye 1989; Belsky 1999). Securely attached infants learn to trust and rely on the caregiver (Clarke-Stewart and Hevey 1981) and develop independence (Sroufe 1983). Insecure-disorganised infants experience neglect and abuse, and fail to predict how their caregiver will respond to their needs. They are fearful of their caregiver, appear to be dazed and often display repetitive behaviours such as rocking (Soloman and George 1999). These infants' approach–avoidance behaviour is considered by Soloman and George (1999) to be an adaptive response to a distress-ful attachment relationship. Interestingly, disorganised attachment has been considered using a genetic approach by considering the **DRD4 gene** (see Box 3.6).

Box 3.6 The role of the DRD4 gene in attachment

In recent years geneticists have examined the relationship between specific genes and attachment styles. A good example of a gene–environment 'evocative relationship' involves the development of personality during childhood (see Chapter 1: 'Behavioural genetics'). In relation to attachment behaviour babies who smile and act sociably elicit positive reactions from others that reinforce their genetic predisposition to be 'easy to get on with' babies. Research by Lakatos et al. (2000) found that infant attachment to the caregiver at 12–13 months was influenced by the gene DRD4. This is important in the production of dopamine (a chemical messenger carrying signals between nerve cells). Researchers looked at DRD4 in detail, in particular its structural form. It was found that the common form it takes is a '4-repeat allele'. The other form it can take is a '7-repeat allele' (DRD4-7R; see Figure 3.8). It was found that the 7-repeat allele is more common in infants who show a disorganised pattern of attachment (or 'D-infants'). Disorganised/ undifferentiated (D-dyad) infants fail to fit into any of the above categories and are very difficult to settle into a normal day-to-day pattern of feeding, sleep and bonding. They are also very wary of strangers. We all possess two alleles of each gene (one set from each parent) and the chance of having at least one 7-repeat allele is 71 per cent for D-infants and 29 per cent for non-D-infants. Lakatos et al. (2003) further found that the 7-repeat DRD4 allele influenced wariness of strangers. The DRD4 gene is a good example of an evocative relationship with the environment because the parents have a large hand in how they interact with the infant, which may or may not reinforce the infant's pattern of attachment. It is worth pointing out that such research on single genes and personality is not without its critics. In 2004 Bakermans-Kranenburg and van Ijzendoorn were unable to replicate Lakatos et al.'s findings in their 2000 study. Instead they concluded that it is difficult to attribute a 'simple genetic explanation' to something so complicated as attachment, in particular one that shows a disorganised pattern. Bakermans-Kranenburg and van Ijzendoorn argued that it is important to explore interactions between genetic vulnerabilities and environmental risks. Bakermans-Kranenburg and van Ijzendoorn (2006) revealed a genetic–environmental interactive involvement in children displaying exter- nalising behaviours (e.g., problem and difficult behaviours). Children who had the DRD4-7R combination but sensitive and responsive mothers showed the least externalising behaviours. For those, however, who had insensitive and unresponsive mothers, the level of externalis- ing behaviours was extensive. Their findings support there being a genetic–environmental interaction for disorganised attachment and the presence of externalising behaviours. Adults with DRD4-7R who had experienced unresolved loss or trauma in childhood showed the highest level of parental depression and marital discord unlike their DRD4-7R counterparts who had a good childhood (Bakermans-Kranenburg et al. 2011).

While the research of Lakatos and colleagues suggests a strong involvement of the DRD4-7R gene in disorganised attachment, the work of Bakermans-Kranenburg and van Ijzendoorn shows this to be attenuated when environmental factors are taken into consideration such as maternal sensitivity.

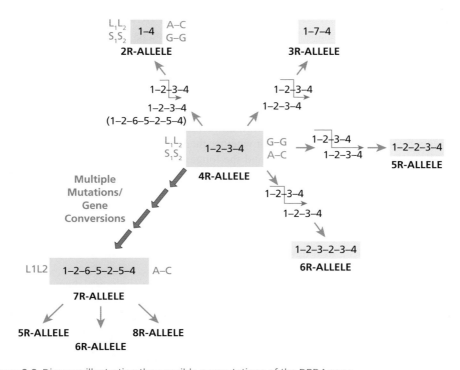

Figure 3.8 Diagram illustrating the possible permutations of the DRD4 gene.

When it comes to attachment, as we have seen, there is evidence of an intergenerational effect. It is well established that the attachment style of infants is closely related to the childhood attachment style of their parents (Bretherton and Munholland 1999; Thompson 2006a). Furthermore, parental recollections of their childhood attachment experiences show similarities to those of their offspring (Grossmann et al. 2005). Bowlby argued that internal working models should be stable across generations, which makes sense, as individuals draw on their own working models.

However, cross-culturally, there are problems with Ainsworth's classification. Although most infants do fit in with these categories, a small minority do not. A higher percentage of insecure-resistant attachments, for instance, has been found in infants nurtured in Israeli kibbutzim (or collective farms) and for many Japanese children than elsewhere. For many children from Northern Germany insecure-avoidant attachment is the most common pattern observed. Why the difference? The way children initially interpret the strange situation is a product of their experience. Kibbutz children spend a great deal of time with their caregiver but sleep in a communal setting – hence secure attachment may be influenced by sleeping arrangements. Japanese children rarely sleep apart from their parents before the age of eight years. When left alone to sleep they demonstrate more distress. Nevertheless, there are other cultures where parents, who are constantly available, have secure attachments with their children such as Australia, South Africa and Brazil (Harrison and Ungerer 2002). It appears that factors likely to influence a secure attachment between caregiver and child are the attendance to needs and comfort inherent within the attachment relationship. Thus far we have addressed the behaviours important within attachment relationships. In the next section the impact of attachment for future socioemotional behaviour is considered.

Influences of attachment on socioemotional development

Bowlby believed that the relationship between the infant and its mother during the first five years of life was crucial to socialisation. He believed that disruption of this primary relationship could lead to a higher incidence of juvenile delinquency, emotional difficulties and antisocial behaviour. To examine this contention, Bowlby interviewed 44 adolescent juvenile delinquents who were referred to a child protection programme in London and residing in a clinic because of their stealing activities. They were regarded as thieves. Bowlby selected another group of 44 children with no criminal record to act as 'controls.' He interviewed the parents from both groups to establish whether their children had experienced separation during the early years of development and the longevity of this separation. Bowlby found that a significant proportion of 'juvenile thieves' (32 per cent) developed **affectionless psychopathy** (a condition compromising the child's ability to care about or feel affection for others) due to what he referred to as maternal deprivation and separation. The juveniles demonstrating affectionless psychopathy were those residing in the clinic. None of the controls demonstrated this. He reported his findings in a publication called the *Forty-Four Juvenile Thieves* in 1944. Hence, according to Bowlby, a great deal of criminal behaviour can be traced back to a disrupted early attachment process.

In a similar vein, Harry Harlow demonstrated permanent psychological damage in his rhesus monkeys if they were deprived of any maternal input for longer than three months. Harlow argued that this would be equivalent to six months in humans. Both Bowlby and Ainsworth support the view that **maternal deprivation** has an impact on the developing child. In the Attachment Theory/**Maternal Deprivation Hypothesis**, it is argued that the child's social understanding of the world develops as a consequence of early interactions with the mother (i.e., the caregiver). Later on at around two years of age the child begins to form attachments to others who also provide a secure base from which to explore and return back to.

According to the Maternal Deprivation Hypothesis, breaking the maternal bond with the child during the early stages of its life is likely to have serious effects on its intellectual, social and emotional development. It should be noted here that researchers often fail to make the important distinction between what is meant by deprivation and the concept of **privation** (see Box 3.7).

Box 3.7   Deprivation and privation

Michael Rutter (1981) has argued that if a child fails to develop an emotional bond this is privation whereas deprivation refers to the loss of or damage to an attachment. From his survey of research on privation, Rutter proposed that it is likely to lead initially to clinging, dependent behaviour, attention-seeking and indiscriminate friendliness, then, as the child matures, an inability to keep rules, form lasting relationships, or feel guilt. Rutter also found evidence of antisocial behaviour, affectionless psychopathy, and disorders of language, intellectual development and physical growth in cases of privation. Rutter argues that these problems are not due solely to the lack of attachment to a caregiver figure, as Bowlby claimed, but to factors such as the lack of intellectual stimulation and social experiences that attachments normally provide. In addition, such problems can be overcome later in the child's development, with the right kind of care. Bowlby's Maternal Deprivation is, however, supported by Harlow's research with monkeys. He showed that monkeys reared in isolation from their mother suffered emotional and social problems in older age. The monkeys never formed an attachment (privation) and, as such, grew up to be aggressive and had problems interacting with other monkeys.

There are other repercussions of insecure attachments for socioemotional behaviour. Sroufe et al. (2005) looked at personal competence and peer approval among preschool children. This was a longitudinal study examining the influence of attachment on social development beginning in infancy and continuing until 19 years of age. They developed objective measures for observing positive, negative and inappropriate emotional reactions during social interactions with other people. The social competence rating scale used was derived by subtracting the number of inappropriate and negative interactions from the number of positive and appropriate interactions. Hence the higher the score on this scale the more socially competent the child is. Those securely attached at 15 months had the highest scores, and by three and a half years they were more likely to be peer leaders in preschool. Low-ranked children were described as unpredictable, loners or chronic whiners. Securely attached preschool children of four to five years displayed fewer negative reactions when approached by other children. They were socially competent and formed close friendships. This behaviour continued at eight and 12 years, and further into adolescence. By 19, securely attached individuals showed mature socioemotional functioning, which was reflected in their ability to maintain long-term family, friend and romantic relationships. They were self-confident, determined and independent.

Attachment in adolescence has become an area of interest to developmental psychologists. The impact of secure attachment on the behaviour of adolescents has been researched in the context of ongoing relationships with their parents (Allen et al. 2003; Kenney and Barton 2003), self-esteem and social adjustment (Cooper et al. 1998). A secure attachment to parents has been linked with adolescent social competency and the ability to form positive relationships (Lieberman et al. 1999). There is an abundance of research findings in support of insecure attachments having negative social effects on future behaviour.

These findings support Bowlby's study of the 44 'juvenile delinquents' who experienced insecure attachments during their stay in care. The same attachment categories to those identified for caregivers and their six year olds by Main (1985) were also found among adolescents: secure, dismissing-avoidant, preoccupied-ambivalent and unresolved-disorganised. La Greca and Harrison (2005) examined the differences between adolescents of 14–19 years old who were in romantic relationships with those who were single. They found that those who were single were more likely to have social anxiety issues. The onset age for romantic involvement is also related to problem behaviour. Females who became romantically involved at a younger age often had adolescent pregnancies and problems associated with school and at home (Florsheim et al. 2003). Furthermore, such girls were often disengaged from school work and participation in the classroom (Buhrmester 2001).

A study conducted by West and Farrington (1973) examined the influence of family and social background on young boys aged eight to nine in the London area. This longitudinal study became known as the Cambridge Study. The boys were interviewed and given a set of IQ and personality tests to complete. Parents and teachers were also interviewed and asked to provide information about these boys. They found a relationship between low intelligence and offending behaviour. Those boys who scored low on IQ tests and exhibited offending behaviour also demonstrated poor school performance and difficulty understanding abstract concepts. Many of these boys came from problem families and experienced rejection or neglect. Browne (2013) concluded that positive attachment to parents or carers in childhood is paramount in ensuring a crime-free future. Further discussion of problems in adolescence will be addressed in Chapters 7, 8, 10 and 11. Attachment plays an important role in how children and adolescents process socioemotional information. Belsky et al. (1996) found securely attached individuals were far ahead of those who were insecurely attached in their ability to recall positive events. In fact, insecurely attached individuals recalled significantly more negative events.

Attachment theory has much support but not everyone agrees with Bowlby's understanding of attachment and some have offered criticisms of his work (see Box 3.8).

Box 3.8　Criticisms and responses to Bowlby's critics

During his lifetime, and subsequently, Bowlby's ideas have received their fair share of criticism. Below we outline four main criticisms that have been levelled at Bowlby's work and consider some of the responses.

1. The debate is not about the quality of institutional care:
   Complaints about a lack of interaction with young children in institutions being harmful are nothing new. Skeels (1936) and Spitz (1945) argued the same in the 1930s. When arrangements were made for toddlers who were left alone in an institution nursery to be raised by 'feeble-minded' women their IQs rose.
2. The gender roles debate:
   Complaints were made that Bowlby's theory encouraged women to stay in the home and allowed men to take back jobs occupied by women during World War Two. Bowlby's publication, however, was six years after the war had finished. Bowlby's work was also criticised for reinforcing traditional views of gender roles (but nowhere does Bowlby say parenting 'must' be the mother's task; just that a single reliable presence is needed).
3. A key issue concerns how permanent the effects of maternal deprivation are. Bowlby argued that they were permanent and almost impossible to reverse.

Evidence for long-term effects is mixed. Freud and Dann (1951) found that children in concentration camps until three years of age showed rapid improvement and few problems once released. Koluchová (1976) found that twins raised in a cellar for seven years had no discernible negative effects by adulthood. Skuse (1984) claimed that even in extreme cases of deprivation (more accurately called privation where something has never been known rather than known and then removed, as in deprivation – see Box 3.7), only subtle effects are found. In less extreme cases Robertson (1956, 1958a, 1958b, 1958c) found that the effects of temporary institutional care lessened if children visit the place first, are given a familiar daily routine and had discussed what was happening with their caregiver first.

4. Reasons for separation:

Michael Rutter (1976) studied boys aged 9–12 years on the Isle of Wight and in London and found that separation due to death or illness of the caregiver caused only a very slight inclination in antisocial behaviour, whereas a high-stress family environment (e.g., parents always arguing; parental absences other than for illness/death) is more clearly associated with antisocial behaviour. Therefore, according to Rutter, it is stress, and not the strength of maternal bond, that leads to antisocial behaviour. Stress associated with lengthy separation may be the cause of problems rather than maternal deprivation. Aversive early-life experiences can, however, have negative effects no matter how good the intervention is. For example, Romanian orphans adopted by UK families during the 1990s had a good prognosis when adopted before two years of age (Rutter et al. 1998). Tizard and Hodges (1978) studied institutionalised children in care for up to the first four years of life. These children could be placed in one of three categories: remained in the institution, were adopted, or were restored to their natural parents. In the case of institutionalised children there were very few or no attachments and poor peer relationships at 16 years. For those adopted, while good attachments were made there were some problems with peer relationships. Finally, for those restored to their parents, it was found that they formed relatively poor attachments and had problems with peer relationships. Hence it is not always easy to overcome a lack of early attachment.

Despite criticisms of Bowlby's attachment theory, it remains an important concept within developmental psychology. It continues to initiate research examining the impact of positive and negative attachment styles on the socioemotional development of the individual.

Summary

- New-borns have an innate capacity to form attachments with their caregivers (usually the parents and the mother first). This innate capacity to form an attachment with the caregiver arises out of a need to be nurtured to ensure their survival. They are born with innate competencies such as being able to imprint on their caregiver's face, face recognition ability and simple approach–avoidance arousal states.
- The new-born's ability to distinguish facial stimuli from non-facial stimuli has clear advantages in enabling the formation of a bond with the caregiver. New-borns therefore have innate but rudimentary mechanisms, called conspec and conlern, to enable facial processing. Conspec processing enables a 'primitive' representation of a face to develop whereas conlern allows for the refinement of such representations to occur. Recognising the caregiver's face helps the developing infant to form

(continued)

(continued)

a bond. Infants use another innate ability to aid in the formation of bonding to the caregiver – this is the ability to show approach or avoidance behaviours. When infants are distressed they exhibit avoidance behaviours, the most obvious being crying. When they are contented they display approach behaviours such as smiling and looking at the caregiver. These socially facilitating behaviours are performed as a means of encouraging the caregiver to want to nurture them (feed, comfort and provide security).

- Approach–avoidance behaviours give rise to the six universal emotional expressions of happiness, fear, anger, sadness, disgust and surprise. Infants have to learn how to regulate or modulate their emotions and how they are expressed. When the secondary emotions of empathy, guilt, embarrassment, pride and shame develop at about 18 months, new ways of emotional modulation occur.
- Bonds with the caregiver are referred to as attachments. Ainsworth found three attachment dyads: one secure (B-dyad) and two insecure (A-dyad and C-dyad) ones. B-dyad infants form strong attachments and seek security from the caregiver. A-dyad infants (insecure avoidant) ignore the caregiver, showing no distress at her leaving or any attempt at contact with her when she returns. C-dyad infants (insecure resistant) are wary of the caregiver, unphased when she leaves them and resist contact on her return. D-dyad infants (disorganised/disoriented) are difficult to console or settle into set routines.
- Belsky (1997) and Chisholm (1999) examined the different attachment types and related this to their later reproductive strategy styles. Securely attached individuals engage in supportive long-term relationships with partners. Insecure-avoidant adults engage in sex in long- or short-term relationships and have more break-ups. Insecure-resistant individuals are less likely to be romantically involved or have children themselves.
- Infants who have secure attachments with their caregiver form internal working models of a caregiver who is reliable and will always be there to comfort them. These working models form out of many memories developed over a period of time concerning their interactions with their caregiver. Internal working models provide an evaluation of the nature of the relationship between the infant and caregiver.
- Bowlby claimed that infant attachments formed are stable throughout the lifespan – from the cradle to the grave. There have been criticisms of this point of view. Research shows that an insecure attachment can change to a secure one provided changes to the nurturance received are positive. Intergenerational transmission of attachment styles can be seen in caregivers and their parents as well as their own offspring.
- A secure infant attachment relates strongly with the development of a socially confident and well-rounded adolescent. Insecure attachments alternatively lead to a troubled child and adolescent. These individuals have problems forming lasting social relationships with peers and potential romantic partners. They are more likely to become 'juvenile delinquents' and engage in other types of antisocial behaviour. Hence the type of nurturance received and attachment formed in infancy has more than a short-term effect. An insecure attachment compromises socioemotional development throughout the lifespan.

Questions for discussion

1. Are babies born to make attachments?
2. Developmentalists have identified four main attachment styles (secure; insecure avoidant; insecure resistant; disorganised/disoriented). Suggest what each style would predict in terms of the forms of adult romantic relationships that are later formed.
3. Make a list of the typical behaviours seen when children demonstrate self-conscious emotions such as guilt and shame.
4. Bowlby's quote, 'From the cradle to the grave', has important implications for our understanding of stable attachment styles. What does he mean by this? Critically examine the significance of this in the intergenerational transmission of attachment style?
5. According to Johnson and Morton 'conspec' is an innate but immature mechanism enabling new-borns to process facial stimuli. Critically examine what Johnson and Morton mean by 'innate but immature'. Can you think of other explanations for why babies tend to focus on their caregiver's face?
6. Explain what we mean by socially facilitating behaviours. Critically examine the importance of these behaviours in the initial stages of bonding.

Further reading

If you are interested in exploring in more detail the connection between schemas, attachment and family contexts, as well as the contribution of schemas in socioemotional development, look at:

- Arnold, C. (2010). *Understanding Schemas and Emotion in Early Childhood.* London: SAGE Publications Ltd.

If you are interested in understanding more about the importance of attachment in the development of personality using neurobiological, interpersonal and intrapsychological explanations, look at:

- Hart, S. (2008). *Brain, Attachment, Personality: An Introduction to Neuroaffective Development.* London: Karnac Books Ltd.

If you are interested in examining a synthesis of scientific knowledge about children's emotional development that integrates current and classical research in more detail, look at:

- Music, G. (2016). *Nurturing Natures: Attachment and Children's Emotional, Sociocultural and Brain Development.* London and New York: Routledge, Taylor and Francis Group.

If you are interested in knowing more about a unique integrative approach to attachment and the self and how relationships between caregivers, siblings and friends develop throughout the lifespan, look at:

- Rosen, K. (2016). *Social and Emotional Development: Attachment Relationships and the Emerging Self.* Basingstoke, UK: Palgrave MacMillan.

Contents

Introduction   109

Jean Piaget   110

Lev Vygotsky   112

Neo-Piagetian accounts   113

Information-processing accounts   115

Influence of social interaction on the epigenetic landscape: Piaget, Vygotsky, neo-Piagetian and information-processing   121

Communication   123

Evidence for the cognitive–social connection   133

Summary   139

Chapter 4

Cognition and communication

4

What this chapter will teach you

- The relevance of cognition (perception, memory, thought and language) to social development.
- Piaget's and Vygotsky's accounts of cognitive development and their relationship to social development.
- The importance of Neo-Piagetian accounts.
- Information-processing accounts of cognitive and social development.
- The acquisition of language in children.
- Chomsky's concept of a language acquisition device and universal grammar.
- Bruner's language acquisition support system.
- The role of executive function in helping to control aggressive responses.

INTRODUCTION

The processing of information from our environment occurs in two ways – sensation and perception. Sensation occurs first when stimuli in our environment are picked up through our sensory systems and in particular by our five traditionally recognised sensory organs: eyes (for vision), ears (for sound), nose (for smell), mouth (for taste) and skin (for touch). Stimuli are picked up by these sensory organs and transformed into a code that the brain can interpret. This interpretation is known as perception. It is through the process of perception that we can understand what is happening around us and respond appropriately.

As we saw in Chapter 3, the new-born has some innate abilities to enhance their prob-ability of survival. Despite the initial limitations of these abilities, infants are able to perceive their immediate environment to a level that promotes bond formation with their caregiver. If perception involves the interpretation of stimuli, then this understanding must involve some form of limited thought that is stored for future reference – hence memory formation. Furthermore, we would expect there to be some comprehension of some aspects of language used by the caregiver, even if this is initially limited to the emotional emphasis of the spoken word.

In this chapter we will explore how these four areas of cognition (perception, memory, thought and language) play an important role in social development. It is important to have an understanding of both cognition per se and its role in communication in order to fully comprehend social development. Although Swiss developmentalist Jean Piaget is often con-sidered to be the father of our understanding of cognitive development, it is clear that he also considered social development. It was Russian-born Lev Vygotsky, however, who incor-porated the importance of the social environment and social interaction into his theoretical framework of how infants and children learn and communicate (see Chapter 1). Of relevance to both Piaget's and Vygotsky's accounts of cognitive development is the notion of the 'epi-genetic' landscape introduced by Conrad Waddington in 1957 (see Chapter 1). This involves the shaping of our genetic constitution, which can vary as a consequence of our (social) environment. The impact of the epigenetic landscape is of particular importance to a child's adaptiveness for pedagogy. This, in turn, influences all aspects of the child's cognition used in understanding and adjusting to the social world – and ultimately their social behaviour. Information processing is another approach to understanding how children learn; focusing on how memory, thought and language are used by children to solve problems (see Chapter 1).

Language also plays an important role in the development of our social skills. Language acquisition develops within a social context and is used as a means of communication with others. Infants initially communicate with the caregiver using babbling and cooing noises but this quickly extends to include actual words. These words eventually form sentences that children use to communicate with their peers. Usage and understanding of language therefore relies on the social context in which it occurs. Moreover, language is intricately interwoven with our emotions and emotional understanding that require an appreciation of the social context out of which they arise.

It is important, first, to consider the impact of Piaget's and Vygotsky's theoretical approaches to understanding how children develop cognitively, which is the topic of our next section.

JEAN PIAGET

Swiss-born developmentalist Jean Piaget began his interest in child development by conduct-ing research on the area of genetic epistemology (i.e., the theory of knowledge and how our biology predisposes us to this). This became his underlying theoretical approach to under-standing the cognitive development of individuals during infancy, childhood and adolescence. It is through his initial research on molluscs that Piaget saw the development of intelligence in humans as a form of adaptation to the environment. Margaret Bell-Gredler (1986) explained Piaget's interpretation of how adaptation to the environment occurs in molluscs. She referred to the change of shell size in molluscs as a consequence of their habitat such that those mol-luscs transported from calm waters to turbulent waters will develop shortened shells. This enabled molluscs to maintain anchorage to rocks during rough seas. Hence, following Piaget's lead, Bell-Gredler (1986) claimed that, 'The organism, in response to altered environmental conditions, constructs the specific biological structures that it needs' (pp. 193–4).

Biological structural changes, Piaget believed, are fundamental to intellectual development. Reference to structural changes can be seen throughout his theory of cognitive development. Moreover, Piaget considered that structural change occurs via a triad of interacting processes that he called **assimilation, accommodation** and **equilibration**. This is best illustrated by Abraham and Renner's (1986) example of students observing the effects of heating a metal can (see Box 4.1).

You may recall from Chapter 1 that Piaget referred to four stages of development that children traverse in a fixed order. (Note that Piaget further divided these into sub-stages). Moreover, he argued that these stages occur universally regardless of ethnicity, and are framed within set age ranges. In the case of the first stage, **sensorimotor**, infants are expected to experience this from birth until about two years of age, by which time the biological structures necessary for the transition to the next stage, **preoperational**, have been appropriately developed. The preoperational stage lasts until the age of about seven and then develops into the **concrete operational** stage. The concrete operational stage continues until about 11 years of age and then develops into the **formal operational** stage, the last stage Piaget considered. This stage continues into adolescence and adulthood. For our purposes clearly the question we need to answer is how does cognition influence or interact with the development of social behaviour? As we can see, Piaget's theory is biologically influenced. It relies upon the maturation of the brain via developing a sequence of **schemas** that allow us to understand our environment. Interacting with the environment, however, is an important aspect of this development. By interacting with the environment through experimentation, either alone or with others, we learn about different phenomena, events and situations. This learning will help us to integrate with others and to develop our social skills as a means of finding our place within society (see Chapter 5 for discussion of the role of Piaget's approach in social cognition). Piaget, however, is regarded by many as a biologist trying to explain psychological phenomenon, unlike our next developmentalist, Lev Vygotsky.

Box 4.1   Abraham and Renner demonstrate Piaget's mechanisms of equilibrium, assimilation and accommodation

If students are presented with a demonstration in a physics class showing a phenomenon that they are unfamiliar with and which they fail to understand, then, according to Piaget, they will need to update their **mental structures** (or mental blueprints as described by Abraham and Renner 1986). Such updating can be seen when students come to understand the physics involved in why a sealed metal can, with a small amount of water, will buckle and fall over when heated. At first the reason why this happens is unknown to these students because their current mental structures are inadequate to explain what they observe. According to Piaget there are three mechanisms involved in updating mental structures: assimilation, accommodation and equilibration. These mechanisms constantly interact so as to compare incoming information with what is already known. It is through the mechanism of equilibration that differences between old and new information can be self-regulated. Equilibration, therefore, is a biological function enabling an individual to maintain a steady state but, at the same time, allowing for new experiences. Applying this to our example of the classroom demonstration, students find the new information confusing and need their teacher to explain what this means. It is through teacher interaction and explanation that they can learn and construct new mental structures. This revision of mental structures is an ongoing process of equilibration. There are, however,

(continued)

(continued)

two other mechanisms operating in tandem that enable equilibration to occur: assimilation and accommodation. In the case of assimilation new information is merged into the existing mental structure, which represents the individual's current understanding of the world. This current understanding of the world is what Piaget referred to as a schema. Infants, for example, have simple sensory and motor schemas that they draw upon in order to respond to stimuli in their immediate environment – tasting and touching objects to attain a sense of what these objects are. Once an understanding is mastered, the infant progresses to the next cognitive stage (see Chapter 1). In our classroom example, students assimilate this new information without having to change it provided they already have a schema containing some knowledge about metal objects. So, in effect, this information is incorporated into existing schemas. In some situations, however, information is so novel that there are no existing schemas into which it can be assimilated. This is when the mechanism of accommodation takes over. Accommodation works by changing the schema. These new schemas therefore replace the old ones and, in so doing, reorganise our mental structures. An infant, for example, modifies its action of trying to pick up a small object with the whole hand to using a thumb and finger action. Students, in our example above, if they have not already developed a schema for understanding how metal objects are affected by heat, will develop a new schema to explain this.

According to Piaget, reorganising our mental structures is what enables us to progress from one stage of cognitive development to the next. This is what developing our intelligence or cognitive acumen is all about. Finally, Piaget considers intelligence as the human way of adapting to the environment. Just as molluscs can change their shell size to adapt to turbulent waters, humans can increase their intellect as a means of adapting to, and surviving in, their ever-changing environment.

LEV VYGOTSKY

Russian-born Lev Vygotsky had a very different approach to Piaget. He proposed a social developmental theory of learning whereby social interaction is central to cognitive development. Biological and cultural development do not occur in isolation (Driscoll 1994) but are interdependent. Vygotsky's far-reaching theory consists of three interactive aspects: the influence of culture, language and the zone of proximal development. He believed that a child requires a certain level of biological maturity in order for social development to occur. It is social interaction and language, however, that drive this development further. Hence it is culture, expressed through social interaction and language, that provides the motivation to develop cognitively beyond the constraints of our biology. Coupled with our human predisposition to engage in social interaction and respond to social demands, our cognitive learning excels. Vygotsky emphasised this increase in cognitive potential through what he referred to as the zone of proximal development. The zone of proximal development has a lower and upper limit that differentiates between what the child can manage by itself and what it can achieve when guidance from others is at hand. A task that is too difficult to complete alone successfully becomes achievable through verbal instruction or demonstration. Frede (1995) illustrates the zone of proximal development in action by referring to a task of classification. A teacher observes a child who has divided shopping items into fruit and non-fruit but believes that this classification can be made more sophisticated with her help through pretend play. She pretends to operate the cash-till but points out to the child that in order to put items into bags they need to be sorted into foods that require refrigeration or can be stored away in cupboards. With her assistance the child learns to categorise foods according to the type of storage required. The child's ability to perform this task was in the upper limit of the zone of proximal development. With instruction and demonstration the child acquired a new form of understanding food items. If the child were to repeat this task, it would now come into the remit of the lower zone of proximal development. In another example of adult–child task collaboration, Radziszewska and Rogoff (1988) found more efficient route planning of a shopping spree than was observed in a child–child dyad. There was far more backtracking and disorganised planning for the child–child dyad. What is more, the child who planned the shopping route with the adult was able to show transference of this cognitive skill to other similar tasks. Clearly, children learn valuable skills when they receive a little help along the way.

The notion of scaffolding, first introduced by Jerome Bruner in 1976 (see Chapter 1), refers to the modification of support levels that children require. As they can successfully complete some tasks without the help of an adult, the level of scaffolding required for these tasks is minimal. In cases where the task is beyond the child's ability, more scaffolding is necessary. Hence, the extent of scaffolding input required changes as a child's level of task performance success alters. Wood et al. (1976), in a classic study, examined the effects of physical and verbal scaffolding on children aged three and five. Their task was to build a pyramid using interlocking wooden blocks. The teacher demonstrated how the blocks could be connected and offered verbal encouragement to the children. She made the task less daunting by providing children with a series of steps that, when followed, made it easier to understand what was required of them. The teacher monitored each child's progress and, based on how they were doing, constantly revised her assistance to suit the level of headway shown. As the children progressed towards being independent learners, the teacher's input was decreased.

The zone of proximal development allows children to alter their epigenetic landscapes through social interaction (see Chapter 1). Social interaction is key to providing the child with the support required to develop both cognitive skill and understanding. Vygotsky was interested in how people connect with each other and with their overarching cultural environment. In particular he focused on how we manipulate all aspects of language, within a given culture, to mediate our social environment. Children therefore use these tools as ways of communicating their needs. For Vygotsky, these tools would become internalised in such a way that led to higher thinking abilities. Hence, he believed that thought and language co-exist with each other. Driscoll (1994) pointed out that in Vygotskian understanding of egocentric speech in three- to seven-year-olds this arises out of social speech and its internalisation (see Table 1.4, Chapter 1). Vygotsky is clearly a psychologist concerned about the influential impact of the social environment on a child's cognitive development.

During the late 20th and early 21st centuries, a number of developmentalists have modified many of Piaget's original concepts. Such developmentalists are known collectively as neo-Piagetians.

NEO-PIAGETIAN ACCOUNTS

Neo-Piagetian theorists continue to adopt Piaget's view of cognitive development progressing unevenly in a stage-like manner. Like Piaget they also argue that there are biological limits on what children can achieve at different ages – thereby placing brain maturation at the forefront of development. They too advocate that thinking reflects developing internal mental structures, albeit using different terminology (e.g., Pascual-Leone talks of M-space). Developmentalists of a neo-Piagetian persuasion adopt a more culturally attuned approach and consider individual differences as important. French-born Juan Pascual-Leone (1970) proposed that there are underlying gradual biological maturational changes occurring to the

Plate 4.1 Parents helping their children to complete the homework set. Vygotsky considered that there is a human predisposition to engage in social interaction and that this greatly aids cognitive and social development. (Shutterstock 111297197.)

capacity of short-term memory (or working memory, see information-processing accounts). This means that the capacity of working memory defines the upper limits of problem-solving ability in children. He referred to this as **mental space,** or M space for short, and accounted for Piaget's stages as a gradual continuous change in M space (Case et al. 1982). Increases in M space enable children to perform more complex tasks more quickly. Concrete operational tasks all require about the same amount of M space (Pascual-Leone 1970). Chi (1978), for example, showed that when asked to repeat a string of digits after a delay, children of 5 years repeated four, whereas those aged 11 repeated six.

Canadian psychologist Robbie Case (1998) has pointed out that the complexity in thinking, for example, increases with age. This is due to increasing brain maturity and resultant improvements in strategies for learning. Such improvements include attending to salient aspects of information and applying sophisticated methods of categorisation. As a consequence, cognitive processing becomes more efficient and faster with age. This explains why children in the first two years of their development acquire so much knowledge about the world around them. It also explains why older children can think faster than younger children – partly due to their ability to keep more concepts simultaneously in memory.

Neo-Piagetians also consider the role of **domain specificity** to explain the unevenness of development of different types of cognitive skill. The concept of domain specificity addresses the workings of the mind as modular, such that there are different cognitive faculties operating independently of one another and developing at different times. According to this view we have modules responsible, for example, for the processing of numerical, linguistic and facial information. Neo-Piagetians therefore consider information-processing accounts but they also use principles outlined in social-cognitive approaches such as those of Vygotsky.

An important neo-Piagetian was Annette Karmiloff-Smith who argued against **modularity** as the only explanation for cognitive development. She claimed that when developmental disorders are taken into account the notion of domain-specificity breaks down (Karmiloff-Smith 1998). She argued that development arises as a consequence of gene, brain, behaviour and environmental interactions that shape the epigenetic landscape (Gottlieb and Lickliter 2007).

The different modules in the brain are specialised in processing specific types of information that, according to Karmiloff-Smith (1996), appear relatively late on in development. Hence developmental disorders occur during development and traverse many module boundaries. In the case of autism, for example, there are other deficits such as odd patterns of visual search and multi-tasking in addition to the typical reports of impaired social cognition (Elsabbagh and Johnson 2007). Similarly, Karmiloff-Smith (2007) argued that, despite being good at processing social cues, children with Williams syndrome have a host of other impairments that a domain-specific approach has difficulty explaining. Instead, she advocated a **domain-relevant** approach that takes account of:

- Biological constraints of neural activity.
- **Cross-domain interactions** occurring over developmental time.
- Constant change occurring over developmental time.
- Domain-relevant circuits dominating and therefore becoming specialised over developmental time.

There is overlap between many neo-Piagetian approaches and information-processing – our next approach.

INFORMATION-PROCESSING ACCOUNTS
In the words of Klahr and MacWhinney (1998), the information-processing approach

views the mind as a symbol-manipulating system through which information flows, that often uses flowcharts to map the precise series of steps individuals use to solve problems and complete tasks, and regards cognitive development as a continuous process.

This sounds very complex but in essence what Klahr and MacWhinney are referring to here is the transformation from sensation to perception. Models of information-processing describe how data from our sensory organs are coded, transformed and organised by the brain in a format that can be readily interpreted. We call this perception. The preferred method of representing such series of events is the flowchart. Flowcharts can be created to illustrate attention/perception, memory, thought and language. Figure 4.1 illustrates a classic example of an information-processing flowchart – the Baddeley and Hitch model for **working memory**.

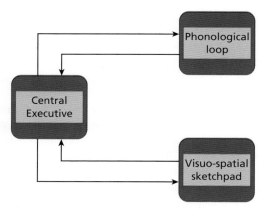

Figure 4.1 Baddeley and Hitch's (1974) model of working memory. (Taken from Taylor 2015.)

In this model, two important sub-components of memory (the phonological loop and the visuo-spatial sketchpad) are controlled by the **central executive**. The central executive allocates information to be processed by the phonological loop and visuo-spatial sketchpad. These, in turn, process respectively auditory and visual information.

The use of flowcharts is particularly helpful in illustrating the steps children take to solve problems and complete given tasks. This can be demonstrated clearly in a problem task set by Thornton (1999) known as 'building a bridge across the river'. School children of different ages were compared on their ability to successfully build a bridge using a pile of blocks varying in size, shape and weight. A river was painted on the floor, its breadth carefully measured such that only two of the blocks when put together could possibly cross it. This means that children have to use some of the blocks as counterweights. In Thornton's study the older children successfully built bridges by using blocks as counterweights; however, only one of the younger children (aged five) was able to do this after repeated attempts of pushing two planks together and pressing down their ends to keep them in place. Through trial and error her efforts eventually paid off and her prior attempts helped in understanding why this counterweight approach was a successful method. These findings raise the question of why the older children could do this easily. Does a child's ability to solve problems simply increase with age?

In common with Piaget, the information-processing approach considers individuals as active in their learning and attempts at understanding their environment. In the case of information-processing, memory, perception, attention, language and thought are considered to be similar at all ages during the lifespan but are present to a lesser or greater degree. Hence, unlike Piaget, there are no discrete stages of development in the information-processing approach – it is a continuous process. American psychologist Robert Siegler (1998) claimed that information-processing theories share key assumptions:

1. Thinking involves information processing, therefore associated processes and structures should be emphasised.
2. It is important to provide a detailed account of these processes and the cognitive changes they cause.
3. These cognitive changes result from a process of self-modification where children connect their own actions and activities to the outcomes that follow. This then leads to changes in their thinking and behaviour. Taking the example of working memory (see Figure 4.1), information held in a short-term memory (or working memory) has a limited life-history unless mental strategies such as rehearsal are performed. The central executive determines what information to attend to and coordinates the incoming information to form connections with existing knowledge. Moreover, this selects, applies and monitors the strategies required to enable the information to be held longer in working memory. The longevity of the information is further increased by transference to long-term memory. This basic structure is similar throughout the lifespan but its capacity increases to allow for more complex forms of information retention. The same can be said for the structure of the entire mental system.

The physical system changes in some fundamental way that allows greater efficiency of mental processing and speed of response. One explanation for this pertains to the restructuring of the nervous system through the formation of new synaptic connections (see section on 'Biological and behavioural genetics perspective', Chapter 1). During the lifespan, and in particular in infancy and childhood, new synapses are formed through a process known as '**blooming**' at the same time as redundant synaptic pathways are disconnected, referred to as '**pruning**'. The addition and subtraction of synaptic connections via these two processes helps to clean-up the '**wiring diagram**' of our brain. Pruning begins at 18 months and continues steadily throughout childhood. A main consequence of this is the creation of more efficient and faster cognitive processing.

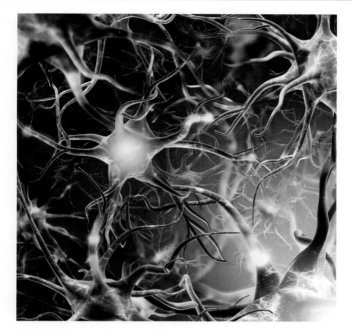

Plate 4.2 Neuron making synaptic connections. (Shutterstock 376647661.)

According to Gopnik et al. (1999), the number of synapses formed by two or three years of age is around 15,000 per neuron. The average adult brain has fewer connections per neuron – in fact the infant has twice as many. Between infancy and adulthood there is a considerable degree of synaptic pruning. Blooming and pruning, in addition to the acquisition of new strategies for learning and retaining information, combine to create an efficient cognitive processing system. This can be observed in infants and children as they develop their abilities at problem-solving and increase their memory performance. Studies have shown that attention management and memory improve with increasing age (see Box 4.2).

Problem-solving abilities also improve as children acquire new strategies. Siegler (1994) proposed that these strategies emerge through experience and experimentation such as trial and error. Siegler introduced four rules by which children learn about number and positioning of weights (i.e., pegs) on a balance scale:

- Rule I involves the number of weights and considers only one dimension. For example, how many pegs should go on the balance scale?
- Rule II is a transitional rule. Here the child judges on the basis of number with the exception of circumstances where the same number of weights appears on each side of the fulcrum. Under these circumstances distance from the fulcrum is considered.
- Rule III is a concrete operational rule. In this rule the child will take both distance from the fulcrum and weight into account simultaneously, except when the information is conflicting. Under circumstances of conflicting information, such as if the side with the weights closer to the fulcrum has more weights, the child resorts to guesswork.
- Rule IV is aligned with formal operational thought where the child acquires an understanding of the formula needed for calculating the combined effect of weight and distance (i.e., distance × weight for each side).

Plate 4.3 Picture of the type of scales used by Siegler.

Box 4.2   Age improves cognition

Infants become better at managing their attention and at attending to aspects of their immediate environment. Slater et al. (1996) showed new-borns two rod pieces above and below an occluding box until they stopped looking at it (see Figure 4.2).

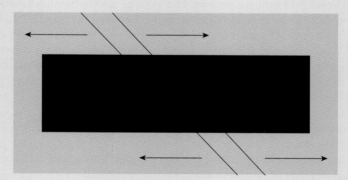

Figure 4.2 Example of the rods and occluding box format. (Taken from Johnson and Aslin 1996.)

Looking time is a measure used to determine when an infant stops showing interest in the object it is observing (see Figure 4.3). This is often referred to as habituation of looking and is commonly used as part of the habituation paradigm (see Box 2.1, Chapter 2).

Slater et al. then showed infants displays where the rod was complete or in two separate pieces by leaving a gap to suggest a broken rod. They demonstrated that it takes new-borns three to four seconds to habituate and recover to novel stimuli. This increased to between 5 and 10 seconds for infants aged four and five months. In other words, it took longer for the older

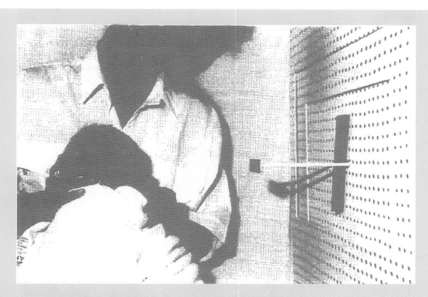

Figure 4.3 The display presentation. (Taken from Slater et al. 1996.)

infants to observe a complex stimulus and then recognise that it is different from the previous one. According to Frick et al. (1999) this is because the older infants have difficulty disengaging their attention from interesting stimuli. By four to six months the infant's attention becomes more flexible (Atkinson 2000).

Memory also improves with age. Infants can remember visual stimuli, such as a photograph of a face, for longer (Pascalis et al. 1998). Pascalis et al. showed that infants of three months remember photographs of faces for 24 hours unlike the 12-month infant who does so for a few weeks.

These studies provide support for increasing age being an important factor in cognitive development and the mastery of skills enhancing problem-solving ability.

Siegler concluded that children perform on this and similar tasks by using these rules in a progressive order. Nevertheless, Siegler acknowledges that the logical sequence of these rules depends on the level of skill and practice experienced. Moreover, he claimed that children will use a variety of problem-solving strategies and select the most successful one that becomes the predominant tactic. Siegler refers to this methodology as the **'overlapping waves' theory**. According to Siegler, children who fail to solve problems do so because they fail to search for pertinent information that is central to solving the task at hand or are unable to maintain more than one or two bytes of information simultaneously in memory. Support for these explanations comes from Vurpillot (1968) and Flavell (1970). Vurpillot recorded the eye movements of children ranging in age from 3 to 10 while spotting differences between two similar pictures of houses. Older children methodically scanned and compared the two pictures unlike preschoolers who were unable to search systematically for the relevant details. In the case of remembering words, preschoolers rarely used rehearsal strategies whereas 8 to 10 year olds repeatedly said the words under their breath (Flavell 1970).

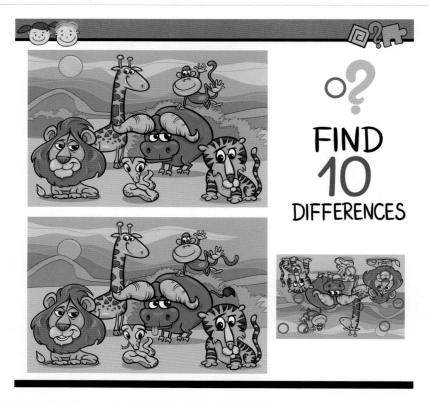

Plate 4.4 Spot the difference task. (Shutterstock 259865099.)

Different strategies for learning information have been identified by American-born Robert Gagné in 1977. Gagné (1977) said:

> *These [cognitive] theories propose that stimulation encountered by the learner is transformed, or processed, in a number of ways (. . . commitment to short-term memory, conversion to long-term memory, and the retention and retrieval of that information) by internal structures during the period in which the changes identified as learning takes place.*

> *(p.13)*

What Gagné means by 'in a number of ways' refers to the different strategies used to commit information to short-term memory and convert this to long-term memory for its retention and future retrieval. Gagné refers to 'conditions of learning', which encapsulate several types or levels of learning. Each type of learning requires different forms of instruction and relates closely to the conditions necessary for this learning to occur. Internal conditions refer to the capabilities already mastered by the individual whereas external conditions are the instructions provided by the mentor (Driscoll 2000). For example, when a mentor provides instruction on how to solve a task various internal learning processes are activated to aid in the accomplishment of learning outcomes. According to Gagné et al. (1988) instructions are designed to trigger the internal processes of learning into action.

Table 4.1 Gagné's nine types of instruction.

Type of instruction	Resulting learning process
Gaining attention by providing the learner with a stimulus signalling the presence of an upcoming instruction.	Increased attention.
Informing the learner of the task objective so that they will be aware of what the forthcoming instruction enables them to do.	Heightening expectancy.
Stimulating recall of prior learning is effectively asking for the retrieval of existing knowledge.	Retrieval from working memory.
By presenting the stimulus the content is made visible.	Calls upon pattern recognition processes and heightens selective perception.
Providing learner guidance helps to advise on ways of learning information.	Methods of learning information such as the use of rehearsal and encoding techniques.
Eliciting performance encourages learners to respond thereby demonstrating learning.	Heightens retrieval.
Providing feedback helps the learner gauge their performance level.	Reinforcement enables the learner to correct errors.
Assessing performance provides further feedback to learners thereby helping to improve performance and reinforcing successful performance.	Responding to feedback and the retention of successful performance strategies.
Enhancing retention and transfer enables the learner to practise and generalise their new-found skills.	Retention, retrieval and generalisability.

Gagné defined nine ways of transferring memory events from short-term to long-term memory (see Table 4.1 above).

These four approaches (of Piaget, Vygotsky, neo-Piagetian and information-processing) to cognitive development suggest that learning takes place within the confines of an epigenetic landscape. Moreover, that the epigenetic landscape can be influenced by the way in which learning is mediated – through social interaction and instruction for example. This social influence is important it would seem in determining the epigenetic landscape – as discussed next.

INFLUENCE OF SOCIAL INTERACTION ON THE EPIGENETIC LANDSCAPE: PIAGET, VYGOTSKY, NEO-PIAGETIAN AND INFORMATION-PROCESSING

We have already alluded to the concept of an epigenetic landscape in relation to how our development can be excelled, which has been discussed in detail in Chapter 1. In this section we will consider the impact of social learning on cognitive development and vice versa.

One of Piaget's lesser-known contributions to developmental psychology is his assumption of a strong connection between biological and psychological development. He claimed that the pre-existing mental structures of the developing infant constrain what can be created from experiences within the environment. The epigenetic landscape can be understood metaphorically by picturing a landscape featuring hills and valleys. By taking into consideration the prevailing environmental conditions, such as wind direction, a rolling ball can go in one of a number of directions downhill. The ball (which represents the child's development) of course will be pushed along in the direction of the wind's force.

So what does this mean in relation to Piaget's theory of cognitive development? The structure of the landscape according to Piaget is restricted by the structure of knowledge existing in the new-born – in other words, the schemas inherent within the sensorimotor stage. The schemas described in the sensorimotor stage are limited and comprise of simple reflex actions, which nevertheless enable the developing new-born to thrive. The schemas of the sensorimotor stage develop and become refined as the infant interacts with the environment through processes of assimilation, accommodation and equilibration (see Box 4.1). By the end of the sensorimotor stage the original schemas have changed to unrecognisable proportions such that the infant is said to have progressed to the next stage of development (i.e., the preoperational stage). A landscape analogy could be the shifting of the hills and valleys as a consequence of a natural weathering and other geological changes. This means that the ball's progression might take a different direction due to these resulting landscape changes. In Piaget's theory, it is knowledge (attained through interacting with the environment) that modifies schemas and ultimately the structure of the mental landscape.

Although Vygotsky does not refer to the epigenetic landscape, his concept of the zone of proximal development alludes to the importance of adult instruction and demonstration provided within social interactions. This will ultimately influence the direction of learning and the skill-set attained. While biological maturation provides the impetus for learning, it is the zone of proximal development that enables cognitive development to excel further. The quality and nature of this social interaction can either facilitate or impede learning. It can be surmised that learning is a product of our biology (genetic endowment) and culture (through social support/scaffolding). In order, however, to be able to learn effectively the developing child needs to develop appropriate social skills to extract the social message from the social interaction. This binds cognition and social skill development together in such a way that these are interdependent upon each other.

Neo-Piagetian approaches such as that of Pascual-Leone refer to M space to describe underlying maturation changes occurring to increase the capacity of short-term memory. As children age, this M-space capacity increases to enable the extensive processing required for more complex tasks. This is a bit like how the memory cache operates in computers. When a computer programme is running that requires vast amounts of memory, a central executive equivalent allocates more memory so that the programme can operate efficiently. Modern cognitive psychologists see this as analogous to human information processing.

In the case of information-processing, reference is made to an epigenetic landscape in terms of processes and structures involved in the management of information and how this is then translated into knowledge. These structures have been described in flowchart format while the processes are outlined as the mental strategies adopted to learn information.

We can see that all three approaches to cognitive development (Piaget's and Vygotsky's theoretical approaches and the information-processing approach) outline structures and processes enabling learning to occur. There are, however, differences between the three approaches. Such differences concern how the relationship between cognition and social development is perceived. Vygotsky, more than Piaget, emphasised this connection.

In relation to information-processing, Gagné also recognised an important relationship between socially derived learning and cognitive processing. He described how external conditions, such as instructions offered by a mentor, activate internal processes of learning. There have been many studies demonstrating the connection between cognition and social development, which we will return to when considering the research evidence.

Another facet of cognition is verbal and nonverbal language development. We will consider language development in relation to our ability to communicate thoughts and emotions in the next section.

COMMUNICATION

Communication is a process of imparting information about one's feelings, thoughts and needs using sounds, gesticulation, words or behaviour. Note that this definition suggests communication is a combination of nonverbal and verbal means of information transfer. Certainly during the early months of infancy much communication with the caregiver is through making sounds, smiling, crying and eye gazing (see Chapter 3). Smiling is seen as important in the coordination of vocalising (Yale et al. 2003), and stems from the general emotional arousal state of approach (see Chapter 3). In infants nonverbal communication dominates and is used to manipulate the caregiver into wanting to fulfil its needs. The antecedents of verbal communication are present during infancy (Adamson 1995) but the caregiver plays an important role in developing this innate capacity to communicate further. Goldin-Meadow (2006) emphasised the importance of gesturing and displaying facial expressions as aids to developing infant skills of nonverbal communication. In the early months of infancy, the caregiver shows objects to their three- to four-month-old baby who then learns to respond by six months using smiles, gestures or kicking actions. Pointing gestures begin at about six months but infants are still unable to follow a pointing gesture given by the caregiver – this occurs at 12 months. Pointing gestures are an important form of nonverbal communication as it develops a sense of shared attention (or joint visual attention) between infant and caregiver. Joint visual attention enhances the development of verbal communication as infants learn to associate an object with its name (Golinkoff and Hirsh-Pasek 1999). Pointing during joint attention provides infants with a new-found freedom of self-expression as they can share their intentions with others (Tomasello et al. 2007). Pointing can be used as an action to share an interest in a particular object with the caregiver. This is considered to be a **declarative statement** hence the label **protodeclarative**. This is different to **protoimperative** pointing where the infant wants the caregiver to do something such as retrieving an unreachable cuddly toy (Bates et al. 1989).

Infants, as we discovered in Chapter 3, have an innate predisposition for sociability (Fantz 1961). Some developmentalists would argue that they have an innate predisposition to acquire verbal communication or language. This is supported by the seemingly infinite forms of sentence structures children rapidly learn to construct – some of these sentences they self-create without having heard them uttered ever before. Before this happens, infants go through a phase of practising sounds of the language they are subjected to. Babies as young as five months have the ability to distinguish the difference between sound-bites such as 'bah' and 'gah' known as **categorical speech perception** (Moffitt 1971). In Moffitt's study he allocated babies to one of three groups, each of which heard a series of short auditory clips:

1. heard 60 repetitions of 'bah' then 10 repetitions of 'gah';
2. heard 60 repetitions of 'gah' then 10 repetitions of 'bah';
3. heard 70 repetitions of 'bah'.

Plate 4.5 Mother and child sharing attention. (Shutterstock 129083705.)

Using heart rate as an indicator of discriminatory ability, Moffitt found that babies in the first two groups had an increase unlike those in the third group (who had no change). Note that increase in heart rate suggests the babies were aware of a change in the sound during conditions 1 and 2 ('bah' to 'gah' and vice versa). Moffitt concluded that babies had an innate ability for categorical speech perception. Others have also demonstrated this ability in babies of one month using single consonants (Aslin et al. 1998; Miller and Eimas 1994). Categorical speech perception appears to be restricted by the early language the infant hears. There is a developmental timeframe depicting sensitivity to learning the language the infant is subjected to and this occurs early in infancy. Babies respond early on to the language they hear by practising vowel-like sounds first then progressing to strings of consonant–vowel combinations. In the case of the former, known as '**cooing**', babies make sounds by combining the same vowel such as 'oo' or 'aa' during social interactions with their caregiver. In the case of the latter, strings of consonant–vowel sounds such as 'dadada' or 'mamama' are repeated and are referred to as '**babbling**'. Stoel-Gammon and Otorno (1986) claimed that this is due to brain maturation since babies all over the world show the same time course for cooing and babbling.

By 12 months babies are stringing together **phonemes** (i.e., distinct units of sound used to form words) to form non-words – known as patterned speech. Patterned speech and learning real words overlap in the infant's developmental timeframe. According to Fenson et al. (1994), at about 17 months toddlers can understand 50 to 100 words, but utter their first words earlier than this at 10 to 15 months. Beyond 15 months, however, the **naming explosion** occurs rapidly. As many as 900 words are known by the age of two, which increases to 8,000 by six years of age (see Box 4.3). This naming explosion is impressive as indeed is the relatively rapid acquisition of the rules of grammar. How children learn language is a question that has been addressed by various researchers using different theoretical stances (see Chapter 1). In our next section we explore the ways in which children acquire language.

Plate 4.6 Children learning words in the classroom. (Shutterstock 342056471.)

Box 4.3   Age and extent of word learning

In nearly all languages the first words learnt refer to important people (e.g., mum or dad), then to objects that move (e.g., car or ball), and to familiar actions (e.g., bye-bye, up or more), and to the outcomes of familiar actions (e.g., dirty, wet or hot). Among the first fifty words learnt by 18-month-olds there is rarely any reference to things that remain still like a table or vase (Nelson 1973). About 65 per cent of the fifty words acquired pertain to the naming of objects (nouns) and 14 per cent to actions (verbs). The reason for this has been attributed to nouns being easier to learn conceptually and the fact that, before verbs can be fully appreciated, children need to make connections between objects and their actions (Huttenlocher and Lui 1979). Not all findings are consistent with this. For example, Huttenlocher et al. (1987) demonstrated that children learn verbs reflecting their daily activities, while Bloom (1998) found that in children from nine months to two years of age nouns represented a third of the words they knew. Also there are cross-cultural differences where for some languages (e.g., Japanese) verbs have a more dominant status than nouns (Hoff 2005).

In two-word utterances smaller, less important, words such as articles (e.g., the, a) and prepositions (e.g., on, after) are left out. This **telegraphic speech**, as it is called, sounds a bit like a telegram and begins between 17 and 24 months of age. From this age between one to three words a month are learned. Fenson et al. (1994) claimed that as cognition (e.g., memory, categorisation and representation skills) develops further children can add between 10 and 20 words a week to their vocabulary. By two to three years of age children can put together simple sentences in a meaningful way (following rules of grammar – subject-verb-object). By three and a half years children acquire many rules but are prone to over-generalisation (e.g., I goed, I rided). Between four and five years of age they can use embedded sentences like 'I think he will come too' and indirect objects like 'He showed his friend the present'.

(continued)

(continued)

The practical side of language, that is the **pragmatics** (i.e., context), develops in a skilled manner. Here, the child has to learn how to use language across different situations. Pragmatics of language is subtle but, if incorrectly used, can cause embarrassment. Pragmatic skills are in place by 10 years of age and tend to follow after a good understanding of language and grammatical rules has been acquired.

Good pragmatic skills enable children to adapt to the needs of listeners and to be more precise about what they are trying to communicate (Deutsch and Pechmann 1982). Furthermore, conversational strategies become more refined, such as knowing how to make polite requests (Axia and Baroni 1985) and understanding the differences between what one says and what one means (Ackerman 1978). In adolescence a good pragmatic skill set enables teenagers to master irony and sarcasm (Winner 1988) and the nuances of language necessary in the interpretation of literary works. Acquiring good pragmatics allows adolescents to vary their language style according to the situation (Obler 1993), even to moderate their language complexity to a level suitable for whom they are in communication with (e.g., using simple language to talk with young children). One important pragmatic skill, however, is the ability to listen to others when in conversation. Communication is a two-way process, so it is important to be able to listen as well as to speak. When participating in a conversation, it is important to identify the cues for speaking and listening – if these are ignored, the person might be considered as rude or liking the sound of his or her own voice.

Hence children learn language through interacting with others. They also learn important lessons concerning how it should be used in conversation with others in different situations and circumstances.

The acquisition of language in children

Many developmentalists support a socially derived explanation of how children acquire an extensive vocabulary. Smith (2000), for example, claimed that children form associations between the object and its label, and further consider the similarity of features across objects. This eventually leads to a form of categorisation based on the similarity of object characteristics such as shape and number of legs. According to Skinner (1957), learning words and forming sentences using grammar happens as a consequence of operant conditioning (see Chapter 1). In other words, as infants make sounds parents reinforce those that most resemble a word using hugs, smiles and positive interaction. In a similar vein, Whitehurst and Vasta (1975) claimed that complex utterances like whole phrases and sentences are acquired through imitation, which can also be combined with reinforcement. Hence the caregiver can point at an object and say the name so that the child will gradually learn to associate the sound pattern with the object.

Tomasello (1998), however, believes that labelling objects is more to do with using social cues, like pointing, provided by the caregiver. In this way children remember the word given to the object of their joint visual attention with their caregiver (see Box 4.4). Adults, therefore, interact with infants in an important way and it has been shown that four-month-old infants will gaze in the same direction that adults are looking. Adults will often label what they see. Such joint attention often leads to infants talking at an earlier age (Dunham and Dunham 1992).

Box 4.4   Importance of joint attention in language acquisition

Of the different aspects of joint attention, pointing is considered to be the best early behavioural indicator of understanding social interactions between caregiver and infant. Pointing indicates three types of joint attention. First, pointing could be a request for an object or for someone to perform a specific action (protoimperative); second, it might guide the attention of the caregiver so as to share the moment (protodeclarative); and third, it might provide information concerning an object's location (Tomasello 2006). The timing in which pointing occurs has been associated with language development (Goldin-Meadow and Butcher 2003). Pointing, however, is just one facet of joint attention and, although important for language development, it is joint attention per se that plays a significant role in the course of acquiring verbal language. Joint attention serves to increase an infant's learning of object naming but also suggests the beginnings of developing an understanding of people's mental states (Carpendale and Lewis 2004; Racine 2004; Wittgenstein 1958). Interestingly, Gallagher (2004) considers that the link between mental state and overt behaviour requires a social context because, without it, the action can be ambiguous. Gallagher provides the following example,

> you see my right arm, with open hand drop through the air, but nothing else that would provide the context for what it means, . . . it could mean many different things . . . Without the context, my intention is simply not clear to anyone . . . watching me, or trying to interact with me.

> (p. 211)

Dropping of the right hand might, for example, indicate the start of a race – but only if the context is correct. In the context of children learning language, this implies that they must become competent socially by understanding different types of shared interaction before they can learn the words (Racine and Carpendale 2007a; 2007b). Moreover, directing a caregiver's attention by pointing depends on prior experience of this nature – a shared interaction and an anticipated outcome. Tomasello et al. (2005) believe that infants must have a degree of understanding of the intentions of others in order to acquire the skills of language. Racine and Carpendale (2007) consider this degree of understanding to be limited to routines shared with the caregiver that provide a context of anticipated outcomes. Moreover, this is a necessary interactive platform in the development of language. Another way of considering the importance of joint attention is to perceive it as an activity that helps to progress social development. In this case social understanding is not a prerequisite for engaging in joint attention. Joint attention might simply be based on an action that is reinforcing – the caregiver points to something interesting and worth having a 'looki look'. Moreover, by doing so the infant learns about others in addition to acquiring new labels for objects.

Joint attention plays an important role in how infants acquire words for objects. Even when children acquire a substantive vocabulary, gesturing such as pointing is often used in tandem with stringing words together (Adamson 1995). It is not surprising therefore that joint attention is developed early on in social development as it enables infants to interact with the caregiver who then provides the social linguistic scaffolding that language acquisition requires.

At 6 months infants become interested in social turn-taking games like peek-a-boo. This demonstrates that from an early age infants are already engaging in the important element of language that is turn-taking and attention. This form of word learning is known as **ostensive communication** and only appears easy because it is supported by specific cognitive mechanisms. But learning by ostension is not straight forward. When a parent points at a furry creature and calls it a cat, for example, there is nothing in the act of pointing that tells the child the parent is referring to the type of animal rather than describing its coat. In fact, according to American developmentalist Ellen Markman (1992) for this to work the child has to make three assumptions about the word-naming process. These are known as **whole object**, **mutual exclusivity** and **taxonomic assumption**. By using these three assumptions, young children are able to make good guesses as to the word's meaning.

In the case of the whole object assumption the child assumes that when an object is named the person is referring to the whole object and not its component parts. Moreover, when an object is named the child assumes the person is referring not to that specific object (e.g., Smelly the cat), nor to its general category (e.g., a mammal) but to the basic level (e.g., categories containing items resembling each other such as all cats) (Rosch 1975). Markman demonstrated this in an experiment whereby three-year-olds were presented with an array of objects, some familiar (i.e., cups) and some unfamiliar (i.e., tongs). When shown a 'tong' they were told that it was a 'biff' and asked to collect more 'biffs'. They collected more tongs by relying on the whole object assumption. When, however, a pewter cup was referred to as 'biff', they collected examples of objects made of pewter. Markman claimed that under such circumstances children use the mutual exclusivity assumption. In other words, young children when introduced to a novel word label (i.e., 'biff') will know that the word is not referring to the familiar object (i.e., cup). Therefore they select the unfamiliar trait, or part, of the object (i.e., pewter) and look for other objects showing the same characteristic as a token of the novel word label (Markman and Wachtel 1988).

The mutual exclusivity assumption means that children come to assume that words refer to entirely separate (non-overlapping) categories, meaning that objects have just one name. Under the mutual exclusivity assumption, children as young as 16 months learn that an object cannot have more than one label. This helps children to map novel labels to novel objects simply through the exclusion of already known labelled familiar objects (Markman 1990). Hence according to Markman et al. (2003) this assumption 'allows children to overcome the whole-object assumption thus freeing them to acquire words for parts, substances, and other properties' (p. 242). Moreover, mutual exclusivity helps children to infer correctly what novel word labels are referring to when circumstances are ambiguous such as in the absence of pointing and other joint-attention behaviours.

The taxonomic assumption plays an important role in differentiating between objects as individuals or as members of the same kind. This assumption enables us to 'individu-ate' objects belonging to the same group (e.g., to distinguish Ginger my cat from Smelly the next-door neighbour's cat). The taxonomic assumption, however, assumes that children learn an example of the category in question and will then formulate a hypothesis about what the defining characteristics of that category are. Preschoolers are open to overgener-alisation (e.g., dogs are sometimes called cats) but, as they get older, they will eventually revise their hypothesis according to the same characteristics shared by objects. Markman and Hutchinson (1984) considered the way in which children organise objects when a novel label is provided. For example, when children were presented with 'dog', 'dog food' or 'cat' and asked to categorise them, they would put 'dog' and 'dog food' together – hence relying on a thematic connection between 'the dog and its food' rather than a taxonomic one (i.e., the dog and the cat share the same characteristics). (Note that for Huttenlocher et al. (1987), a thematic connection is a means of extending the word label to include other factors associ-ated with the object. Hence, a child who points at the fridge and says 'milk' is not indicating that 'fridge' and 'milk' are the same thing but rather 'my milk is in there and I want some'.) When, however, children were given a novel label for 'dog' such as 'dax', and asked to find another 'dax', they then selected 'cat' – hence relying on a taxonomic connection rather than a thematic one. Research findings by Markman and her colleagues seem to suggest that all three assumptions work in tandem, and that young children tend to generalise labels for objects according to the whole object and taxonomic assumptions.

Children, however, also rely on other social cues. When adults use a new label while looking back and forth between the child and object, the label in this case refers to the action associated with the looking behaviour (e.g., come, help or play) and not the object itself

(Tomasello and Akhtar 1995). It would appear that the behaviourist model of association formation does not necessarily hold up, especially when we consider the extent to which children make assumptions based on a shared attention. If the caregiver, for example, introduces a novel word for a new toy, the child will assume it is the name of the toy provided that attention is focused on the toy (Baldwin 1995). Furthermore, if a novel name for the toy is provided by the caregiver, the child will look to see the direction of eye focus to attain joint visual attention. All-in-all the above factors seem to suggest an innate language knowledge, which becomes even more apparent as children acquire grammar (see Box 4.5).

Box 4.5   The innateness of learning grammar

American linguist Noam Chomsky (1957) observed that children learn language rapidly and with relatively few errors. It occurred to Chomsky that this could not simply be a feat of trial and error and reinforcement as suggested by Skinner. This led Chomsky to believe that language skill must be etched into the structure of the human brain given the complexity involved in comprehending grammar. He claimed that infants are born with a **language acquisition device** (LAD), a biologically based innate system containing rules common to all languages. This enables children to understand and speak in a rule-orientated manner once they have acquired a reasonable vocabulary. To illustrate this Chomsky provided an example where the placement of the word 'is' changes the meaning of the sentence: 'The boy is playing marbles' changed to 'Is the boy playing marbles?' Now consider the complexity of the next statement where the word 'is' appears twice: 'The girl who is wearing a wedding dress is playing darts'. Which 'is' needs to be moved in order to create a question? 'Is the girl who wearing a wedding dress is playing darts?' is clearly grammatically incorrect. Children usually do this 'statement to question transformation' task correctly (Crain and Nakayama 1986). If this was learnt by the process of trial and error, children would be expected to make many more errors than they do. This begs the question of why children make few errors on this task. Chomsky believes that this is because children perceive utterances as hierarchically structured noun and verb phrases. Hence, in our example, 'The girl' is a noun phrase and 'is playing darts' is the verb phrase. 'The girl who is wearing a wedding dress', because 'who is wearing a wedding dress' is saying something about the girl rather than the action she is performing, is thus the noun phrase. Because the question requires the child to ask what the girl is doing (the verb phrase), the 'is' that is moved has to be the one that relates to the verb phrase. It is interesting that the majority of people are unaware of these rules but implicitly use them. Turning statements into questions is not something the linguistic environment provides and nor do parents teach their children about verb and noun phrases (something that they themselves probably know little about). This knowledge comes from somewhere and Chomsky argues that it is innate. Further support of an innate linguistic knowledge comes from a study by Hirsh-Pasek and Golinkoff (1991). They demonstrated that infants of 13–15 months, still at the one-word stage of language, had no problem discriminating between similar-sounding but syntactically-distinct phrasing. They were shown footage of two versions of Cookie Monster and Big Bird from Sesame Street. There was a voice-over that said, 'Oh look! Big Bird is washing Cookie Monster! Find Big Bird washing Cookie Monster'. Infants spent longer looking at the screen that matched this action rather than a similar action of Cookie Monster washing Big Bird. This suggests that they can understand the different roles of subject, verb and object before being able to string words together. Finally, Chomsky argues that language learning is supported by a language organ that contains knowledge of **Universal Grammar** (UG) underlying all languages. All languages have a subject (S), verb (V) and object (O)

(continued)

(continued)

and all languages have structures performing the function of nouns, verbs, adjectives and prepositions. According to Chomsky these structures exist as part of the new-born's innate knowledge of language contained in UG. Languages vary syntactically where the position of S, V and O differs. For example, 180 languages (45 per cent) such as German have SOV arrangements, 168 (42 per cent) such as English have SVO structures and 37 (9 per cent) have VSO combinations of which Gaelic is one such language. Less common combinations include VOS (12, 3 per cent) and OVS (5, 1 per cent) languages. Moreover, in 96 per cent of languages, the subject is placed before the object. When a child is subjected to a specific linguistic experience, Chomsky proposes that one of many **mental switches**, called parameters, is activated. This parameter setting increases the rate of language learning. Hence UG informs the child about S, V and O but the parameter activated triggers the appropriate combination setting.

Although many developmentalists subscribe to the Chomskian model of language development, this view is not universal and recently some researchers have challenged it (Sampson 1997). Clearly, although influential, Chomsky's model of language acquisition remains contentious to some developmentalists.

Despite the possible existence of an innate UG, the importance of social interaction in language development cannot be ignored. Even Chomsky suggests that the social linguistic environment plays an important role in switching on the correct parameter (see Box 4.5). The way the caregiver communicates verbally with the child has been shown to influence language acquisition. This form of speech between caregiver and child (or **Adult–Child (A–C) speech**) was initially referred to as **motherese**. During episodes of A–C speech, the utterance is raised by about an octave in pitch and slows down in such a way as to create swooping contours that babies find interesting. Adults are unaware that when they adopt an A–C mode of speech they stretch and exaggerate the acoustic components so that the infant pays attention to these components and can form 'maps for speech'. Hence, A–C speech allows infants to identify the individual acoustic components and can be seen as a kind of scaffolding (see Box 4.6).

Plate 4.7 Noam Chomsky. (Shutterstock 125767211. Credit: deepspace/Shutterstock.com.)

Box 4.6   A–C speech makes things simple

According to Messer (1994) adults do modify their speech when using 'motherese' to communicate with young children. Messer highlighted a number of important measures in speech and
compared these for Adult–Child (A–C) and Adult–Adult (A–A) speech:

Syntax	A–C	A–A
Mean length of utterance (MLU)	3.7 words	8.5 words
Verbs per utterance	0%	81.5%
% of utterances with conjunctions	20%	70%
(since, because, then)		
% of pauses at end of sentence	75%	51%
Speed, words per minute	70	132

A–C speech has a higher pitch, a greater range of pitch and is simpler in meaning. The mean
length of utterance is shorter and simpler. It is more likely to be in the present tense, easier to
process, is slower, has more repetitions and an exaggerated form. It contains more concrete
nouns, uses proper names and uses special words like 'teddy, 'doggy' and 'wee-wee'.

It appears that infants respond to sound patterns, or what is known as the **prosodic characteristics** of speech, even before they can speak themselves. These prosodic characteristics
are unrelated to individual words but related to the general pattern of sound. Stern (1983)
found that when infants were inattentive, parents would alter the pitch of their voice by
conforming to a pattern of rising and falling pitch. By doing this they capture the attention
of their infant. Using A–C speech also helps infants to identify the individual words in a sentence. (Note that it is necessary for infants to be able to identify individual words that they
hear prior to producing the words themselves.) According to Gleitman (1990) infants can
do this because they are predisposed to attend to smaller segments of speech, which is what
happens during episodes of A–C communications – syllables are stressed. Infants cleverly
achieve this through the identification of words marked by pauses before and after. These
words are then divided into smaller units that are emphasised in A–C speech – so helping
infants to locate where they are. Gleitman claims that the caregiver speaks loudly at particular points in the conversation, which he calls bootstrapping.

Messer (1981) showed that during A–C speech words for objects receive greater emphasis and are spoken the loudest. Caregivers therefore provide useful cues enabling infants to
identify important words in the conversation. The more the caregiver speaks or reads to the
infant, the greater the infant's acquisition of new words. Hart and Risley (1995) found that
parents with professional careers spoke more frequently and for longer durations with their
children than those from low-income families. They found a large margin of difference in the
level of vocabulary acquisition between children from high and low-income families – with
children from high-income families developing more extensive vocabularies. Hence, socioeconomic class can have a serious impact on language acquisition.

Many developmentalists recognise the importance of the linguistic environment a child is
exposed to but simultaneously assume we are biologically prepared to learn verbal communication (Tomasello 2003). Bloom and Tinker (2001) argue that this is connected with other
aspects of development. From an interactionist point of view, language acquisition occurs

within a context of other behavioural developments such as the ability to interact with others and the formation of goal-oriented behaviour. Interactionists have been interested in the relationship between the environment and biology, so much so that Bates and Goodman (1999) refer to this as unravelling the 'nature of nurture' (p. 33). Social interactionist Jerome Bruner (1983) adopted the view that the environment provides the child with a **language acquisition support system** (LASS). The LASS refers to the acquisition of language in younger children as a consequence of receiving help from older children and adults. According to Bruner, language development in very young children is facilitated primarily by their caregivers. He advocates that a child, regardless of age, can understand complex information. He stated in 1960, 'We begin with the hypothesis that any subject can be taught effectively in some intellectually honest form to any child at any stage of development' (p. 33). This occurs through the concept of the **spiral curriculum**. At first information is structured in such a way that complex concepts are simplified to the child's level of understanding. Once the child understands this, the content of the information can be stepped up to a more complex level when returned to at a later date. This means that the complexity of information taught gradually increases, which is why Bruner labels this the spiral curriculum. In relation to language acquisition there are different ways LASS can be put to use. For young children, caregivers can facilitate language acquisition by:

- Playing nonverbal games such as 'peekaboo' or 'patty-cake'. Through these games, children learn structural elements of spoken language like, for example, the rules of turn-taking (Garvey 1990). Caregivers help toddlers to acquire these social skills by repeating the dialogue and providing pauses that they will fill with the appropriate response until their child can do this of their own accord.
- Using A–C speech (see Box 4.6) provides the bootstrapping required for language acquisition (Gleitman 1990). If the child fails to understand what is being communicated, the caregiver adjusts the speech to that which is understood – this provides further support for the notion of scaffolding.
- Using expansion and recasting helps the child to elaborate their simple sentence structures. In the case of expansion, the caregiver will imitate and add to what the child has said – hence expansion. This helps to increase the child's vocabulary (Weizman and Snow 2001). According to Tomasello and Farrar (1986), this is also a way of engaging the child further and providing scaffolding. Recasting reframes the incomplete sentence made by the child to a more complex grammatical format. If the child comments on the action of a pet, such as 'Doggy drinks', the caregiver might respond in the tone of a question. For example, 'What is the doggy drinking?' The scaffolding here involves the correction of the child's utterance and guidance towards appropriate use of language.

The approach of Burrhus Skinner (1957) to language acquisition is an environmental one, encapsulated in his behaviourist perspective. Skinner suggested that the environment is the key factor for a child's ability to learn how to communicate verbally. This is down to the process of reinforcement provided by the caregiver's persistence at reinforcing selected cooing and babbling noises. The caregiver reinforces these noises by responding with soft vocalisations or saying the word he or she believes to be what the infant is trying to communicate. This is a loop that is repeated such that a connection between making the noise and receiving the caregiver's approval becomes cemented. It is these close approximations to what the caregiver believes to be communicated that eventually become shaped to sound like the correct utterance. Language acquisition cannot, however, be simply explained by using a behaviourist approach. Observations of caregivers reveal that they are not discriminative in what they reinforce. Moreover, the rate of language acquisition is more rapid than can be explained by reinforcement and imitation.

Research concerning language competency suggests a robust connection between cognitive and social development, which we will explore further in the next section.

EVIDENCE FOR THE COGNITIVE–SOCIAL CONNECTION

An interaction between cognitive and social development works in both directions, whereby social skills can help academic achievement and cognitive abilities can promote a better understanding of social communication. Ten Dam and Volman (2007) claimed that social skills are paramount in enabling adolescents to succeed in everyday-life situations such as the workplace. The impact of good social skills on academic and professional pursuits is sometimes underplayed and should be considered more carefully in the guidance offered to adolescents (Elias et al. 1997). Elias et al. (1997) claimed that, '[W]hen schools attend systematically to students' social and emotional skills, the academic achievement of children increases, the incidence of problem behaviors decreases, and the quality of relationships surrounding each child improves' (p. 1).

Social development involves the application of social skills and, as discussed in Chapter 3, this begins early on in life. Both Bowlby (1969/1982) and Ainsworth and Bowlby (1991) demonstrated the impact of attachment and the nature of this attachment on future social development across the lifespan (see Chapter 3). The effects of early childcare on the development of cognition, language and problem-solving have been demonstrated by numerous researchers (Bradley 1993; Landry et al. 2006; Tamis-LeMonda et al. 2001). Although Bowlby and Ainsworth emphasised the importance of the primary caregiver, a number of studies have suggested that nursery care can be beneficial to both cognitive and socioemotional development. Some studies have reported a link between the quantity of nursery care received by infants and later cognitive abilities. For example, the National Institute of Child Health and Human Development Early Child-Care Research Network (NICHD ECCRN 2000) considered infants (from birth until 17 months) and toddlers (between 18–35 months) receiving nursery care or care at home in relation to their later academic/language performance at four and a half years. The NICHD ECCRN (2000) found that more nursery care in infancy co-occurred with poorer academic scores but in toddlerhood this increased language skill acquisition. These findings, however, are open to debate.

In some studies high-quality nursery care enhanced the development of social and academic skills prior to attending school (Lamb and Ahnert 2006). Cote et al. (2007) found evidence of good nursey care promoting cognitive and academic performance. Cote et al. also found that good nurseries can benefit social development. There is disagreement, however, among researchers concerning the benefits of nursery care in promoting social development, especially when such care occurs very early on in infancy and takes up many hours in the day (Belsky 2001; Cote et al. 2008; Nomaguchi 2006). There have been studies to show that the extent of time spent in care settings correlates with behaving negatively – that is the longer children spend in nurseries the more social problem behaviours they exhibit (Magnuson et al. 2007). Developmentalists, when researching this area, consider the quality, quantity and the type of care experienced. Sammons et al. (2002) found that children who had experienced more nursery care before reaching two years and five months demonstrated a higher level of cognitive functioning on starting school. Sylva et al. (2004) supported these findings by showing that primary school children were reaping academic advantages. It is important to acknowledge that many studies have also shown the quality (in addition to quantity) of care to be just as influential in the development of socioemotional skills.

Longitudinal studies examining socioemotional development in children have found that the quality of childcare plays an important role here (Howes 2000; Votruba-Drzal et al. 2004) and this positive finding also extends to cognitive-linguistic skills (Burchinal and Cryer 2003; Montie et al. 2006). Despite the emphasis that Bowlby and Ainsworth placed on the primary caregiver, interestingly, Sylva et al. (2011) found that it does not necessarily follow that children in nursery care from an early age are disadvantaged. If they receive good quality care, their socioemotional and cognitive development can be facilitated.

Plate 4.8 Learning in the nursery. (Shutterstock 447240148.)

Recent research, however, shows how a child's individual characteristics can influence the effectiveness of childcare. Belsky and Pluess (2012) found that a child's temperament interacted with the quality of care provided. Babies, less than six months of age, considered to be 'difficult' and rated as having a negative emotional disposition, proved to be sensitive to the quality rather than quantity or type of care received. Belsky et al. (2007) found that children with a difficult temperament in infancy showed more problem behaviours through-out their schooling years if their quality of care had been low. If, however, their care was of a good quality they experienced fewer behavioural problems than other children (Belsky and Pluess 2012).

The influence of the child's social environment will also impact on the development of socioemotional and cognitive skill acquisition. The effects of support outlined in Vygotsky's approach imply that social and cognitive development is entwined in the learning process and very much depends on the social environment of the child. Vygotsky's zone of proximal development enables a social dialogue between mentor and learner in such a way that it heightens the cognitive experience. Effectively a child can master academic skills more quickly through a social interface. Being able to attend to and store information are clearly important processes involved in our ability to learn in both socioemotional and cognitive domains (Bell and Deater-Deckard 2007). Attention and memory are considered to be higher-order cognitive processes, often referred to as **executive functions** (EF). Executive function is influential in orchestrating our thoughts, emotions and directing our behaviour (Miyake and Friedman 2012). Executive function is involved in the following cognitive processes:

- verbal skills
- problem-solving
- decision-making
- nonverbal communication
- understanding social cues
- understanding the perspective of others
- egocentric speech in the form of self-talk used in the delay of gratification
- the control of impulses
- self-awareness

Executive function consists of a system of components including working memory (WM) which, in turn, consists of the phonological loop and visuo-spatial sketchpad and a central executive (CE) (see Figure 4.1). Diamond et al. (2007) examined the 'Tools of the Mind Curriculum', a programme devised to improve WM and induce increased self-control. The programme focused on 40 different activities designed to improve preschoolers' EF. The tasks were associated with improving the memory and attention of these children and adopted techniques of self-regulatory speech. Children were taught to regulate their behaviour by talking to themselves – a form of egocentric speech. Diamond et al. claim that the 'Tools of the Mind Curriculum' programme is a successful way of improving the social behaviour of preschool children at risk of developing problem behaviours.

Moreover, EF enables us to react to stimuli in our environment and be selective in our behaviour towards these stimuli (Diamond 2013). Blair and Razza (2007) found an association between EF and school functioning, whereas McQuade et al. (2013) showed a link with socioemotional development. Noble et al. (2005) reported that EF development is particularly sensitive to social factors. Other studies have identified different social factors, such as disadvantaged families causing instability and chaotic family environments, in the development of EF performance (Bernier et al. 2010). Under these circumstances, Vandenbrouke et al. (2016)

found that parental stress in low socioeconomic status (SES) (and other high-risk factors such as single parenting and low level maternal education) families was negatively associated with high EF performance ability. Hence, in these families, preschool children scored low on EF tasks such as digit and word recall, backwards digit recall and the odd one out. Executive function is clearly important in academic performance (Bull, Espy and Wiebe 2008). Disruption of EF features strongly in the early onset of conditions such as autistic spectrum disorder (ASD) and attention-deficit hyperactivity disorder (ADHD) (Semrud-Clikeman et al. 2010) (see Chapter 5). Executive function development is also found to be lagging behind in children exhibiting aggressive behaviours (see Box 4.7).

Zelazo and Carlson (2012) distinguished between '**hot**' and '**cool**' **executive function**. Hot EF is aroused by emotional and motivational factors that make it difficult to delay gratification. Cool EF, alternatively, stems from cognitive abilities to use working memory and processes of inhibition and cognitive flexibility to make effective decisions. Zelazo et al. (2005) claimed that aggressive behaviour might tap into hot EF. Furthermore, Kim et al. (2013) found a positive relationship between cool EF and academic achievement and a relationship between hot EF and socially disruptive behaviour in three and five year olds. The process of inhibition in cool EF is important in childhood aggression, primarily because it suppresses one action in favour of another. If the inhibition process is not functioning optimally then there is likely to be an immediate hot-headed response (such as physical aggression). Recently, Poland et al. (2016) have suggested that cool EF plays an important role in inhibiting childhood relational and physical aggression.

Box 4.7   Executive function (EF) in aggressive children

Displays of aggressive behaviour in children have been linked to poor academic, social and psychological development (Montroy et al. 2014). This has been explored further specifically in relation to executive function (EF). Executive function consists of different subcomponents, but the most commonly researched is that of working memory (the component that deals with information by holding and transforming it). Researchers such as Goldstein et al. (2014) showed the importance of working memory and processes such as inhibition (the ability to suppress one response in preference to another one) and cognitive flexibility (ability to shift across perspectives) in goal-directed behaviour. It was a study by Allan and Lonigan in 2014 that showed a connection between inhibition (poor EF performance) and aggression in children. Aggressive behaviour takes on different forms and is likely to have a variety of underlying causes. A study by McQuade et al. (2013) demonstrated a relationship between various forms of aggression in relation to EF. Increased physical and relational (non-physical but can cause psychological problems) aggression in 9 to 12 year olds was linked to poor working memory. Both of these forms of aggression can be reactive in response to another person's behaviour or proactive by initiating the aggressive episode to another person. Relational aggression has been linked to higher cognitive function unlike physical aggression that is considered a triggered uncontrolled response.

These findings show a link between poor EF performance and aggressive behaviour in children. In particular, physical and relational aggression was associated with poor working memory function.

Clearly the social environment a child experiences is important to executive function. It is in impoverished social environments that social and cognitive problems are more likely to occur. But if Vygotsky is correct in his notion of the zone of proximal development, then parental and teacher 'scaffolding' will enhance academic and social competency and thereby promote positive behaviour (see Box 4.7). Children who are considered popular, for example, have higher levels of both cognitive and social problem-solving skills. Moreover, they show less aggression than those rejected and neglected by their peers (Dodge et al. 1983). Although Dodge et al. found evidence that popular adolescents may also use less aggression than their rejected and neglected counterparts, it is important to note that at this age aggression is sometimes used for status-gaining ends. There have been various initiatives to enhance youth development through coordinated social, emotional and academic learning in American schools and communities (Greenberg et al. 2003).

There has been a strong surge towards **social and emotional learning** (SEL) in school and community settings as a means of providing the necessary support that Vygotsky talked about in his theory of cognitive development. Some of these initiatives involve the following:

- a coordinated approach to planning and organisation within schools (Cook et al. 2000);
- the creation of schools as a place of learning through the support of the family and community – this might involve more contact and connectedness via class meetings and community-based activities (Solomon et al. 2000);
- improvements to the way teachers teach by enhancing their instructional mentoring to learners and increasing the involvement of family members (Hawkins et al. 1999);
- introducing smaller classroom numbers so that there is more accessibility and time to interact with teachers and for peers to interact with each other – this helps provide a classroom culture of guidance and the scaffolding required for learning (Bryk and Schneider 2002).

Provided such initiatives are long-term they work. These initiatives are more successful when increased family and community input are involved. Weissberg and Greenberg (1998), for example, found that students are more likely to follow positive social and health behaviours when there is greater support and involvement from the family and community. In 2011, Durlak et al. conducted a meta-analysis of 213 school-based SEL programmes. This involved 270,034 children and teenagers (kindergarten to high school students). Durlak et al.'s findings demonstrated that, where SEL programmes were successfully implemented, these children and teenagers showed significantly improved social and emotional skills. Moreover, there were improvements in overall attitude, behaviour and academic performance. This study provides sound evidence that SEL programmes do help to improve children's and teenagers' life skills and academic potential.

The idea behind such initiatives is to create a social environment inside and outside of school that is conducive to learning (the family environment providing appropriate scaffolding for learning such as language, see Box 4.8). Bronfenbrenner (1979), in his ecological approach (see Chapter 1), also acknowledged important linkages between family and school environments, enabling both social and cognitive development to interface.

Bandura (1986) also alludes to the important link between social and cognitive development in children by considering a triadic relationship between:

1. what the child observes within the environment;
2. cognitive abilities;
3. social factors inherent within a classroom context.

Bandura explained this further by emphasising how each of these three facets influences the others by causing interdependent change (see Chapter 1).

Plate 4.9 Activities creating community cohesion. (Shutterstock 78237505.)

Box 4.8   Does parental help with homework improve learning?

As children are expected to learn outside of the school environment, teachers set their pupils homework. Cooper et al. (1998) have demonstrated the value of completing homework in academic progression for children attending secondary school rather than for those of younger years. Parental involvement in their children's education has meant that parents are more likely to provide help when their children find homework difficult. Estrada et al. (1987) provided evidence of the positive effects for academic progression when parents support their child in the completion of homework. The benefits of helping the child with homework extended to behavioural adjustment and the initiation and maintenance of peer relationships (Johnson and Jason 1994). This may be the case for a multitude of reasons. The first is that the mentor relationship inspires the child to become enthusiastic and pleased at overcoming the challenge encapsulated in the homework set (Nolen-Hoeksema et al. 1995). A second reason proposed is that the parent helps the child to understand the homework challenge and to find a solution. In this case the parent promotes autonomy in understanding and being able to represent the problem in a format that makes sense (Landry et al. 2000). The third relates to the importance of emotional support provided by parents when the child is trying to solve the homework problem. If too much emotional support is provided in the form of praise then this can be disadvantageous (Fagot and Gauvain 1997). Furthermore, in cases where parents themselves have emotional problems, then this can have a negative effect. Murray et al. (1996) found that inadequate maternal interaction during a bout of postnatal depression predicted poor cognitive performance up to five years of age. In most cases, however, when considering the nature of parental support given to the child during a homework session, Nolen-Hoeksema et al. (1995) found that parental interaction fostering enthusiasm and autonomy of understanding enhanced academic achievement. Furthermore, a non-coercive parenting style offering support and undivided attention promoted positive emotional and behavioural wellbeing. This area of research provides strong evidence for Vygotsky's notion of scaffolding in the zone of proximal development.

Considering the first point raised by Bandura, children observe what is going on socially around them and often learn by imitating the behaviours of others. Want and Harris (2001) believe this ability to imitate is important in the development of cognitive skills used in understanding causal reasoning. This means that children can calculate what made a person behave and act in the way they did by observing a catalogue of events (pre and post the actions performed). This aspect of reading the situation is linked with social cognition, which we will be discussing in the next chapter. It is clear that the development of cognitive skills through observation enables some form of learning. This is the case whether or not the learning is socially desired, as highlighted in Bandura's Bobo doll study (see Chapters 1 and 2).

The link between cognitive and social development has been explored by studies looking at delayed social development and the impact this has on academic achievement. Malecki and Elliot (2002) showed that the level of social skill attainment could be used to predict academic achievement. This finding has also been repeated in other studies (Caprara et al. 2000; Mitchell and Elias 2003). Herbert-Myers et al. (2006) claimed that the acquisition of social and language skills at an early age will increase levels of social competency. Social competency will then have an impact on the acquisition of cognitive skills – further cementing the link between social and cognitive development.

The interaction between social and cognitive development is complex but areas of research addressed here suggest that the two are deeply interwoven and difficult to unravel. Social and cognitive development is especially important in how we learn to communicate with others and, as we have seen, communication is complex. It involves both nonverbal and verbal communication, which develops and becomes refined as we progress from infancy to childhood to adolescence.

Summary

- Some developmentalists, such as Jean Piaget, emphasise the physical environment and the child's interaction within it. Others, like Lev Vygotsky, emphasise social and cultural settings as important routes to the attainment of knowledge during childhood. While Piaget introduces the concept of schema to explain the changing cognitive landscape of the child's brain, Vygotsky uses the notion of the zone of proximal development. Neo-Piagetians such as Juan Pascual-Leone referred to there being M space that increases in capacity with age. Those supporting an information-processing account of cognitive development claim there are structures that become more sophisticated, and functions which operate more efficiently, with age. According to Robbie Case, as M space increases with age, children learn to solve problems in ways that are consistent with the different stages outlined by Piaget. Karmiloff-Smith introduced the domain-relevant approach to explain how genes, the brain, behaviour and the environment interact to influence our development. Domain-specific modularity, she argues, does not explain the deficits seen in many developmental disorders such as autism and Williams syndrome.
- Piaget, Vygotsky, Neo-Piagetians and the information-processing approach all incorporate the idea of brain maturation, whether it is via schemas, the zone of proximal development or structures (e.g., M space). These depend on there being

(continued)

(continued)

an epigenetic landscape whereby the contribution of our genes and how these interact with the environment influences the pathway of development. Vygotsky describes the social environment as providing children with the necessary social support for learning beyond the limits of their genes. This point, where social support helps children learn beyond the limits imposed by their genes, is the zone of proximal development.

- Communication is more than verbal language – it involves all the nonverbal nuances that enable people to exchange information. Infants develop their skills of communication by using joint visual attention to enhance their verbal language learning. Attaining joint visual attention involves the use of various gestures and eye focusing to summon the caregiver's interest. The most commonly used gesture is pointing. Pointing has three functions in attaining joint attention: protoimperative (requesting an action); protodeclarative (showing the caregiver something of interest); and to share information about an object's location. Pointing at objects and providing a label helps the infant to learn new words.

- This type of word learning through pointing is known as ostensive communication but only works because of underlying cognitive mechanisms. The child has to make three assumptions. Ellen Markman claimed that children adopt the principle of mutual exclusivity – they assume the word refers to separate non-overlapping categories. The whole object and taxonomic assumptions are the other two. For the whole object the child assumes the word and object pointed at is referring to the whole object and not its parts. The taxonomic assumption refers to categories containing objects that are similar.

- Noam Chomsky introduced Universal Grammar (UG) to explain language acquisition and why its development is unstoppable in all countries. Although UG is an innate mechanism, the social linguistic environment plays a pivotal role in activating the correct language parameter. Chomsky argues that UG contains innate knowledge of information about the structuring of grammar such as how nouns, verbs, adjectives and prepositions are used. Moreover, all languages make use of the subject (S), verb (V) and object (O) but the ordering of these in sentences varies.

- Adult–Adult (A–A) speech is generally rapid and has a different emphasis on word pronunciation than Adult–Child (A–C) speech. A–C speech contains fewer words per utterance, longer pauses and not as many words per minute. A–C speech has a higher pitch and is simpler in meaning but takes on an exaggerated form. Infants respond well to the sound patterns inherent in A–C speech, which are known as prosodic characteristics. A–C speech, initially referred to as 'motherese', enables the infant to mark out the beginnings and endings of words and to extract the important points in the conversation, which Gleitman has called bootstrapping.

- Underlying cognitive processes enhance social developmental skills but social developmental skills also improve cognition. Scaffolding in the form of social interaction also plays an important role in further developing cognitive skills. Cognitive development in the form of executive functions (EF), such as attention and memory, are sensitive to social factors including the socioeconomic status (SES) of the parents. Aggressive behaviour has been linked to poor academic, social and psychological development in which EF is a major factor.

Questions

1. How does joint attention, in particular pointing, help infants learn language?
2. The A–C speech pattern is said to be universal. What might this suggest? Why is A–C speech so effective in helping infants to learn language?
3. How does Vygotsky's notion of the zone of proximal development differ from Bruner's notion of scaffolding?
4. Critically evaluate how Karmiloff-Smith's domain-relevant notion differs from domain-specificity.
5. Critically evaluate how Bruner's LASS differs from Chomsky's LAD.
6. Critically assess whether language would progress successfully if caregivers failed to communicate using A–C speech.

Further reading

If you are interested in a guide providing information about cognition and language within a holistic context of child development and a fuller account of the relationship between communication difficulties and social risk factors accounting for poor educational outcome, look at:

- Hayes, C. (2016). *Language, Literacy and Communication in the Early Years: A Critical Foundation.* Northwich, UK: Critical Publishing.

If you are interested in good coverage of the issues involved in child development including cognition and language, look at:

- Parke, R.D. and Gauvain, M. (2009). *Child Psychology: A Contemporary Viewpoint.* New York: McGraw Hill.

If you are interested in children's thinking from the early to the teenage years contextualised within cognitive topics such as perception, language, memory and problem-solving, look at:

- Siegler, R.S. and Alibali, M.W. (2005). *Children's Thinking* (4th Edn). Upper Saddle River, NJ: Prentice Hall.

If you are interested in the progression of mind development from conception to adolescence examined using research and theory, look at:

- Thornton, S. (2002). *Growing Minds: An Introduction to Cognitive Development.* Basingstoke, UK: Palgrave Macmillan.

Contents

Introduction   143

What is theory of mind?   144

How different types of theory of mind operate together   149

Perspective-taking and egocentricity   157

What helps us to develop a theory of mind?   159

The biology of social cognitive skills: mirror neurons and simulation   166

The case of autism   169

Summary   172

Chapter 5

Development of social cognition

Theory of mind

What this chapter will teach you

- Theory of mind (ToM) and how it develops.
- How false belief tasks can help us to understand the development of ToM.
- An understanding of the potential neurological bases of ToM.
- The tripartite model of ToM including cognitive, affective and conative components.
- An understanding of Selman's Developmental Stage Theory of Perspective-Taking.
- The concept of empathising and systemising systems.
- How autism spectrum disorder may be related to problems with the development of ToM.

INTRODUCTION

Fantz (1961) claimed that infants have an innate predisposition to be sociable beings (see Chapters 3 and 4). This implies that we are biologically designed to interact with other social beings. In order to do so we need to be able to understand each other. Social cognition enables us to understand and socially interact with other humans. One important aspect of understanding other people is the ability to comprehend what causes them to behave in the way that they do. We formulate hypotheses about other people's behaviours which, although occasionally incorrect, more often than not are well-founded. Our ability to do this apparent 'mindreading' is referred to as naïve psychology or theory of mind (ToM, see below). We are not at the mercy of our prevailing environment, as we are active agents guided by emotions, beliefs, thoughts and goals. This knowledge is put to good use through the formulation of hypotheses about people's behaviour and what they might do next. It is believed that our ability to do this is not derived from direct experience but rather draws on mental constructs that enable us to make inferences about the behaviours being observed. Clearly, having an understanding of other people's intentions is advantageous during any stages of the lifespan. Theory of mind might be limited in infants but, as we have already seen in Chapter 3, understanding the caregiver's intentions helps them make predictions about what to expect next. In order to achieve this they draw on a 'working model'. Here, infants fathom the care-style of the caregiver by observing the behavioural responses to their display of socially facilitating behaviours. The working model developed depends largely on the infant's interpretation of the caregiver's response. As discussed in Chapter 3, Ainsworth outlined different caregiver–infant interaction types, of which the secure attachment mode was the best for ensuring infant survival. Moreover, this secure attachment type was based on a positive working model resulting from interpretations of the caregiver's responses to the infant's display of behaviour. Therefore, it would seem, infants are capable of understanding the intentions of their caregiver, suggesting they have developed a ToM, albeit a limited one.

Understanding people's different mental states is not as simple a feat as it would appear. Theory of mind involves a complex mental calculation that children appear to grasp more and more as the brain develops. This is strongly linked with the development of mirror neurons in the brain, which we will return to later in this chapter. First, we need to explore what is meant by ToM and the emotional and cognitive forms it takes.

WHAT IS THEORY OF MIND?

British psychologist Simon Baron-Cohen (2001) defined **theory of mind** (ToM) as,

> *being able to infer the full range of mental states (beliefs, desires, intentions, imagination, emotions, etc.) that cause action. In brief, having a theory of mind is to be able to reflect on the contents of one's own and other's minds.*
>
> *(p. 176)*

This definition appears straightforward enough but what ToM entails is actually quite complex. The underlying complexity of cognitive ability required to successfully perform ToM tasking is phenomenal. By considering a simple example of a ToM-related task, the extent to which a full understanding of a statement is required (including the translation of another person's held belief) will become apparent. Consider the following example: 'Kangaroos are large rodents' – clearly a factually incorrect statement and easily judged as so. This becomes somewhat more complicated, however, when it becomes part of another person's belief system such as: 'Mary believes that kangaroos are large rodents'. Whether this is a true statement is difficult to ascertain for several reasons. First, it depends on who Mary is and, second, the statement has two components – the propositional content (kangaroos are large rodents) and an attitude towards the content (Mary believes it to be true). This means that the statement can be true despite the content being false. Moreover, as pointed out by Whiten and Byrne (1988), we are aware that other people can maintain different beliefs and feelings to the ones we hold and so can use these to manipulate or deceive us. Therefore, an additional level of interpretation is required where judgements about genuine incorrectness or intentional deceit are necessary. Telling the truth is a case of stating what is known, unlike lying, which takes account of the other person's mental state. Whiten and Byrne referred to the manipulation of others involving deceit as **Machiavellian intelligence** (a term they attribute to Cambridge philosopher Nick Humphrey (1976)). Interestingly, tests for ToM were initially developed to determine whether non-human primates have the ability to 'mind read' (Premack and Woodruff 1978 – see Box 5.1).

An understanding of ToM must therefore involve the realisation that other people have their own unique stance about the world. The American philosopher and cognitive scientist Daniel Dennett, in 1996, suggested that there are different levels used by people to interpret their world: physical, design and intentional stances. In the case of the **physical stance**, people use physical laws to make predictions about actions observed (e.g., gravity causes objects to fall down to earth). The **design stance** differs in that it is used to predict how designed things work, and this can include nature (e.g., the skin when pierced will bleed or press a button and the computer boots-up). The **intentional stance**, however, is very different from the physical and design stance as it involves judgement about goals and desires. This stance is reserved for understanding people and animals. The ability to attribute intentions to others is clearly a component of ToM. Very young children and individuals on the autism spectrum find the intentional stance difficult and tend instead to make physical- and design-based predictions about people. This will be returned to later on in the chapter.

Box 5.1   Non-human primates as 'mindreaders'

The term 'theory of mind' rose out of the research on chimpanzees by Premack and Woodruff in 1978. This was followed by researchers such as Whiten and Byrne (1988) who were interested in how non-human primates behave in ways that are advantageous to themselves. These behaviours often took the form of tactical deception, in other words, 'acts from the normal repertoire of [an] agent, deployed such that another individual is likely to misinterpret what acts signify, to the advantage of the agent' (Byrne and Whiten 1991, p. 127). Byrne and Whiten took this behaviour to indicate evidence of ToM and made references to the development of a 'Machiavellian intelligence'. Machiavellian intelligence was a term coined by Nick Humphrey in 1976 and tested by experiments involving deceit. Deceit is used to conceal actions, emotions or objects from others. Byrne and Whiten (1991) describe a chimpanzee stand-off where one chimp, who was approached by a rival from behind, was in a fearful emotional state but could be seen disguising this through the manipulation of his lips. Once the new lip configuration showed fearlessness, this chimpanzee turned to face his aggressor. Another example of deceit involved a subordinate chimpanzee with an obvious penile erection that he showed to a nearby female. When the dominant male approached, however, he dangled his arm over the erection as a means of concealing it (Whiten and Byrne 1988). This action helped avoid a violent confrontation, demonstrating that the subordinate chimpanzee 'knew his place' in the hierarchy. This suggests that he understood the consequences his actions might cause and how to avoid this. Is this evidence of a ToM? Experiments on counter-deception demonstrate that chimpanzees can change their behaviour depending on the actions of others.

Menzel (1974) devised an experiment where only one chimpanzee called Belle was informed of the location of hidden food. Belle wanted to share this information but changed her behaviour when another chimpanzee, called Rock, refused to share the food. Instead Belle sat on the food until Rock left. Only then did she uncover the food and began eating. This was short-lived as Rock returned and pushed Belle away. Belle waited for her opportunity

(continued)

(continued)

to have some food when Rock looked away. What was interesting and provided insight into Rock's 'state of mind' was the fact that he would walk away looking disinterested, but aware that Belle would try and take some food. When she did, he would quickly turn and head back towards her just at the point when she uncovered the food.

Another area demonstrating ToM is called righteous indignation – a reaction to having been deceived. Juice was served as a treat to a chimpanzee, which was dropped accidentally on one occasion by the researcher. On another occasion, a second researcher deliberately poured the juice onto the floor. The chimpanzee was allowed to choose which researcher should give the juice next time – unsurprisingly the researcher who accidentally dropped the juice was chosen, suggesting the chimp disliked the individual who purposely deprived it of a drink (Whiten 1993).

These studies suggest that chimpanzees do have a ToM. In their natural everyday behaviour they use deceit and show Machiavellian intelligence. In their natural and experimental environment chimpanzees show evidence of 'righteous indignation' to those who deceive them. This surely suggests that they have a relatively well-developed ToM (Byrne and Workman 2014).

According to Dennett, we rely on a rather complex level of intentionality comprehension. Furthermore, an understanding of the social environment increases as children begin to grasp ToM. In other words, as children experience their social world their ability to understand it improves, and this coincides with a maturing ToM and use of the intentionality stance.

Plate 5.1 Showing concern for another. (Shutterstock 492270820.)

Dennett refers to 1st, 2nd, 3rd and 4th orders of intentionality, which increase in their levels of difficulty and in the cognitive ability required to interpret what is going on. Dennett provides the following interpretation of these levels as:

(1st) I believe something.

(2nd) I believe you believe something.

(3rd) I believe that you believe that I believe something.

(4th) I believe that you believe that I believe that you believe something.

A sense of how difficult a 4th interpretation order is can be seen in the example of the story of sweet-sharing in Lance and Colin (see Box 5.2).

Box 5.2   The story of sweet-sharing in Lance and Colin

As children Lance and his brother Colin were given a bag of sweets every Sunday, which tended to contain an odd number of sweets. This meant that one of the brothers would have one more sweet than the other. Colin, the oldest of the brothers, had the task of counting the sweets and putting them into two separate bags. Many times he would ensure that he had the bag containing the extra sweet. Lance was unaware of this until one day he realised what Colin was doing and demanded that he swapped bags with Colin. Knowing that Lance would select his bag Colin had to think of a different strategy, which he did by putting the extra sweet into what would have been Lance's sweet-bag. Many times Lance would select Colin's bag of sweets, which now contained one sweet less, until one day he realised what Colin was doing. Lance therefore now selected his original sweet-bag that contained the extra sweet. Once again Colin had to switch strategies by putting the extra sweet into his original sweet-bag. Lance was once again unknowingly insisting on having the sweet-bag containing one sweet less. This continued until he realised his brother had shifted strategy and was once again swindling him out of one sweet. Colin then changed the strategy by putting the extra sweet into Lance's sweet-bag which Lance eventually 'cottoned on to'. At this point the whole system began to break down as neither brother was capable of tracking where they were in this game of leap-frog.

This example, based on a true-life experience of one of the authors, describes the development of a belief-system from the 1st to 4th order of intentionality. This, although a mundane example, illustrates the complexities involved in ascertaining a 4th order understanding of intentionality (and also illustrates how this thinking can be useful when gaining resources). It is no wonder that young children who have grasped an understanding of 1st order intentionality find it difficult to succeed on a 2nd order of intentionality task, let alone a 4th order.

According to Leslie (1994), the ability to infer mental states from other people's behaviour (that is a theory of mind) is driven by a **theory of mind mechanism** (ToMM). Additionally, Baron-Cohen suggests that the ToMM must be able to represent the full range of mental states, including those that he refers to as the **epistemic mental states** (see Figure 5.1). Baron-Cohen claims that this mechanism must enable us to understand the connection between mental states and actions that follow. The ToMM does just that. **Referential opacity** is a key property of epistemic mental states as it allows us to suspend the normal truth relations encapsulated in propositions (see Box 5.3).

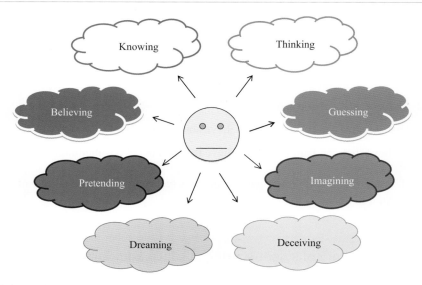

Figure 5.1 Examples of epistemic mental states.

Box 5.3   Referential opacity: a facet of ToMM

Baron-Cohen provided examples to illustrate how referential opacity operates as a means of enabling us to suspend truth relations in the following propositions.
     Example one (a biblical reference):

'Joseph's brothers thought they were bowing down to the prime minister of Egypt' – can be true while
     'Joseph's brothers thought they were bowing down to their brother' – may be false, even when the prime minister of Egypt is the same person as Joseph.

Why? They do not know that their brother Joseph has become the prime minister and nor do they recognise him. The term 'thought' is the 'attitude' that the brothers hold towards the proposition. It is the entirety of the statement that has to be considered for its truth or falsity.
     Example two (a fairy-tale reference):

'Snow White thought the woman selling apples was a kind person' – can be true while
     'Snow White thought her wicked stepmother was a kind person' – may be false, even when the woman selling apples is the wicked stepmother.

This type of deception is often appreciated by children as young as four. They seemingly comprehend what is going on in a pantomime – by shouting 'he's behind you'. It is referential opacity that enables this understanding early on in childhood.

     The ToMM allows the developing minds of children to use their mentalistic knowledge in a structured theoretical-like way. This was highlighted by Wellman in 1990 who illustrated

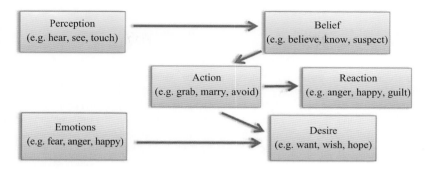

Figure 5.2 Pathways of action and reaction originating from perception and emotions. (Adapted from Wellman 1990.)

how our perceptions and basic emotions feed into our belief and desire systems resulting in an action and a reaction. Figure 5.2 illustrates how these facets interact.

We will address different facets of ToM considered by Wellman (1990) in the next section.

HOW DIFFERENT TYPES OF THEORY OF MIND OPERATE TOGETHER

Wellman's Human Theory of Mind provides insight into how our emotions and perceptions interact to influence our behaviour. As children develop, their emotions stabilise and their perceptions modify due to increased experience within the social environment. Both perceptual and emotional development feed into the social behaviour of children. If, for example, a child likes the smell of some doughnuts then he will want his mother to buy some. If the mother refuses then he might cry and stamp his feet in protest. With increasing age and experience of the social environment, his perceptions and emotional responses change, leading him to realise that he needs to modify his responses (e.g., by asking politely).

It is clear that perception and emotion play important roles in ToM. Perception, however, as we have seen from Wellman's model, also influences action. Emotion is important in ToM, especially empathy. Empathy has been described as an emotional response expressed towards another person experiencing pain (both physical and emotional) – as if to experience the pain ourselves. It is the experience of empathy that enables us to sympathise and exhibit altruistic behaviour towards the person in pain. On seeing a concussed elderly lady in the street, for example, most of us would stop to help her. Empathy has an important role in understanding other people's emotions. This is one reason why it helps us to interpret the underlying intentions of others from their behaviour. Theory of mind can be represented as a facet of empathy that overlaps with perspective taking (i.e., the ability to understand different points of view within a situation) which, in turn, overlaps with cognitive empathy (i.e., the ability to understand the emotions of others) (see Box 5.4 and Figure 5.3). As perception and emotion are key components in the development of a mature theory of mind, the bifurcation into cognitive and emotional ToM makes perfect sense.

Box 5.4   The relationship between ToM, perspective-taking and cognitive empathy

Davis and Stone (2003) argue that understanding the beliefs of others is not a guarantee for understanding emotions. Moreover, the understanding of emotions does not necessarily lead to the activation of empathy which, in turn, is not a guarantee of sympathy and other prosocial behaviour. Dvash and Shamay-Tsoory (2014) claim that 'empathy is the link between knowing the thoughts and feelings of others, experiencing them, and responding to others in caring, supportive ways' (p. 282). They argue that ToM is a facet of an individual's ability to infer the emotions of another. Empathy enables us to comprehend and feel for another. Davis (1994) describes empathy as the reactions we have towards the experiences we observe in others. Some researchers perceive empathy as a cognitive process – referred to as cognitive empathy. **Cognitive empathy** involves making inferences about the emotional aspects of another person. It implies that we cognitively recognise someone else's emotional state. In order to do this other processes are involved such as **perspective-taking** and ToM (Eslinger 1998; Shamay-Tsoory et al. 2004). Some researchers consider perspective-taking and cognitive empathy as the same thing (e.g., adopting someone's point of view). Gery et al. (2009) claim, however, that perspective-taking is important for ToM and is one way of obtaining cognitive empathy. There are other ways of attaining cognitive empathy, however, such as looking at facial expressions, recalling similar emotional events, imagining equivocal emotional events and assuming the observed person's emotional state is the same as one's own.

While ToM, perspective-taking and cognitive empathy overlap in that they are all required for social cognition, they also operate independently and are therefore separate processes.

Empathy, however, has also been considered in terms of two related human abilities: cognitive and **affective (or emotional) empathy**. As previously pointed out, cognitive empathy plays an important role in mental perspective-taking. Affective empathy, however, involves the 'vicarious sharing of emotion' (Smith 2006, p. 3). Affective empathy, according to Davis (1996), is what motivates us to behave in **prosocial** ways towards our kin and allies. It is important, however, that we are able to separate our own emotions from experiences of empathic ones. (Note that we appear to have evolved mechanisms to enable us to do this – see the section on the biology of social cognition on p. 166.)

Affective empathy plays an important role in moral development (see Chapter 10) and in the inhibition of aggressive behaviour (see Chapter 11). Plutchik (1987) sees affective

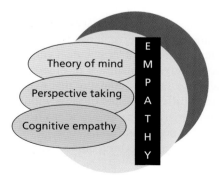

Figure 5.3 Venn diagram representation of empathy and ToM.

Plate 5.2 Showing signs of affective empathy. (Shutterstock 160499429.)

empathy as, 'the fundamental basis for social bonding between parents and children' (p. 44). Not all researchers accept that there are two forms of empathy (e.g., Strayer 1987), and some suggest that it makes more sense to separate empathy from 'pure emotional empathy' (Eisenberg 2000). In the case of pure emotional empathy, the cognitive and affective components are integrated and, according to Davis (1996), may regulate each other. Smith (2006) proposed that these two components, although separate, are complementary processes.

With the onset of sophisticated neuroimaging techniques introduced to the study of phenomena, such as ToM, researchers have increasingly suggested a separation between a cognitive ToM (ascertaining cognitive beliefs from the minds of others or '**mindreading**') and an affective ToM (ascertaining the emotional states of others, which may or may not activate our own emotions such as empathy – see Box 5.4) (Shamay-Tsoory and Aharon-Peretz 2007; Hein and Singer 2008). Much research has focused on cognitive ToM. A research paradigm, known as **false-belief tasks**, relies on asking children two fundamental belief questions concerning the current state of mind of the person in question. The most famous of these tasks is that of two dolls called Sally and Anne (see Box 5.5).

Box 5.5   False-belief tasks used to test for cognitive theory of mind

According to Wellman, by two years of age children understand others through their own desires. By the age of three this progresses to include an understanding of a person's desire and their beliefs about the world. Children at this stage in their development of theory of mind (ToM) perceive beliefs as a blueprint of the real world rather than a mere interpretation of the real world. At four years of age, however, they come to realise that beliefs are not mere

(continued)

(continued)

replicas of the world but are synonymous with interpretations that can be correct or incorrect at times. Hence Wellman sees ToM as becoming progressively more sophisticated with increasing age and experience with the social environment. Wellman makes the analogy to a scientist who has a theory, tests it and obtains more information that may or may not fit the existing information. This, he believes, is what children do. There is a consensus amongst researchers that children below the age of three fail to succeed on ToM tasks because they do not understand that others may have a different belief system to their own. Moreover, four-year-olds may not perform as well as five-year-olds. One way of investigating children's understanding of cognitive ToM (i.e., an understanding of another person's belief system and intentions) is to test their knowledge of false-belief. In order to do this Wimmer and Perner (1983) developed the famous Sally-Anne Test.

The test goes like this: Sally has a basket, Anne has a box. Sally has a marble and puts it into her basket, then leaves the room. Anne takes out Sally's marble and puts it into her box. Sally comes back and wants to play with her marble. 'Where will Sally look for her marble?' Most children under four years of age will say 'in her basket' as they understand that Sally believes that is where it is. As a rule children younger than four cannot do this task successfully because they fail to realise the implications of having a false-belief.

Perner et al. (1989) adopted the 'Smarties' test. Here the child is shown a Smarties tube and is asked, 'What do you think is inside?' The correct answer is 'Smarties'. They are then shown inside and, to their surprise, it contains pencils. The experimenter then closes the tube and asks the child two belief questions. 'When I first showed you this tube what did you think was in here?' The child correctly answers 'Smarties' as there is no reason to suspect anything else. 'And when the next child comes in (who hasn't seen the tube) what will he think is inside here?' The correct answer is 'Smarties', which is the false-belief held. Again children of four and above can perform on this task successfully. However, younger children incorrectly answer 'pencils'. False-belief tasks place an understanding of ToM at four years of age but, for some researchers, ToM is not fully acquired until four or five years. Chandler and Sokol (1999), for example, claim that children's understanding of how other people's 'minds' operate develops long after the acquisition of false-belief comprehension.

In a study by Carpendale and Chandler (1996) children between five and eight years viewed an ambiguous drawing of a rabbit or duck face. They could successfully identify two interpretations. When asked what 'Anne' would see they answered either the rabbit or duck or that they did not know. When pressed further they failed to explain why it was difficult to predict someone else's interpretation. With increasing age they found it easier to respond to this question. This implies that there is more to learn post false-belief acquisition. Moreover, it could simply be beyond children of this age to extrapolate their success at false-belief tasks to other contexts. This can be observed in Harris et al.'s (1989) study of Ellie the elephant. Children were informed that Ellie liked to drink Coke but the can of Coke she was given contained milk. They were asked how she would feel when given the can of Coke (before drinking from the can). 'Happy' is the correct answer as Ellie still believes that there is Coke in the can. Four-year-olds answered incorrectly by saying 'sad' whereas five-year-olds said 'happy'. The connection between false-belief and emotion may take longer to acquire than false-belief and behaviour (Sally-Anne task). Nevertheless, false-belief tasks have helped researchers to develop a timeframe of when different aspects of ToM are understood by children.

Dennis et al. (2013b) have, however, taken this differentiation between cognitive and affective ToM further by proposing a **tripartite model of ToM**: cognitive ToM, affective ToM and conative ToM. Cognitive ToM refers to research concerned with 'reading the mind' and experiments on false-belief. Research on affective ToM draws upon emotional expression displayed in faces and considers the emotional persona we express for others to see – or emotive communication that can even involve deception. In the case of conative ToM, however, we use social communication as a means of influencing another person's cognitive and emotional state. Such strategies used to influence the cognitive and emotional states of others might include praise or criticism for instance. Dennis et al. employed different ways of testing for cognitive, affective and conative ToM in children with traumatic brain injury (TBI), as discussed in Box 5.6. Dennis et al. (2013b) studied the differences between cognitive, affective and conative theory of mind using stimuli that helped to separate the three facets of ToM (see Figure 5.4). What is clear about understanding cognitive, affective and conative ToM is our ability to suspend the normal truth relations held within propositions. This is only possible by understanding epistemic mental states using referential opacity (as discussed in Box 5.3).

Box 5.6   Testing the tripartite model of ToM: cognitive, affective and conative

The cognitive ToM task is typical of the false-belief method used (see Box 5.4). In Dennis et al.'s (2013b) study, a new dimension of Jill being present while Jack moves the ball was added (this additional format was based on a previous study by Dennis et al. 2012). In Figure 5.4, in frame A, Jill places a ball in the blue hat. Jack, in frame B, however, moves the ball into the red hat while Jill is absent. This is the typical false-belief format but, for some conditions, Dennis et al. (2013b) have Jill watching Jack move the ball. In frame C the false-belief question is asked, 'Where does Jill believe her ball to be – in the red or blue hat?' Children who can successfully perform on false-belief tasks are said to have accomplished cognitive ToM. Children who understand false-belief will answer that Jill believes the ball to be in the blue hat if she was absent when Jack made the switch, but in the red hat if Jack was observed making the switch.

In the case of the affective ToM task, Dennis et al. (2013a) presented traumatic brain injury (TBI) children with 25 short auditory narratives of which there were five per emotion of sadness, disgust, happiness, fear and anger. An example of a narrative might be 'Mary ripped her favourite dress. If her mother saw this Mary would not be allowed to wear it to church'. Children are asked how Mary was feeling inside (the emotional condition) and how Mary's faced looked (the emotive condition). They had to select the correct facial expression from an array of faces depicting different emotions. The ToM question relates to the emotive communication portrayed to the mother. As Mary did not want her mother to know she had ripped her dress she would have to display a deceptive emotional expression – this is measured by the 'look on the face' question providing a deceptive representation from that experienced inside. The emotional expression scores represent how the individual in the narrative feels inside and its depiction in the facial expression (this acts as a control).

Conative ToM is tested using two characters depicted within a number of different situations. One situation described by Dennis et al. (2001) involves fixing a bicycle (see bottom panel of Figure 5.4). These pictorial situations have a narrative presented in audiotape format. The utterance of the speaker varies according to a neutral, ironic criticism or empathic intonation. Sally informs John that 'he has done a good job of fixing the bicycle' (Dennis et al. 2013b, p. 29). There are three scenarios: literal truth, ironic criticism and empathic praise. In the literal truth scenario, the complement is consistent with John doing a good job of fixing the bicycle. Sally in the ironic criticism scenario is of the opinion that John is failing fast at fixing the bicycle and

(continued)

(continued)

tells him so – a negative evaluation. In the case of the empathic praise scenario, Sally thinks John is failing at fixing the bicycle but intends to provide John with a positive evaluation to convey encouragement. Children were informed that fixing the bicycle was the task goal and the outcome was depicted in one of the three pictures in the bottom panel of Figure 5.4. They were also provided with information about Sally (e.g., she liked to talk to people or she liked to annoy people or she liked to cheer people up). Children were also told what was said by Sally to John (e.g., 'you did a great job'). Dennis et al. asked the children probing questions concerning the beliefs of Sally and her opinion of John, as well as her intentions conveyed by her utterances towards John. This latter point has two intended outcomes: what Sally wanted John to think about the event and what she wanted John to think about himself. The literal truth scenario acts as a control, while the ironic criticism and empathic praise provide a negative and positive second-order intention towards John respectively.

Dennis and colleagues have shown that these different types of ToM tasks are useful in measuring success rates in children with traumatic brain injury. Their general finding is that children with TBI have a lower threshold for perturbation of affective and conative than cognitive ToM tasking. Put simply, this means that TBI impacts more negatively on emotionally and behaviourally related theory-of-mind tasks while leaving cognitive ToM ability more intact. Their findings are more detailed and beyond our examination here (for further discussion refer to Dennis et al. (2013b) 'Cognitive, affective, and conative theory of mind (ToM) in children with traumatic brain injury'). For the purposes of our discussion here, their methods of inquiry for ToM-related tasking is a very useful way to investigate children's acquisition of all three types of theory of mind.

There are alternative ways of investigating theory of mind to the classical false-belief tasks such as the Eyes Test by Baron-Cohen et al. in 1997. This research has led to differences in male and female processing styles known as **systemisers** and **empathisers** respectively, which we will explore next.

The Eyes Test: an alternative way of testing for theory of mind

A different method used to understand the ability of children to read the emotions of others was introduced by Baron-Cohen et al. in 1997. They designed the 'Reading the Mind in the Eyes Test' (Eyes Test) to measure how successful we are at judging people's mental states from pictures of their eye region only. In their study participants were presented with 25 photographs of the eye region, each with two trait descriptors. In a later study Baron-Cohen et al. (2001) used four trait adjectives such as 'reflective, 'aghast', 'irritated' or 'impatient' with only one being correct (as depicted in Figure 5.5 – you might like to try this for yourself). Participants were asked to select which of the traits they believe to be correct. As this is a difficult task to do, a special child's version was also developed. Baron-Cohen et al. (2001) suggested that being able to 'read' the emotion depicted in the eyes is an important skill required for effective social cognition. The Eyes Test is designed to enable participants to put themselves into the mind of the person so that their mental state can be predicted. Baron-Cohen et al. (2001) describe this task as 'an advanced theory of mind test' (p. 241). The Eyes Test reveals that girls are superior to boys at gauging the emotional state from the eye strip presented. Such sex differences in the ability to read emotions in others have been highlighted in Baron-Cohen's research on empathisers and systemisers.

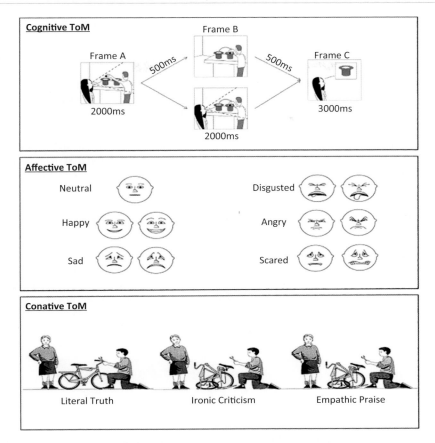

Figure 5.4 Stimuli and descriptions of the different types of ToM tasks (Used with permission.)

In his book in 2003, *The Essential Difference: Male and Female Brains and the Truth about Autism*, Baron-Cohen explores the tendency of males to be superior at systemising and females to have an advantage when empathising (see Figure 5.6). In the case of systemising, the individual expresses an urge to analyse how things work and the underlying principles involved in the behaviour of the system studied. Empathising, however, is

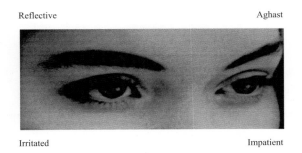

Figure 5.5 An example from the Eyes Test. (Used with permission.)

very different. People who score highly on empathising are particularly good at reading the emotions and thoughts of other people (and respond to other people using appropriate emotional responses). Empathising is a way of understanding the mental state of another person and in so doing being able to predict their behaviour and emotions.

It is interesting to note that individuals on the autism spectrum tend to score highly on systemising (possibly analogous to Dennett's design stance). They also tend to be male. Furthermore, males tend to be 'systemisers', leading Baron-Cohen to suggest that symptoms of autism such as communication deficits might be an extreme form of the male brain. More will be said about the autism spectrum later in this chapter. Figure 5.6 demonstrates that individuals vary in terms of their ability to empathise and systemise and that in some extreme cases there may be a 'trade-off' between the two.

In a study by Stannage and Taylor (2012) gender differences associated with empathy, systemising and the recognition of emotion were examined using three tests: Empathy Quotient (EQ), Systemising Quotient (SQ) and Reading the Mind in the Eyes Test (RMET). It was anticipated that there would be a positive relationship between EQ and RMET and a negative relationship between SQ and RMET. In support of Baron-Cohen, they found that females had higher empathy and emotional recognition scores than males, and that males had higher systemising scores than females. This was borne out by multivariate analysis of variance, which detected a gender difference on the EQ and SQ but not on the RMET. Analyses produced weak positive correlations between scores on the EQ and the RMET, and the SQ and the RMET. The only significant positive correlation found, however, was

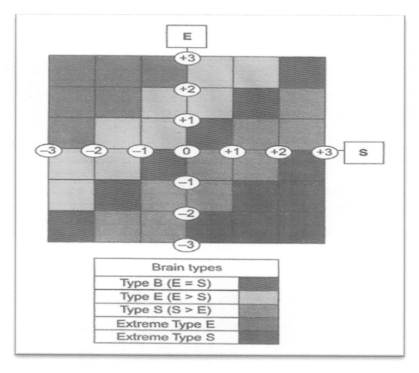

Figure 5.6 Diagram illustrating the empathising (E) and systemising (S) brain types. The numbers represent standard deviations. Type E = female brain; Type S = male brain; Type B = balanced brain. (Used with permission.)

between the SQ and RMET for male participants. Regression analysis showed SQ scores for males was the best predictor of their level of performance on the RMET. They suggested that it is possible that males and females use different skills to recognise emotion on the RMET. Furthermore, findings suggest, in contrast to Baron-Cohen's conclusions, that emotion recognition might rely on more than empathy alone. This might explain why there was no gender difference on the RMET and why, for males, SQ and RMET correlated positively. This suggests that an element of systemising might help when examining the eyes to ascertain the underlying emotion portrayed. A link between empathy and emotion recognition, and systemising and emotion recognition, was found by Besel and Yuille (2010) but they only used the six universal emotions. Stannage and Taylor expanded this to include the epistemic emotions in the RMET and provided support for Besel and Yuille's findings. Moreover, Penton-Voak et al. (2007) conducted a similar study to Stannage and Taylor but used line drawings that lacked validity.

It appears that theory of mind is far more complex than original conceptions of ToM suggested. We have also seen how ToM is today considered a facet of empathy. Moreover, ToM overlaps with perspective-taking (see Figure 5.3). Perspective-taking is an important skill that children need to acquire for social cognition and therefore social development. But what exactly is perspective-taking and how do researchers investigate this? We will consider perspective-taking and its relationship with Piaget's notion of egocentricity next.

PERSPECTIVE-TAKING AND EGOCENTRICITY

One perspective-taking approach linking with an emotional-cognitive theory of mind was developed by American-born Robert Selman in his 'Developmental Stage Theory of Perspective-Taking' (1971b). He proposed a five-stage model to describe the development of perspective-taking throughout the lifespan, but concentrating primarily on its point of origin in childhood (see Figure 5.7). Selman's approach very much relied on reading different stories to children about a specific character and how others would react to this character's actions in a given situation. This was designed to examine how children perceive situations and the many permutations of those situations held by other people. Selman would ask questions about the story read to the children. An example of a story is that of Holly, an eight-year-old who enjoys climbing trees. Despite being a good tree climber she falls out of the tree. Her father observes the event and is obviously worried, even though she appears unhurt, and asks her to promise him that she will stop climbing trees. Although she promised her father that she will no longer climb trees, she has the dilemma of whether to rescue her friend's kitten, which is stuck in the tree, or to keep her promise. Stories like this example were read to children, who then answered a series of questions such as, 'Should she climb the tree?' 'What will her father do when she climbs the tree?' and 'Will her friend understand her position?' Selman found that their answers and the justifications given were age-dependant. From his data he was able to devise a stage approach to perspective-taking based on the maturity level of the child. As is the case with any stage approach introducing age as a defining criterion, there will be overlaps of ability in different stages – hence an age overlap across stages.

As we can see from Figure 5.7, Selman's understanding of perspective-taking is a lifespan approach, although most of the learning takes place in childhood and adolescence. It is strongly associated with being able to understand the mind of another person and how this impacts on their behaviour. His stage approach, however, also pays lip-service to the influence of the social environment and the restrictions this might impose on how we respond across different situations.

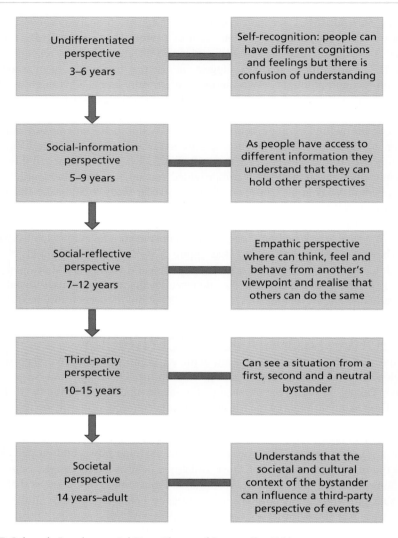

Figure 5.7 Selman's Developmental Stage Theory of Perspective-Taking.

The role of perspective-taking is also addressed in Piaget's stage-theory of cognitive development, in particular during the preoperational stage (see Chapters 1 and 4). The defining characteristic of the preoperational stage is what Piaget refers to as **egocentric thinking**. Children between two and six years of age are locked into the preoperational stage of cognitive development. Here, egocentric thought parallels theory of mind in that children of this stage and age group find it difficult to understand the possibility that another person can have a different mental state to their own. They believe that others maintain beliefs about the world that mimic their own. One typical Piagetian egocentric thinking task involved the presentation of a landscaped model that contained three mountains of differing colour and feature. In Piaget and Inhelder's (1956) task a small doll was placed at one end of the mountains and the child stood at the other. The child was asked what the doll can see (see Figure 5.8).

Figure 5.8 Diagram representation of the three mountains model.

As the younger children might have struggled to provide a verbal response, Piaget instead presented them with ten different photographs from which they selected the one they felt represented the doll's view of the landscape. He found that children aged in the preoperational stage performed poorly at this task, often selecting their own view rather than that of the doll. In other words these children fail to decentre or adopt a shared understanding of the world. This is a difficult perspective-taking task and it is not surprising that other researchers have taken issue with the methodology used. Newcombe and Huttenlocher (1992) found that very young children can successfully solve this problem once the task is made more child-friendly. For example, if the scenario is made to appear like a game where a 'robber' doll has to hide from a 'police' doll behind a set of walls, then most three-and-a-half-year-olds can successfully place the 'robber' doll appropriately out of the 'police' doll's view (Hughes 1975). It appears that Piaget had underestimated the ability of young children to entertain a ToM. Flavell (1981) also demonstrated this by holding a card so that the child saw a different side to the other person. Three-year-olds realised that they would not be seeing the same thing as the other person – hence recognising the other person's point of view.

As we have seen, children as young as three can perform successfully on belief and false-belief tasks. Wellman, Cross and Watson (2001) analysed the results of 178 studies of theory of mind using a meta-analysis research approach. This meant that only studies comparing like-with-like were considered. Moreover, the variables controlled for and the methodology adopted in these studies were the same. They found that children improved on their performance of false-belief tasks from three to five years of age.

There is clearly a connection between perspective-taking and ToM as demonstrated in Figure 5.3. It is clear that in order to develop a mature ToM it is necessary to be able to perspective-take. But how do we develop a theory of mind in the first place? Is this an innate feature or something we learn through our social interactions? In our next section we will consider such social interactions.

WHAT HELPS US TO DEVELOP A THEORY OF MIND?

The impact of theory of mind on social behaviour is profound. We constantly rely on social cognition (in particular our ToM skills) on a daily basis across many types of social situation. A social cognitive skill that is necessary for social communication must, it would seem, arise from a biological predisposition to understand the minds of others. (A point we will return to later in this chapter). Indeed Herba and Phillips (2004) acknowledged the continuous development of speed and accuracy in recognising facial expressions from childhood to adolescence (see Chapter 3 for discussion of face recognition). Blakemore and Choudhury (2006) make a further claim of the adolescent brain being particularly sensitive to social cognitive input. They suggest it is during this period of brain maturation that sensitivity to stimuli of a social cognitive nature is heightened. It is interesting that adolescence is a time when teenagers are forming relationships both of a friendship and romantic nature (see Chapter 7), and developing their self-identity and place in the world (see Chapter 8). Adolescence also coincides with much physiological change as a consequence of the onset of puberty (see Chapters 7 and 12). As we have seen, however, theory of mind begins to develop prior to adolescence and some children are better at it than others. It has been suggested that this development might relate to the nature of communication provided by the caregiver.

Influence of the caregiver

Research considering the effects of caregiver verbalisation of feelings and their causality on ToM development in infants has provided interesting insights. Findings show that, the more feelings are verbalised, the greater the understanding of false-belief tasks is. Verbalising feelings and their causality is referred to as **internal-state language**. Dunn et al. (1991) showed a positive correlation between caregiver verbalisations about feelings (and their causality) and later increased understanding of false-belief ToM tasks in their infants aged 40 months. Caregivers who are good at verbalising feelings and their causality have been labelled as showing **maternal mind-mindedness**. Meins et al. (2002) argued that maternal mind-mindedness towards their infant at six months helped improve ToM performance at 45–48 months. This maternal mind mindedness is shown through their use of internal-state language such as commenting on what they believe to be the infant's state of mind and emotion. For example, 'You really enjoyed that stewed apple dessert didn't you. I can see you liked it as you are smiling and looking happy'.

In recent years researchers have turned their focus to exactly how internal-state language is related to the development of ToM. In a study by Meins et al. (2006) seven-to-nine-year-old children were given two different ToM tasks: creating a narrative for a wordless picture book and providing a description of their best friend. Both tasks involved the use of a ToM but might also tap into their usage of internal-state language.

Meins et al. (2006) argued that providing a book narration for animals and characters in the story might not require internal-state language because children do not normally associate animals and fictitious characters with feelings. This therefore suggests that children are less likely to apply internal-state language to the book narration task but tend to use this form of verbalisation towards their friends – hence there being a positive correlation between ToM and internal-state language for descriptions of friends. They failed, however, to find an association between ToM and internal-state language across both tasks, which is interesting considering maternal mind-mindedness (shown in the form of internal-state verbalisation) by the caregiver promotes theory of mind development in the child. Meins et al. (2006) concluded that internal-state verbalisation must operate separately from their ability to represent these internal states. The research clearly demonstrates that internal-state language helps to increase theory of mind ability (Dunn et al. 1991; Meins et al. 2002). In addition to the caregiver, siblings also play a role in the development of ToM.

Influence of siblings

Findings from false-belief studies (see Box 5.5) suggest that there are individual differences in the acquisition period for ToM – occurring between three and five years of age. The most likely age of ToM acquisition is four years (Astington and Gopnik 1991; Perner et al. 1987; Perner et al. 1994). Interestingly, however, Hughes and Cutting (1999) suggest that

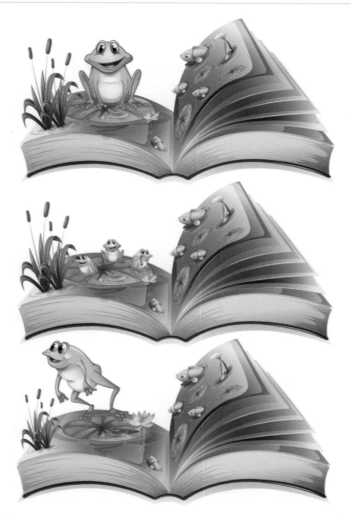

Plate 5.3 Example of a picture book coming to life in the imagination of a child. (Shutterstock 380064697.)

variations in levels of conversation across different families influence preschoolers' development of ToM. Perner et al. (1994) reported that there was a relationship between ToM development and the absence or presence of siblings. They found that having one sibling was a good influence for ToM development, more so than being an only child. This advantage, however, decreases when there are a large number of siblings. The age of the sibling had no impact on performing false-belief tasks. There is disagreement regarding the influence of sibling number and age in relation to ToM development. Jenkins and Astington (1996) argued that it is the number of siblings rather than their age that is important in ToM development. Ruffman et al. (1998) found that having older and many siblings increases performance scores on false-belief tasks. Among preschoolers, Cutting and Dunn (1999) failed to find a correlation between false-belief performance and having siblings in low-income families; a finding that was confirmed in a study by Cole and Mitchell (2000) of children between three and five years of age. This might be taken as suggesting that in more wealthy families having a number of siblings can be beneficial because they are not competing for the same resources.

Having at least one sibling within the age range of 12 months to 12 years helps improve ToM performance (Peterson 2000). Peterson and McAlister (2006) studied three-to-five-year-olds and found that their ToM performance increased when they had at least one sibling who was also a child, than those whose siblings were either infants or adults, or who were only children. In an Iranian study by Farhadian et al. (2011), only children were found to perform lower on ToM tests than children who had one sibling or those with two or more. They found that the most influential family members were the caregivers, especially the mother who was likely to be in the home. This was found to influence sibling ToM development more than sibling interactions.

Ruffman et al. (1998) claimed that the advantages of having siblings in the development of ToM relates to the types of interaction experienced. Older siblings, they argue, assist in the development of ToM via pretend play (see Chapter 9) and through the provision of an open forum for discussing feelings. Peterson (2000) agrees that there is more opportunity for play and discussion when there are siblings around. Furthermore, Peterson (2000) suggests that siblings assist in learning how to understand the perspectives of each other and facilitate the development of imagination.

Research findings suggest that both caregivers and siblings are influential in the development of ToM. Farhadian et al.'s (2011) findings show that siblings in Iran influence the development of ToM in a similar way to those living in the West. An interesting question is whether there are any cross-cultural differences in the development of ToM – discussed next.

Influence of culture

Research on false-belief understanding has been explored predominantly in US and European cultures (Wellman 2012). Where there has been cross-cultural research the focus has been restricted to the acquisition of false-belief understanding. The results here are mixed. A study comparing children from five different cultures (including Canada, Peru and India) found

Plate 5.4 Two brothers sharing their thoughts. (Shutterstock 90210835.)

evidence for the acquisition of false-belief understanding showing a universal timescale of development (Callaghan et al. 2005). Despite this, however, developmentalists have found variations in age acquisition of false-belief understanding (up to two years) across similar neighbouring cultures – including Italy with Britain (Lecce and Hughes 2010) and Japan with Korea (Oh and Lewis 2008). Astington (2001) argues that this is 'the danger in letting a single task become a marker for complex development' (p. 687). Hence, it is important to consider ToM as being more than just false-belief understanding.

Wellman and Liu (2004) demonstrated that different aspects of ToM acquisition can be time-scaled. Children of three, four and five years old were tested on five types of ToM task:

1. diverse desires (e.g., 'you might have a different desire to me');
2. diverse beliefs (e.g., 'you might have different beliefs about an event to me');
3. knowledge access (e.g., 'you might know something to be true but I don't know that');
4. false-belief (e.g., 'you might know something to be true but I might believe something different');
5. real-apparent emotion (e.g., 'you might feel sad but show a different emotion').

They found that children acquired an understanding of diverse desires before they understood the implications of diverse beliefs. Diverse beliefs, however, was understood before they were able to access the knowledge held by another person when it was different to their own. Only once this was acquired could they progress to fathoming the false-belief task. The older children found this easier to comprehend than the younger ones in this study. The most difficult ToM task was the ability to differentiate between real and apparent emotion – this could only be achieved when all previous four types of ToM task were successfully accomplished. Using this five-step scale of ToM development, Wellman et al. (2006) compared Beijing preschoolers who spoke Chinese with those in the US who were English speakers. US preschoolers mastered diverse desires, followed by diverse beliefs, then knowledge access, then false-beliefs, and finally real–apparent emotion. This pattern was found in English-speaking Australian preschoolers (Peterson and Wellman 2009) and those

Plate 5.5 You really don't mind me going out with your ex-boyfriend? (Shutterstock 179690219.)

in Germany (Kristen et al. 2006). Wellman et al.'s (2006) Chinese cohort, however, had the diverse beliefs and knowledge access order reversed. These differences were accounted for by Wellman et al. as being due to 'culturally shaped differences in input' (p. 1080), which impact on the development of ToM.

A study comparing the acquisition of knowledge and belief understanding in three- and four-year-old Australian and Iranian preschoolers found there to be a difference in how quickly these facets of ToM were acquired. The Iranian preschoolers were faster at mastering knowledge access tasks but slower to pass diverse belief tasks when compared with their Australian counterparts (Shahaeian et al. 2014a). These differences in performance were explained by socio-cultural variations between Iran and Australia. In a similar study, Shahaeian et al. (2014b) demonstrated that Iranian children aged between three and nine years scored similarly over all for ToM, but showed more understanding of knowledge access and sarcasm than their Australian counterparts. The Australian children, however, demonstrated more understanding of diversity of beliefs and desires. They claimed that these findings suggest universal similarities but also culturally influenced aspects of social cognitive development.

An example of a cultural difference is the extent to which caregivers differ in their level and nature of interaction towards offspring. There is much research showing the diversity of ways in which caregivers from different cultures interact with their infants (Bornstein et al. 2012; Richman, Miller and LeVine 1992, 2010). Furthermore, these differences reflect the individualistic and collectivist cultural divides. In the case of **individualistic cultures**, such as many countries of the West, children are socialised to be independent thinkers, to create their own ideas and express their thoughts and feelings openly (Greenfield et al. 2003; Nisbett 2007). Hence, they are more likely to challenge existing ideas and form their own beliefs. In contrast, children from **collectivist cultures** are taught to respect their elders who have volumes of valuable experience and knowledge from which they can learn (Johnston and Wong 2002). They are encouraged to conform to the rules, mores and the traditions of their culture. Shahaeian et al. (2011) argued that in Iran children are taught to learn the 'correct way' of thinking about issues. Such differences in socialisation might explain why children from individualistic cultures acquire an understanding of diverse beliefs more quickly than those supporting collectivist ideals. This may also account for why children from collectivist cultures acquire knowledge access ability more quickly than their individualistic counterparts. These explanations can account for the differences between Iranian and Australian children found in the two studies by Shahaeian et al.

Despite some cross-cultural variations in the developmental order in which facets of ToM occur, there is more similarity than there are differences. Children, regardless of culture, are likely to demonstrate prosocial behaviour, morality and the increased sharing of possessions as ToM matures (see Box 5.7). The downside, however, is that their ability to deceive, show aggressive behaviour and to bully can also escalate as ToM improves (see Box 5.7).

Box 5.7   Good and bad aspects of superior theory of mind acquisition

Theory of mind (ToM) has been linked with the ability to form good social relationships. One of the foundations for a good social relationship is the ability to show prosocial behaviour. Prosocial behaviour involves providing helpful and positive acts towards other people and is very much a promoter of social acceptance. Moore and Macgillivray (2004) have linked prosocial behaviour to ToM. In Thompson et al.'s (1997) study children between three and five years old were presented with the opportunity to share or not share their stickers. They established that the preschoolers with a more developed ToM were happy to share their stickers with their play partner. According to Hoffman (2000), knowledge about how others think and feel is important in prosocial behaviour because it enables one to reflect on the needs of others and to provide care. Turiel (1983) argued that by three or four years of age children have an understanding of justice and are able to differentiate these rules from other social rules. Children at these ages are therefore able to make moral judgements about moral issues that are relevant to them (more will be said about this in Chapter 10). Young children, despite understanding moral rules, have not yet established how a moral 'wrongdoer' should feel. They focus on the personal gain acclaimed by the perpetrator and say that they feel happy. Older children, however, understand the harm committed against the victim and feel that the perpetrator should feel sadness or guilt. Children who found it easy to make attributions of 'moral emotions' towards specific types of behaviour (e.g., should feel bad about intentionally breaking a cup) tended to show prosocial behaviour towards their peers. Malti et al. (2009a) used information provided by teachers to identify children of six years old who were either prosocial or aggressive in their behaviour. Children who were considered to be prosocial were more likely to make moral-based emotional attributions of behaviour than those identified as aggressive. Moreover, Gummerum et al. (2008) found that moral-based emotional attributions predicted prosocial sharing behaviours. It was noted by Repacholi et al. (2003) that children who use clever but dishonest methods to deceive others, often referred to as 'Machiavellian', tend to have a well-developed ToM. They are also good at spontaneously lying (Sodian et al. 1991). Children who act aggressively towards their peers have also been found to have a good ToM (Gasser and Keller 2010). Gasser and Keller believed that having a well-developed ToM places them at an advantage in that they know how the other children think and feel. This knowledge helps them to strategically attain their own goals. Gasser and Keller also considered that child bullies demonstrate a good understanding of the minds of others but fail to make appropriate attributions of moral-based emotions. Malti et al. (2010) concluded that there is a specific deficit of moral competency in children who exhibit aggressive behavioural problems. They further speculated that aggression that is planned ahead (i.e., proactive aggression) is related to superior social cognitive skills.

These studies demonstrate how ToM might be used in a positive or negative way depending on the child's inclination to be good or bad.

Interestingly, however, their ability to tell '**white lies**' (false statements aimed at deceiving the listener for a good reason) can be considered as a form of prosocial behaviour. Telling a white lie can be used to improve or protect another person's feelings. A number of studies have examined this, including three we describe below. In the 'reverse rouge task', an adult who was about to have a photograph taken had a red mark on the forehead (Talwar and Lee 2002).

Children of three to seven years had to say whether the adult was ready to have their photo taken. The older children were more likely to say the adult was ready as they did not wish to hurt the adult by saying they had a mark on their forehead. In another study by Talwar et al. (2007) children were given a disappointing gift. The disappointing gift was a bar of soap instead of an attractive toy. They found that the children responded most of the time by saying they liked the gift. Talwar et al. found that the telling of white lies increased with age. Furthermore, Banerjee and Yuill (1999) found that children of 10–12 years of age told a white lie even if it meant they would forgo exchanging the disappointing gift for an attractive one. Finally, in Fu and Lee's (2007) art-rating task, children were asked to score a piece of artwork when the artist was present or absent. Children of five years plus provided increased scores for the artwork when the artist was present rather than when absent. One question we might ask is, are these examples of the child being sensitive about the feelings of others?

Plate 5.6 Adult with a red mark to the forehead – ready or not for a photo? (Shutterstock 35480431.)

Bloomfield et al. (2002) presented children with a fictitious vignette of a person receiving a disappointing gift. When the children were asked how the protagonist will react to the gift, the older children of nine years believed that the person would say they liked the gift and would pretend to be happy. Younger children generally believed that the protagonist would be upfront and admit to not liking the gift. According to the findings of Gnepp and Hess (1986), children of 8 to 10 years of age predicted that the person in the vignette would tell a white lie in order to protect the other person's feelings and that it is okay to do so (Heyman et al. 2009). Hence it appears that children of this age are already showing a marked improvement in their social cognitive skill-set. Not only are they comprehending first-order representations (i.e., understanding another person's mental state based on behavioural cues) but also second-order representations (i.e., understanding how the person's response to the gift would affect the mental state of the person who gave the gift). This is quite a complex ToM capability.

Thus far we have considered factors that might help to develop our social cognitive skills (in particular theory of mind). But are there any underlying biological explanations for why we acquire this ability? This is the topic of our next section.

THE BIOLOGY OF SOCIAL COGNITIVE SKILLS: MIRROR NEURONS AND SIMULATION

Patients who have experienced destruction of specific parts of the brain provide researchers with information about the workings of the brain. Adolphs et al. (1995), for example, studied a 30-year-old patient referred to as S.M. An area of S.M.'s brain known as the **amygdala** was destroyed by a metabolic disorder. The main function of the amygdala (see Figure 5.9) is in the perception and experience of negative emotions like fear and anger. In S.M.'s case,

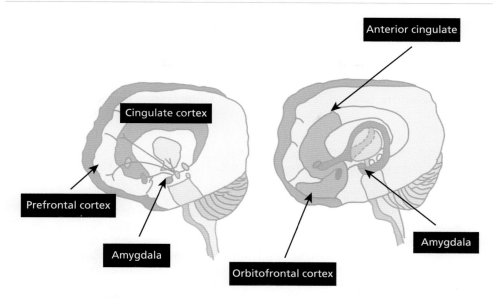

Figure 5.9 Drawing of the brain depicting areas associated with mirror neurons. (Taken from Taylor 2016.)

recognition of fear in photographs of emotional faces was difficult. Moreover, S.M. failed to experience emotions such as fear. Findings such as these are interesting and provide insight into the association between perception and action. Studying brain deficits such as amygdala malfunction in patients adds to our knowledge of the neural foundations of emotional processing (including an understanding of the emotional states of others). For S.M., understanding the emotional states and intentions from other people's behaviour was difficult. Although some facets of theory of mind remained intact, the quality and depth of understanding others was seriously compromised.

Technological advances in brain-scanning techniques such as fMRI and **PET** provide information about areas of the brain involved in social cognition. Interestingly, brain scanning has been used to investigate the areas of the brain that light-up during tasks of simulating actions performed in the first or third person. In order to simulate such actions on a daily basis, an orchestration of different facets of social cognitive skills is used. According to Decety and Ingvar (1990), performing a simulation task in the first person (i.e., from one's own perspective) requires less effortful processing than when carried out in the third person (i.e., someone else's perspective). They describe the simulation as a 'conscious reactivation of previously executed actions' that have been stored in memory.

Hesslow (2002) showed that the motor areas of the brain (**fronto-parietal**) become activated during performance on simulation tasks that required participants to imagine themselves carrying out a task using an observed person's current mental state. It was interesting that this pattern of activation resembled that shown when the action was actually performed. Moreover, this activation resembled real-time activity. Such simulation studies have informed researchers as to how we interpret the mental states of others. In addition to human studies, researchers have also considered simulation in non-human primates. Rizzolatti et al. (1996) studied monkeys mimicking the actions of other monkeys while attached to an electrophysiological apparatus. They found that two areas of the brain would become activated: the premotor cortex and the superior temporal sulcus. Neural activity of a specific area of the premotor cortex called the F5 area became active. These neurons are referred to as **sensori-motor neurons** or 'mirror neurons' for short. These **mirror neurons** were activated whether the monkeys performed or observed the action. In fact, some of these mirror neurons only code for the inferred goal of the action rather than the action itself. This means that, in a sense, mirror neurons are involved in a simulation of the internal state of another. Of interest to our discussion here, however, is the importance of mirror neurons for social cognition (see Box 5.8).

Box 5.8   The role of mirror neurons in social cognition

One interesting question we might consider is whether imagining the emotions and pain experienced by another person activates our own mirror neurons. Answers to this question are at the heart of theory of mind. Levenson and Ruef (1992) discovered that when two people experience the same emotion they are more in tune with understanding each other's intentions. This appears to have support from fMRI scans. Mimicking or merely observing facial emotional expressions will increase neural activation in areas of the brain used for understanding what these expressions mean. Additionally, the premotor cortex used in physically portraying emotional expression is activated. This suggests that the same pattern of neural activation occurs when we physically experience the emotional expression as well as observing or mimicking it. As we discussed earlier, theory of mind overlaps with empathy (see Figure 5.3). Morrison et al. (2004) investigated the relationship between imagining and physically experiencing another's pain. In their study they compared the neural pattern of activation for the physical experience of pain with the observation of someone else experiencing the pain. fMRI scans were administered while participants experienced a sharp probe similar to a needle prick. In another condition participants watched a video of someone else having a sharp probe applied to the hand. In both of these conditions a similar pattern of neural activity occurred in the **anterior cingulate cortex** (ACC) and **anterior insula** (see Figure 5.9). This might be taken as evidence that when we observe pain in another, at some level we really 'feel it'. This would suggest that the same neural activity pattern occurs either when we experience pain or someone else does. So how then do we know when we are experiencing pain rather than merely observing it in another? In the study by Morrison et al. it was found that there are qualitative differences of ACC activation in the first and third person. It is believed that this might be a mechanism enabling the differentiation between experiences of our own distress and empathy towards another person's pain. According to Decety and Jackson (2004), when we empathise with others it is important to be able to separate our own feelings from those of the other person – hence why there is a qualitative difference in neural pattern activation. Knowing the difference between the two is supported by the role of the **right inferior parietal cortex**. This is responsible for enabling us to keep a log of the actions self-produced separate from those performed by others (Blakemore and Frith 2003). This information is taken further by Saxe and Wexler (2005) who suggest that the right inferior parietal cortex is specifically involved in ToM. This area of the brain is activated when actions simulating another person's perspective are executed and not for one's own behaviours. This finding extrapolates to imagining how another person feels in an aversive situation but not when it is imagined for ourselves (Jackson et al. 2005).

It is clear that mirror neurons play an important role in the development of theory of mind.

Although the findings from neuroscience provide empirical support for the involvement of mirror neurons in how empathy is experienced, there is some concern expressed by researchers such as Lamm and Majdandžić (2015) that the implications of these results have been, at times, misinterpreted (see Box 5.9).

> **Box 5.9   Concerns about mirror neurons**
>
> Lamm and Majdandžić (2015) have raised some concerns over the findings from neuroscience about the relationship between mirror neurons and empathy. There is neuroscientific evidence that the same neural structures in the brain are activated when we empathise with an individual, and when we directly experience the emotion experienced by the person we are empathising with. Lamm and Majdandžić noted that we should be cautious when making claims that there is a shared neural route for experiencing our own emotions and those of others such that we can empathise with their personal distress. One reason why we should be cautious, they argue, is down to methodological limitations such as interpreting what overlapping fMRI activations mean: this does not necessarily suggest the same neural pathways are active (Gill-Spector and Malach 2001). Furthermore, the spatial resolution of fMRI is of relatively low fidelity making it difficult to distinguish neural firings. Logothetis (2008) made the important point that, when using scanning techniques such as fMRI, the analysis of observations are correlational in nature – hence, neural activations co-occurring during empathy are often assumed to have a causal relationship. This may well be the case but there is no sure way of knowing. fMRI has been used to examine empathy in relation to negative emotions such as pain. Perry et al. (2012), however, compared empathy for joy and for distress in the hope of finding different neural activation pathways. They found overlapping patterns of activation, which were more pronounced for empathising with distress. Morelli et al. (2014) found a difference in activation patterns between empathy for pain and anxiety when compared with happiness. Lamm et al. (2015) also found a different pattern of activation for empathy of pleasant and unpleasant emotional states. Such research is beginning to unravel neural activation patterns for the empathy of different emotions – there is still a way to go if concerns of correlational effects are to be resolved. Lamm and Majdandžić (2015) also pointed out that mirror neurons might not be necessary for empathy. Research findings suggest that empathy cannot be fully explained by mirror neuron activity. They argue that there are robust evolutionary roots accounting for automatic responses of empathy towards others, but that these relate to learning, nurturance, socialisation and culture instead of 'hard-wired mirroring' (p. 20). Moreover, Engen and Singer (2013) discussed the malleability of empathy resulting from changes to situational factors.
>
> The concerns expressed by Lamm and Majdandžić (2015) are important and should be kept in mind when interpreting the findings from neuroscience. Although neuroscientific findings have provided much insight into how the brain works and, in particular, which areas of the brain become activated during episodes of empathy, there is still more research needed to establish a clear link between correlation and causation.

Despite these concerns, similar patterns of activation of mirror neurons are observed in different individuals under the same experimental conditions. There is a population of individuals, however, for whom mirror neuron function is quite different. Interestingly, such people also have problems with understanding the mental states of other people and consequently find ToM-related tasks challenging. These individuals are on the autism spectrum and are of particular interest to our discussion on theory of mind. The case of autism will be considered in our next section.

THE CASE OF AUTISM

For over 60 years clinicians have relied upon a manual to diagnose a variety of psychological conditions. This is known as the **Diagnostic Statistical Manual of Mental Disorders** or **DSM**. In version four of the DSM (DSM-IV) individuals could be diagnosed with one

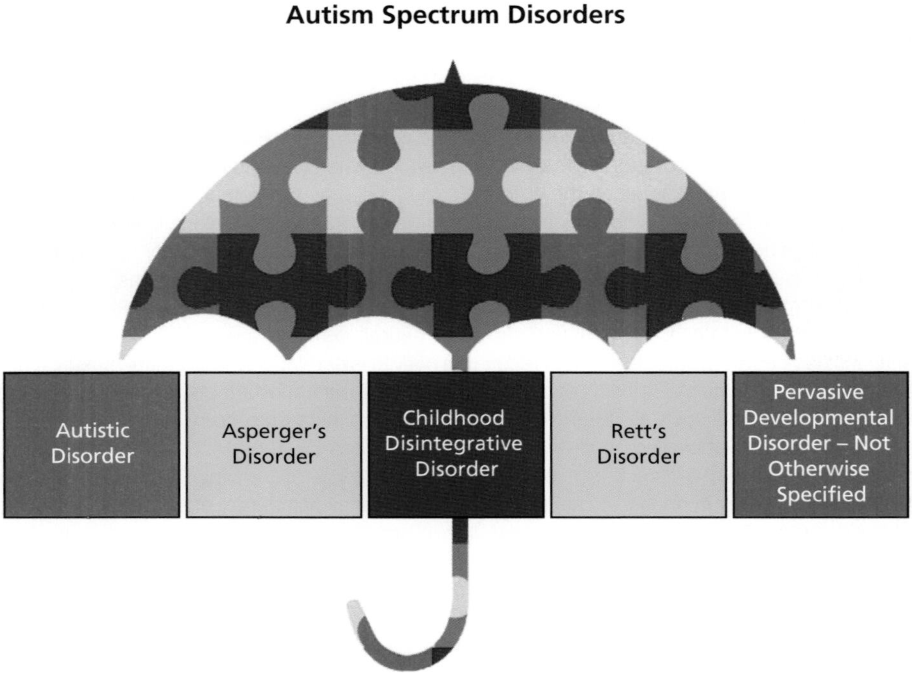

Autism Spectrum Disorders

Plate 5.7 Umbrella of autistic spectrum disorder. (Shutterstock 228337870 – labels added.)

of five separate autistic related disorders (see Plate 5.7). As it was difficult to separate these diagnoses, the 2013 revised edition, DSM-5, combined the different disorders under the umbrella of '**autism spectrum disorder**' (**ASD**) – hence there now exists a continuum ranging from more impaired to less impairment. Autism spectrum disorder was first identified by Austrian-American psychiatrist Leo Kanner in 1943, the diagnostic criteria of which was refined by later researchers. There are a multitude of deficits including problems of social communication and interaction as well as restricted and repetitive patterns of behaviour. The severity of these problems is graded according to three levels of help required: Level 3 (requiring very substantial support); Level 2 (requiring substantial support) and Level 1 (requiring support). The level of support required is assessed according to the extent of interference to daily life that the symptoms cause. The Autism Society of America provided a list of the traits illustrative of the condition (see Box 5.10).

Box 5.10   List of traits provided by The Autism Society of America

The following traits provide an insight into the symptoms experienced by many individuals on the autism spectrum. These traits are quite diverse and are not all necessarily experienced by every individual.

- Resistance to any changes of routine.
- Problems in expressing their needs so they often resort to gesturing instead of verbalisation.

- Tendency to repeat word phrases as they lack ability for responsive language.
- Showing inappropriate emotional expressions such as laughing or crying for no reason.
- Prefers own company.
- Tantrums.
- Problems of integrating with others.
- Avoids affection such as cuddling or being cuddled.
- Little or no eye contact.
- Odd play behaviour.
- Spinning, rocking, head-banging or hand-twisting behaviour.
- Odd attachments to objects.
- Over-sensitivity or under-sensitivity to pain.
- No real fear of danger.
- Unresponsive to verbal cues, often appearing to be deaf despite normal hearing.
- Difficulty relating to people, severe impairment to social interaction.

As we can see, The Autism Society of America has listed many of the symptoms known to inter-fere with individuals' daily life. This is, however, by no means an exhaustive list of symptoms.

The following quote by van Krevelen-Wing (1991) encapsulates the essence of having ASD:

The low functioning child with autism lives in a world of his own. The high functioning child with autism lives in our world but in his own way.

(Cited in van Krevelen-Wing 1991, p. 99)

Autism spectrum disorder is considered to be a developmental disorder arising from neu-rological or brain deficits. This ultimately causes behavioural problems and difficulties in communication and interacting within a social context. Researchers Nishitani et al. (2004), Oberman et al. (2005) and Theoret et al. (2005), for example, using fMRI, found evidence of mirror neuron dysfunction in individuals diagnosed with ASD. This implicates the neural system in the social impairment seen in individuals with ASD. Strong evidence for a genetic cause comes from identical and fraternal twin research. If one identical twin is diagnosed with ASD, the likelihood of the other of the pair developing ASD is 76 per cent, for same sex fraternal twins this is 34 per cent and boy–girl fraternal twins 18 per cent (Frazier et al. 2014). Frazier et al. also point out that girls are less likely to be diagnosed with ASD than boys. A theory as to why boys are more likely to be diagnosed with ASD has been put forward elo-quently by Baron-Cohen (2003) when he discussed differences between the male and female brain (see earlier). According to Baron-Cohen, due to differences occurring during foetal development girls are born with a superior ability to develop empathising skills. In contrast, boys are born with a greater potential to develop systemising skills. Extreme systemisers (who according to Baron-Cohen are poor at empathising) are those who become diagnosed as being on the autistic spectrum – hence more boys than girls are placed on the spectrum.

Baron-Cohen (1995) refers to the inability of individuals to realise others have different thoughts, plans and perspectives to their own as '**mindblindness**'. As discussed earlier in this chapter, mindreading is the intentional stance described by Dennett. As you may recall, adopting a physical or design stance as described by Dennett will not get us very far in under-standing other people's behaviour because this fails to explain human behaviour and mental states. In contrast, the ability to mind-read helps us to communicate and make sense of the intentions behind utterances and actions. This ability appears to be absent in individuals on the lower end of the ASD continuum. Those who are situated at the higher end of the ASD continuum can interpret stimuli in terms of goals and desires by using words such as 'want', 'desire' or 'like'. Moreover, they can understand that desires might have repercussions for specific emotions such as feeling happy because they received a present. However, even those at the higher end of the ASD continuum, according to Leekum (1993), have difficulty showing joint attention behaviour and gaze monitoring (see Chapter 4). False-belief tasks have been used to examine the extent to which children with ASD can appreciate that others might entertain a false-belief. In Wimmer and Perner's (1983) and Perner et al.'s (1989) studies it was shown that children on the ASD continuum failed to answer belief questions correctly. For example, they found it difficult to take account of 'Sally's' belief (see earlier). Moreover, these children consistently answered 'pencils' to the two belief questions in the 'Smarties' task. Children with ASD answered these questions by considering their own knowledge rather than their own previous false-belief or someone else's current false-belief.

An inability to 'read the mind' of others is a deficit that has major repercussions in children and adolescents with ASD. It makes social interaction and communication with others extremely challenging and often isolates these individuals from the general population. It demonstrates just how important social cognition is when it comes to navigating the complexities of social life. This deficit in ToM might be likened to an earlier stage in our ancestry prior to this 'evolutionary development'. In fact, the ability to 'mind-read' is considered by many to have been a major 'step forward' in hominin evolution. Although it is likely that other non-human primates have developed a degree of ToM (see Box 5.1), our hominin ancestors took this ability to a new dimension. In addition to being able to predict the behaviour of others, the ability to mind-read may also have been important in the evolution of human language. This may well have enabled our ancestors to communicate and socially interact within and between small tribal groups. In particular, the development of an advanced ToM, and the complex language that accompanied it, allowed for division of labour and social exchange (Ridley 1996; Renfrew 2009).

Summary

- Social cognition can be defined as the ability to socially interact and communicate with other people. Theory of mind (ToM) is an important aspect of social cognition. Theory of mind is defined as the ability to infer the different mental states (e.g., beliefs, intentions and emotions) of others based on their behaviour. It involves the ability to reflect on what is in one's own and other people's minds. As ToM develops, children become aware that other people might entertain different feelings and beliefs to their own. It becomes even more complex when others try to deceive us – referred to as Machiavellian intelligence.
- Dennett introduced three levels of understanding the world: physical, design and intentional stances. While physical and design stances can explain many phenomena in our world, it is only the intentional stance that allows us to understand the 'minds' of people. Dennett argued that we have four orders of intentionality, which increase in complexity and become more challenging to interpret.

  o (1st) I believe something.
  o (2nd) I believe you believe something.

○ (3rd) I believe that you believe that I believe something.

○ (4th) I believe that you believe that I believe that you believe something.

- A theory of mind mechanism (ToMM) enables us to infer the mental states of others. This allows us to understand the full range of mental states, which also includes epistemic mental states (such as knowing, thinking, pretending, imagining and believing). Referential opacity is the ability to suspend truth relations held within a statement. It is this that is a key property in interpreting epistemic mental states.

- Wellman's Human Theory of Mind makes connections between our perceptual and emotional pathways and how these interact to influence the way we behave. Emotion influences ToM, in particular empathy. Empathy is an emotional response shown towards a person in pain – we sympathise. Empathy is important in understanding other people's emotions, which, in turn, helps us to interpret intentions behind the behaviour. Theory of mind has been represented as a facet of empathy and, moreover, interfaces with perspective-taking. Dennis and colleagues (2013), in their tripartite model, suggested we have cognitive ToM, affective ToM and conative ToM. Cognitive ToM relates to 'reading the mind' using false-belief experiments.

- False-belief tasks are used to test aspects of cognitive ToM. In Wimmer and Perner's (1983) Sally-Anne Test, children have to determine where Sally will look for a marble that (unbeknown to Sally) Anne has moved from a basket to a box. Children between three and four understand what Sally believes to be the case, which is that the marble is still in the basket. Younger children fail to realise Sally's false-belief.

- The 'Reading the Mind in the Eyes Test' was introduced by Baron-Cohen as a measure of our ability to judge mental states from pictures of the eye region only. Participants are given a choice of four adjectives describing the mental state depicted in the eyes. This ability helps us to interpret the emotional state of another person.

- Perspective-taking overlaps with ToM. Selman (1971) introduced a time-line for the acquisition of perspective-taking in his five-stage model. Selman showed that perspective-taking increased in profundity with age. Furthermore, perspective-taking increasingly becomes influenced by the social environment. Piaget also considered perspective-taking in his experiments on egocentricity. He believed that children between two and six years in the preoperational stage of cognitive development are very egocentric in the way they think.

- It has been found that the caregiver's verbalisations about feelings and causality help increase their children's understanding of false-belief. Maternal mind mindedness communicated through internal-state language helps children to understand the connection between mental state and emotion. This, in turn, increases ToM ability. Interestingly, telling white lies (false statements aimed at deceiving others) has been connected with being prosocial. The purpose of telling white lies is to protect another person's feelings and to make them feel better. Children as early as five years are capable of telling white lies in order to spare another's feelings.

(continued)

(continued)

- There is evidence that social cognitive skill ability has a biological foundation. The amygdala (part of the brain) plays an important role in the perception and experience of negative emotion – hence being tuned into other people's emotional states. fMRI and PET scans have highlighted areas of the brain active during social cognition. Neural activity in an area of the prefrontal cortex (which contains 'mirror neurons') increases when performing or observing an action. Some mirror neurons code for inferred goal of the action only. Activity of mirror neurons in social cognition (e.g., the experience of pain or observing someone else's pain) occurs consistently in the anterior cingulate cortex (ACC) and the anterior insula. Qualitative differences of ACC activation in the first and third person, however, allow us to differentiate between self-distress and another person's distress.
- Individuals with autism spectrum disorder (ASD) find social cognition problematic. Due to the symptoms incurred by having ASD, they experience problems of social communication and interaction as well as a multitude of behavioural deficits. Autism spectrum disorder is considered to be a developmental disorder arising from neurological or brain deficits. Mirror neuron dysfunction appears to be the root-cause of social impairment observed in people with ASD. Performance on false-belief tasks is poor as children with ASD struggle to realise that others have different mental states and belief systems to their own.

Questions for discussion

1. Explain the importance of having a social cognitive skill-set and what happens when it is dysfunctional.
2. There are different types of theory of mind. What are they and how have researchers studied them?
3. Describe how individuals with ASD have problems understanding others.
4. Critically assess the evidence that there is a biological basis to the development of a theory of mind.
5. Critically examine the limitations of using fMRI in our ability to understand the nature of mirror neurons.
6. Critically consider Baron-Cohen's notion that males are superior at 'systemising' and females are superior at 'empathising'. Can you think of any limitations to this view?

Further reading

If you are interested in exploring the cognitive basis of theory of mind using research findings from other disciplines such as neuroscience, developmental and comparative psychology, look at:

- Apperly, I. (2012). *Mindreaders: The Cognitive Basis of 'Theory of Mind'*. Hove, UK: Psychology Press.

If you want to examine social cognition using social neuroscience, cultural psychology and applied areas of psychology, look at:

- Fiske, S.T. and Taylor, S.E. (2008). *Social Cognition: From Brains to Culture*. New York: McGraw-Hill.

If you are interested in exploring empathy from the perspective that it is hard-wired and is at the heart of what makes us who we are, using a novel approach of setting out six life-enhancing habits of extremely empathic individuals, look at:

- Krznaric, R. (2015). *Empathy: Why It Matters, and How To Get It*. London: Rider.

If you are interested in exploring human existence prior to written records using findings from archaeology, geology, evolution, prehistoric art, social anthropology, radiocarbon dating and DNA examination, look at:

- Renfrew, C. (2009). *Prehistory: The Making of the Human Mind*. New York: The Random House Publishing Group.

Contents

Introduction   177

Changes to the family over time   178

Social functions of the family   186

Parental discipline and parents as
role models   187

Effects of family biology on the social
development of children   201

Summary   206

Influence of the family

6

What this chapter will teach you

- Knowledge of different types of family structure.
- How parents act as socialising agents affecting the child's behaviour.
- An understanding of how differing parental discipline styles affect child development.
- The intergenerational transmission of hostile attributional bias.
- The relationship between family biology and the social development of children, especially with regard to mental health issues and antisocial behaviour.

INTRODUCTION

In the early stages of a new-born's life the central focus of attention is most likely to be the caregiver who provides a sense of comfort and safety in addition to the life-saving provisions of food and drink. As we have seen in Chapter 3, the new-born has an innate skill-set to ensure bond formation with the caregiver. Therefore, during the early months after birth, attachment to the caregiver is the most important adult relationship. This caregiver–infant relationship remains central for months to come although increasingly there is more contact with other family members. According to Bronfenbrenner's contextual perspective, the immediate social environment impacts on the development of the infant. Bronfenbrenner (1979) argued that this occurs through a system of interfacing environmental layers beginning with the microsystem and mesosystem, followed by the exosystem and macrosystem. In his ecosystem model, Bronfenbrenner describes micro-, meso-, exo- and macro- systems, like layers of an onion, enveloping the child who sits at its centre (see Figure 1.5, Chapter 1). The relevancy of Bronfenbrenner's model to our discussion about the influence of the family on the developing individual becomes clear when we consider the first social environmental layer, the microsystem, surrounding and influencing the infant. The mesosystem allows for other microsystems to become integrated, such as the extended family and close friends. Bronfenbrenner's eco-system model considers the influence of the family on the child's development but, more importantly, it emphasises the impact of a social milieu on the way we are socialised. Our parents are informal social agents who teach or socialise us to adopt the rules, mores, values and attitudes representative of our society. This intergenerational transmission of societal values encourages us to become 'good citizens'. Socialisation by our parents (and family) is the driving force ensuring the continuation of society's rules, mores, values and attitudes. Socialisation, as a function performed by the family, is therefore central in developing law-abiding children who later become society's citizens. The extent of impact the family has over the developing child depends on how we consider the family. Do we view the family as a unit consisting of parents and offspring or is it more extended than this? Throughout history conceptions of the family have changed. This means that family members, who could poten-tially influence a child's development, might differ as a consequence of the timeframe being considered. We will begin by briefly considering what it is to be a family between the 18th and 21st centuries. We then move on to discuss the family's involvement in the socialisation of the child. It is clear that the structure of the family influences the dynamics of the interac-tions between its members. This is why consideration of changes over the centuries to the structure of the family is important in our discussion of how it influences social development in children. Moreover, the different types of family will also have an impact on children's development. The 20th century, in particular, has seen many technological developments that have changed the way we live.

CHANGES TO THE FAMILY OVER TIME

Before industrialisation many families obtained subsistence and wealth from herding ani-mals (i.e., pastoral societies), a practice that was controlled primarily by men. This resulted in men having authority over the family hence maintaining a **patriarchal system** (Quale 1992). This patriarchal family system influenced the inheritance dynamics between siblings, leading to patrilineal inheritance patterns. This meant that the family's wealth was handed down the male generations – sons to sons. No doubt such inheritance patterns acted as bar-riers to the female siblings and forced them to adhere to the wishes of older brothers and behave according to their social expectations. It was originally believed by sociologists that during pre-industrialised Britain the dominant family format was the **extended family**. The extended family, also referred to as the 'joint family system', arose out of early marriages for women resulting in co-residency with the husband's family (Kertzer and Barbagli 2002). This meant that the wife had to reside with multiple generations of the husband's family or **patrilocality**. In addition to family members, for wealthy families servants also resided under the same roof (and in many cases were involved in the socialisation of children). Early marriages enabled these multi-generational families to develop and thrive.

Murdock and White (1969), however, have argued that a **nuclear family** structure was at the core of many of these extended families during this period. Conversely, the nuclear family structure or 'simple household system' derived from marriages between men and women who were of an older age. Under these circumstances a separate household, post marriage, was established, an arrangement that is referred to as **neolocality** (Kertzer and

Plate 6.1 Extended family together. (Shutterstock 671780899.)

Barbagli 2002). A woman's age at marriage, therefore, can be seen as an important deter-minant of family structure (late marriages would mean there was less time to establish extended families). It was at the time of the Industrial Revolution (1750–1850) that people began to leave rural areas and move to cities in the hope of new work prospects. This means that the division of labour between husband and wife increased as they shifted from extended to nuclear family units and, in many cases, the husband worked while the wife managed the home (Gottlieb 1993). This exaggerated the differences between men and women and led to role separation based on stereotypes of what it is to be masculine or feminine respectively. **Masculine** and **feminine roles** within the nuclear family arose as a 19th-century change from an agricultural to an industrial based household. The nuclear family structure continued to thrive and became the norm in the 20th century (see Box 6.1). Gottlieb (1993) argued, however, that while the nuclear family became the norm in the 20th century, it was historically rare during medieval Britain and the rest of Europe. This is because, for most people, it was necessary to live in an extended family due to the high mortality rate resulting from disease (e.g., Black Death), malnutrition (e.g., poor crop pro-duction) and social problems (e.g., poverty due to high taxes).

Box 6.1   Extended versus nuclear families

An extended family structure had advantages over the nuclear form, especially prior to the industrial revolution. For example, having more family members provides a stronger workforce such that common objectives are easier to achieve. A family is considered as consisting of two or more individuals related by blood or marriage. Hence, it can be seen that the greater the number of family members working together, the more effective the

(continued)

(continued)

family becomes in providing both practical and emotional support to all of its members. In the case of the nuclear family unit, where there are fewer members, the greater is the parental effort required to raise each child. This means that as we have seen a shift from extended families to smaller nuclear families the socialisation of each child has become restricted to its parents.

The 20th century saw many technological and social changes that impacted on the structure of families and the relationships between family members. One of the biggest changes during the 20th century was an increase in the number of women entering the workforce at all levels. This led to a less differentiated and more egalitarian relationship between males and females within the family. Where there was once an obvious family role division based on masculine and feminine characteristics there was now, for example, more sharing of childcare responsibilities between men and women. Advances in medicine and technology have improved the general health of people in the 21st century, such that more people are living longer and fewer infants are dying of disease and malnutrition (see Box 6.2). It is not uncommon to hear of octogenarians living healthy lives. Interestingly, the oldest woman alive in 2017 is Nabi Tajima aged 117.

Box 6.2   Mortality of the young

According to collaborative research by the Plimoth Plantation and the New England Historic Genealogical Society, the average life expectancy at birth in late 16th- and early 17th-century England was 39.7 years. An individual who reached 30 was expected to live until 59. Infant mortality was common during this period. It has been estimated that more than 12 per cent of infants would die within one year of being born. Moreover, two per cent of live births resulted in death on the day of birth and three per cent more during the first week. Even beyond infancy and into childhood and adolescence the dangers of mortality were ever present. By the age of six, 31 per cent would have died and a further 24 per cent between seven and sixteen years of age. This calculates at 60 out of 100 live births dying before sixteen years of age. With such high mortality rates it is not surprising that women tended to give birth six to seven times. These high mortality rates remained constant until the end of the 19th century, but dropped with the introduction of new medical interventions – especially with the advent of antibiotics and improved levels of hygiene. These medical interventions have lowered infant mortality worldwide. In a longitudinal study, UNICEF (2015) documented that the infant mortality rate per 1,000 live births worldwide has dropped from 63 (in 1990) to 32 (in 2015). If industrialised nations are considered alone this reduces to 12 deaths per 1,000 live births. In a longitudinal study the United Nations *World Population Prospects* (2015) shows the lowest mortality rates to occur in Luxembourg (1.58 per 1,000) and the highest in Angola (96.22 per 1,000). They further state that the worldwide infant mortality rate currently stands at 49.4 per 1,000 live births. Although there is wide variation across different countries, this rate has decreased since 1993 figures. For the under-fives, the mortality rate in Turkey, for instance, is 13.5 but it is 6.5 for the US. For the UK it is 4.2 per 1,000 but 2.7 for Japan (WHO 2015).

   The mortality figures have seen a decrease, especially during the 20th century with the advent of antibiotics and other hygiene measures introduced at the time. There are still variations in the mortality figures across countries but these rates have come down even since the 1990s.

In contemporary Western societies there are many types of family relationships, even though we tend to have a stereotyped opinion of what the family should be like. Frequently, when we consider a family, we assume that this is based around a monogamous marriage between one woman and one man. **Monogamy** is the most common relationship in Britain and other Western societies. This, however, is not uniform across non-Western societies. In some African and Middle-Eastern societies a man having more than one wife is considered to be the norm (known as **polygyny**). Less commonly in a small number of societies it is permissible for a woman to have more than one husband (known as **polyandry**). The demographics (e.g., social group, religion, ethnicity and social class) of spouses tend to be similar, which is known as **endogamy**. This is an important factor as it reinforces the social status of the spouses and ensures their children maintain this level of recognition. In the case of **exogamy** the marriage of two individuals can cross the barriers often imposed between different social groups. Historically, exogamy has been found to be more common in villages than towns due to population limitations. It is also more common among royalty where choices are limited. There can be problems arising from such marriages, especially the hostility that can arise between the relatives due to differing demographics.

It would appear that in the 21st century, the nuclear family is the norm across most societies but it is not the only viable family format that works efficiently (Eshleman and Bulcroft 2010). Today we see a range of family structures including same-sex parents and blended (or reconstituted) families and single-mother units. Despite this variety, stereotypical views of the family remain as that of a small unit (mother, father and children) residing together under one roof. According to the Office for National Statistics, Families and Households (2015), the average number of children for married couples in the UK is two (see Figure 6.1).

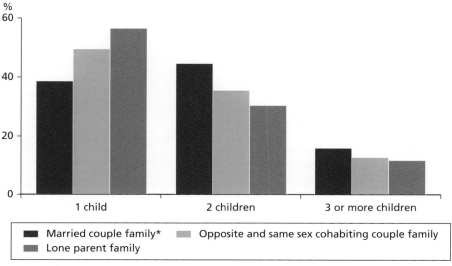

* In the case of married couple families, opposite and same sex married couples are included. For cohabiting couple families opposite sex and same sex couples are considered.

Figure 6.1 Represents the number of dependent children for different family type in 2015.

This average number of children for married, cohabiting and lone families is compounded by the fact that divorce and remarriage rates have created a new **blended** (or **reconstituted**) **family** structure. Often in blended families there are children from previous marriages who now live as step-brothers and sisters. Divorce and blended family rates have increased during the 20th and 21st centuries as a consequence of social reform laws making it easier for women to leave their husbands – something virtually impossible for women to do in 17th-, 18th- and 19th-century Britain. In England and Wales divorce rates have seen substantial increases since 1933 (see Figure 6.2 comparing marriages and divorce rates, and Figure 6.3 showing divorce figures between 1973 and 2013 – Office for National Statistics 2015). Over the years there has been a rise in the number of blended families, but since 2001 figures have dropped (see Table 6.1). In the case of married couples, stepfamily arrangements have dropped by 6,000 and significantly from 285,000 to 203,000 for cohabiting couples in 2001 and 2011 respectively.

Figure 6.2 Number of marriages and divorces, 1933 to 2013.

Figure 6.3 Divorce rates by sex, 1973 to 2013.

Table 6.1 Families with dependent children by family type and stepfamily or non-stepfamily status. England and Wales, 2011.

Family type	Stepfamily or not	2001	2011
All couples	Non-stepfamily	4,130,000	4,280,000
	Stepfamily	631,000	544,000
Married couples	Non-stepfamily	3,673,000	3,469,000
	Stepfamily	346,000	340,000
Cohabiting couples	Non-stepfamily	457,000	811,000
	Stepfamily	285,000	203,000
Lone parents		1,616,000	1,951,000
All families		6,376,000	6,774,000

The formation of blended families generally means that two nuclear families come together to form a new nuclear family structure. Children from both marriages have to learn to live together and adjust to the new adult in the family and to each other. These children have a new status – that of step-brother or sister. Some of the pitfalls of blended families are:

- Too many simultaneous changes can cause children to feel unsettled.
- The new 'mum' or 'dad' may find it difficult to love the other's children.
- Finding time to experience life all together can be challenging.
- Different parenting styles can confuse the children and cause negativity.
- Ignoring one's own children can occur if the partner makes ultimatums.
- Respect for each other is not always forthcoming.
- Affection given to the partner's children might not be returned immediately.

Ryan and Claessens (2012) studied the effects that divorce/separation and remarriage have on the development of young and older children. Children of married parents (who then divorced when their children were in their first year of school) demonstrated the most profound behavioural changes in later years. In the case of blended family formations, Ryan and Claessens found that, provided children integrated quickly, there were fewer behavioural problems. While most stepparents treat their stepchildren with appropriate levels of care and affection, Elliott and Richards (1991) found that some stepfathers had a negative effect on the behavioural scores of their stepchildren. Baydar (1988) previously found that remarriage had more of a negative impact on the child's behaviour and emotional development than divorce. These studies suggest that stepfamilies can hinder children from developing their full potential. This might be a consequence of the potential pitfalls outlined earlier. Pryor and Rodgers (2001) claimed that a low level of cohesion inherent in blended families is a likely factor contributing to problems seen in the children. In fact Fine et al. (1993) found that stepfathers rarely involved themselves in the activities of their stepchildren, which increased the distance between them. The children from same-sex families appear to fare better than those from blended family set-ups.

Plate 6.2 An example of a blended family where both partners had children from previous relationships. (Shutterstock 18324832.)

Same-sex family structures have risen in the UK since the introduction of civil part-nerships under the Civil Partnership Act of 2004. This allowed same-sex couples to attain the same legal rights as those granted for civil marriage. This also meant that they were able to obtain parental responsibility for a partner's children (*BBC News* 31 March 2004). The Marriage Act (2013) legalised same-sex marriage in England and Wales, which com-menced in 2014. Manning et al. (2015) reviewed the effects of having two same-sex parents on their children's well-being. They found that the academic performance of these children

Plate 6.3 An example of a lesbian couple with daughter taking a nap together. (Shutterstock 301072733.)

was similar to those from **heterosexual** partnerships. This included a range of factors such as scores for reading and mathematics, educational attainment and behaviour in school (looking for correctness of behaviour and extent of trouble-making in school). Rosenfeld (2010) found evidence of highest school performance from children in different-sex families and lower among same-sex couples – but these findings were a result of socioeconomic status rather than family structure.

Fedewa and Clark (2009) found no significant differences in social adjustment behaviours between kindergartners from same- or different-sex couples. Wainright and Patterson (2008) found that the quality and quantity of peer relationships is the same for teenagers across same- or different-sex couples. Furthermore, Wainright et al. (2004) showed that teenage girls from same- and different-sex families had similar scores for the incidence of depression and level of self-esteem. Gartrell and Bos (2010) also found similar incidence levels of child **Attention Deficit Hyperactivity Disorder** (ADHD) and teenage anxiety and depression regardless of having a same- or different-sex family background. There are numerous studies demonstrating that behavioural adjustments were similar across family types (Farr and Patterson 2009; Ryan 2007; Tan and Baggerly 2009). The evidence suggests that children and teenagers from same-sex families are no more disadvantaged than those living in a heterosexual family arrangement.

Regardless of family type (e.g., same- or different-sex marriage or blended), the structure tends to conform to the nuclear family unit. Nevertheless, it is normal for extended family members to also help in the upbringing of children. Grandparents from both sides of the family, for example, play important roles in childcare by volunteering their time to take their grandchildren out for the day. Moreover, they offer advice to their own children on how to nurture their grandchildren. Other extended family members such as uncles and aunts also provide support to their nephews and nieces. Hence, the nuclear family today has retained some features of the extended family structure and has developed into what is called the **modified nuclear family**. Extended family members often live close by to each other in the modified nuclear family of today. The family, therefore, plays a pivotal role in how children develop socially and behave in society (although some would argue it is peers who do – see Chapter 7). The family provides an important base for social functions which we will consider next.

SOCIAL FUNCTIONS OF THE FAMILY

The family can be considered as the core 'nurturance centre' in the upbringing of children. Hence, the family performs a number of social functions impacting on their developing off-spring. From the point of view of systems theory (see Chapter 1), the family is considered as a unit of socialisation (Parke 1988). Here, the family in its entirety should be considered for its performance of social functions instead of analysing separate interacting 'subsystems' of the marital context, parent–child relationships and sibling affiliations (Minuchin 2002). A systems-theory approach considers the family as a dynamic unit, changing as it develops and reacts to different situations (Kerig 2008; McHale 2008). This has an impact on the socialisation of the child, not just by the parents, but by all family members. As outlined in the systems theory approach, the family is a unit and so there is a network of viable interactions between family members. All family members are involved in the reinforcement of the intergenerational transmission of familial and societal values. According to Fiese (2006) and Cicchetti and Toth (2006), all families have their own rituals, whether this be in the form of religious teachings or simple everyday greetings and dinner arrangements. (For example, some families hug each other when they arrive home whereas others frown upon this overt form of affection). These rituals serve to promote the family's socialisation functions.

In Bronfenbrenner's ecosystem model, the family is considered as an informal agent of socialisation. Sometimes referred to as primary agents of socialisation, it is the people who are closest to the child who help to shape future social behaviour. This, therefore, includes family members and **fictive kin** (e.g., friends of the family who are affectionately referred to as 'aunt' or 'uncle'). It is, however, the parents who are normally associated with the early stages of the socialisation process. Through socialisation a child learns the social behaviours considered acceptable by society across different situations and contexts. (For example, cursing is generally unacceptable behaviour). At later stages of socialisation, the onus shifts to formal **social agents** such as different institutions within society, including schools, places of employment, religious establishments, mass media and the various branches of the law. (For example, talking when the teacher is talking is unacceptable). There is, however, a more subtle socialising agent – that of social class (see Box 6.3).

Box 6.3   Social class as a socialising agent

The social standing of an individual in terms of economic and educational allegiance is referred to as social class. Social class, as a socialising agent, can be divisive. Social class in Britain historically divides into three groups: working, middle and elite class. With each class comes a host of differing values, mores, norms and attitudes. This can cause differences in opinion of what is important and how one should behave socially. For example, children from working-class families might bring different expectations to children from middle-class families as to the purpose of education. This may lead to lower expectations from the (middle class) teacher as to how far the children will progress in education. This, in turn, means that children from working class families from the outset may have lower expectations about progressing to higher education.

Despite the importance of social class and formal social agents, the main focus of this chapter is informal social agents – that is the family in the zone of Bronfenbrenner's microsystem. The family, however, is more than just a strong socialising agent. There are a multitude of social functions that the family is expected to perform. These include the following:

- parental care and love that help to pre-adjust a child for life (see also Chapter 3);
- emotional support;
- parents as role models;
- learning starts in the home (see also Chapter 4);
- teaching children morals;
- parental discipline;
- parental supervision;
- control over 'wild' adolescents;
- siblings as role models.

In this section we will consider four of the above social functions performed by parents: parental discipline, parents as role models, teaching children morals and parental emotional support.

PARENTAL DISCIPLINE AND PARENTS AS ROLE MODELS

It is important that parents instil social values in their children. This is not always an easy task and can sometimes involve the use of negative forms of persuasion such as punishment. Children, however, do need to learn what socially acceptable behaviour is and to uphold the social values of their society. The parents' role is to provide their children with guidance and defined boundaries of what they can and cannot do. When children fail to follow this guidance and contravene the boundaries, parents need to provide discipline. Discipline is important in the upbringing of children, especially during the early years of development. Discipline can be used to help improve the child's emotional, intellectual and social

Plate 6.4 Example demonstrating the differences across social class. (Shutterstock 266637398.)

behavioural developmental trajectory. There are different types of discipline, which research has shown have different effects on the development of social skills, behaviour and morality. Hoffman and Saltzstein (1967) argued that the best approach is to use **induction** as an approach to discipline and a method of instilling good 'moral fibre'. Parents who use induction as their method of discipline use reasoning skills to enlighten their child about behaviour and consequences. For example, taking grandmother's milk money to spend on sweets means she will be deprived of milk. The focus of this style of discipline is to make children understand the consequences of their behaviour for others.

Hoffman (1977) identified three types of discipline used by parents: **power assertion**, **love withdrawal** and induction. Both power assertion and love withdrawal can have negative consequences in the socialisation of children. Power assertion uses physical punishment, threats, maternal deprivation and criticism as means of controlling a child's behaviour. In the case of love withdrawal, the child receives non-physical forms of disapproval such as the deprivation of affection. These classifications were modified in 1983 by Maccoby and Martin who argued for there being two types of parental interaction. Maccoby and Martin labelled these as affection and control. Both affection and control are dimensional. At one end of the affection dimension is acceptance and warmth while at the other end is rejection and hostility. In the case of control, this is demanding and restrictive versus undemanding and permissive. These two forms of interaction combine to create four different parenting styles of discipline: **authoritative**, **authoritarian**, **indulgent** and **neglecting**. In the case of authoritative discipline (equivalent to induction), a balance between accepting and demanding is achieved thereby providing an effective tool in promoting self-control and self-confidence. The opposite is true of authoritarian discipline where the extremes of a rejecting and demanding approach tip the balance in favour of a power assertion style.

This is a negative parenting style of discipline leading to poor moral development and a child with low self-esteem. Just as a neglecting style of interaction (rejecting and undemanding) leads to poor socialisation so does an indulgent one (accepting and undemanding). Support for Maccoby and Martin's disciplinary typologies came from a study by Weiss et al. (1992)

Plate 6.5 Father telling his daughter that her rough play hurt her little brother. (Shutterstock 193825739.)

Plate 6.6 Daughter being threatened with physical punishment by her mother. (Shutterstock 462874042.)

in which an authoritarian approach among preschoolers led to poor socialisation and moral development. An example of this is that being shouted at led to resentment rather than compliance. This was a longitudinal study of child development but the results were clear; harsh discipline is associated with later aggressive behaviour exhibited during kindergarten. These disciplinary styles differ in their consistency, intensity and frequency. It is, however, inconsistent and erratic disciplinary practices that have plagued dysfunctional families, such as families renowned for having delinquency issues (see Box 6.4).

Box 6.4   The discipline–delinquency connection

Children whose parents adopted an authoritarian or neglecting style of discipline have a tendency to indulge in later deviant behaviour. Patterson (1986) found evidence to link children's social behaviour with the type of discipline experienced in early childhood. Children, for example, who lied, stole, set fires and were overactive (referred to as 'stealers'), tended to have parents who were uninvolved, lax or inconsistent in the way they 'dished out' punishment. In the case of 'social aggressors' (i.e., children who teased and hit their siblings and exhibited tantrum behaviour), their parents made unobtainable demands and unreasonable commands. These parents used coercive interactions to manipulate their children into behaving in ways consistent with their ideals. These findings corroborated how authoritarian and neglecting interactive parental styles of discipline have negative outcomes for the child's social behaviour. Rejection is a potential source of future delinquency. In 1983 Rutter and Giller outlined five adverse familial factors likely to cause future social behavioural problems in children. These factors are parental criminality; intra-familial discord; disciplinary inconsistencies across parents; large family size and low socioeconomic status. These five adverse factors collectively impact on the child's social development. Of relevance here is the effect of inconsistent punishment. Rutter and

(continued)

(continued)

Giller found that both inconsistent and harsh punishment influence a child's social behaviour, including increased levels of aggression and antisocial behaviour. Inconsistent harsh punishment creates aggressive and hostile children (Gershoff 2002; Patterson 2002). The situation is worse when the parent–child relationship lacks any warmth and love (Caspi and Moffitt 2006). In line with previous findings by Patterson (1986), the parents of aggressive children tended to be inconsistent and unpredictable in their methods of disciplining inappropriate behaviour and in reinforcing prosocial actions (Patterson 2002). This ineffective parenting can create further problems that can 'lead to cycles of mutually coercive behaviour' (Parke and Gauvain 2009, p. 536). The consequence of this is that children produce coercive behaviour themselves in order to achieve what they want – such as having tantrums until the parent gives in and the child has won. Coercive behaviours can be used on other members of the family such as siblings. This can escalate even more when the older sibling has delinquent tendencies because younger children often model their behaviour on older siblings (Slomkowski et al. 2001). The coupling of rejecting approaches to discipline and sibling discord fuel the probability of problem behaviour in the future (Garcia et al. 2000). These problems, however, do not stop here. These early problems set up precedence for an intergenerational transmission of hostile and ineffective parenting. Scaramella and Conger (2003) showed how these patterns of parental nurturance remained alive and well in later generations of parental disciplinary style.

Research findings suggest that the type of discipline adopted by parents is important. The best, as we have discussed previously, is the authoritative (or induction) model. There is clear evidence that other types of discipline can cause future social behavioural problems.

Other experts have made use of a different labelling system for disciplinary styles such as that introduced by Welch (2010). Four styles of discipline were identified (which correspond well with Maccoby and Martin):

1. authoritative (parents provide clear boundary rules and explain why aversive behaviour is wrong, avoid 'spanking' and provide support);
2. authoritarian (firm, overly restrictive rules; lack warmth; use of 'spanking');
3. **lax or permissive** (hardly any rules and no discipline for misbehaving children);
4. **unresolved discipline** (hardly any rules and very little emotional support provided).

As found by Maccoby and Martin in 1983, Ginsburg et al. (2009) agree that authoritative discipline promotes moral development and prosocial children. McKee et al. (2007) claim that parents who use authoritarian discipline believe this to be an important method of instilling morals in their children but the research suggests differently. Children subjected to overly restrictive rules and a cold environment are more prone to delinquent behaviour (see Box 6.4). Physical punishments in the guise of spanking, as performed in authoritarian approaches, promote antisocial behaviour – the antithesis of the parental desired outcome. According to Berlin et al. (2009), the use of **spanking** gives the wrong message. Children associate spanking with behaving in ways to avoid it rather than for the reasons why the behaviour is wrong. Moreover, parents who adopt spanking as their method of discipline can be used as role models. Here, children model their behaviour on their parents and use violence as a way of resolving interpersonal issues. Bandura demonstrated this in his Bobo doll experiment (see Chapters 1 and 2 for a description of this experiment and a critique of the methodology).

There is debate, however, regarding the effects of moderate spanking on the social development of children. Larzelere and Baumrind (2010) discussed whether the concept of negative effects of 'spanking' children has scientific evidence to support the claim. Their findings have uncovered some support for the use of spanking. Box 6.5 addresses the current debate of whether spanking should be prohibited or used on a conditional basis.

Box 6.5   'Spanking': to use or not to use?

Those who advocate the use of conditional spanking believe that it can be an appropriate form of physical discipline. Supporters of conditional spanking are in agreement with advocates in favour of spanking prohibition that 'overly severe and abusive corporal punishment' (Larzelere and Baumrind 2010, p. 58) is not the answer and causes further problems of behaviour. The crux of the debate is whether or not spanking always causes harm. Larzelere and Kuhn (2005) defined conditional spanking in terms of physical punishment used to support other forms of discipline such as reasoning or time-out tactics. This was primarily for children who continued to show defiance but was used in a controlled manner. This was compared with other forms of physical punishment and was found to fare well in situations of non-compliant and antisocial behaviours. They concluded that conditional spanking used for defiant children worked best when other tactics failed. Roberts and Powers (1990) conducted a series of clinical studies concerning the effects of spanking children with defiant behaviour such as conduct disorder, oppositional defiant disorder and attention deficit hyperactivity disorder. Their studies showed spanking to be a non-abusive form of discipline. Furthermore, it is an effective form of discipline for children with behavioural problems who were at high risk of later delinquency and criminal involvement. Roberts and Powers argued that spanking often plays a supportive role in order for non-physical punishment such as reasoning and time-out to work effectively. For non-clinical children, they argued that levels of cooperation can be maintained using a 'two-swat spank'. For those who no longer need to be spanked, a non-physical punishment such as reasoning is then used. Larzelere and Baumrind (2010) have argued that where studies have found spanking to cause negative effects, the comparisons have generally been made between different levels of spanking – some quite severe. Comparisons have not been made between never-spanked and conditional spanking. Hence, the adverse effects arise out of levels of spanking used, and given that, in some cases, it is used inappropriately and frequently, the negative effects are likely to be significant. When conditional spanking is compared with spanking prohibition, a reduction of antisocial and defiant behaviours can be seen for defiant children who fail to respond to non-physical forms of discipline.

Larzelere and Baumrind (2010) have helped to add scientifically based research findings to the debate on whether spanking is necessarily a bad thing. When used appropriately, it helps to control defiant children who would otherwise veer towards an antisocial lifestyle. Of course this whole debate may become redundant as some countries have made spanking illegal.

A lax or permissive style of discipline also encourages children to misbehave at the onset of childhood and continues throughout adolescence. In the case of unresolved discipline, children have no guidance or boundaries set to help them understand what is considered as appropriate behaviour. They are in many ways rejected, as parents provide very little, if any, emotional support. These children often develop antisocial behavioural problems that can lead to contact with different branches of the criminal justice system.

Closely associated with rejecting parents is the lack of monitoring of their children's activities, whereabouts and choice of peers. Ineffective parental supervision has been linked to delinquency (Patterson 2004). By failing to supervise their children, parents might be initiating a trajectory of delinquent behaviour. According to Ladd (2005), this onset of a delinquent pathway instigates further problems such as rejection by non-delinquent peers at school.

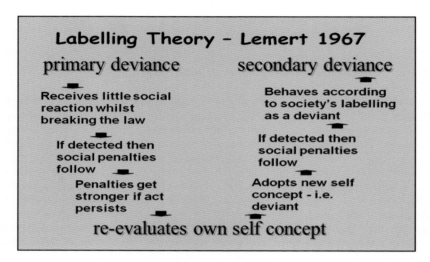

Figure 6.4 Lemert's Labelling Theory. (Taken from Taylor 2016.)

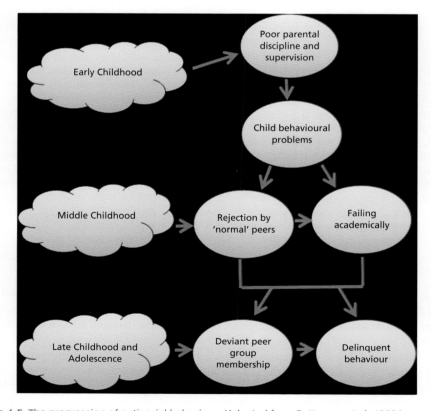

Figure 6.5 The progression of antisocial behaviour. (Adapted from Patterson et al. 1989.)

This then encourages these now labelled antisocial children to seek like-minded peers and spiral downwards into a life of deviancy (Coie 2004). Lemert (1967) described this process using a series of stages in his **labelling theory** perspective (see Figure 6.4).

Patterson et al. (1989) considered the effects of early childhood experience in the home and its impact on later delinquency. They perceived a progression of child conduct problems causing later academic failure and peer rejection to joining deviant peers and committing social transgressions – a process not unlike the labelling theory proposed by Lemert (see Figure 6.5).

Possibly one of the most important socialising factors performed by parents involves teaching children 'right from wrong'. In other words, parents are expected to instil an understanding of morality and promote moral behaviour – as discussed next.

Parental (and family) influence on moral reasoning

Developmentalists are interested in how children acquire moral behaviour through studying the development of **moral reasoning**. Stage theorists such as Piaget believe that moral reasoning and intelligence co-vary such that low intelligence hinders the development of moral reasoning. Piaget developed three stages of moral reasoning that are linked to his four stages of cognitive development (see Chapters 1, 4 and 10). He defined three stages of moral development: moral realism, egalitarianism and equity (see Figure 6.6). More will be said about the theories underlying moral development in Chapter 10.

Various researchers have found that adolescent and adult offenders have low levels of moral reasoning comparable with that expected of children in the pre-conventional stage of cognitive development (Nelson et al. 1990; Smetana 1990). Low levels of moral reasoning

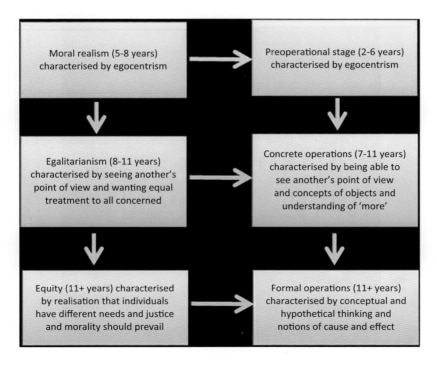

Figure 6.6 The mapping of Piaget's moral stages with cognitive development.

are also shown to be related to decreased feelings of guilt following transgression (Ruma and Mosher 1967). Nelson et al. consider moral reasoning as an aspect of social cognition, which plays a hand in how social information is processed. This is an important point that has been studied by looking at patterns of moral reasoning within families. Speicher (1994), for instance, showed that the level of moral reasoning attained by an adolescent in the family was strongly related to the parents' level of moral reasoning. The level of cognitive empathy (see Chapter 5) expressed by parents predicted their children's sharing and compliant behaviour. Whether this arises as a consequence of an interaction between passive, active or evocative genes (see Chapter 1) and the environment, or by parents teaching specific moral suppositions is difficult to know (Scarr and McCartney 1983). Scarr and McCartney argued that it is more likely that there is a combination of biological and socio-environmental factors operating here. Interestingly, Walker and Taylor (1991) previously found that the highest levels of moral understanding belonged to children who had experienced supportive interactions with their parents.

According to Strassberg et al. (1994), this implied that parents (and family per se) also shape the cognitive and social information-processing styles of their children. This is apparent in studies demonstrating the 'hostile attributional bias' (Crick and Dodge 1996). The **hostile attributional bias** (termed by Nasby et al. in 1979) refers to an overemphasis of hostile intention assigned to other people's behaviours. According to Waldman (1988), aggressive children and those who have been rejected by their parents often demonstrate this type of negative mind set (see Box 6.6). More will be said about this in Chapters 10 and 11. Hence, in addition to providing children with emotional (e.g., comfort, nurturance and love) and practical (e.g., shelter, clothing and food) support, the family shapes the way children think about others.

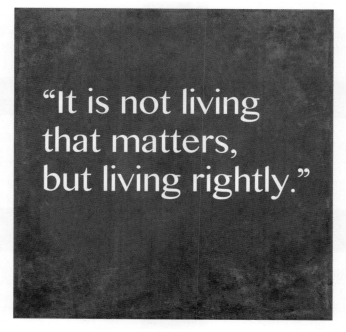

"It is not living
that matters,
but living rightly."

Plate 6.7 Inspirational quote by ancient Greek philosopher Socrates. (Shutterstock 187234400.)

> ## Box 6.6   Generations of negative outlook: hostile attributional bias affects social behaviour
>
> You may have noticed that hostility tends to run in families. Why should this be the case? Research into what is now termed **intergenerational transmission** demonstrates that when parents reject, neglect and abuse their children such children are likely to continue with this parenting pattern. Hence, intergenerational transmission leads to a cycle of negativity. This cycle of negativity is shown through the hostile attributions made about other people's intentions from their behaviour. The use of hostile attributions is just one aspect of social information processing but, as we will see, it plays a role in shaping the child's cognition (Strassberg et al. 1994). If a child perceives other children as pretending to be friendly, for instance, it may put a negative spin on the intended social interaction. Researchers have investigated hostile attributional bias in children's interpretation of stories describing ambiguous intent (Crick and Dodge 1996). Quite often these stories describe actions such as a child breaking a cup while looking in a cupboard or leaving a toy on the floor causing someone to trip over. The connection between aggressive children who have rejecting parents and their level of hostile attribution is apparent – these children will put a negative spin on a story containing ambiguous intent (Waldman 1988). Securely attached children are far less likely to do this.
>
> Researchers have also considered the effect of parental support and style of discipline on children's moral reasoning. Palmer and Hollin (1997), for example, found that university students who perceived their parents as providing positive nurturance tended to have a mature level of moral reasoning. In a later study conducted in 2000 they also found an association between poor moral reasoning skills and an inclination towards making hostile attributions of other people's intentions. Moreover, adolescents in their study with a history of parental rejection self-reported higher rates of delinquency. It would seem that a complex interaction exists between parental rejection and the continuation of a cycle of negative social-cognitive processing (Palmer and Hollin 2000).
>
> The findings are clear – negativity crosses the generations from parent to child to grandchild. When a child uses hostile attributions towards other playmates, for instance, social exchanges can become antagonistic – in some cases resulting in antisocial behaviour.

The support provided by families can vary both quantitatively and qualitatively and this, in turn, may have either a positive or negative impact on the child's development. For example, parents who ridicule their child in times of crisis can thwart the development of social identity and self-esteem. A child's social identity and self-esteem can impact on future social behaviour and their life choices within society. As mentioned previously, families vary in the way support is given to the developing child. This includes the way family members interact with each other and the general dynamics within the extended family network. Bornstein (2002) argued that children who are actively encouraged to participate in discussions and decision-making by their parents are more likely to develop higher levels of moral reasoning. It is important, argued Bornstein, that parents use appropriate probing, paraphrasing and asking questions to ensure that their children understand the situation. By doing this their children's level of moral reasoning is facilitated further. If the child experiences positive interactions within the family then it is likely to develop more socially acceptable behaviour. A supportive chat with mum, for example, may help to resolve conflict during puberty. This chat, however, has other implications – by giving her daughter emotional support mum is creating an affectionate bond between them, and this does not go unnoticed by the daughter

Plate 6.8 An adolescent's hostile attribution of a friend's intention behind the gift of a plant. (Shutterstock 411105970.)

who responds positively towards her mother. Kochanska and Aksan (1995) found that a mutual expression of affection between mother and child helped to instil moral standards in preschoolers. The converse is also true, however. In our next section we will address parental emotional support for the child and how this influences a child's future social behaviour.

Parental emotional support

How family members interact has a profound influence on the developing child. These social interactions can be influenced by many factors including social class and gender. Komarovsky (1964) found differences in communication between husbands and wives depending on social class. Husbands from lower working classes failed to express their emotions to their wives in times of trouble, unlike their middle-class counterparts who did so easily because of their higher standard of education. A study by Rubin (1976) found that the ideal husband for wives in a middle-class family was described as a good communicator. In contrast, their working-class counterparts were happy if their husbands went to work and drank only a small

Plate 6.9 Happy parents on whom to model male and female behaviour. (Shutterstock 46432435.)

amount of alcohol. These differences in attitude and expectation influence the way in which partners interact. This, in turn, provides children with a social model of how men and women are expected to behave.

As pointed out by Bandura (1986) in his Cognitive Social Learning approach, children will model their behaviour on what they see occurring within their family context. According to this approach, sons model their behaviour on how dad behaves while daughters imitate the mother's actions. The notion of 'romantic love' can also affect the nature of interaction between husband and wife. If there is a deep underlying emotional connection between the spouses then this provides a positive foundation for offspring to model their emotions on. Not all marriages are based on romantic love; some are arranged by the parents to form economic alliances. Although, more often than not, these marriages are successful, there are cases where the relationship interactions between husband and wife are confined by a loveless match, which can create a negative family environment for the children. Such arranged marriages were common in late 18th- and early 19th-century Britain (Lystra 1989). Of course, such arrangements remain acceptable in some Asian and African cultures today.

The relationship between parent and child shows asymmetry of power and competence (Maccoby 1992). This makes perfect sense given that the child is in its early days of development. It is during the early stages of development that support provided by the family helps the child to learn and develop a self-identity (see Chapter 8). Developing a self-identity also involves an understanding of gender. The understanding and development of gender identity and gender role is not to be confused with sex identity. In the case of the latter, a biological cause accounts for what it is to be of the male or female form (see Chapter 12). Unlike sex role identity, the recognition of a gender assignment is socially-driven and influences the social behaviour of children (see Chapters 8 and 9). Gender identity is established through socialisation processes – hence individuals come to perceive themselves as having either **masculine** or **feminine traits** (see Box 6.7).

Box 6.7   The socialisation of gender-specific behaviour

One question we might ask is how do we come to develop an understanding of our own gender? Slaby and Frey (1975) identified three stages that children go through in order to develop an understanding of gender: **gender identity** (i.e., I label myself as boy or girl); **gender stability** (i.e., I understand I will always be a boy or a girl) and **gender consistency** (i.e., others retain their gender even when they dress as the opposite sex). According to Kohlberg (1966) in his **Gender Consistency Theory**, gender identity is established through imitating the behaviour of same-sex individuals. Martin and Halverson (1983) introduced a **Gender Schema Theory** where children acquire rules or schemas that provide a framework for how females and males should behave. The Social Cognitive Theory (SCT) (Bussey and Bandura 1999) places the social environment as the main factor in shaping gender-specific behaviour. Family members, for example, reinforce gender-specific behaviour and this, coupled with observational learning, means that children will later imitate the observed behaviours of same-sex parents. The SCT combines the theories of Gender Consistency and Gender Schema. In the case of the latter, a girl, for example, who wants her bedroom decorated, is likely to want colours normally associated with femininity such as pink. She is therefore acquiring schemas associated with being a girl. The SCT claims, however, that children rehearse in their minds what they observe and then select which behaviours to copy. According to the SCT, children model on same-sex individuals first and then ask questions later. Parents have ideas about what toys are gender-appropriate and which forms of play are acceptable. For example, most parents are more permissive about rough-and-tumble play in boys than they are for girls and use expressions such as 'boys will be boys' and 'I don't think that's lady-like' to reinforce gender-appropriate play. In a longitudinal study by Fagot and Leinbach (1989) they found that children who were good at labelling picture portraits as boys or girls tended to show gender-appropriate behaviour which, in turn, reflected the behaviour of their parents. Fagot and Leinbach found that, by 28 months of age, children could easily perform this gender-labelling task. Moreover, the earlier children developed this ability the more 'gender-appropriate behaviour' they showed and the greater their sex-role discrimination. Parents were more positive towards their child if he or she demonstrated gender-related play. Fathers tended to have more traditional attitudes about how their daughter should behave and the expectations they had of them. Langlois and Downs (1980) found mothers gave a warmer response than fathers towards their children even when they played with 'gender-inappropriate toys'. This was not the case for fathers who showed disapproval – some even ridiculing their child for choosing such 'inappropriate' toys. In the case of boys, other male playmates showed disapproval when they saw their friend playing with toys for girls such as dolls. Siblings as well as peers provide reinforcement for play with toys classed as same-gendered and, in so doing, further socialise each other (see Chapter 7). According to Parke (2002), mothers are less influential in gender socialisation than fathers.

Hence, research has shown that parents subtly shape their children to adopt appropriate gender roles by the way they react to their children's behaviour (Leaper and Friedman 2007).

The role that siblings play in the socialisation of gender has been researched by McHale et al. (2001). By adopting a longitudinal research approach they were able to establish whether the personality traits of the first-born influence the development of the gender-specific behaviour of the second-born. They found that there were stronger modelling behaviours between the siblings than those between the child and its same-sex parent. The order of this influence was always in the direction of the second-born modelling on the first-born. The impact of having sisters or brothers was different in terms of developing more feminine or masculine qualities (Rust et al. 2000). Rust et al. found that sisters enhanced the development of more feminine qualities while brothers stimulated masculine traits. Other pairings fostered stereotypically feminine play such as sister–sister and older sister–younger brother couplings. Brother–brother pairs promoted masculine play (Stoneman et al. 1986). Fewer gender stereotypes were found among children with older opposite-sex siblings.

The nature of parent–child relationships in relation to the level of parental support has been studied by numerous developmentalists. East (1991), for example, observed the level of support provided by parents to their school-aged children. The parent–child agreement about the level of support given was analysed. Interestingly, differences in the level of agreement about the perceived support provided varied depending on whether children were described as sociable, withdrawn or aggressive. The findings suggested that girls who are withdrawn and boys who are aggressive perceive less support from their father relationships. The mothers of aggressive and withdrawn children perceive there to be less support in their relationships with their children. Fathers, however, only perceive this to be the case with aggressive children. In contrast, in the case of sociable children, there was strong agreement between parents and child concerning the level of perceived support given and received. Other studies have considered parent–child interaction in terms of the effects it has on social adjustment to school and, in particular, making and keeping friends (see Box 6.8). The research suggests that the way parents interact with their children has a profound effect on the development of future social skills. Interestingly, it appears that the social functions of the family have a cross-cultural consistency.

Box 6.8   How parental interactions impact on the social-skill development of their children

Studies have revealed the effects that parents have on the developing social skills of their children. Parent–child relationships, for example, even influence a child's ability to adapt to the school environment. Barth and Parke (1993) made observations of how parental interactions

(continued)

(continued)

with their preschool children during physical play sessions affected later social adjustment in school. During play sessions with their preschool children, parents who were too controlling caused the child to resist parental demands. The quality of interaction between mother and child was found to influence interpersonal skill ability. In a study by Kochanska (1992), 75 five-year-old children were observed for their quality of interaction with their mother and peers. The mother's influence style strategy predicted the nature of the influence style their children used with peers. If the mother forced her child to play with a toy in the way she did, for example, then this negative control was used by the child as a method of influencing peers. Likewise, frequent commands lacking clarity resulted in less prosocial interactions with peers. The best outcome of articulate and non-coercive interaction styles occurred when the mother used polite guidance. Baumrind (1972) observed three-to-four-year-olds in the home and at nursery school. She rated children for self-control, tendency to approach new situations positively, self-reliance and the ability to express warmth towards other children. Baumrind also assessed the parents using four criteria:

- control (extent of parental influence over their child's activities and the way dependent and aggressive behaviour coincided with their own);
- maturity demands (the pressure placed on the child to perform at his or her ability level);
- communication (level of explanation given as to why the child should obey and how considered the child's opinions are);
- parental nurturance (level of warmth and compassion exhibited).

Three groups arose from these ratings.

- Group 1, the children were mature and competent scoring high on these criteria. They had parents who also scored high on their criteria.
- Group 2 were moderately self-reliant and self-controlled but experienced apprehension when faced with new situations. They also showed little interest in interacting with other children. They had controlling parents who failed to listen to their child's opinions or show any warmth or affection.
- Group 3, however, were the most immature and scored low on self-reliance and self-control. They were also highly dependent on their parents and retreated from new situations. They had overly affectionate parents who failed to provide boundaries through absent control and demand.

Hence, the best parents provide a warm and caring home environment but reward responsible behaviour and encourage self-reliance.

In 1959 Barry, Child and Bacon identified six core cross-cultural dimensions of child rearing. These included:

1. Nurturance – children are taught prosocial behaviour enabling them to care for and help others such as dependant and younger family members.
2. Obedience – children are taught that they should obey their elders.
3. Responsibility – children are taught to take responsibility for their fair share of jobs within the family environment.
4. Self-reliance – children are taught to be independent of others such that they can assist in sufficing their own requirements and taking care of themselves.

5. General independence – children are taught to become independent from domination, control and supervision.
6. Achievement – children are taught to aim for and entertain high standards of performance.

Given the cross-cultural consistency of social functions performed by families, it raises the question of the extent to which there are biological undertones driving the behaviours of family members per se. Not just in the social functions they perform, but at a more individual level of how these are implemented. The intergenerational transmission of rejecting behaviour, for instance, could be derived at a genetic level just as easily as it can socially. This is the topic of our next section.

EFFECTS OF FAMILY BIOLOGY ON THE SOCIAL DEVELOPMENT OF CHILDREN

Bronfenbrenner placed the child at the centre of his Ecosystem Model. Despite Bronfenbrenner's model addressing the layers of social influence impacting on the developing child, he acknowledges the importance of the various behavioural predispositions (courtesy of our genes) already apparent in the new-born. The innateness of these predispositions must come from somewhere and that somewhere is our parents and grandparents and their parents before them. An important question is to what extent can we map the behaviours of children historically to their family-tree?

As Plate 6.11 shows, it is easy to trace physical characteristics that we inherit from our extended families, such as hair colour. This raises the question of whether we can also trace behavioural characteristics back to our family tree, and how might we go about this? One obvious approach to this is to consider famous individuals from well-documented families such as royalty. King George III, for example, had a medical ailment known as porphyria, which is an inherited metabolic condition causing a multitude of symptoms including moments of insanity. Various symptoms of porphyria can be traced from King George to members of the British royal family. Two of his great granddaughters, Princess Victoria and

Plate 6.10 Older sibling looking after her younger sister. (Shutterstock 431666662.)

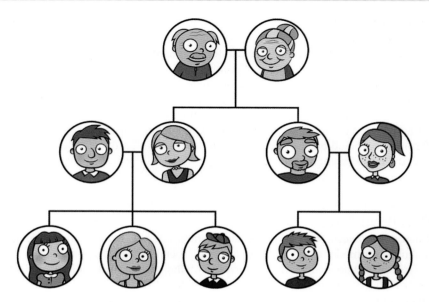

Plate 6.11 Cartoon vector illustration of a three-generation family tree – depicting inheritance of hair colour. (Shutterstock 205791736.)

Princess Charlotte, for example, also suffered from this mood-altering malady. This example illustrates how a physiological condition passed down from one generation of family members to another can have an impact on behaviour. This also demonstrates the complex relationship between our biology and our behaviour. There are other examples of inherited conditions that impact negatively on behaviour such as **bipolar depression** and **schizophrenia** (both considered by psychiatry to be mental health conditions). It is easier to examine the nature of 'bad' genes on behaviour across generations than it is to investigate how 'good' genes are passed down from one family member to another (probably because deleterious genetic effects are more salient). As we discussed in Chapter 1, behavioural genetics has been an informative approach to understanding how genes are passed on from one generation to the next and the likelihood of family members inheriting various behavioural problems. A sparsely studied area is depression in children. There is evidence, however, that children of parents suffering from chronic depression tend to have areas of the brain with lower activation than their counterparts (Embry and Dawson 2002). In contrast, research shows that short-term parental depression fails to have the same impact on brain activity suggesting more of an environmental influence. Hence the relative contributions of nature and nurture to child behaviour (especially when things go wrong), is very difficult to disentangle (Gottlib et al. 2006).

One way forward in understanding how family biology influences the development of social behaviour in children is to consider the likelihood of related family members experiencing the same behavioural problems. This provides us with what is known as a **comorbidity likeness**. As we have already seen, the chances of a child developing signs of depression increase if the parents suffer from depression themselves. Identical twins have the same genes so it follows that if one twin has a behavioural problem we can expect the other to develop the same problem. In reality, however, this is not always the case. Given that identical twins share 100 per cent of their genes, they are likely to be more behaviourally similar than when compared with their other siblings (this is because the other siblings share only 50 per cent of their genes by common descent). German-born Johannes Lange (1931) made an interesting observation about our genes and the environment. He said, 'The natural tendencies one is born with, the surrounding world he grows up in, these are essentials, these are destiny'. This statement is spelling out the notion that although we are born with traits, during development these can be influenced by our environment. This is known as the biosocial interactionist approach (see Chapter 1 for further discussion). You may recall from Chapter 3 that the inheritance of a 7-repeat allele form of the DRD4 gene is linked to behavioural characteristics observed in so called 'D-infants'. These D-infants are apparently difficult to cajole. Interestingly, however, the impact of this gene can be attenuated given the right environmental response. In families that demonstrate patience and perseverance, children with this form of the DRD4 gene show a lesser degree of disorganised behaviour. Hence, we need to be careful when we discuss the effects of genes on behaviour. Genes do not determine behaviour, but rather genetic differences between individuals can contribute to differences in their behaviour. Change the rearing environment, however, and the effects of the genes can be reduced or even reversed.

An interesting question posed by Plomin et al. (2008) is whether the effects of heredity become more or less pertinent as we age. As we continue to develop, our experiences with the environment are likely to be different to those of our parents. It is for this reason that many people would answer that the effects of our heredity depreciate as we age. Counterintuitively, Plomin and co-workers (2008) found that siblings tend to become more similar as they age, and this is especially the case for identical twins. This might be taken as suggesting that some of our genes act to influence behaviour later in life. Interestingly, Plomin et al. have also uncovered evidence that siblings growing up in the same family are no more alike than individuals nurtured by other families. They describe this as being due to the effects of a non-shared environment – even siblings housed under the same roof will have different experiences and will interact with environmental factors differently. The non-shared environment is an important factor in behavioural genetics that can be used to account for how the effects of our genes might be reduced or even reversed (see Box 6.9). Another account of the relationship between genes and environment during social development is provided by Judith Rich Harris' Group Socialisation Theory, which describes the strong influence of peer-shared environments (see Box 6.9 – see also Chapter 7).

Box 6.9 The effects of shared and non-shared peer environments on our behaviour

Twin and adoption studies were initially designed to separate the effects of shared heredity over a shared family environment. Plomin and Daniels (1987) argued that many of these studies instead found overwhelming support for family resemblance being down to a shared heredity and not to a common family environment. In relation to many personality disorders and alcoholism, a shared heredity and not a shared environment explains much of the resemblance between biological parents and offspring. The empirical evidence suggests that a quarter of the variance in cognitive ability in children is due to a shared environment (which becomes negligible after adolescence). According to Plomin et al. (2008), the influence of the environment cannot be ignored but it is the non-shared rather than the shared environment that plays an

(continued)

(continued)

important role in shaping our behaviour. Effects of the non-shared environment are estimated by ruling out (technically 'controlling for') the influences of heredity and having a shared environment. Adoptive siblings correlate with their adoptive parents at +0.25 for cognitive ability. Given that these children are unrelated genetically to their adoptive parents, then this positive correlation must be due to having a shared environment. In order to identify non-shared environmental factors, it is important to concentrate on environments specific to the child rather than looking at features shared by siblings. Siblings have separate lives (Dunn and Plomin 1990) and socialise with different peer groups. According to Harris (1995), children develop their identity and personality as a result of a nature–nurture interaction. As children age the parental influence for this attenuates. Research supports there being a 50 per cent genetic contribution towards differences in personality across siblings (Plomin 2011) but very little impact from parenting. Hence, Harris asks what of the remaining 50 per cent? Harris explains this diversity of personality and social development as resulting from the impact of peers (see Chapters 7 and 12). Children aspire to and are socialised by their peers. Her Group Socialisation Theory accounts for this by children conforming to the norms and attitudes of their peer group (they know only too well the consequences of not doing so).

Findings suggest that a non-shared environment is more influential in shaping children's behaviour than a shared home environment. Heredity and a non-shared environment impact on personality and social development across siblings more so than sharing their home setting. Siblings have different experiences and associate with different peers who, according to Harris, have a stronger socialising influence on how they behave socially.

There have been studies exploring the 'inheritance' of **antisocial behaviour** in families across the generations – the notorious Juke family is one such example (see Box 6.10).

Box 6.10   The notoriously bad Juke family

During the 19th century the Juke family became famous for producing generations of 'deviants' who caused constant problems for the police in New York State. The family tree of the Jukes was examined by American sociologist Richard Dugdale who later wrote of them in his book, *The Jukes: A Study in Crime, Pauperism, Disease and Heredity* published 1877. He used a survey method in which questions about family demographics such as income and education, heredity, intelligence and the nature of criminal activity were addressed. In his investigation, Dugdale found connections between crime and pauperism. There was an abundance of prostitution and illegitimate offspring across the generations. Many of the illegitimate offspring were neglected and uneducated. A connection was also made between exhaustion and self-indulgence, which he believed interfered with any ability to make reasonable decisions. Dugdale traced the Juke family tree back to the 1700s. In Dugdale's search he discovered that the first Juke member had both legitimate and illegitimate children (totalling six girls and two boys). There were incestuous relationships and two of his sons illegally married his daughters. Dugdale continued following this line until there was a total of 709 Juke family members. Of the 709, 540 were of Juke blood and 169 from reconstituted families. Out of 535 children, 335 were born legitimately, 106 illegitimately and 84 unknowns. He concluded that heredity was a key player in physical and mental capacity but behaviour was shaped by the environment and not physical or mental capacity. In Dugdale's view both environmental and hereditary factors conspired to create this antisocial family. Moreover, the heredity produced an environmental context that perpetuated that heredity. American eugenicist Arthur Estabrook reanalysed Dugdale's data in 1916. His findings and conclusions favoured a more pronounced heredity influence over the behaviours and decision-making capacity of the Juke lineage. He proposed that families such as the Jukes should be prevented from having offspring because of their genetic predisposition towards criminality. He claimed that the implementation of social improvement policies would be ineffective for families like the Jukes and instead advocated that they should be sterilised – very much in keeping with the view of a number of eugenicists of the time.

Dugdale's study is an example of interesting historical research that alludes to there being passive, active and evocative gene effects on the behaviour of this family. Estabrook's reanalysis of the data, however, promoted an extreme genetic rhetoric.

The Juke family is not the only one to be examined across the generations. More than 100 years later, following the development of modern genetics, Brunner et al. (1993) discovered a mutated gene that apparently contributes to the development of criminality. A Dutch family passed a mutated gene down the generations that influenced the production of **monoamine oxidase A** (or MAOA). Low levels of MAOA were found to be associated with aggressive criminal behaviour. Brunner et al. found that the males across the family lineage were deficient of MAOA and, as a consequence, secreted low concentrations of serotonin (5-HIAA). Low levels of 5-HIAA are associated with impulsive aggressiveness (reacting aggressively before thinking), thereby providing a link between antisocial behaviour and genes. This Dutch family had a long history of antisocial behaviour and violence.

Another way of exploring family antisocial behaviour is to consider the impact of criminal activity of family members on other related kin. In a study of 1,349 boys in Glasgow, Ferguson (1952) found a relationship between the number of relatives with criminal tendencies and the percentage of boys who later committed crime. If one family member was convicted, crime level rose from 9 per cent (no family member convicted) to 15 per cent. This figure doubled when two family members were convicted and increased further to 44 per cent when three or more were convicted. Interestingly, committing crime depended on who in the family was an offender.

Plate 6.12 Family of antisocial sons. (Shutterstock 12774139.)

If the father was an offender then the likelihood of the son committing a crime was 24 per cent. This increased to 33 per cent when the family offender was an older brother and 38 per cent if he was a younger brother. The conclusion drawn by Ferguson was that criminality is linked to male family offenders. He further speculated that this increase in offending is a result of sibling modelling and socialisation (this will be discussed further in Chapter 7).

Farrington et al. (2001) found similar results in their longitudinal study of 1,517 boys. They looked into the history of these boys' families and found that 117 families in total had criminal records. Some 597 arrests (43 per cent of arrests) came from these identified criminal families. If one relative was arrested there was a strong possibility that another family member would have a similar fate. Moreover, fathers with an arrest record tended to be married to mothers who were also criminal. Extended family members who had arrest records could often be traced back to the criminal behaviour of their grandparents. All family members influenced these boys but it was the father's criminality that had the largest impact. Farrington et al. claimed that there is a host of nurture-linked explanations but there must come a point when we need to ask where this criminality originates from. Does nature drive nurture or nurture drive nature? This is a very difficult question to answer.

Many of the family studies, including twin studies, have considered the inheritance of behavioural problems arising out of psychological and medical conditions such as depression, schizophrenia, autism and antisocial behaviour. There are studies examining the more positive outcomes of genetic transmission such as musicality, artistry and other special talents. Studying positive behaviour such as being sociable in relation to our genetic inheritance is less common. Possibly the consideration of the non-mutant form of the DRD4 gene provides us with an explanation of why some new-borns are more sociable than others. This gene contributes to the predisposition of new-borns to behave in a sociable way. They are less temperamental in their behaviour and are often referred to as 'easy babies' (see Chapter 3). Even here, however, there is a strong environmental influence. Happy babies encourage others to respond in a friendly way, which further reinforces the predisposition to be happy.

It is clear that the family's biological heritage provides future generations with predispositions to behave in a particular way. How this behaviour is progressed, however, very much depends on a multitude of interactions within a familial context. Both our genes and the environment interact to influence the social development of the child.

Summary

- There are two major types of family unit: the extended family and the nuclear family. The extended family comprises the parents with their children residing alongside other family members such as uncles, aunts and grandparents. Nuclear families consist only of parents and children. The modified nuclear family is a reformed version of the original nuclear family where extended family members live close by but under a separate roof. In Britain, most relationships are monogamous, where marriage occurs between one man and one woman. Some cultures conform to a polygynous relationship structure where men have more than one wife, or polyandrous where women have more than one husband.
- One of the most important functions of the family is socialisation. Parents and other family members are considered as informal socialising agents who teach their children the values, mores, attitudes, norms and customs representative of their society. In doing this parents are teaching their children how to become good

citizens by behaving in socially acceptable ways condoned by society. Other social functions performed by the family include guidance in moral behaviour, providing emotional support, providing suitable role models for children to imitate and enforcing discipline when required.

- Providing discipline is important as it sets boundaries for children. There are different types of discipline that can have positive or negative effects on the socialisation process. Physical punishment is used in the power assertion form of discipline. Love withdrawal is non-physical disapproval such as affection deprivation. Induction is the best form of discipline and is analogous to authoritative discipline, a term used by Maccoby and Martin (1983). This discipline enables parents to reason with their child so that it is clear why the behaviour is inappropriate and has to be checked. Authoritative discipline is associated with children who develop a mature moral understanding and theory of mind. Authoritarian, indulgent and neglecting types of discipline all result in inappropriate socialisation.
- Discipline is used to help instil morals. A lack of parental supervision is associated with rejecting parents. This has been linked to delinquency. A lack of supervision provides children with opportunities to associate with others who have delinquent tendencies leading to a deviant lifestyle.
- The socialisation of moral reasoning is an important role undertaken by parents. Effective and appropriate socialisation of moral behaviour results in well-adjusted prosocial children. If this is performed inappropriately then it can result in children with low levels of moral reasoning. Parents shape the way their children view the world. Making hostile attributions of other peoples' intentions from their behaviour occurs in children who have rejecting, neglecting or abusive parents.
- Bandura's (1986) Social Cognitive Learning approach is important in explaining how children learn about gender appropriate behaviour. Children not only model on the same-sex parents but will imitate the behaviours of their siblings.
- Cross-culturally, families appear to nurture their children in similar ways and this includes the social functions performed by the family. This might suggest there are underlying biological influences to the way families developed. Bronfenbrenner in his Ecosystem Model placed the child at the centre of layers of social influence, believing that the child is responsive and born with predispositions to behave and interact with others in a certain way.
- Some researchers have considered family histories in relation to antisocial behaviour. Dugdale in 1877 thoroughly investigated the family tree of the antisocial Juke family. Throughout the family tree, traced back to the 1700s, were antisocial members known to the police. Dugdale concluded that heredity played a role in physical and mental capacity but the environment shaped behaviour.
- Farrington et al. (2001) conducted a longitudinal study of 1,517 boys and looked at their family history. Of the families studied, 117 were identified as having numerous criminal records and 597 arrests came from these identified families. Farrington et al. found a connection between family member arrests and delinquency among the boys. Although Farrington et al. acknowledge the importance of nurture they also argue that there must be a point where nature begins the cycle of criminality.
- In relation to social development within the family it is clear that nature and nurture are so intricately woven together that it is difficult to differentiate the effects of either independently.

Questions for discussion

1. Discuss two important social functions performed by the family.
2. We tend to think of the family as comprising of the husband, wife and a couple of children. What other forms of family structure are there? Are there likely to be any problems concerning children's integration into these other types of family?
3. In what ways can family members (in particular the parents) influence the moral reasoning of younger children?
4. Critically evaluate differences between the underlying factors of authoritative and authoritarian discipline responsible for the varying trajectories seen in the social development of the child.
5. Critically consider the notion that antisocial behaviour runs in families. What does this mean? Discuss this using evidence from studies looking at heredity.
6. Critically examine the evidence against the use of 'spanking' as a form of discipline.

Further reading

If you are interested in understanding what good parenting means and why the 21st-century ideal of parenting may be profoundly wrong, look at:

- Gopnik, A. (2016). *The Gardener and the Carpenter: What the New Science of Child Development Tells Us about the Relationship Between Parents and Children.* New York: Farrar, Straus and Giroux.

If you want to understand how children process elements of socialisation through their own experiences in the home, school and neighbourhood, and learn social norms, values and self-identity through these experiences, look at:

- James, A. (2013). *Socialising Children.* Basingstoke, UK: Palgrave Macmillan.

If you are interested in understanding how behavioural genetics operate in humans and animals, look at:

- Plomin, R., DeFries, J.C., McClearn, G.E. and McGuffin, P. (2008). *Behavioral Genetics* (5th Edn). New York: Worth Publishers.

If you want a guide that provides practical and clinically sound information on how to tackle common problems encountered by families, look at:

- Powell, J. (2013). *Introducing Family Psychology: A Practical Guide.* London: Icon Books.

Contents

Introduction 211

Different types of relationship 212

Children socialise each other 221

Peer acceptance using sociometrics 226

What does sociometrics tell us
about the unpopular? 234

In-group/out-group effects amidst a
backdrop of national attitudes 236

Summary 240

Chapter 7

Influence of peers and friends

INTRODUCTION

In Chapter 6 we considered the various social functions performed by the family, in particular the parents. One of the important social factors we discussed was the role of the parents in socialising their children to behave in ways considered to be socially appropriate. Socialisation is a complex process involving children being taught the mores, values, norms, attitudes and culture representative of the society in which they live. Hence, it is important that parents and other family members perform this duty effectively so that their children can develop into 'good citizens'. But is the family the only socialising agent?

According to Bronfenbrenner, the family is placed close to the child in the microsystem of his Ecosystem Model. The family is not the only informal socialising agent in the microsystem however. Bronfenbrenner was insightful enough to realise that children form close bonds with each other and such relationships are influential when it comes to social behaviour. This is seen clearly during play (see Chapter 9). Even with evidence of how children influence each other, the family, especially the parents, have been perceived as taking prime position as informal socialising agents. This 'nurture assumption', however, was challenged in 1995 when American psychologist Judith Rich Harris published a ground-breaking article in *Psychological Review*. Harris disputed the notion of parents being the main contributors in the socialisation of their children by suggesting that children socialise other children. This was depicted in her Group Socialisation Theory (GST), which described children as socialising powerhouses. They do this, according to Harris, by forming groups of solidarity with their own set of norms and value system. At first the GST was ridiculed by stout supporters of the traditional view of the family as central informal socialising agents.

In recent years, however, GST has received acclaim as a consequence of increasing empirical evidence in support of Harris' approach (see later). Children forming bonds and friendships with other children also have consequences for the development of self-concept, self-esteem and gender identity. Peer relationships and group membership binds children and adolescents together in terms of attitude similarity and common interests. These intergroup attitudes develop such that positive views are perpetuated towards other group members but negative ones towards group outsiders. This can be problematic and, in the extreme form, can initiate prejudice and negative behaviour towards those perceived as outsiders. The school playground, in particular, can exacerbate differences between groups, resulting in an 'in'- and 'out-group' mentality. A group dynamics approach using sociometric methods can help us to understand the formation of this mentality. A sociometric status approach can be very informative as to how different roles are distributed amongst peers and the status value they carry – for example, who is popular. This will be discussed in relation to peer groups and the consequences that peer relationship status has on the development of future social behaviour. First, however, a discussion of the different types of relationships possible will help us to understand the nature of the 'glue' that binds both children and adolescents together.

DIFFERENT TYPES OF RELATIONSHIP

As infants develop their social skill set they begin to forge relationships extending beyond their family context (Dunn 2004). These new outside-of-the-home relationships serve an important role in the development of social behaviour. When these interpersonal relationships are examined it becomes apparent that they contain a multitude of dimensions that combine to influence the nature of the relationship formed. These dimensions include the following:

- diversity of interaction within relationships
- quality of relationship
- reciprocity or complementarity
- intimacy
- interpersonal perception
- commitment

Different relationships will vary in their level of interactive style and content. This will influence the quality level of the relationship and the purpose it serves. The more intimate the relationship then the more likely there is to be commitment and reciprocity. Moreover, close relationships often bring individuals together who have different strengths and weaknesses.

Plate 7.1 One child consoling another. (Shutterstock 37698100.)

This complementarity of need fulfilment develops further as relationship intimacy increases. We all perceive other people in different ways. For some, a person might be perceived as strong willed, whereas to another the same person could be viewed as lacking will-power – it is all relative to how we perceive ourselves. Relationships can be long- or short-term. Furthermore, the nature of a relationship between two people progresses out of a history of their interactions. This means that mum, for example, may be perceived as the caregiver during infancy but a mentor in later years. As we saw in Chapter 3, Weiss (1974) outlined differences between relationship forms and the functions they serve, which are worth reiterating here:

- attachment relationships provide security (e.g., mother-child, see Chapter 3);
- social network relationships provide a shared interpretation of experiences and companionships (e.g., students attending the same class might share anecdotes about the lecturer);
- caregiving relationships provide a sense of being needed (e.g., a community nurse visiting a patient of many years);
- kin relationships provide individuals with a reliable alliance (e.g., brothers coming to the aid of each other during an aggressive argument);
- mentor relationships offer guidance (e.g., a teacher might suggest possible career opportunities);
- other relationships might provide individuals with feedback of worth and competency.

The formation and function of peer and friend relationships is considered to overlap with sibling relationships (see Chapter 6). Dunn (1983) considered sibling and peer interactions to be similar; arguing that in both cases there is a high frequency of interaction, uninhibited emotional response, an interest in each other, imitation of behaviour and attachment towards one another (see also Hartup 1975).

Plate 7.2 Two young children enjoying each other's company while sitting on a hay-stack. (Shutterstock 214114069.)

They both show negative reactions when apart and do their best to be together; they help and cooperate with each other and provide sympathy; they provide defence for each other when faced with threats; have a shared language understood by no one else and, when they do argue, issues are resolved openly and quickly. As we have seen in Chapter 6, siblings will model on each other (not always for the good) and contribute towards the socialisation of gender (McHale et al. 2001). Moreover, siblings reinforce which toys are gender-appropriate and therefore are good to play with. Sibling relationships can be very intimate, especially when they share the same bedroom, toys and friends – this enables them to know each other well and to make all types of comparison. According to Dunn and Kendrick (1982), siblings tend to engage in play that allows them to imitate each other and share similar emotions. Sibling interactions can be considered to be of a reciprocal, complementary or conflicting/ rivalry nature. Gass, Jenkins and Dunn (2007) suggest that the nature of sibling interaction can be related to temperamental or personality characteristics. This interaction is likely to impact on how different activities are time-allocated (Shanahan et al. 2007). Siblings who maintain reciprocal interactions tend to have a similar temperament (Meadows 1986) and do similar play activities simultaneously or in turns such as chasing each other or rough and tumble games (especially seen in boys). Reciprocity interactions often give way to complementarity. In a play interaction for example, one sibling will do something different that coordinates well with the actions of the other. This can be seen in role-play games such as doctors and nurses – one sibling would be the nurse and the other the patient. Despite the difference in play behaviours seen, there is coordination enabling the progression of the game. Under conditions of sibling rivalry, there is often competition for parental attention as they may feel a sense of differential treatment by their parents (Dunn 1999). This is likely to create a negative relationship between siblings (Stocker et al. 2002).

A longitudinal study conducted by Dunn et al. (1994) demonstrated that sibling conflict during childhood was a good predictor of emotional problems. Stocker et al. (2002) claim that preschool sibling conflict predicted adjustment problems at school. Lawson and Mace

Plate 7.3 Two young siblings fighting. (Shutterstock 90285622.)

(2008) argue that sibling rivalry may have a profound effect on social and personal develop-ment. Moreover, the extent of sibling rivalry is influenced by family characteristics such as parent–child discord, which can then lead to depression (McHale et al. 2007). Other family dynamics include the family demography such as birth order, gender combinations, family size and the age gaps across siblings. In the case of birth order, first-borns have to readjust from being an only child and attaining full parental attention to sharing that attention with the second-born. This invites unpleasant emotions such as aggression, which can be directed towards the new sibling. It is largely the emotions of the older sibling that impact on the nature of sibling relationship exhibited. As younger siblings develop their social and cog-nitive skills, they become an equal partner in joint play activity (Meadows 2010). Sibling rivalry, not only in the case of vying for parental attention but in areas of niche picking, can cause sibling de-identification (Whiteman et al. 2007). This means that siblings will avoid making comparisons with one another, and consequently avoid any rivalry, by defining them-selves using different spheres of competency, interests and specialisms. This is more likely when there is a narrow age-gap difference and siblings are of the same gender. Interestingly, younger siblings are more likely to be influenced by their older siblings in the nature of friendships they form with other children (Tucker et al. 1999).

According to Furman and Buhrmester (1992), sibling conflict decreases as youngsters progress through the teenage years and their relationships become more egalitarian and recip-rocal. Siblings, however, also become less close due to their diverse and differing social networks. We must not lose sight of the fact that siblings have separate lives (Dunn and Plomin 1990) and tend to socialise with different peer groups but, as we have seen, younger siblings are very much influenced in their peer relationships by their interactions with older siblings. Thus far, we have considered the different types of relationships possible and the important influence that siblings have on future peer and friend relationships. Is there, however, a difference between peer and friend relationships? Also, if there is, when do we consider a peer relationship to be a friendship bond? This is the topic of our next section.

Peer and friend relationships

Interestingly, the type of sibling relationship experienced during childhood is likely to influence the type of individual selected as a friend. Older siblings are often encouraged to look after their younger brothers or sisters, especially in the school playground, and are expected to allow them to 'tag along' with their own friends (Meadows 2010; Rothbaum and Trommsdorff 2007). It is not surprising, therefore, that friendships formed bear a resemblance to the friends of their older siblings. There is an important difference, however, between what we mean by peer and friend relationships. Peers are considered to be individuals who generally share social characteristics such as age, social background and status. Their level of interactive discourse is one of equality. It is highly likely that, with increasing age, individuals will come to belong to more than one peer group. Children, for example, will point out who they especially like and others who they have to sit next to in class and regard as schoolmates. Moreover, they reserve the term 'friends' for those they especially like and play with. If peers are those who share common characteristics, then a friend can be considered as someone you like to be with and have affection for. In other words, we can have an attachment bond with special peers we call friends. A quote by Aristotle précises what it is to be a friend: 'A single soul dwelling in two bodies' (Aristotle 9, cited by Diogenes Laërtius).

The transformation from peer to friend has been examined using a timeframe outlined by developmentalists based on years of research (see Figure 7.1). According to Schneider (2000) it is during the period of 18–36 months that specific friendships are formed, suggesting a transformation timeframe from peer to friend status. If friendships made during this timeframe are maintained and surpass the three-year-old threshold then, according to Howes (1996), such relationships will aid in the acquisition of later social skills. Howes and Phillipsen (1998) argue that the level of complexity seen in play during toddlerhood can be used as a predictor of prosocial behaviour shown in childhood. Furthermore, this can also predict the level of social withdrawal and aggression displayed at nine years of age. Schneider suggests friendships formed after three years of age tend to be more stable. Dunn (2004) points out that between 50 per cent and 70 per cent of friendships formed by one or two years of age are more than temporary, with most lasting beyond a year and others several years. These childhood relationships are often considered to be precursors of friendship formation in later life. Developmentalists suggest that the nature of friendship expectations vary with age. For three- to seven-year-olds the objective of friendship is to be able to play together successfully. This objective changes with age. At 8 to 12 years of age being accepted by playmates of the same gender becomes central to any friendship. By 13 to 16 years, social skills have developed and become complex, which is reflected in friendship goals.

Here, we find that adolescents experience physiological changes with the onset of puberty, which feeds into the development of **self-identity**. Friends can be very helpful in developing an understanding of the self. Sometimes, by providing compliments about their friend's appearance, for example, they can help to improve **self-esteem**. During this time there is an increased interest in the formation of cross-gender relationships. Although the preference for peers to parents is established at an early age, it is during adolescence that relationships with peers and friends become pivotal in the social life of teenagers (see Figure 7.2).

As we can see from Figure 7.2, during the ages of one and two infants' preferences for being in the company of their parents is higher than it is for their peers. This is most likely a consequence of the caregiving roles that parents perform, given that infants at this age are still developing their locomotive skills and rely heavily on their caregivers (see Chapter 3). It is interesting that one of the things that caregivers do is to introduce their children to other children of a similar age – who might later become their peers. This coincides at around the age of

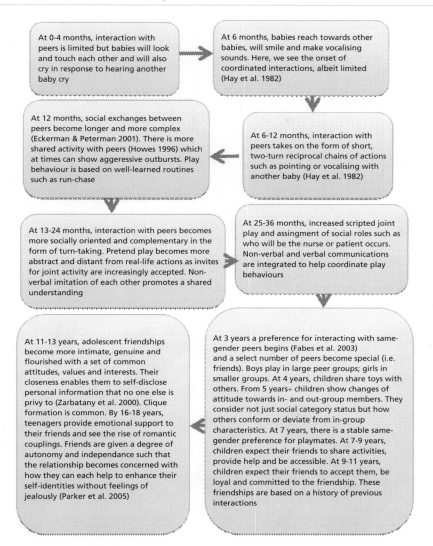

At 0-4 months, interaction with peers is limited but babies will look and touch each other and will also cry in response to hearing another baby cry

At 6 months, babies reach towards other babies, will smile and make vocalising sounds. Here, we see the onset of coordinated interactions, albeit limited (Hay et al. 1982)

At 12 months, social exchanges between peers become longer and more complex (Eckerman & Peterman 2001). There is more shared activity with peers (Howes 1996) which at times can show aggressive outbursts. Play behaviour is based on well-learned routines such as run-chase

At 6-12 months, interaction with peers takes on the form of short, two-turn reciprocal chains of actions such as pointing or vocalising with another baby (Hay et al. 1982)

At 13-24 months, interaction with peers becomes more socially oriented and complementary in the form of turn-taking. Pretend play becomes more abstract and distant from real-life actions as invites for joint activity are increasingly accepted. Non-verbal imitation of each other promotes a shared understanding

At 25-36 months, increased scripted joint play and assingment of social roles such as who will be the nurse or patient occurs. Non-verbal and verbal communications are integrated to help coordinate play behaviours

At 11-13 years, adolescent friendships become more intimate, genuine and flourished with a set of common attitudes, values and interests. Their closeness enables them to self-disclose personal information that no one else is privy to (Zarbatany et al. 2000). Clique formation is common. By 16-18 years, teenagers provide emotional support to their friends and see the rise of romantic couplings. Friends are given a degree of autonomy and independance such that the relationship becomes concerned with how they can each help to enhance their self-identities without feelings of jealously (Parker et al. 2005)

At 3 years a preference for interacting with same-gender peers begins (Fabes et al. 2003) and a select number of peers become special (i.e. friends). Boys play in large peer groups; girls in smaller groups. At 4 years, children share toys with others. From 5 years+ children show changes of attitude towards in- and out-group members. They consider not just social category status but how others conform or deviate from in-group characteristics. At 7 years, there is a stable same-gender preference for playmates. At 7-9 years, children expect their friends to share activities, provide help and be accessible. At 9-11 years, children expect their friends to accept them, be loyal and committed to the friendship. These friendships are based on a history of previous interactions

Figure 7.1 Timeframe of peer to friend transformation.

two–three and, as we can see from the graph, interest in peers becomes aroused and overtakes preferences for caregiver contact. This difference peaks, according to Ellis et al.'s (1981) data, at seven to eight years of age where peer preference is heightened to about 70 per cent and adult preference takes a hit at 10 per cent (that is a 60 per cent difference in favour of peers). As we can see from the graph, this preference difference continues to increase until seven to eight. Peer preference takes a dip between nine and ten and plateaus at eleven–twelve years of age, but continues to remain significantly above that of the parents. Larson (1997) showed this trend continuing into pre-adolescence and adolescence (10–15 years of age). Moreover, teenagers prefer to be with their friends or spend time alone rather than with adults. This trend is cross-culturally consistent although American adolescents spend double the time communicating with each other than do Korean or Japanese teenagers (one hour per day).

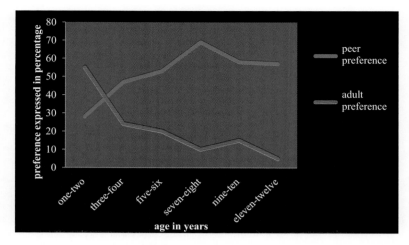

Figure 7.2 Depicting peer and adult preferences across age. (Adapted from Ellis et al. 1981.)

Plate 7.4 Teenage girls in pyjamas giving a friend a make-over at sleepover. (Shutterstock 930543.)

Ellis et al.'s findings support the view that children enjoy being with other children and forging different types of relationships with them. Dunn (2004) regards these relationships as acquaintances with a history of common interactions impacting on each other's future social behaviour. Ross et al. (1992) describe these early encounters between toddlers as positive and negative exchanges that later combine to form the basic elements of peer friendships. These early relationships can be of the dyadic or triadic structure (Ishikawa and Hay 2006), suggesting that toddler social interactions are more complex than researchers initially thought.

An interesting question is when do peers transform into friends? Figure 7.1 suggests that the magic age of peer to friend transformation is around three-years-old (although the longevity of friendship might not necessarily be life-long). Although children understand this transformation they have difficulty explaining why a friend is a friend. Rubin (1980, p. 11) demonstrates this in the following excerpt:

Interviewer: *Why is Caleb your friend?*
Tony: *Because I like him.*
Interviewer: *And why do you like him?*
Tony: *Because he's my friend.*
Interviewer: *And why is he your friend?*
Tony (with   *Because – I – choosed – him – for – my – friend.*
mild disgust):

It is apparent that Tony is providing a circular explanation to why he is friends with Caleb but fails to see this when he presents his reasons. As yet Tony has not learned the qualities inherent within a friendship such as intimacy, commitment and reciprocity. As previously discussed, the expectations of friendships change, however, as do friendship obligations. This is particularly so when contrasting 10–11 year olds with 16–17 year olds. As many as 80 per cent of 10–11 year olds considered friendship to be a matter of 'being nice and helping each other out'. This figure decreased significantly to 11 per cent for 16–17 year olds. For 62 per cent of these teenagers the focus of obligation should be the provision of emotional support rather than just being nice. This contention was shared by only 5 per cent of 10–11 year olds (Smollar and Youniss 1982; Youniss 1980). With age and cognitive maturity the individuals' underlying reasoning supporting these views changes. The youngsters believed that if you are nice to your friends they will be nice in return. The reasoning for the teenagers is socioemotionally more mature – claiming that if you provide emotional support your friend will be happier, which is mutually beneficial. This is something that girls are more likely to do than boys (Ladd 2005). Clearly, being nice and providing emotional support are characteristics important in friendship maintenance but children have to make friends first and then adapt to the changing nature of friendship characteristics. For most children this is easy to achieve (see Box 7.1).

Box 7.1   The making and keeping of friends

An interesting question that developmental psychologists have pondered is what skills do children need in order to make and retain friends? One important factor appears to be how easily children can communicate with one another. Researchers have examined key elements of friendship by recording children in play with their friends and with peer-strangers. Gottman and Parker (1986) used two groups of children: those who played with their friends and those who played with peer-strangers (see also Parker and Gottman 1989). Of those peer-stranger pairings considered the most likely to form future friendships, a high degree of positive interactions, communication, exchange of information and rule-making, and the resolution of issues of difference were found. We should bear in mind that in some respects this is a circular answer because children who get on well will spend more time together (Dunn 2004).

Friends do have moments of disagreement but what is important is how they then proceed to resolve their differences. Friends are more likely to use reasonable and justifiable ways of resolving issues than non-friends and, in so doing, they ensure their friendship is

(continued)

(continued)

maintained (Bowker et al. 2006). Friendship over time will become more intimate, show increased self-disclosure of personal information and knowledge of each other's strengths and flaws (Dunn 2004; Ladd 2005). Despite changes of friendship goals throughout the lifespan, close friends remain close. The goal for three- to seven-year-olds is coordinated play, whereas for those aged eight to twelve this is acceptance by same-gender peers. In the case of 13–17-year-olds, the emphasis shifts to shared understanding and development of the self. This involves the sharing of intimate details of one's desires for the future with the person who knows you best – your best friend.

Not all children, however, manage to keep their friends. This could be for a multitude of reasons, as was shown in an American study of 216 children between the ages of eight and fifteen attending a summer school camp. In this study Parker and Seal (1996) considered the common patterns of friendship shown between children. From this they identified different subgroups of friendship formation and breakup (see Table 7.1).

As we can see from Table 7.1, it would appear that children have already developed different personality traits that influence the type of friendships they make. This implies an interactive style already in situ from a young age. An interesting question arises here regarding the extent to which a child's personality develops out of interactions with the caregivers or through interactions with peers. The family is traditionally considered to be the main informal socialising agent impacting on the child's behaviour (see Chapter 6). However, as we saw earlier, this '**nurture assumption**' was challenged by Judith Rich Harris in 1995 in her **Group Socialisation Theory** (GST). We will now focus our attention on the evidence that children are the main informal socialising agents of other children.

Table 7.1 The five subgroups of common friendship patterns.

Subgroup 1 made friends easily but the social ties showed decreased stability.	These children were labelled as playful teasers and tended to be untrustworthy, liked to gossip, were bossy and behaved aggressively.
Subgroup 2 made friends easily but maintained their existing friendships.	They were not bossy but nor were they 'pushovers'.
Subgroup 3 broke-up with their friends and failed to replace them (this means that in some cases individuals ended up without friends).	These children engaged in playful teasing but were caring and shared with others – however, they were considered to be 'show-offs'.
Subgroup 4 tended to have a stable number of friends but also added new ones.	These children were an honest group but, despite a reduced inclination to tease group members, they were less caring towards each other.
Subgroup 5 had no friends.	These children were seen as preferring to play alone and were shy and timid – the reality was that they felt lonelier than the other children.

CHILDREN SOCIALISE EACH OTHER

Friendship, as we have seen, is a positive interpersonal relationship built around recipro-cal interactions (Shantz 1983). It involves intimacy with one or more peers and is often synonymous with social achievement such as social competency and positive state of mind (Hartup 1978). Friendship is considered to be the most ubiquitous form of human relationship. It is therefore unsurprising that friends have a significant impact on our social behaviour. According to Corsaro (1981), in childhood it is friends who help each other to develop social skills through play (see Chapter 9). During adolescence friends provide instruction on issues such as aggression and sexual relationship management (Hartup 1978) and offer an emotional support system.

In Chapters 3 and 6 we discussed the important role played by caregivers, especially in infancy, a time when infants learn a great deal from their parents. Caregivers are there to pro-vide the initial impetus for learning language and useful social skills. Caregivers also help in coaching their children to develop successful peer relationships that can act as a springboard from which to develop more advanced social skills (Ladd and Pettit 2002). If caregivers provide the springboard then who is it that propels the child into developing advanced social skills and modified attitudes, values, norms and behaviour? Judith Harris (1998, p. 147) said the following:

> *Children are born with certain characteristics. Their genes predispose them to develop a certain kind of personality. But the environment can change them. Not 'nurture' – not the environment their parents provide – but the outside-the-home environment, the environment they share with their peers.*

Harris argued that the internal working model developed during the caregiver–infant attach-ment is only applicable for this coupling, hence having no generalisability value to any other type of relationship formed. When Lamb and Nash (1989) looked at the data obtained using the 'strange situation' experiment (see Chapter 3), they concluded that:

> *Despite repeated assertions that the quality of social competence with peers is deter-mined by the prior quality of infant–mother attachment relationships, there is actually little empirical support for this hypothesis.*
>
> *(p. 240)*

Harris concluded from the attachment research that having a secure attachment with the mother, for example, does not necessarily imply that all familial interrelationships will be of a secure nature. There is likely to be more than one internal working model representative of our relationship with each individual encountered (see Box 7.2).

Box 7.2   Little 'savages' who were gentle towards each other

The importance of a peer group can be traced back to a classic study by the daughter of Sigmund Freud, Anna Freud, and her colleague Sophie Dann. Six war-traumatised Jewish orphans from the Nazi 'show camp' called Theresienstadt were observed by Freud and Dann in

(continued)

(continued)

a donated Sussex home. Theresienstadt was referred to as a show camp because it appeared in propaganda film footage to show the world 'how well inmates were treated'. Of interest to Freud and Dann was what helped these children, who were deprived of their parents, to survive the bleak conditions of Theresienstadt. While in the camp these orphans were looked after by other prisoners but ultimately they had been neglected. When they arrived in England they lacked basic speech and language abilities, which Freud and Dann interpreted as a result of deprivation as babies. Given their life circumstances at Theresienstadt, it was unlikely that they were able to form attachment bonds with other adults. These children were only three years old, the oldest nigh on four years of age. It is most likely that they never knew their parents; failed to form attachments with plausible substitute caregivers; experienced little stimulation (certainly had no toys); were moved around to different places; and only knew a few swear words. When they lived in Sussex, all the children were hostile to adults but showed solidarity towards each other. According to Freud and Dann (1951), 'The feelings of the six children toward each other showed a warmth and spontaneity that are unheard of in ordinary relations between young contemporaries'. In adult life all six orphans were found to have formed successful relationships.

This classic study shows how, when it comes to resilience, peers can substitute for absent parental caregivers.

The orphans studied by Freud and Dann were deprived of adult attachments in their harsh environment, which must have appeared to them as an uncaring world full of uncaring adults. Instead they became attached to each other, thus developing the concept that 'children are caring'. Their close bonds to each other were clearly demonstrated at meal times when Anna Freud commented that they would pass food on to the neighbouring child before claiming it for themselves. This self-sacrifice and making sure the others are okay first is a sure sign of a loving and caring attachment. In commenting on the work of Freud and Dann, Harris pointed out that each child was responding to the perceived neediness of the other children. This research suggests that, not only can children form attachment substitutes with each other, but they also developed different internal working models – adults are uncaring but children care. Harris would argue that these children were influencing one another in the way they behaved towards other adults (e.g., hostile) and other children (e.g., caring). This is but one example of evidence supporting Harris' contention that children socialise each other. This is the essence of her controversial Group Socialisation Theory. We will now look more closely at the implications of the GST.

Group Socialisation Theory (GST)

Harris argued that children initially develop their own identity and personality due to 'nature' (i.e., genetic make-up) and 'nurture' (i.e., how their biological parents bring their children up). (It should be noted that although we tend to use the term 'caregivers' to describe those who bring up children these days, Harris' model is concerned with biological parents). With age, however, parental influence diminishes greatly as peer group influence grows. She also argues that studies by developmentalists have underplayed the influence of genes in the equation. Numerous research findings support a 50 per cent genetic influence on personality and social behaviour but have failed to provide evidence of any substantial impact of parenting on the developing child. This means that 50 per cent of variation in a child's social development could be explained by heredity. But what of the remaining 50 per cent? From this Harris deduced that as the home environment was having a limited impact on the way children develop socially, then the 'nurture' influence must be coming from peer interactions. Studies by Plomin (2011) have demonstrated that the parental environment fails to make siblings any more similar to one another (Plomin and Daniels 1987). This finding, however, does not preclude parents from having an influence on their children's social development. Parents think they interact and influence their offspring equally but this is not a view shared by the children themselves. Moreover, this does not hold true from the ratings of parental interactions with their children obtained through observational studies (Reiss et al. 2000). In fact, Plomin (2011) argues that parents provide different nurturing environments for each of their children. This means that they create partially non-shared environments for each child even within the home setting. Parental influence, it would seem, is to fashion offspring to be different from themselves and their other children. But this conflicts with much of the research addressed in Chapter 6 showing strong correlations between parent–child attitudes and social behaviour. In relation to such correlational research, Harris points out that there are a number of inherent weaknesses (see Box 7.3).

Box 7.3   The 'nurture assumption' and those misleading correlations

Prior to Judith Rich Harris' GST, a vast number of developmental studies based around correlational measures were taken as suggesting that much of a child's social behaviour arises from modelling of parental behaviour. Typically, parents and offspring were observed or completed personality inventories in the home environment. The observation of a positive correlation between, for example, a high hostile score for father and son would be taken as evidence that the son modelled his hostile behaviour on the father. Likewise a high score on anxiety for mother and daughter would be taken as indicating that the latter had modelled her behaviour on the former. Hence, many developmentalists considered there is strong evidence that children acquire much of their behaviour and attitudes from observations of their parents. A position that Harris describes as 'the nurture assumption'. The question is, does such a conclusion based on correlational measures stand up to scrutiny? Harris criticises such studies on a number of logical and methodological grounds. The most important of these are as follows.

- Almost none of these studies distinguish between environmental and genetic influences (that is, each child shares 50 per cent of their genes by common descent with each parent).
- They do not distinguish between parent to child effects and child to parent effects (e.g., an anxious child can lead to anxiety in the parent).
- Researchers do not distinguish between the child's behaviour inside and outside of the home (which may be very different).
- In correlational studies a large number of parental and child variables are compared. This is more likely to result in some comparisons being statistically significant (given this, it is important that the threshold level of significance is raised to reduce the likelihood of spurious correlations but detect robust ones).

Due to these problems with such correlational designs, Harris considers that the findings are often interpreted in ways that support the nurture assumption whereas, in actual fact, they do not (Harris and Workman 2016).

In Box 7.3 we see how misleading correlational studies can be. Correlational studies are often used to show how two separate variables apparently influence each other (e.g., move together in the same direction or show the inverse). The more sweets eaten, for example, the more tooth decay. This appears to be a sound explanation but there could be other reasons too, such as poor enamel formation, the consumption of sweet drinks using a straw or the inheritance of mum's 'rotten' teeth. Harris and Workman (2016) provide a good example of how misleading correlations can be. Harris asks us to entertain the correlation between the frequency with which the family eats together and a teenage family member keeping out of trouble. If the correlation suggests that eating together protects the teenager from becoming delinquent, then what is this actually saying? It provides us with little control or information about inherited genes (such as conscientious parents having conscientious children), or teenagers being welcomed to the dinner table because of their good behaviour (i.e., what Harris calls child-to-parent effects). These other explanations take a back-seat at the expense of researcher assumptions favouring the notion that children regularly pick up behavioural patterns by modelling on their parents. This error is compounded by increasing the number of comparisons between parent and child behaviours, thereby increasing the likelihood of finding parent–offspring behaviours or attitudes that correlate significantly. (In order to compensate for this, the threshold significance level should be increased to make it more difficult for results to be significant – but for most correlational studies this is rarely done).

It appears that correlational studies therefore provide little in the way of concrete evidence for the notion that parents have a profound influence on their children's social behaviour through modelling. Evidence suggests that genes account for around 50 per cent of the differences in personality traits between children (Plomin 2011). Harris claims that of the remaining 50 per cent variation nearly all of this arises out of peer influence. She also claims that there are good reasons for learning from peers because parents make for poor role models. Children imitating their parents' behaviour are very likely to be ostracised from their peer groups – so most children avoid behaving that way. To be successful amongst peers the goal must surely be to behave like a child; to behave like one's peers. And this is what they do and why peer socialisation matters more. There are various reasons Harris puts forward as to why children might have evolved to favour socialisation from their peers in preference to their parents. Learning from peers, for example, adds variation to their knowledge base; even though this information is present in the child's culture, not all parents will access this. This means that other children might be aware of this information, which they then share. In our evolutionary past the chances of parents surviving was less than that of peer survival (given that there were more peers), which meant that peers were more likely to be available to learn from. Most importantly, however, is the competing parental and peer interests shown. What parents want their children to know might not necessarily be best for them. If children were to learn and behave in ways parents want them to, the result could be peer excommunication. Hence children's preferred models are other children.

In order to fit in children need to first figure out what sort of people they are. They make social comparisons with other children and from this decide which social category or group they want to belong to. Once they have made their decision, they then learn what the group norms, values and attitudes are and behave in the same way as the other members of their selected social category. Children's groups do this by adopting the **majority-rules rule** (see Box 7.4).

Plate 7.5 Teenage friends conforming to their group dress code. (Shutterstock 387546337.)

Box 7.4   You do as we do or go!

Have you ever wondered why some children either fit in easily or are bullied into leaving a peer group? Most children are good at judging which social category best describes them. They are also very resourceful at seeking out other peers who fit the same social category, and then they join with their seemingly similar peers. For some children, however, they have not selected wisely and find their mismatched peers are ousting them from the group. Why is this the case? What are they doing wrong? Children's groups use the majority-rules rule. This means that newcomers have to conform to the behaviour exhibited by the majority in the group. If the child hates 'skipping' but this is what members of the group like to do, then she has to either learn to like this game or leave the group. Moreover, if a child speaks German but the majority of children speak English, then this child has to quickly learn the language of the peers or find other children who speak their native tongue.

Harris argues that the majority-rules rule is a strong socialising mechanism used by children to ensure all members willingly conform to the group norms.

In support of Harris' theory it has been documented that children in the early stages of school do use social comparison with their peer group members as a way of developing their self-concept and for self-evaluation (Harter 2006). Furthermore, Harter (2006) believes that making social comparisons will provide an indication of their self-esteem such that favourable appraisals with peers increase self-esteem. In contrast, negative appraisals can have deleterious effects for the developing self-esteem. It is important, however, to note that children also learn things from their parents that they bring into the peer group. If, children speak the same language, then the language parents taught them is retained. This is highly likely as most children live in the same culturally defined neighbourhood. Here we expect the parents to speak in the same manner as the parents of their children's peers. Children, however, have different experiences within their peer group from those in the home environment. In contrast to home experiences, Group Socialisation Theory (GST) predicts that peer-group experiences will have long-term consequences for how the child behaves in different contexts. According to GST, behaviour learned away from the home environment can enter the home but the reverse is not permitted. Behaviours acquired outside of the home will take precedence even when the two environments overlap. Take the example of Tom falling over and hurting himself at the family barbeque in front of his peers. He may feel like crying and might even begin to shed a few tears but as soon as he sees his peers then all efforts not to cry are made. Tom's peers are dictating his behaviour and not his parents. We also have to bear in mind that similarity of behaviour across different contexts will be due, in part, to genetic factors (Saudino 1997). American-born Kimberly Saudino (1997) reported that children who are of a shy and quiet disposition tend to show these qualities outside of the home. This uniformity of behavioural response can be explained by their innate temperament.

Peer group versus social category?

Recently Harris has re-developed GST. In her book *No Two Alike*, Harris extends our understanding of how children socialise each other by accounting for why, despite being socialised by their same-gendered peers, they continue to develop personalities and social behaviours that are different from one another. In this book she endeavours to explain how children can become similar to their peer group at the same time as being different. In Harris' first book, *The Nurture Assumption*, she referred to the term 'peer group' as influencing children's behaviour. In a recent interview with Lance Workman in 2016, however, she confessed that this was misleading. Instead she feels that the term 'social category' would have been more appropriate as it is 'an abstract concept, not necessarily an actual group of children' (p. 2), which is the driving force gelling peers together.

The GST remains a contentious approach that continues to divide many developmentalists. Despite this, there have been attempts at synthesis between the views that either parents or peers act as the main socialising agents. Jay Belsky claims that the two viewpoints can co-exist. In 2005 Belsky argued that children might vary in their susceptibility to parental influence and this could be a form of adaptation. In other words, being more susceptible to parental influence might be better suited in certain types of environment. He gives the example of a stable world where very little alters across the generations. Under these circumstances it would make perfect sense to defer to the experts – that is the parents. Alternatively, in a changing world, the strategies for survival provided by parents could become readily outdated and therefore ineffective. Being influenced by new strategies, such as those advocated by peers, might be more beneficial to survival. But what if there is a combination of these two world situations – long periods of little change followed by quick successions of change. This, he argues, would favour not one type of child who follows in the footsteps of his parents or by those paved by peers. Instead, a reproductive strategy of having many children, some of whom are more susceptible to parental influence (i.e., best when the world is stable) and others less so (i.e., best when the world is unstable), would be more successful. In an evolutionary sense this would secure the passing of parental genes down the generations as at least one offspring is likely to survive and have children of their own. Belsky advocates therefore that parents are important for those children genetically predisposed to be influenced by them. At the same time, however, parents are not as important to those children who are less susceptible to their influence. This is an interesting approach and might account for contradictions found amongst the socialisation literature. Regardless of whether developmentalists agree or disagree about who are the main informal socialising agents, it remains clear that peers and friends have an important role throughout an individual's lifespan. In our next section we will explore just how important it is to be accepted by our peers using a **sociometric approach**.

PEER ACCEPTANCE USING SOCIOMETRICS

Peers are considered to be individuals who are part of the same societal group and who have certain characteristics in common such as age, gender, year at school or status (e.g., top at sport). Peers also have individual traits that are similar, which is why, according to

Plate 7.6 The most popular child in class. (Shutterstock 314220080.)

McPherson et al. (2001), the adage 'birds of a feather flock together' rings true. Children and adolescents can be categorised according to specific characteristics such as age and gender (Maccoby 1990). With increasing age, however, this becomes less important such that homogeneity of peers is decreased during adolescence (Lempers and Clark-Lempers 1993). Moving into adulthood, peer social networks become less gender dependent as men and women integrate socially and perhaps become romantically involved. There is some evidence of homogeneity in personality and social behavioural characteristics among peers but this is less robust than it is for ethnicity (Urberg et al. 1997). This suggests that individual peer characteristics are not static over the lifespan but instead become modified as a consequence of life experience (e.g., a new career involving a change to the age demography of co-workers). In **dyadic peer relationships** peers are considered as equals. They expect to receive and give the same amount of support and affection to one another. If this peer relationship is imbalanced then its natural course is to terminate at some point down the line (Neyer et al. 2011). Equality matching underlies both peer group and dyadic peer relationships. In a classroom situation, for example, Joey might help Billy with his algebra on the basis of sitting next to each other. Likewise, Billy might help Joey with his spelling. By virtue of sitting next to each other they can more readily strike up an equitable social exchange. In the case of a group of teenage peers grape-picking in France, the norm might be to go out in the evening at the end of the week for a congratulatory drink in celebration of their hard week's work. Teenagers declining the offer and therefore contravening the group norm would be perceived as a non-team player. This equality matching is persistent throughout the lifespan.

According to Hinde et al. (1985), peer relationships rise steadily from 75 per cent in childhood to 80–90 per cent during adolescence; a time when teenagers interact with a greater number and diversity of peers. Adolescence is a time when teenagers spend more time with their peers and devote considerable attention towards obtaining social acceptance from them (Brown 2011). Social acceptance by our peers is important as it provides a great deal of information about ourselves such as how we differ from peers seen as popular. Our social comparisons are more often than not based on how we compare with our peers, and

Plate 7.7 Peers rated as the top student or with outstanding sport skills. (Shutterstock 244517776.)

if they are rejecting us then this is saying that we are not good enough to be part of their group. It is therefore unsurprising that teenagers focus much of their time on being liked and accepted by their peers.

There are different ways of ascertaining how well children and teenagers are received by their peers but a simple and easily administered method is just to ask them. For this, developmental psychologists adopt sociometric techniques. When using sociometric techniques, researchers ask children and adolescents to rate their peers on a number of scales such as helpfulness, friendliness, aggressiveness and intelligence. These ratings are collected and counted and used to develop a character profile of individual peers. Peers alternatively could be nominated for their likeability and desirability as a friend (Ladd 2005). This process of sociometry provides data as to a child's or teenager's peer status. It is a non-biased way of attaining 'insider' knowledge about specific individuals. Children know other children, and teenagers know other teenagers, in greater depth than teachers or other adults because of their frequency of interaction and shared experiences. The nomination of peers undertaken through asking children and teenagers to select two or three peers they particularly like and the same number of those disliked, provides researchers with scores that they can add together. The total number of 'likes' and 'dislikes' obtained for all participants provides researchers with a peer hierarchy such that there will be popular children and teenagers ranging down the ranks to least popular. Popular children have the least number of negative nominations but by far the most positive ones. They are perceived as being assertive, competent and friendly, and as having good social skills. Black and Hazen (1990) noted that they can integrate in play with other children easily without interrupting the state of play. Their good social skills enable them to communicate well and set the norms within their peer groups – something that individuals with poor nominations fail to do. Some developmentalists, however, argue that being popular does not necessarily come labelled with positive traits. Cillessen and Mayeux (2004) and Cillessen and Rose (2005) argue that some popular children and teenagers can be manipulative and have less attractive personality traits such as being arrogant, over-dominant and aggressive. For these researchers, the route to popularity can take a number of pathways. Ladd (2005) and Parke and Gauvain (2009) have outlined other types of peer labels depicted in Table 7.2.

Peer status is influenced by a number of factors that we will explore one by one.

Social-cognitive skill competency

According to Rubin et al. (2006), the ability to initiate conversations and other forms of positive interaction is probably at the top of the list – in other words it is important to have effective cognitive and social skills. A child who joins a peer group and shows interest in its members by asking questions politely will be received more positively by the other children. Therefore, having good social skills will help in the quest for peer acceptance. Another factor that plays a key role in how children react towards each other is the processing and interpretation of social information.

Social information processing

It is important that a child interacting with new peers can actually understand what is being communicated to them. If the intentions behind the communication are misunderstood then problems can arise in a child's response. Crick and Dodge (1994) devised a model of social information processing (see Figure 7.3).

Table 7.2 Different types of peer labels.

Popular peers	These individuals receive the most positive nominations making them popular with their peers. They tend to have many friends and are liked by many peers.
Average peers	These individuals receive both positive and negative nominations making them not as popular or as disliked as some peers. They have friends but are not as well liked as peers rated as popular.
Neglected peers	These individuals receive fewer nominations per se. Despite being isolated and more withdrawn than other peers, they are not necessarily disliked.
Controversial peers	These individuals split the field by being liked by as many peers as they are disliked.
Rejected peers	These individuals tend to be disliked by more peers than they are liked.
Aggressive rejected peers	These individuals are considered to be aggressive by their peers and therefore rejected. They lack self-control and often have behavioural difficulties.
Nonaggressive rejected peers	These individuals are rejected by their peers but, unlike aggressive rejected peers, they display anxiety, social incompetence and withdrawal from social interaction.

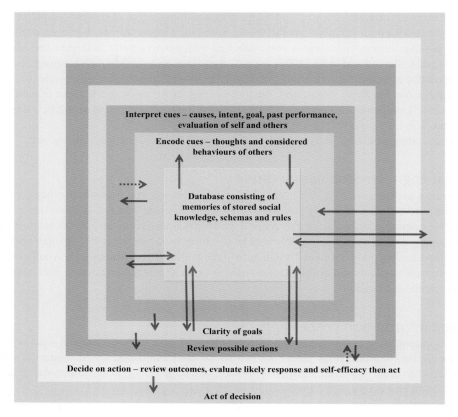

Figure 7.3 Social information processing model. (Adapted from Crick and Dodge 1994.)

As we can see from Figure 7.3, there are six decision-making stages (starting at the centre and working outwards) that children must make. The appropriateness and helpfulness of these decisions depend very much on the database (centre of the diagram) attained through interactions between cognitive development and the impact of learning and socialisation processes. Children who have, for example, assimilated a great deal of social knowledge through experiences with their social environment will understand the behaviours of others and make better informed decisions. This model outlines how children might make informed decisions about joining in to play with other children. At any of the six steps it is possible that a child may make the incorrect decision. Let's take the example of John who wants to play marbles with a group of boys. He watches them play and notices that one boy beckons him to come over. John encodes the boy's gesture as positive (step 2) and using step 3 he decides that he wants to be friends with these boys. After reviewing what he should do and how the boys might react (step 4), John decides to approach the boys. John's decision to be friends allows him to show his interest in their game by commenting on how good their marbles look (step 5). John takes the opportunity to join in when the boy who beckoned him over asks if he wants to play (step 6). It is equally possible that a child with poor social skills misses the friendly cues and ends up taking affront by the fact that he was not asked to play. Such a hostile reaction might lead to further hostility or being 'sent to Coventry'. Therefore, being socially incompetent could mean that such children become ostracised from playgroups through their own

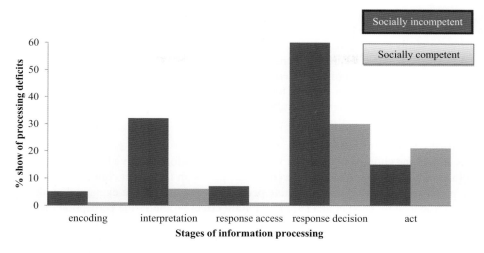

Figure 7.4 Social competency with level of social processing skills. (Adapted from Dodge et al. 1987.)

misjudgements of other children's behaviours or simply by focusing incorrectly on the wrong social cues. Either way these children have a poor social skill set (see Figure 7.4).

Figure 7.4 shows the robust connection between thought and behaviour. Good cognitive understanding and interpretation of social information promotes appropriate action. Any deficits, however, in social processing can lead to inaccurate decision making and inappropriate responses towards others. In Figure 7.4 we see that socially incompetent children display a higher percentage of processing deficits during most of the information-processing steps defined in Crick and Dodge's 1994 model. We can see, for example, that socially incompetent children have a higher percentage of inefficient encoding of social information. In other words, they come to code the social information incorrectly (e.g., they encrypt an accidental shove as being deliberate). This then becomes interpreted as a consequence of a hostile intent. Such encoding and interpretation can lead to an antisocial response.

What we have discussed thus far in this chapter would suggest that popular children are considered to be socially competent and those rejected by peers as socially incompetent. Does it follow therefore that rejected peers are lonelier as a consequence of this peer status? Bukowski et al. (2007) found that unpopular children such as those rejected by their peers

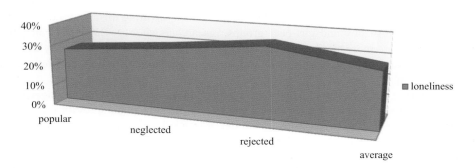

Figure 7.5 Levels of loneliness according to peer status. (Adapted from Asher et al. 1984.)

experienced the most isolation and loneliness due to being ostracised. Asher et al. (1984) uncovered an interesting trend with regard to the degrees of loneliness experienced by peers of different status (see Figure 7.5).

As expected, just over 30 per cent of rejected peers experience loneliness compared with just below 30 per cent of neglected peers. Popular peers experience loneliness the least but surprisingly they are not lagging too far behind the average child who is not popular, neglected or rejected. Another factor influencing peer status is physical attractiveness.

Physical attractiveness

Just as infants and children of three years show preferences for attractive faces (Langlois 1986; Langlois et al. 2000), so do older children and teenagers. In fact, older children and teenagers much prefer to spend time with attractive peers. This can, in part, be explained by the 'halo effect' introduced by Dion et al. (1972). The **halo effect** promotes the perception that physically attractive people possess a positive personality and social traits such as being friendly, competent, prosocial individuals. In short, because they are good looking then everything else about them is positive. Langlois et al. found that physical attractiveness is very important in both childhood and adolescence. Children perceived as attractive are rated as being socially competent and more socially appealing when compared with less attractive children. This can be seen in adolescent romantic pairings too. The advantages of being considered an attractive child is seen in the positive ways other people respond during social exchanges. Popular children tend to be physically attractive and have good interpersonal skills. They are also emotionally well-adjusted and more intelligent. These traits, however, could have developed as a consequence of being treated more favourably than their less attractive counterparts rather than because they are inherently good-looking. Our last but equally important factor impacting on peer status is gender.

Influence of gender

It is commonly observed that boys prefer to play with other boys and girls prefer their playmates to be girls. Interestingly, there is a timeframe for this apparent childhood sexism. Children typically prefer to play with peers of the same gender between 7 and 12 years of age (Harris 1998). There are exceptions to the rule such as circumstances bringing a boy and girl together through their shared commitments but even here the friendship is often kept a secret. Children who associate only with the opposite gender are generally frowned upon and considered to have poorer social skills and academic ability. These children often rate themselves as having low self-esteem. On the positive side, Zarbatany et al. (2000) showed that boys who played with boys but also had girls as friends believed the closeness with their best same-gender friend increased. Despite earlier studies reporting differences between the structure and size of boy and girl peer groups, researchers such as Bagwell et al. (2000) argue that there are more similarities than previously thought. The interactive styles across gender peer groups are also similar with both showing tendencies towards competitiveness and cooperation.

Adolescence is a period marked by considerable biological change to the teenager's body and brain, as the release of sex hormones trigger the onset of puberty. With the onset of puberty come changes in perceptions of the opposite gender. Teenage boys and girls find each other interesting and are mutually attracted to one another. This is a time when romantic relationships form and discontinue. Carver et al. (2003) looked at the longevity of adolescent romances (see Figure 7.6).

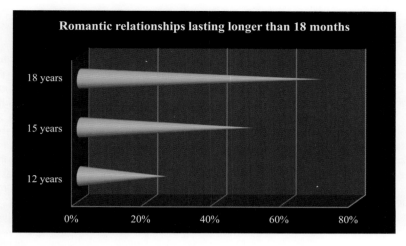

Figure 7.6 Longevity of teen romances. (Adapted from Carver et al. 2003.)

We can see from the graph that just over 20 per cent of romantic relations among 12-year-olds lasted longer than eighteen months. This increases for the 15-year-olds to just below 50 per cent and for the 18-year-olds to less than 70 per cent. Furthermore, they found that 20 per cent of teenagers (14 years and below) had romantic relationships lasting more than eleven months. These relationships can be rewarding by providing a sense of peer group inclusion, self-esteem and competency (Connolly et al. 2004). Other researchers, however, have shown that over-dating can be detrimental to the formation and quality of long-term adult relationships (Collins and Van Dulmen 2006). Davies and Windle (2000) added that early onset dating can be a trigger in the development of behavioural problems in the future. Adolescent romances are generally regarded as a good thing and a forerunner to later romantic relationships.

It should be noted that, thus far, we have focused on sociometric popularity. Developmentalists, however, have made a distinction between sociometric popularity and perceived popularity. This distinction goes a long way towards explaining why sociometrically popular children and adolescents can actually possess negative traits and behave in negative ways. So what is the difference between sociometric and perceived popularity? As we have previously discussed, sociometric popularity is based on a nomination system of 'liked' and 'disliked' peers. These are the peers who we want to be friends with. Perceived popularity, however, focuses on popularity in terms of achievements, positions, possessions and activities indicative of social prestige and social influence (Eder 1985). The nature of social prestige can vary from athletic ability to academic achievements to physical attractiveness with fashion sense. Social prestige can also include traits (e.g., leadership qualities, self-confidence, winning disputes and immunity from ridicule) that enable an individual to express social dominance (Eder and Kinney 1995). Alsaker (1989) claimed that the ability to protect oneself from ridicule has a clear influence over emotional well-being. This can, however, be a double-edged sword. If this state of emotional well-being is achieved through dominance and aggression it can lead to other problems such as learning ability (LaFontana and Cillessen 2002; Moody et al. 2011; Salmivalli et al. 2000). Interesting research has been carried out on the distinction between sociometric and perceived popularity, which we should bear in mind when interpreting the general findings on popular and unpopular peers (see Box 7.5).

Box 7.5   The sociometric/perceived popularity distinction

Using sociometry, peers with the most positive nominations are popular and, although they tend to have good leadership skills, they also know how to compromise in order to maintain group cohesiveness (Lease et al. 2002; Wentzel et al. 2004). In the case of perceived popularity assessment, psychological traits such as 'easy to push around', 'kind and trustworthy', 'initiates fights', 'bad at handling teasing' and 'stuck up' are used as indicators of social functioning. Social functioning is an important factor for perceived popularity and comprises a balance between acceptability and dominance. Adequate levels of dominance involve the ability to attain and command the attention, compliance and respect from others (Lease et al. 2002). Paikoff and Savin-Williams (1983) noted that, during early adolescence, teenagers adopt activities as a means of attaining social dominance. Even when children tease and joke and engage in rough-and-tumble play they are trying to establish their social dominance or 'pecking order'. They do this, however, in a socially acceptable way that allows them to assess their peers' level of resistibility towards domination (Eder 1987). Those skilled at managing peer teasing and winning at rough-and-tumble play, as well as refraining from being dominated, are perceived as popular provided they can do all of this without offending and becoming disliked by others (Eder 1987). As pointed out by Rabiner and Gordon (1992), however, such individuals need to be socially competent to orchestrate these goals effectively. Parkhurst and Hopmeyer (1998) assessed the nominations provided by 727 students in the 7th and 8th Grades using both sociometric and perceived popularity methods. Students who were sociometrically popular were considered as kind and trustworthy; more so than those who scored high on perceived popularity only. Those who scored high on perceived popularity only were judged as initiators of fights and were stuck up. They were also poor at handling teasing and were certainly not easy to push around. Students who scored high on both sociometric popularity and perceived popularity were considered to be kind and trustworthy but, at the same time, were not easy to push around and were just as likely as the average scorers to start fights and be stuck up. These findings support the view that perceived popularity correlates more with social dominance than sociometric popularity, and that the two popularity measures do not always correlate well with each other (Cillessen and Mayeux 2004; Parkhurst and Hopmeyer 1998).

We can see that there is a distinction between sociometric and perceived popularity measures in terms of the criteria being considered as popular. This difference can also be used to account for why not all popular children and adolescents are prosocial and can indeed behave in antisocial ways towards their peers.

In the next section we explore what happens to individuals who are unpopular or who have been rejected by their peers and the opposite gender by returning to sociometrics. Can such individuals still be part of a peer group?

WHAT DOES SOCIOMETRICS TELL US ABOUT THE UNPOPULAR?

Children and adolescents who are unpopular with their peers are often excluded from joining in any group activities. Their opportunities for forming friendships are considerably reduced, as indeed is the sampling pool of peers that they can approach. Unpopular children and adolescents are normally those who are rejected. As we saw earlier, there are two categories of rejected peers: aggressive and non-aggressive. Rejected peers experience loneliness more than individuals in any other peer status group (see Figure 7.5). For non-aggressive rejected peers this loneliness is greater because they often have the additional problem of experiencing verbal and/or physical victimisation in the form of bullying (Ladd 2005). A **protective factor** for these peers is to have a stable friendship even if it is just the one. The difference between having one friend or no friends can decrease the self-reported levels of loneliness, therefore buffering the peer from being bullied (Parker and Asher 1993).

Being rejected by peers can have long-lasting effects on social development and academic achievement. This can be the case for both aggressive and non-aggressive rejected peers. In the case of non-aggressive rejected peers, their situation is often such that they become targets of abuse by fellow peers. Boys can be physically attacked and harmed if they refuse to cooperate with their bullies (Perry et al. 2001). However, this cooperation often heightens the humiliation they experience. Girls, alternatively, have a different *modus operandi*. Failure to comply with peer requests could result in exclusion from events or defamation of character by spreading lies, rumours or innuendo (Ostrov and Crick 2006). Either form of victimisation can have devastating short-term and long-term consequences for social development. As well as loneliness, these peers often feel increasingly anxious and depressed (Nangle et al. 2003). Anxiety and depression coupled with loneliness will have more of a negative impact on social skill development and self-esteem evaluations the longer it continues (Goldbaum et al. 2003). These experiences of the non-aggressive rejected child and teenager can lead to academic issues where they fail to attend school or spiral into severe anxiety and depression, both known to interfere with concentration and learning.

What of the aggressive rejected peer? Does this individual experience a similar outcome? The research findings suggest that these peers do not experience as much loneliness as those who are non-aggressive. Rejected peers can and do make friends but these friendships are often based on aggressive rejected peers. These friendships tend to be less satisfactory and of a poorer standard with increased conflict (Poulin et al. 1999). These aggressive rejected peer friendships often spur each other's deviant behaviours according to Bagwell 2004 (see Box 7.6).

Box 7.6   A case of criminal-minded peers: child-killers Thompson and Venables

Robert Thompson and Jon Venables murdered the toddler James Bulger in 1993. The boys became friends and would spend their time together watching videos of films showing violence. Psychologists believed they had been influenced by these films and in their fantasy world wanted to perform scenes of violence on another child. Their opportunity came when they played truant from school and frequented the shopping precincts. It was in one of these precincts that they came into contact with two-year-old James Bulger. They held the boy's hand and led him on a long trek across Bootle in Merseyside. His body was later found on a railway track covered in bruises and coloured paint. He had been violently kicked, punched and stoned. Thompson and Venables were close friends but psychologists believe that it was Thompson who was the more dominant partner in the dyadic relationship. It was he who encouraged Venables to perform violence. It is clear that both boys were deviant and criminally inclined. They influenced each other to behave in deviant ways – perhaps ways that would not have been possible had each acted alone. They were certainly rejected by their peers and were considered as odd. It is not surprising therefore that the two became friends. Two rejected peers forming their own deviant dyadic friendship. Although both boys were incarcerated they were eventually released with new identities. As far as we are aware, since

(continued)

(continued)

being released, Thompson has not contravened the law. Not so for partner in crime Venables who was imprisoned in 2010 for using child pornography.

The importance of who one chooses to become friends with is clearly pertinent in this case example. Rejection by peers has a profound effect on social development. An interesting question, however, is why do peers reject specific individuals? Perhaps Thompson and Venables were rejected for their deviant and aggressive tendencies? Perhaps peer rejection is not responsible for antisocial pathways taken by some rejected peers (especially aggressive ones) – instead they already have these tendencies, which other peers pick up on and want to avoid.

It is interesting (as we have seen in Box 7.6) that two aggressive rejected children, Thompson and Venables, found they shared deviant values, mores, norms and attitudes and, together, exhibited antisocial behaviour. Although this was a dyadic friendship the same thing can happen among deviant peer groups only scaled up. Different peer groups will have their own values, mores, norms and attitudes that all members abide by. This is what gels members together and creates an **in-group mentality**. Members of the same group will show favouritism and an affinity towards each other. Other children and adolescents who are not part of the same group are perceived as outsiders or belonging to the out-group. Members of the out-group are often perceived in negative ways but the key perception is that they are very different from individuals comprising the in-group. This perception of difference is often at the heart of inter-group peer aggression resulting in intentions to harm members of the out-group. The impact of in-group/**out-group mentality** will be explored next within the context of prejudiced attitudes towards different ethnic groups and the impact of national attitudes on the development of social behaviour.

IN-GROUP/OUT-GROUP EFFECTS AMIDST A BACKDROP OF NATIONAL ATTITUDES

Peers who are part of a group conform to the norms and values set by its members. These norms and values can be conventional thereby reflecting mainstream cultural views. Alternatively, they can be of a deviant and criminal nature that contravenes the predominant views within society. The predominant views within society reflect nationally held attitudes and, as we have seen, the family is responsible for socialising their children to adopt socially appropriate behaviours (at least in the early years of development, see Chapter 6). According to Hirschi's Social Bond Theory (1969), conforming to the norms and attitudes of deviant and criminal peer groups occurs when such individuals have little attachment and commitment to mainstream society. This implies that children and adolescents who join these groups have been rejected by 'normal' peers. The **Social Bond Theory** appears to provide a good explanation for the social behaviour of these children and adolescents. It should be noted that the Social Bond Theory can also be applied to the development of positive social group norms. There are four facets to this theory:

1. attachment
2. commitment
3. involvement in activities
4. common value system to the attached society or subgroup fraction (see Box 7.7).

Box 7.7 Social Bond Theory in action

Why do certain individuals associate with delinquent peers? According to LaGrange and Raskin (1985), this might be because weak social bonds with parents and strong social bonds to deviant peers make individuals more likely to gravitate towards delinquent behaviour. Hindelang (1973) claimed it is attachment to delinquent peers rather than conformity to mainstream norms and values that increases the likelihood of behaving antisocially. These findings support the four facets of Hirschi's Social Bond Theory. Hirschi stated that the less attached a child or teenager is to mainstream society, the more motivation there is to join a deviant peer group. These children and teenagers will show their allegiance by adopting the norms and value system representative of the deviant peer group they have joined. This allegiance is further tested by being involved in the group's activities – and if this happens to be burgling residential property then this is what the new member will do. What about gang warfare? Is it the same process that drives members of different gangs towards fighting each other? The Social Bond Theory accounts for how children and teenagers can easily become drawn into joining deviant peers (especially if they are rejected by other peers) and acquiring the deviant norms and values, and behaving in ways reflecting these. Gang members see other members of different gangs as out-groups. Because members of out-groups are different and espouse alternative norms and values, they are often perceived as rivals. This, in turn, spurs on their aggressive behaviour towards each other. In-group members, however, are treated with respect.

The Social Bond Theory offers an explanation of how individuals, who feel unattached to mainstream society and rejected by their peers, explore deviant peer groups and join gangs.

The in-group/out-group divide plays an important role in how peers respond to one another. Muzafer Sherif (1954) demonstrated in his '**Robbers Cave**' study how boys could become so well integrated with fellow in-group members that they failed to notice their prejudice towards out-group members (see Box 7.8).

Box 7.8 Journey to prejudice by the Robbers Cave boys

In a ground-breaking social psychology experiment, 22 boys from white middle-class backgrounds attended a Boy Scouts of America camp located in the Robbers Cave State Park in Oklahoma. These boys were strangers to one another and were randomly assigned to one of two groups. The brief was to encourage boys from each group to bond with other members of their group. Bonding was helped by providing common goals requiring each member's cooperation, discussion, planning and execution of action. Each group was unaware of the others and developed its own group norms, which were cemented through joint activities such as swimming and hiking. Members of each group voted for a group name that was then stencilled onto their shirts ('The Rattlers' and 'The Eagles'). Competitive games were arranged by Sherif with the two groups engaging in activities such as tug-of-war and baseball. At the end of a host of competitions the winning group was awarded a trophy but there were medals awarded to individual winners also. The losing team failed to receive any prizes. During this competition phase, The Rattlers spoke of their victory and did things such as putting their flag on the pitch and making threats to anyone who removed their flag. Such verbal threats and name-calling were common but, as time went on, the prejudice shifted to activities such as burning the Rattlers' flag and, in return, the Rattlers' ransacking the

(continued)

(continued)

Eagles' cabin. Both groups became physically aggressive towards each other. During the cooling off period each boy had to list a series of traits depicting their group and the other group. The boys depicted their own in-group favourably but the out-group using discriminatory terms.

This study demonstrates the strong influence that being part of an in-group has on social behaviour, even when the individuals were randomly assigned to these groups. There is a sense of comradery with those perceived as the same but rivalry against those perceived as different.

It is astonishing how discriminatory people can behave towards those perceived to be in the out-group. Polish-born social psychologist Henri Tajfel (1963) found strong evidence that those perceived to be in the out-group can be punished even at the expense of a cost to the in-group. In his study children were given the option of either providing members of the in-group with 20 coins and the out-group with 15 or 15 coins to the in-group and eight to the out-group. Interestingly, children chose to give their in-group peers fewer coins just so that they could give out-group members even fewer. In choosing the second option, these children intentionally deprived out-group members of coins at the expense of possibly receiving more for their in-group peers.

In-group/out-group attitudes prevail within society as a whole. Quite often these attitudes are based on stereotypes or preconceived beliefs about individuals, different countries and ethnic groups. Stereotypes become a problem when they are based on negative, unfounded and biased prejudices that cause people to behave inappropriately and discriminately towards a selected few. Prejudicial attitudes by children towards others from different ethnic groups often reflect opinions harboured by their parents. This means that these individuals might see anyone different as a threat to their norms and values. In recent years there has been a large increase in the number of asylum seekers travelling from the Middle East to Europe in order to escape the atrocities of terrorism and warfare. This has led to a change in the population mix in countries such as France, Germany and the UK. During this period a rise in hate crimes has been documented in these Western European countries. It seems likely that here we are witnessing an extreme example of hostility towards a perceived out-group (see, for example, The Leicester Hate Crime Project, Chakraborti et al. 2014). The perception of negative attributions associated with the out-group can be exacerbated if this group is seen to be resistant to integration.

Despite evidence of ethnic integration, older generations tend to maintain their traditions and own norms, values, mores and attitudes alongside those of the host country (Banks 2008). For some people this difference is perceived as threatening to their own lifestyle and community demography, such that they discriminate against 'these newcomers'. It is important to stress that such prejudicial attitudes are not representative of national attitudes but rather of the few who express extreme **xenophobia** (i.e., a dislike of people from other cultures). Intervention programmes, developed to reduce prejudicial attitudes and discrimination, have been employed in schools to educate the young before they succumb to such attitudes. This will be considered next.

Intervention programmes to reduce prejudice

How do we address prejudicial attitudes towards different ethnic groups? There are three components to prejudice:

- the way we think about different ethnic people;
- the way we feel towards different ethnic people;
- the way we behave towards different ethnic people.

Therefore, when we consider intervention programmes to reduce prejudice towards children and adolescents of different ethnic backgrounds, these three components need to be addressed. Interestingly Becky Slack, correspondent for *The Guardian* in 2014, reported the following,

> *Our education system has a key role to play in the creation of social trust and community spirit. More and better teaching of history, culture and non-mainstream languages will enable our people to become more culturally aware, cohesive and tolerant . . . longer-term strategic planning around school places . . . integration of minorities would address challenges.*

Slack is commenting on the importance of educating children to understand other children of different ethnicity. In Box 7.9 we describe some of the educational programme initiatives to reduce prejudice towards children from ethnic minority groups.

Box 7.9   How can we reduce prejudicial attitudes to different ethnicities in schools?

Educational prejudice reduction programmes are based on the notion that contact with other ethnic minority children helps to break down barriers of misunderstanding and negative stereotypes. Through cooperative learning, discussions amongst peers and appropriate instruction embedded within a multi-cultural curriculum, it is possible to reduce prejudicial attitudes. One approach to this is to have peers involved in shared learning and discussions about tension-provoking issues that create divisions. For example, if John can openly discuss past historical events like slavery with Adrian, who is black and had ancestors who were enslaved, then this is a good start towards building bridges. By having such discussions between the two boys, it is hoped that the ability to perspective-take and empathise is increased. In 2013 a study conducted in Belfast, Northern Ireland, was part of the 'Promoting Reconciliation through a Shared Curriculum Experience Programme'. A two-year evaluation focused on the challenge teachers faced when it came to addressing controversial issues with children attending primary and secondary schools. With 840 children from 27 primary and secondary schools, teachers delivered 12 lessons over six months about Catholics and Protestants in a curriculum-only or a contact-and-curriculum basis. During these lessons the children learned about people from different religious backgrounds in a shared learning context. With teachers acting as facilitator, in-group attitudes were questioned, which allowed children to have more of an understanding and positive outlook towards those considered in the out-group. Souweidane (2012) conducted 'An Initial Test of an Intervention Designed to Help Youth Question Negative Ethnic Stereotypes' among 192 high school students. These students came from two schools that differed in their preponderance of Arab American and Jewish American students. The approach used was to challenge prejudicial stereotypes and develop perspective-taking by using media to discuss stereotypes. The results were promising in that there was improvement in levels of tolerance, more positive interactions and reduced negative stereotyping. There were also improvements to critical thinking that, according to Walsh (1988), is important in reducing prejudice. The discussions amongst peers helped them to confront and consider their negative ethnic stereotypes – such peer-based learning was effective in changing attitudes.

There have been many successful initiatives undertaken to reduce prejudicial attitudes towards ethnic minority groups. Success is mostly achieved when the young are targeted through education to nip negativity in the bud.

As we can see in Box 7.9, it is possible to reduce prejudicial attitudes towards ethnic minority groups by focusing on children and adolescents. When children and teenagers understand that individuals in the perceived out-group camp are really quite similar to themselves there is a shift towards positive attitudes and a reduction of negative stereotyping.

Summary

- Interpersonal relationships have the following dimensions: many types of inter-action, quality of the relationship, intimacy, reciprocity or complementarity, commitment and interpersonal perception. Different types of relationship will have these dimensions to varying degrees. As a relationship becomes more intimate, the complementarity of need fulfilment increases. Weiss (1974) outlined different types of relationship: attachment, social network, caregiving, kin, mentor and types providing feedback of worth.
- Peers share social characteristics such as age and status. They are perceived as equal. An attachment bond can occur between special peers referred to as friends. Special friendships are seen to form during 18–36 months but ones that develop after three years of age are longer lasting. Of friendships formed by one or two years, 50–70 per cent are more than temporary – some lasting beyond a year or more. At eight to 12 years being accepted by same-gender playmates is central, but by 13–16 friendship goals become complex as social skills mature. By 16–18 years teenagers expect emotional support from their friends.
- Five subgroups of common friendship patterns were found in children attending a summer school camp: subgroup 1 made friends easily but social ties were unstable; subgroup 2 made friends easily but maintained their existing friendships; subgroup 3 broke-up with their friends and failed to replace them; subgroup 4 had a number of stable friends and added new ones; and subgroup 5 had no friends. They linked personality traits to the type of friendships formed.
- Socialising children to accept society's norms and values is traditionally considered to be the role of the parents – hence the 'nurture assumption'. Judith Rich Harris, however, has challenged this view with her Group Socialisation Theory (GST). She argues that peers and friends have a significant influence on social behaviour.
- Support for Harris comes from parents being poor role models for how children should behave when interacting with their peers. If children imitated their parents' behaviour then the chances are they would become ostracised by their peers. To interact suc-cessfully with peers they need to behave like children – i.e., like their peers.
- Belsky (2005) considers there to be circumstances where some children are more socially influenced by their parents (i.e., generally during times of environmental stability) than others. During times of instability, however, he believes it pays chil-dren to be influenced by their peers. An appropriate adaptation to times of stability followed by instability would best suit a reproductive strategy whereby parents had a number of children (i.e., some of whom were more susceptible to parental influ-ence and others susceptible to peer influence).

- Sociometric techniques are informative methods of determining which peers are most popular and liked. This is carried out by asking children and adolescents to rate their peers using a number of dimensions such as friendliness or aggressiveness. Another way is to ask peers to nominate other peers for their likeability and desirability as a friend. By using the nomination approach it is possible to categorise peers according to peer status such as popular, average, neglected, controversial, rejected (aggressive rejected and non-aggressive rejected peers).
- Sociometric findings suggest that popular peers are rated as being highly socially competent and hence are well received by their peers. Unpopular peers are prevented from joining peer group activities. These peers are normally rejected and this can have detrimental effects on social and academic development.
- Members of groups tend to develop their own norms and values that impact on how they behave socially. Hirschi's Social Bond Theory of 1969 explains why members of a group are closely knit. In-group and out-group prejudice was highlighted in a study by Sherif (1954) called 'Robbers Cave'. Boys were divided into two groups and were unaware of each other until they went into competition. They developed their own norms and values and bonded well to the extent that their group (i.e., the in-group) was perceived as superior to the out-group.
- Attitudes towards out-group members can become so extreme that it can lead to xenophobia. We see this in prejudicial attitudes and negative stereotyping towards ethnic minority groups. This, however, can be remediated through educational programme initiatives. The ideology behind such initiatives is to heighten awareness of cultural differences (and similarities) so as to better understand one another. The best time for such initiatives during the lifespan is in childhood and adolescence.

Questions for discussion

- Sociometric methods are considered to be useful in understanding how peer relationships form. What do you think might be the strengths and weaknesses of these methods?
- What impact do sibling relationships have on social development?
- What causes peers to join specific groups?
- Critically consider the underlying mechanisms involved in in-group and out-group member behaviour.
- Critically evaluate the notion that xenophobia is in some way related to the pressures of our evolutionary past.
- Critically examine what determines which peers come to be regarded as popular, rejected or neglected. Consider your discussion by asking if there are real differences in appearance and behaviour of these peers.

Further reading

If you are interested in exploring the implications of peer rejection in more detail, look at:

- Bierman, K.L. (2004). *Peer Rejection: Developmental Processes and Intervention Strategies.* New York, NY: Guilford.

If you are interested in understanding in more detail how relationships among siblings, peers and friends link with the family and other socialising agents such as education, law and culture, look at:

- Bronfenbrenner, U. (2005). *Making Human Beings Human.* Thousand Oaks, *CA:* Sage Publications.

If you are interested in understanding in more detail children's early friendships and the significance this has on development and well-being, look at:

- Dunn, J. (2004). *Children's Friendships: The Beginnings of Intimacy.* Oxford: Blackwell.

If you are interested in why one expert considers that peers have more of a socialising impact on the way children behave than parents, look at:

- Harris, J.R. (2009). *The Nurture Assumption (2nd Edn).* New York, NY: Free Press.

Contents

Introduction 245

Self-concept and how
developmentalists study it 246

Concept of gender identity 258

Summary 264

Chapter 8

Development of self-concept

What this chapter will teach you

- The four interrelated facets of the 'self' – self-understanding, self-esteem, self-concept and self-regulation.
- How visual self-recognition and self-understanding develop in young children.
- How adolescents begin to label the 'self' using abstract and idealistic terms and then develop an advanced level of self-consciousness.
- The relationship between self-esteem and behaviour.
- The relationship between self-regulation and achievement.
- How gender is socially constructed and forms a part of our self-identity.

INTRODUCTION

Self-concept is used to describe how people think about themselves. Given there are many ways of thinking about ourselves, it is not surprising that the list of traits and categories capturing what it is to be 'me' or 'you' appears to be infinite. You might describe yourself as being female and perhaps add that you are, for example, 'on the short side'. These descriptions refer to physical attributes shared by the social category you consider yourself to be in. While physical attributes appear to be easy to pigeon-hole, behaviourally related traits are more profound and might cross over into other social categories. In order to decide which social categories best define us, we make cross-references to other people such as their dress-code, gender and hobby interests. Cross-referencing is one way of making evaluations about ourselves. In the psychological literature these evaluations are referred to as self-esteem and, as such, are influential in the perceptions developed regarding our self-concept. The developing self-concept is a dynamic process because it changes across the lifespan – these changes are, in part, age related. As a child develops so too does the brain and neural landscape. With increasing changes to brain and neural topography (such as new synaptic connections), cognition and socioemotional understanding can develop further. Cognitive and socioemotional development occur as a consequence of environmental factors (such as parental and peer influence) interacting with biological ones leading to neural maturity. As we saw in Chapters 6 and 7, in Bronfenbrenner's Ecosystem Model both the caregiver and peers are considered to be informal socialising agents. Informal socialising agents not only teach right from wrong and appropriate social behaviour, but also act as a guide for self-esteem and self-concept management. These two aspects of identity formation vary considerably throughout the lifespan but we will concentrate on infancy, childhood and adolescence. The main reason for focusing on these earlier periods of the lifespan is because it is during such periods that we see developmental strides – one of which is the formation of self-concept.

The development of self-concept begins early and, as we shall see later in this chapter, developmentalists have devised ingenious measures to test the point at which infants can recognise themselves (e.g., the 'mirror test'). Preschoolers have concrete understandings of the self, based primarily on observable attributes such as name and possessions (Keller et al. 1978). Eder (1989) found, however, that preschoolers can make statements about their emotions, attitudes and beliefs, as can be seen in two and a half year olds referring to being happy playing with their friends. Eder (1990) alludes to these insights as evidence of preschoolers' understanding their own psychological attributes and demonstrating a sense of self-control. Despite preschoolers obsessing over ownership of possessions, some researchers argue that this is not necessarily selfish behaviour but rather the beginnings of differentiating between self and others. Brownell and Carriger (1990) consider this as contributing towards social skill development as it allows preschoolers to practise the art of cooperation and to iron out problems that might occur during social interaction. In middle childhood (7 to 11) individuals begin to use psychological traits to describe themselves in ways often linked to self-esteem. According to Damon and Hart (1988), school children become aware of their strengths and weaknesses and readily inform us of what they are good at doing. Advances in cognition of the adolescent see further change during this period of the lifespan. Adolescence is a time when teenagers begin to develop an organised system where principles become more integrated. Self-statements tend to be positive and moral understanding more developed.

Different approaches to understanding the mind, such as the hypercognitive system, have contributed towards our comprehension of how our development of the self is monitored across the lifespan. An important aspect of self-concept is gender identity, which we considered briefly in Chapters 6 and 7. Given the importance placed by developmentalists on understanding gender we will concentrate on this topic as an example of self-concept. In order to do this we need to first understand what developmentalists mean when they refer to self-concept.

SELF-CONCEPT AND HOW DEVELOPMENTALISTS STUDY IT

It is difficult to separate self-concept from how it is researched by developmentalists. Our intention therefore is to discuss simultaneously self-concept and the studies designed to investigate it. Different facets of the self are interrelated. These facets of the 'self' help to promote personality integration and the essence of what it is to be 'me' or 'you'. In Box 8.1 we consider four facets important in the development of the self.

Plate 8.1 The faces of different selves. (Shutterstock 426978934.)

Box 8.1 Facets of self-development

The 'self' is made up of different interrelating components such as self-understanding, self-esteem, self-concept and self-regulation (Santrock 2008). While the self can be construed as the combination of all the traits of a person, this develops from self-understanding. Once this has been achieved then self-esteem helps to develop our self-concept. Importantly, by being able to self-regulate our social behaviour, we can control what we do without reliance on others. Self-understanding can, in part, be defined as the social roles and social categories that we belong to (Harter 2006). Mary, for example, who attends Art College, considers herself as a female student. Andrew, alternatively, sees himself as a budding male football player as he plays at county level. These can be considered as **global evaluations**. Self-understanding, according to Damon and Hart (1988), also serves to develop our very own identity. Dusek and McIntyre (2003) claim that self-esteem and self-concept are often used interchangeably but the two are different. Self-esteem, for example, involves making global evaluations about ourselves. We do this by drawing upon questions of our self-worth and the image we have of ourselves and portray to others (our self-image). By feeding stray cats, Anne's self-image, for example, is that of a caring person. Self-concept, according to Harter, relates to more specific evaluations of different domains of our life. These evaluations might relate, for example, to talents such as a world-class dancer, being academically advanced for one's age or possessing physical beauty. Hence, self-esteem refers to global evaluations while self-concept relies on making domain-specific evaluations. Self-regulation is akin to a monitoring system that keeps track of our feelings, thoughts and behaviours. We have goals that we would like to attain but, in order to do so, a checking system is required to ensure we achieve our aims appropriately. Self-regulation therefore provides us with a mechanism of self-control. Interestingly, Schunk and Zimmerman (2006) found that high-achieving students tend to be better at self-regulation than their low-achieving counterparts.

Concept of self, it would seem, is part of an integral system where we acquire understanding, make global and domain-specific evaluations and monitor our thoughts, feelings and behaviour. This is an ongoing process that changes with increasing age and the type of goals we set ourselves.

As we have seen in Box 8.1, self-understanding, self-esteem, self-concept and self-regulation are key factors involved in how we develop our personality and identity. These will be discussed in turn by drawing upon research findings from studies conducted by developmentalists.

Self-understanding

The level of **self-understanding** varies across the lifespan. It also becomes easier to research with increasing age due to cognitive development. Examining how well developed self-understanding is during infancy can be a challenge for researchers given the limitations of infant verbal communication (Thompson 2006a). Nevertheless, an ingenious but simple method used by researchers is to obtain a baseline of self-attentiveness and positive response to one's mirror image. Mascolo and Fischer (2007) noted that being attentive and positive towards one's image in the mirror develops at three months of age. Recognition of physical features during infancy, however, occurs much later than this at two years of age (Thompson 2006a). The '**mirror test**' has become a standard technique for ascertaining an infant's level of visual self-recognition. Here, the caregiver applies a dab of rouge to her infant's nose while the researcher observes and records the frequency with which the child touches its nose. The infant is then placed in front of a mirror while the researcher again records the number of times the nose is touched. Of particular interest to researchers is whether nose touching increases when the infant sees itself in the mirror. The level of nose touching is an important measure used in the mirror test as it allows researchers to gauge an infant's **visual self-recognition**. The idea behind this relates to there being self-understanding if infants try to wipe the rouge away. If they do, then this indicates that they perceive the rouge as a violation of their understanding of the self – rouge on the nose is not normally there.

According to Lewis and Brooks-Gunn (1979), infants less than a year old fail to recognise their own image in the mirror. They further found that for some infants between 15–18 months of age the onset of self-recognition has begun. It is not until two years of age that most of the infants pass the mirror test. These findings are similar to those found by Amsterdam in 1968 (see Figure 8.1).

Hence, Hart and Karmel (1996) believe that a rudimentary form of self-understanding (i.e., visual self-recognition), begins at 18 months. Courage, Edison and Howe (2004) tested infants aged between 15–23 months on three separate measures: visual self-recognition on

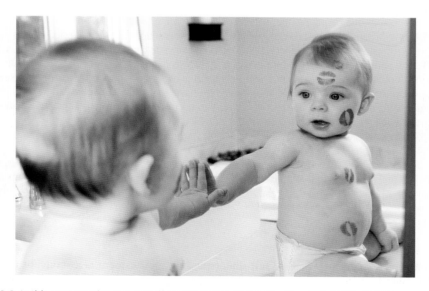

Plate 8.2 Is this me? Do I have red stuff on me all the time? (Shutterstock 375184510.)

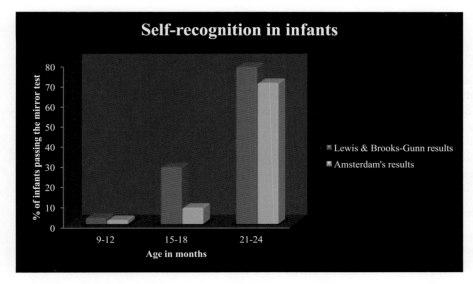

Figure 8.1 Comparison between the Lewis and Brooks-Gunn study findings and the Amsterdam study findings. (Adapted from Santrock 2008.)

the mirror test; reference to the 'self' using personal pronouns; and self-identification from photographs. Courage et al. showed that infants of this age group passed on all three measures. As far as Lewis (2005) is concerned, this demonstrates the formation of mental states of the self. Lewis suggests that 'they are objects in their own mental representation of the world' (p. 363). This is borne out by the references that three year olds use to label their appearance (e.g., me-nice), emotions (e.g., I like), possessions (e.g., toy mine) and the monitoring of ability (e.g., me do) (Bullock and Lutkenhaus 1990; Fasig 2000; Thompson 2006a).

By childhood great strides in self-understanding are achieved. In early childhood, children can communicate using verbal language (albeit limited). This cognitive development means that self-understanding can be investigated in other ways than by focusing on visual self-recognition. Researchers can now conduct interviews with children. According to Santrock (2008), five aspects of self-understanding have been obtained from interviewing young children (see Table 8.1).

By middle to late childhood self-understanding develops alongside a maturing social cognitive system (see Chapter 5). The development of social cognition enables children to consider other people's perspectives and to engage in taking turns of speaking and listening during verbal discourse. According to Santrock (2008), this lifespan period can be defined by five major changes occurring in the child (see Table 8.2).

Self-understanding during adolescence, not surprisingly, is profound given it is a time of much physical development and change. With further increases of cognitive/social cognitive maturity, teenagers are armed with more knowledge about who they are. Santrock (2008) outlines four defining aspects of self-understanding at this juncture of the lifespan (see Table 8.3).

As we have seen, self-understanding is important in developing a self-identity and personality. There are other important aspects aiding the development of the self. We will now turn to self-esteem (and self-concept).

Table 8.1 Aspects of young children's self-understanding.

Self, mind and body are blurred concepts	Children tend to perceive the self as an aspect of their body. They describe the self in terms of shape, colour and size.
Use of concrete descriptors	Children use concrete terms as a form of self-definition. Harter (2006) notes that preschool children might define themselves by referring to what they can do or which school they go to. Children of 4–5 years make use of socioemotional descriptors. In this case a child might refer to feeling scared about the monster in the cupboard.
Use of physical descriptors	Children use physical descriptions to differentiate their appearance from others. References to height and colour are often made.
Use of active descriptors	Children often refer to their activities to define themselves such as learning ballet or judo.
Overestimate the positive traits	According to Harter (2006), children overestimate what they know, feel and can do because they have not as yet acquired the ability to separate what they wish for from what is the case. Furthermore, they fail to differentiate the ideal self (i.e., what they would like to be) from the real self (i.e., what is the case). This stems from poor social comparison ability.

Table 8.2 Aspects of older children's self-understanding.

Psychological descriptors	Children of 8–11 years tend to define themselves using psychologically derived traits. This is a progression from the use of concrete descriptors seen in younger children. Hence children can perceive themselves as popular with, or rejected by, their peers, for example.
Use of social descriptors	Harter (2006) found that children consider themselves as part of a social network of friends and peers – often referring to different social groups.
Use of social comparison	Social comparisons are increasingly made to other children. Such comparisons revolve normally around different abilities such as writing or numerical skills. Children of 7 and above will use social comparisons as part of their self-definition.
Separation between real and ideal self	According to Harter (2006) differences between what can be done (real self) and held aspirations of what can be achieved (ideal self) are now understood.
Realistic sense of competency	Children develop a more realistic sense of their abilities due, in part, to increased social comparison and cognitive/social cognitive development.

Self-esteem (and self-concept)

As we have outlined earlier, self-esteem and self-concept are closely intertwined in definition by virtue of both involving evaluations of the self (see Box 8.1). Self-esteem provides us with global evaluations of ourselves. This is achieved through using information regarding our self-worth and self- and public-image portrayal (our **self-image**). By dancing in the streets

Table 8.3 Aspects of teenagers' self-understanding.

Labelling of the self in abstract and idealistic terms	Teenagers tend to use two levels of self-description. By using abstract descriptors they can consider themselves in terms of non-concrete traits such as, 'I am European'. Idealistic descriptors alternatively involve definitions of the self using references to how they would like to be perceived by others.
A new level of self-consciousness	Teenagers can be considered as egocentric due to their over-preoccupation and self-conscious awareness of, for example, what they look like or how popular they are.
Multitude of self-contradictions	As the self can be defined using a multitude of roles arising out of the various friend and peer relationships, these can cause contradiction and conflict. This, according to Harter (2006), contributes to an understanding that life is not straightforward and there are shades of grey. Nevertheless, teenagers will entertain different selves depending on the situation and context at a given period of time. Eventually these seemingly unstable selves become integrated creating an organised understanding of self. The development of real and ideal selves can cause conflict for teenagers. The notion of possible selves can create a timeline of what 'I can be in the future' or 'what I will try and avoid being' (Dunkel and Kerpelman 2004). Positive future possible selves will create a positive state of mind. Likewise, negative ones will encourage a negative state of mind.
Self-unification	Self-understanding becomes integrated as teenagers develop an organised view of the self by eliminating major inconsistencies previously entertained.

Mary's self-image, for example, is that of a carefree person. Marsh (1990) provides a hierarchical structure of **general self-esteem** (see Figure 8.2). In the case of self-concept, Harter argues that specific evaluations are made about various domains such as talent, academia, popularity with peers or physical prowess. Therefore, this implies that, while self-esteem refers to global evaluations, self-concept evaluations occur at a domain-specific level. Self-concept refers to the perceptions we hold regarding our characteristics and self-esteem is merely the emotional reaction to the evaluations of the self-concept. There is a debate as to whether the two are separate or unidimensional.

Rosenberg (1985) supports the view that self-esteem and self-concept are integrally related, providing a consistent perception of the self. Demetriou (1993), alternatively, argues in his **hypercognitive system** that the two are separate entities and organised in a hierarchical way – this is something we will return to later in this chapter. For our purposes here, we will adopt a unidimensional approach.

An interesting question we can ask is just how important is self-esteem in our everyday lives? Does having high self-esteem make us happy while low self-esteem causes depression and self-loathing? There is strong correlational evidence suggesting happiness comes with high self-esteem. But, for many of the other variables tested such as academic performance level, perceived physical attractiveness and sexual relationship formation, the correlations between one's own and other people's attributions of oneself are surprisingly low. This suggests that how we perceive ourselves varies somewhat from the ways in which other people do. The problem with researching self-esteem is the correlational design used to ascertain whether two variables are associated and progress in the same direction (see Chapter 2). This means that an association between self-esteem and agoraphobia, for example, lends itself

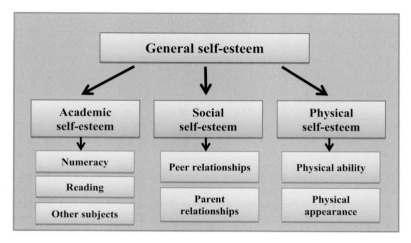

Figure 8.2 Hierarchical structure of general self-esteem.

to two possible interpretations and is a bit like the chicken and egg conundrum. Teenager Shyama might have low self-esteem because she finds it difficult to go out and see her friends or, because of her low self-esteem, she just fails to muster enough courage to go outside. Both are equally plausible explanations. Research findings indicate that high self-esteem correlates significantly with happiness (Baumeister et al. 2003). Furthermore, this supports findings from a cross-cultural study of 13,000 students from 49 universities spanning 31 countries (Diener and Diener 1995). They found a robust cross-cultural relationship between happiness and high self-esteem. Caution in interpreting this finding is needed as the same methodology problem arises. Correlational-based data should not be interpreted as providing causal associations. An adolescent might be happy due to positive reports from his sport's teacher.

Plate 8.3 Teacher's admiration for star footballer. (Shutterstock 274439507.)

Frequent positive reports might also help to increase his appraisal of self-esteem. In this case, his self-esteem and levels of happiness rise as a consequence of having favourable reports from the teacher in charge of sports. Hence, self-esteem and happiness are linked by virtue of positive feedback from a teacher.

Self-esteem is a dynamic process that changes across the lifespan. Harter (2006), for example, claims that young children tend to overestimate their ability and generally have inflated perceptions of themselves (this is for a number of factors such as appearance, talent and academia). This changes, however, when children reach the age of eight. At this age children develop a more realistic appraisal of what they are capable of achieving (Harter 2006). Robins et al. (2002) conducted a study of self-esteem evaluation using a five-point scale where '1' represented 'strongly disagree' and '5 strongly agree' to set statements. The study consisted of 326,641 individuals varying in age from 9 to 90 years of age. For our purposes the findings of interest in this study are the differences in self-esteem evaluations between children and adolescents (see Figure 8.3).

The drop in self-esteem scores during adolescence is unsurprising given that there are many physiological and psychological changes experienced by teenagers. These changes can alter and conflict with previously held evaluations of self-esteem. Puberty, for instance, initiates bodily configurational changes that might not reflect the self-image a teenager wishes friends and peers to perceive them as having. Despite this, there is research to suggest that most adolescents have a positive self-image. More than three quarters of teenagers in a cross-cultural study held a positive self-image (Offer et al. 1988). In the case of children below eight years, as we have seen, overestimating their self-esteem and self-image is highly likely. As Harter (2006) reports, however, children beyond eight are good at judging themselves and often form a positive profile that correlates well with other peers' evaluations – for example, Erika is very good at yodelling and so say all her peers.

One plausible explanation for why there is a sudden drop in self-esteem in adolescence pertains to what Graham (2005) refers to as '**empty praise**'. Empty praise in childhood can lead to overestimations of self-esteem. Graham argues that children often receive praise from their parents even though performance is mediocre at best. This praise is used as feedback in the development of the child's self-esteem. Progressing from school to college or

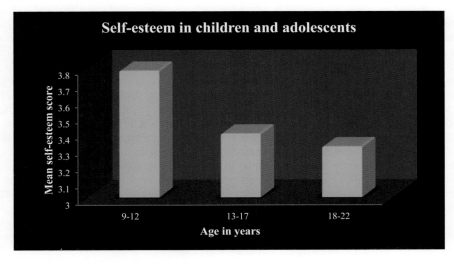

Figure 8.3 Levels of self-esteem in children and adolescents.

university, the now teenager might find the tasks set are challenging and difficult to pass or that there are, for example, many boys who are superior at scoring goals in a game of football. This realisation that they are not quite as good as mum or dad made out can cause self-esteem to fall. Interestingly, levels of self-esteem appear to vary cross-culturally. In two cross-cultural studies it was shown that teenagers from the US have higher reported levels of self-esteem than those from Japan, Germany and Russia (Little et al. 1995; Little et al. 2003). But it was the fact that teenagers in the US showed incongruences between self-esteem and performance levels that was important here and supported the notion of 'empty praise'. Unlike their adolescent counterparts from Japan, Germany and Russia, teenagers in the US showed a mismatch between self-esteem and actual ability. For teenagers from Japan, Germany and Russia their self-esteem evaluations were more realistic and robustly correlated with school performance – suggesting a socialisation package devoid of empty praise (Little et al. 1995; 2003). Despite the fall in self-esteem during adolescence (see Figure 8.3), Powers et al. (1989) claim that self-esteem rises for most teenagers as they develop pride in their achievements and self-confidence. According to Offer et al. (1988), it is a time of optimism.

It has been suggested that high self-esteem often leads to happiness and good academic performance while low self-esteem can predict a pathway to depression and criminality. How empirically supported this bifurcation actually is has been examined by numerous researchers. One approach has been to increase the self-esteem of children and teenagers who have low self-evaluations (see Box 8.2).

Box 8.2   Ways of improving the self-esteem of our children

Increasing the self-esteem of children and teenagers is assumed to improve their life outcomes such that they obtain greater academic success and are mentally healthier. But to do this it is important that the causes of low self-esteem and the areas of competency are identified: providing social approval; providing emotional support; learning to take responsibility and control over the direction of one's self-esteem; set aims for achievement; and establish optimal strategies of coping. Without due attention to these factors, the lessons for self-esteem improvement become less effective. Harter (1990) claims the early interventions of the 1970s and 1980s failed because they did not consider the causes of self-esteem depreciation. Interventions should therefore include space for reflecting on the causes of low self-esteem but also the areas of ability. Emotional support is not always forthcoming from the parents for a variety of reasons including neglect, so it is important to receive this from another source. Often this can be obtained from a teacher or mentor who encourages the child or teenager to do well. Failing this, an adult who is close to the child or teenager such as a grandparent or friendly neighbour can provide the emotional crutch and incentive needed in order to improve self-esteem. Having good friends and peers can also be a help. Encouragement should be given to take responsibility for developing one's self-esteem by developing a sense of self-confidence. Baumeister et al. (2003) claim that achievement through reasonable goal setting will also improve self-esteem. Bednar et al. (1995) point out that facing up to one's problems rather than avoiding them is more effective in the long term in the development of self-esteem. By facing challenges children and teenagers learn effective coping strategies for dealing successfully with potentially stressful situations.

The five outlined factors considered necessary for devising successful interventions makes perfect sense. It is no good teaching children and teenagers ways of improving their self-esteem without getting to grips with why it is low in the first place.

It is interesting that there is a common assumption that high self-esteem promotes good performance at school. Is this true, however? The findings do not suggest this is the case, as was eloquently expressed by Baumeister et al. (2003) who found, 'only modest correlations between school performance and self-esteem, and these correlations do not indicate that high self-esteem causes good performance' (p. 1).

In their article in *Scientific American*, 'Exploding the self-esteem myth', Baumeister et al. (2005) present empirical evidence showing that high self-esteem is not necessarily the answer to personal success. They responded to the assumptions of the 1980s that raising the self-esteem of teenagers reduces criminality, under-achievement, drug abuse and unplanned pregnancies – views espoused by State Assemblyman John Vasconcellos. Baumeister et al. (2005) are critical of the ways in which self-esteem data are collected. The commonly adopted method involves asking participants to disclose information concerning how they feel about themselves. Researchers, for example, commonly find robust links between physical attractiveness and ratings of self-esteem. For Baumeister et al. (2005) this positive link could have more than one causal effect. Those who are physically attractive receive positive treatment by others such that a 'halo effect' (i.e., good-looking people must have many other positive traits) is occurring. Baumeister et al. (2005) also argue, however, that those high on self-esteem could be singing their own praises including their physical appearance.

Diener et al. (1995) obtained self-esteem ratings from participants in their study who were also photographed. These photographs were distributed to a panel of judges who rated them for physical attractiveness. When the scores for the photographs were compared with their corresponding self-esteem ratings no significant correlation was found. This suggests that evaluations of physical attractiveness are independent of self-esteem per se. It is interesting to note that those who rated themselves highly for attractiveness also considered themselves to have boundless self-esteem. These findings suggest that people like to rate themselves in a positive light. But what of those with low self-esteem? Baumeister et al. (2005) suggest a floccinaucinihilipilification ('the habit of estimating things as worthless') effect is occurring here. This refers to individuals who consistently make evaluations of themselves and everyone and everything as worthless or negative. Floccinaucinihilipilification implies that individuals who are negative about themselves will continue this negativity into all aspects of their lives and, in so doing, provide researchers with misleading information that low self-esteem equates with disagreeable consequences. Another assumption from the self-esteem literature is that high self-esteem promotes good academic performance and interpersonal skills (see Box 8.3).

Box 8.3   High self-esteem and all is good?

Pottebaum et al. (1986) were interested in whether we can predict future academic performance based on levels of self-esteem. They tested over 23,000 high school teenagers attending the 10th grade (15 years of age) and repeated this procedure for 17 year olds in the 12th grade. Self-esteem failed to be an effective predictor for academic performance and achievement. Other studies like this one have uncovered similar findings. This implies that an injection of self-esteem contributes little to increasing academic performance levels and, in some cases, it can be detrimental. These findings generalise to the workplace and later employment in that positive self-promotion does not lead to successful careers. In a study by Buhrmester et al. (1988) it was shown that self-ratings for four of five interpersonal skills measured

(continued)

(continued)

differed from ratings provided by room-mates. Only for one interpersonal skill was there a significant correlation with high self-esteem and this was the ability to initiate relationships. This suggests that high self-esteem provides an individual with the impetus to make the first move. Other researchers such as Bishop and Inderbitzen-Nolan (1995) found no correlation between self-esteem and popularity rankings amongst the sample of 542 fourteen year olds (in the ninth grade). This dispelled the assumption that popular children are high in self-esteem and those of low self-esteem have poor social interactions with others. Another assumption made is that low self-esteem encourages aggressive behaviour. Baumeister et al.'s (1996) review of studies examining the relationship between self-esteem and aggression led to the conclusion that it is not individuals with low self-esteem who tend to be transgressors but rather those who have too much self-esteem. Using an indirect measure of self-esteem, Olweus (1986) focused on personality characteristics such as anxiety and insecurities of bullies at school. The consensus view was that bullies portray themselves as aggressive and tough but inside they are plagued with anxiety and insecurity. Olweus dispelled this outdated assumption by finding that bullies have very few anxieties and insecurities. In fact, the bullies studied by Olweus were more assertive and sure of themselves – hence indirectly informing us that they were certainly not short of self-esteem. It appears that creating high self-esteem in individuals is not the panacea for reducing aggressive and violent behaviour.

The evidence paints a picture about high self-esteem that contradicts a commonly held assumption – that it promotes positivity and improves our abilities. If, anything, high self-esteem can contribute towards an inflated perception of the self and create individuals who are too sure of themselves leading to a desire to control and dominate those they feel are less confident.

As we can see in Box 8.3, high self-esteem does not necessarily promote positive outcomes and appropriate behaviours. When it comes to self-esteem, it appears that either too little or too much can be a bad thing.

The perceptions we have of our attributes are encapsulated within our self-concept. These can be changed by our emotional responses directed at our beliefs about ourselves. Hence self-esteem can influence our self-concept just as our self-concept impacts on our self-esteem. The interplay between self-concept and self-esteem, and self-understanding, can be controlled through the process of self-regulation. Self-regulation involves the cognitive monitoring of the way we think, feel and behave as we strive to fulfil our goals. Self-regulation will be considered next.

Self-regulation

Self-regulation is about monitoring our feelings, thoughts and behaviours using self-generated control mechanisms. The monitoring of how we think, feel and behave enables us to achieve our goals. Monitoring can be considered as a mechanism of providing feedback on how well we are doing in accomplishing our goals. If we go out for a three-course dinner every day then achieving a goal of losing weight is likely to be compromised. Self-regulation therefore involves the interplay between monitoring and controlling our thoughts, feelings and behaviours. Schunk and Zimmerman (2006) found that individuals who consistently self-regulated their behaviours achieved their goals more readily than those incapable of monitoring and controlling what they did. This extended into the classroom context where high achievers engaged frequently in self-regulation and low achievers failed to do so. This means that high achievers are more attuned with their goals and adopt methods of achieving them (Schunk and Zimmerman 2006).

The focus of self-regulation differs throughout the lifespan. The main focus for infants is emotional regulation (see Chapter 3). Kopp (1987) claims infants between 12–18 months self-regulate their behaviours, feelings and thoughts by feedback from their caregiver. This process enables infants to comply with caregiver requests and to learn to behave appropriately. Between the ages of two and three years, children internalise the expectations of the caregiver such that they no longer require external monitoring. This means that an understanding of the rules is beginning to take shape. Children still have a long way to go in terms of self-regulation. They can be unaware of the dangers imposed by risk-taking behaviours such as playing near a cliff-top or failing to apply the 'Green Cross Code'. They also find it difficult to delay their gratification as was seen in the 'marshmallow' experiment by Walter Mischel and co-workers in 1972 (see Chapter 2). Preschool children become increasingly better at self-regulation and can often avoid distracting behaviours that would take them away from their goals (Thompson 2006b). According to Laible and Thompson (2007), children of middle to late childhood become self-disciplined at managing their feelings, thoughts and behaviours, thereby increasing social competency. Increased self-regulation, according to Durston et al. (2006), is due to developmental advances in prefrontal cortex activation. This prefrontal cortex activation promotes more effective self-regulation and self-control. In adolescence there is further brain development that improves cognition, therefore enabling teenagers to exert more control and balance of the equation between delayed gratification to achieve long-term goals and immediate gratification to fulfil 'here and now' goals. Mary, for example, decides to stay at home and study for future exams rather than to go clubbing with her friends.

Self-regulation, in terms of monitoring and controlling behaviour, has been incorporated into a **mind-mapping theory** introduced by Demetriou (1993). This theory is designed to provide an architectural account of how the mind works. It is a complicated theory with many levels, systems and principles describing how information is processed. Of relevance to our discussion of the self, however, is the hypercognitive system.

Hypercognitive system

The term 'hypercognitive' refers to 'higher than or going beyond'. When Demetriou (1993) introduced the hypercognitive system, he outlined two levels of knowing. The first level of knowing involves the processing of input from the environment by domain-specific mental processing structures. This means that learning occurs as a consequence of independent specialised structures in the brain that selectively process information. It is because these brain structures process information within their remit only that they are referred to as domain-specific. The second level of knowing involves the output instructions of the input (i.e., information) processed by domain-specific processing structures. This means therefore that information processed from the first level is used as a basis for instructing what we should do next. It is analogous to a global self-instruction guidance system – hence hypercognitive (see Figure 8.4).

The hypercognitive system comprises self-awareness and self-regulation, as well as knowledge and strategies for self-regulation. It organises, guides and controls behaviours – a bit like a monitoring system or a programme in a computer. Given the nature of what the hypercognitive system does, it has a working hypercognitive component allowing for an on-line constant monitoring system. **Working hypercognition** enables people to monitor their thoughts and to regulate these thoughts in response to their current goals. There is also **long-term hypercognition**. This analyses the products of working hypercognition using learned knowledge and rules. There are three types of knowledge but only one is relevant to our discussion of the self – the cognitive self-image. The cognitive self-image contains representations that we have of ourselves like, for example, 'I am good at solving Sudoku

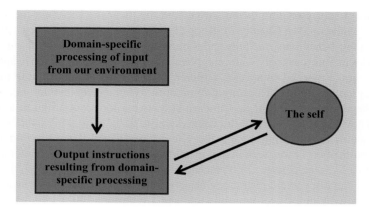

Figure 8.4 The relationship between levels one and two of the hypercognitive system.

problems' or 'I find mental arithmetic taxing'. As we discussed previously, these self-images can change with age as our global self-concept is being constantly revised. Our global self-concept comprises different representations such as academic, social and the physical self (see Figure 8.2), which subdivide further still. These undergo modification as we age and become more realistic such that children who overestimate how good they are at certain activities will eventually have a reality-check when they encounter other children who are better than they are. The emotional reaction to this (i.e., self-esteem) might also take a hit as older children receive more feedback from social referencing. The hypercognitive system is an informative way of understanding how self-regulation might operate.

The relationship between self-understanding, self-concept and self-esteem is very much influenced by factors such as age (as we have already seen) and gender identity. It is the concept of gender identity that we will consider next in relation to self-concept and how this influences our social behaviour.

CONCEPT OF GENDER IDENTITY

Gender is one example of a social category that we become aware of early on in our development. Gender is a culturally defined social category used to distinguish between femininity and masculinity. This is not to be confused with biologically driven sex divisions of female and male. Individuals are born female or male (with the exception of hermaphrodites who are born with ambiguous genitalia) but become feminine or masculine through complex developmental processes occurring early on in the lifespan. In Chapter 6 we considered how a gender identity develops and the theoretical approaches accounting for how this occurs (see Box 6.5). In this chapter the intention is to consider the other aspects of gender-concept formation that influence social behaviour. One such area is the development of gender typing. Gender typing can only occur once a child has figured out that she is a girl or he is a boy. Once this has been established the child is likely to be receptive to further socialisation processes. Gender role models portraying socially acceptable feminine and masculine behaviours provide children with gender-based beliefs. These gender-based beliefs are based on **gender stereotypes**. Gender stereotypes are widely held beliefs about female and male traits. One way of examining gender stereotypes is to present individuals with adjectives commonly associated with males and females who then categorise them accordingly. Williams and Bennett (1975) studied this by asking a large group of individuals to categorise adjectives

Plate 8.4 A girl's and boy's stereotype of what it is to be mum and dad. (Shutterstock 195221240.)

as either female or male. They found that 90 per cent of the adjectives were categorised as typically female or male. There was strong agreement across participants suggesting a robust effect of socialisation. Ruble (1983) repeated this exercise and found adjectives of ability, personality and social behaviour typically describing female and male stereotypes (see Box 8.4). As this study was conducted during the 1980s some of these categorisations are likely to be out-of-date in 21st-century Western cultures.

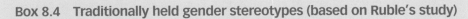

Box 8.4   Traditionally held gender stereotypes (based on Ruble's study)

Plate 8.5 Stereotype of a boy. (Shutterstock 321791933.)

Plate 8.6 Stereotype of a girl. (Shutterstock 265780853.)

(continued)

(continued)

active	aware of others' feelings
adventurous	considerate
aggressive	creative
ambitious	cries easily
competitive	devotes self to others
dominant	emotional
independent	enjoys music and art
leadership qualities	excitable in crisis
likes maths and science	expresses tender feelings
makes decisions easily	feelings hurt
mechanical aptitude	gentle
not easily influenced	home oriented
outspoken	kind
persistent	likes children
self-confident	neat
skilled in business	needs approval
stands up under pressure	tactful
takes a stand	understanding

Ruble et al. (2006) discuss how, within cultures, there tends to be agreement as to what constitutes appropriate gender-role behaviour. Western ideals of masculinity conform to stereotypes of men controlling their surroundings, of being dominant, independent and competitive across many spheres of everyday life. Females are still perceived as providing emotional support to family members, passive and non-aggressive, and emotionally laden during stressful situations. The gender divide is still apparent in the workplace as demonstrated by adult and children occupational stereotypes of nurses and doctors for example ('female' and 'male' posts respectively). Variations of gender-role behaviour occur across cultures also. In countries such as Saudi Arabia, Iraq and Taiwan gender-role divisions are particularly inflexible and adhere to traditional perceptions of how woman and men are expected to behave. Such rigidity of gender-role behaviour occurs less in the West. According to Leaper et al. (1999), children of American families are socialised more flexibly for gender-role behaviour and, as a consequence, develop less rigid gender stereotypes. Basow (1992) describes how in American families girls are now socialised to be assertive and less timid while boys are socialised to be more emotionally expressive.

An important question is do children share these **gender-role stereotypes** and, if so, when do they develop? Kuhn et al. (1978) studied two and a half year olds. They found that, even by this age, children entertain different expectations for boys and girls. Moreover, they found some agreement among boys and girls as to how the genders differed. Boys and girls both agreed that girls like to play with dolls, help their mother, cook, clean, talk, refrain from

Plate 8.7 Father showing his emotional side. (Shutterstock 222895396.)

hitting others and confess to needing help. There was agreement again between boys and girls regarding their views about boys – boys like to play with cars, help their father, build things, and are quick to remind you that they can hit you. The positive traits that each gender was perceived as having included: girls look nice, they like to give kisses and avoid fighting; boys are hard workers. The negative traits aimed at the opposite gender included: girls perceive boys as mean and weak and like to fight; boys perceive girls as being slow and crybabies. During this age in the lifespan each gender perceives the opposite gender as negative but its own as positive (analogous to out-group and in-group attitudes – see Chapter 7). Children at kindergarten (five year olds) had similar gender-role stereotypes to fourth and fifth graders (nine and ten year olds) in the US, England and Ireland (Best et al. 1977). Best et al. also found that the male stereotype developed earlier and was more robust than the female stereotype. There was more agreement over the male stereotype, which raises the question of why should this be the case? One possibility is that the female role is more flexible and diverse than that seen for males – females after all can be child bearers, mothers, cooks, house cleaners as well as working wives.

Although gender-role stereotypes are socially defined, researchers have examined whether they are founded on true differences between males and females. Empirical support for some of these stereotypes can be seen in the preferences children have at an early age (see Box 8.5 and Figure 8.5). Whether gender-role stereotypes are valid is neither here nor there because what is important is the extent to which people believe they are true and use them. These gender-role stereotypes are so inherently engrained through socialisation that we behave according to their predicted expectations. This influences the way we behave and how we socially interact with the same and the opposite gender. The gender-role stereotype profile becomes a fixture of how we want to behave. This suggests that our social behaviour is nurture-driven. But is it? What are the real differences between males and females (see Box 8.6)?

Box 8.5   Some stereotypes reflect preferences shown by young children

When we consider gender differences we examine the actual disparities between males and females on variables such as behaviour and ability. Eagly (1995) suggests that, based on statistical findings from meta-analyses (i.e., the pooling of findings of studies researching the same variables), there are genuine behavioural differences across the sexes. This implies that gender-role stereotypes are not entirely inaccurate. Eagly and Wood (1999) further claim that evolved behavioural differences interact with environmental factors that cue sex-typed responses. We must be cautious, however, as there are fewer differences than there are similarities and, where there are differences, the size effect is small. Fagot (1974) found differences between boys and girls aged between two and three years in their preferences for specific types of toy. Fagot and Leinbach (1989) found that the onset of gender-typed play occurs by 28 months. This suggests they have developed gender-appropriate preferences before playing with their same-gendered peers. Serbin et al. (2001) confirmed that there are differences in preference choices for toys, with girls being far more inclined to choose dolls than boys. They found this preference for dolls by girls can be seen as early as one year of age (see Figure 8.5). This difference in preference for toys increased further by a year and a half to two years of age. Moreover, by this age boys were showing heightened interest in toys that moved such as trucks and cars. These children were expressing a preference for toys considered to be gender-appropriate. Research by Baron-Cohen (2003) and Stannage and Taylor (2012) suggest that boys are more likely to be 'systemisers' and girls to be 'empathisers' (see Chapter 5). Systemisers are interested in how things work – the mechanics of objects such as fire-engines. Empathisers, alternatively, are more focused on caring and nurturing behaviours such as feeding dolls. Deloache et al. (2007) describe boys as developing intense interest in specific gender-appropriate toys much more than girls do, which continues into early adolescence. The choice of playmate in three- to four-year-old preschoolers demonstrates a same-gender preference. Furthermore, choices for bedroom décor were also consistent with gender-role stereotypes (Rheingold and Cook 1975). Although a survey found that 50 per cent of women and girls described themselves as tomboys by showing a distinct liking for male pursuits and activities (Morgan 1998), at puberty they reverted to traditionally feminine pursuits and social behaviour (McHale et al. 2004).

Toy preference is a good indicator of gender-role stereotype acquisition. Gender-appropriate toy preferences develop despite parental socialisation input, which suggests that there are both nature and nurture forces operating in the formation of gender stereotypes.

Box 8.6   Real differences between males and females?

Researchers have found real differences between males and females in four main domains: cognition, socioemotional development, physical/neurological development and vulnerability to atypical development. All four domains influence the way we develop and make use of our social skills. Girls develop physically and neurologically before boys – they tend to walk earlier and begin puberty at an earlier age. As boys increase in age they develop stronger muscles enabling them to perform better in sports activities. In terms of influencing social behaviour, girls are likely to be more mature than boys at an earlier age. Boys, alternatively, are likely to show more physical prowess, which could be a talking point during social interactions. Vulnerability to atypical development such as physical and cognitive disabilities (e.g., reading and speech-related problems) puts boys at more risk than girls and is likely to have profound effects on social development. In relation to cognition, females exhibit small but robust superiority for verbal ability. Speech onset is earlier in girls who tend to have extensive vocabularies and higher reading scores

(Halpern 2000). Moreover, girls have faster access to information (semantic in particular) stored in long-term memory. Boys out-perform girls in geometry (Halpern 2004; Hyde 2005). This gender gap increases further from the age of 12. From 10 onwards boys score higher on visual-spatial skills (Voyer et al. 1995). This genuine advantage shown by males is reflected in the stereotype of females being poor map readers. Females find mental rotation tasks (e.g., moving an image mentally from one rotation to another) challenging (Choi and Silverman 2003; Liben 1991). Another domain where there are genuine differences between males and females is socioemotional development. Coie and Dodge (1997) found males to be more physically and verbally aggressive than females. This begins early on in childhood with boys tending to be both aggressors and victims of aggressive acts. Females engage in more covert and relational aggression such as ignoring and undermining other peers (Crick and Rose 2000). Females tend to be more sensitive to subtle nonverbal cues than males (McClure 2000), which can be a blessing in situations of potential conflict. There is a host of subtle personality differences between the genders. Males, for example, score higher on assessments of risk-taking behaviour (Byrnes et al. 1999), assertiveness and global self-esteem (Costa et al. 2001). Females score higher on anxiety and agreeableness (Costa et al. 2001). Due to their higher scores on agreeableness, girls comply more readily to adult demands. They also show nurturing behaviours to younger children. Males have more permissive attitudes towards casual sex.

We should bear in mind that, when considering such differences between the genders, we are dealing with broad group means. As we will see in Chapter 12, individual differences are much larger than group differences. Moreover, all these differences have underlying biological causes but are exaggerated by socialisation processes and gender-role stereotypes. This provides us with an insight into the nature-driven aspects of social behaviour.

In Box 8.6 we can see that there are some genuine nature-driven differences between males and females. These differences are usually cemented further by nurture-driven processes such as differential treatment by parents, extended family members and peers (see Chapters 6 and 7). While there are gender differences, many of the gender-role stereotypes fail to have empirical support.

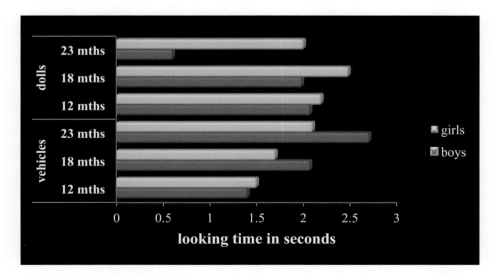

Figure 8.5 Toy preferences begin as early as one year: girls spend more time looking at dolls while boys spend more time looking at vehicles.

Self-concept, and aspects of it such as gender identity, influences how we perceive ourselves, which, in turn, shape our social skills set. Our self-concept and social development are intertwined through a continual process of self-regulation. Perceiving ourselves negatively might impede our ability to socially interact effectively with others. Alternatively, a positive self-concept might encourage favourable social interactions with our peers.

Summary

- There are four different interrelated facets of the 'self'. These four facets include self-understanding, self-esteem, self-concept and self-regulation. Self-understanding derives from social roles and categories we consider ourselves to be a part of. Self-understanding helps us to develop our own self-identity. Self-concept relates to specific evaluations of the various domains of our life while self-esteem consists of global evaluations of ourselves using self-worth and self-image. Self-regulation is a process of monitoring and up-dating our feelings, thoughts and behaviours.
- Researching self-understanding in very young infants is a challenging task. This is because their verbal communication has yet to develop, which is why developmentalists have designed experiments using nonverbal measures of response. The most widely used is that of the 'mirror test'. The infant has a spot of rouge applied to the nose and is observed to see how often the infant touches its nose. Thompson (2006a) places the ability of infants to recognise their physical features at two years. The mirror test allows researchers to gauge when infants attain visual self-recognition. Adolescents can label the 'self' using abstract and idealistic terms and have a more advanced level of self-consciousness.
- A hierarchical structure of general self-esteem developed by Marsh (1990) provides a breakdown of the various areas of self-esteem. While some researchers would consider this as part of self-concept, others categorise it as a part of self-esteem. According to Marsh there are three components to general self-esteem: academic, social and physical self-esteem. All three interact to influence our social behaviour but social self-esteem is concerned with peer and parent relationships, hence taking a more direct route in influencing our social interactions with others.
- Self-esteem is higher in children than it is for many adolescents. This drop has been explained as arising from the phenomenon of 'empty praise' in childhood; parents praising their children even when it is undeserved and performance is mediocre. Children come to realise that they have overestimated their abilities when they move on to colleges and universities, at which point self-referencing with others becomes heightened.
- Self-regulation involves the interplay between monitoring and controlling our thoughts, feelings and behaviours. High achievers tend to engage in frequent self-regulation, which keeps them more attuned with their goals. Low achievers fail to do this. Self-regulation in its format varies throughout the lifespan. For infants, the self-regulation of emotions is important at this stage in the lifespan. Being able to use feedback from the caregiver helps infants to develop and comply with their caregiver's requests and rules. These requests and rules become internalised by two to three years of age so that children require fewer reminders of how to behave.
- Self-regulation, in terms of monitoring and controlling processes, has been incorporated into Demetriou's (1993) architectural account of how the mind works. In particular the hypercognitive system is of relevance to our understanding of how the

'self' is developed. There are two systems involved here: the first involves domain-specific mental processing structures and the second the output instructions derived from domain-specific processing. The hypercognitive system comprises of self-awareness and self-regulation as well as knowledge and strategies for self-regulation. Demetriou refers to a working hypercognitive component that is continually monitoring and regulating our thoughts in the context of our current goals. Long-term hypercognition analyses the outcome of working hypercognition using knowledge and rules stored in our memory. Knowledge in the form of cognitive self-image provides us with the existing representations we have of ourselves (e.g., I'm good at singing). These can change throughout the lifespan.

- Gender is an important social category that we become aware of very early on in our development. Gender is a part of our self-identity – how we consider ourselves. Hence we can consider ourselves as masculine or feminine. Gender is socially defined and not to be confused with biologically driven sex categories of female and male. Gender-concept formation is influenced by gender typing but only once the child has established he is a boy or she is a girl.
- Two and a half year olds entertain different expectations for boys and girls. They also agree on how boys and girls differ. They agree on what are gender-appropriate toys and on the gender-role behaviours exhibited by boys and girls. Eagly (1995) concludes that there are some genuine behavioural differences between the genders.
- There are real differences between females and males in four domains: cognition, socioemotional development, physical/neurological development and atypical developmental vulnerability. Halpern (2000) found that girls have superior verbal ability. Boys out-perform girls on geometry. Girls are poor at mental rotation tasks. Boys are more physically and verbally aggressive than girls. Girls are more sensitive to subtle nonverbal cues. Boys score higher on assertiveness and self-esteem and on risk-taking behaviour. Girls score higher on agreeableness and anxiety.
- Despite some differences in cognitive and socioemotional development, males and females share more similarities.

Questions for discussion

1. Explain how the mirror test is used as a measure of self-recognition and how this, in turn, helps us to gain some insight into self-understanding.
2. Present arguments both for and against the notion that self-concept and self-esteem are really the same thing.
3. Discuss both the strengths and weaknesses of the notion that gender-role stereotypes reflect real life.
4. Critically examine why self-esteem appears to be one important factor predicting life success. You might want to consider in your answer the function of self-esteem in the development of individuality.
5. Critically discuss the notion that gender-role stereotypes are derived from innate predispositions.
6. Critically review the contribution of a hypercognitive system to help guide the development of the 'self'.

Further reading

If you are interested in exploring the advantages and disadvantages of having too little and too much self-esteem, look at:

- Baumeister, R.F., Campbell, J.D., Krueger, J.I. and Vohs, K.D. (2005). Exploding the self-esteem myth. *Scientific American,* 292(1), 70–7.

If you are interested in exploring how self-understanding serves to develop our own identity, look at the classic work of:

- Damon, W. and Hart, D. (1988). *Self-understanding in Childhood and Adolescence.* New York: Cambridge University Press.

If you are interested in understanding how self-concept is monitored and developed within the architecture of the mind, look at:

- Demetriou, A. and Kazi, S. (2013). *Unity and Modularity in the Mind and the Self: Studies on the Relationships Between Self-awareness, Personality, and Intellectual Development from Childhood to Adolescence.* London: Routledge, Taylor and Francis Group.

If you are interested in exploring a biosocial account of sex differences/similarities and how these impact on self-development, look at:

- Wood, W. and Eagly, A.H. (2012). Biosocial construction of sex differences and similarities in behaviour. In J.M. Olson and M.P. Zanna (eds). *Advances in Experimental Social Psychology* (Vol. 46, pp. 55–123). London, UK: Elsevier.

Contents

Introduction   269

Different understandings of play   270

What is play?   277

Play enhances social skill development   281

The group dynamics of play and
social networking   287

Summary   294

Chapter 9

Social development through play

What this chapter will teach you

- How many psychologists, including Freud, Erikson, Piaget and Vygotsky, have all considered the functional significance of play.
- How ethologists such as Eibl-Eibesfeldt perceive play as providing young animals (including humans) with a vehicle from which to acquire information through exploration.
- There are a number of classification systems for different forms of play.
- Different types of play help in the development of specific skills, such as solving puzzles, aiding cognitive abilities.
- Learning the rules of a game aids social and moral development.
- How social dominance hierarchies develop within play groups and cliques.

INTRODUCTION

Play is often considered a trivial activity that children engage in, either alone or with other peers. The fact that play is considered a trivial activity may well reflect the commonly held belief that children just engage in play for the fun of it; that it has no obvious benefit except to provide a sense of happiness. Researchers, however, have unpacked a multitude of functions that play serves for the developing child. Play, for example, develops cognitive skills that may have been selected for in our evolutionary history. The main focus of this chapter will be on the relationship between play and the development of interactive social skills and communication with other children (both verbally and nonverbally). This extends to the group dynamics involved in group play observed in children and the extensive social networking activities pursued by adolescents. What attracts children to join particular play groups and adolescents to seek specific types of social networks will be considered in terms of similarity of socialisation experiences.

Play is a topic that has received considerable attention from many psychologists in the 19th and 20th centuries such as Herbert Spencer (1855), Karl Groos (1901), Sigmund Freud (1920), Jean Piaget (1962) and Lev Vygotsky (1967). It is not surprising therefore that a variety of definitions of play have developed. Hence, play means different things depending on the theoretical approach taken to understanding it. In this chapter play will be considered in the light of social learning and bonding with other children. One approach is to consider play as a prerequisite for future social relationships. Empirical support for this supposition will be explored. Another interesting conception of play is whether pretend play impacts on a child's further development or whether it is an epiphenomenon of the factors driving development. Clearly play is an important activity for child development. Play behaviour has a significant role in the development of future social behaviour – an important aspect of play that we will examine empirically. Evolutionary psychologists have compared animal play behaviours with that of humans and have found some startling similarities, especially among the primates. First, however, to get a feel for how play has been considered, we need to review the theories of key psychologists, educationalists and philosophers throughout the centuries.

DIFFERENT UNDERSTANDINGS OF PLAY

Play has a long history of explanation; dating back on record to Greek philosophers such as Plato (427–348 BCE). Plato in his work *Laws and the Republic* provided justifications for the use of play in education rather than a theoretical account of play.

Coming forward 2,000 years, English philosopher John Locke (1632–1704), like Plato, believed that play had an important role in education. He expressed his views in his work

Plate 9.1 Statue image of Greek philosopher Plato. (Shutterstock 421938271.)

Thoughts Concerning Education. Unlike most thinkers of his time Locke considered that 'carrots were better than sticks' when it came to education. He was, for example, a strong believer that corporal punishment had no place in education since it acted as a demotivator. The acquisition of virtue and being wise was best attained through non-coercive means such as recreation (i.e., play). Swiss-born Jean-Jacques Rousseau (1712–1778) wrote in his work *Emile* in 1762 that children traverse distinct stages of development and that play was an instinctive form of sensory and physical growth. Rousseau claimed that play activity provided educational instruction that would benefit the child's learning. Plato, Locke and Rousseau's views of play as a facilitator of learning were taken on board by Anglo-Irish Richard Lovell Edgeworth (1744–1817) and his daughter Maria Edgeworth (1768–1849). Their book entitled *Practical Education* (1798), contained empirical information based on structured observations of domestic education. From their observations they outlined how best toys might be employed in the educational process and play in childhood experimentation and attainment of scientific discovery.

Plate 9.2 Picture of Jean-Jacques Rousseau. (Shutterstock 81842470.)

German-born Friedrich Fröbel (1782–1852) is considered to be an educationalist and the initiator of the concept of the **kindergarten** (literally 'child garden' or nursery). He described how objects normally associated with play could be incorporated into sessions of learning. This was not a ground-breaking revelation. However, his insistence of play being at the fore-ground of children's education was. Fröbel was key in the formation of games and the play apparatus, which he referred to as 'gifts' and 'occupations' respectively. He wrote a manual for mothers to use as a guide, offering suggestions on how they should play with their children (e.g., 'Mother's Songs, Games and Stories'). Furthermore, Fröbel in his *Education of Man*, written in 1826, made it clear that 'play at this time is not trivial, it is highly serious and of deep significance' (p. 55).

German-born philosopher Friedrich von Schiller (1759–1805) wrote about the functions of play in his *Letters on Aesthetic Education*. Schiller claimed humans have a tendency to act on impulse as a consequence of their predisposition to perform behaviours that increased the probability of their survival. (Note that this notion of the survival value of play preceded Darwin's *Origin of Species* by at least half a century.) In the case of play behaviour, he argued that it was an impulse 'to extend enjoyment beyond necessity' and to stimulate imagination. For Schiller necessity referred to the struggle for survival. He provided the example of a lion who occasionally roared purely to release surplus energy. Therefore an animal whose survival needs were satiated could release its surplus energy in the guise of play. This play would be a paler imitation of behaviours used in survival activity. English sociologist and philosopher Herbert Spencer (1820–1903) postulated in his *Principles of Psychology* (1855) that surplus energy is expended by the child in acts of play behaviour. According to Spencer, given that offspring needs are sufficed through parental care, youngsters can engage in play behaviour.

Karl Groos (1861–1946), a contemporary of Spencer, came from Germany and also supported a biologically driven explanation of play. He considered play in animals and play in

Plate 9.3 Kindergarten – a legacy left by German educationalist Friedrich Fröbel. (Shutterstock 400303387.)

humans in his books *The Play of Animals* and *The Play of Man* respectively. Groos (1901) claimed that playful behaviour, which appeared as similar to adult activity but was executed imperfectly, might be an instinctive act. The function of this playful behaviour is to imitate and practise the skills necessary for adult life. This way of thinking about play was also championed by American philosopher John Dewey (1859–1952). According to Dewey, children were provided with play objects that, in our evolutionary past, would have promoted survival. Hence, the throwing of sticks for fun recapitulates the pastime of using sticks to help hunt prey. Given that the throwing of sticks is an action no longer required as a means for obtaining food, it now serves as a source of pleasure. Dewey described play in relation to work in his book *How We Think*, published in 1909. He believed that play is secondary to work and that play eventually gives rise to socially suitable adult occupations. He seems to be suggesting here that play is a prerequisite for future adult roles in the workplace. Dewey (1916) said '[i]t is the business of the school to set up an environment in which play and work shall be conducted with reference to facilitating desirable mental and moral growth . . . to introduce plays and games, handwork and manual exercises. Everything depends upon the

Plate 9.4 A boy uses a stick as a weapon while in play. (Shutterstock 59148031.)

way in which they are employed' (p. 230). This contention was adopted by Italian education-alist Maria Montessori (1870–1952). Montessori adopted a stage approach consisting of a series of **sensitive periods** when individuals were most receptive to learning specific types of information. These sensitive periods (see Table 9.1), she argued, are genetically programmed blocks of time when a child is motivated to master specific tasks (e.g., to master language, a skill that is difficult to acquire at a later time in the developmental timeline).

The 20th century saw the rise of psychoanalysis championed by Austrian-born Sigmund Freud (1856–1939). Freud considered play as therapeutic and outlined his psychoanalytic view of play in his work *Beyond the Pleasure Principle* (1920). He observed children in pretend play where they imagined themselves in different roles such as a soldier or dancer and acted out behaviours they believed characterised these roles. Sometimes children pretended to be someone or something else such as an animal. Freud interpreted these pretend play episodes as a way for children to express indirectly any pressing fears or anxieties they might have. He argued that children would repeat such play actions (i.e., described by Freud

Table 9.1 Montessori's sensitive periods of reception to specific forms of learning.

Sensitive period for small objects (interest in the details)	Children between 1–2 years are fixated on minute details. They explore their environment and may put objects into the mouth as a means of establishing object details.
Sensitive period for order	Children in their first year strive to categorise their experiences. This becomes easier to do when there is an element of order. They want consistency in order to construct a mental image of the world. If consistency is not forthcoming this can be upsetting for the child. Order helps to promote an organised mind. They make use of their hands to grasp objects; open and close things; placing objects inside containers and piling objects. These movements become refined during the next two years of development. They want things to be ordered and set routines. The breaking of routines leads to tantrums.
Sensitive period for walking	Locomotive skills and coordination increases leading to the ability to walk at around 12–15 months. Once walking is achieved, children enjoy the change from being helpless to being actively engaged in exploration.
Sensitive period for language	Learning language begins at birth and continues to at least six years of age. An infant hears the caregiver's voice and attempts to imitate lip and tongue movements. By six years an extensive vocabulary is acquired but the learning of language continues throughout childhood. Parental communication facilitates language acquisition.
Sensitive period for social aspects of life	Between two and a half and three years, children become aware of being part of a group. They show interest in other peers of similar age and through play will learn to cooperate. They model on the social behaviour of adults and acquire group social norms. Children learn norms, mores, values and manners. They strive to be accepted by others.
Sensitive period for learning through the senses	All sensory information combines to promote greater understanding of the environment. Montessori calls these, 'the instruments of man's intelligence'. Exploration using all the senses promotes development.

Plate 9.5 A therapist engages a girl in play as a means of overcoming anxieties over insects. (Shutterstock 425856214.)

as the **repetition compulsion**) in an attempt to re-experience and consequently resolve or control a difficult situation – hence drawing upon the **pleasure principle**. For Freud, play is a part of the pleasure principle, which is eventually replaced by the **reality principle** and, in so doing, gives rise to the ability to reason. In Freud's psychoanalysis (see Chapter 1) there are different stages the child progresses through, each with its own anxieties, which, in turn, are expressed in play. A boy who throws his sister's doll against the wall, for example, is expressing his feelings of jealousy harboured towards his sibling. In his subconscious mind this is what he would ideally like to do to his sister. Advocates of psychoanalysis and post-psychoanalysis such as Erik Erikson (1902–1994), like Freud, perceive play as an important part of social adjustment. Erikson introduced his conception of psychosocial development (see Chapter 1) where the developing individual traverses through stages, each with their own conflicts and contradictions in need of solution. Play therefore enables adjustment by allowing the child to resolve and overcome tensions and anxieties experienced.

Jean Piaget (1962) perceived play as a means of advancing a child's cognitive development (see Chapters 1 and 4). The play context is a safe haven for children to practise their newly acquired skills. Piaget's theory of cognitive development provides a backdrop from which to consider the functions of play (see Box 9.1).

Box 9.1   Piaget's stages of play

In 1952 Piaget observed play during preschool and the early school years. In particular he was interested in **symbolic play**. This is when children transform objects and the environmental context into creative scenarios and symbols to use during play. He divided symbolic play

(continued)

(continued)

into two main stages according to age: up to four years and from four to seven years. These stages had sub-stages. In stage 1 he outlined three sub-stages that are best considered using examples.

During the first sub-stage labelled 'projection of symbolic schemas onto new objects', children apply familiar schemas to new objects. Piaget gives the example of an 18 month old imitating the sound of crying to her toy dog then to her toy bear. By 19 months she made her hat cry. At 21 months children use objects to imitate actions they have seen another person perform such as rubbing the floor with a seashell (having watched the cleaning lady wash the floor). The second sub-stage is called 'separation of index and action', and it is here where the child shows the identification of one object with another. For example, Sarah at 27 months holds a brush over her head and labels it an umbrella. At four years and three months Sarah pretends to be a church by making noises resembling bells. Both examples involve reconstructive imagination. The third sub-stage called 'combination of symbols' is when children now transpose real scenes with imaginary ones. Sarah uses an empty match box as a bath and a blade of grass as the thermometer. When she first puts the blade of grass inside the box she says it is too hot but, on repeating this action, she then declares that it is all right. It is at this sub-stage that children come to understand unpleasant situations through imaginary play and this allows them to emerge victorious against potential threats (e.g., the water being too hot). In stage two symbols become more constrained by reality. The method of play becomes ordered and an exact replica of reality, as do the social roles depicted in symbolic play. There are games following rules by the age of seven, which continue to be the dominant form of play in middle childhood. Harry Sullivan (1952) argues that this form of play can offer a child attachment and security. It can also provide children with a platform for future social acceptance, intimacy, friendship and sexual relations. According to Piaget it is during this stage that children become involved in game play where there are explicit rules to follow, more than two sides, competition and a consensus of determining the winner. These games are important to social behaviour as they provide opportunities for selecting who will be on the same side – thus affirming friendships and social pecking orders.

Piaget's observations show that children below four years engage in play that is highly imaginative and symbolic. As children have had more experience with their environment and developed an understanding of reality, their play behaviour reflects this in the guise of ordered and structured games. Ordered and structured games tend to help children develop their social skills.

Lev Vygotsky (1896–1934) offers a perspective of play that involves his theory of cognitive and social development (see Chapters 1 and 4). Vygotsky highlights the importance of play in language development and how children come to understand their external world. During play children are in constant dialogue with themselves or with others such as their peers. When children engage in conversation with themselves while in play they use **inner speech**. This 'inner speech' is spoken out loud and is considered as being egocentric. This is often witnessed when children talk themselves through their play activity – it is almost like providing instructional guidance on how to perform an action. Mimicking what adults do is often reflected in their inner speech (e.g., when playing the role of mum a young girl might say 'Now brush your teeth before going to bed'). Through play children can perform different roles and experiment using language. These different roles and language styles are performed by children in order to imitate their parents which, in turn, allow them to practise their social skills. Vygotsky (1930) also informs us that by re-enacting different roles children are able to mimic and create a new reality paralleling their needs and

Plate 9.6 Children at play within the context of the early 20th century. (Shutterstock 238329868.)

interests. This reality, however, is bounded by the cultural context such that the way play is expressed differs across cultures and even within a culture over time (even if the motives and the essence of play remain constant).

Thus far we have explored the different perspectives of play and what it serves. Why there are so many different explanations for play behaviour might best be answered by exploring the various proposed functions of play.

WHAT IS PLAY?

Play is said to promote:

- social skills
- cooperation and team work
- mastery and control
- emotional regulation
- cultural and gender norms
- communication
- imagination
- physical skills.

Sutton-Smith (1994) believes that play enables children to rehearse the behaviours and roles that may feature strongly in adult life. Ethologists such as Irenaus Eibl-Eibesfeldt (1967) perceive play as an '**experimental dialogue**' with the environment. 'Lower species' that are highly specialised animals, such as many insects, have a rigid script to follow (i.e., behaviour is based on instinctive actions), which means there is no time for play – hence the saying, 'as busy as a bee'. Animals with a larger brain, however, show a great deal of flexibility through learning. Play therefore is a means of adapting to changing environmental circumstances and the more flexible the animal the more we see play behaviour. Humans are an example of a highly flexible species. Flexibility, however, is associated with a long period of maturation and dependency on the caregiver (Reynolds 1976). This means that children have time on their hands in which to learn and develop their skills through play. Moreover, play is more often social than solitary and prepares children for future adult social roles. Play therefore offers children a vehicle for which to explore their surroundings, and learn about others and, more importantly, themselves. Through developing social skills and cooperation with others, play also promotes both prosocial and antisocial behaviour. As play can help to develop a number of different skills, this implies that there are many defining facets of play (see Box 9.2).

Box 9.2   Defining facets of play

There have been many descriptions of play, but the general consensus is that play behaviour involves the following facets.

- It has to be enjoyable and perceived positively by the child.
- It has no extrinsic goals but rather is driven by intrinsic motivations.
- It is inherently unproductive.
- It is spontaneous and has to be voluntary.
- It involves the child being actively engaged.
- It is differentiated from what is not play but nevertheless has links with the development of language and social roles, creativity and problem solving.
- It contrasts with other states of being such as work. Bruner (1972) claims there are sharp distinctions between play and work in technological societies such as the West but play in traditional societies mimics work. The children of African pygmies, for example, tend to show play behaviours that model on adult working lifestyles. The children will emulate adult hunting behaviour by playing with sticks or climbing trees, which eventually evolve into the real deal.

In the West it is clear that play behaviour is very different to the working activities seen in adults. The play behaviour seen in children has no obvious and immediate objective and yet it helps promote social skill development.

Three important theoretical approaches within developmental psychology have contributed to our understanding of play (see Figure 9.1).

Psychodynamic
Play provides catharsis. It uses fantasies and wish fulfilment as seen in symbolic play.

Social learning
Play encourages reinforcement, imitation and vicarious learning. This is seen in parallel and cooperative forms of play.

Cognitive psychology
Play promotes languages and communication skills as well as developing visual and intellectual abilities. This is seen in solitary and social forms of play.

Figure 9.1 Three important areas of theoretical contribution to play.

American sociologist Mildred Parten (1932) developed a classificatory system of children's play. Parten observed the social play behaviour of children aged between two and five years. From these observations she surmised there are six **categories of play** that children can use in different combinations. These six categories of play outlined by Parten are still used today (although new categories have subsequently been added). In Box 9.3, the six original categories of play defined by Parten are described.

Box 9.3   Mildred Parten's six categories of children's social play

Parten acknowledged there are different forms of play in which children regularly engage. Sometimes more than one form of play is shown in unison. Parten's classification of play is widely used although there are other classificatory systems of play. The following is a description of the six types of play.

- **Unoccupied play** – the child is not engaged in play as it is commonly understood. Observations of the child reveal behaviours such as standing in one spot, looking around the room, or performing movements with no apparent goal.
- **Solitary play** – the child engages in play independent of others. This is commonly observed in two and three year olds who enjoy playing alone unlike older preschoolers.
- **Onlooker play** – the child watches while other children play. As the child has an active interest in the play of others it is different from unoccupied play.
- **Parallel play** – the child can be seen to play separately from others, although the toys are similar and are used in a manner that mimics the other children's style of play.
- **Associative play** – this form of play involves social interaction with others despite a lack of organisation. Children engaging in this form of play are more interested in each other than they are in the play behaviours performed.
- **Cooperative play** – there is considerable social interaction with peers in this form of play. Often in a group, these children gain a sense of group identity and participate in organised play activity. Cooperative play is less common in preschool children (Santrock 1999).

Although these six types of play are generally mutually exclusive children can switch or perform them in unison. Socially cooperative play becomes commonplace as the child ages.

There have been other classifications of play such as the five types of play advocated by Moyles (1989). Moyles labels these forms of play as follows.

1. **Physical play** – this involves exercise play (e.g., climbing, dancing and cycling); fine-motor practice (e.g., colouring books, sewing and toy construction); and rough-and-tumble activities (e.g., chasing, wrestling and kicking) with friends or siblings for instance.
2. Play using objects – this is seen in infants as grasping, mouthing, hitting and dropping. This would be described by Piaget as sensorimotor play. Toddlers explore objects by arranging, sorting, classifying and through building and construction. Older children are likely to form narratives around their play with objects.
3. Symbolic play – this often involves the use of language and the representation of objects as having other functions (as we saw in Box 9.1). According to Christie and Roskos (2006), symbolic play enhances language and literacy skills in young children. This extends to numerical skills as this play can involve counting activities (Carruthers and Worthington

2006). Matthews (2011) claims that drawing is an evolved type of symbolic representation that can be seen in symbolic play. Kirschner and Tomasello (2010) researched the influence of joint music-making on the development of spontaneous cooperative and prosocial behaviour. They found that 96 four year olds showed increased cooperation and prosocial skills in comparison to a control group who were not involved in joint music-making.

4. **Pretence/socio-dramatic play** – play involving pretence has been shown to enhance social, cognitive and academic performance. Whitebread and Jameson (2010) found that pretence play improved deductive reasoning skills as well as social competency in impulsive young children. The socio-dramatic play helped to self-regulate the behaviour of these impulsive children. Despite pretence/socio-dramatic play being considered as 'free play', Berk et al. (2006) found that children follow social rules predicting how the character they are pretending to be would behave. According to Berk et al., this form of play increases a child's level of social responsibility.

5. **Games with rules** – young children enjoy following the rules of games and sometimes invent their own. Rule-based games can involve physical activity such as hide-and-seek and playing catch. As children grow older, however, rule-based games become more intellectually stimulating such as a game of cards and computer games. Games with rules are essentially social in nature, which helps to develop children's social skills. These games usually involve turn-taking and obtaining an understanding of the other participants' perspective on the game (DeVries 2006).

Moyles' 1989 categories of play is not the only alternative classificatory system of play behaviours. Bobby Hughes (2002) introduced 16 types of play (see Box 9.4).

It becomes apparent from Parten's, Moyles' and Hughes' categories of play behaviour that children acquire many cognitive and social skills by playing either on their own or with others. Even play that enhances cognitive abilities will influence social skills development. It is play that ultimately has the biggest impact on social skill development that we are interested in here. In our next section we will be looking at studies showing how play helps promote social skill acquisition.

Box 9.4   Hughes' 16 types of play

1. Symbolic play enables children to exert control, exploration and understanding within a safe context (e.g., a match-box could resemble a bath).
2. Rough-and-tumble play involves close encounters with peers and is more to do with playful fighting enabling children to gauge their relative strength and resolve (e.g., having fun during a chase).
3. Socio-dramatic play is the enactment of real-life experiences in the social, domestic or personal domain (e.g., mother going to the shops).
4. Social play involves rules and social interaction (e.g., playing a game).
5. Creative play involves the transformation of information such that new responses can occur (e.g., making a toy from twigs).
6. Communication play is based on playing with words and using language to create something (e.g., making jokes and rhymes).
7. Dramatic play is used by children to dramatise events that they are not privy to (e.g., presenting a TV show).
8. Deep play enables children to experience potentially threatening events by conquering their fears (e.g., balancing on a branch of a tall tree or lighting fires using matches).

9. Exploratory play allows children to manipulate objects to gain information (e.g., bridge building from blocks).
10. Fantasy play enables children to reinvent the real world in their own way (e.g., driving an expensive sports car).
11. Imaginative play allows children to warp the conventional rules of how the physical world operates (e.g., pretending to be an aeroplane).
12. Locomotor play is based on movement occurring in all directions for no real purpose (e.g., running around).
13. Mastery play demonstrates a child's control over the environment (e.g., making dens using branches).
14. Object play is reflected in the infinite use of hand-eye movements involving objects (e.g., novel use of a paintbrush).
15. Role play is used to express different ways of being (e.g., dialling on the telephone or emulating a driver).
16. Recapitulative play enables children to explore their past through rituals, story-telling, rhymes and history (e.g., can access the play of human evolutionary stages).

Hughes' categories of play are diverse but do overlap with previous understandings of the functions of play and play behaviour classifications. Note, his final recapitulative category is considered to be controversial (some would suggest imaginative) by many developmentalists.

PLAY ENHANCES SOCIAL SKILL DEVELOPMENT

The influence of play in promoting cognitive, physical and socioemotional development is apparent even during infancy. Furthermore, different types of play help to promote distinct abilities. Puzzle-solving games, for example, are more likely to aid in the development of cognition whereas ball games promote physical strength and hand-eye coordination. In this section, however, we are interested in different types of play that help to promote social development. Carpenter et al. (1998) claimed that the imitation of others begins in infancy as early as 12 months. This imitative learning enables infants to acquire the rule-governed conventions that are culturally permitted. A study by Casler and Kelemen (2005) demonstrated how rigidly preschoolers will adhere to the assigned functions of objects and how they are used by others (when a child plays with a phone, for example, she treats it as a phone). Through observation and imitation the function and purpose of an object remained set. Rakoczy et al. (2008) introduced two- and three-year-old children to a novel and simple rule-governed game called 'daxing'. The children were shown the correct way to play the game but also an accidental mistake where the researcher said 'whoops'. The children later demonstrated that, not only did they know the rules of the game, but also they were aware when these were contravened by another person. They were quick to point out to the person that they were playing daxing incorrectly. Hence imitative learning helped these children to learn the game, which ultimately gave them the confidence to point out to others when they played the game incorrectly. Imitative learning in a play situation was influencing their social skills. Rakoczy (2008) took this a step further by introducing two and three year olds to a pretend play scenario. The researcher showed a series of objects such as a wooden block that were given fictional identities such that different coloured blocks served as different objects. Hence a green block was a bar of soap used to wash oneself and a yellow block was a sandwich – these were the rules of the pretend play. When a third person incorrectly applied the rules (e.g., washing with the 'sandwich'), these children were quick to criticise and to point out how the blocks should be used, again demonstrating competency of understanding the pretence game and confidence to correct the wrongdoer.

Rakoczy's study demonstrates that pretend or socio-dramatic play (Moyles 1989), or creative-symbolic play (Hughes 2002), can be seen to occur in children of only two years of age. Pretence play, however, can take on many guises such as substituting the function of an object for something different (as we have seen) or pretending to be an object that bears no relation to the real world (e.g., pretending to be a ship). Young children often have problems understanding the perspective of others (see Chapter 5), which can be problematic when they are asked to describe what they see in a picture and how that could be different for the person sitting opposite. A picture of a cow standing would be a cow lying down with legs upright for the person sitting opposite the child (Flavell et al. 1983). Such perspective problems are less apparent in pretence play given that children's actions bear no resemblance to the real world. This means that children do not have to consider if the stick really is a sword as well as a piece of branch from a tree. Perner et al. (2003) believe that children are likely to perceive their pretend play as them acting both in a real and pretend world. They argue that children assign the 'stick' to the real world and the 'sword' to the pretend world. Therefore children, when engaging in pretend play, have two separate descriptions for identifying the same object – real versus pretend. Wyman et al. (2009) provide evidence suggesting that, by the age of three years, children can entertain multiple pretend identities for an object.

Many developmentalists have turned their attention to investigating whether there is a connection between emotional understanding, social cognition and social interactive play behaviour. Denham (1986) examined children's emotional understanding using a variety of puppet vignette tasks. Emotional reactions to these puppet vignettes and to other children were observed. These reactions were considered as good indicators of social cognitive ability that, in turn, predicted social behaviour. This meant that appropriate emotional reactions formed a good basis for social cognitive development and therefore positive responses to other children. A lesson taken from Denham's findings is that being aware of, and able to interpret, other children's emotions promotes key play skills such as sharing toys, initiating play and avoiding conflict. Malti et al. (2009b) considered the level of social cognitive development as measured by moral explanations provided by children towards others who violated hypothetical rules. They found that such measures correlated significantly with teachers' previous ratings of prosocial behaviour. In support of these findings, Mathieson and Banerjee (2011) found evidence that emotional understanding and moral explanations of transgressions during play positively related to teacher ratings of **social play**. Such sociomoral explanations allowed children to reduce peer conflict during play. Children who were good at reducing peer conflict also received more sociometric nominations of being the most-liked peer. Mathieson and Banerjee conclude that emotional understanding is at the heart of children developing good social interactive play skills. Poor emotional understanding can lead to disconnected play where children withdraw or wander around aimlessly. Clearly having specific social skills promotes effective play. Play, however, allows children to practise these social skills and to develop them further within a safe context (see Figure 9.2). Play among siblings also provides opportunity for the discussion of feelings and thoughts, and for conflict resolution (Hughes and Ensor 2005). Hughes and Ensor believe this improves social awareness, which, in turn, develops social cognition (see Chapter 5).

As they develop children incorporate emotional responses and their linguistic abilities into their play. In the case of emotion, Bruner et al. (1977) showed that smiling and laughter are strongly indicated in play. To begin with children might show vague gestures that are indicative of happiness. As children become more active in creating situations for humour they also engage more fully in physical play. When children develop further they increase

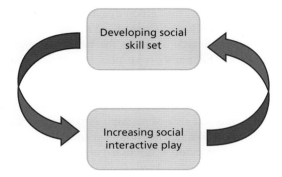

Figure 9.2 The social skill – play – social skill development relationship.

their remit of what they find funny. With further cognitive development, children can understand more and extend their play to new areas of experience. Laughter indicates joy and is reflected in their play behaviour. Gestures of happiness such as smiling and laughter are present in the early stages of play development and continue to be modified by interpersonal and environmental contingencies. Happiness and play co-occur during shared attention and awareness, and become increasingly linked in episodes of communication. There are three types of **social play with language**:

- spontaneous rhyming and word play;
- play with fantasy and nonsense;
- play with speech acts and discourse conventions.

According to Bruner et al., children have a tendency to imitate the rhyme of others even when they fail to totally understand what it means. How words sound is often played upon. Children also enjoy nonsense stories and will find ways of distorting and exaggerating how something is supposed to be. They often have silly names for their friends such as silly-face or dumb-head. Their understanding of nonsense stories is demonstrated through laughter and giggling. An example by Bruner et al. is a boy telling a story to his friend about a thanksgiving turkey. The turkey was caught, patched up with a bandage and cooked but it flew out of the window. Both boys found this amusing and giggled. Play with conversation can only occur once the idea of false assertions is understood. Davidson (1967) found this type of play to be fully understood by about three years of age. Davidson found that, of three siblings who engaged in none-serious speech with their mother who was misnaming things, it was the oldest child (aged three years and two months) who understood the joke even when mother kept a serious face. The second oldest sibling (aged two years) understood the play on words but only when the mother showed an amused facial expression. The youngest (aged 22 months) failed to comprehend the funny side of this non-serious speech.

Play helps to promote social development whether this occurs in a solitary context or within a group situation. When play occurs in a group context, however, there are within-group dynamics that each child has to contend with. As we have seen in Chapter 7, Judith Rich Harris made use of her Group Socialisation Theory to help explain the behaviour of children in groups. Children are drawn towards groups that maintain similar norms, values and attitudes to those they are accustomed to (simply because children from similar neighbourhoods will have experienced a common form of socialisation). In addition to group norms, values and attitudes there are other group dynamics taking place such as who is the 'leader of the pack' and who is the 'leader's right-hand person'. There are other social roles children and adolescents might entertain such as the best builder of dens if the group is involved in outdoor activities. Children's **group play** and adolescents' **social networking** will be explored later in the chapter.

It is interesting that children showing atypical development, such as those on the autism spectrum or with Down syndrome, tend to demonstrate play behaviours differently from their 'normal' peers. This is an important area of research as it provides us with information on how factors, such as play, impact on social development and what happens when play behaviour fails to follow the standard trajectory – discussed next.

Social development amongst atypically developing children

As we have seen, play contributes an important element to the development of social skills. We have also seen how play comes in many different guises, each with its own impact on the socially developing child. Atypical development in children can be classified into four different groups:

1. genetic disorders such as Down syndrome and Williams syndrome;
2. disorders showing behavioural deficits such as autism spectral conditions;
3. mental retardation;
4. environmentally triggered disorders such as foetal alcohol spectrum disorders.

As there has been extensive research on the play behaviours of children on the autism spectrum disorder (ASD) and those with Down and Williams syndrome, our focus here will be on these three disorders. Boucher (1999) discussed the importance of play in children's acquisition of social skills, focusing on the safe and supportive context it provides. Pellegrini and Smith (1998) previously considered play as providing children with an opportunity to hone their social skills. In the case of children with ASD, core deficits involve communication and social behaviour. Children with ASD show impairment in social interaction as well as creative-symbolic play (Mitchell and Ziegler 2007; see Box 9.5), which suggests that this form of play might have a role in the development of social skill acquisition. According to Van Berckelaer-Onnes (2003), it is during the first 12 months of life that deviations in play behaviour can be observed and these continue throughout childhood. During exploratory play and the manipulation of objects, Van Berckelaer-Onnes claims that the features of this form of play are very different in children with ASD. Children with ASD tend to prefer a limited array of objects and often become occupied with a part of the object (Freeman et al. 1979). Moreover, it has been noted by Williams (2003) that they prefer to use their senses of touch and taste at the expense of visual sensation. Given that they also prefer to be focused on one object for a long time and often engage in non-play-like behaviour, their play development becomes impeded (Van Berckelaer-Onnes 2003).

> ### Box 9.5 The social development and pretend play link in children on the autism spectrum
>
> Baron-Cohen (1987) found that the inability to engage in creative symbolic play and imitative play was a good indicator of children falling somewhere on the autism spectrum rather than having other forms of learning disability. In support of this, Mundy et al. (1987) found that

children on the autism spectrum who were unable to understand and to show/share gestures with others scored low on measures of symbolic play. Moreover, the number of symbolic acts during play is related to the frequency of occurrence of joint attention with another person (Sigman and Ruskin 1999). Charman et al. (1997) found that developmentally delayed infants aged 20 months are able to present at least one example of an **object substitution** such as a banana for a telephone. This was not the case, however, for infants on the autism spectrum, despite prompting and role models providing examples of object substitution. One explanation pertains to an inability to separate descriptions for identifying the same object – real versus pretend. More recently, Hobson et al. (2013) demonstrated that impaired symbolic play might be related to deficits in language and social interaction skills rather than deficits in pretend play per se.

As we can see, pretend play influences social development but it is also influenced by social factors such as social interaction, communication, joint attention and language. For those children on the autism spectrum, however, having deficits in the aforementioned skill set may well lead to problems in the development of pretend play.

Williams et al. (2001) found ASD children's symbolic play behaviour to be less spontaneous than that of non-ASD children and it appeared to follow a learned script. In a similar vein, their play with objects tends to be more restricted, simpler and reliant on static mental representations resulting from limited information for cognitive processing (Szabó 2014). Hughes (2010) argues that children in general who have impairment to sensory, social and intellectual capacity gravitate towards solitary and parallel play. The more cognitively powered forms of play such as symbolic play using objects tend to occur less frequently.

Interestingly, children with **Down syndrome** (DS) are more socially engaged than are those of a similar age on the autism spectrum. Furthermore, they are similar to typically-developing children in the number of times they spontaneously engage in functional play (i.e., play with objects according to their original function). When involved in symbolic play with objects, children with DS rely on processes of imitation, unlike typically-developing children who base their play on symbolic properties of objects – i.e., imaginative or pretend play (Wright et al. 2006). They suggest that the cognitive style of DS children is that of imitation and attention to social cues. Wright et al. further suggest that this might explain why they are more successful on object search and symbolic play tasks than would ordinarily be expected. The fact that children with DS are better at paying attention to social cues and being socially engaged than those on the autism spectrum might be one explanation as to why their symbolic play performance scores are higher.

Symbolic play is a sophisticated form of play utilising profound cognitive ability (Karmiloff-Smith 2002; Wolfberg 2003). Previous studies on children with DS have illustrated that they are able to engage successfully in symbolic play (Hill and McCune-Nicolich 1981; Motti et al. 1983). Hill and McCune-Nicolich (1981) explored the connection between symbolic play and cognition. They found a clear positive relationship between cognitive age and symbolic play. Wright et al. (2006) provided evidence that children with DS rely on imitation and focus on visual social cues to direct their symbolic play. A study conducted by Cicchetti and Sroufe in 1976, however, suggests otherwise. Their findings showed that the play behaviour of children with DS follows the same developmental trajectory as typically developing children, albeit considerably delayed.

A similar conclusion was drawn by Layton et al. (2014) who studied the play behaviours of Chinese toddlers diagnosed with DS. The main objective of their study was to compare DS Chinese toddlers with a control group who did not have DS. The toddlers with DS showed the same play behaviours as the controls that were matched for level of cognitive function.

The toddlers with DS, however, exhibited more pre-symbolic than symbolic play behaviours at later ages than their control counterparts. For example, at stage IV (19–22 months) pretend play normally becomes more extensive, such as pretending to feed a doll using a spoon. In Layton et al.'s study, stage IV symbolic play behaviours occurred at 17 months for the typically developing children but between 22 and 27 months for those with DS. Hence, when matched for cognitive ability, the DS children were functioning at the same stage of play as their typically developing counterparts. When matched for chronological age, the DS toddlers were lagging behind.

Children with Williams syndrome (WS) show a different set of symptoms and deficits from those with ASD and DS. Williams syndrome is a genetic disorder caused by a deletion on chromosome 7q11.23 (Osborne 2006). Children with WS exhibit relatively normal language but have profound intellectual deficits. Finn (1991) stated that 'People with Williams syndrome are smart and mentally retarded, gifted and inept at the same time' (p. 55). Despite having a restricted comprehension of social norms they are considerably friendly and sociable towards others. They have, in fact, been described as overly-friendly and even hypersociable (Jones et al. 2000). So might this be a problem in the way they approach others and socially interact – perhaps in their play behaviour? Social interaction tends to be prolonged and intense, and is initiated earlier than that seen in typically developing children. In a study by Dodd et al. (2010) ten Australian preschool children diagnosed with WS aged three to six years participated in a play session conducted in a room equipped with unobtrusive cameras and other recording devices. Due to its interesting findings, this study is worthy of some consideration. Each play session comprised of two non-social and two social components. The non-social components were designed to assess how forthcoming the child was to engage in a novel environment by playing with toys in the play room at arms-length from the caregiver – known as free play. After three minutes of free play a stranger entered who initially sat down making no eye contact with the child. After 30 seconds the stranger made eye contact and greeted the child. After an additional 30 seconds there was further interaction. Then a 'cupboard task' was introduced as part of the non-social component after free play. Here the stranger asked the child if he or she would like to play 'hide and seek' and suggested the cupboard would make a good place to hide. Again this game was introduced to assess the child's willingness to play with a stranger in a novel environment.

The social component was designed to see how interactive the child was with a stranger whose face was covered (as a way of preventing eye contact). Hence, following the hide and seek game, a second stranger entered the room whose face was covered. This stranger sat down and after 30 seconds said 'hello'. No further interaction was made unless the child initiated contact. The findings showed that WS children approached the toys more quickly and played for longer than the controls. The WS children engaged with the first stranger prior to being greeted unlike the controls. After the stranger said hello, more WS children than the controls continued to interact with the unfamiliar person. Furthermore, WS children were willing to initiate interaction with a stranger prior to any greeting and regardless of any eye contact being made. The WS children would even initiate interaction with the first stranger before they introduced toys to play with whereas the controls were more likely to engage with the stranger after a greeting and the provision of toys.

This study supports one of the key deficits seen in children with WS. They are over-friendly and like attention, which can be problematic in their play relationships with other children. According to the URMC website (2017), WS children prefer the attention of adults and can struggle to comprehend the social cues of their peers but they can be taught to develop appropriate play and friendship skills. Hence, there is often a developmental lag in their ability to play and interact with children of their own age. It is interesting to note that it was a study of play behaviour that allowed us to understand further the nature of social deficits found in WS children.

Despite children with atypical development finding it difficult to develop play-related behaviours, most eventually gravitate towards some form of group dynamics.

THE GROUP DYNAMICS OF PLAY AND SOCIAL NETWORKING

We have already seen how both good social skills and the ability to produce socio-moral explanations for transgressor behaviours contribute towards being nominated as most-liked peer. Group dynamics also influence popularity within play groups and established adolescent social networks. Each member of a group has his or her own role to perform and status to maintain within the group. How role and status are assigned depends on many factors but the level of social skill competency is one that we will consider here. Social skill competency derives from a host of factors such as socialisation and social interactive experience (e.g., as experienced in play). Children and adolescents who feature highly in the status ranks within a play group or social network respectively, are likely to be respected for the social skill competency that they bring to the group. Children's social groups are renowned for having hierarchical structures and norms that undergo change when interests become modified as a consequence of increasing age.

Plate 9.7 Teenager with many friends within his social network. (Shutterstock 75092971.)

Plate 9.8 An example of how a children's play group might be hierarchically structured. (Shutterstock 180180962.)

Plate 9.9 A teenage girl ostracised by her peers. (Shutterstock 491323459.)

Children and adolescents become preoccupied with the social impact their actions have on others while away from the prying eyes of adults. This preoccupation can be shown through behaviours that flitter between play actions and actions serving to create positions of power within a group. These social preoccupations also provide them with the opportunity to adapt to the changing dynamics occurring within a given group. According to Jarrett and Maxwell (1999) children and adolescents use play and social networking as a means of acquiring social skills concerning how to treat peers. For Erikson (1950), learning to anticipate and cope with change is an important factor enabling the progression through his stages of psychosocial development (see Chapter 1). Children and adolescents do this through practising playful scenarios that they find enjoyable. If play in groups with peers helps children to develop social skills that can be useful in later life, what then happens to those who are ostracised?

An interesting study by Watson-Jones et al. (2015) examined the behaviours of children who have been ostracised by their in-group. In their study 176 children aged five and six years were randomly assigned to either a 'yellow' or a 'green' playgroup in order to engage in a two-minute group Cyberball virtual ball-tossing game. Hence each child perceived there to be an in-group and an out-group. There were four conditions:

1. children ostracised from the in-group;
2. children included in the in-group;
3. children ostracised from the out-group;
4. children included in the out-group.

Children who were ostracised were excluded from playing in their playgroup. Based on previous research findings, Watson-Jones et al. predicted that children would model their behaviour on their peers. This might include playing and performing specific activities and gestures observed by their peers in an effort to feel part of the group. In their study the facial expressions, postures, gestures and anxiety expressed in speech were considered. Children who were ostracised by the in-group exhibited far more behaviours indicative of increased anxiety – even more than those who were excluded from the out-group. Furthermore, these children made more of an effort to imitate the actions of in-group members after being shown a video of them performing a 'hand and object signal' conveying a group convention. This imitation was performed even more extremely by the ostracised children than the non-ostracised children in the original in-group. For the children excluded and included by the out-group there was no difference in the level of imitative fidelity shown. According to Watson-Jones and Legare (2016), 'The psychological experience of being ostracized by in-group members is aversive. Even young children are highly motivated to engage in behaviors such as group rituals to re-affiliate with other group members'.

Forsyth (2010) points out how individuals have always felt the need to belong to a group even if their individuality is sacrificed for a 'group-think' mentality. Children especially want to be part of a group and are pleased to be sought out by others (Forsyth 2010). Children in groups feel valued unlike those who are ostracised and who, as a consequence, suffer loss of self-esteem (see Chapter 8). Could social play serve an adaptive function? As we saw when we considered ethological approaches earlier, it is likely that play helps us to develop and practise social skills. In Box 9.6 we consider the benefits derived from playing in groups.

Box 9.6   The benefits of playing in groups

Playing alongside peers helps children to increase their knowledge set concerning social roles and rules. Important social skills developed include the following.

- Group play teaches children how to work collaboratively with their peers. Here they learn the importance of their input for group success.
- Group play provides an improved sense of self. This develops through peer-related social interaction serving to create a context where self-expression is encouraged. It also helps to define their role within the group.
- Group play provides children with interpretations of the different aspects of adult life and the activities adults perform.
- Group play provides a link with culture such that play behaviours reflect cultural norms.
- Group play provides children with the foundation for the development of social behaviour and personality traits.
- Group play allows children to develop their social roles which, in turn, stimulate further socialisation.
- Within group play children are provided with models to learn from – hence social learning (Bandura and Walters 1963).
- The level of social information each child has will help establish the play group's organisation. When a child lacks social information then group dynamics relegate that child to a position of submissive acceptance of other group members' ideas. If, however, the child brings to the group the essential social information then he or she can be more selective in accepting the ideas from other group members. This helps promote self-esteem and can lead to group leadership.

These are just some of the benefits to being part of a group. It is not surprising therefore that peers want to be perceived as part of the in-group and are willing to adopt the norms, values and behaviours enacted by group members.

As we see from Box 9.6, there is much to be gained from being involved in social play within a group context. In adolescence the nature of play is manifested differently. This tends to be in the form of leisure pursuits that are interesting and of the teenager's choosing. This can be pursued alone or within a group context. Young adolescents tend to be involved in **cliques** based on friendship (Schneider 2000). According to Kindermann et al. (1995) cliques can range in number of friends from between three to nine members, generally of the same gender. These cliques serve to facilitate psychological well-being and provide a context in which to gain coping skills against stressful situations (Rubin et al. 2006; Salkind 2008). During the mid-adolescent years these cliques give way to crowd formation defined by common attitudes and activities (e.g., the football team). Crowds are also defined by specific stereotypes (e.g., 'swots', 'jokers' or 'nerds'). Rubin et al. believes that crowd affiliation is an automatic process where teenagers are assigned by agreement of the peer group rather than by self-allocation. By late adolescence the social networking of teenagers reverts back to a clique structure of mixed-gender friendships and romantic dyadic relationships. Adolescent social networks provide an important role in supporting friends by enhancing their social functioning and academic performance (see Box 9.7).

Box 9.7   The support provided by social networks

Providing social support to our friends encompasses a range of factors, which is why Tardy (1985) introduced a series of specific dimensions.

- 'Direction' refers to the support provided or received.
- 'Disposition' refers to the accessibility of support.
- 'Content' refers to the nature of support received and who provides this support.
- 'Evaluation' refers to the level of satisfaction with the received support.
- 'Network' refers to the individuals in the group.

Malecki et al. (2000) developed the Child and Adolescent Social Support Scale as a reliable tool to assess the level of perceived support from parents, teachers, friends and peers. The scale touches on issues such as emotional (e.g., trust and empathy), informational (e.g., advice), appraisal (e.g., providing evaluative feedback) and instrumental (e.g., prosocial behaviours) support and is therefore useful in gauging levels of support from social networks.

As can be seen, social networks provide an abundance of support enabling teenagers to develop their social skills further and to be buffered from the stresses of adolescence.

Returning to our question of whether social play could serve an adaptive function, research findings suggest this is the case. When all the benefits attained through social play and social networking are taken into consideration, social interaction within play groups and social networks provide members with the support they need to develop. Ethologists have considered the benefits acquired by animals that play-fight versus those who are deprived of this behaviour. For example, the domestic rat is considered to be one of the most playful of animals. If, however, the rat is play-deprived through having been reared in isolation or with

Plate 9.10 Rats are renowned for playing. (Shutterstock 472740154.)

drugged rats, it succumbs to fits of rage or fear when faced with a potentially threatening or stressful situation. These behaviours can be reversed once the rat is allowed to play for one hour per day (Potegal and Einon 1989). Play has been found to have the most robust influence over rates of rat brain growth (Ferchmin and Eterovic 1982). There is evidence showing how the deprivation of play-fighting can have similar effects in primates including humans (Pellis and Pellis 2009; Saunders et al. 1999). There appears to be an exception to the rule – meerkats (see Box 9.8).

Box 9.8   Are meerkats the exception to the rule about play-fighting?

Lynda Sharpe who studied play behaviour in Kalahari meerkats was interested to see whether play behaviour was a way of learning combat skills for survival (i.e., the practice theory) or for cementing friendships (i.e., the social bond theory). Meerkats live in a close-knit group but 80 per cent of the pups are from the group's dominant pair (Griffin et al. 2003). This means that if other meerkats want to breed they have to displace the dominant couple and to do this it is important to have fighting skills. Sharpe (2005) observed the play-fighting behaviours of the young meerkat pups and noticed that some played more than others. She found that the amount of, and expertise at, play-fighting bore no relevance to how good they were at fighting in adulthood. Nor did play behaviour reduce levels of aggression amongst the meerkats (Sharpe and Cherry 2003). Meerkat pups that played were just as likely to be recipients of aggression as those who refrained from play. Sharpe (2005a, 2005b) also failed to find evidence for the social bonding theory. Meerkat pups that played more often were no more committed to their group and playmates than non-playing pups; nor did they show more affection by grooming the others; nor were they more likely to team up with a favoured playmate than one they had rarely played with.

It is interesting how these observations go against general research findings of there being benefits to play-fighting. The consensus is that play-fighting offers practice skills for hunting and dominance assertion in adulthood. It is possible that meerkats gain from play behaviour in ways that we do not yet understand.

Meaney et al. (1991) found evidence of there being chemical changes to a young animal's brain during stress that makes them less sensitive to stress hormones. The implication of this is that the youngster will recover more quickly from a stressful and threatening situation – the advantages for the animal are clear. Furthermore, Siviy (1998) argues that play activates the same neurochemical pathways as stress and perceives play behaviour as a mechanism for priming or fine-tuning their stress response. Although there is evidence for this in monkeys it has not yet been substantiated in humans.

Interestingly, one of the world's leading experts on play behaviour, Peter K. Smith, considers that while play is important in human development he also concedes that we still do not have a full understanding of its function in our species (Smith 2010). Smith has developed the concept of 'play ethos', which can be thought of as a 'strong and unqualified assertion of the functional importance of play, namely that it is essential to adequate (human) development' (Smith 2010, p. 28). This means the notion that play serves a well-established function in human development is an assumption for which there is no conclusive evidence. In fact, the observations of Smith and his co-workers suggest that, in terms of development, play is no more effective than structured training.

Despite Smith's reservations, Bekoff and Allen (1998) argue that play enables animals (including humans) to read the intentions of others, and Biben (1998) claims it boosts confidence. We have certainly seen evidence to support both points of view in children's play. There are clearly parallels between most primates and humans in terms of play-fighting behaviours (especially between males). One of the useful benefits of play-fighting for young animals is that they practise skills that enable them to assert their dominance over others. This can be seen to some degree in children and adolescents when they play with others within a group context. Children as young as 16 months will establish a **social dominance hierarchy** (Hawley and Little 1999). According to Hawley (2007), children become increasingly expert at judging their status within the group even if they start off by overestimating their position. Social dominance can be decided within the first 45 minutes of meeting. Pettit et al. (1990) found this to be the case among first grade (six years) and third grade (eight years) boys who within 45 minutes developed an organised group structure. Having an organised hierarchical group structure reduces aggression among members. This operates because high-ranking members can resolve potential conflict among the lower ranks using threat postures. Hawley and Little (1999) claim that among highly structured groups children and adolescents rarely show aggressive behaviour.

There are other reasons for hierarchy formation in groups. One such reason pertains to the division of labour where lower-ranking members do most of the work and high-ranking ones take on leadership roles. Furthermore, those in higher-ranking positions are more likely to be in receipt of resources when these are limited (Hawley 2007). Even among nursery school children the higher-ranking receives more privileges. Higher-ranking teenagers attending summer camp were found to receive the biggest pieces of cake and slept in the best outdoor locations such as being nearest the camp-fire (Savin-Williams 1987). Dominance hierarchies benefit the higher-ranking children and adolescents.

But how do children and adolescents determine their social role within the group structure? Jockeying over specific social roles within groups can be a constant tension and opportunity for ongoing competition. More flexible groupings might, however, allow children to rotate roles in their play behaviours. Children can alternate between playing roles such as leader or the bully when given the opportunity. Most play groups and social networks have more than one social role available to its members. As mentioned earlier in Box 9.6, the more social information an individual brings to the group, the more likely they are to have a high ranking status. There are different types of social information possessed by the individual that can influence the social role attained within the group. Using sociometric methodology, Vitanova (1976) identified three types of **child leader**: organisational, informative and communicative. In the case of the organisational function the child leader coordinates different aspects of the play to increase joint activity. The information function of the child leader encourages the acquisition of new relevant knowledge that can be utilised by the group. For the communicative child leader the role is to ensure group cohesiveness using prosocial skills and friendliness.

Dijkstra et al. (2012) claim that, despite individuals in cliques and play groups having similar social status, status differentiation can still emerge (Closson 2009). For some cliques there is a rigid hierarchical structure due to there being a diversity of social status among members. For other cliques there is a small range of social status differences that results in an egalitarian format. Garandeau et al. (2013) found increased levels of bullying in the classroom among adolescents when there was a **status hierarchy divide**. In the case of clique aggression, Closson (2009) found it was associated with higher status hierarchies (more will be said about aggression among peers in Chapter 11). According to Lindenberg (1996), adolescents feel the need to increase their status among peers and therefore compete in order to acquire it. This might have an impact on the level of aggression exhibited as it reflects power and dominance over lower-ranking peers (Cillessen and Mayeux 2004; Dijkstra et al. 2009). Kwon and Lease (2007) argue that, in most cliques and play groups, members offer support, acceptance and social bonding, thereby providing a safe atmosphere with minor disputes over status. These cliques tend to be egalitarian. Interestingly, Pattiselanno et al. (2015) argue that it is possible that cliques could potentially become more hierarchical or more egalitarian as time progresses as members embrace the social normative behaviour of other members. Hence, for hierarchical cliques, aggressive behaviour might not be the norm and so this deters members from using aggression to acquire status. In the case of egalitarian cliques, adolescent members might imitate the normative aggressive behaviours observed as a means of improving their status. This implies that social networking behaviour might be more dependent on selecting appropriate behaviours and adhering to the socialising effect of group norms.

As we can see, the dynamics operating within play groups and the social networks of adolescents are complex. These dynamics have a strong influence over how children and adolescents interact with each other. These group dynamics can be seen to operate when children are immersed in social play and when adolescents are engaged in maintaining their social networks.

Summary

- Throughout the centuries there have been philosophers, psychologists and educationalists who have contributed to our understanding of what play is and the functions it serves. Fröbel pioneered the concept of the kindergarten and introduced guides for mothers on how they should play with their children – still very much in use today.
- Freud and Erikson perceived play as an important part of adjustment, while Piaget saw play as a facilitator of cognitive development. Piaget described in detail the functions of symbolic play and connected this with his stage approach to cognitive development. Vygotsky related play to cognitive and social development by highlighting the importance it has in language acquisition and in understanding the external world. He described how children talk themselves through their play activity and use it to mimic the roles played by adults.
- Play promotes a variety of different social skills and other skills feeding into social development. Such skills include cooperation and team work, mastery and control, emotional regulation, communication, imagination, cultural and gender norms and physical skills. Ethologists such as Eibl-Eibesfeldt perceive play as an experimental dialogue with the environment where 'lower species' have rigid scripts unlike humans who show greater flexibility. Play provides developing children with a vehicle from which to acquire information through exploration.
- Mildred Parten was the first to devise a classification of children's play: unoccupied, solitary, onlooker, parallel, associative and cooperative play. Moyles identified five forms of play: physical, play using objects, symbolic, pretence/socio-drama and games with rules. Hughes, however, uncovered 16 different types of play, many of which overlapped with Parten's and Moyles' classifications.
- Play promotes cognitive, physical and socioemotional development (the latter of which is apparent during infancy). Different types of play help in the development

of specific skills, such as solving puzzles, aiding cognitive abilities. Researchers see imitative learning as a way in which children come to understand rule-governed conventions that are culturally bound.

- Perner et al. (2003) claim children perceive their pretend play as part of the real and pretend world. For example, a stick is a stick in the real world but in pretend play it is a sword – hence children can entertain multiple pretend identities for an object. Children on the autism spectrum have difficulty using objects in a pretend manner. Researchers argue that this might be related to their deficits of communication, language and social interaction. Children with Down syndrome are more socially engaged than those on the autism spectrum. This is reflected in their superior skills of symbolic play. They do, however, rely on imitating the behaviours of other children at play demonstrating how socially attuned they are.

- A connection between emotional understanding, social cognition and social interactive play has been found by Denham (1986). Denham found that being aware of and able to interpret other children's emotions promoted prosocial behaviour and key play skills such as sharing toys. Furthermore, the moral explanations children give to peers who violate the rules of play match teacher ratings of prosocial behaviour. These socio-moral explanations allow children to reduce peer conflict during play. Emotional understanding therefore helps children to develop good social interactive play skills.

- As children grow older they play in groups, which later become smaller-numbered cliques. Adolescents become involved in social networking, usually belonging to a number of cliques of close friends. These groups and cliques usually comprise of individuals who have high- and low-ranking status. In hierarchically structured play groups and cliques there are children and adolescents who take prime top position and strive to maintain their high status. Play groups and cliques can also be more egalitarian where all members are of similar status ranking. The social dynamics of play groups and cliques can change but have a profound effect on how high- and low-ranking members are treated. Children who have been ostracised from their in-group will make every effort to closely imitate the actions of in-group members in order to ensure they follow the group's conventions and hopefully be allowed back in.

- There is a need to be part of the group or clique, even if it means a compromise such as sacrificing individuality for a 'group-think' mentality. This raises the question of whether social play serves an adaptive function. This could be the case given the benefits of playing in groups and being part of a social network. The main benefit is the support provided by group and clique members. Ethologists claim that in the animal kingdom social play provides the young with opportunities for practising survival skills. This can be seen through play-fighting. One expert, Peter K. Smith, however, has argued that there is a 'play ethos'. This means that the notion of play serving a well-established functional role in human development is equivocal.

- A social dominance hierarchy occurs within group and clique contexts. Six and eight year olds decide on social dominance within 45 minutes of meeting each other for the first time. Having an organised hierarchical group structure has been found to reduce aggressive outbursts among members. There are three types of

(continued)

(continued)

child leader according to Vitanova (1976): organisational, informative and communicative. Organisational leaders coordinate different aspects of play to create a joint activity. Informational leaders gather information that can be effectively utilised by the group. Communicative leaders promote group cohesiveness using prosocial skills.

- Play groups and cliques provide children and adolescents with support, acceptance and social bonding. They also buffer from the stresses of everyday life and provide a safe-haven to practise social skills.

Questions for discussion

1. Compare and contrast two types of play. What are the implications for social development for your chosen types of play?
2. What do we mean by pretend play? What does this form of play entail?
3. Can social play serve an adaptive function?
4. Critically examine the notion that the ethological approach has helped us to produce a better understanding of human social play.
5. Consider the different classifications of play and critically examine the view that play constitutes practise for later adult behaviour.
6. Critically examine how the study of children with atypical development can make a valid contribution towards understanding the interaction between play behaviour and social development.

Further reading

If you are interested in exploring the importance of symbolic play in the development of social skills in more detail, look at:

- Bornstein, M.H. (2007). On the significance of social relationships in the development of children's earliest symbolic play: an ecological perspective. In A. Göncü and S. Gaskins (eds), *Play and Development: Evolutionary, Sociocultural and Functional Perspectives.* New York: Lawrence Erlbaum Associates.

If you are interested in exploring how the deprivation of play-fighting in primates (and in humans too) can affect social development, look at:

- Pellis S. and Pellis V. (2009). *The Playful Brain: Ventures to the Limits of Neuroscience.* Oxford, UK: Oneworld Press.

If you are interested in exploring how group play interventions can improve social skills, look at:

- Reddy, L.A. (2011). *Group Play Interventions for Children: Strategies for Teaching Prosocial Skills.* Washington, DC: American Psychological Association.

If you are interested in the functional value of play in human child development (including the adaptive value) and the importance of contemporary and classic research in fuelling the debate of a 'play ethos', look at:

- Smith, P.K. (2010). *Children and Play.* Oxford: Wiley-Blackwell.

Contents

Introduction   299

Theories of moral development   301

The influence of moral (i.e., prosocial)
judgements on how we behave   335

Summary   338

Chapter 10

Moral development and prosocial behaviour

What this chapter will teach you

- Knowledge of the theoretical stage approaches to moral development of Piaget, Freud, Kohlberg and Eisenberg.
- Knowledge of other approaches such as that of Bandura, social constructivism and evolutionary psychology.
- From a social constructivism perspective, an understanding of the three domains of social knowledge: moral, conventional and personal.
- From an evolutionary psychology perspective, an understanding of how rules concerning our development of morality arose in our hominin ancestors in relation to reciprocity, devotion and deference.
- The positive relationship between the development of prosocial behaviour and moral emotional attributions.

INTRODUCTION

The word morality comes from the Latin *moralis* referring to custom. Custom is defined as a widely accepted way of behaving within society and is governed by set rules, beliefs, values, mores and attitudes. Specific rules or customs can become set in law through regulatory legislation, thereby enforcing a convention. This means that specific actions, such as driving a car on the wrong side of the road, are regulated in law and are punishable by the legal system. Within a social context, conventional behaviour is driven by implicit laws of custom. For example, when a person is speaking it is accepted that it is polite to listen and not to interrupt until they have finished. Most individuals within society conform to these rules and follow the set conventions regarding personal and social behaviour. There are, however, cross-cultural variations regarding these rules and some take the form of laws, taboos and religious tenets (Chasdi 1994).

Convention, however, contrasts with moral considerations that are intrinsic to the behaviours performed. Harming others as a consequence of our actions, for example, is a moral issue. Many moral issues are therefore not arbitrary nor are they determined by cultural precepts – although, as we have seen, legal conventions can derive from moral issues. Children therefore need to understand what constitutes **moral behaviour**.

In each culture children are guided in the development of their moral behaviour by parents as part of the socialisation process (see Chapters 3, 5 and 6). How this is achieved will be considered using psychological theories of moral development such as the stage theory approaches of Piaget, Kohlberg and Gilligan. These stage theorists offered accounts of how children develop their moral reasoning in a set progressive order. Freud also offered a stage theory account of moral development; however, he focused on emotional rather than cognitive aspects of how children acquire morals. Freud also considered the stages to occur in a set progressive order.

Children learn how to behave in ways condoned by society. This is supported through the socialisation process carried out by parents (see Chapters 3, 5 and 6), later by peers (see Chapter 7) and by institutions such as schools and the legal system. This is nicely exemplified in Bronfenbrenner's Ecological Model (see Chapter 1). Behaviour that is condoned by society includes those responses considered to be prosocial (which is the antithesis of antisocial behaviour). Prosocial behaviour is succinctly defined as actions intended to help others. Not all condoned behaviours, however, are prosocial in nature (e.g., playing the star role in a play at the expense of another child). Eisenberg offers a stage model by focusing on prosocial behaviour in relation to 'doing the right thing' (behaving morally). Unlike Piaget, Kohlberg and Gilligan, Eisenberg's stage account, although progressive, allows for children and adolescents to return to any stage at any time. In contrast to a stage approach, Bandura provides a social cognitive interactionist perspective. Once considered as a behaviourist, Bandura realised reward and punishment was too simplistic an approach to explain children's acquisition of complex behaviours such as moral understanding. He therefore became an advocate of the interactionist approach. Here he emphasised the influence of personal, cognitive, behavioural and environmental factors interacting interdependently (see Chapter 1).

A different theoretical approach is that proposed by social constructivists. Social constructivism focuses primarily on differences between children's understanding of conventional and moral transgressions. The acquisition of moral behaviour occurs at a surprisingly young age as was demonstrated by Nucci and Turiel (1993) (see also Smetana 1993). In order for the child to avoid committing social transgressions parental guidance is necessary and, according to many developmentalists, it is this that helps to develop and refine a rudimentary capacity for moral reasoning. Not all developmentalists, however, subscribe to this view (e.g., those adopting a nativist approach and some constructivists). The constructivist approach has helped developmentalists understand how children construct their social knowledge according to a social-cognitive domain. This consists of three separate sub-components: moral, conventional and personal.

It has been debated whether humans have an innate propensity to behave morally. This is exemplified by the evolutionary psychology approach. The evolutionary psychology literature suggests that morality evolved as a consequence of kin selection and group reciprocation arising in early hominins (i.e., those species considered as directly ancestral to humans) living in close knit groups. These close knit groups are likely to have been made up of extended families and **fictive kin** (i.e., individuals who are close friends and are considered as family). To evolutionary psychologists children develop moral codes due to factors that are ultimately related to passing on their genes (or what would have done so during our evolutionary history). Hence, behaving well towards 'kith and kin' is likely to aid us in passing on our genes either directly or indirectly via reciprocation.

We will begin our discussion of the theories of moral development by focusing on stage approaches.

THEORIES OF MORAL DEVELOPMENT

Believing it is wrong to hit your nursery school friend on the grounds that they refuse to share their toys with you provides developmentalists with insight about the child's attitude towards this particular issue. Learning about the contribution of attitudes that children develop about specific situations can help us to understand their behaviour. Hence, the child in our example refrains from using physical violence to attain toys because he or she reasons that it is wrong to hit another child as this can cause harm. Reasoning is the cognitive element of an attitude and elicits predispositions to behave in certain ways. Attitudes are considered to comprise of three interdependent components.

- Cognitive component – pertaining to the way we think about a moral issue.
- Emotional component – pertaining to the way we feel about a moral issue.
- Behavioural component – pertaining to the way we act towards a moral issue.

We have to bear in mind of course that, although these three facets appear separate, they interact. The emotional component, for example, always contains a cognitive element. This can be seen, for example, when attributing blame in the case of guilt. When considering how we develop morally, it is important to keep in mind all three components of an attitude (or disposition). As with any type of attitude, a moral attitude can be riddled with inconsistencies such that the three components are dissonant to one another. A child, for example, might know and therefore think it is wrong to steal her playmate's ice-cream cornetto but feels like having it anyway. So she behaves in a manner consistent with a bully who grabs the ice-cream away (even though she knows it is wrong). Stealing an ice-cream is more likely to be seen in younger children as they have yet to learn how to control their desires and develop a social system of behaving appropriately. Turiel (2015), however, has argued that older children and adults can sometimes violate moral principles when it comes to social behaviour. On some occasions exceptional violations are judged to be warranted (Turiel 2015). Turiel's understanding of moral acquisition in children is based on the social domain theory, which will be discussed later under the theoretical approach of constructivism.

Moral development in children will be considered using a stage approach, advocated in different ways by theorists Piaget, Kohlberg, Gilligan, Freud and Eisenberg.

Stage theorists

Jean Piaget

In his 1932 book, *The Moral Judgement of the Child*, Piaget considered morality as consisting within a system of rules akin to judgements of justice and equity. He adopted a bio-cognitive approach to understanding children's moral thinking and considered brain maturity and cognition to underlie moral development (Piaget 1965). In fact, he was later to publish his famous stages of cognitive development in the 1950s (see Chapters 1 and 4). Piaget used two

Plate 10.1 Hands off, this is my ice-cream now! (Shutterstock 294313766.)

methods to investigate how children come to understand and reason about events: games of marbles and moral stories. In the case of games of marbles, Piaget observed boys between 3 and 12 years of age playing marbles with other children. He was interested in the extent to which they understood the rules of the game and how important they believed it was to follow those rules. Hence, he wanted to establish whether there were differences according to age in the way children reasoned about the rules of the game. It was through observations and interviews with the boys that Piaget discovered differences between younger and older

Plate 10.2   Children playing a game of marbles. (Shutterstock 113496667.)

children's levels of understanding of the games they were playing. Piaget found that pre-school children (0–5 years of age) had no preconception of how a game of marbles should be played but instead enjoyed rolling the marbles for the fun of it. In middle childhood (5–10 years of age), children were keen to win and were competitive in how they played. He observed that they followed the rules avidly. At this age children were unaware that the rules of playing marbles are flexible and can be modified as long as every other player agreed with the proposed changes. Piaget's findings suggest children between five and ten years of age have not yet fully grasped that some rules involved in playing rule-bound games are conventional. As children reached the ages of ten upwards, Piaget demonstrated that they understood it was okay to change some game rules provided there was a consensus between all players regarding how the game will be played in future. Based on his observations and interviews with the boys playing marbles, Piaget proposed three stages of moral development (see Table 10.1).

Table 10.1 Piaget's stages of moral development.

Stage and years	Description
Pre-moral period (0–5 years)	During this period children show very little understanding of rules. There is also limited understanding of the different aspects of morality.
Heteronomous morality or moral realism (5–10 years)	Children tend to be inflexible in their thinking such that they perceive rules as being static. They believe that rules are devised by important people and therefore must be obeyed regardless of the circumstances. They have not yet grasped that sometimes telling a white lie can make another person feel better. Children consider the objective outcomes from actions and not the underlying intentions as a determinant of how bad behaviour is. There are two important characteristics influencing their moral reasoning: expiatory punishment and notions of fairness. Expiatory punishment describes a direct mapping between bad actions and the extent of punishment deserved. In other words, the naughtier the behaviour, the greater the punishment should be. For example, a child who breaks a bottle of milk should be smacked. There is no understanding, however, that the punishment should fit the crime committed. Children during this period believe in fairness. Hence, if a child misbehaves they will always be punished in some way. This supports the idea of immanent justice. Morality is therefore very much dependent on external rules, which Piaget refers to as **heteronomous morality**.
Autonomous morality or moral relativism (10 years upwards)	Children are able to think more flexibly about rules and moral issues. They understand that moral rules derive out of relationships. They come to realise that not everyone has the same moral standards. Importantly, they realise that many of the rules of morality can be broken. There are situations where it is okay to tell a lie, for instance, which is characterised by a profound understanding of the needs of others. Children now make decisions concerning the wrongness of a behaviour based on the intentions of the person rather than the outcomes of the action. Children's judgements are now based on moral correctness and justice. They believe in reciprocal punishment rather than expiatory – hence, the punishment should fit the crime. They realise that not everyone gets punished when they should be as they manage to avoid it. This means that justice is not necessarily immanent. Children attain **autonomous morality** – right and wrong have been internalised.

Piaget's approach to understanding moral development focuses primarily on moral thought, thereby addressing the cognitive element of a moral attitude. As we saw from Table 10.1, young children are guided by the consequences of behaviour rather than the intentions behind actions. An example of this would be John who accidentally breaks 15 cups when compared with Henry who breaks one cup while reaching for something forbidden. Young children who are still in the heteronomous stage of morality would regard John as the naughtier of the two. Children who are still heteronomous thinkers also believe in immanent justice. Belief in immanent justice influences the way the child thinks about misdemeanours. They believe that if an individual's actions go unpunished then their behaviour cannot be considered as being wrong – hence, punishment should be forthcoming immanently. Children who are autonomous thinkers are able to empathise with John and imagine how he feels. They also realise that punishment can be meted out if someone else such as a parent or teacher witnesses the misdemeanour. Furthermore, they realise that the misdemeanour has to be serious enough to justify being punished for. Hence, there is an understanding of which behaviours are wrong and are deserving of punishment but also that punishment could be delayed.

The second method adopted by Piaget to investigate moral understanding and reasoning used moral stories (e.g., the story of John and Henry). These moral stories helped Piaget to ascertain when children shift from basing their moral judgements on the consequences of behaviours to the intentions behind people's actions (see Box 10.1).

Box 10.1 Consequential to intentional reasoning using moral stories

Piaget used moral stories as a way of investigating how children reason about misdemeanours. As we have seen, Piaget describes children in the heteronomous stage of moral development as basing their decision of what is naughty behaviour on the consequences. This means that if John breaks many cups and Henry breaks only one then John is more culpable. In this case, they see the result in terms of quantity (i.e., the number of cups broken). As far as these children are concerned, it does not matter if John accidentally broke all the cups and Henry only broke one while doing something forbidden. Children in the autonomous stage have a different focus. They believe that what is important is why and how the cups were broken. In John's case it was an accident and there was no intention to do it. For Henry, he was already doing something he was not supposed to. Let's see how Piaget concluded this from his moral stories (adapted from Piaget 1932, pp. 122 and 129).

> John gets called down to dinner. As he enters the dining room he opens the door, which knocks over 15 cups balanced on a tray, causing them to break. John had no idea that the cups were behind the door.
> Henry tries to get some jam out of a top cupboard while his mother is out. Despite climbing up onto a chair he still had trouble reaching the jam. While he was trying to get hold of the jam he knocked a cup over, which fell to the floor and broke.

Children were asked a series of questions about both boys' actions. From their responses it was clear that they understood what was going on but those in the heteronomous stage consistently indicated that John should be punished because he broke more cups than Henry, even though they understood that his actions were accidental.

Piaget used many different moral stories and found that the responses children gave could be divided according to the moral stage of development they had reached. Those in the heteronomous stage relied on judgements of wrongdoing and punishment based on the consequences of misdemeanours, unlike children in the autonomous stage who based their judgements on the intentions behind the actions.

There is research by Hamlin (2013) suggesting that even babies are capable of taking intentions into account when making moral evaluations. This was studied by using preferential looking and reaching. When puppets were used to portray helping or hindrance behaviours, infants preferred looking at puppet characters who behaved in a prosocial manner. Hamlin, however, points out that we have to be careful about how we interpret such findings. Moreover, the incorporation of intentions when making moral judgements generally occurs later in middle childhood (Cushman et al. 2013; Killen et al. 2011). Piaget believed that moral reasoning develops from cognitive advancement in relation to social issues such as cooperation, mutual give-and-take and negotiation. Piaget's methodology has, however, been criticised (see Box 10.2).

Box 10.2   Did Piaget get it wrong in the way he investigated moral judgement?

Piaget introduced the use of moral stories as a method of investigating what children base their moral judgements on. By presenting different stories to children he was able to ask them questions about the characters in the story and what they had done (see Box 10.1). He also asked them which of the characters were in the wrong and should be punished. Using this method he was able to ascertain what children of different ages based their moral judgement on – the outcomes or intentions of the behaviours described. Using this approach he was able to divide children according to what stage of moral development they had reached – heteronomous or autonomous (see Table 10.1). Piaget's use of moral stories has been an innovative way of investigating children's moral development. It is still a method that many researchers use, although with different presentation permutations. Researchers have, however, questioned Piaget's notion of the age at which children make moral judgements based on intention. Piaget places this ability at about ten years of age. Researchers such as Chandler et al. (1973) place this ability at six years of age. Chandler et al. presented moral stories using a videotape format rather than reading them out to children. This they believed helped younger children to use other visual information such as facial expressions signalling the underlying emotion felt – hence accounting for why children of six years used intention in their moral judgements. The content of the moral stories used by Piaget has been criticised on account of mixing two aspects of the storyline – the outcome of the action and the actor's intention. By separating good and bad intentions from good and bad outcomes, children of younger years can base their moral judgements on someone's intention (Bussey 1992; Helwig et al. 2001). Hence, when the cup-breaking scenario is presented differently, such as the child breaking five cups while helping his mum do the dishes or while trying to reach for a forbidden biscuit, children understand

(continued)

(continued)

the significance of intention in moral decision-making. According to Helwig (2008), there are many factors influencing children's moral judgements that Piaget's structure of moral stories had been unable to decouple.

Children are capable of understanding much more about moral behaviour and moral reasoning than previously thought. While moral stories, first used by Piaget, are a useful experimental paradigm, improvements to the presentation and content have shown that children use intention at an earlier age than suggested by Piaget.

Early critics of Piaget, such as Weston and Turiel (1980), demonstrated that children of three years have no problem with changing the rules of a game as long as other players agree. Moreover, they remind us that children regardless of age can refuse to obey the rules. Further critics of the moral story approach point out that the emphasis placed on the consequences encourages children to think that the negative outcomes are driven by negative intentions. Resolve this by making the intentions clear and children as young as three are able to divorce intentions from outcomes (Nelson 1980). If, it is argued by Nelson, Piaget had emphasised intentions in his moral stories then his timeframe of progression from heteronomous to autonomous morality would have occurred at an earlier age. On the issue of punishment, Irwin and Moore (1971) found that three year olds can separate out concepts of deserved and undeserved punishment.

Piaget is considered as having a structural-organismic approach (as discussed in Chapter 1). This is reflected in his stage approaches to moral and cognitive development. He conceived cognitive development as an organised biological process and emphasised the importance of brain maturity. As children traverse through the stages of cognitive development their moral understanding is likely to be influenced by their level of cognitive understanding. In effect, children's ability to comprehend moral and conventional rules becomes more sophisticated as they master skills of cognition.

Another influential stage theorist is Lawrence Kohlberg who provided an understanding of how children acquire moral reasoning.

Lawrence Kohlberg

Kohlberg (1969, 1985), like Piaget, advocated a stage approach to understanding the development of moral reasoning (more correctly justice reasoning). Kohlberg interviewed mainly boys ranging in age from 10 to 17 in a longitudinal study of 20 years. He presented these children with stories of moral dilemmas faced by the characters depicted. In particular, one of Kohlberg's moral dilemmas has been well cited – that is the case of Heinz whose wife is dying of cancer. In this dilemma there is a drug developed by a local chemist that could save her life but the chemist asks for an extortionate amount of money that is beyond what Heinz can afford. The chemist is non-compromising and refuses to accept half the amount of money he is asking for (nor will he allow Heinz to pay the remainder at a later date). One night Heinz breaks into the chemist store and steals the drug. Kohlberg developed this scenario in order to examine the quality of moral reasoning and how it changes with age. He wanted to know what the children thought about Heinz's actions. In particular, he wanted to know what made them think about Heinz's actions in the way that they did. In effect,

Kohlberg's interest lay with how children reasoned about people's transgressions. To find out how the children reasoned about the different dilemmas presented, Kohlberg asked two important questions:

'Did Heinz do the right thing?'

'If so, why do you think this? (If not, why do you think this?)'

Kohlberg found that there were differences of response to these questions due to the age of the children. On the basis of the children's answers Kohlberg devised three levels of moral reasoning ability that divided into stages; all told there were six stages (see Figures 10.1, 10.2 and 10.3). Children were allocated to a specific stage when their responses to the dilemma questions consistently corresponded with the arguments expected at that stage (referred to as the child's modal stage). Kohlberg argued that these levels and stages occur in a set order. Hence, children have to traverse the first level and stage before progressing to the next.

Level I

Pre-conventional morality

Children up to the age of nine years, still attending primary (elementary) school, have not yet developed their own code of morality. The moral code of these children is shaped by the moral standards expressed by adults and the consequences incurred for breaking them. Hence, authority is meted out by someone else and the child's moral reasoning is founded on the consequences experienced by obeying or breaking the rules specified by the authority figure.

Stage 1 – punishment–obedience

Children are in the early years of primary school. The child is oriented towards obedience and punishment; will avoid physical punishment; shows deference to authority figures (including parents); is egocentric and finds it difficult to take others' perspective into account. Hence, the child behaves appropriately to avoid being punished. As far as the child is concerned, a person who is punished is punished because they must have done something wrong.

In relation to the Heinz dilemma, they fail to see shades of grey. Heinz should not steal the drug because he will be punished by going to prison.

Stage 2 – self-interest

Children are in the later years of primary school. The child makes choices based on what is the right behaviour necessary to satiate his/her own needs without incurring punishment; presence of egalitarianism and moral reciprocity (e.g., I'll help you if you help me); punishment inflicted as vengeance for a misdemeanour.

In relation to the Heinz dilemma, he should steal the drug because by doing so he will be happier for saving his wife's life, despite serving a prison sentence.

Figure 10.1 Kohlberg's levels and stages of moral development: **pre-conventional morality**.

Level II

Conventional morality

Children of ten years of age and adolescents attending secondary/high school should have developed conventional morality. The term 'conventional' signifies moral thinking generally found in society. Adolescents and adults begin to internalise moral standards depicted by valued adult role models. While the rules of authority become internalised, there are no questions asked concerning their validity. Moral reasoning reflects the norms inherent in the group of which the individual is a member.

Stage 3 – interpersonal accord and conformity

This stage is also referred to as the 'good boy/good girl' attitude. The child, adolescent or adult is oriented towards conforming to the expectations of peers and society. Being a model person in the eyes of others, a willingness to please and follow the rules to gain approval take precedence. Can entertain many different perspectives; understands the motivation behind others' behaviours. There is forgiveness rather than revenge.

In relation to the Heinz dilemma, he should steal the drug as this is what his wife would expect of him. He will not be thought of badly if he steals the drug but will be regarded as inhuman if he does not.

Stage 4 – authority and social-order maintaining

This stage is also referred to as law and order morality. The child, adolescent or adult makes moral choices based on beliefs of what is right and wrong in the eyes of society. Rules are there to be followed to maintain social order, uphold the law and avoid feelings of guilt. Those who transgress the law should be punished and authority should not be questioned.

In relation to the Heinz dilemma, he should not steal the drug as stealing is prohibited by the law. Given the law is there to maintain social order, breaking it could cause others also to break laws which can lead to chaos.

Figure 10.2 Kohlberg's levels and stages of moral development: **conventional morality**.

Kohlberg's approach focuses on the cognitive element of moral attitudes. In the pre-conventional level, children know the rules but think it is wrong to break those rules mainly because of the consequences incurred to them. In the conventional level, children, adolescents and adults know the rules and believe it is important to follow them (especially in stage four). In stage three they behave in ways that are socially expected and base their judgements on what others might think of them – for instance, individuals should behave in ways that make them happy. For example, it would look bad if they thought that Heinz should not steal the drug to save a life. In stage four, the emphasis is on obeying the law. It is not until the postconventional level that individuals have acquired full morality and cannot go any further. Kohlberg believed there to be a difference between stages five and six in the breadth of conception concerning universal principles but failed to obtain consistent and significant empirical evidence for this. As a consequence, he labelled stage six as a theoretical stage and focused on scoring responses up to stage five instead (Colby and Kohlberg 1987). Kohlberg claimed that his methodology of using the interview approach to obtain responses to the

Level III

Postconventional morality

This level is not reached by many adults. However, some reach stage 5 but very few enter stage 6. For this reason, stage 6 is considered to be hypothetical. This level is highlighted by moral reasoning based on individual rights and justice. Self-chosen principles are used in making moral judgements.

Stage 5 – social contract

The individual's behaviour is governed by universal moral principles. The social contract consists of norms and values that are followed by citizens of the society in which they inhabit. Individuals become loyal to the social contract and use democratic means in order to change laws. There is a genuine interest in ensuring the welfare of other people. Personal values might sometimes conflict with the law which, in turn, can conflict with moral principles and individual rights. Retribution can be seen as neither rational nor just.

In relation to the Heinz dilemma, there are two possible responses. He should steal the drug as the right to live outweighs any laws. He should not steal the drug because the chemist has the right to be paid for his efforts in making the drug.

Stage 6 – universal ethics

This stage is also referred to as principled conscience. The individual makes moral choices based on beliefs of self-selected ethical principles pertaining to his/her own conscience. These ethical principles pertain to matters such as equality, respect and justice. Other people's interests should be considered even if it can lead ultimately to civil unrest. Very few people acquire this stage of morality but a few who have include Mother Teresa, Gandhi and Martin Luther King.

In relation to the Heinz dilemma, there is more than one possibility. Heinz should not steal the drug as to do so contravenes the rule of honesty and respect. Heinz should steal the drug because saving another person's life outweighs the chemist's property rights. Heinz should not steal the drug and accept that we all die at some point.

Figure 10.3 Kohlberg's levels and stages of moral development: **postconventional morality**.

dilemmas failed to differentiate between stages five and six. Controversially it should be noted that Kohlberg claimed that a greater proportion of males reached stages five and six than females.

Kohlberg's theory has received much criticism, especially from Carol Gilligan (1982, 1996) who accuses his methodology as being gender-biased. Gilligan argues that men adhere to more **universal ethical principles** whereas women prefer to base moral judgements on an **empathic/caring model** where the effects of judgements on people are more important. Males are therefore more abstract and females more concrete in their moral reasoning and decision making. Gilligan also maintains that Kohlberg has over-emphasised the importance of justice as a main theme in moral development at the expense of factors such as empathy, caring and sympathy. She basically argues for a care perspective where communication, concern for others and social interactions and relationships with others lie at the heart of moral decision making. Gilligan's perspective has also been criticised by Jaffe and Hyde (2000) who argue that she overstates the gender difference. In fact they found that both males and females use care-based reasoning for interpersonal dilemmas and justice reasoning for dilemmas of a societal nature. Gilligan's criticism has been attenuated by developmentalists such as Hyde (2007) and Walker (2006). In addition to Gilligan's misgivings there have been other types of criticism aimed at Kohlberg's methodology (i.e., how individuals are assigned to a stage and the absence of a focus on moral behaviour); the absence of reference to familial and peer influence on moral development; and to evidence for universality (see Box 10.3).

Box 10.3   Criticisms of Kohlberg's theory

Despite empirical support for Kohlberg's theory there has been a variety of criticisms of his approach. In particular there have been criticisms directed at his methodology. Walker (2004), for instance, claims there is too much emphasis on moral reasoning and very little on moral behaviour. Bandura (2002) argues from a social cognitive point of view that individuals tend to engage only in harmful behaviour once they have morally justified why it needs to be undertaken. Hence, immoral behaviour becomes justified by social concerns and morally just reasons for acting that way. The assessment of Kohlberg's dilemmas has been criticised on the matter of scoring difficulty (Rest 1986). Rest (1979) found that individuals do not always progress through the stages in a set order. People in one situation might base a decision on principled reasoning (Level III) but revert back to conventional reasoning under different circumstances. Moreover, people flitter between postconventional and conventional reasoning across different dilemmas. Rest devised an alternative way to assess moral development called the Defining Issues Test (DIT). This is used to determine which moral issues are important to the situation under consideration. A series of dilemmas is presented with moral issues that could be taken into consideration. For example, by using the Heinz scenario, Rest adds further information that should be considered such as the importance of obeying laws or whether Heinz should risk being injured whilst being chased as a burglar. Rest also presented six stories where children had to rate the most significant issue in each story and consider its importance in their judgements. They were then asked to make a list of the four most important issues. Rest et al. (1999) claim this is a more reliable means of tapping into people's moral cognition. Also, findings from Smetana (2006) and Turiel (2006) supporting a difference between moral and social conventional reasoning (see Box 10.7), is largely absent in Kohlberg's approach. Although Kohlberg has been criticised for using a cross-sectional design (see Chapter 2) where children of different ages were interviewed instead of adopting a longitudinal study following the same children until reaching adulthood, Colby et al. (1983) did find that children traverse the stages in a set order. It is worth noting that Colby et al. made use of a longitudinal study involving 58 males over a 27-year span who were tested six times during this period. Another criticism that has been levelled at Kohlberg is the absence of familial and peer influences in his theory of moral development. Hoffman (1970) describes inductive discipline (also known as authoritative discipline) as helping children to learn about the consequences their own behaviour has on others. This form of discipline has a positive influence on children's moral development. Gibbs (1993) also highlights the fact that parental moral values influence the moral reasoning of their children. There is consensus among developmentalists, however, that peers do have an influence on the direction moral reasoning takes. There is some evidence for the universality of Kohlberg's stages but researchers argue that his theory of moral reasoning is not a universal one. It is culturally biased (Miller 2006, 2007; Wainryb 2006). A meta-analysis of 45 studies in 27 different cultures, however, provided support for Kohlberg's first four stages in the order described (Snarey 1987). As for stages five and six, there was inconclusive support for their universality. In a study of 20 adolescent male Buddhist monks in Nepal justice was not found to play a central role in their moral judgements but rather compassion and the prevention of human suffering (Huebner and Garrod 1993).

Even with all these criticisms, Kohlberg's theory has validity and empirical support – certainly for the first four stages. Furthermore, his theory remains widely respected and used as a point of reference in explaining how moral reasoning progresses across the lifespan despite concerns over his methodology and absence of familial and peer influences.

Both Piaget and Kohlberg focus on the cognitive element of a moral attitude. When we do something that is wrong there is often an emotion such as guilt or shame associated with knowing we have behaved inappropriately or a belief that we have behaved inappropriately. This was demonstrated in a study by Kochanska (see Box 10.4).

Box 10.4   Guilt or shame associated with doing something wrong (in this case believing that a transgression had occurred)

Researchers such as Kochanska have observed how children react when they feel guilty. Kochanska et al. (2002) tested whether 106 children of 22, 33 and 45 months experienced emotions of remorse, guilt or shame. Children were presented, for example, with the researcher's favourite stuffed animal toy cherished from childhood. Each child was instructed to be careful with the toy. The toys were 'rigged' to self-destruct as soon as the child handled them. The reactions of the youngest children showed a look resembling guilt such as frowning and fretting. At 22 months, Kochanska et al. (2002) believe it is difficult to separate guilt from shame as infants of this age fail to fully understand what they have done wrong. These infants' behavioural and emotional signs of discomfort, however, are considered as precursors of future guilt. In the case of the older children, overt reactions of frowning and fretting appeared to be masked by more subtle cues of guilt such as postural changes, hanging the head low, squirming and emotional discomfort and upset. It is also possible, however, that they experienced less guilt in the situation than the younger children. Bodily tension depicted by postural changes, for example, was the only type of behaviour that showed a significant increase with age. When children were tested at a later date (now aged 56 months), a difference in approach/avoidance of forbidden toys was observed. Children who exhibited less guilt when younger were more likely to play with the forbidden toys. In contrast, those children with an extreme guilt response avoided the toys in question. Kochanska et al. also found a difference in the extent of guilt expressed by boys and girls where girls showed more guilty reactions. These gender differences continue into middle childhood (Zahn-Waxler 2000). Such gender differences might be a consequence of different expectations of gender behaviours during the socialisation process. Kochanska et al. (2002) also studied the relationship between guilt and fearfulness using observational data. Maternal reports were considered and included observations of their children now aged 56 months. They found that children rated as having a fearful temperamental disposition as infants (e.g., showing avoidance of playing with forbidden toys) were also subject

(continued)

(continued)

to guilt proneness. The opposite was true for fearless children who approached playing with the forbidden toys. These findings have been supported using physiological measures, such as skin conductance level (SCL) and heart rate (HR) to record levels of fear (Baker et al. 2012). Baker et al. (2012) found that observed fearlessness in infancy predicted low levels of SCL arousal to fear and guilt.

This study demonstrates a consensus in the way children respond to having done something wrong. Children who showed excessive guilt were more likely to be fearful of playing with forbidden toys in the future. In this study the child had done nothing wrong but was made to believe that he or she had. For this reason there have been some concerns expressed over the ethics of the study. These children were subjected to a situation causing considerable distress resulting in negative emotions of guilt and fearfulness.

Sigmund Freud is an example of a stage theorist who focuses on the feeling or emotional aspect of moral development.

Sigmund Freud

Freud, the founder of psychoanalysis, believed that moral development occurred as a function of our emotions. The emotion of guilt and the desire to avoid feeling guilt is what drives our moral development. Freud described three facets of personality development (id, ego and superego) that interact in ways that help to develop a moral conscience (see Chapter 1). The 'id' encompasses our instinctive and selfish desires and operates at an unconscious level.

Plate 10.3 Baby boy with a guilty face. (Shutterstock 210536248.)

The 'ego' develops as a 'go-between' between the id and 'superego' and operates at a conscious and preconscious level (see Figure 10.4). The superego is important in the development of morality as Freud considered this to be our conscience. The superego has two main facets called the 'ego ideal' and 'conscience' and operates largely at an unconscious and preconscious level (although it partially operates at a conscious level). According to Freud, the ego ideal is mediator between parental expectation and feedback concerning correctness of their child's behaviour and the child's sense of pride and personal worth. Alternatively, the conscience acts as a punisher of wrongful behaviour and makes the child feel guilty and worthless.

The formation of these facets of personality is related to Freud's fixed **psychosexual stages** of development proposed in 1905. Freud's psychosexual stages are based on a fixation of **libido** relating to different parts of the body. Freud describes libido as sexual drives or instincts and it is this that becomes associated with different parts of the body, potentially providing pleasure or frustration or a combination of the two. These areas of the body are considered to be erogenous zones. He believed that our lives are balanced between tension and pleasure – the tension mounting due to bounds of sexual energy or libido which, when released, provides a sense of pleasure. In Freud's definition of sexual energy, he uses 'sexual' to describe pleasurable actions and thoughts. The id is considered to be the facet of our personality development concerned with our primary wishes, such as wanting to take a toy from a shop. The id is usually in conflict with social demands and what it desires. Both the ego and superego develop to mediate the desire for gratification posed by the id and to channel this in ways that are socially acceptable. The gratifications of the desires posed by the id are channelled into different areas of the body at different stages of psychosexual development (see Table 10.2). Each psychosexual stage has a specific conflict that the child must resolve. To resolve the conflict the child must expend sexual energy. If too much energy expenditure occurs at a particular stage, then it is possible that the characteristics of the stage in question become a fixation. This fixation can influence the psychological development of the child in later life.

As we can see in Table 10.2, during the phallic stage the child identifies with the same-gendered parent in order to reduce any anxiety experienced, to avoid feeling guilty and to maintain parental affection. This identification with the same-gendered parent promotes the

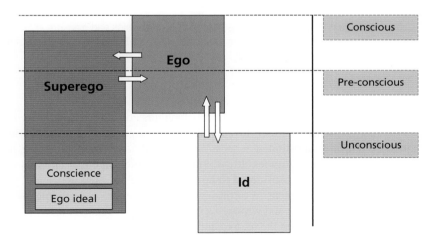

Figure 10.4 Freud's three facets of personality.

Table 10.2 Freud's psychosexual stages in relation to the id, ego and superego.

Psychosexual stage	Description
Oral (0–1 year of age)	Libido is focused at the baby's mouth. Satisfaction is derived by putting objects into the mouth such as the breast. Oral-oriented activity includes sucking, biting and feeding from the breast. Fixation at this stage results in an oral personality, where oral behaviours such as nail-biting and thumb-sucking occur more frequently in times of stress. The ego is beginning to develop.
Anal (1–3 years of age)	Libido is focused on the anus. Satisfaction is derived from defecation. The ego has developed enabling the child to realise he or she has desires. These desires can be in conflict with restrictions imposed on their behaviour such as during potty training. Harsh or too early potty training regimes can lead to an anal retentive person whose pleasure derives from 'holding on to their faeces'. Anal expulsive individuals, who experienced a liberal potty training regime, derive pleasure from 'sharing their faeces'.
Phallic (3–5/6 years of age)	The genitals become the libido focus. Awareness of physical sex differences means that a series of emotional conflicts occur. In girls this is encapsulated in the Electra complex and in boys the Oedipus complex. In boys, pleasurable desires are directed at the mother but they fear castration from their father should he find out. To resolve this boys imitate their father's behaviours and identify with him. By identifying with the father they are adopting his values, behaviours and attitudes. This results in a male gender role and feeds into the ego ideal representative of the superego. In the case of the Electra complex, girls desire their father but on realising they have no penis they develop penis envy and want to be a boy. Girls resolve this conflict by repressing their desires towards their father and substituting their wish for a penis with the desire to have a baby. After blaming their mother, girls repress their feelings and take on the female gender role. The superego develops during this stage.
Latent (5/6 years of age to puberty)	The libido is dormant and hidden. Defence mechanisms help to repress libido by involvement with other activities such as hobbies. Energy is channelled towards learning new skills and associating with the same gender.
Genital (puberty to adult)	Libido is directed towards heterosexual relationships and pleasure is derived through intercourse. Fixation and unresolved conflict during previous stages may result in sexual perversions.

internalisation of this parent's moral standards of behaviours considered right or wrong. It is these moral standards that help further develop the child's superego. As the child develops further, parental control is substituted with **self-control** attained by conforming to societal norms, values, mores and attitudes. It is during the phallic stage that children develop their superego. The superego is considered to be the centre of our conscience and plays an important role in moral development. We consider 'the conscience' as a guiding force in an individual's sense of what is right and wrong. As far as Freud was concerned, our conscience arises out of the interplay between the id, ego and superego but it is the superego that is the powerhouse of our moral decision-making in our everyday lives. The contribution of the interplay between the id, ego and superego, and the superego per se, to the development of our conscience can be explained as follows.

- The interplay between the id, ego and superego helps us to develop a sense of how to resolve conflicts of when it is acceptable to release or repress our libido and the form it should take.
- The interplay between the id, ego and superego helps the superego to develop the moral principles that our conscience is founded on.

Freud's perspective of how moral development occurs is difficult to test empirically. It is an interesting approach to understanding children's moral developmental pathway but it is difficult to ascertain if a baby experiences conflict between desire and social demands during the oral stage. Observations of children's behaviour might provide some support for what Freud advocates but then their behaviours could equally be explained in many other ways. In fact, Freud's theory of moral development does not really lend itself to scientific testing and, as such, it has received much criticism (Stevens 2008).

Developmentalists such as Nancy Eisenberg have also concentrated on the 'feeling' aspect of a moral attitude but in a very different manner to Freud. Eisenberg focuses on the role played by empathy in prosocial behaviour. In this way Eisenberg's stage approach considers the emotional aspect of moral development as well as moral action in the guise of prosocial behaviour – discussed next.

Nancy Eisenberg

As we have seen in Chapter 3, the emotion of empathy is important to how we respond to the distress experienced by other people. It helps to provide a standard of how we should behave socially towards others and respond to their needs in times of distress. According to Eisenberg et al. (2002) empathy comprises both an emotional state and a cognitive element. These two elements enable us to ascertain the covert psychological perspective of another person. Eisenberg et al. argue that appropriate moral behaviour arises through understanding the full range of emotional states experienced by others and being able to effectively foresee which actions would be most beneficial for their well-being. Actions that help another person are referred to as prosocial behaviours.

Prosocial behaviour involves helping an individual or an animal in need. Often prosocial behaviour is considered to be synonymous with acts of altruism. There is a difference, however, between the two. In the case of altruism, an action is performed to help someone else at some cost to the donor. It is a voluntary act and generally considered to be motivated by a selfless concern for other individuals (e.g., saving a stranger from drowning). Prosocial behaviour, alternatively, need not have a cost to the donor. Eisenberg et al. (2006) regard **altruistic acts** as behaviours performed strictly to help another person without concrete rewards (see Figure 10.5). It might be argued, however, that the rewards received derive from the satisfaction that **internalised values** and goals have been fulfilled or the approval of others received.

Eisenberg (1986) asked children to respond to stories that caused a dilemma – to choose between self-interest and helping another person. By helping another person the protagonists in these stories compromise their self-interest pursuits. One example of such a story was that, on the way to a party, a child sees another child who has fallen and hurt himself. If the child (i.e., the protagonist) stops to help out then he will be late and therefore misses the party food. What should he do? How the child responds to this sort of scenario was found to be age-dependent.

Eisenberg showed that children between three and seven years of age respond to hypothetical dilemmas using so-called hedonistic reasoning. This implies that their reasoning about the dilemmas is based on prosocial acts that would ultimately benefit the protagonist.

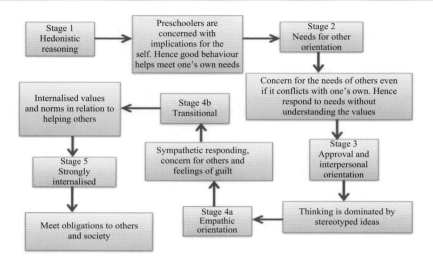

Figure 10.5 Eisenberg's (1986) prosocial reasoning chart.

Eisenberg et al. (2006) found that young children are capable of showing prosocial behaviour but it is not until reaching early adolescence that truly altruistic actions are performed (see Table 10.3).

According to Eisenberg, the moral reasoning ability of children develops early on in childhood (see Figure 10.5 and Table 10.3). How children think, feel and reason about moral events, for the most part, is a good predictor of how they will behave. This is, however, not always the case as can be seen from research on attitudes per se. The thinking and feeling components of an attitude can be incongruent with the behaviour exhibited. A teenager, for example, might believe it is wrong to steal money from friends and feels bad about doing so but nevertheless continues this behaviour to cover the costs of a smoking habit. Hence, the thought and feeling towards a moral wrongdoing are consistent but the behaviour is in opposition to the cognitive and emotional components of the moral attitude.

In a classic longitudinal study (between 1928 and 1930) Hartshorne et al. observed 11,000 children in a variety of contexts including the school and home environment. They placed these children in a variety of situations tempting them to steal, lie or cheat. In one example, children were given a test and the opportunity to self-mark their performance. This provided them with a temptation to over-inflate their marks. Unbeknownst to the children, their papers had been duplicated before being returned to them for marking. From their observations Hartshorne et al. concluded that it was a tall order to find a completely honest or dishonest child. They claimed that this is because the children's judgements and behaviours were situation-specific. The children showed inconsistency across many of the situations. For example, a child cheating on self-marking could be honest or dishonest in one of the other moral dilemmas presented in a different situation. Cheating became common practice when friends pressured them to behave this way, but the probability of not being caught was also influential. Their findings suggest that situational factors are influential in the development of moral behaviour. Moreover, various situational factors, such as peer pressure, can also influence the degree of morality shown. Generalising from Hartshorne et al.'s findings, it appears that most people think it is okay to cheat or lie under certain circumstances, especially when there are temptations.

Table 10.3 Age demarcation for prosocial and altruistic acts. (Adapted from research by Belsky and Domitrovich 1997; Eisenberg et al. 2006; Hay and Cook 2007; Warneken and Tomasello 2006, 2007).

Age	Description
Neonate–six months	Shows empathy to another's distress by crying and being upset; shows positive emotional displays to others such as smiling; becomes involved in social games.
Six months–1 year	Shows affection to familiar individuals; shows active engagement in social games and performs sharing behaviours.
1–2 years	Comforts others in distress; knowledge of caregiving skills; shows knowledge of rules in games involving cooperation; follows simple requests; shares toys with adults; shows helping behaviours; able to feel embarrassment, empathy and envy.
2–3 years	Shows increasingly more caregiving and helping behaviours; tries to protect others; offers helpful advice; tells others of his or her intention to help; expresses knowledge of tasks; begins to feel emotions such as guilt and shame; shows postures resembling pride on successful task completion.
3–7 years	Increasingly performs many types of prosocial acts.
3–11 years	Increased recognition of the needs of others despite any conflict with own requirements.
6–17 years	Subscribes to stereotypical definitions of good and bad actions and uses this to determine when prosocial and non-prosocial behaviour is justified; being accepted and receiving approval is important.
10–17 years	Experiences of pride or guilt following the consequences of their own actions become refined in the way they are openly expressed – more likely to follow conventions of appropriate social expression; shows increased empathy with others in a variety of situations.
14–17 years	Justification of helping others based on internalised values and notions of rights and dignity; self-respect based on living up to own values; belief in personal and social obligations.

Hartshorne et al.'s research was tapping into the notion of whether honesty is a result of a general personality trait or dependent on aspects of a situation. This divide is sometimes referred to as generality–specificity. Burton (1963) re-analysed their data and found that honest behaviour was not merely rooted within the situational context but is, in fact, part of an underlying general personality factor. Rushton et al. (1983) applied the principle of aggregation to Hartshorne et al.'s data. Aggregation is a procedure used for statistical analysis where an average is taken from multiple measurements. This is more reliable than using any one single measurement from the set in question. Rushton et al. concluded that there are robust associations between behaviour and moral traits. One such example they used is altruistic behaviour for five tasks and the child's reputation for exhibiting altruistic tendencies – this correlated at +0.61, which is significant. This result suggests that both general and specific measures tap into this form of measured altruism.

There have been other approaches to understanding moral development such as that proposed by Bandura (1986). In our next section we move away from stage theoretical approaches to consider Cognitive Social Learning Theory (see Chapter 1).

Cognitive Social Learning

Albert Bandura

Bandura (1991), and more recently Grusec (2006), claim that being able to exhibit self-control in an effort to resist temptation is an important factor in behaving according to one's moral principles. Being able to ignore pressures that encourage cheating, lying and stealing, for example, can, in part, be explained by self-control (see Chapter 8). Of course it also depends on how important the act of cheating is to the child – having a forbidden toy to play with might be perceived as a cheat worth doing. If given self-instructions to exert patience and self-control, children can deal with temptation more effectively. In a study by Mischel and Patterson (1976) children were given a monotonous task to perform but adjacent to them was a talking mechanical clown. This clown was heard enticing children to play with it. For the group of children trained to covertly say 'I'm not going to look at Mr Clown when Mr Clown says to look at him', their self-control was heightened. They managed to ignore the clown and continue performing the monotonous task they were asked to do. In contrast, the children in the control group, who did not receive such self-instruction, were less likely to resist the clown's beckoning. These findings support Bandura's Cognitive Social Learning Theory (see Chapter 1) of 1986.

Bandura argues that resisting temptation and showing self-control strongly links with cognition. Cognition forges the link between moral behaviour and environmental experiences (Grusec 2006). The relationship between the environmental context, cognition and behaviour is fundamental to Bandura's approach to understanding moral development. In his theory, there are two aspects of importance:

- **moral competence** – an individual's ability at performing moral behaviours;
- **moral performance** – an individual's performance of moral behaviours across situations.

In the case of moral competence, the individual has a set of social skills, awareness of social rules regarding moral behaviour, emotional regulation skills and cognitive understanding enabling the construction of moral behaviours. Moral performance, alternatively, involves behavioural responses that are motivated by social incentives and rewards for behaving in morally appropriate ways. Bandura (2002) acknowledges the important interaction between social and cognitive factors, both implicit and explicit, in the development of self-control. Bandura perceives self-regulation as the important factor in moral development rather than advanced reasoning. He states that in development of a

> *moral self, individuals adopt standards of right and wrong that serve as guides and deterrents for conduct. In this self-regulatory process, people monitor their conduct and the conditions under which it occurs, judge it in relation to moral standards, and regulate their actions by the consequences they apply to themselves.*
>
> *(Bandura 2002, p. 102)*

Bandura (2002), however, argued that individuals tend to perform morally unsound behaviours as a consequence of using their own forms of moral justification. By doing this it is possible to condone immoral behaviour using moral justifications such as social concern and just reasons for acting that way. This is a form of moral disengagement that Bandura uses to explain how good people can act in cruel ways (see Box 10.5).

Box 10.5   The role of moral disengagement

Moral disengagement is used to describe the process of convincing oneself that ethical standards do not apply in a particular context. This is achieved by divorcing moral reactions from inhumane behaviour. We are socialised to behave according to the mores, beliefs, values and morals of our respective society. The socialisation process is so strong that, for the majority of us, if we behaved in a morally unacceptable way we would subject ourselves to varying forms of self-condemnation (i.e., guilt). We use self-sanctions and activate self-control mechanisms driven by a self-regulatory system that promote socially acceptable behaviour. Self-regulatory mechanisms, however, need to be activated to ensure that we do not become morally disengaged from inhumane conduct (Bandura 1986). There are different ways that moral disengagement can occur. Harmful, dangerous and antisocial acts can be reasoned as being honourable and used as a moral justification for their enactment. Also, by divorcing oneself from the agency of action, this diffuses and displaces one's responsibility. Using the dehumanisation of victims and attributing blame to them for their suffering is a form of moral disengagement seen throughout history all too often. During Hitler's reign the Jews were scapegoated and blamed for the poor economy in Germany. Dehumanising them morally justified their suffering in concentration camps and allowed Hitler and his regime to morally disengage from the Holocaust they caused. Another more topical application of moral disengagement is terrorism. Here, 'moral justification sanctifies violent means' (Bandura 2004, p. 124). History shows us that terrorists indoctrinate people with a good moral compass to do inhumane acts using righteous ideologies, acting in the name of God or Allah, or perpetuating nationalistic agendas. Terrorists act aggressively in order to implement social change or obtain social power but use principles of religion or a political agenda to effectively morally disengage. As the intensity of aggressive and violent behaviour increases so does the level of moral disengagement. These are extreme examples but moral disengagement can also be used to account for school bullying. In a Swedish study by Thornberg and Jungert (2013), 372 children aged 10 to 14 years completed a questionnaire. The aim was to establish how different forms of moral disengagement were influenced by gender, age, behaviours of bullying and defending victims. Boys expressed significantly more moral justification and victim attribution in relation to bullying when compared with girls. Boys bullied more than girls but age had little influence. Younger children and girls tended to show more defending behaviours of those subjected to bullying. Diffusion of responsibility and victim attribution played no role in defending behaviour towards victims. This study demonstrates that moral disengagement is 'alive and well' among bullies in the playground.

Moral disengagement has been used to explain how individuals can easily lose their moral compass, allowing them to behave in inhumane ways. Common moral disengagement strategies used by bullies in the school environment appear to be moral justification and victim attribution.

According to Kopp (2002), self-regulation is achieved first by adult control and then by self-control. At 12–18 months, infants go through a control phase where their behaviour is modulated by adult instruction on how to behave. This gives rise to the self-control phase, where infants begin to submit to caregiver demands without having to be constantly reminded of how they should behave. The ability to behave appropriately without reminders runs in parallel with cognitive development such as executive function (see Chapter 4). During the self-regulation phase, children are able to apply strategies developed (as cognitive development advances) to direct their behaviour and increase their self-control. This means infants can delay their need for gratification as they develop their ability to self-regulate behaviours. Vaughn et al. (1984) demonstrated this in a study where infants of 18, 24 and 30 months of age could only hold out from touching a forbidden object for 20, 70 and 100 seconds respectively. Kopp (2002) found an increasing time value of self-regulation ability across preschool children using this same design. One question we might ask is, is it the case that when children acquire self-regulation their capacity to behave morally is enhanced? (See Box 10.6.)

Box 10.6   Is self-regulation the key to behaving morally?

Children reach the self-regulation phase between four and five years of age (although there is some variation from one child to the next). During development self-regulation appears to go hand-in-hand with self-control. According to Kochanska (2002), the acquisition of **self-regulatory processes** helps create a child who has a robust sense of moral-self. Kochanska further claims that such children have internalised the social and moral rules endorsed by their parents and follow the socialisation guidelines more closely. By conforming to these rules, children have sometimes to forgo their own gratifications and even make conscious efforts to activate their self-control. Caregiver input can help children to control their behaviours by teaching them how they should behave. One way of doing this is to ensure they learn the boundaries of what is permissible and what is not. Kuczynski et al. (1997) argue that by meting out punishment simultaneously with the transgression, caregivers are providing the child with clear boundaries regarding which behaviours are right and which are wrong (see Chapters 5 and 6). It is also important that the caregiver shifts from a physical to a verbal-based form of control, such as the use of explanations for why certain behaviours are wrong. This then enables children to exert the same type of congenial control measures towards their peers. This form of positive interaction between caregiver and child also promotes the development of a higher conscience (Kochanska et al. 2008). While these findings are interesting and provide support for the importance of caregiver and child interactions in the development of self-control and a higher conscience, they rest on correlational data (see Chapter 2). The problem with correlational data is that they do not provide a causal explanation, and so these findings describe the relationship between two or more factors only. Another important point is the relevancy of self-control in making moral judgements but not necessarily for behaving morally. The evidence for there being a change to moral behaviour as a consequence of developmental transformation to a child's self-control is limited. If we consider Mischel's Marshmallow task, discussed in Chapter 2, some children found it difficult to wait a few minutes in order to receive two marshmallows instead of one. These children, who ate the marshmallow straight away, found it a problem to delay their gratification, even knowing that they could have an extra one if they did so. This experiment was a good test for self-control but it does not inform us further about moral behaviour – along lines of rights, fairness and the welfare of others. If there had been another variable involved here, such as causing deprivation to another child by eating the marshmallow straight away, then we may have been able to connect self-control with some aspect of moral behaviour (the other child's welfare, for example).

Self-regulation helps to promote self-control. Correlational studies suggest that this relies on the socialisation provided by caregivers and the type of punishment meted out. While self-control can be an important factor in the nature of our moral judgements made, there is little clear evidence to suggest that it will directly influence our moral behaviour. Clearly, self-control is an important aspect of how we behave but more research is needed to make a direct connection with morality.

Another theoretical approach to understanding moral development in children arises from social constructivism. This approach highlights the ability of children to understand the difference between conventional and moral transgressions. First, however, it is important to understand what is meant by conventional and moral behaviour (see Box 10.7).

Box 10.7   What are the differences between conventional and moral behaviour?

According to Turiel (1983), societal conventions are shared uniform rules for behaviours arising out of the social milieu. These social conventions are the standards held within society designed to maintain social organisation. It is important to remember that, although many conventions are arbitrary, in that there is nothing inherently correct or incorrect about the behaviours they define, this is not always the case. According to Witherell and Edwards (1991), conventions are regarded as arbitrary by people outside of the social system in question. This is very different for people living within a social system as they perceive many conventions as being non-arbitrary. Hence, not all conventions are arbitrary as some function to enable people to live together more harmoniously. For example, many conventions provide predictability and a sense of order to what would otherwise be an essentially chaotic social life. Social institutions such as schools and hospitals function effectively (for most of the time) due to having conventions that provide organisation. In fact, societies function as a consequence of having a multitude of organised systems based on conventions (Nucci 2010). The underlying function of conventions in society therefore is to enable individuals and organisations to communicate and coordinate effectively (Witherell and Edwards 1991). Conventions, grounded in law, are there to protect us from endangering others as well as ourselves. An example of this is driving on the correct side of the road, because ignoring this rule is likely to lead to road accidents. Following legal conventions is therefore important and involves moral considerations. Social conventions concerning how males and females should dress, however, are less important and are subject to cross-cultural variations. While men in England and Wales do not generally wear dresses, in Scotland wearing the traditional kilt is not uncommon for men and nor is it considered to be an essentially feminine dress code. Hence, based on dress code alone, we can see how conventions are arbitrary and socially defined even within similar social systems. Social conventions are different to moral considerations. Moral considerations arise from the behaviours performed such that they are intrinsic to the interaction between individuals. An example of a moral issue occurring during a social encounter with an individual would be if we caused harm, as a consequence of our actions, to the person. Most moral issues are not considered to be arbitrary and remain separate from aspects of our culture. That is not to say, however, that moral issues fail to influence our legal conventions. Turiel (1983) argues that moral instruction (e.g., it is wrong to 'mug' someone in the streets) arises out of factors inherent within social interactions. In other words, in our example, it arises out of the interaction between the potential transgressor and potential victim.

Conventional behaviour derives from a rule-based understanding of what is considered to be appropriate ways of behaving. These rules are subject to cultural and legal expectations. Moral behaviour, alternatively, is driven by what is believed to be right or wrong behaviour. It has particular relevance to how we act towards others during social encounters. Causing others harm is fundamental to moral issues.

Social constructivism

Social constructivists are interested in the ways children and adolescents describe the differences between **moral** and **conventional transgressions**. Studies by social constructivists into how children and adolescents understand moral and conventional transgressions has led to a theory of moral development that is different to traditional stage approaches. Social constructivists believe that conforming to the social rules and how society expects its citizens to conduct themselves influences our behaviour. These conventions (i.e., shared behaviours outlined by the enveloping social system) become socially accepted over time and set the standards within society. As mentioned earlier, these conventions can be considered to be arbitrary because there is nothing to say that they are inherently wrong or correct − hence they are socially defined. Behaviour considered to be morally appropriate is dependent on people's actions and the consequences these actions have for others. In particular, moral conduct takes account of whether actions performed cause harm to other individuals and, in so doing, violate their rights.

Social constructivist Elliot Turiel (1983) argued that moral behaviour is driven not by external factors such as culture, religion or a social milieu, but by the contents of a social relationship. Thus, for instance, to what extent do children know that hitting another child during a play session will cause harm to that child. Children, for example, are told to play nicely by their caregiver. Prosocial behaviour is not always forthcoming from young children but, as they grow older, they begin to see the merits of being helpful and kind to each other. Being prosocial is often associated with moral behaviour such as children sharing their toys and helping a child who has fallen over.

Turiel devised a list of characteristics that can be used to separate moral from conventional transgressions:

- increasingly wrong and punishable;
- universally agreed;
- independent of authority such that moral transgressions are wrong regardless of laws.

By applying Turiel's characteristics, researchers have found that young children readily differentiate between moral and conventional violations (Nucci and Turiel 1993; Smetana 1993; Nucci 2001).

Plate 10.4 A boy misbehaving in class. (Shutterstock 389722207.)

Plate 10.5 Boy helping his friend to finish the race after having fallen over. (Shutterstock 380643181.)

The **moral/conventional paradigm** has been used by many social constructivists to examine children's understanding of the difference between the two concepts. This has been investigated by examining the reasons children give for why a moral transgression is more serious than a conventional one (see Box 10.8). Consistently it is found that children use the concept of harm as an explanation for why a moral transgression is wrong. Alternatively, in the case of conventional transgressions, children agree that it is okay to break a convention if no harm is done. These findings are representative of toddlerhood, childhood and adolescence regardless of religion or nationality (Hollos et al. 1986; Nucci 2001; Yau and Smetana 2003). Moreover, children with cognitive and developmental anomalies (e.g., those on the autism spectrum) show a similar pattern of response on this task (Blair et al. 2001; Smetana et al. 1999). There are, however, some children who are exceptions to this pattern. Children exhibiting antisocial behaviours, such as those seen in **conduct disorders** and attention deficit hyperactivity disorder (ADHD), fail to show the same pattern (Blair 1997). This has led some researchers to perceive the moral and conventional separation as having innate roots (Dwyer 2006; this will be considered later in the chapter).

Box 10.8 The moral/conventional paradigm and the findings

Turiel (1979) developed the moral/conventional task, which is a simple experimental paradigm used to test children's understanding of the differences between prototypical moral and conventional transgressions. Children were presented with a series of prototypical examples of both moral and conventional transgressions. They were then asked a series of questions to ascertain the reasoning for their responses. Questions included:

(continued)

(continued)

- Is the behaviour wrong? If yes, then how serious is it?
- Does the transgression depend on a rule being broken? Does it depend on an authority figure announcing the rule?
- Does the rule apply to everyone or to a select few people?
- Is the rule justified? Is the rule there to prevent harm, protect justice and the rights of others?

By asking children these questions (in child-friendly language) Turiel uncovered a difference in the reasoning used for moral and conventional transgressions (Nucci and Nucci 1982; Nucci and Turiel 1978; Smetana 1981). Turiel (1979, 1983) maintains that children construct the moral/conventional distinction by interacting with the social environment. In a study by Nucci et al. (1983), preschool children were presented with a moral and a conventional issue. The excerpt for the moral issue was as follows:

Researcher:	'Did you see what just happened?'
Child:	'Yes. They were playing and John hit him too hard.'
Researcher:	'Is that something you are supposed to do or not supposed to do?'
Child:	'Not so hard to hurt.'
Researcher:	'Is there a rule about that?'
Child:	'Yes.'
Researcher:	'What is the rule?'
Child:	'You're not to hit hard.'

The researcher goes on to ask if it would be okay to hit someone if there was no rule to say you cannot, to which the child replies no. When asked to give her reasons why, she said it would hurt the boy. A very different response is given to a conventional issue. When asked about children being noisy, she believed the rule should be followed but if it was not there then it would be permissible to be noisy.

Such studies have found that, for prototypical moral transgressions, children identified the issue of harming a person as a key factor. These transgressions were considered to be more serious and independent of an authority figurehead. For older children notions of justice and rights were added to the mix. Prototypical conventional transgressions (such as shouting in class) were judged as less serious and contravened rules determined by an authority figurehead such as a teacher. Reasoning for these transgressions did not appeal to concepts of harm, justice or rights.

The moral/conventional paradigm is widely used by social constructivists. It is a simple procedure and has helped developmentalists to understand the differences in reasoning children use when separating moral and conventional transgressions.

Moral transgressions elicit faster and more extreme evaluations by children, which appears to be a universal phenomenon (Van Bavel et al. 2012). This fits in with the assumption that we have a fast-tracking system for processing moral information. Some developmentalists have argued that we possess **'uniquely primed moral computations'** that operate when individuals are presented with a moral transgression (Cushman et al. 2006; Hauser 2006; Waldman and Dieterich 2007; Moore et al. 2008). This means that we are primed to process morally related information quickly without too much thought. Thus, morally related information, such as a moral transgression, is processed largely on an automated basis. Evaluations and judgements require little computation as we have a unique fast-tracking system for processing morally related information. Some developmentalists further claim that domain-specific moral computations occur when we make judgements concerning moral transgressions – but not when dealing with conventional transgressions.

Smetana and Braeges (1990) used the moral/conventional paradigm to test when the ability to differentiate between moral and conventional transgressions first emerges. They found that children as early as three years and three months knew the difference between the two types of transgression, and that this was the case across many different cultures (Nisan 1987). In a study of Amish adolescents, Nucci and Turiel (1993) found that even 'when God said it was okay to hit another person' these teenagers maintained that hitting was morally wrong. Their findings suggest that a separate cognitive domain for morality is at work here. Despite being religious and believing the word of God, these teenagers still maintained a belief that aggressive behaviour is wrong even when God gives permission for its use. The Amish teenagers effectively had a robust understanding of what constitutes a moral or conventional transgression – akin almost to an 'instinctive gut feeling'.

Preschoolers tend to focus on issues of physical harm as the determining factor as to whether a moral transgression has occurred (Smetana 1985). Older children, alternatively, will focus on other factors within the moral domain such as a sense of fairness and how behaviours influence outcomes (Nucci 2001). Although there is evidence that people have a sense of fair play (Henrich et al. 2006), the way 'fairness' is understood and implemented does tend to vary cross-culturally (Hauser 2006). The ability, however, to separate moral and conventional transgressions is ubiquitous. This has led to the notion of there being a distinct cognitive domain for processing moral-based stimuli (Dwyer 1999; Nichols 2004).

As children are not passive recipients of information provided during their socialisation experience we would expect them to interpret and reflect on information received, so much so that they can select the social rules they wish to accept (Neff and Helwig 2002; Wainryb 2006). Neff and Helwig (2002) argue that individual differences with regard to the social rules accepted emerge out of an interaction between cultural practices and the extent to which individuals comply with these. Moreover, this allows for there to be different takes on the meaning of social values, norms, mores, attitudes, rules and behaviours encapsulated within the socialisation process. These different perspectives are likely to influence the development of different cognitive domains. This idea of different cognitive domains is encapsulated in the **social-cognitive domain theory**. According to social constructivists who advocate social-cognitive domain theory, children construct their social knowledge according to three different domains: **moral**, **conventional** and **personal** (see Table 10.4).

In Table 10.4 the moral and conventional domains corroborate previous findings from studies using the moral/conventional paradigm (see Box 10.8). In support of previous research findings, children making judgements about moral transgressions will consider these to be wrong regardless of rule presence or absence. Also, in contrast to conventional transgressions, children judge moral wrongdoings as more serious and wrong (Davidson et al. 1983; Nucci and Weber 1995; Smetana and Bitz 1996; Turiel 2008). There is also agreement with previous research showing that children base their judgements for moral transgressions on the extent of harm and injustice caused by the perpetrator's actions. In contrast, the basis for judgements for conventional transgressions rest on social norms, rules and social expectations that underlie our social conventions (Davidson et al. 1983; Nucci and Weber 1995; Smetana 1985; Turiel 2008). Older children find it easier to consider events that have overlapping domains. Hence, they are able to identify and extract the moral and conventional elements co-residing within events. Moreover, they can reason about them – something that younger children find difficult to do (Crane and Tisak 1995; Killen 1990).

Table 10.4 The three domains of social knowledge – moral, conventional and personal. (Adapted from Killen and Smetana 2014; Nucci 1981; Smetana 1981, 2006, 2013; Thornberg 2010; Turiel 1983, 2006, 2015.)

Domain	Content	Judgement base
Moral	Notions of welfare, justice and human rights influence our behaviour across social relationships (universal and culture-free).	It is wrong to cause harm to another person – is an example of a moral judgement.
Conventional	Notions of agreed and uniform social behaviour defined by society (culture dependent).	Not showing a professional respect by using their first name instead of their title is an example of a conventional transgression. It is defined by a social standard quite independent of any interpersonal effect caused by such an action.
Personal	Notions of behavioural choice and preference that the person considers to be outside of any social regulation. Personal domain behaviours can be prudential (i.e., cause harm to the self) or non-prudential (i.e., do not cause harm to the self) (culture dependent).	Behaviours performed are likely to be judged as a personal choice and preference (e.g., selection of friends and music). Some personal preferences can cause self-harm (e.g., heavy drinking) but are considered okay by the actor because they do not put anyone else in danger.

In relation to the third domain in Table 10.4, children consider both moral and conventional transgressions relating to their own personal issues as increasingly wrong (Nucci 1981). Tisak (1993) showed that moral transgressions continue to be rated higher on the scale of 'wrongness' than transgressions of a prudential (self-harm) nature. Adult constraints placed on the way children and adolescents should behave are accepted when they involve the moral and conventional domains, but those directed towards the personal sphere tend to be disputed, especially if the behaviours cause no harm. Under these circumstances children and adolescents think they should be at the helm of decision making (Killen and Smetana 1999; Nucci et al. 1996). Nevertheless, when behaviours are of a prudential nature (can cause harm) then children believe that adults should intervene as a voice of authority and regulation (Smetana 1989; Smetana and Bitz 1996; Tisak 1993). An example of this might be a parent catching their child smoking. During the latter years of childhood and adolescence, however, teenagers increasingly believe that they should be able to regulate their own behaviour even in cases of a prudential nature (Smetana 1989; Smetana and Bitz 1996).

Decisions within the moral, conventional or personal domain often occur within the school context. Children and adolescents consider school rules concerning moral issues as the most important (Nucci 1981). According to a study by Smetana and Bitz (1996) rules of a moral and prudential nature were perceived in a positive light. As expected, transgressions of a moral or prudential nature were perceived more negatively than conventional or personal wrongdoings. Smetana and Bitz found that conventional transgressions were judged more harshly than personal wrongdoings. Conventional rules per se were perceived more positively than personal rules. This could be interpreted as individuals preferring others to follow conventional rules rather than self-made rules. When **personal transgressions** are made, however, these are down-played. As the school experience is an important and long-term factor in the lives of children, it makes sense to examine how school rules are perceived. In a Swedish study conducted by Thornberg (2008a) two elementary schools were considered. Thornberg was interested to see how school rules were interpreted within a moral, conventional and personal domain framework. Thornberg uncovered a five-rule classificatory system of school rules (see Figure 10.6). These rule categories partially overlap and reflect the different levels and complexity that underlie most school rules. Some of the different categories of school rules can be more readily associated with moral rules while others are associated with conventional rules. Based on Thornberg's findings (see Figure 10.6), relational rules can be viewed as being morality-driven while rules of etiquette and structuring define what the socially accepted conventional behaviours are. The different school rule categories are not necessarily mutually exclusive. For example, etiquette and relational rules can overlap such that profanities aimed at school peers can be a verbal form of bullying behaviour and therefore contravene a relational rule. At the same time, however, unnecessary usage of swear words in conversation can be considered an infringement of an etiquette rule.

Thornberg (2008b) demonstrated how primary school children vary in their reasoning about the different types of school rule categories. Children consider relational rules as

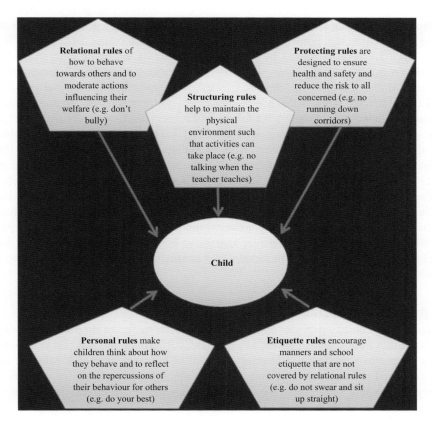

Figure 10.6 Five-rule classificatory system of school rules.

being important because they refer to moral issues such as harm and promoting equality. Structuring and protecting rules were also perceived as important due to having a courtesy and protection value for children and adults working within the school environment. In the case of structuring rules, children maintained that transgressions of this order interfere with the smooth running of school lessons and activities designed to benefit them. Etiquette rules were of least importance and perceived as being pointless. Thornberg (2010) found children of 10 to 13 years of age to be aware of all types of school rules and their attitudes towards school rules to be category linked – hence, for example, having positive attitudes to relational rules. If children perceive many rules as pointless they could become sceptical of the whole system of school rules.

As we have seen, it is clear that children understand the difference between moral and conventional transgressions from as early as three years and three months of age (Smetana and Braeges 1990). Moreover, this ability occurs at about the same age across many different cultures (Nisan 1987). They also understand the reasoning behind having moral and conventional rules in place, not only in the school environment but in the home and in society at large. These social rules influence not only the way children behave but how they want to behave. The socialisation process is partially responsible for children's social behaviour. Parents teach their children what is socially appropriate behaviour and why some actions are wrong and therefore contravene social moral codes of practice. Although caregivers socialise their children through reward and punishment schedules, verbal reasoning and by providing appropriate role models (see Chapters 1, 3 and 6), the socialisation process extends beyond the home environment. Children are socialised in the school environment and, as we have seen from Thornberg's work, are subjected to school rules crossing the moral, conventional and personal domains. In Chapter 7 we saw how children are also socialised by their peers outside of the home environment; what Judith Harris referred to as Group Socialisation Theory. According to Bronfenbrenner's Ecosystem Model there are informal (e.g., caregivers, extended family and friends) and formal (e.g., advocates from the educational and legal system) socialising agents. The informal socialising agents occupy the micro- and mesosystem, whereas formal socialising agents span across the exo- and macrosystem (see Chapter 1, Figure 1.5). Bronfenbrenner places the child at the centre of these layers of socialising systems as he believes that the child brings his or her own inherited factors into the mix. These influence the way the child engages with the environment (see Chapter 1). This also helps explain why some children are more likely to exhibit prosocial behaviours while others tend towards aggressiveness (see Chapter 11). But an interesting question we might ask is why do we tend to follow a prosocial rather than an antisocial behavioural model? Although aggression will be covered in the next chapter, we will consider aggressive behaviour in as much as it can provide an explanation for why most of us behave in a prosocial manner – discussed in our next theoretical approach.

Evolutionary psychology

Evolutionary psychology provides an explanation of how rules and simple systems of order may have arisen in our ancient ancestors (see Box 10.9). This might suggest that **hominins** (i.e., those species considered as directly ancestral to humans) have long been inclined to follow rules and to behave in a manner that encourages individuals to live together cooperatively. This would surely mean that we have long had the capacity to develop prosocial behaviour and show a sense of morality.

Plate 10.6 Imaginary depictions of how caring behaviour towards an ill friend might have been demonstrated by cave dwellers. (Shutterstock 125253950.)

Box 10.9   Evolved rule-abiding hominins: the role of kin selection and reciprocal altruism

A short lesson about our evolutionary ancestors will help us to understand why a system of simple order and rules were necessary for their survival. About 4.2 million years ago, our hominin ancestor *Australopithecus* moved away from trees and began to live mainly on the savannah plains. A gracile *Australopithecine* (i.e., less robust features) gave rise to species of the genus *Homo* about 2.5 million years ago. According to Workman and Reader (2014) fossil records suggest *Homo sapiens* evolved from the earlier *Homo erectus* around 150,000 years ago. Fossil and artefact records suggest that *Homo sapiens* lived in small groups of between 20 to 200 individuals – mainly in groups of extended families and close friends. By living together in small groups, survival under harsh environmental conditions was possible. Tasks such as hunting and gathering food sources were a cooperative and organised affair. Hunting and gathering food in groups could only work effectively if the individuals cooperated with one another. Based on extant forager societies it is likely that group members failing to find food would be provided with food by others. It is also likely that there would be an understanding that these members would be expected to reciprocate the favour at a later date (again based on studies of extant forager societies). There are two concepts that can be used to explain the helping behaviours of extended family members and close friends: kin selection and reciprocal altruism respectively. The concept of kin selection was introduced by Hamilton (1964) to help explain

(continued)

(continued)

why, in addition to parental aid, individuals are also likely to aid other relatives (e.g., nephews and nieces) because they share genes by common descent. Hence, we are able to pass our genes on either directly via offspring or indirectly by helping other relatives. Note that, according to Hamilton, the amount of aid we give will diminish as do the proportion of genes shared between two family members.

The concept of **reciprocal altruism** was introduced by Trivers (1972) to help explain hominin social evolution. He made a number of prerequisites for the evolution of reciprocal altruism (RA):

- the cost of performing an altruistic act is less than the (deferred) benefits;
- RA encourages reciprocation to friends;
- RA encourages the detection of group members trying to cheat the system;
- RA leads to the development of an emotional system of empathy and morality (both underpinning reciprocal altruism).

When considering the development of human laws, both cooperation and reciprocal altruism are often found to be at the heart of rule-making. Trivers (1985) argues that the pressures of living in social groups on the open savannah contributed to the formation of moral codes.

Moral codes to this day are entwined in our socially defined laws. Humans, as did early hominins, need to have social order to be able to live together peacefully. To evolutionary psychologists cooperation and reciprocation are two important driving forces underlying the development of moral codes and prosocial behaviour.

Plate 10.7 Imaginary depictions of how cave dwellers might have conversed peacefully by the campfire. (Shutterstock 208334998.)

Social conventional behaviours define how we should behave in different situations and contexts. These social conventional behaviours tend to be prosocial but there are pockets within any society where individuals tend towards antisocial behaviour. Fagan and Tyler (2005) discuss the influence of **legal socialisation**, where family members, peers and the neighbourhood moderate how children and adolescents are socialised into accepting prosocial values and behaviour. If families, peers and the neighbourhood favour antisocial values and behaviour then socialisation is likely to go against the more widely accepted conventions of behaving in a prosocial way. Prosocial behaviour is, in part, learned through socialisation and features strongly in what it is to be moral (see Chapters 6 (parental socialisation) and 7 (peer socialisation)). Evolutionary psychologists, however, have considered how prosocial behaviour might have arisen in our evolutionary past. Trivers (1985) acknowledged the importance of the existence of **free-riders** or cheats during hominin evolution who exploited moral codes such as sharing and cooperating with others. In smaller group sizes it was easier to identify those individuals who chose an antisocial pathway, leading them to be ostracised from the group. Moral codes and simple laws might have been developed as a means of negating the impact of free-riders (Krebs 1998, in press).

Behaviours considered to be prosocial tend also to be influenced by moral principles. Other behaviours labelled as antisocial, deviant, immoral and criminal (or any combination) are perceived as inappropriate and in some cases contravene the **human moral code**. Behaviours that contravene the human moral code (and the law) are universally regarded as heinous acts, such as murder and rape. These serious acts against the human moral code are referred to as *mala in se* **crimes**. The human moral code is not something we readily learn but instead arises out of what appears to be an innate capacity for empathy towards others' suffering. Many religious scriptures are designed, in part, to ensure people do not contravene human moral codes. Examples include the 'Ten Commandments' in Christian religions and the 'Five Pillars' of Islam. Whether moral principles arose from religion or whether they pre-existed religious practice is a contentious issue. The literature concerning the advent of laws, however, tends to suggest that some kind of social order pre-existed many religions practised today (examples include 'The Code of King-Ur-Nammu', which is the oldest known law code from Mesopotamia dating to 2100–2050 BCE and 'The Code of Lipit-Istar' outlining the legal code prevailing in all aspects of Sumerian society and culture of the 19th century BCE). Evolutionary psychologists have tackled the question of whether the development of morality preceded law and possibly religion. Some evolutionary psychologists have focused on how the human brain evolved mechanisms for processing moral decisions.

Ruse and Wilson (1985) argued that we are born with innate dispositions shaped by our genes that influence us towards prosocial and moral behaviour (and, as we have already seen, such behaviours help us to survive therefore passing on our genes to the next generation). It is interesting to note that inbreeding is not a particularly suitable reproductive strategy for promoting the viability of our offspring and, according to Ruse and Wilson, this would not make genetic sense. They argue that specific **epigenetic rules** ensure that we avoid sexual relationships with our own kin. It is no surprise therefore that incest is not only a moral taboo but is against the law. Such epigenetic rules are influenced by our genes but reinforced by our environment. Ruse and Wilson also argue that epigenetic rules encourage morally correct behaviour accounting for why incest is considered to be immoral across many different cultures. Ruse and Wilson's notion of epigenetic rules, however, has been widely replaced by Dennis Krebs' (1998) views on the evolution of morality (see Box 10.10).

Box 10.10   The evolution of morality

Dennis Krebs (1998, in press) expanded the epigenetic-rules approach of Ruse and Wilson by suggesting three pathways influencing the course of moral development:

- reciprocity;
- devotion;
- deference to authority.

Reciprocity contributed towards the creation of a prosocial culture and enabled hominins to identify free-riders responsible for causing a feeling of injustice. With the formation of robust bonds with a partner, as a way of ensuring paternity, devotion arose. Robust bonds and devotion increased the longevity of relationships which, in turn, helped ensure offspring survival. In the case of deference to authority, institutions such as law and religion have substituted the role played by the 'alpha male'. In Krebs' view, the social hierarchy in the times of our ancestral hominins had dominant males (i.e., alpha males) who commanded the deference of group members. To challenge such males would have had serious consequences such as fighting to the death. Instead of showing deference to alpha males, we now have the institutions encapsulated within our society to obey. This is different to the point raised about moral transgressions being 'independent of authority'. If a new ruling is introduced in law that is considered to be morally defective, then individuals can act in ways to defy the ruling as the moral principle stands alone, independent of the authority issuing the ruling. Showing deference to authority, however, is to obey those in charge to avoid chaos and anarchy.

Hence, according to Krebs, reciprocity, devotion and deference all served to develop laws and increase the likelihood of us behaving morally (unless the laws were in conflict with moral principles).

There is an important element of moral development and that is how we feel about the moral decisions we make. As we have seen earlier in this chapter, a moral attitude is interplay between how we think, feel and behave. Evolutionary psychologists have drawn upon other areas of psychology such as biological findings to help inform an evolutionary account of moral development. Biological measures of empathy have shown that this is expressed at a very young age indeed (see Chapters 3 and 5). In Radke-Yarrow and Zahn-Waxler's (1986) study, when babies were shown faces expressing pain, their stress levels rose. They concluded that the onset of moral universals occurred at a very early age. Hoffman (2000) claims that new-borns crying in response to hearing other babies cry is an example of a biological predisposition to show empathy towards others.

Zahn-Waxler et al. (1998) believe there is an underlying genetic basis for prosocial behaviour. Based on twin studies they found that the empathic tendencies of identical (i.e., **monozygotic**) twins resembled each other's more closely than fraternal (i.e., **dizygotic**) twins. Davis et al. (1994) had previously found this to be the case for prosocial behaviour. However, according to Hastings et al. (2005), prosocial behaviour and empathy are not simply a product of our genes but rather a complicated interaction with various nurture-driven factors such as caregiver support and the use of authoritative discipline (see Chapter 6). This is highlighted in a study of preschool identical twins by Deater-Deckard et al. (2001). They found that prosocial behaviour was shaped by environmental influences such as caregiver responses and how discipline was meted out.

Neurological research findings provide insight into the roots of prosocial behaviour and have also been influential in evolutionary psychological explanations. The use of brain scanning techniques has informed neuroscientists of structures and neural pathways that become activated when moral decisions are being made. While it is only to be expected that different situations and different responses are accompanied by different patterns of brain activation, scanning the brain informs neuroscientists of designated areas of brain activity for morally related decision-making. This might be taken as evidence that our brains have evolved in such a way to deal with moral issues. In a study by Decety and Chaminade (2003), PET scan imagery of the brain showed neural structures such as the amygdala becoming activated in response to sad stories.

Figure 10.7 An example of a moral dilemma used to separate moral-personal from moral-impersonal decision-making: the cases of Denise and Frank. (Based on Hauser, M.D., Cushman, F., Young, L., Kang-Xing, K. and Mikhail, J. (2007). A dissociation between moral judgements and justifications. *Mind and Language*, 22, 1–21.)

Greene et al. (2001) looked at the areas of the brain activated using fMRI scanning under conditions of **moral-personal** and **moral-impersonal** decision-making. Participants were presented with a range of moral dilemmas varying in the degrees of personal contact the protagonist had with potential victims resulting from their moral decision-making. One example of a moral dilemma provided a scenario of a runaway train that was on course to kill people if no action was taken to change its direction (see Figure 10.7). Denise, who is one of the passengers, could switch the train on to a different track thereby killing one person instead of five people. In another example, Frank could throw a large object off the footbridge to stop the train in its track from killing five people. The only large object to hand is a fat man standing next to him.

Greene et al.'s (2001) findings show there are differences in brain activation (using fMRI) across moral-personal and moral-impersonal decisions. They were able to locate areas of the brain more active under moral-personal decision-making (e.g., the **medial frontal gyrus**, the **posterior cingulate gyrus** and the **angular gyrus** – note that a gyrus is a 'ridge' on the cortex of the forebrain). Activation of these areas suggests there is more 'emotional arousal' when making decisions of a moral-personal nature. (It should be noted, however, that the mapping between fMRI findings and emotional arousal is not perfect.) From an evolutionary psychological perspective this makes sense as it may well have paid our ancestors to have developed mechanisms to avoid physically harming members of our own group (who tended to be relatives and close friends). Hence, making moral-personal decisions to harm others would require extreme circumstances such as immediate threat. Note that in the Frank scenario no such circumstances arise.

Another area contributing towards an evolutionary account is that of temperament, which will be discussed in more detail in Chapter 12. Young et al. (1999), for example, found that young children of two years of age, who were more able to inhibit undesirable responses, became increasingly more upset at another's distress than their counterparts who were less inhibited. Also children better capable of emotional regulation showed more consoling behaviour.

Moral development is a combination of a complex interaction between nature and nurture. It appears that infants are endowed with a predisposition to behave in a prosocial way

Plate 10.8 Decision to fight must ensure the survival of both self and friend. (Shutterstock 335741567.)

and to develop empathy for others in distress. Both prosocial behaviour and the ability to experience empathy are important for developing a sense of morality. Children, however, develop their understanding of morality and what constitutes moral behaviour partly through socialisation. Behaving morally (by showing prosocial behaviour) plays an important role in social development. In our next section we will explore just how much of an impact prosocial behaviour has on the way children and adolescents behave socially towards one another.

THE INFLUENCE OF MORAL (I.E., PROSOCIAL) JUDGEMENTS ON HOW WE BEHAVE

An interesting question we might ask is whether prosocial behaviour is facilitated by children's competency at making moral judgements and their capacity to care about the welfare of others? Research by Arsenio et al. (2006) suggests that children's moral judgements and moral emotional attributions are important in later prosocial or antisocial behaviour. Moral judgements and moral emotional attributions are considered to be associated with either actions of an immoral or moral nature in others (Malti et al. 2009b). Nunner-Winkler (2007) believes that children base their moral emotional attributions of others' internal states (e.g., negative emotions such as sadness, guilt and shame) on what they perceive is the motivation behind the action. Young children perceive transgressors as being happy because of the benefits transgressors receive. As children grow older they have a more in-depth understanding that moral transgressions can cause harm to others and are therefore serious wrongdoings. According to Turiel (2002), older children no longer attribute happiness to transgressors but instead assign moral emotions such as sadness or feeling guilty.

Malti et al. (2009a) found a positive relationship between prosocial behaviour and moral emotional attributions. They concentrated on six-year-old children with a teacher-assessed record of behaving in either a prosocial or aggressive way. Children who were rated as prosocial were more likely to attribute moral emotions to transgressors than those considered by teachers to be aggressive. Moreover, Gummerum et al. (2008) found that children who made moral emotional attributions were more likely to show later sharing behaviours with peers during play. Back in 1996, Miller et al. found a positive link between effective moral reasoning skills and prosocial behaviour among four-to-five year-olds.

Children are socialised not only by their family but by peers and friends (see Chapter 7), so it makes perfect sense that they associate with peers and friends who are similar in social outlook (including their behaviour). Dishion et al. (1996) showed that when adolescents associated with peers of an aggressive tendency they also behaved antisocially. According to Fabes et al. (2012), this is because exposure to aggressive peers provides these teenagers with a set of norms and values regarding how they should behave – in this case socialising them to behave negatively. Barry and Wentzel (2006) showed that this was true of children who adopted the attitudes and behavioural styles of their peers. Therefore peer affiliations have a profound effect on how children and adolescents behave. Sullivan (1953) and Youniss (1980) connected positive social adjustment and the acquisition of morality to the nature of peer social interactions. Youniss (1980), for example, argued that when peer interactions were cooperative, reciprocal and mutual, then individuals were more likely to consider concepts of justice, kindness and concern for others. Peer relationships have a two-prong contribution to the development of prosocial behaviour (Berndt 2002):

- good peer relationships are promoted by prosocial behaviour;
- good peer relationships determine prosocial behavioural outcomes.

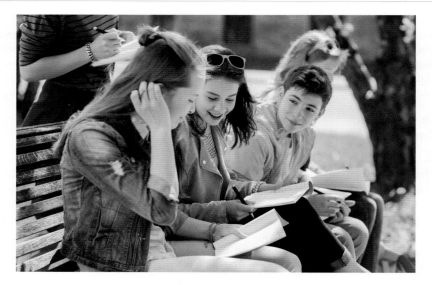

Plate 10.9 Group of teenagers happily helping each other out with school work. (Shutterstock 496115566.)

Fabes et al. (2003) used a sociometric approach to ascertain how often children of low or high prosocial ratings interacted with peers who were likewise rated as low or high on prosocial behaviour. They found it was rare for children of low prosocial skills to interact with others scoring high (i.e., this occurred in about 5 per cent of their interactions). In contrast, highly rated prosocial children socially interacted with peers of a similar status for 20-25 per cent of their social interactions. This figure was the same for the low prosocial ranking children. Fabes et al. (2012) were interested in whether the level of prosocial peer affiliation could be used as an indicator of the emotional quality experienced by children (mean age of just over four years) with their peers a semester later. They found that affiliation with prosocial peers enhanced positive emotional experiences. This suggests that peers can have a positive influence on social development.

Children's responses to moral transgressions inflicted on a third party have been used as an experimental approach to ascertaining a child's understanding of moral norms. Very little is known about how children respond to situations where harm is being inflicted on another individual. Vaish et al. (2011) considered three year olds' responses to violations committed against a victim using puppets (a design adapted from Rakoczy et al. 2008) (see Box 10.11).

Box 10.11   Puppet theatre – protagonists and victims

Vaish et al. (2011) adopted an interesting approach to test whether children are likely to intervene when a 'victim puppet' had its belongings destroyed by a 'puppet protagonist' or had similar but irrelevant objects destroyed. Hence, there were two conditions: harm and control respectively. They hypothesised that children would intervene more often in the harm condition than the control condition, simply because the actions of the puppet protagonist were morally wrong rather than just negative. Vaish et al. also hypothesised that under conditions where the victim puppet is absent when the transgression occurs, children are more likely to 'tattle' on the protagonist. Furthermore, they claimed that children would show prosocial behaviour and sympathy towards the victim puppet on her return. Their findings demonstrated that children did intervene on behalf of the absent victim puppet by tattling on the transgressor and exhibited prosocial behaviour towards the victim on her return. Such behaviours were more apparent in the harm condition.

This study shows that children of three years of age understand and apply their moral norms to a third party. They also punish those transgressors by tattling on them. Their prosocial behaviour towards the victim puppet in the harm condition shows a concern for her well-being.

A similar type of study was conducted by Palmer et al. (2015) on children and adolescents who were shown scenarios of verbal aggression between individuals from different groups (in-group and out-group):

- an in-group aggressor and an out-group victim;
- an out-group aggressor and an in-group victim.

Palmer et al. were interested in the development of prosocial bystander intentions as a function of the following factors:

- group membership;
- in-group identification;
- group norms;
- social moral reasoning.

They found that younger children prioritised social moral reasoning more than teenagers when it came to justifications for their bystander intentions. Teenagers in contrast, prioritised psychological reasoning for their bystander intentions, which reflected being part of a group and identifying with the group's norms. Palmer et al.'s findings suggest that children (in contrast to teenagers) are more likely to exhibit prosocial behaviour regardless of peer group allegiance and adoption of group norms. This suggests that children are less likely to follow group norms if they conflict with moral and conventional rules. For teenagers, the rejection of group allegiance and group norms becomes more difficult as it appears that they invest more psychologically. Moreover, in support of these findings, Palmer et al. found that bystander intention was influenced by whether or not the in-group member was the victim of verbal aggression by an out-group member. When an in-group member was the victim of verbal aggression from an out-group member, the bystander was more likely to express an intention to intervene. According to Rutland et al. (2010), there is a careful balance to be had between showing loyalty to the group and following moral principles. Mulvey (2016) showed that young children judged both moral and conventional transgressions towards an out-group member as more acceptable than such transgressions towards an in-group member. Moreover, Mulvey typically found that conventional violations are deemed less severe, but are still wrong. These findings suggest that conventional violations are often deemed permissible in the absence of a rule, unlike moral violations – hence supporting previous findings such as those by Smetana in 1983.

Social development is influenced by many different factors but there is evidence for moral reasoning and the level of morality acquired as playing important roles in how we behave towards others. There is some evidence of moral behaviour being rooted in the development of emotions such as empathy, guilt and shame. Although the development of guilt and shame require input from our caregivers, empathy appears to be present in new-borns, albeit in a rudimentary form (see Hoffman 2000). This suggests we might have a predisposition towards feeling sympathy for others in distress. Socialisation by parents promotes the development of moral thinking, feeling and behaviour in young children that continues into adolescence. This does not necessarily mean that teenagers will continue to be morally inclined and behave in a prosocial manner as peers also influence socialisation (more will be said about aggression and bullying behaviour in Chapter 11).

Summary

- Moral considerations are intrinsic to the behaviours performed such that causing harm to others is considered morally wrong cross-culturally. When broken they constitute a moral transgression. The conventions within society are there to maintain social organisation. These conventions are arbitrary and socially driven. When broken they constitute a conventional transgression.
- Stage theorists such as Piaget, Kohlberg, Freud and Eisenberg outline a series of universal stages that children traverse. Piaget focused on the cognitive value of a moral attitude. Based on observations of rule-governed games and responses to moral stories, he devised a three-stage theory: pre-moral, heteronomous and autonomous. In the heteronomous stage, children (5–10 years) are inflexible thinkers and see rules as static. They view outcomes of behaviour to justify their wrongness. In the autonomous stage, children (10 years upwards) think more flexibly about rules and moral issues and can make decisions about the wrongness of behaviour based on intentions of the person rather than outcomes.
- Kohlberg also concentrated on the thinking aspect of moral development by focusing on moral reasoning. He presented boys of 10–17 years of age with a series of moral dilemmas. From these dilemmas he devised a three-level six-staged theory. The first and lowest level of moral reasoning is pre-conventional morality (consisting of two stages). The child is oriented towards obedience and punishment and will show deference to authority figures. The next level is referred to as conventional morality (consisting of two stages). The child conforms to the expectations of society and peers and makes moral choices based on beliefs of right and wrong. Level three is called postconventional morality (consisting of two stages). The child makes moral choices based on ethical principles such as equality, respect and justice.
- Freud considered the emotional component of moral development. Guilt and the desire to avoid feeling guilt drive moral development. Different facets of personality (id, ego and superego) interact to develop a moral conscience that is driven by a series of psychosexual stages: oral, anal, phallic, latent and genital.
- Eisenberg advocates that prosocial decision-making develops once an understanding of emotional states is achieved. Her five-stage model begins with hedonistic reasoning where the child is only concerned with behaviours meeting his or her own needs. In stage two, the child becomes concerned with the needs of others even if they conflict with their own. In stage three, the child's thinking is dominated by stereotyped ideas. In stage four (a) sympathetic responding, a concern for others and feelings of guilt arise in the child. Stage four (b) is considered a transitional stage where values and norms relating to prosocial behaviour become internalised. Stage five shows that these values and norms have become strongly internalised.

- Bandura's Cognitive Social Learning Theory offers a behavioural approach to moral development. Being able to exert self-control as a means of resisting temptation is important in behaving morally. Self-control protects us from the pressures of lying, cheating and stealing. Two aspects of importance include: moral competence (ability to perform moral behaviours) and moral performance (performance of moral behaviours in different situations). These interact to promote self-control.

- Social constructivists, using the moral/conventional paradigm, have shown that young children understand the difference between moral and conventional transgressions. Children identify harm to a person as important when justifying judgements about moral transgressions. Older children add notions of justice and rights into the mix. Conventional transgressions are considered as less serious and only undermine authority figures making the rules. Children identify rule-breaking when justifying judgements about conventional transgressions. Three domains of social knowledge are identified: moral, conventional and personal. The moral domain is based on universal and culture-free factors. The conventional domain is culture dependent and involves agreed social behaviour driven by society. The personal domain is culture dependent but involves behavioural choice and preference separately from any social regulation.

- According to evolutionary psychologists having rules encouraged small groups to live together cooperatively and harmoniously. Trivers introduced reciprocal altruism to account for the evolution of moral development. Here, individuals engage in acts of apparent altruistic cost whereby the benefit was later reciprocated by another. Hence, moral codes and prosocial behaviour are driven by cooperation and reciprocal altruism. Krebs suggests there are three evolved routes to moral development: reciprocity, devotion and deference. Reciprocity created prosocial behaviour through sharing and helping out others. Devotion encouraged strong bonds with a partner that helped enable offspring survival. Deference to an authority figure gave rise to institutions such as law and religion.

Questions for discussion

1. Compare and contrast the theoretical approaches to moral development of Piaget and Kohlberg.
2. How do the three components of an attitude (i.e., thought, feeling and behaviour) feature in our moral development?
3. Bronfenbrenner addresses the importance of informal (i.e., caregivers, family and close friends) and formal (i.e., education, law, media and culture) socialising agents in our development. Provide examples of how both informal and formal socialising agents help to promote moral behaviour.
4. Critically consider what evolutionary psychology has taught us about how moral development might have initially begun.
5. Critically assess the validity of a moral/conventional paradigm. What does this method tell us about children's understanding of morality?
6. Critically examine the contribution of self-control in the development of a moral compass.

Further reading

If you are interested in exploring in more detail the topic of why good people are capable of doing cruel things and how they can selectively disengage from moral behaviour, look at:

- Bandura, A. (2016). *Moral Disengagement: How People Do Harm and Live with Themselves.* New York: W.H. Freeman and Co Ltd.

If you are interested in exploring in more detail how developmental psychology can provide a research-based approach to moral development that teachers could use in an educational setting, look at:

- Nucci, L. (2010). *Nice Is Not Enough: Facilitating Moral Development.* Upper Saddle River, NJ: Pearson.

If you are interested in exploring in more detail the criticisms of Kohlberg's theory and responses to these, look at:

- Rest, J., Narvaez, D., Bebeau, M.J. and Thoma, S.J. (1999). *Postconventional Moral Thinking: A Neo-Kohlbergian Approach.* New Jersey: Lawrence Erlbaum Associates.

If you are interested in challenging the view that there has been a moral decline from one generation to the next, look at:

- Turiel, E. (2015). *The Culture of Morality: Social Development, Context, and Conflict.* Cambridge, UK: Cambridge University Press.

Contents

Introduction 343

What is antisocial behaviour? 344

When antisocial behaviour becomes
a Disruptive Behaviour Disorder (DBD) 346

Neurodevelopmental disorders 354

Different types of aggression 361

Bullying, the bullies and their victims 365

An evolutionary psychological
perspective 379

Gangs 381

Summary 384

Antisocial behaviour

11

What this chapter will teach you

- What antisocial behaviour is and its links with delinquency.
- An understanding of the two main DBDs, Oppositional Defiant Disorder and Conduct Disorder, and the neurodevelopmental disorder, Attention Deficit Hyperactivity Disorder.
- How aggression can be reactive (impulsive and uncontrollable and unreasoned) or instrumental (controlled and premeditated) and how it differs across gender.
- Different types of bullying such as physical, verbal and cyberbullying.
- Knowledge of the relationship between perpetrator and victim, including the fact that victims can also be bullies.
- The bully–delinquent link and possible causes such as school and media.
- The relationship between aggression, bullying and the structure of gangs.

INTRODUCTION

In contrast with prosocial behaviour discussed in Chapter 10, in this chapter our focus shifts to children and adolescents who behave antisocially towards their peers. In every society there are individuals who resort to antisocial behaviour for various reasons – to gain status and kudos or to manipulate others in a bid to attain what they want. Children and adolescents are no exceptions here. There are some children and adolescents who behave beyond society's level of tolerance and resort to varying levels of aggressive behaviour, which can escalate into delinquency and other atypical behaviours. Antisocial behaviour does not always involve overt aggressive behaviour but can be considered as the antithesis of prosocial behaviour (see Chapter 10). Clearly, exhibiting antisocial behaviour and behaving aggressively deviate from societal norms of how we should behave. Despite this, however, developmentalists have shown that most children at some point in their development use physical force against other children (Hay et al. 2000; Tremblay 2000). There are some children and adolescents with behavioural disorders who are more prone to behaving antisocially. As these children have behavioural problems that interfere with their capacity to behave in a disciplined and prosocial way, it is important to describe their symptoms, which can lead to disruptive antisocial, aggressive and delinquent behaviour. Such children and adolescents are also prone to bullying other children within the context of school and outside of the school ground. Children and adolescents, however, do not have to have a behavioural disorder in order to behave aggressively.

Developmentalists have researched different types of responses seen among individuals inclined to resort to aggression. In order to do this we will consider the two main forms of aggression: reactive and instrumental. It should be noted that, despite this main distinction, there have been variants in the terminology of the different forms of aggression. Terms such as hostile, relational and proactive have been introduced, which we will also consider. Bullying has not escaped categorisation. Bullying can involve different forms of aggression that in children and adolescents tend to be physical and verbal. Bullying has been classified by Smith (2016) into six types varying in the nature of aggression exhibited: physical, verbal, social exclusion, indirect, cyberbullying and, finally, bias-prejudiced, which can take the form of all the others.

Within a school context, the victim is often subjected to bullying behaviour by a gang of children or adolescents. There is often a leader of the gang who has supporting followers (see Chapters 7 and 9). School experiences of bullying will have an impact on how children and adolescents perceive the world around them, their society and, ultimately, on how they respond to it socially. There is a wider issue concerning why children and adolescents behave antisocially within the school context, which we will explore. Hence, we will also explore aggressive behaviour in light of individual and contextual factors. Examples of contextual factors include the impact of television, film, Internet violence and violent video games on levels of aggression (see also Chapter 13). Are bullies influenced by such visual media and, if so, how is this reflected in their behaviour towards their victims? Alternatively, individual factors, such as temperament and personality traits and types, could be influential in why children and adolescents behave antisocially. Both individual and contextual factors will be discussed in relation to possible causes of why some children and adolescents follow a path of antisocial behaviour.

Before we can address definitions and typologies of different forms of aggressive and bullying behaviours, it is important to clarify what we mean by behaving antisocially. Moreover, we need also to consider how antisocial behaviour encompasses actions of an aggressive and bullying nature.

WHAT IS ANTISOCIAL BEHAVIOUR?

From a legal perspective antisocial behaviour involves 'the day-to-day incidents of crime, nuisance and disorder that make many people's life a misery – from litter and vandalism, to public drunkenness or aggressive dogs, to noisy or abusive neighbours' (Home Office 2014, p. 1). Developmentalists consider antisocial acts as being destructive or troublesome behaviours directed at others. Antisocial acts can, however, be in the guise of an illicit or a licit behaviour that is also considered to be morally offensive. Hence, a licit antisocial action may well be within the confines of the law but contravenes a culture's moral code. The opposite is also true where an illicit antisocial behaviour contravenes the law but is not regarded as breaking the moral code. A teenager, for example, who 'deals' cannabis to children on the streets, is not only performing an illicit antisocial act but an act considered to be morally offensive by many people. In contrast, a child who bangs on a neighbour's door late at night and runs away is behaving antisocially but is not committing a crime. To some this would not even be considered a moral transgression. It can, however, become a moral transgression if the behaviour is continuous and causes the neighbour psychological distress leading to a mental health issue. Antisocial behaviour can also be considered as **deviant**. The majority of people might find an individual living in a grave yard as a deviant lifestyle choice but also antisocial if he or she leaves cigarette butts lying next to graves. As Taylor (2016) points out, 'Differentiating between criminal behaviour and what is simply considered antisocial, deviant or morally offensive behaviour is a difficult task' (p. 49).

Children and adolescents who perform illicit antisocial behaviours are labelled as **delinquents**. Delinquent behaviours performed by a young person may vary from those referred to as 'petty criminal acts' to more serious criminal transgressions. When forensic psychologists describe delinquency, however, they are generally referring to 'minor crime'. These include:

- shoplifting
- petty burglary
- criminal damage
- vandalism
- handling of stolen goods
- assault

Delinquency therefore does not always involve aggressive behaviour as, in some cases, the outcome is destruction of property. In 2005, BBC News reporter Peter Gould described the existence of a British **'yob culture'** consisting of drunken youths who took to the streets fighting with each other and innocent bystanders. These youths failed to respect the law and the rules of orderly behaviour. According to the Ministry of Justice in 2008 (cited in Leapman 2008), youth crime statistics show a rise in delinquent acts performed by 10–17 year olds. Delinquency committed rose from 184,474 in 2003 to 222,750 in 2006. It is the more violent and aggressive delinquent acts that have seen steep rises over the years. These findings have been corroborated by numerous sources such as Home Office Statistics (showing, for example, that during this period an offence was committed every two minutes by juvenile delinquents aged between 10–17 years). In 2011 a large number of individuals (many of a young age) rioted in the streets of London and other major British cities. There was criminal damage to residential and commercial properties with many individuals smashing shop windows and looting for self-gain. There has also been a trend of **'happy slapping'** where young people use their mobile phones to photograph victims being attacked by receiving slaps to the head (Youth Justice Board 2009). Furthermore, a Mori poll carried out for the Youth Justice Board found that 22 per cent of these youths had also used their mobile phones to send antisocial texts and voicemails to people. These varying acts of delinquency can cause physical and psychological harm to victims. While physical harm is the result of an aggressive act, psychological harm is more debatable. For our purposes here, we will consider psychological harm as being caused by an aggressive act, whether performed through direct contact or more distantly using social media. An interesting question is whether children and adolescents who behave aggressively to others have a developmental disorder that puts them at risk of not controlling their aggressive impulses effectively. This is the topic of our next section.

WHEN ANTISOCIAL BEHAVIOUR BECOMES A DISRUPTIVE BEHAVIOUR DISORDER (DBD)

As any parent knows, children and teenagers will sometimes behave in antisocial ways. This is only to be expected and is even outlined in a table listing the **standardised age-related behaviours** by Gelfand et al. (1997). These age-related behaviours set a normative pattern of how the majority of children are expected to behave (see Table 11.1). These behaviours are often considered as undesirable but nevertheless are to be expected from developing children and teenagers (even though some of the behaviours might be illicit). This makes it difficult for caregivers to ascertain when their child is demonstrating problem behaviour. How can caregivers and practitioners know when children and teenagers are 'going through a phase' (albeit an undesirable one) of normal expected behaviour rather than problematic antisocial behaviour? There is a cluster of problems that have been referred to as **disruptive behaviour disorders (DBDs)**. Children and teenagers diagnosed with DBD often exhibit a range of problems with overlapping characteristics. Within the category of DBDs two common conditions are recognised: Conduct Disorder (CD) and **Oppositional Defiant Disorder (ODD)**. Attention Deficit Hyperactivity Disorder (ADHD) was considered as a DBD in version four of the Diagnostic Statistical Manual (DSM-IV-TR) but was recently moved to 'Neurodevelopmental Disorders' in version five (DSM-5). This change was administered to reflect the way ADHD is now conceptualised and it will be discussed separately under **neurodevelopmental disorders**.

The deciding criteria concerning when antisocial behaviour might be considered as a DBD are:

- onset age – the earlier the antisocial behaviour commences the more likely there will be a problem;
- frequency – the more often the antisocial behaviour occurs the more likely there will be a problem;
- longevity – the longer the antisocial behaviour continues the more likely there will be a problem.

In 1993 Moffitt introduced two typologies of antisocial behaviour in adolescents: **adolescence-limited** and **life-course-persistent**. These typologies differ in a number of ways, but the two dividing factors are the age of onset and the longevity of the antisocial behaviour exhibited. Individuals classified as life-course-persistent engage in antisocial behaviour from a young age (usually from the age of 10) that continues into adulthood. Their behaviours are supported by the nature of their **criminogenic environment**. In the case of individuals classified as adolescent-limited, antisocial behaviour occurs as a consequence of a maturity gap in their teen years (i.e., they are immature). This maturity gap encourages them to mimic the antisocial behaviours exhibited by other antisocial adolescents, especially when they see the rewards gained by behaving this way. It has long been noted that the longevity of antisocial behaviour depends on its onset – the earlier it first occurs the longer it will continue (Farrington 1983; Loeber 1982). Furthermore, families who encourage antisocial models of behaviour are more likely to have children who will behave antisocially (Patterson 1982, 1986; Patterson et al. 1989). This finding of a distinction between early and late onset antisocial behaviour continues to be an important area of research (Schulenberg and Zarrett 2006). Roisman et al. (2004) support previous findings that early onset antisocial behaviour persists into adulthood. Roisman et al. also found that there are likely to be mental health problems occurring concurrently. Such individuals also exhibit problems in forming social and sexual relationships with others. Often early onset

Table 11.1 A table of standardised age-related undesirable behaviour.

Age	Description of age-related undesirable behaviour
1 ½ to 2 years	Over activity, inattentiveness, wanting continual attention, defiance, expression of temper tantrums, experience of specific fears.
3 to 5 years	Over activity, defiance, wanting continual attention, expression of temper tantrums, experience of specific fears, negative outlook, over-sensitivity, make up lies.
6 to 10 years	Over activity, expression of temper tantrums, experience of specific fears, over-sensitivity, make up lies, achievement problems in school, jealousy, reserve outlook.
11 to 14 years	Expression of temper tantrums, over-sensitivity, achievement problems in school, jealousy, reserve outlook, moodiness.
15 to 18 years	Achievement problems in school, truancy from school, drinking, smoking and using drugs, early sexual activity, minor law transgressions such as shoplifting and trespassing, a depressed outlook.

antisocial behaviour occurs in children as a consequence of an inability to control aggressive outbursts. We will consider Oppositional Defiant Disorder as our first DBD.

Oppositional Defiant Disorder

Oppositional Defiant Disorder (ODD) has been defined by DSM-5 as 'A pattern of angry/irritable mood, argumentative/defiant behavior, or vindictiveness lasting at least 6 months . . .' (American Psychiatric Association 2013).

In DSM-5 the common symptoms of ODD are divided into three categories (see Table 11.2).

The DSM-5 outlines two other categories of symptoms: disturbed behaviour is linked with the child's distress or distress shown by others and that behaviours occur independent of a psychotic episode, depression or substance use. Furthermore, symptoms exhibited can be categorised as mild (confined to one situational context), moderate (exhibited in at least two situational contexts) and severe (exhibited in three or more situational contexts). Children diagnosed with ODD tend to be regarded as exhibiting less severe behaviours than those with a Conduct Disorder (CD) diagnosis (see Conduct Disorder). The social skills of

Table 11.2 The criteria used by DSM-5 to describe ODD symptoms.

Categories of symptoms	Descriptions
Angry/irritable mood	Easy to annoy, regular loss of temper, regularly shows anger and resentfulness.
Argumentative/defiant behaviour	Regularly argues with others including those in authority, refusal to obey or follow rules or comply with requests, intent to annoy others, refusal to take the blame for own errors or misdemeanours.
Vindictiveness	Showing spitefulness and vindictiveness twice within a six-month frame.

Plate 11.1 The face of a defiant teenager. (Shutterstock 58601296.)

children with ODD appear to be more impaired than those of their CD counterparts but they nevertheless perform better at school. Children with ODD misbehave and show disobedience towards others. They also exhibit defiance and hostility towards others simply for the sake of it. Common cognitive symptoms include difficulty in concentration and not thinking before speaking. They frequently feel frustrated and annoyed. As well as problems of making and maintaining friendships they also experience a loss of self-esteem. This can lead to social isolation and problems at school. It has been found that two-thirds of children who receive treatment for their symptoms of ODD are symptom-free after three years. Such treatments include **psychotherapy** such as counselling or **cognitive-behavioural therapy (CBT)**, which helps to reshape the thinking patterns of the child. Family therapy is also used as a way of improving interactions and communications within families. Parent management training enables parents to reshape their child's behaviour positively. The alternative route is to use medication normally given to those with ADHD or depression in order to attenuate the more distressing symptoms. If the symptoms and diagnosis of ODD are ignored, it is possible for these children to progress to CD – thirty per cent according to Connor (2002). Cohen and Flory (1998) alternatively argued that only a small proportion of these children ever cross the CD boundary. Causal explanations for ODD will be addressed in Box 11.1.

Box 11.1   What causes ODD?

Explanations for why ODD develops include genetic, physiological and environmental factors. In the case of genetic factors, children with ODD tend to have family members who experience many different types of mental illness such as mood, personality and anxiety disorders. First-degree relatives who have a mental illness including ODD, CD or ADHD, depression, anxiety or a personality disorder, increase the likelihood of ODD onset. If a sibling has the disorder then the chances of developing it increases. This suggests a genetic element causing an individual to be susceptible to acquiring ODD. There are a multitude of physical explanations influencing the development of ODD. Using the startle reflex (blink responses) as a way of investigating fearlessness in children with ODD, van Goozen et al. (2004) found that those with ODD had a lower startle response to emotional slides. These children were also assessed using the delinquency subscale of the Child Behavioural Checklist (CBCL), a test devised by Achenbach (1991). van Goozen et al.'s findings suggest that the more delinquent these children were the less of a startle response they exhibited to negative emotional slides – which suggests an underactive amygdala. Other physiological measures such as skin conductance, heart rate and cortisol levels are lower in children with ODD compared with control groups. These measures in combination have led to the 'fearlessness theory of antisocial behaviour' (Raine 1993). According to this theory, reduced skin conductance and heart rate reflect low levels of fear. Because children with ODD tend to be fearless they are more likely to instigate fights. van Goozen et al. (1998) studied boys with ODD with a mean age of 10 years. They measured cortisol levels in samples of saliva. The boys were divided into four groups according to their level of disruptive, aggressive and anxiety behaviours ascertained using the CBCL. The four combinations were: high aggressive and anxiousness; high aggressive–low anxiousness; low aggressive and anxiousness, and low aggressive–high anxiousness. van Goozen et al. (1998) presented ODD boys with conditions that increased their frustration. With increased frustration their anger escalated and so did their heart rate and blood pressure. They found that cortisol increased during stressful conditions when the boys were classified as highly aggressive, disruptive and anxious. Cortisol levels decreased for the boys who were highly aggressive and disruptive but not anxious. This is an interesting finding and highlights a developmental continuity between children with ODD and antisocial adults. Other physical measures show that children with ODD have differences in neurotransmitter levels. In particular, they have low levels of serotonin and noradrenaline that might, in turn, be responsible for low sensitivity to punishment. This accounts for why individuals make poor judgements about which behaviours are inappropriate. There might also be problems in specific areas of the brain involved in executive function, such that control over motivations and emotional behaviour become impaired. Environmental factors involving the child's home-life suggests that marital discord and general familial chaos significantly increase ODD symptoms. Observing violence or being exposed to it encourages destructive and reckless behaviours and can also correlate with the onset of ODD. There are other environmental risk factors for ODD. A stressful environment, dysfunctional family, inconsistent discipline, exposure to violence, alcohol or drug abuse, parental abuse, neglect and rejection can all trigger or influence onset.

There are many factors influencing the onset of ODD. There appear to be underlying genetic causes but this alone does not explain all the symptoms. Clearly a disruptive home environment greatly increases the risk of developing ODD.

The second DBD condition we will consider is referred to as Conduct Disorder (CD). Of the two DBDs and the neurodevelopmental condition ADHD, CD is considered to be the most serious and disruptive. This will be considered next.

Conduct Disorder (CD)

Conduct Disorder has been defined by DSM-5 as 'A repetitive and persistent pattern of behaviour in which the basic rights of others or major age-appropriate societal norms or rules are violated' (American Psychiatric Association 2013).

In DSM-5 the common symptoms of CD are divided into four categories (see Table 11.3). There are, however, two other sections: the behaviour causing disturbance also affects social, academic or occupational functioning, and if an 18 year old fails to meet the criteria for anti-social personality disorder then he/she will receive a diagnosis of CD.

Table 11.3 The criteria used by DSM-5 to describe CD symptoms.

Category of symptoms	Description
Aggression to people (and animals)	Intimidation and bullying, cruelty to people and animals, regularly causes physical fights, stealing/mugging, use of weaponry to cause harm to others, coercive sexual activity.
Destruction of property	Fire-setting with intent to cause damage and harm, deliberate destructiveness to property.
Deceitfulness/theft	Delinquent acts such as breaking into houses, buildings or cars, other delinquent acts include stealing such as shoplifting and forgery, lies as a way of attaining goods or getting out of obligations.
Serious violations of rules	Disobeys parental rules before 13 years of age by staying out at night, truancy from school before 13 years of age, running away from home overnight or once for a lengthy amount of time.

The occurrence of CD in children has been estimated at approximately 5 per cent. From parental reports, findings suggest that about 50 per cent of children between four and six years of age have caused damage to property, stolen money, told lies and refused to follow rules at some point in their development (Achenbach 1997). Achenbach, however, points out that, for most of these children, such behaviours disappear by late adolescence. In cases where such antisocial behaviour continues and escalates well into adolescence, these individuals are often referred for therapeutic intervention (Achenbach 1997). Individuals with CD perform a wide range of antisocial behaviours that violate both moral and conventional rules (American Psychiatric Association 2000). According to Sterzer et al. (2005), behaviours can range from less serious (e.g., swearing and exhibiting temper tantrums) to more serious antisocial acts (e.g., vandalism and assault). According to DSM-5, practitioners can specify whether the onset of CD occurred in childhood prior to 10 years of age or during adolescence (i.e., no symptoms before 10 years of age) or an unspecified onset. Furthermore, there are other specifications that can be recorded such as the level of prosocial emotions present (e.g., lack of remorse, guilt and empathy; lack of concern about performance ability and shallow presentation of emotional expression). As is the case with ODD and ADHD (discussed next), symptoms can be mild, moderate or severe. In cases of a severe diagnosis, extreme harm to others occurs.

Although some of the above behaviours are not unique to children and teenagers diagnosed with CD (see Table 11.3), the sheer intensity, frequency and longevity of these actions is a feature of such individuals. Studies have found that individuals with CD fail to develop a mature moral compass and lack the ability to demonstrate empathy for others. Moreover, they are incapable of showing appropriate levels of guilt for the destruction they cause to others (Cohen and Strayer 1996; Frick and Silverthorn 2001; Obradović et al. 2007). Deficits in empathy and guilt contribute towards a poorly developed conscience. Barkley (1990) argued that these characteristics result from a deficiency in developing rule-governed behaviour and self-management skills (Rhode et al. 1993). Such deficiencies in the development of rule-governed behaviour and self-management skills in children and teenagers with CD can be exhibited in the form of insufficiently controlled **behavioural excesses** and **behavioural deficits**. Based on the common descriptions of CD behaviours, it is possible to separate these

Plate 11.2 Child contemplating stealing grandmother's coins for the electricity meter. (Shutterstock 218105845.)

into behavioural excesses and behavioural deficits (see Table 11.4). Note that while many of the listed characteristics in the behavioural excesses category are specified in DSM-5, not all those mentioned under behavioural deficits are. Instead these characteristics are a conglomeration of the many findings from research and parental reports.

One area of research focuses on the underlying physiological factors causing behavioural excesses seen in children and adolescents with CD. Such research has uncovered two motivational systems considered to be involved in the regulation of approach and

Table 11.4 CD behavioural characteristics.

Behavioural excesses
Aggression – physically attacks others, is verbally abusive, causes criminal damage and vandalism, sets fires, is revengeful, shows cruelty to animals.
Non-compliance – breaks rules, fails to follow orders, is defiant, performs the opposite of that asked.

Behavioural deficits
Moral behaviour – little remorse is shown, lacks concern for others, poorly developed conscience.
Social behaviour – unable to form bonds with others so has few friends, lacks affection, has little in the way of problem-solving skills, acts aggressively and impulsively, unable to cooperate, is an attention-seeker, poor conversation skills.
Academic performance and schooling – have poor reading and numerical skills, lagging behind academically, poor at new information acquisition, truant.

withdrawal behaviour in response to various environmental stimuli (Depue and Collins 1999; Gray 1982). These are referred to as the **behavioural inhibition system (BIS)** and the **behavioural activation system (BAS)** (more recently the behavioural approach system). The BAS activates approach, happiness and motor activity and BIS activates avoidance, inhibition and anxiety. High levels of BAS activation has been used to help account for the behavioural excesses seen in CD (Quay 1993; Muris et al. 2005). More specifically, high levels of BAS and low levels of BIS could be used to help explain CD behaviours (Carver and White 1994; Newman et al. 1997; Quay 1993, 1997). Thrill-seeking and a lack of

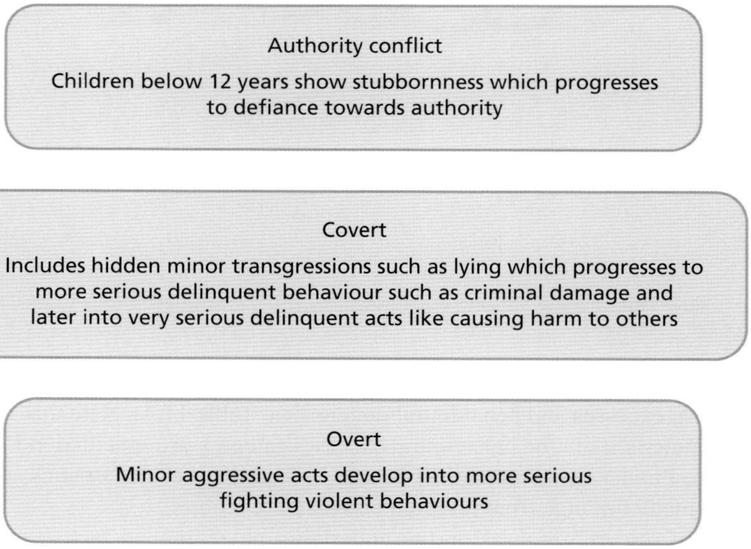

> **Authority conflict**
> Children below 12 years show stubbornness which progresses to defiance towards authority

> **Covert**
> Includes hidden minor transgressions such as lying which progresses to more serious delinquent behaviour such as criminal damage and later into very serious delinquent acts like causing harm to others

> **Overt**
> Minor aggressive acts develop into more serious fighting violent behaviours

Figure 11.1 The three developmental pathways to delinquency.

sensitivity to punishment, often seen in children and adolescents with CD, has been explained as problems of both the behavioural inhibition system (BIS) and the behavioural activation system (BAS). According to McBurnett (1992), these systems are part of the **septo-hippocampal structure** of the brain responsible for the regulation of fear and anxiety. It has been suggested by Quay (1988) that an overactive BAS compels the child to seek rewards and thrills while an underactive BIS reduces the experience of fear and anxiety.

There are other explanations for what causes of CD that will be considered in Box 11.2. An interesting longitudinal study focusing on approximately 1,500 boys living in the inner-city of Pittsburgh uncovered three developmental pathways that delinquents diagnosed with CD follow (see Figure 11.1).

Box 11.2   What causes CD?

Different explanations of how CD develops have been put forward. There are theories claiming that individuals with CD have a disposition towards developing a specific type of temperament – an antisocial one. In a classic longitudinal study by Thomas and Chess (1986) 136 two-year-old children living in New York could be classified under three basic types of temperament. Sixty-five per cent of the children were classified into one of these three categories, but the remaining 35 per cent failed to fit one category exclusively. Of the 65 per cent, 10 per cent were 'difficult' children who cried, were easily frustrated such that they commonly experienced tantrums and had negative moods. Fifteen per cent were considered as 'slow to warm up' children who were slow to adapt to changes and had low activity levels. Forty per cent were perceived as 'easy' children. Thomas and Chess found that 70 per cent of the difficult children developed behavioural disorders ranging from depression to CD.

According to Keenan and Shaw (2003), several studies have shown a link between an irritable temperament and having conduct problems. Temperament can therefore be considered as a biological risk factor for the development of CD in children. As we have seen in Chapter 3, the DRD4-7-repeat gene has been implicated in the development of a difficult temperament. Another gene known as monoamine oxidase type A (MAOA) has been associated with aggressive behaviour and violence (Feresin 2009; Kim-Cohen et al. 2006). The MAOA gene plays an important role in the metabolism of neurotransmitters that, if poorly regulated, can cause problem behaviour. The MAOA gene codes for an enzyme called monoamine oxidase A. This enzyme degrades neurotransmitters such as dopamine, noradrenalin and serotonin. If a mutation in the gene causes a deficiency in this enzyme, then high levels of neurotransmitters remain in the brain causing excessive impulsive behaviour, hypersexuality and violence (Hunter 2010). Furthermore, in support of the notion that genetic factors are involved in the development of CD, there is a higher concordance for antisocial behaviour in identical twins than there is for fraternal twins (Eysenck and Eysenck 1975). Moffitt (2005) claimed there is robust evidence based on twin and adoption research that CD is heritable. In a study of twins by Jaffee et al. (2003), the child-rearing environment (e.g., maltreatment) interacted with a high genetic risk for CD by 24 per cent, but by only 2 per cent in cases of low genetic risk. This provides evidence of a gene–environment interaction (Dodge and Rutter 2011) and implies that the risk of developing CD can be attenuated if positive changes are made to child-rearing practices (Odgers et al. 2007). Other deficits are associated with CD such as poor verbal skills (Lynam and Henry 2001). According to Dodge (2006) children who have problems using language to assert themselves have a tendency to do so using aggressive social interactions. Individuals with CD have poorly developed executive functions (Hobson et al. 2011; Ishikawa and Raine 2003). Executive function, as we

(continued)

(continued)

discussed in Chapter 4, is important for reasoning, problem solving, maintaining attention and concentration, and achieving goals using appropriate channels. Performing executive-related tasks successfully is linked with effective frontal lobe function. Family factors such as attachment, the type and consistency of disciplinary actions and family dynamics (e.g., atmosphere and extent of marital discord) have been shown to influence the extent of CD symptoms. Scott et al. (2011) showed that the type of attachment representation a child has of the caregiver independently predicts CD symptomology regardless of the quality of parenting provided. This means that how the child perceives the attachment rather than the nurturing received is more important to the development of CD behaviours. Frick (1993) found that harsh and physically abusive discipline and parental inconsistency in punishment meted out linked positively with CD behaviours. This was especially played out when parents were rejecting and authoritarian (Frick 1993). Cummings and Davies (2002) claim that marital discord and disharmonious dynamics occurring in families affects the child's ability to regulate their emotions, which ultimately influences their behaviour. Children who see violence in the family become fearful but control their reactions by denial. This then leads to a lifelong problem of appraising social situations correctly and using appropriate social problem-solving skills. It can also lead to modelling the behaviour of the aggressor. Jaffee et al. (2003) also point out that, in situations of abuse, children are unable to effectively regulate their anger responses, which provides them with a model of violent responding when stressed. They argue that this can result in CD.

There are a number of possible factors that together enhance the problematic behaviours seen in children with CD. There is much evidence to suggest that a temperamental issue is the prime driver of CD symptoms. A gene–environment interaction, however, is strongly implicated in the symptoms of CD.

NEURODEVELOPMENTAL DISORDERS

Neurodevelopmental disorders consist of a collection of conditions characterised by developmental deficits. These deficits typically cause impairments to a child's personal, social and academic functioning. Dysfunction can take the form of specific limitations to learning and executive functions or global impairments of communication and intelligence per se. Examples of neurodevelopmental disorder include Attention Deficit/Hyperactivity Disorder (ADHD) and Autism Spectrum Disorder (ASD). Here we will consider ADHD as ASD was previously discussed in Chapter 5.

Attention Deficit Hyperactivity Disorder

Attention Deficit Hyperactivity Disorder is defined in DSM-5 as 'A persistent pattern of inattention and/or hyperactivity-impulsivity that interferes with functioning or development' (American Psychiatric Association 2013). There are two aspects to the disorder: inattention, and hyperactivity and impulsivity. In DSM-5 there are nine criteria meeting the inattentive aspect of ADHD (see Table 11.5).

DSM-5 also outlines nine criteria meeting the hyperactive-impulsive aspect of ADHD (see Table 11.6).

Children and adolescents under 17 years must show six out of nine from the inattentive and/or hyperactive-impulsive lists of symptoms. The age of onset has been increased under DSM-5 from 7 to 12 years of age and the level of severity can be considered as mild, moderate or severe.

Table 11.5 The criteria used by DSM-5 to describe the inattentive symptoms of ADHD.

Inattentive symptoms
Inaccurate schoolwork due to poor attention to details and careless error making.
Lacks ability to maintain attention during the performance of various tasks such as reading and focusing on content in classes and conversations.
Mind not focused on what is being said during conversation hence appearing to not listen.
Fails to engage in the completion of tasks and to follow instructions.
Problems of organising tasks causing poor time management and sequencing tasks in an ordered way.
Problems sustaining mental effort as seen in schoolwork, form completion and writing reports – such tasks are often avoided.
Loses items needed for task and activity completion.
Easily distracted by unrelated thoughts and other forms of distraction.
Shows forgetfulness in daily activities, for example, forgetting to run an errand.

Table 11.6 The criteria used by DSM-5 to describe the hyperactive-impulsive symptoms of ADHD.

Hyperactive-impulsive symptoms
Constant fidgeting, which might include tapping hands and restlessness when seated.
Finds it difficult to sit still in class and often leaves the seat unoccupied.
Active when it is inappropriate such as running about the classroom.
Problems with engaging in activities quietly.
Constantly active and is often compared to being 'driven by a motor'.
Finds it difficult to refrain from blurting answers out and finishing other people's sentences.
Problems in waiting for one's turn.
Excessive talking.
Interrupts others and may intrude by taking over the activity.

Barkley (2006) described ADHD as a common childhood psychological disorder and compares the behaviour of individuals diagnosed with it with the behaviour of non-ADHD children (see Table 11.7).

Children exhibit these symptoms to varying degrees as indicated in Table 11.7, but they are far more frequent in children diagnosed with ADHD. Children with ADHD, where the predominant problem is inattention, find it difficult to focus on one task and very often become bored within a couple of minutes of beginning the task. Hyperactivity, as an **externalised behaviour,** is often expressed by moving around and fidgeting with objects. Those

Plate 11.3 Boy behaving disruptively in class. (Shutterstock 68372572.)

Table 11.7 Symptoms of ADHD (Barkley 1990).

Symptom	ADHD per cent	Non-ADHD per cent
Fidgets	73.2	10.6
Refuses to remain seated	60.2	3
Distracted	82.1	15.2
Problems in turn-taking	48	4.5
Shouts out answers	65	10
Problems following instructions	83.7	12.1
Problems maintaining attention	79.7	16.7

Failure to complete tasks	77.2	16.7
Fails to play quietly	39.8	7.6
Excessive talking	43.9	6.1
Interrupts others	65.9	10.6
Inability to listen	80.5	15.2
Keeps losing things required for task completion	62.6	12.1
Involves oneself in physically dangerous pursuits	37.4	3

who are inclined towards impulsivity will often act before thinking about the consequences of their actions. Hence, children with ADHD can be diagnosed as:

- ADHD-C – combined presentation (both inattention and hyperactivity/impulsivity);
- ADHD-PH or ADHD-HI – predominantly hyperactive or predominantly hyperactive–impulsive presentation;
- ADHD-I – predominantly inattentive presentation.

While the symptoms outlined in Table 11.7 occur to varying degrees, the most problematic behaviours experienced by these children relate to the inability to respond to discipline and having a low frustration tolerance level (Faraone and Doyle 2001). They find it difficult to obey the rules, which can lead to episodes of aggressive behaviour (Barkley 1998). The causes of ADHD tend to be both biological and psychological (see Box 11.3) such that methods of treatment often involve a combination of medication and behaviour therapy.

Box 11.3 What causes ADHD?

There have been many different explanations of how ADHD develops. One argument is that brain damage has occurred, either pre- or post-natally, for example, by injury or oxygen deprivation (Banerjee et al. 2007). Eme (2012) presented evidence to show that at least 30 per cent of children who had experienced traumatic brain injury developed ADHD at a later stage. Studies have shown there to be a reduction of volume in specific areas of the brain in children diagnosed with ADHD. Reduced volume has been found in the left side of the **prefrontal cortex** (Krain and Castellanos 2006; Malenka et al. 2009). The prefrontal cortex is implicated in the coordination of complex cognitive behaviour, decision-making and the moderation of social behaviour (Yang and Raine 2009). According to Miller, Freedman and Wallis (2002), individuals with ADHD have problems involving the orchestration of thoughts and actions required for achieving goals. Problems associated with the prefrontal cortex lead to deficits of executive function (see Chapter 4). Malenka et al. (2009) further showed there to be thinning of the **posterior parietal cortex** when compared with controls. This area of the brain is typically involved in planned movements, attention and spatial navigation. Problems associated with the prefrontal and posterior parietal cortex are clearly reflected in the symptoms observed in individuals with ADHD. These findings

(continued)

(continued)

support the earlier work of Zametkin et al. (1990) who performed PET scans on ADHD and non-ADHD individuals. They found that the areas of the brain involved in the control of attention and motor activity showed the largest reductions of glucose metabolism. Moreover, there was less activity in the **frontal-limbic system**, which plays a role in arousal and reward. Findings from all studies combined suggest there is a defective inhibitory system causing individuals to be more active and less sensitive to positive reinforcement. Chandler et al. (2014) found impairment to executive function as a consequence of problems involving neurotransmitter pathways in the brain such as those for dopamine and norepinephrine. Both dopamine and norepinephrine are responsible for modulating a variety of functions such as executive control, motivation, motor control and responsiveness to rewards. Chandler et al. conclude that problems to the dopamine and norepinephrine pathways are strongly indicated in individuals with ADHD. Goos et al. (2007) argue that there is a tendency to inherit ADHD. From twin studies, researchers have found that children with ADHD inherit the condition from their parents in 75 per cent of cases (Burt 2009; Neale et al. 2010). Nolen-Hoeksema (2013) found that siblings of those with ADHD are three to four times more likely to develop the condition. Gizer et al. (2009) identified genes directly involved in dopamine transmission and, as we have seen earlier, dopamine dysfunction is implicated in ADHD. Genes associated with ADHD have also been found (Gizer et al. 2009). Nikolaidis and Gray (2010) found that the 7-repeat variant of the dopamine receptor D4 (as in DRD4-7R) causes behavioural attention deficits typical of ADHD.

Environmental factors have also been implicated in ADHD. Alcohol consumption during pregnancy causes foetal alcohol spectrum disorders that, according to Burger et al. (2011), sometimes include ADHD or similar symptoms. Eubig et al. (2010) found that toxic substances, such as lead or polychlorinated biphenyls, can cause ADHD symptoms. Smoking tobacco during pregnancy can increase the risk of ADHD (Abbott and Winzer-Serhan 2012). Various infections during pregnancy have also been associated with increased likelihood of developing ADHD (Millichap 2008). Millichap and Yee (2012) suggested that a minority of children develop ADHD or symptoms like ADHD when exposed to artificial food dyes and preservatives – but findings linking diet and ADHD are inconclusive. Family factors have also been considered as causal in escalating the symptoms of ADHD. Critical, unaffectionate, disapproving and disciplinarian mothers have been considered as part of the problem. Weiss and Hechtman (1993), however, suggest that this is more likely to be a response to the child's ADHD rather than the cause. The **diathesis-stress theory** was developed by Bettelheim (1973) as a possible explanation for ADHD. This theory proposes that the child develops a predisposition to be hyperactive which, when coupled with inappropriate parental nurturing, exacerbates the problem.

A multitude of possible causes have been proposed. There is evidence showing ADHD is caused by certain gene combinations. Furthermore, problems in brain neurotransmitter pathways can cause executive function deficits. It is also clear, however, that environmental factors can exacerbate such biological factors.

As is the case with many disorders and conditions, there is a preponderance of boys diagnosed with ADHD. Nevertheless, when girls are diagnosed with ADHD or any one of the DBDs, they express the symptoms more severely. This has been described by the notion of the **gender paradox** first introduced by Taylor and Ounsted (1972). Interestingly, Taylor and Ounsted found that the gender that expresses the condition most frequently is not the gender that exhibits the most serious symptoms. Likewise, Loeber and Stouthamer-Loeber (1998) found that children with disruptive behaviours tend to be boys but girls who do have such problems exhibit more extreme traits. There are well-established gender differences in personality factors (as measured by the 'Big 5' personality factors – see Chapter 12). Females perform differently on the five dimensions of this personality test. They are less likely to be verbally and physically aggressive and certainly score lower on risk-taking behaviours than males (Coie and Dodge 1997; Byrnes et al. 1999). Moreover, their global self-esteem and assertiveness scores are lower than those for males (Costa et al. 2001 – see Chapter 8).

At this point, given their overlap, you might be wondering why there are two separate categories of DBDs. Moreover, why is it that ADHD as a neurodevelopmental disorder can also have similar characteristics? While the symptoms of ADHD can be problematic and troublesome, they are not as severe and devastating to others as the DBDs. In fact, what seemingly links ODD and CD is the poor development of morals and empathy towards the plight of others. Despite this, Uekermann et al. (2010) reported that children with ADHD exhibit emotional deficits and reduced levels of empathy. These children have further problems of theory of mind (ToM) (Uekermann et al. 2010). Perner et al. (2002) studied ToM in children at risk of ADHD and found deficits are related to executive control dysfunctions. Shoemaker (2009) discussed important links between empathy, moral understanding and accountability for one's behaviour. He argues that in order to be accountable for a transgression there are three considerations that an individual should respond to:

- recognise and appreciate the distress associated with injuries and harms for what it is;
- understand what it is like for the injured or harmed party;
- feel what the injured or harmed party feels in being so affected.

(Shoemaker 2009, p. 448)

Shoemaker further argues that to be morally accountable for one's actions does not rely on an intellectual ability to comprehend moral principles but requires empathy. In the case of individuals with ODD or CD, their symptoms prevent them from empathising with others. In contrast, individuals diagnosed with ADHD have intellectual disabilities that should not interfere with their ability to empathise.

According to Pardini and Fite (2010), what separates ODD and CD from ADHD is the outcome in later life with regard to features such as criminality and general mental adjustment. Pardini and Fite (2010) found, for example, that a diagnosis of CD is also a robust predictor of future antisocial behaviour. They found that children with symptoms of ADHD, if left untreated, were more likely to develop behaviours typical of ODD and CD than non-ADHD children. Moreover, children diagnosed with ADHD and ODD were more likely to experience social difficulties and problems of internalising values, beliefs, mores and attitudes taught through the socialisation process. Pardini and Fite (2010) also included a trait measure of callous-unemotional (CU) in their study, which had an additive effect on the symptoms of ADHD, ODD and CD. The CU trait in effect was strongly associated with persistent and serious criminal behaviour in the boys they studied over a two-year follow-up period. In the case of ADHD, Pardini and Fite's (2010) findings indicated that these children's symptoms, although not predictive of criminal involvement, can be seen as a developmental precursor of conduct problems (especially symptoms of hyperactivity and impulsivity). The inattentive aspects of their symptoms can also cause future academic problems.

Developmentalists, however, have found that the symptoms associated with ADHD puts individuals at risk of criminal behaviour (Savolainen et al. 2010; Savolainen et al. 2012). Young (2007) reported that two-thirds of juvenile offenders in Britain are diagnosed with ADHD. Rosler et al. (2004) believe the increasing numbers of individuals diagnosed with ADHD who have a criminal record is due to educational failure. It has been argued by Groman and Barzman (2014) that, despite the propensity towards deficits of moral reasoning, this is not necessarily the cause of their criminal behaviour.

Furthermore, they believe that individuals with ADHD have reduced empathy resulting from their condition. This, in turn, they argue, is important in the socialisation process and for moral development.

As discussed in Chapter 10, prosocial behaviour is strongly connected with a sense of morality and the ability to use moral reasoning as a means of moderating behaviour. Behaving aggressively can be perceived as the opposite of prosocial behaviour. This suggests that individuals, whose *modus operandi* is to adopt aggressive styles of social interaction, are likely to be at a low level of moral development. Furthermore, they are less likely to demonstrate empathic responses to others experiencing personal distress. It appears that underdeveloped moral reasoning and a limited empathic response coupled with impulsive actions influences aggressive and violent behaviour.

Do children and adolescents with DBDs (and also ADHD) develop into adult criminals?

It is interesting how many of the characteristics of the disruptive behaviour disorders (DBDs) and ADHD overlap with the thinking process that typifies the criminal personality described by psychiatrist Samuel Yochelson and clinical psychologist Stanton Samenow in 1976. According to Taylor (2016),

The criminal personality acts as a template for guiding the behaviour and the cognitive and emotional processes of criminally inclined individuals, which in turn determines and manages their lifestyle.

(p. 231)

Yochelson and Samenow classified 52 typical errors of thinking (see Box 11.4 for a sample of these) by individuals with a tendency towards having a criminal personality. These errors can be clustered into three groups:

1. Criminal thinking patterns – wanting to exert power and control over others, lying and demonstrating a lack of sense of time.
2. Crime-related thinking errors – related specifically to criminal behaviour, delusions about invulnerability to being caught and consequently punished, such **cognitive distortions** enable them to engage in aggressive and criminal acts.
3. Automatic thinking errors – lacking in empathy, secretive and trusting no-one.

Box 11.4 Examples of thinking errors of the criminal personality (based on Yochelson and Samenow 1976)

- Lying – creates a false reality to maintain control.
- Failure to put oneself in another's position – helps maintain a self-centred approach such that effects from actions on others are ignored.
- I can't – used as an excuse to avoid accountability.
- Failure to consider injury to others – fail to admit the injury caused to others and sees self as a victim.
- Lack of trust – difficulty trusting others but expect to be trusted.
- Lack of time perspective – want immediate gratification.

- Ownership – take what is wanted but owned by others (think they have the right to do what they want).
- Corrosion – eliminates deterrents so that desire to behave antisocially exceeds any deterrent.
- Cut-off – eliminates deterrents from equation of behaving antisocially.

Individuals with a criminal personality, and children with any of the DBDs, tend to make attributions of hostile intent when trying to understand the behaviour of others. Such individuals often have empathy and theory of mind deficits (see Chapter 5). There is current debate as to whether CD, in particular, is an early development of **antisocial personality disorder (APD)** diagnosed in adults. The emotional, cognitive and behavioural traits are very similar. Moreover, these traits overlap with the thinking errors committed by individuals harbouring a criminal personality. It is important to note, however, that the evidence of there being a progression from DBDs to APD is limited. Furthermore, while some individuals with APD adopt a criminal lifestyle, having APD is a personality problem and not a criminal issue per se. Some individuals with APD also ultimately develop a criminal personality. What is clear, however, is that for many individuals with DBDs there is an overlap in behavioural deficits with APD.

Individuals with DBDs typically exhibit high levels of aggression. Researchers have outlined different types of aggression, which will be discussed in our next section.

DIFFERENT TYPES OF AGGRESSION

Aggression has been considered by forensic psychologists as any behaviour that is performed with the intention of causing physical or psychological harm to others. **Violence**, alternatively, refers to behaviour by persons against persons or to their property with the intent to threaten, inflict physical harm or cause criminal damage. The two forms of behaviour are very similar, however, whereas all violent acts are aggressive, aggressive behaviour causing psychological harm (e.g., threats to reputation and **cybercrime**) are not always violent. As a rule, violent behaviours causing harm to others or damage to their property are punishable by law whereas harmful behaviours that are aggressive but lack physical violence are not necessarily punishable by law.

Crick and Dodge (1996) argue that there are two main categories of aggression.

1. **Reactive aggression** is an automatic response that is impulsive, uncontrollable, spontaneous and unreasoned.
2. **Instrumental aggression** is a controlled response that is calculated, reasoned and premeditated.

These two types of aggression are referred to as the **reactive–instrumental dichotomy**. Tapscott et al. (2012) point out that the reactive–instrumental dichotomy can include other defining aspects such as information processing. This is an important point, for, as we have seen in Chapter 5, some individuals are prone to interpreting the actions of others using hostile attributions. If Tommy, for example, interprets Jack's rough and tumble behaviour incorrectly as threatening, then he is more likely to react in a negative manner, possibly even starting a fight. Cornell (1996) further claims that this dichotomy is not a mutually exclusive one. In other words, reactive aggression can turn out to be instrumental and vice versa. Tapscott et al. claim that there are four possible combinations of reactive and instrumental aggression.

1. Purely reactive – for example, Jack bangs into Tommy resulting in him dropping his ice-cream, which triggers Tommy to hit Jack.
2. Reactive-instrumental – for example, when Tommy hits Jack back he then proceeds to steal his pocket money.
3. Instrumental-reactive – for example, Tommy steals Jack's mobile phone from his school-bag but is seen by John who is consequently punched in the face by Tommy.
4. Purely instrumental – for example, Tommy trips up Jack in order that Jack drops his mobile phone, which Tommy had hoped would happen so that he could steal it.

According to Parke and Gauvain (2009), there are changes occurring in the pattern of aggressive behaviour shown across infancy, childhood and adolescence. Based on cumulative findings from a number of studies, they outlined the development of aggressive behaviour according to age (see Figure 11.2). Whereas preschool children are more likely to use instrumental aggression as a means of attaining toys, older children (above three years) adopt a more hostile approach when they come into conflict with others (Dodge et al. 2006). These hostile approaches were personally driven whereby the victim was ridiculed, criticised, gossiped about and called names. The difference, however, that Dodge et al. found between the two age groups lay in the fact that the younger group were physically fighting over things whereas the older group were using verbal aggression. This suggests the older children had further developed their language skills and were better at interpreting the intentions of others. Interpreting the intentions of others would have helped them to understand how the effects of their hostility affect the targets of their hostility.

This shift, according to Ferguson and Rule (1980), is considered to be a consequence of advances in social cognition (see Chapter 5). They point out that older children are better able to identify another child's intent to hurt them and so are more likely to adopt a direct assault on the individual rather than an indirect one involving their possessions. Even though children's social cognitive skills develop, there are those who fail to correctly infer the intentions of peers. The use of hostile attributions often occurs when situations are highly ambiguous such that the peer's behaviour could be interpreted as prosocial or aggressive. According to Dodge and Frame (1982), boys who are aggressive are likely to commit more unprovoked aggressive acts towards peers. At the same time, however, they have an increased probability of being at the receiving end of aggressive attacks by others. Levels of aggression remain fairly consistent over time such that young children who are aggressive are likely to act aggressively throughout the lifespan (Dodge et al. 2006). This was demonstrated by Huesmann et al. (1984) who, in a longitudinal study of over 600 eight-year-old children, found aggressive individuals to have remained so at the age of 30 (they also had a more extensive offence record – see Figure 11.2).

The notion of there being two broad forms of aggression (hostile and instrumental) has been challenged. Bushman and Anderson (2001), for example, are not supportive of a **hostile versus instrumental aggression dichotomy** and have argued that it is 'time to pull the plug' on this division. They agree that, historically, this dichotomy has aided the development of theories concerning aggression but argue it no longer provides a good descriptor of the different forms aggressive behaviour takes. Bushman and Anderson also believe that such a dichotomy becomes unnecessarily confounded by notions of whether the aggressive action was autonomous or considered, and whether the act was driven by one or more motives.

Developmentalists such as Vitaro and Brendgen (2005), however, suggest that a distinction between reactive and proactive aggression is an effective approach to understanding aggression in children. Reactive aggression is a defensive or retaliatory response to a provocation. Proactive aggression, alternatively, is enacted to attain a goal. Hubbard et al. (2010) reported that most studies indicate the presence of both types of aggression in children to

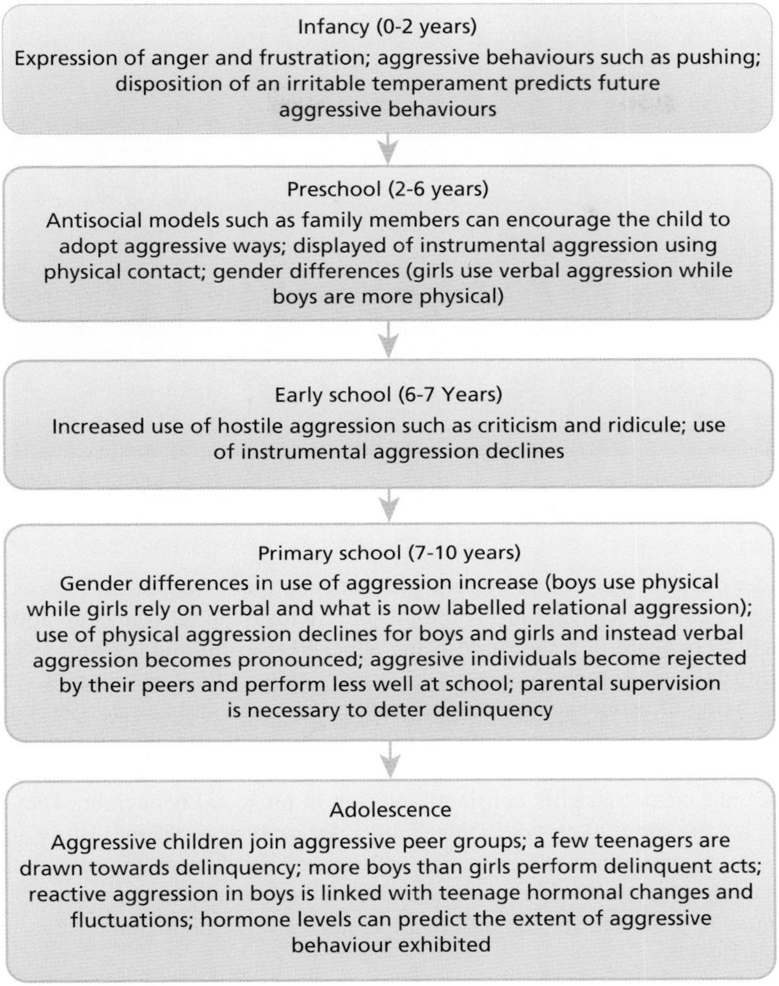

Figure 11.2 Aggressive behaviour through infancy, childhood and adolescence.

varying degrees. They suggest it might be more fruitful to think of aggression as being a continuous dimension instead of discrete categories. Having distinctions of aggression is currently an area of debate.

Most people assume that boys are more aggressive than girls. But does this assumption stand up to scrutiny?

Gender differences in forms of aggression

A number of developmentalists have examined the relationship between gender and rates of aggression. Huesmann et al. (1984) found that boys clearly show higher rates of aggression than girls. As we can see from Figure 11.3, boys leap-frog girls in the extent of aggressive behaviour shown. Maccoby (1998) claims the gender difference in aggression exhibited during infancy is minimal but the divide increases at the onset of toddlerhood where boys are far more involved in aggressive events.

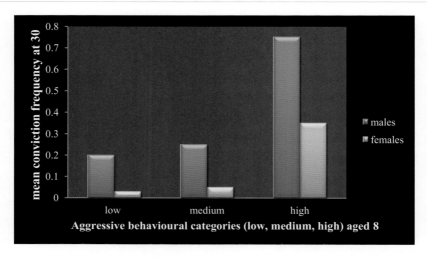

Figure 11.3 Childhood aggression and adult convictions. (Adapted from Huesmann et al. 1984.)

This gender difference is a cross-cultural phenomenon seen in countries such as the UK, US, Japan, New Zealand, Kenya, India, Ethiopia and Switzerland (Dodge et al. 2006). Boys are more likely to retaliate in response to being attacked (Darvill and Cheyne 1981); more physically confrontational; more frequently physically aggressive (Ostrov and Crick 2007) and more approving of using such overt aggression (Huesmann and Guerra 1997). Girls are more likely to resolve conflict using methods of negotiation and strategies that attenuate the likelihood of aggressive behaviour (Eisenberg et al. 1994). This difference in conflict resolution style does not mean that girls constantly engage in prosocial behaviour. They too can be aggressive but are more likely to do this using **relational aggression** (Ostrov and Crick 2007). Relational aggression involves tactics such as causing damage to peer relationships through tarnishing other girls' reputations and ostracising them from the group (Xie et al. 2004). In Figure 11.4 we can see the difference in use of aggression among boys and girls from a study in the US.

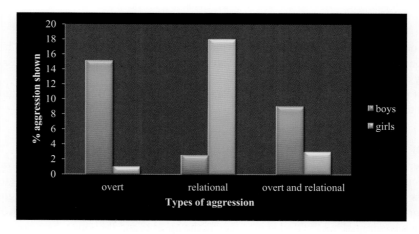

Figure 11.4 Type of aggression in boys and girls. (Adapted from Crick and Grotpeter 1995.)

An important type of aggressive behaviour occurring during childhood and adolescence is **bullying**. This is especially a problem of the school playground but occurs in other spheres of social life. As with aggressive behaviour per se, there are different types of bullying behaviours as there are different types of bully. This will be the topic of our next section.

BULLYING, THE BULLIES AND THEIR VICTIMS

There is a general consensus that bullying is a form of aggressive behaviour that is repeated over time and targeted towards a victim who has less power than the aggressor (Olweus 1999). Smith and Sharp (1994) define bullying simply as the 'systematic abuse of power', which 'repeatedly and deliberately' (p. 2) causes harm to others. How we define bullying has changed over the years, especially since the advent of technological developments in **social media**. In recent years, for example, we have seen the rise of **cyberbullying** (Bauman et al. 2013 – see later). When we consider bullying behaviour in childhood and adolescence, we have an image of bullies in the playground targeting specific children who are in some way vulnerable or different. Bullying as a concept came to prominence in the book *Tom Brown's School Days* written by Thomas Hughes in 1857 (see Box 11.5).

Box 11.5 Excerpts from *Tom Brown's School Days*

Tom Brown's School Days heightened readers' awareness of the bullying behaviours occurring within the school environment. Prior to this the term bullying was unknown. The story is about a boy called Tom Brown who attends Rugby school. When Tom first arrives at Rugby school he makes friends with Harry East who has been at the school already for six months. Harry provides Tom with helpful advice about dress code and how to endure the bullying that newcomers to the school automatically receive. Both Tom and Harry are model pupils and do well academically and in sport. In his second year, Tom enters the lower fourth form, a class that is dominated by bullies. Tom and Harry begin to become disillusioned by the school system and begin to cheat and ignore their duties. They ignore many of the school rules and behaved inappropriately. Although Tom and Harry have misbehaved, they also do good things for the younger pupils of the school. They try to get rid of the custom of 'fagging'. This is where the younger boys have to do all kinds of errands for the older boys and wait on them hand and foot. The older boys tend to bully the younger ones. One particularly bad bully they encounter is Flashman. Tom and Harry decide to oppose Flashman by going on strike and locking themselves inside their room. When they eventually come out Flashman regularly torments them and tarnishes their remaining school days. Tom says, 'Flashman was about 17 years old, and big and strong of his age . . . a formidable enemy for small boys' (p. 178). As far as the Head of House was concerned it was commented that, ' . . . there's a deal of bullying going on . . . Bullies are cowards' (p. 123).

On one occasion Tom is burned in front of a fire-place by Flashman because he refuses to give him a sweepstake ticket for the favourite horse to win in a horse race. After being bullied for so long Tom and Harry eventually persuade other boys, in the lower forms, to join them in their strike. With the help of an older boy called Diggs, Flashman's control wanes.
These literary excerpts demonstrate that bullies are often big and strong and their victims are small and easy pickings. *Tom Brown's School Days* helped to illustrate the imbalance of power between aggressor and victim that often occurs within a school environment.

But bullying is not restricted to the school environment – bullying happens in common social meeting points such as shopping precincts, sports and dance clubs. Moreover, bullying is not restricted to the young as there are many examples of adult bullies 'picking on' employees in the workplace. Bullying in the school environment occurs in many countries, but it was first seriously researched in Scandinavia by Swedish-born Dan Olweus in 1973. Since then, however, there have been many studies in countries of the East such as South Korea and Japan (Smith et al. 2016).

It was Olweus who first devised a self-report questionnaire allowing children to document their personal experiences of bullying. There are other means of establishing the nature of bullying via the use of sociometric approaches (see Chapters 7, 9 and 10). Sociometric approaches provide children with the opportunity of nominating peers for various different status categories such as being popular and liked or being the school bully and disliked. The approach of nominating peers for status of bully or victim, for instance, was first adopted in Finland during the 1980s by Kirsti Lagerspetz. It was Salmivalli et al. (1996) who used this method to separate out the different types of role held by bullies within the group. Furthermore, Veenstra et al. (2007) used the nomination procedure to ascertain details about dyadic relationships. Questions were asked such as 'who do you bully' and 'who are you bullied by'. Such information is valuable for understanding the intricate interaction between victim, perpetrator and victim-perpetrator, which we will discuss later in this chapter.

As we have seen in Chapters 7, 8 and 9, bullies can sometimes be popular children, high on self-esteem, who are liked by their peers and are popular group members. Bullies tend to operate in groups that have a hierarchical structure of dominance (see Chapter 9). Salmivalli et al. (1996) described three roles often seen in these groups, the:

1. ringleader who is in charge of the bullying;
2. assistant who helps the ringleader carry out the bullying;
3. reinforcer who 'eggs on' the bullying by laughing and jesting.

Smith (2016) argues that ringleader bullies perform well on tasks involving theory of mind, which provides them with the upper hand in understanding how their victims feel and in the identification of their victims' vulnerabilities. This makes it easier for them to devise a plan of how to hurt their victims effectively. Smith refers to this as '**cold cognition**'. Peeters et al. (2010) used the sociometric approach on 13-year-old Dutch children to establish any differences between those nominated as being bullies. Three different subgroups of bullies arose from these nominations:

1. popular with good social cognition;
2. reasonably popular with average social cognition;
3. unpopular with low social cognition.

Those who are unpopular tend to be rejected and ostracised to groups of equally disliked peers – many of whom lack social skills (Cook et al. 2010).

There are different types of bullying behaviour, which parallel the categories of aggression. Björkqvist et al. (1992) claimed that, in addition to physical and verbal bullying, as we have seen for aggressive behaviour, there is also indirect and relational bullying. Smith (2016) describes the main typologies of bullying used by studies conducted in the West (see Table 11.8).

In Table 11.8, cyberbullying is considered a form of indirect and relational bullying that has only become seriously recognised since 2006 (Zych et al. 2015). Rivers and Noret

Plate 11.4 A bully showing threatening behaviour. (Shutterstock 135976247.)

(2010) describe the initial communicative format of cyberbullying as emailing and texting messages. This has become more extensive with new technologies such as the smartphone and network site developments for social communication and connecting with other people. These offer new pathways for cyberbullies to operate and hide under. Based on the typologies in Table 11.4, what can we say about the demography of bullies? There are age and gender differences in relation to when bullying is at its peak and the type of bullying behaviour seen across gender (see Box 11.6).

Table 11.8 Different types of bullying commonly used.

Types of bullying	Description
Physical	Punching, kicking, hitting and taking or damaging victim's possessions.
Verbal	Taunting, teasing and using threatening language.
Social exclusion	Excluding victim systematically and directly from being involved with peers.
Indirect	Informing other peers not to engage with someone, spreading nasty untruths.
Bias or prejudice-based[1]	This includes racial, faith-based, sexual and homophobic harassment.
Cyberbullying[2]	This occurs via the use of electronic devices such as emailing, texting, phoning, instant messaging, chat-room networking, social networking and sending inappropriate pictures or video clips.

Box 11.6   The demography of bullies

Monks et al. (2002) used the term 'unjustified aggression' to describe bullying during infancy that occurred in preschool establishments such as nurseries and kindergartens and later in infant schools (see also Vlachou et al. 2011). Bullying involving a victim target is seen during the ages of seven and eight in primary school settings. This tends to be of a physical nature but shows a shift towards indirect and relational bullying beyond this age (Rivers and Smith 1994). According to Eslea and Rees (2001) bullying reaches its climax between the ages of 11 to 14 years. Cyberbullying, alternatively, often continues longer (Tokunaga 2010) and in some cases into adulthood. Although bullying attenuates in the later years of schooling, there is evidence to show that it infiltrates university settings (Cowie and Myers 2015). As we have seen for aggressive behaviour per se, there is a gender difference in the way bullying is meted out. Boys are more frequently involved in bullying behaviour but both boys and girls are equally on the receiving end of victimisation. Boys in groups tend to use their physical might whereas girls perform indirect and relational bullying tactics (Besag 2006). Both adopt verbal bullying and cyberbullying. Barlett and Coyne (2014) found that girls perform more cyberbullying tactics using social networks up to their early teenage years but boys are likely to escalate this form of bullying into late adolescence. Children who have disabilities are more likely to be targets for bullies, but interestingly they can also be bullies. Van Roekel et al. (2009) found that, in various European countries, children who have special needs issues are between two and three times more at risk of being victims of bullying and at having a participatory role in meting out bullying tactics. It has been speculated that this might be a result of having specific characteristics making them likely targets. Moreover, they might have behavioural problems such as ADHD, CD or ODD (discussed earlier) causing them to express aggression or behave in ways invoking an aggressive response from others (i.e., a **provocative victim** – see later). Ethnic bullying is a problem in schools; where individuals are bullied on account of their different ethnicity. In the US, Pepler et al. (2006) found that children of an ethnic minority origin were twice as likely to be bullied as those from non-ethnic minorities. They also found that 44 per cent of children and 33 per cent of adolescents who were victims of ethnic bullying reported bullying others using the same excuse. In the UK, a survey by 'Ditch the Label' in 2016 found that 1.5 million young people were bullied, and for those of ethnic minority origin this was higher. The chair of Bullying UK, Anastasia de Waal, claims that 'Even though we have made tremendous progress, bullying is still a major issue in schools and there's still a lot around race' (Sanghani 2016). According to Barchia and Bussey (2007), children who are bullies are more likely to morally disengage. This means that bullies are able to continue bullying free of guilt and self-censure (Bandura 2001). They do this using different strategies such as introducing moral justification for their behaviour, minimising their personal responsibility and blaming their victim (Bandura 2001). Bandura (2001) argues that moral disengagement increases with greater aggressive and violent behaviour (see Chapter 10). Hymel et al. (2005) found that bullies were more likely to have positive attitudes towards bullying behaviour.

As we can see, the type of bullying and cyberbullying adopted varies between genders. Moreover, there are differences in the peak age of bullying and cyberbullying that are gender related. Some children become targets because of their disabilities and others due to their ethnicity.

Most children and teenagers, however, refrain from bullying behaviour, and even when they do not, it is generally short-lived or a one-off event. An interesting question therefore is what makes some children and teenagers bully others? According to Salmivalli (2010), children who enjoy bullying do so for purposes of asserting and advertising their dominance within their peer group. This commonly occurs in mid-adolescence coinciding with puberty (Ellis et al. 2012). Children and teenagers who are members of an antisocial in-group (indulging in bullying behaviour) follow the group's norms, and if the norms are to bully out-group members then this is what they will do (see Chapters 7, 9 and 10). For some in-group members such behaviour is a way of self-protection against becoming victimised themselves (Fox and Boulton 2006). Moreover, Caravita et al. (2009) argued that a high status and popular peer is good to have on your side.

The relationship between victim and perpetrator is a complex one. In some cases, as we have seen in Box 11.6, the victim can also be involved in bullying others. In some cases victims provoke others into bullying them – known as provocative victims. Provocative victims behave in a manner that encourages others to respond negatively towards them such as being bullied. These victims tend to possess a number of characteristics that cause classroom disruption and single them out as being different. This cluster of traits often results in rejection by their peers and 'invites hostility' from others (see Chapters 7 and 8). Provocative victims can, however, have characteristics that overlap with those of pure bullies such as low levels of tolerance for frustration as well as high levels of dominant, antisocial and aggressive behaviour. There is also an overlap with passive victims where low self-esteem, social anxiety and a sense of being unpopular with peers is common. Randall (1997) described the provocative victim as the one 'everybody loves to hate' (p. 94). Some of the characteristics described can be seen in children who have attention deficit disorder (ADD without the symptoms of hyperactivity) or even ADHD.

This suggests that there is something about the victim that bullies object to. But we can equally ask if there is something about bullies that distinguishes them from other peers. As discussed previously, rejected peers tend to be ostracised from mainstream peer groups, and will, as a consequence, gravitate to other like-minded and rejected individuals. However, some bullies, as we have seen earlier, are popular and have good social cognitive skills. This would suggest that there are individual differences of personality and temperament across the different types of bully. Equally there are likely to be individual differences across different types of victim that lend themselves to being bullied (as is the case for provocative victims) (see Box 11.7).

Box 11.7   Differences between victims, bullies and provocative victims

There is a complex social interaction taking place between bullies and victims (including pro-vocative victims). The nature of such interactions depends, in large part, on individual factors. Risk factors of being bullied include those with special educational needs (Nabuzoka and Smith 1993), delayed developers (Carney and Merrell 2001), those with physical problems, children with an ethnic minority background (Smith and Sharp 1994) and children who contravene gen-der stereotypes – such children are called names like 'sissy' (Robertson and Monsen 2001). Pikas (1989) described two types of victim: those whose behaviour is independent of being bul-lied and those whose behaviour is a major factor in provoking an aggressive response. Victims who 'provoke' bullying often have behavioural problems causing them to be disruptive in class and outside of class such as ADHD. Carney and Merrell (2001) suggest that these individuals quite often receive negative responses from most peers. As victims per se tend to have poor self-assertive behaviours, Smith and Sharp (1994) argued that they find it difficult to deal with the bullying and instead give in to the bullies. This response reinforces the bullies' behaviours such that they find bullying rewarding. In this way, the behaviour of most victims contributes to their victimisation. Sharp and Cowie (1994) outlined four types of victim responses to bullies: passive unconstructive; passive constructive; aggressive; and assertive. Passive unconstructive responses describe the victim as ignoring the bullying but giving in to the bully's demands. Passive constructive responses take the form of avoiding the confrontation and seeking support. Aggressive responses are counterproductive as they escalate bullying behaviours. The assertive response is considered to be the most effective where the individual stands his or her ground in a calm manner refusing to meet the demands of the bully. This is most effective in preventing bullying in the future. For victims from happy families their sense of helplessness is exaggerated because they have never needed to acquire social skills to deal with situations of conflict.

What can we say about bullies? It has been suggested that there may be genetic factors operating here; factors that influence emotional regulation, social cognition and even person-ality. Sutton and Keogh (2000) studied 9 to 12 year olds in Scotland for their Machiavellian attitudes (the ability to understand the way others think and to use this as a means of manipu-lating them). They found that bullies had far more Machiavellian attitudes than those children who refrained from bullying others. Similarly, Andreau (2004) discovered that bullies and victims of 9 to 12 years of age, from Greece, tended to be negative about human nature and expressed more Machiavellian attitudes. Other factors such as higher levels of impulsivity in bullies were found by Jolliffe and Farrington (2011). Muñoz et al. (2011) identified callous-unemotional traits as being important for predicting bullying behaviour. Deficits in moral development are more commonly found in bullies (Gini 2006). Ringleader bullies are found to have good social cognitive skills (e.g., theory of mind) and these, coupled with Machiavellian attitudes, makes them good at social manipulation (Sutton, Smith and Swettenham 1999).

Despite there being differences between victims, bullies and provocative victims, there are also some overlapping features. The behaviours of victims can initiate further bullying and can help to reward bullies into continuing their harassment of their targets. There are different types of victims as there are bullies and it is this that makes the relationship between the two a complicated affair.

There are additional factors influencing the risk of being a victim or a bully. The family can be an influential factor in how an individual behaves (see Chapter 6). Three family fac-tors arose out of discussions within a focus group conducted by Bibou-Nakou et al. (2012). Their focus group consisted of 13- to 15-year-old Greek pupils who were instructed to talk about their home life. Living in a home environment presenting problems as well as issues of control and child abuse figured highly as family factors contributing towards being bullied or bullying others. Olweus (1978) discovered that over-controlling and over-protective mothering created shy and unassertive children – traits that put them at risk of being bullied. Resilience to bullying, however, was promoted by having a mother and siblings who showed affection and by a home environment with a good atmosphere (Bowes et al. 2010).

Rutter and Giller (1983) outlined five key adverse factors that are causal in delinquency but can just as easily influence the development of bullying behaviour. As discussed in Chapter 6, these include the following factors:

- parental criminality;
- intra-familial discord;
- inconsistencies in response to unacceptable behaviour;
- family size and siblings;
- socioeconomic status.

Peers are also very influential (see Chapter 7). Peers with poor social skills, less liked or rejected by others are at greater risk of being bullied (Fox and Boulton 2006; Cook et al. 2010). Having many friends or at least one popular friend, however, attenuated this risk. For many victims of bullying it can be difficult to shake-off the label of victimhood. Boulton (2013), for example, found that 11–13 year olds were less likely to interact with a newcomer to the school when informed of their previous school victimisation. This was explained by Boulton as the possibility of the victim status being associated with them, leading to their victimisation also. According to Caravita et al. (2009), bullies tend to be rejected during the infant and junior school years, but on reaching adolescence their status position can become more favourable. This was not so much that they were liked but rather were perceived as being popular. Bullies who are also victims tend to have all the characteristics of both bullies and victims, but also have the lowest self-esteem scores and academic level of ability (Cook et al. 2010). Bowes et al. (2009) connected family factors with the risk of becoming a bully, the neighbourhood with becoming both a bully and victim, and the school with developing into a victim. School factors, however, have been considered as influential in the development of bullies in particular. Schools and school processes will be considered next.

Schools and school processes

Bronfenbrenner considered the influence of school and school processes as part of the microsystem of his Developmental Ecosystem Model (see Chapter 1). The school environment is a place where peers form social bonds and friendships. As we have seen in Chapter 7, peers have a strong socialising influence on each other. The school environment, however, is a focal point where many peers from different social backgrounds will meet and form friendship bonds. In addition to this, the school will have an identity of its own, which children and teenagers will either embrace or reject.

Acceptance of the school's identity and what it stands for (including rules and norms) will foster a strong sense of belongingness and social bonding. Weak bonds of attachment and level of commitment to the school are likely to be associated with delinquency and bullying. Children and teenagers who reject their school are likely to form bonds with each other (as pairings or groupings) and become antisocial-prone. As the school is considered a place of teaching the mores, rules, values, beliefs and attitudes of mainstream society, by rejecting these individuals are refusing to conform – something that Bronfenbrenner accounts for in his Ecosystem Model (see Chapter 1).

Plate 11.5 Boy refusing to conform to school rules. (Shutterstock 312216818.)

Other factors influencing an attachment to the school arise from school processes and the school itself. Such school processes can also affect school achievement. Rutter et al. (1979) examined 12 inner London schools with high delinquency levels in their *Fifteen Thousand Hours* study. They found that high delinquency rates were associated with the admittance of low ability pupils. They considered factors associated with school processes rather than the school per se and the ability of pupils therein. These factors included the extent of absenteeism, how individuals behaved in school classrooms and playgrounds, the level of academic achievement and the preponderance of delinquency. Rutter et al. (1979) considered a multitude of variables under the banner of school processes (see Box 11.8)

Box 11.8   Factors considered under the banner of school processes

In their classic *Fifteen Thousand Hours* study, Rutter et al. (1979) found that delinquency was linked to a number of factors occurring within the school classroom. Teachers with high autonomy in how they prepared their courses had the authority to teach what they saw fit. Hence, pupils in classes of low ability might not have received as much attention and challenges as those of higher ability. There was a variation in the standard of discipline meted out: for some teachers giving extra work as punishment compared unequally with those who demanded the child remain behind after class to write lines. When teachers failed to provide any positive feedback to work submitted by their pupils, a sense of achievement was lost. This was especially so if negative feedback was consistently forthcoming and outweighed the positive things these pupils had achieved. Teachers with low expectations of their pupils' ability to look after school items, such as books and pens, reinforced the negativity these children felt. It was found that pupils of 'low ability' tended to bond with each other forming stable groups.

How teachers respond to their pupils in terms of punishment and feedback impacts on their pupils' self-perceptions. This extends further to what teachers teach and how they do it.

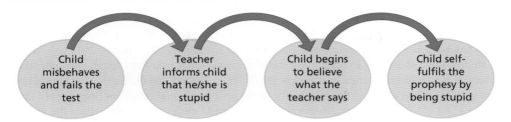

Figure 11.5 Demonstrates how the self-fulfilling prophesy works.

Hirschi (1969) claimed that the risk of delinquency during adolescence is linked with academic failure, which, in turn, is influenced by school processes. Hargreaves (1980) showed that streaming (clustering children of similar ability together in the same class) in schools is one causal factor in the formation of delinquent groupings among pupils. This means that pupils with higher academic ability are segregated from those who are of a lower academic standing. This can create an atmosphere of the 'swots' and 'snobs' versus the 'remedial' streams; thereby creating a **self-fulfilling prophesy** of 'I am clever' and 'I am stupid' respectively (Figure 11.5). Clearly, such self-fulfilling prophesies feed into the development of self-concept and self-esteem (see Chapter 8). This sense of rejection increases the likelihood of a disregard of school rules and further increases the appeal of behaving antisocially and bullying others.

In Bronfenbrenner's model the macrosystem refers to the cultural context encompassing the child such that identification with specific groups shapes the attitudes and values embraced by individuals. The conflict between middle-class school ideals and working-class values is just one example of a problem that arises at the level of the macrosystem. Social class clearly contributes to differences in attitude towards schooling and school ethics. Hence, children from working-class families, for example, are likely to identify with being working class. These aspects of Bronfenbrenner's model are relevant when we consider why some children and teenagers reject the philosophy of the school.

Schools and social class

Neill (2005) conducted a survey of the number of schools that experienced problem behaviour from the pupils attending. The survey showed that such behaviours were rife in schools sited in areas where socioeconomic status was low. Neill further found that weapons were more likely to be brought into schools in the London area by students receiving free school meals. Being in receipt of free meals, according to Hobbs and Vignoles (2007), is a good measure of low family economic status. A connection between receiving free meals and coming from a low family economic status makes sense. Neill's findings of a link between having free meals, coming from a family of low economic status and carrying weapons must be carefully considered. Clearly there is not a causal relationship between receiving free meals and carrying weapons. Rather, receiving free school meals is an indication of living in a family of low economic status and, for various complex reasons, this increases the likelihood of carrying a weapon. Hence, removing free meals could not seriously be considered an important contingent measure for improving the behaviours of these children. Neill (2005) has further speculated that carrying weapons might be a consequence of failing to integrate and endorse 'middle-class' ideals. Hence, these individuals reject the school's academic ideology and follow a delinquent one.

In Britain, class differences can lead to entirely different expectations and this, in turn, can be a cause of conflict. School achievement among 'white working-class' children has become a concerning issue (Cassen and Kingdon 2007; Strand 2014). A series of studies have shown that social class has significant input into the educational outcomes achieved by children (Demie and Lewis 2010a, b, c; Strand 2014). Babb (2005) reported that working-class children are less likely to achieve good qualifications from school than their middle-class counterparts. A report by Demie and Lewis (2014) highlighted the lack of aspiration amongst the white working-class children studied. They considered a lack of education among the parents of these children as a causal factor underlying low aspirations for performing well at school. Demie and Lewis (2014) quote the comments of a head teacher that 'Many . . . parents are young with a legacy of hostility to the school. They do not feel themselves to be stakeholders in education, rather, that sending their children to school is just something they have to do, and "even stepping over the threshold" of the school is a barrier for some parents' (p. 5).

These working-class children, for example, are more likely to want to follow in the footsteps of their parents. Hence, Demie and Lewis believe that parental attitudes to education influence their children's learning and aspirations. In their report, Demie and Lewis found that parents felt the educational curriculum did not meet the needs of their children. Many parents emphasised the importance of apprenticeships, working in an office or a factory without having to study further. These attitudes can be seen to reflect a culture of entering the workforce following schooling.

In contrast, 'middle-class' children often anticipate entering university at the end of their school life. This difference in expectations can, in some cases, lead to conflict in the classroom. Evans (2006) claims white working-class boys have a 'street' reputation to maintain which includes concepts of masculinity that contrast with expected classroom behaviour. She further claims that such behaviours in the classroom contrast with the ethos of education and prevent others from learning. Differences in socialisation regarding attitudes espousing the benefits of education between the working- and middle-classes has been a topic of debate. In Britain, the issue of differences between working- and middle-class attitudes towards education has been put to Parliament in the House of Commons in a question raised by Professor Denis Mongon (2014). He said, 'If you are working class and successful, you have got to abandon your mates and your community, because our system requires you to move on and be different. It is a big cultural ask for some youngsters at that very tense teenage point'.

School-based anti-bullying programmes

Many schools from a variety of countries have introduced anti-bullying interventions. The question is, do these actually work? In 2011, Marie Ttofi and David Farrington conducted a meta-analysis of 44 studies of such school-based programmes in order to answer this question. The meta-analysis revealed that, on average, following the introduction of such programmes, there was a decrease in the rate of bullying by 20–23 per cent. Furthermore, levels of victimisation decreased by 17–20 per cent. Ttofi and Farrington noted that the duration and intensity of a programme was directly related to its effectiveness. Hence, those schools that took such interventions seriously and continued with them for lengthy periods were the most successful. Anti-bullying programmes that were particularly successful were those that made use of firm discipline, increased and effective playground supervision and meetings with the parents of child bullies and child victims.

The media

In Bronfenbrenner's model, the exosystem impacts on the child from across a wide set of factors such as the mass media, extended family and welfare and legal services. One aspect of this that can impact negatively on the behaviour of children and teenagers is the media. This is especially the case in those who have a predisposition to behave aggressively and antisocially (see also Chapter 13). Studies of how the media influences children and teenagers have focused primarily on screen violence in the forms of film and television. Friedrich-Cofer and Huston (1986) found that the relationship between watching filmed violence and levels of aggression was small but robust. Huesmann and Eron (1986) found that, for children aged between 8 and 12 years, boys were more influenced by television violence than girls. They found, however, that other factors such as being low academic achievers, unpopular with peers and a tendency towards behaving aggressively interacted with the effects of television violence. In 1991, Wood et al. studied the effects of exposing children and teenagers, within a school context, to aggressive and non-aggressive films. They divided the children and teenagers into two groups after viewing the film footage. One group was allowed to play with their peers in an observation room containing a one-way mirror, so that researchers could code their behaviours for any signs of aggression. Members of the other group returned to their classroom and were allowed to interact with peers who were uninvolved in the experiment. Wood et al. found a marginal effect of watching aggressive film footage on the aggressive behaviour towards peers. They concluded that, after many viewings of aggressive film footage, there was a cumulative effect on levels of aggression in children and teenagers.

Plate 11.6 Young children scared by the violence they are viewing on the television. (Shutterstock 511895011.)

Plate 11.7 Negative media messages. (Shutterstock 413784919.)

With increased use of the **Internet** and social media, questions have been asked about how these relatively new media formats impact on the social development of children and adolescents (see Chapter 13). Researchers are particularly interested in how these media are used negatively as is the case for cyberbullying.

Until recently, cyberbullies generally sent emails and text messages to their unsuspecting victims. These contained nasty snippets of information that could be of a personal (by someone known to the victim) or impersonal (random) nature. This meant that if someone known to the victim was sending nasty emails or texts then this would contain specific information arising out of the relationship between the cyberbully and the victim. Recently, however, technology has developed further so that mobile phones and iPads can be used to take photos or record people, which might later be exploited. Additionally, it is now easy to connect with the Internet and use instant messaging and the numerous social networking sites to target victims – hence the term cyberbullying. Cyberbullying has received much international interest. So much so that numerous cross-cultural studies exploring the nature of this type of bullying have been published.

Genta et al. (2009) researched cyberbullying in countries such as Italy, Finland, England, Spain and Bosnia-Herzegovina. Cross-cultural studies such as this reveal Italian students, for instance, are more involved in cyberbullying than Spanish and English students. Hinduja and Patchin (2008) identified a number of factors initiating cyberbullying. These include:

- more time spent on the Internet;
- involvement in various on-line activities;
- likelihood of participating in more traditional forms of bullying behaviour;
- school problems;
- assaultive behaviour;
- increased use of illegal substances.

In 2010 Patchin and Hinduja added that cyberbullies tended to have low levels of self-esteem. Pyżalski (2012), however, found that self-reports of self-esteem in cyberbullies who attacked many different types of victim was higher. Other profile factors have been investigated such as loneliness – the rationale being that because they have no friends they spend longer on the Internet. This was ruled out by Şahin (2012) who found that loneliness was not a useful predictor of cyberbullying. Interestingly, Calvete et al. (2010) found personal predictors such as attitudes justifying the use of violence and behaviours like proactive aggression as being important in understanding why these individuals enjoy cyberbullying. They also found that contextual factors like being exposed to violence and less perceived support from friends were influential promoters of cyberbullying behaviours. Ang and Goh (2010) argue that low levels of empathy are also associated with individuals who commit cyberbullying. Cyberbullies also tended to have problems bracketed under the conduct disorders (including behavioural problems of hyperactivity).

Guarini et al. (2012) looked at the prevalence of traditional forms of bullying and cyberbullying in Italian secondary schools. Of interest here, they found the following:

- The mobile phone was most commonly used by Italian teenagers to perform electronic aggression directed at their classmates.
- There was little difference between boys and girls for cyberbullying.
- Cyberbullying was more common among teenagers than younger pupils.
- Boys had higher self-esteem in all spheres than the girls.
- Loneliness was more of a factor for girls than boys.
- Girls had a more positive perception of their school regarding academic support than boys.
- Lower perceptions of self-esteem related to school predicted cyberbullying.
- Higher perceptions of self-esteem for peer relationships increased the risk of cyberbullying.

Emler and Reicher (1995) introduced the **Reputation-Enhancement Theory (RET)**. Advocates of RET argue that individuals choose a self-image or identity that they then present to others. If the feedback is positive or in some ways heightens an individual's prestige or self-esteem, then it is maintained. The RET can be applied to bullying behaviour in children and adolescents. The self-image or identity that bullies present is maintained as it plays a role in establishing peer status (Juvonen et al. 2003). The RET can also be applied to cyberbullying. Here, cyberbullying is a way of communicating and seeking approval from peers that helps to develop an identity. Melotti et al. (2009) apply the Reputation-Enhancement Theory as follows:

> *The internet, as a means of communication, becomes therefore fundamental for "publicising", divulging acts of bullying and "creating" an audience which contributes to strengthening the bully's identity.*
>
> *(p. 49)*

New forms of technology have replaced the likes of film, television and magazines in how they influence individuals' social behaviour. While, for most of us, this technology has been embraced in a positive way, there are those who use it to harass others in the guise of cyberbullying. The influence of media on social behaviour will be addressed in more detail in Chapter 13.

Factors associated with bullying other children or being victimised have also been studied using a behavioural genetics approach (see Chapters 1 and 14) – this is our next topic.

Genetic effects

Research was conducted in England and Wales using a behavioural genetics approach – known as The Environmental Risk (E-Risk) Study. This involved the examination of 1,000 twin pairs (fraternal and identical) between 9 and 10 years of age. Findings suggest a robust genetic influence on who is likely to be victimised or to turn into a bully (Ball et al. 2008). Ball et al. argue that genetic influences are manifested through personality expression, social cognitive skills and level of successful emotion regulation. Nevertheless, the environment interacts with genetic factors, which enable some children to develop resilience against victimisation. Bowes et al. (2010) argue that a warm, happy and positive home-life goes a long way in protecting children against the harshness of being bullied at school.

Research on the extent of bullying behaviour and the likely victims of this has been conducted in schools in Canada. A rate of one in three adolescent students in Canada reported being bullied (Molcho et al. 2009). In the 2001 Ontario Student Drug Use Survey of over 4,211 participants, a quarter reported being bullied at school at least once (CAMH 2001). There were more male victims than females at 26.9 per cent and 22.3 per cent respectively. Interestingly, a third of these students admitted to having bullied someone at school, again males scoring higher rates than females (40 per cent and 24 per cent respectively). In the Quebec Study of New-born Twins (QSNT) childhood development was examined by considering both environmental and biological factors. The objective was to try and separate the contributions of environmental and biological factors using a variety of measures. One of these was to consider the relationship between bullying and victimisation. Children aged 5, 18 and 30 months were evaluated using different behavioural and physiological measures. The attitudes and behaviours of the parents were also taken into consideration as a possible influential social factor. In total there were 662 families of twins born in the Montréal area between 1995 and 1998. These twins were tested regularly and continue to be part of this longitudinal investigation.

Boivin et al. (2013a) collated the data concerning twins' peer difficulties while in kindergarten (796 twins), Grade 1 (948 twins) and Grade 4 (868 twins). The findings suggest a robust contribution of genetic factors in continuous peer difficulties. Boivin et al. (2013b) found a strong gene–environment correlation linking disruptive behaviours to peer relationship difficulties. Moreover, this was mainly accounted for by genetic factors. In an interview Boivin said 'We know that it's behaviour that drives the peer difficulties . . . It's the genetic factors that underlie the tendency to behave in a certain way that explain how the group reacts to the child and then rejects and victimizes the child' (McQuigge 2013).

In Boivin et al.'s (2013b) study, strong evidence for a child's genetic makeup having an impact on the type of interactions encountered with peers was found. Victimisation at school was considered to have roots in the child's and teenager's genes. In this research 800 pairs of identical and fraternal twins were studied over a five-year period. Self, peer and teacher evaluations of the school experience, including kindergarten, Grade 1 and Grade 4 were analysed. The findings provided a strong association between genes and peer interactions. Furthermore, specific behaviours are influenced by a child's genetic makeup. Specific behavioural states such as being aggressive, impulsive and hyperactive combine to isolate children in addition to physical characteristics (e.g., appearance).

Using identical twins from the Québec Study, Vitaro et al. (2016) considered the exposure of 'deviant' friends on the influence of teenagers' aggressive behaviour. In this study 201 pairs of identical twins were rated individually and as a pair by their teacher for physical aggressive behaviour. Their findings suggest that there has been an overemphasis on peer influence on aggressive behaviour. Instead there are underlying genetic effects on physical aggression and aggressive peers selected as friends.

It is interesting to note that many children with DBDs and ADHD have problems at school and with academic achievement. Given their disruptive behaviours, they are often perceived as problematic and of low ability, which also leads to a self-fulfilling prophesy of being a 'problem' or a 'stupid' child or teenager. Frequently they are at the receiving end of aggression and, as discussed earlier, tend to be provocative victims. They can also, however, be rejected by peers and isolate themselves from mainstream school ideals leading to seeking out like-minded peers. This may also lead to gang membership – a topic we will return to.

For some developmentalists, understanding aggression and morality together is best explained using an evolutionary psychological perspective. This is somewhat different from the more traditional social information approaches previously discussed.

AN EVOLUTIONARY PSYCHOLOGICAL PERSPECTIVE

As you will recall from Chapter 10, evolutionary psychologists have suggested that certain aspects of moral behaviour may be the outcome of evolved predispositions. In order to explore this notion further, some developmentalists have considered aggression in the light of evolutionary theory. Prosocial behaviour enables us to work well together but, from a gene-centred perspective, according to Pinker (1997), ultimately we promote our self-interests. Integrating well into social groups is considered to be an adaptation helping us to survive – it is therefore a means to self-preservation and potentially to passing on our own genes. Why this should be the case comes down to the old adage that there is safety in numbers. If you have others to help you, then your chances of survival increase. In addition to this mutually beneficial integration found in social groups, other aspects of evolutionary theory can account for facets of our social behaviour. According to Hawley (1999), socially dominant individuals within a social group might use coercive strategies (e.g., threatening others or simply taking what is wanted) as a way of ensuring they have full access to resources (i.e., **resource control theory**). Resource acquisition can also occur by using prosocial behaviour. The balance between resource control and prosocial behaviour has been studied in preschool children by Hawley (2002). The type of strategy employed by these children can be divided into subgroups that have their origins in the personality traits present. This further interacts with the success of the strategies adopted (Hawley 2003). Hawley (2003) compared four types of strategists: **bistrategic controllers** (use coercive and prosocial strategies); **coercive controllers** (use coercive strategies); **prosocial controllers** (use prosocial strategies) and **non-controllers** (use neither strategy; see Box 11.9).

As bullying is ubiquitous, Volk et al. (2012) consider whether there is a biological predisposition towards developing into a bully (see the section on genetic effects earlier). They point to bullying as an evolutionary adaptation (see Chapter 1). According to Dawkins (1989), a behaviour that is considered as an evolutionary adaptation must have arisen either through natural selection or sexual selection. This means that there must be a genetic component to the development of the behaviour. It is likely that when there is genetic involvement in the development of responses, this will involve a number of genes. In a similar vein to Hawley, Volk et al. conclude that bullying in young children serves the same functions as dominance and social resource control (see Box 11.9). Volk et al. further consider bullying as advantageous to some adolescents and that many of these teenagers are socially skilled and reasonably clever. They view adolescent bullying behaviour as a successful evolutionary adaptation rather than being maladaptive.

Box 11.9　Hawley's study on the advantages of different children's strategies for getting what they want: an evolutionary perspective

Hawley (2003) compared the strategies used by 163 children recruited from six different pre-schools in Connecticut, US. Children were of different origins: 90 European-American, 46 African-American, 21 Hispanic-American and 6 Asian-American with an average age of just over four years. Girls comprised 54.6 per cent and boys 45.4 per cent. Teacher descriptions of prosocial and coercive behaviours were used to classify children according to their resource control strategies adopted. Other measures were taken including an aggression scale and a child interview that considered language skills, moral cognition and emotion, and self-reports of problem-solving strategies and who they like the most. Hawley found that of the four types of strategists more girls and boys were 'bistrategic' and 'prosocial controllers'. There was no significant difference in the number of boys and girls who were 'coercive controllers'. In the context of aggression, Hawley found that the aggressive children were a heterogeneous group; where some were morally underdeveloped whereas others were not. Two groups of aggressive children were found, however: unskilled and socially skilled bistrategic controllers. Teacher ratings of coercive control were associated with aggressive behaviour. Prosocial control across gender was associated with relational aggression. A difference was found between children in their beliefs of wrongness to take something and the reasons for this as a consequence of moral maturity. Nevertheless, it was found that increased aggressiveness in girls was associated with moral maturity. Furthermore, the relational aggression used by girls is a way of sufficing their social intimacy status, and this relies on superior social understanding of how relationships work. Hawley's findings also show that the bistrategic children were consistently the top scorers on moral measures. This adds credence to the findings discussed earlier that ringleader bullies have a well-developed theory of mind (see also Box 5.7). Using sociometric analysis, adolescent bistrategics are the most preferred peers and have high status (Hawley 2002). Coercive controllers are the least preferred. Non-controllers were likely to provide rules as reasons for why a moral transgression was wrong. They have also been found to be the least socially active and most withdrawn from social engagement (Hawley 2003). Prosocial controllers were not as morally developed as bistrategic children and were average scorers on the question asked about the wrongness of taking things. Hawley, however, found that these children scored highly on agreeableness using the 'Big-5' (see Chapter 12). These findings are consistent with an evolutionary perspective. It is self-preservation that guides us towards resource-directed behaviour, and using more than one strategy in order to achieve this makes perfect sense.

Balancing coercive strategies with prosocial ones ensures the best for self and group interests. Moreover, children who are bistrategics have well-developed social skills and social understanding of others' intentions and goals. This clearly helps them to operate within social group norms and at the same time achieve personal gain.

According to Ellis et al. (2012), **risky teenage behaviours**, such as aggression and drug use, are often viewed as maladaptive and arising out of poor socialisation or disturbed developmental factors interacting with a biological propensity to behave this way. However, risky behaviours, they argue, enable teenagers performing them to attain dominance and kudos, despite the dangers experienced and the harm done to others (Gallup et al. 2011). For these adolescents risky behaviours cannot be equated with being maladaptive. An evolutionary psychological perspective provides a way of considering these behaviours as adaptive to the environmental conditions faced by the individuals concerned (see Box 11.10).

Box 11.10   Is risky behaviour adaptive or maladaptive?

Using an evolutionary psychological model helps developmentalists, such as Ellis et al. (2012) to understand why adolescents perform risky behaviours both to themselves and towards others. It is important to understand what the goals of adolescents are. According to evolutionary psychologists, adolescence is a time of impressing the opposite sex to attain reproductive status. In order to accomplish this, both physical and social skills are required as a means to accessing the desired commodity – having a romantic partner. Also, bodily changes are occurring in teenagers as they reach puberty. Puberty is a phase when peers compete to attain status and resources. Performing risky behaviours might be one way of attaining these goals by way of increasing social and sexual kudos. For example, the underlying motivations for drinking games, fighting and daredevilry serve to attain admiration from peers and social status. Bullying others serves a function for the individual concerned and, if stopped, the successful strategy for gaining social and sexual recognition might be lost. Therefore, evolutionary psychologists perceive the environmental conditions under which risky behaviours operate as important to whether they are adaptive or maladaptive. For example, in an environment where adolescents perceive there to be little control over the predictableness of the changes occurring around them, performing risky behaviours would seem to be an adaptive response. If, by bullying, a teenager accrues benefits, then this strategy can be considered a good adaptation. If, however, the costs clearly exceed the rewards, then performing risky behaviours is a poor solution and a maladaptive strategy for the individual. Ellis et al. also highlight the impact of the mismatch between the current and ancestral environment (i.e. the **mismatch hypothesis**). If we consider, for example, the type of environment that adolescents would find themselves in during the ancient past, this is likely to have been very different from current practices whereby they are cooped up in a classroom with 30 other teenagers. It is difficult to know precisely how teenagers lived during ancestral savannah dwelling times, but such close classroom contact would not have been an option. So perhaps it is not surprising that, in current times, this forced close proximity with other youngsters can lead to aggression. Hence, due to this mismatch between the environment in which we evolved and the current environment, we may see an increase in the likelihood of bullying.

Evolutionary psychologists provide a different perspective on the causes of behaviour such as bullying. It is difficult, however, to provide definitive proof of some of their conclusions such as those related to the mismatch hypothesis simply because we lack precise information about the social landscape of our savannah dwelling ancestors.

Aggression and bullying are social problems that, in their extreme form, can be seen in gang behaviour. Many gangs are made up of male adolescents. We will consider the social behaviour of members of violent and aggressive **gangs** next.

GANGS

Thornberry et al. (2003) point out that peers will imitate each other, even in the case of antisocial behaviours. If friends therefore indulge in delinquent behaviours such as truancy from school or stealing money, then it is highly likely that others will follow suit. This can also lead to joining gangs. Thornberry et al. argue that children and teenagers who are associated with gangs are more likely to engage in violent activity. In fact, Spergel et al. (1989) found members of gangs to be three times more likely to commit violent offences than those who were not affiliated to such groups. While children or teenagers are members of a gang they commit more violent behaviours but this decreases on leaving (Thornberry et al. 2003).

Plate 11.8 Violent gangs confronting each other on the street. (Shutterstock 474591934.)

Various studies have shown that African American mothers who have little social support and are struggling financially are prone to stress that, in turn, can lead to ineffective parenting skills. This is likely to have an impact on the social behaviour of their children – in many cases leading to aggressive behaviour and to joining gangs (Farver et al. 2005; Tolan et al. 2003). It is difficult to know the exact number of gangs but statisticians have made estimates (see Box 11.11).

Box 11.11　Violence through gangs and knife-crimes

In the US, Egley (2002) found that there are as many as 24,000 gangs with memberships in the region of 750,000 – mostly aged 17–18 years. Latest statistics based on the Federal Bureau of Investigations, released in 2016 by the Statistic Brain Research Institute, show that the number of gang members has increased to 1,150,000 (40 per cent of whom are under 18 years of age). Female membership, as expected, is lower than that of males (8 per cent). In 2007 the Metropolitan Police estimated there to be 171 gangs in London alone. In Glasgow the Strathclyde Police estimated 170 gangs with 3,500 gang members in 2008 (Trueman, The Learning History Site 2016). Topping (2011) interpreted Scotland Yard figures of knife crime injuries in London as having risen from 941 to 1,070 between February and April in 2011. The Metropolitan Police reported 1,157 knife crimes in London between 2010 and 2011. In 2011 Gavin Berman compiled a document for Members of Parliament that reported that 18 per cent of offensive weapon possession was in the hands of juveniles aged between 10 and 17 years.

Although there are fewer violent gangs in Britain (even when we add the various numbers of gangs from different cities) than the US, it still presents itself as a social problem. This is especially so when weapons such as knives are carried and used to threaten other children and teenagers living locally.

There have been a number of speculations regarding the reasons why children and adolescents join gangs. For Lauber et al. (2005) this is a consequence of a disorganised neighbourhood suffering from economic deprivation. In these environments it is not uncommon for other family members to be involved in gang activity (Matza 1969) where drug use is rife and peer-pressure strong. Lauber et al. also argue that joining a violent gang offers an individual a gang identity (such as being brave or tough) for which they offer their loyalty in return. Dishion et al. (2005) have outlined other contributory factors encouraging gang involvement:

- failing academically at school;
- peer rejection;
- exhibiting antisocial behaviour.

Garbarino (2001) believes that parents simply ignore what their children become involved in because they might not like what they find – they appear to be in denial of reality. Garbarino provides the example of two outcasts from the Columbine school who became notorious mass killers (see Box 11.12).

Box 11.12   The Columbine High School massacre: deadly tracks of outcasts Harris and Klebold

Garbarino (2001) argued that the activity of children and teenagers is often hidden from their parents. Parents, however, often do not want to know what their children get up to. Eric Harris and Dylan Klebold are good examples of where information about them was ignored. At 18 they were members of the 'Trenchcoat Mafia' (although there is some debate as to whether they were part of a Goth subculture). For a school assignment they composed a video of them walking down the corridors of their school shooting at other students. They even put information on the Internet bragging about their accomplishment at building four bombs. This information was passed on to the Sherriff's Department, which subsequently dismissed it. The seeds of their destructive intent were evident but nobody picked up on it. In 1999, prior to entering their school, Harris and Klebold set off two small fire bombs to keep firefighters and emergency staff busy. They then entered Columbine High School, set off two bombs at the cafeteria section of the school and shot dead 12 of their classmates and a teacher fleeing the building. They left 24 wounded and then they shot themselves. Bai et al. (1999) commented that they had been heavily influenced by video games, 'obsessed with the violent video game *Doom* – in which the players try to rack up the most kills – and played it every afternoon' (p. 24).

These adolescents were considered to be gifted but were victims of bullying over a four-year period. They were ostracised by their peers and considered as 'the losers of the losers' (Lynch 2014).

Taylor (2016) addressed why children and teenagers join gangs by adopting two prominent theories: Social Bond Theory and Social Learning Theory. The Social Bond Theory implies that children and teenagers become drawn into gang membership by their association with deviant peers. It is through the association with deviant peers that norms, values and behaviours adopted tend towards deviancy. Moreover, these norms, values and behaviours are consistent with the gang they drift into and become socially bonded with. Sutherland (1939) argued that juveniles living in a bad neighbourhood and attending ineffective schools are likely to interact with older delinquent children, thereby adopting their deviant attitudes. This means law-abiding values are substituted for delinquent ones. These children and teenagers drift into a lifestyle of delinquency and gang loyalty through 'techniques of neutralisation'. These techniques involve the denial of injury they cause their victims; denial of there being any victims; condemnation of those who accuse them and using their peers as an excuse for doing what they did. In the case of Social Learning Theory individuals seek membership of deviant gangs as a family substitute. Often children and teenagers who join these gangs feel rejected by their family, school, peers and the community. Members of deviant gangs provide these disaffected children and teenagers with rewards for behaving in accordance to their group norms and provide a sense of belongingness (Taylor 2016).

Children and adolescents become radicalised by gang members who encourage them to contravene mainstream cultural norms, values and behaviour. There is a question of whether these individuals are already prone to aggressive and delinquent tendencies or if they drift into deviant ways of perceiving how interpersonal relationships operate. Whatever the answer, it is clear that such individuals develop antisocial ways and deviate from the path of condoned social behaviour.

Summary

- Antisocial behaviour is considered to be destructive and troublesome. Not all anti-social behaviour breaks the law but it can be considered as morally offensive if a culture's moral codes are contravened. At the same time, antisocial behaviour that contravenes the law does not necessarily cause moral offence.
- Children and teenagers sometimes behave in ways that parents consider to be antisocial. Most individuals grow out of these behaviours but not all. There are developmental conditions known as disruptive behaviour disorders (DBDs) where individuals frequently exhibit problem and aggressive behaviours long-term. As a rule, the earlier the onset of antisocial behaviour the more problematic it is.
- Conduct Disorder (CD) and Oppositional Defiant Disorder (ODD) are examples of DBDs. Individuals with CD tell lies, steal, refuse to follow rules and behave aggressively. Individuals with ODD can be defiant, hostile, argumentative, resentful, angry, spiteful and vindictive. An example of a neurodevelopmental disorder is ADHD. Individuals with ADHD are impulsive, inattentive and underachieve academically.
- Aggressive behaviour is considered to be antisocial and designed to cause physical or psychological harm. Violence refers to behaviour by persons against persons with intent to threaten or inflict physical harm. All violent acts are aggressive but not all aggressive acts are violent (e.g., cybercrime). Aggression can be of a reactive (automatic, impulsive, uncontrollable and unreasoned) or instrumental (controlled, calculated, reasoned and premeditated) nature.
- Bullying is an abuse of power and performed deliberately to cause harm to others. Sociometric approaches ask children to nominate peers they consider as popular or disliked. Through the sociometric approach, it was found that bullies can be popular and have good social cognition; reasonably popular with average social cognition or they can be unpopular with low social cognition. Those who are unpopular tend to be rejected and ostracised.
- Bullies tend to be in groups that have a hierarchical structure of dominance. There are three roles: the ringleader who is in charge of the bullying; the assistant

who helps the ringleader and the reinforcer who encourages the bullying often by laughing and jesting. In addition to physical and verbal bullying there is also indirect and relational (personal) bullying. Smith (2016) describes six types of bullying: physical, verbal, social exclusion, indirect, bias or prejudice and cyberbullying.

- Cyberbullying is a form of indirect and relational bullying. Originally this was carried out by emailing and texting but, as technology developed further, new devices such as the smartphone and network sites provide another avenue for cyberbullies.
- Victims can also be bullies. Some victims provoke others into bullying them and are called provocative victims. There is something about them that bullies dislike. Victims per se tend to have poor self-assertive behaviours that reinforce bullies to bully further (as it is rewarding). Victims tend to be unpopular and suffer low self-esteem. They tend to have poor social skills and are less liked or rejected by others.
- Viewing violence on television, film or in magazines can increase aggressive behaviour in children. Development of technology means that individuals have access to mobile phones, iPads and smartphones, all of which can be used to record violence or for cyberbullying. Low empathy levels are associated with cyberbullying.
- Evolutionary psychologists offer a different way of considering risky behaviours such as bullying. They consider whether these behaviours are adaptive or maladaptive and use the mismatch hypothesis to help explain how these behaviours might have arisen.
- Members of gangs are three times more likely to commit violent acts than those who are not part of a gang. It has been argued that coming from a disorganised neighbourhood increases the likelihood of joining a gang. Three factors encouraging gang involvement include: poor academic performance, peer rejection and behaving antisocially.

Questions for discussion

1. In what ways are physical and relational aggression different?
2. What are the differences between bullies, victims and provocative victims?
3. What is cyberbullying? How does it differ from other forms of bullying?
4. Critically discuss how Social Bond Theory and Social Learning Theory differ in their account of how individuals become involved in gangs.
5. Consider whether the traits common to the conditions of ADHD and CD really differ. Critically discuss if an argument can be made that they are really slightly different forms of the same disorder.
6. Critically assess the findings that there are underlying genetic effects for being bullied by peers at school.

Further reading

If you are interested in exploring interpersonal functioning within groups and, in particular, the aggression–adaptation link from a multi-interdisciplinary approach, look at:

- Hawley, P., Little, T.D. and Rodkin, P. (2007). *Aggression and Adaptation.* Mahwah, N.J.: Lawrence Erlbaum.

If you are interested in exploring serious child and adolescent conduct problems and how this progresses into delinquency, look at:

- Lahey, B.B., Moffitt, T.E. and Caspi, A. (2003). *Causes of Conduct Disorder and Juvenile Delinquency.* London: The Guilford Press.

If you are interested in understanding school bullying through the integration of research, theory and practice in more detail, look at:

- Smith, P.K. (2014). *Understanding School Bullying: Its Nature and Prevention Strategies.* London: Sage.

If you are interested in exploring state-of-the-art research into cyberbullying and the development and evaluation of the various interventions designed to prevent and stop it in its tracks, look at:

- Völlink, T., Dehue, F. and Mc Guckin, C. (2016). *Cyberbullying: From Theory to Intervention.* Abingdon, Oxford: Routledge, Taylor & Francis Group.

NOTES

1 Here Smith includes 'bias or prejudice-based' bullying but it should be noted that this form of bullying is different from the other categories. Bias or prejudiced-based bullying can take on the form of all the other categories of bullying – an individual can be physically or verbally bullied, excluded from social events, ostracised indirectly or receive emails containing bullying content.
2 Note that cyberbullying is also different as it describes the medium (online) – and it can be verbal, social exclusion or indirect as well.

Contents

Introduction   389

Temperament – the precursor
to personality   391

The relationship between temperament
and personality   393

The structure of personality   394

Evolution and individual differences   396

Personality and social development   397

Personality stability over the life span   403

Are there reliable gender differences
in temperament and personality?   406

Summary   411

Chapter 12

Individual differences

Temperament and personality

12

What this chapter will teach you

- The relationship between temperament and personality.
- The notion of multiple intelligences including social aspects of behaviour.
- The nature of the Big 5 personality factors or dimensions.
- The person–situation debate.
- How stable or plastic are personality factors as people age.
- How children change in terms of personality as they enter adolescence.
- Evidence that there are subtle gender differences in personality traits and where these arise from.

INTRODUCTION

When we talk about individual differences we are normally referring to the way that people vary in terms of **temperament** and **personality**. But what exactly are temperament and personality and how do they differ? As we will see, **personality factors** such as levels of extraversion, conscientiousness and agreeableness are largely social variables. Individuals vary greatly along these dimensions. But why do we vary in our responses to others and when does this variability emerge during development? In this chapter, drawing on material considered in previous chapters, we examine the biological and environmental roots of individual differences in social development. In order to do this we consider the structure of personality, evolutionary approaches and behavioural genetics, before finally examining how personality changes with age by taking a life-span approach to end this chapter. In addition to temperament and personality, some psychologists who are interested in individual differences concentrate on variability in levels of intelligence. Although there are debates concerning the precise definition of intelligence, most mainstream psychologists consider that it includes the abilities of reasoning, planning and problem-solving. These factors might appear to have little to do with social development but, since the mid-1980s, a number of experts have begun to expand the concept of what constitutes intelligence, taking it into areas related to social behaviour. In particular, Harvard developmentalist Howard Gardner has developed the argument that standard intelligence tests measure only a small sub-set of human intellectual abilities. For the most part this chapter is concerned with individual differences related to personality, but to begin with we will briefly consider intelligence in Box 12.1.

Box 12.1   Social development and multiple intelligences

According to Howard Gardner, how well we deal with the environment and with other people are also forms of intelligence. Gardner (1983, 2010) suggests that we should expand the concept of intelligence to **multiple intelligences**, which cover eight separate human abilities that we all vary on.

1. Linguistic (ability to use language(s)).
2. Logical-mathematical (ability to reason mathematically).
3. Visuospatial (ability to visualise and manipulate objects in space).
4. Musical (ability to perceive and produce music).
5. Bodily-kinaesthetic (ability to control body movements).
6. Interpersonal (ability to understand others).
7. Intrapersonal (ability to understand oneself).
8. Naturalistic (ability to understand the natural world).

Note that only the first three of these are normally assessed in IQ tests. Furthermore, because in Gardner's scheme these eight abilities are independent, he claims it is possible to be highly intelligent socially (numbers 6 and 7) without being considered intelligent in the traditional academic manner (1, 2 and 3). If Gardner's concept of multiple intelligences is correct, then schools and colleges currently only measure a small proportion of children's intellectual abilities. In particular, they are missing out on social aspects of intellectual development. We should also bear in mind, however, that Gardner's concept of multiple intelligences has not gone unchallenged. In fact, three main criticisms have been made. First, other researchers have found high positive correlations between different aspects of intelligence, suggesting an underlying general intelligence that they all draw on (Geake 2008). Second, it might be suggested that what Gardner has really done is to redefine all abilities as forms of intelligence (Sternberg 1991). If this is the case then he has simply expanded the meaning of the word intelligence. Third and finally, Gardner has never produced a reliable test of these eight forms of intelligence (Waterhouse 2006). This final point means that some of the intelligences he includes are really rather ephemeral concepts – if they do not lend themselves to measurement then how can we call them forms of intelligence?

Despite the criticisms, many developmentalists agree with Gardner that what intelligence tests measure is really quite restricted when we look at children's abilities to deal with the world they encounter (including of course the social world).

TEMPERAMENT – THE PRECURSOR TO PERSONALITY

Temperament refers to specific characteristics of an individual that are considered to have a biological input. Such **temperamental dispositions** include 'the domains of activity, affectivity, attention, and self-regulation, and these dispositions are the product of complex interactions among genetic, biological, and environmental factors across time' (Shiner et al. 2012, p. 437). They are known as temperamental dispositions because such emotional responses appear very early in development. A child's temperament helps to shape their eventual personality due, in part, to the way they engage with their social environment and the responses they evoke from others (Rothbart 2011; see also Chapter 3). Individual differences appear virtually from birth, and over the first few months of life quite clear differences in proneness to distress, approach, frustration and positive affect can be observed (Rothbart 2011). When presented with novel objects at six months infants vary in how rapidly they approach these. The amount of smiling and laughter at this age reliably, if modestly, predicts levels of extraversion (see later) when measured at age seven (Rothbart et al. 2000). Towards the end of the first year of life, individual differences in levels of observable fearful inhibition to novel stimuli appear. This means that some infants who previously approached new objects now begin to become more wary of them. Levels of approach at this age reliably, if once again modestly, predict a number of features of personality later in life such as levels of empathy and guilt.

Some developmentalists suggest there are three broad temperamental dimensions very young children vary along (Rothbart 2011; Rothbart and Bates 2006; see Table 12.1). Being at the extremes of each of these dimensions has been linked to both positive and negative psychosocial development in later life. To complicate matters, psychosocial problems can often be the outcome when infants score highly on one dimension but are low on another.

Plate 12.1 Toddler showing fearful inhibition when meeting a GP for the first time. (Shutterstock 237486490.)

Table 12.1 Three broad temperament dimensions. (Based on Rothbart and Bates 2006.)

Temperamental dimension	Description	Predictor of life outcomes
Extraversion/ surgency	Level of motor activity, positive emotionality, impulsivity/risk-taking.	High levels of extraversion/surgency, when combined with low levels of effortful control, are associated with the development of later social behaviour problems.
Negative affectivity	Tendency to show fear, sadness, anger, frustration and discomfort.	High negative affectivity predicts both internalising problems (such as anxiety and depression) and externalising problems (such as aggression).
Effortful control (self-regulation)	Attention focusing and shifting, perceptual sensitivity, inhibitory and activational control.	High effortful control is linked to positive development, including high levels of social competence. Those low on effortful control have difficulty regulating their arousal levels and consequently become easily agitated.

Looking at each dimension in turn, extraversion/surgency is a measure of what might loosely be termed confidence (surgency is a technical term used to describe impulsivity, high levels of activity and positive engagement). Clearly, providing this is not taken to an extreme, having a reasonably high level of extraversion/surgency is broadly regarded as a positive feature. In contrast, negative affectivity concerns the level to which a child responds negatively to experiences including social encounters such as meeting people for the first time. Finally, effortful control, which develops over the first four years of life, consists of the ability to inhibit a dominant response in favour of a subordinate response. An example of this might be to get dressed before playing with a favoured toy. Hence, we can think of effortful control as the ability to inhibit a behavioural response that leads to a pleasurable sensation in favour of a response that, despite being less pleasurable, is often more important – even if this other activity is simply sitting quietly. This means that effortful control often involves delayed gratification (see Chapters 4 and 5). Children who develop good early effortful control score highly on measures of social compliance (Rothbart 2011). They also develop a good sense of empathy, guilt and shame. (Note that it might seem odd to suggest that children can develop 'good levels' of guilt and shame, but these feelings stop us from being uncaring to others – psychopaths are generally regarded as lacking such emotional responses.) Children with low effortful control are often perceived as 'difficult' and lacking in concentration by adults.

It is interesting to note that each of these three dimensions has been related to attentional and emotional brain systems in humans and in non-human animals. In particular, the brain system that underlies effortful control is known as the **executive attention system** (Posner and Rothbart 2000; see also Chapter 4). The executive attention system, which involves frontal lobe activity across species, manages what information is held in working memory and how well we maintain focus on this material. This finding supports the notion that temperament is, in part, related to biological factors. In fact, controlled lab tests have related effortful control, at least in adults, to specific genes (Posner et al. 2010, see Box 12.2). While this finding might be taken as support for the notion that temperament is largely inherited, it is clear that, as in all cases, genetic expression is open to environmental influence. Such findings can be used to inform teachers and child-care workers that the emotional responses of young children are not solely the outcome of social learning. Rather, individual differences in the ability to self-regulate responses are to be expected and children who differ in these temperamental dimensions are likely to require different interventions in order to achieve social integration.

Although temperament is perceived as biological in origin, this should not be read as immutable. There is clear evidence that, up to a point, parental response to temperamental dispositions can modulate developmental outcomes. For example, some experts claim that parental warmth can enhance positive emotional reactivity (Lengua and Kovacs 2005). Moreover, some studies suggest that high negative emotional control in toddlers is related to negative parental control (Halverson and Deal 2001). The problem with such findings is that it is difficult to determine which way the causal arrows point. Is it the case, for example, that high offspring negative emotional control evokes negative parental control or does negative parental control increase negative emotional control in children? Most developmentalists today consider that the arrows point in both directions and a complex child temperament/ parenting style interaction leads to the modification of responses in both parties. As we will see later, however, behavioural geneticists consider that early parental behaviour has little bearing on the personality that children eventually develop.

THE RELATIONSHIP BETWEEN TEMPERAMENT AND PERSONALITY

Box 12.2   The nature and nurture of temperament and personality

In Chapter 3 we considered temperament within the context of emotional development and attachment in infancy. The widely accepted typologies of temperament in babies is 'difficult, easy or slow-to-warm-up', each showing mutually exclusive patterns of behavioural responses (Rothbart and Bates 2006; Thomas and Chess 1986). These differences have, in part, been accounted for by the different structural permutations (alleles) of the DRD4 gene (see Chapter 3). Having the 7-repeat allele structure is commonly seen in babies considered as difficult (i.e., the disorganised/undifferentiated D-dyad). We have to bear in mind, however, that, while there is a genetic basis for the development of temperament, personality is very much an outcome of biological factors interacting with early environmental experiences (Rothbart and Bates 2006). Heredity contributes to differences of emotionality, sociability and activity levels observed in the earlier stages of the lifespan.

These characteristics, however, become less influenced by our heredity as diverse life experiences, unique to the individual, shape the development of personality further.

As we have seen, temperament, whilst not 'hard wired', is based around biologically influenced dispositions. How, we might ask, is temperament related to personality? The general view among psychologists today is that personality develops out of an interaction between temperamental dispositions and environmental experience. This environment, of course, includes the social environment and, in particular, parental and peer influence. These are, in essence, large factors of what can be considered the shared and the non-shared environment (see Chapter 1 and later). While temperamental dispositions quite reliably predict later personality development, social experiences can modify or possibly even reverse such predilections. Hence if, for example, a child who at the age of two scores highly on measures of extraversion/surgency and then experiences loss of both parents, she will be less likely to develop into an out and out extravert at the age of 14. In fact, should she then experience deprivation between the ages of 2 and 14, we would not be surprised to find she appears quite reserved at the later age.

THE STRUCTURE OF PERSONALITY

Over the last 100 years, personality psychologists (sometimes, when taken together with those interested in intelligence, referred to as 'differential psychologists') have developed sophisticated tools to uncover what we might call the structure of personality (see Box 12. 6 later). That is, into what constituent parts can we break down aspects of the way in which people differ? Also, does it make sense to break personality down into a number of enduring differing aspects or dimensions? Some psychologists question both of these assumptions (see Box 12.3).

Box 12.3   The person–situation debate

Although psychologists generally consider people to have a number of personality traits, this assumption has been questioned. In fact, some psychologists see temperament and personality as psychological constructs that may change with emerging knowledge. One prominent American personality psychologist, Walter Mischel, for example, has suggested that people behave somewhat differently in different situations (Mischel 1968). They may, for example, be scrupulously honest when dealing with friends and family, but, at the same time, less than honest when completing a tax return. This means that their level of conscientiousness is more plastic than many traditional personality psychologists suggest. Importantly, this is also true of young children in social situations. A child might, for example, never cheat when playing games with peers but might repeatedly do so when playing with siblings – feeling this is 'fair-game' in a family-setting. Due to such findings, Mischel and others consider that features of personality are more plastic and situation-dependent. The extent to which situations or enduring internal factors determine personality is known as the personality traits versus personality states debate – also known simply as the **person-situation debate**. It is important to realise that psychological constructs such as the notion of classifiable traits have been developed in order to help us understand emerging function and dysfunction (e.g., the development of stability and neuroticism).

We need to bear this debate in mind when considering the structure of personality. Despite this emphasis on situational variables, even for Mischel, there is some degree of consistency across situations. Without this we would barely recognise people by their behaviour.

Following a century of debate, most differential psychologists today agree that, while people do vary to a degree from situation to situation, it does make sense to consider a number of dimensions that people vary along and that these are relatively enduring (see later). A commonly accepted scheme considers there are five dimensions to personality (McCrae and Costa 1987). These five dimensions (also known as traits or factors – hence the 'five factor approach' or simply the '**Big 5**') are outlined in Box 12.4.

Box 12.4 The Big 5 factors approach

Since the mid-1980s most personality theorists have reached agreement that there are five dimensions of factors on which people vary (conveniently these factors spell out the word 'OCEAN' to aid memory):

Openness to experience -- Closed-minded

(Adventurous, enjoys new experiences)   (Conservative, set in ways)

Conscientious -- Unconscientious

(Self-disciplined, reliable)   (Impulsive, unreliable)

Extraversion -- Introversion

(Outgoing, sensation seeking)   (Reserved, socially inhibited)

Agreeableness -- Disagreeableness

(Nice, helpful, good company)   (Unpleasant, unhelpful)

Neuroticism --- Stability

(Anxious)   (Calm)

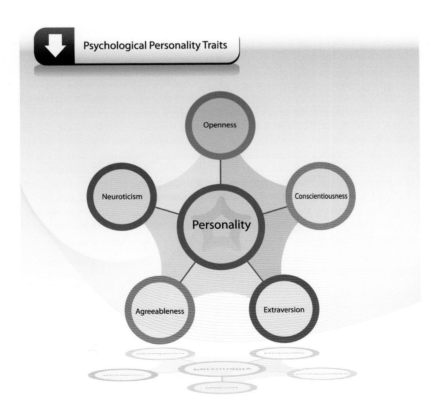

Plate 12.2 The Big 5 **personality factors**. (Shutterstock 79580887.)

EVOLUTION AND INDIVIDUAL DIFFERENCES

Given that life on earth has been evolving for 3.5 billion years, we might ask why have humans not evolved the perfect personality? Why do we differ so much? Surely, after all of this time, we should have evolved the one ideal personality? One way of answering this question is to suggest that variability in personality is free from evolutionary influences. The problem with this argument is the fact that personality factors have a relatively high heritability. In fact, the Big 5 factors vary from around 0.35 to 0.50 in terms of heritability (Plomin et al. 2012; see later). This means that approximately half of the difference between people in terms of things like extraversion and agreeableness can be explained by genetic differences between them. Hence, if genes are involved in personality development, then evolutionary psychologists will have to explain why we have this level of variation. In fact, evolutionists have produced several explanations for this variability, which we consider in Box 12.5.

Box 12.5   Evolutionary psychology explanations for individual differences

Arguably, evolutionary psychologists have made significant contributions to our understanding of many areas of psychology including social, developmental, cognitive and (obviously) biological, but, until recently, they have been less concerned with personality theory. Over the last 20 years they have increasingly begun to consider why, if there is a human nature, this should vary between individuals. In recent years evolutionary psychologists have developed arguments that it may pay us to differ from each other even within a Darwinian framework. Here we consider four of the most influential ones.

Sex and normal variation around the mean

Each organism that reproduces sexually randomly throws away half of its genes and passes the other half on to be combined with those of another individual who has done likewise. This is a very strange way of reproducing but, like most multicellular organisms, humans appear to be stuck with it. This means that gene combinations are broken up and recombined for every individual who is produced. This constantly bringing together of unique gene combinations sets a limit to what natural selection can achieve. It also means that, as with more physical traits such as hair colour and height, we end up with a bell-shaped normal distribution for personality traits. This is particularly the case when several genes are related to a trait. Hence, sexual reproduction is one reason why we find a great deal of variation around that optimum for each of the personality factors, such as level of conscientiousness or extraversion.

Frequency dependent selection

It is important to realise that evolutionary models do not suggest all members of a population should respond to stimuli and social situations in the same way. Quite often how successful a strategy is depends on the strategies that others in the population are adopting. It also depends on the environmental challenges (many of which are unpredictable). It is well established from work on animal behaviour that some 'bold' animals thrive in some environments whereas 'timid' ones thrive in other environments (Dingemanse et al. 2004). Moreover, in a population where most individuals are bold, it then pays a minority to be more timid (and vice versa). This means that as the frequency of one type of 'personality' increases beyond a certain threshold, the benefit of adopting a totally different one increases – hence **frequency dependent selection**. This notion has been suggested as an explanation for the existence of psychopaths. The idea here is that as the vast majority of the population reciprocate kind behaviour, this allows for a small proportion to take advantage by becoming 'free-riders'.

Reactive heritability

The concept of **reactive heritability** is a good example of how nature and nurture can interact to produce personality. In this case natural selection provides each individual with a reasonable range of possible outcomes on each of the Big 5, but these depend, to a degree, on how others react to us. If, for example, a young girl is particularly pretty she may then come to realise that others are likely to be benevolent to her when she smiles and acts in a friendly way. This means that she later scores highly on agreeableness. Likewise, a large well-built boy might learn via feedback from others that people give way to him if he is 'pushy'. Again this may lead him down the path towards being both high on extraversion and low on agreeableness. Evolutionary psychologists and behavioural geneticists call this an evocative relationship between genes and environment (Workman and Reader 2014, see Chapter 1 and later).

Strategic specialisation and family life

One curious finding about families is the degree to which siblings differ from each other. Evolutionists have suggested that one reason for this is having variability allows the family unit to exploit a wider variety of resources. Clearly, having children who are, in turn, imaginative, bold, agreeable and highly conscientious is likely to be a better strategy than having all members demonstrating the same traits. It also means that children are not constantly in competition for family roles. We can think of this as parents not 'putting all of their eggs in one basket'. This of course raises the question - how is this variability in the family achieved? American psychologist Frank Sulloway believes he has provided an explanation. Sulloway, in his book of 1996, `Born to Rebel', suggested that a main source of individual differences in personality within the family is birth order. Sulloway has uncovered strong evidence that firstborns tend to be more conservative and second borns more liberal and rebellious. Interestingly, this movement away from conservatism to rebelliousness increases progressively as we move down the birth order. We might ask why should it be this way around? Sulloway has proposed that different family members fulfil different **ecological niches**. The 'gain resources by pleasing the parents' niche is filled by the firstborn leaving later borns to compete to various degrees in different and more rebellious ways.

Some researchers have criticised Sulloway's findings. Judith Harris, for example, points out that, while his findings are statistically significant, they are also relatively small. Steven Pinker (2002) has even suggested that his theory is incompatible with evolutionary theory. Pinker suggests that successful strategies within the family might not necessarily be successful outside of the family. Parents, for example, provide resources (including affection) regardless of how badly behaved their children are. Non-kin, however, are less likely to be so forgiving. Hence, Pinker considers that we are likely to have evolved different strategies for dealing with kin and non-kin.

Such criticisms need to be considered, but at least Sulloway's findings do attempt to integrate nature and nurture, since in his model their genetic potential is either switched on or off by birth order (Sulloway, 1996, in press).

PERSONALITY AND SOCIAL DEVELOPMENT

You will recall from earlier chapters that theories of development (including personality development) tend to emphasise either biological (nature) or environmental (nurture) factors. As we have stressed throughout, most developmentalists today subscribe to some form of biological and social interactionism (sometimes called **biopsychosocial interactionism** to emphasise the psychological component). The exact flavour of interactionism that developmentalists favour may vary, with some considering that biological factors predominate and others that social ones do. In all cases, however, until the 1990s it was generally agreed that personality is largely formed and stable by the time we reach our 20s. Since the mid-1990s, a number of developmentalists have challenged this view and today those who take a lifespan perspective consider that, while personality becomes more stable as people age, the potential for some degree of change endures into old age (Roberts, Walton and Viechtbauer 2006; see later). This view of development is based on the notion that personality traits are not set in stone but, rather, can be refined by circumstances during our adult lives. Hence, for some life span developmentalists, the personality traits are based around the **plasticity principle**. We will return to this issue of plasticity (and stability) of personality factors after first considering where variability in personality traits originates from. How personality is measured is considered in Box 12.6.

Box 12.6 How personality is measured – the science of psychometrics

Psychometric tests are used to measure personality (and intelligence). The term 'psychometric' literally means 'mental measurement'. Hence, the psychometric approach is concerned with the design and use of tests that measure abilities and aptitude both for the normal population and for those who have specific learning challenges. These tests generally involve self-report questionnaires that require individuals to respond to a set of questions relating to specific aspects of personality. A question relating to extraversion might, for example, ask: 'Would you rather stay in the background at parties?' (YES/NO). In relation to neuroticism a question might ask, 'Do you tend to worry about things?' After completing perhaps a hundred such questions, an individual is then given a score on, for example, each of the Big 5 personality factors. Such psychometric tests are not appropriate for young children, in which case developmentalists often rely on parents, teachers or a trained observer to evaluate temperament/personality. But for those over the age of around 10 years they are generally quite reliable (see below).

All psychometric questionnaires have established high levels of **validity** (do they accurately measure the trait) and **reliability** (for example, would the same person provide the same or very similar answers when given the questionnaire on two occasions).

Here are some examples of the type of questions you might come across in one of these personality questionnaires. Each taps into one of the Big 5 (see if you can work out which one of the Big 5 each question taps into):

1. Do you feel pleased when others fear you?   YES   NO
2. Do you regularly check the doors are locked?   YES   NO
3. Would you lose sleep if you missed a deadline?   YES   NO
4. Do you have many hobbies?   YES   NO
5. Would you describe yourself as the life and soul of the party?   YES   NO

Such tests rely on honesty. In order to ensure this, some contain 'lie detector' questions. In this case when, say, more than one or two of such questions is answered the 'wrong way', then the tester discounts the scores as they are unreliable. These 'lie detector' questions are ones that only 'a saint' would give a particular answer to, such as:

1. Have you ever told a lie to someone?   YES   NO

Sources of variation between individuals

It is well established that individuals vary in terms of personality factors, and that most of these factors are related to social behaviour. But this finding raises another important question – why do individuals vary? Behavioural geneticists rephrase this question as: what are the sources of variation between individuals in terms of their personality factors? You might recall from Chapter 1 that, technically, there are three main components of variation in personality: two of which are environmental and one biological. These are the:

1. shared environment;
2. non-shared environment;
3. genetic components.

(Plomin et al. 2012, see Chapters 1 and 3)

We will consider each in turn, but it is worth noting that each of these overlap with the sources of variation suggested by evolutionary psychologists in Box 12.5.

Shared environmental influences on the development of individual differences

The shared environment is concerned with the effect of growing up in the same family. To work out the effects of the shared environment on personality development, behavioural geneticists compare identical twins reared in the same household with those reared in different households. During the 20th century developmentalists considered that personality is very much affected by this early rearing environment. Many developmentalists argue that the form of attachment children develop has a knock-on effect on how their personality develops. You will recall from Chapters 2 and 3 that, following the work of John Bowlby, Mary Ainsworth suggested there are three types of attachment style (dyads) between primary care-giver and child (Ainsworth et al. 1971). The A-dyad was known as 'insecure avoidant'; the B-dyad was known as 'securely attached'; and the C-dyad was known as 'insecure/ resistant'. Subsequently a fourth, the D-dyad 'disorganized', was added to this list of attachment relationships. Being assessed as forming an A, C or D dyadic relationship is associated with a number of negative outcomes in terms of later relationships (Belsky 1997). Those assessed as fitting into type A generally go on to form ephemeral relationships, and, as such, have low scores on conscientiousness, whereas those of type C tend to over-commit in relationships and demonstrate high levels of neuroticism. In the case of those children experiencing a type D dyadic relationship, in later life they generally are seen as lacking in self-esteem and, as a part of this, are perceived as both high on neuroticism and on introversion (Huis et al. 2011). The fact that three of the four attachment relationship categories have personality problems associated with them might be read as suggesting most children will grow up with social problems. We need to bear in mind, however, that the clear majority of parent–offspring relationships are of the B-dyad (two-thirds). Hence, most children, having formed a secure attachment with their primary care-giver, do not appear to have social personality-based problems that can be traced back to the type of dyad they formed.

Of course regular parent–child interactions continue well beyond this early attachment period, and studies by developmentalists frequently demonstrate significant positive correlations in behaviour and attitudes between the two parties. This might be taken as suggesting offspring model their behaviour on that of the parents. In fact, based on the finding that the nature of the dyadic attachment predicts future behaviour, and that correlations in behaviour between child and primary caregiver are so high, many 20th-century developmentalists concluded that a child's early encounters with her parents has a profound effect on the personality she later develops (Shaffer 2000). Judith Rich Harris has, however, challenged this view. You may recall from Chapter 7 that Harris considers that how parents respond to their children has very little influence on how they 'turn out' (Harris 1995, 1998, 2009).

Non-shared environmental influences on the development of individual differences

The non-shared environment concerns the variation that is left to be accounted for when the shared environment and the effects of the genes have already been assessed. In a nutshell, it consists of those life experiences that occur outside of the rearing environment (home). To Harris, this consists largely of peer relationships. To recap, Harris dismisses the notion that children model their behaviour on their parents because she has major criticisms of studies that base this 'nurture assumption' on correlational studies (see Chapters 1, 2 and 7). In fact, as discussed in Chapter 7, Harris has four main criticisms of such correlational studies.

1. Correlational studies do not distinguish between environmental and genetic influences.
2. Correlational studies do not distinguish between parent-to-child effects and child-to-parent effects (note that this is also the case for the attachment dyads A, B, C and D).
3. Researchers do not distinguish between the child's behaviour inside and outside of the home (which may be very different).
4. Given the large number of correlations performed between parental and child variables, some appear as significant simply due to chance.

In her Group Socialisation Theory (GST), Harris went on to suggest that 50 per cent of the variation between children in attitudes and social behaviour is due to genetic differences between them and most of the remaining 50 per cent can be explained by peer influence (see below). How precisely this peer influence operates was covered in Chapter 7 (at this point you might like to refer back to this material).

Genetic influences on the development of individual differences

Although Judith Harris' GST has been criticised by some developmentalists, the work of behavioural geneticists lends support to her theory. In fact, a large number of studies have converged on the view that the contribution of the three components to individual differences broadly follows the rule of '50-0-50'. That is 50 per cent of the variability is due to non-shared environment, 50 per cent due to genetic differences between individuals and 0 per cent due to the shared (home) environment (Furnham and Kanazawa in press). Even studies that do attribute some of the variation to parental influence still only find around 10 per cent of variability between children in personality factors to be due to the shared environment. This produces a percentage ratio of '50-10-40' (Turkheimer 2000). Astonishingly, and perhaps counterintuitively, this suggests parents only really affect the personality development of their offspring via the genes they pass on to them. Hence, while the nature of the attachment may predict later personality up to a point, this relationship appears not to be based on how the caregiver treats the child but rather based on the genes both parties share. It might also suggest that the 'nurture assumption' really is just an assumption. If Harris is correct then the personality that a child develops is not the outcome of modelling on parental behaviour. This finding is illustrated by a major study review of correlational studies by twin genetics expert John Loehlin of the University of Texas. Loehlin (1992) examined five large-scale twin studies (each from a different country) to establish the degree of similarity they showed on their extraversion and neuroticism scores. In total this gave him a sample size of 24,000 pairs of twins. Additionally, he looked at the similarities between adoptive and non-adoptive parents and their children on these measures. His overall findings are represented in Table 12.2.

Table 12.2 Twin, family and adoption correlations for extraversion and neuroticism. (Based on Loehlin 1992.)

Type of relative	Extraversion	Neuroticism
Identical twins reared together	.51	.46
Fraternal twins reared together	.18	.20
Identical twins reared apart	.38	.38
Fraternal twins reared apart	.05	.23
Biological parents and offspring	.16	.13
Adoptive parents and offspring	.01	.05
Biological siblings	.20	.09
Adoptive siblings	-.07	.11

Looking at Table 12.2, there are a number of features we can consider. First, note that overall correlations for identical twins are close to 0.50 on both extraversion and neuroticism personality traits whereas the correlations are only 0.20 for fraternal (non-identical) twins. These correlations fall only slightly for identical twins reared apart (0.38 for both traits). This means that identical twins reared apart are significantly more similar than non-identical twins reared together. Note also that, while correlations between biological parents and offspring are higher than adoptive (non-biological) parents and offspring (0.16 and 0.13 compared to 0.01 and 0.05), they are still significantly lower than those for identical twins (whether reared together or apart). The miniscule correlations between adoptive parents and offspring for both extraversion

Plate 12.3 Monozygotic twins, sharing all of their genes, look remarkably similar and also show very similar personality profiles. (Shutterstock 201303797.)

(0.01) and neuroticism (0.05) is the strongest evidence that the environment parents/ primary caregivers provide does not play a large role in determining offspring personality development. Based on these and other findings, Loehlin estimates heritability of around 50 per cent for extraversion and 40 per cent for neuroticism. Moreover, he also estimates that most of the remaining variation can be attributed to the non-shared environment, leaving very little of the variation to be explained by the shared (home) environment. One criticism of twin studies (that they are treated similarly due to physical similarities) is considered in Box 12.7.

Box 12.7   Doppelgängers provide validity for twin studies of personality development

The validity of twin studies in assessing the heritability of personality factors has been questioned. One regular criticism of such studies is the notion that, because MZ twins appear to be so physically similar, they are treated more alike (i.e., by parents, siblings and friends) than DZ twins (Anderson 2007; Palmer 2011). Is this criticism valid? A novel way of answering this has been undertaken by behavioural geneticist and twin expert Nancy Segal in her study of **doppelgängers**. As you may know, doppelgängers are unrelated individuals who happen to look identical. Segal reasoned that if people treat identical twins similarly because they are responding to their physical appearance, then doppelgängers should be very similar on personality correlations. In fact Segal (2013) found, when she studied a large sample of doppelgängers from around the world, that the correlations between them on personality dimensions were on average 0. That is, no more similar than two randomly chosen individuals from the general population.

This suggests the similarity in personality between MZ twins does stem from their identical genes rather than from being treated in a very similar way due to their physical similarity.

You might at this point be wondering about the remaining three of the Big 5 factors – openness, conscientiousness and agreeableness? In fact, as Plomin et al. (2012) have pointed out, although behavioural geneticists rarely consider these three other main factors, when they have done so they have produced heritability estimates of 0.45 for openness, 0.38 for conscientiousness and 0.35 for agreeableness. As with extraversion and neuroticism, in all of these cases the remaining variance is almost entirely accounted for by the non-shared environment. Overall, the degree to which people vary on personality factors is accounted for by genetic differences between them that range from 35 per cent (agreeableness) and 50 per cent (extraversion) with an average of 45 per cent. Hence, the notion of a 50-0-50 rule (or possibly 50-10-40) is true when considering extraversion and quite close to correct for the remaining four factors. For most children, the effects of socialisation account for around 50-60 per cent of the variation we see, but much of that variation arises from the non-shared environment rather than from the shared environment (Box 12.8 outlines how genes affect behaviour).

Box 12.8   How do genes affect behaviour?

We have seen that around 40–50 per cent of the variability between individuals can be explained by genetic differences between them. This raises the question, what is the relationship between genes and behaviour? We often read newspaper headlines that suggest scientists have dis-covered a 'gene for' a particular facet of behaviour such as a 'gene for intelligence' or a 'gene for sexual orientation'. We should not be misled by such media simplifications. No single gene codes for a behavioural response in humans. Genes, rather, contribute to differences between individuals and influence behaviour over three different timeframes (Robinson et al. 2008). First, on a moment-by-moment timeframe, genetically influenced brain activity enables individuals to meet environmental challenges and opportunities (including social ones). Hence, when an individual sees someone they are wary of this is likely to place them in an avoidance frame of mind. Second, during individual development, a combination of genetic and environmental input influences the establishment of neural pathways in the brain and this, in turn, leads to some responses being more likely than others. Staying with our example of seeing a person we are wary of, individual responses to this are likely to vary depending on these neural path-ways (note this is not a deterministic relationship but rather a probabilistic one). Hence, as we saw in Chapters 1 and 3, people who have one version of the D4DR gene will be more likely to develop neural pathways that lead to rapid withdrawal. This withdrawal response may, of course, be modified by previous social experiences. Third, and finally, during our evolutionary history, the process of natural selection modified the genetic code in our ancient ancestors to make adaptive responses more likely to the challenges and opportunities of ancestral times. Those individuals who did not show adaptive gene-influenced responses were less likely to pass on their genes to future generations.

We can see that, in order to understand the association between genes and behaviour, we need to consider all three timeframes and realise the complexity of this relationship.

Or do they? As we saw in Chapter 11, antisocial behaviour appears to be, in part, the outcome of parenting style. How can we reconcile these two findings? It appears that, for the majority of children, the shared (largely parentally influenced) environment does not account for differences between children in their general personality factors. There is, however, evi-dence that when we consider extremes of personality and developmental disorders, then parental influence can help to explain a fair degree of the variability (Pergadia et al. 2006). In the case of Conduct Disorder (CD), for example, as we outlined in Chapter 11, if children see violence within the home then this, when combined with the genes they inherit, can lead to them behaving aggressively as a way of resolving social problems (Odgers et al. 2007). This, in turn, leads them down the path of low scores on agreeableness and conscientiousness. It is worth noting that Odgers et al. also concluded that, by altering the home (shared) environ-ment in positive ways, the probability of developing CD is greatly reduced.

This means we can conclude that, while genes are clearly expressed within the environ-ment that parents provide, the effects of the shared environment are more 'visible' at the extreme ends of traits (e.g., in the development of CD). Moreover, the sort of relationships children form outside of the home become increasingly more important than the parental influence in determining differences between children in their personality development.

PERSONALITY STABILITY OVER THE LIFE SPAN

One question that has vexed developmentalists is to what extent are personality traits stable over a life span (see Chapter 3)? One way of studying this is to consider longitudinal studies (see Chapter 2). We can, for example, give individuals a personality questionnaire at differ-ent ages and determine by how much the scores change or remain the same as the participants age. A number of studies have done just this by making use of the Big 5. Box 12.9 considers an important time for change – adolescence.

> ## Box 12.9 Personality development during adolescence: a period of storm and stress?
>
> Adolescence is a period of rapid physical development for both girls and boys. One question we might ask is, is this also a period of rapid change for personality factors? Much of the social developmental research during adolescence has focused on problems that can arise during this period. In summarising the changes that children undergo during this period, Arnett (1999) concluded that, cross-culturally, it is a difficult period in life. For many it is a period both of interpersonal conflict, especially with parents, and of increased risk taking. There is also a decrease in self-esteem between the ages of 9 and 13, especially for girls (Robins et al. 2002). This does, however, begin to rise in late adolescence and continues to rise gradually until the age of 70 (Robins et al. 2002). The increase in interpersonal conflict is associated with a decrease both in agreeableness and in conscientiousness, and an increase in neuroticism (McCrae et al. 2002). Currently there are debates as to the extent to which these, largely negative, changes are the result of biological or social changes in teenagers (McCrae et al. 2002). Undeniably, hormonal changes occur during this stage in life and these steroid hormones are known to affect receptor sites in the brain (Toates 2011). But there are also social changes that can lead to a reassessment of a teenager's role in society (see Chapter 8). Also, as body shape changes, this can lead to a reassessment of personal relationships. Hence, as in all stages in life, we see complex interactions between biological and environmental factors. All of these findings would appear to support the commonly held view that adolescence is a period of 'storm and stress'.
>
> We need, however, to bear in mind that one of the most robust findings in differential psychology is that there is huge variability around the mean. In other words, adolescents vary greatly in the extent to which this period in their lives is a stressful one and many report it to be an enjoyable and relatively stable one (McCrae et al. 2002).

In 2006 Roberts et al. pooled together the results from 92 of these longitudinal studies (covering ages from 10 to 101) and, in so doing were able to provide an answer to the question of how stable personality factors are. Their meta-analysis showed that, while there is a fair degree of stability on each of the five factors, as people age they tend to become more socially dominant (a facet of extraversion), more emotionally stable and more conscientious. These changes are especially associated with the period between adolescence and 40 years of age. Surprisingly, however, not only do we continue to demonstrate personality development beyond our 30s but there is some degree of plasticity which continues into old age. This finding supports the plasticity principle, which suggests personality traits are more plastic than originally thought and open to environmental influence, up to a point, throughout the lifespan. In fact, older people tend to become more agreeable as they age, but they also show a decrease in openness (especially when compared with adolescence) and in social vitality (the second facet of extraversion). Overall, Roberts et al. concluded that people tend towards positive shifts in personality factors as they age. When, however, considering the two sub-divisions of social aspects of personality (extraversion) as they age, while social dominance increases, social vitality decreases. Put simply, older people are more confident socially but are also less likely to be 'party-animals'. A finding that will no doubt be unsurprising to readers. In Figure 12.1 a bar graph for eight age groups illustrates how large a change there is in each of six

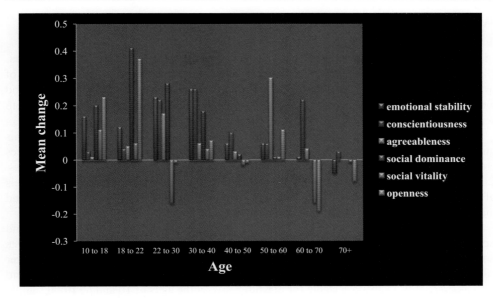

Figure 12.1 Mean-level changes in personality traits across the life course. Note that each bar represents a change during that time period (e.g., age 10 to 18), which can either go up or down. (Adapted from Roberts, Walton and Viechtbauer 2006.)

personality traits (with two measures of extraversion: social dominance and social vitality) and whether they increase or decrease.

One surprising finding with regard to personality is that this has an effect on how long we are likely to live. This is explored in Box 12.10.

Box 12.10   Personality and life expectancy

Personality has a large influence on how we live our lives. You might be surprised to learn that it also has an influence on how long we live our lives. A number of longitudinal studies have established a link between mortality rates and neuroticism and conscientiousness scores on the Big 5. Mroczek et al. (2013) found that older adults who score highly on neuroticism react badly to stressful events and that this, in turn, is related to a shorter life expectancy. Mroczek et al. suggest that this reduction in life expectancy is due to long-term elevated stress hormones leading to cardiovascular dysfunction. In addition to high levels of neuroticism being related to a shorter life expectancy, it was also found that those adults with low scores on conscientiousness have a reduced life expectancy. In this case, however, Mroczek et al. attribute this to the increase in risk-taking behaviours such as increased alcohol drinking and accidents due to impulsive behaviours. For individuals who score highly on conscientiousness, in addition to being less likely to engage in risky behaviour, another benefit derives from the fact that they are more likely to engage in exercise and eat more healthily.

In a nutshell, if you want to live longer then it might be worth at least attempting to reduce levels of neuroticism and increase conscientiousness.

ARE THERE RELIABLE GENDER DIFFERENCES IN TEMPERAMENT AND PERSONALITY?

In 1992 relationship Guru John Gray wrote a bestselling book entitled, *Men Are from Mars, Women Are from Venus*. It became the bestselling self-help book of the 1990s with sales of over 50 million copies. These sales figures suggest that people really do believe men and women are fundamentally different in nature. The question is, does this notion stand up to scrutiny and if so how do these differences develop?

A number of personality psychologists and developmentalists have explored this question. Costa et al. (2001), for example, found small but significant gender differences cross-culturally on the Big 5 with females scoring higher on neuroticism and agreeableness. Likewise, a study by Schmitt et al. (2008), which considered 55 nations, found higher levels of neuroticism and agreeableness in females when compared with males. They also found that males had higher scores on risk-taking behaviour.

The largest study yet undertaken in this area, however, dwarfs those of Costa et al. and Schmitt et al. By making use of modern social media, American personality psychologists Soto et al. (2011) were able to examine personality changes in a cross-cultural sample of over one million children, adolescents and adults. Their main aim was to determine the extent to which personality factors are stable (or plastic) between the ages of 10 and 65 (total sample 1,267,218). In considering this question, however, they also uncovered evidence of gender differences and how these change over this period. Given their huge sample size, they were able to speak with some confidence about gender differences in the Big 5 personality traits. (It is worth noting that in developed countries around 20 per cent of the population is over the age of 65 and hence a sizable proportion did not appear in this analysis.) Below we consider each of the Big 5 in relation both to changes in personality and to gender differences.

Conscientiousness

Here we can see that, during early adolescence, both boys and girls show a reduction in levels of conscientiousness, which then begin to rise in their late teens. From late teens on females are significantly higher on conscientiousness than males with both becoming more conscientious as they age (see Figure 12.2).

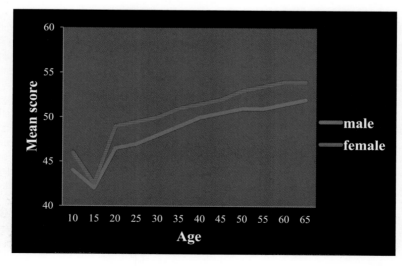

Figure 12.2 Means for overall conscientiousness by age and gender – pink line female, blue line male. (Adapted from Soto et al. 2011.)

Agreeableness

Agreeableness shows a broadly similar pattern of development (and with regard to gender differences) to conscientiousness. Again there is a dip in early teens, which then rises in late teens and this continues to rise through to late middle age. Also, as in conscientiousness, females score significantly higher on agreeableness than males (see Figure 12.3).

Neuroticism

At age 10 males and females demonstrate identical moderate patterns of neuroticism. This then rises quite steeply for females while simultaneously falling for males during adolescence. From 20 to 60+ neuroticism falls somewhat (and more so for women than for men).

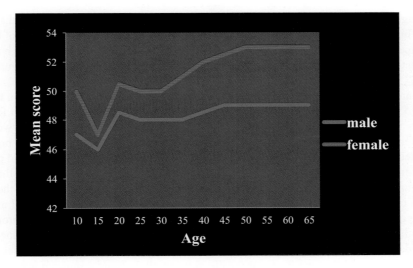

Figure 12.3 Means for overall agreeableness by age and gender – pink line female, blue line male. (Adapted from Soto et al. 2011.)

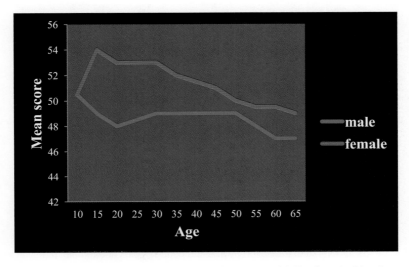

Figure 12.4 Means for overall neuroticism by age and gender – pink line female, blue line male. (Adapted from Soto et al. 2011.)

But note that the lines do not converge and throughout adult life women show higher levels of neuroticism (see Figure 12.4). The finding that females have higher levels of neuroticism during their fertile years fits in quite well with clinical studies that show an increase in mental health issues during these years (Kring et al. 2012).

Extraversion

At age 10 both boys and girls record similarly high levels of extraversion. During the teens these figures fall but more so for boys than for girls (see Figure 12.5). From age 20 on females are higher on extraversion than males (with perhaps some convergence in late middle age).

Openness

At age 10 there is little or no gender difference on ratings of openness; boys then score slightly higher on this trait until late teens when their level of openness falls and that of females rises somewhat. From age 20 on there is a slight increase in openness for both genders but males continue to score higher on this trait than females for much of their adult lives (see Figure 12.6).

In summary we can say the fascinating thing about this large-scale study is that on three of the Big 5 traits the pattern appears to confirm our gender stereotypes of males and females. Females are more agreeable, more conscientious and more neurotic. Anecdotally, we might expect females to be more friendly and helpful than males and to suffer more from problems associated with depression and anxiety. In contrast to these findings, however, (and perhaps counter-intuitively), from mid-teens on females score more highly on extraversion than their male counterparts. Males score higher on openness from late teens on. Neither of these two findings can be said to confirm our gender stereotypes as we might have expected males to be more outgoing then females. Openness would be a difficult one to call and is probably a finding that requires further research. In sum, there are significant gender differences during the development of our personality traits. We should also bear in mind, however, that these differences, whilst significant, are really quite small. In large samples it is possible for two sub-populations to differ significantly on a measure, even when the difference is very

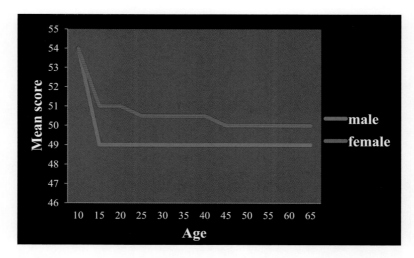

Figure 12.5 Means for overall extraversion by age and gender – pink line female, blue line male. (Adapted from Soto et al. 2011.)

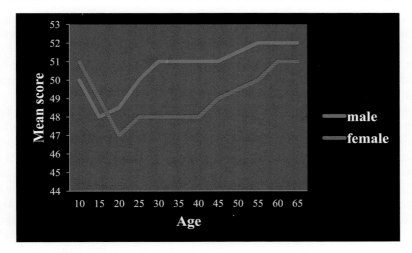

Figure 12.6 Means for overall openness by age and gender – pink line female, blue line male. (Adapted from Soto et al. 2011.)

small, providing it is reliable. We also need to factor in the robust finding that individual differences are much larger than gender differences (Costa et al. 2001; Haslam et al. 2017). Fortunately men and women do not originate from different planets.

Where do gender differences in personality traits originate from?

Whilst the evidence is that gender differences are relatively small, given that they are significant they still need to be explained. So why are females, from their mid-teens on (on average), more agreeable and more conscientious than males, and why are they also more

Plate 12.4 The sex steroid hormone testosterone helps men develop greater upper body strength than women. (Shutterstock 208328110.)

prone to neuroticism? To fully explore such (politically loaded) questions would require a book in itself but we can at least provide a brief summary of the likely causal factors for these gender differences here.

As is the case with individual differences, we can draw on both biological and environmental factors to explain gender differences and, importantly, as we have stressed throughout this book, we need to consider how they interact.

An important biological source of gender differentiation appears to be the sex hormone testosterone (although it could be argued that this is really sex differentiation rather than gender differentiation). Testosterone has both **organisational** and **activational effects** during prenatal and adolescent periods respectively. During the activational stage at around week six of embryonic development, testosterone production in male embryos leads to physical effects (the genital tracts begin to develop along male lines). According to biological psychologists, this increase in testosterone is also the root of psychological effects as areas of the brain are sensitised to respond later to circulating testosterone. At puberty, in males, the testes begin to produce and release into the bloodstream large amounts of testosterone and these again have both physical and psychological effects as upper body musculature develops and libido increases. Hence, this is labelled the activational phase of sex hormones (note that 'female' sex hormones oestrogen and progesterone also have developmental effects during these two phases in girls). The production of testosterone during these two phases of life is triggered by the activity of a single gene on a male's Y chromosome – the SRY (sex determining region) gene (Toates 2011). The fact that males have ten times as much circulating testosterone as females from puberty on has been taken as a causal factor in their higher levels of physical aggression (Archer 2009). This, in turn, might help to explain why, during adolescence, boys become less agreeable and less conscientious than girls. We have to bear in mind here the fact that genes, of course, have both passive and evocative effects on behaviour (see Chapter 1). In the case of passive effects, testosterone may influence areas of the brain (such as the hypothalamus) directly to increase the probability of aggressive response whereas, in the case of evocative effects, a large boy, noticing his increased musculature, might then learn to use this to intimidate others. Some describe this as 'the effects of the effects of the genes' (Plomin et al. 2012). But even if we accept this description, it is clear that the social environment has an input here since the boy's behaviour is, in part, the result of how others respond to him (Eagly and Wood 2013).

Females clearly are also capable of physical aggression but, given they show higher levels of fear response to potentially threatening social situations (Campbell 2018), this might also help to explain why they score higher on agreeableness and conscientiousness (and, arguably, is one of the reasons they score more highly on neuroticism).

American social psychologist Alice Eagly has been influential in the development of a biosocial model of how and why gender differences arise. This means that, while she accepts that there is biological input to gender differences, this difference becomes exaggerated by social and cultural expectations and practices. Eagly and her co-worker Wendy Wood have combined social role theory with evolutionary theory in order to study social development in relation to gender (Eagly and Wood 2011, 2012, 2013). Eagly suggests that girls and women develop social compassion (i.e., showing high levels of agreeableness and conscientiousness) due to an interaction between dispositions and the society's expectations for their role (Eagly and Workman 2008). Males, in contrast, receive feedback from all levels of society that reinforces their view that caring roles are feminine in nature. Eagly and Wood's perspective is a truly interactionist one as it attempts to incorporate biological, cultural and social environmental factors to explain why we see these gender differences in social development.

Summary

- Developmentalists interested in individual differences usually study temperament and personality. Some also consider intelligence. Howard Gardner suggests current views of intelligence should be expanded to consider features such as interpersonal and intrapersonal intelligence. He considers that we each have 'multiple intelligences'.

- Temperament refers to dispositions in attentional, affective and motor responses. These appear very early in development and are considered to be biologically influenced. One scheme considers that there are three broad temperamental dimensions – extraversion/surgency, negative affectivity and effortful control. How very young children score on these dimensions is a good predictor of later behaviour.

- Personality develops out of an interaction between temperament and environmental experiences. Today many personality psychologists consider that there are five main personality factors or dimensions – the Big 5. These five dimensions are openness–closedness, conscientiousness–unconscientiousness, extraversion–introversion, agreeableness–disagreeableness and neuroticism–stability.

- There is a debate among psychologists as to the extent to which behavioural responses are a result of situational variables or personal traits. This is known as the person–situation debate. Despite the emphasis on situational variables by some psychologists such as Walter Mischel, given that people show a fair degree of consistency across situations this suggests that, while our behaviour might vary up to a point between social situations, we do have psychological traits.

- Evolutionary psychologists have developed a number of explanations for why humans differ so much. Their explanations include the fact that sexual reproduction leads to variability; frequency dependent selection suggests that the success of a given strategy (based on personality) may depend on the strategies others adopt; reactive heritability allows for individuals to alter their behaviour depending on how others treat them; and finally, strategic specialisation within families refers to the fact that a family unit is more successful if the offspring take on different roles.

- Psychometric tests have been developed to measure how, for example, people vary on the Big 5. These have to have good levels of validity (do they accurately measure the trait?) and reliability (e.g., would the same person provide very similar answers when given the questionnaire on two occasions).

- Behavioural geneticists divide sources of variability into two facets of the environment – the shared and non-shared environment and effects due to genes. Evidence from twin studies (where the similarity on personality scores between identical twins is compared with that of fraternal twins) suggests that genes account for between 40–50 per cent of the variability between people, and the non-shared environment accounts for much of the remaining variability.

- Genes affect behaviour/personality over three timeframes. First, moment-by-moment responses involve genetically influenced brain activity; second, growth of neural pathways during development affect responses; third, and finally, our evolutionary history created a brain that is likely to develop adaptively flexible responses.

(continued)

(continued)

- Cross-cultural research suggests adolescence is often a period of 'storm and stress' as levels of agreeableness and conscientiousness fall during this time. These do, however, rise at the end of adolescence.
- Recent research suggests personality continues to show a degree of plasticity throughout life and even into old age – a phenomenon known as the 'plasticity principle'. As they age people tend to shift a little towards more 'positive' scores on personality traits. From mid-teens to old age most people become more agreeable and more conscientious.
- Cross-culturally, small but significant gender differences have been uncovered in relation to personality factors. Females are more agreeable, more conscientious and more neurotic. From mid-teens on females also score more highly on extraversion. Males score higher on openness from late teens on.
- Both biological and social factors help to explain these differences. In the case of biological factors, males, with their greater levels of circulating androgens such as testosterone, may become less agreeable and less conscientious (in part due to increases in this hormone during adolescence). It might also be a protective factor for neuroticism however. In relation to social factors, social and cultural expectations are likely to amplify gender differences. Also, according to Eagly and Wood, both genders respond to feedback based on their biological differences to alter their behaviour. This is known as the 'biosocial theory' of gender differences.
- Gender differences are, however, much smaller than individual differences. This suggests the genders are far more similar than they are different.

Questions for discussion

1. Howard Gardner has suggested, in his multiple intelligences model, that we have eight aspects of intelligence. Two of these are intrapersonal and interpersonal intelligence. Devise two questions (as would appear in a personality questionnaire) that might tap into each of these facets of intelligence.
2. Evolutionary psychologists have suggested four reasons why humans might vary in terms of personality. Chose two of these and produce a list of strengths and weaknesses for each of these explanations.
3. Drawing on personal experience, do you feel that gender differences in personality factors really exist? If they do exist, why do they exist?
4. Critically consider the plasticity principle. Why might it be beneficial for adults to continue to develop in terms of personality even up until old age?
5. Why do behavioural geneticists choose to study twins when considering the extent to which genes contribute to differences between individuals? Critically consider the limitations or drawbacks to this sort of research.
6. Critically discuss Judith Rich Harris' Group Socialisation Theory, considering both the strengths and the weaknesses of this theory.

Further reading

If you are interested in understanding the relationship between evolution and individual differences in more detail, look at:

- Buss, D.M. and Hawley, P. (eds) (2011). *The Evolution of Personality and Individual Differences.* Oxford: Oxford University Press.

If you are interested in learning more about the current literature concerning personality, motivation and individual differences including leadership qualities, creativity and emotional intelligence, look at:

- Chamorro-Premuzic, T. (2015). *Personality and Individual Differences* (3rd Edn). Chichester, UK: British Psychological Society and John Wiley and Sons.

If you are interested in learning about the psychology of individual differences in more detail, look at:

- Haslam, N., Smillie, L. and Song, J. (2017). *An Introduction to Personality, Individual Differences and Intelligence* (2nd Edn). Thousand Oaks, CA: Sage.

If you are interested in developing an understanding of the relationship between temperament and personality, look at:

- Rothbart, M.K. (2011). *Becoming Who We Are: Temperament and Personality in Development.* New York: NY: Guilford Press.

Contents

Introduction   415

The development of mass media and
social media   416

Our relationship with the mass media   418

Do individual differences influence our
responses to the media?   440

Summary   444

Chapter 13

The role of
the media

13

INTRODUCTION

Does the mass media play a role in social development, in particular a child's or teenager's self-concept? Research findings suggest it does. Its role in the development of self-concept is a pertinent one as the mass media is constantly sending messages about how we should look and what we should be doing. It also divides people into groups and how they behave by creating in- and out-groups that can be seen in the school environment and out of school. Aspects of how the mass media impact on self-concept, such as the 'ideal girl' and the glorification of being thin (and recently for boys also) will be examined. Another important aspect is the depiction of gender roles and gender stereotypes that impact on social behaviour. Different explanations for why girls are potentially more susceptible to mass media manipulation have been suggested. These include social role modelling and social comparison theory. The reading of glossy magazines has been used as an alternative way for adolescents to make social comparisons (i.e., how they look in comparison with their favourite celebrity), which provides a new source of self-evaluation. Television has also influenced social behaviour by reducing social interaction and social play behaviours in children and adolescents.

The mass media has been a source of socialisation where all too readily specific celebrities are imitated as favourite role models (not all for the good). The Internet (often considered as social media) has also impacted on the way children behave, especially with the advent of Facebook and various chat sites. These sites can be used by some children and adolescents as an alternative to face-to-face social relationships. While this can be a good thing, it can also cause problems, especially in children and adolescents who find interacting with others difficult. It is amongst this vulnerable cohort that paedophiles can use the Internet to groom their potential victims, and gang, cult and politically driven leaders might persuade these children and adolescents to join them. Discussion of 'EU Kids Online' is relevant here, where issues relating to online risks for children are researched by professionals in order to make the social media world a safer place. In Chapter 11 the influence of watching violence on television, films and the Internet, and playing violent computer games, was explored in relation to bullies. In this chapter we will consider such visual media in the context of observed levels of aggression in children per se.

The question of relevance to our discussion on mass media exposure is whether it has a profound impact on the social development of children and adolescents. In fact, research suggests that, due to the many media representations available, the impact it has on an individual's social behaviour will vary greatly. Furthermore, individual differences cannot be ignored here. Children and adolescents, as we have seen in Chapter 12, develop their personalities through various sources including temperamental dispositions. How temperament and personality interact with environmental factors such as exposure to different forms of media therefore contributes to the way social behaviour is shaped. It is therefore important to consider individual differences when evaluating why the social behaviour of a minority of children and adolescents is affected negatively and antisocially. First, however, it is helpful to provide a history of the development of the different forms of mass media. Also, it is important to differentiate between mass media (i.e., media) and social media.

THE DEVELOPMENT OF MASS MEDIA AND SOCIAL MEDIA

When people refer to 'the media' they are generally considering what is more properly called the **mass media**. The mass media refers to the different means of communication used to disseminate information to a very large audience (e.g., newspapers and television). The intention therefore is to provide limited information to a wide number of people – hence the inclusion of 'mass'. In an article posted in February 2016 by Mia Tawile, social media was discussed as being separate from mass media. Tawile (2016) considers mass media and social media as 'sitting on the opposite sides'. As defined previously, she considers mass media as providing a limited amount of information shared with large numbers of people. Social media, alternatively, has bountiful content that can be copied, adapted and shared. The Creative Commons license first developed in the US has been modified for worldwide use. This allows audiences to share the information online and to add to it, thereby making the content malleable. There are still copyright rules applying to the online content. In the case of social media, the audience is not necessarily passive (unlike the more traditional mass media outlets). **Facebook** posts, for example, can be used for the purpose of expressing opinions.

Plate 13.1 Iconic representation of the different types of mass media. (Shutterstock 457708150.)

The mass media includes the following outlets:

- broadcast media – film, radio, recorded music, television;
- print media – books, magazines, newspapers, pamphlets;
- outdoor visual media – billboards, placards, augmented reality advertising (real-time computer-generated input such as video or GPS data projected on a television screen);
- digital media – mobile web serviced through handheld mobile devices (i.e., **smartphones** or mobile phones) and the Internet (i.e., email, **social media sites**, websites, Internet-based radio and television).

Communication has clearly become more complex during our recorded history. Before technological strides were made in the way information is distributed to masses of people, 'word of mouth' was the main source of communication. Although effective, this form of communication is limited to direct contact and interaction with others. The development of writing and reading enabled us to communicate with others indirectly in the form of letters or hand-written books, for example. With the introduction of the first printing press during the Renaissance by German-born Johannes Gutenberg (1398–1468), it was now possible for copy setters to use separate movable metal type. These could be re-used and re-ordered by the copy setters making the whole printing process less arduous. In 1452 Gutenberg printed 200 copies of the **Gutenberg Bible**. It was now possible to extend the writing process of books and leaflets to a mass audience. This type of printing press spread to other European major cities and underwent modifications. Eventually the printing presses would become more sophisticated such that images and colour covered the pages on both sides. The introduction of lithographic machines enabled such printing and these became used in the development of newspapers and magazines in exhaustive numbers to meet the demands of the public (see Plate 13.2).

It was not until the mid-to-late 20th century that printing would develop into a new art form – a period in our editorial history that would become labelled the **Digital Era**. This step forward in how information was disseminated quickly to large audiences was largely due to the development of computers, the introduction of the Internet and the development of mobile phone technology. Within the mass media it is now digital forms that have the

Plate 13.2 An example of a lithographic machine showing the addition of different colours as the paper flows from one roller to another. (Shutterstock 18768442.)

biggest impact on our social development and the way we behave. While it is true that all forms of mass media have impacted on our lives by influencing the way we are informed about the world, it is digital media where we have seen the most poignant influences over our social behaviour. Therefore it is necessary to understand the extent to which it influences us and how invasive this can be.

For some individuals the impact of digital media is considerable such that they succumb to cyberbullying (see Chapter 11). In some cases this has even led to fatalities. For some vulnerable children, the deceit played out by predatory paedophiles in Internet chatrooms has led to them being groomed and abused. For most individuals, however, digital media has offered a new way of living by being able to work in a virtual space away from the confines of the office. It has also changed the way we do things such as shopping from home and operating home appliances from a distance. Children and adolescents can have positive experiences with digital media. There are individual differences in the way we interact with the digital world that will be considered in the context of a media–personality interaction – our next topic.

OUR RELATIONSHIP WITH THE MASS MEDIA

Comstock and Scharrer (2006) claim that children and adolescents living in the US consider the mass media to be important in their lives. This was borne out by a national study surveying 2,000 children and adolescents varying in age between eight and eighteen years (Rideout et al. 2005). Rideout et al. found that participants in their survey regularly spent 44 hours per week on electronic media. Furthermore, they calculated the average time spent per day doing different activities and showed that watching television ranked higher (3.04 hours per day) than being with their parents (2.17 hours) or peers (2.16 hours). Time spent in physical activity was 1.25 hours and pursuing hobbies just reached one hour. Other activities such as

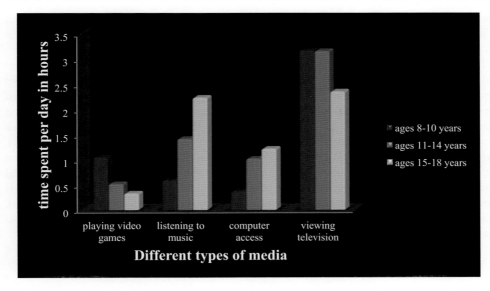

Figure 13.1 Changes in the amount of time spent by US 8–18 year olds on different types of media. (Adapted from Rideout, Roberts and Foehr 2005.)

doing homework or listening to music were under an hour. Rideout et al. also found how age influences the amount of time spent on different types of media (see Figure 13.1).

It is interesting how the focus of attention for different types of media shifts with age. The time spent playing video games decreases with age but listening to music and using computers increase with age. Television features strongly in the lives of 8 to 14 year olds but drops by about thirty minutes for 15 to 18 year olds. Television is by far the most regularly accessed media by the 8 to 18 year olds in this American survey. Other studies have shown that children around the world watch between three and four hours of television every day (Lemish 2007; Roberts et al. 2005; Van Evra 2004).

Influence of television on social behaviour

Television, a 20th-century invention, has been a major influencing factor on the social development of children and adolescents (Dubow et al. 2007). Developmentalists argue that television has also impacted on cognitive development and how this influences social behaviour. Some argue that it can enhance learning while others believe it has a detrimental effect on the learning process as it creates a passive recipient of information. Those in favour of television as a learning medium argue it brings a multitude of information to the immediate environment of the viewer and can also provide visual social cues of prosocial behaviour (Mares and Woodard 2007). In the UK, children's programmes such as *Blue Peter* and *Take Hart* were designed to contain educational content. US programme equivalents include *Sesame Street* and *Reading Rainbow*. Programmes introduced during the 1990s, including the *Teletubbies* and videos/DVDs such as *Baby Einstein* targeted infants (Zack et al. 2009). These programmes typically used music instead of narration to depict images of toys and puppets doing things. Garrison and Christakis (2005) claim that parents believe these programmes would benefit their infants in an educational sense. Moreover, Calvert et al. (2005) argue that parents consider early television and computer exposure as benefitting their infants.

Zimmerman et al. (2007), in their survey of 1,000 US families in 2006, found that parental attitudes fostered the idea that their infants (between 2 and 24 months) would learn from these programmes. These attitudes are unsupported by the evidence presented by a host of developmentalists (Anderson and Pempek 2005; Deocampo and Hudson 2005; Sheffield and Hudson 2006; Suddendorf et al. 2007; Troseth 2003). In fact the findings provide evidence for more learning via face-to-face social interactions than from television (see Chapter 4). Anderson and Pempek (2005) showed that infants were inept at transferring learning from television to real-life events and referred to this as the **video deficit effect**. The psychological evidence supports superior transfer of learning from social interactions with a real live model such as a parent when compared with television (Anderson and Pempek 2005; see Chapter 4). Zack et al. in 2009 investigated whether infants can imitate what they see on television and transfer this to other situations (see Box 13.1).

Box 13.1   Can infants transfer their learning from one format to another?

The question of whether infants can watch something on television and then imitate that action in real life was of interest to Zack et al. (2009). Research suggests that we learn best by face-to-face social interaction. But what if an experimenter performed an action that the infant could imitate that involved either pressing a button on a 3D object or a 2D object on a touch screen? Would there be a difference in the nature of imitative behaviour? Zack et al. presented 15–16 month-old infants with button boxes showing an image of a bus, a fire truck, a duck and a cow pasted onto it (i.e., 3D format) or digital photographs on boxes displayed on a computer touch screen (i.e., 2D format). Each box had a button that when pressed would release an appropriate noise such as a quack for the duck or a siren for the fire truck. In the case of the button boxes the experimenter pressed the button to release the noise made by the object depicted. For the touch screen, a virtual button was pressed by the experimenter to produce the same sounds. Zack et al. found that imitation measures from the baseline reading (i.e., at the beginning of the experiment) were low for both the 3D and 2D objects. However, when tested again in the experimental condition there were improvements in the imitative action of pressing the buttons. There were two experimental conditions: the within-dimension and the cross-dimension. In the case of the within-dimension the action demonstrated by the experimenter was imitated quickly and correctly provided the format remained the same. This was not the case in the cross-dimension condition where the initial format (i.e., 3D or 2D) was changed to the other format (i.e., 2D or 3D) when the infants were tested. It did not matter whether they imitated from the 3D or 2D format first – performance was limited either way.

There was a video deficit effect demonstrated in the cross-direction condition – hence limited transference of learning occurred when the format was changed (see Figure 13.2).

Developmentalists have also focused on the influence of television and literacy. Linebarger (2006) claims that the processing of different types of media draw upon the same underlying cognitive skills. According to Kendeou et al. (2008) these cognitive skills are cross-transferable from one media context to another. This was explored further by Linebarger and Piotrowski in 2009 (see Box 13.2).

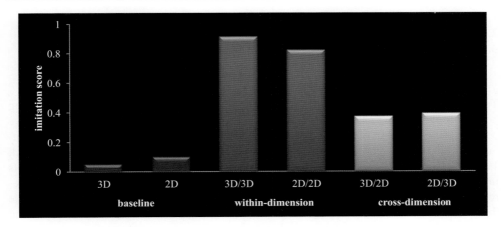

Figure 13.2 Mean imitation score of infants due to baseline and experimental condition.

Box 13.2   Is television a good storyteller?

Televised educational media can be used as an informal educator in the child's home environment. But does the viewing of such televised programmes improve storytelling ability in children? This was investigated by Linebarger and Piotrowski (2009) who studied preschool children's ability to understand stories. This understanding consisted of knowing about the structure of a story, also referred to as **story grammar**. According to Low and Durkin (1998), by understanding the structure of stories children form mental schemas. These mental schemas help children to organise and encode stories, which enable them to retrieve the story line at a later date. Linebarger and Piotrowski claim that by repeatedly showing programmes to children that contained both **traditional narratives** (as seen in typical storybooks with dialogue and the same characters following a linear story progression) and **embedded narrative** (which has a story within a story that becomes a parallel story), they develop a story schema. An example of a traditional narrative might be 'Snow White', whereas embedded narratives may contain more than one storyline as is typical in 'soap operas'. Children were exposed to such programmes for four and a half hours over an eight-week period. This type of programme was found to improve the development of story schema. Having good narrative skills allows children to construct meaning from televised stimuli. Hence, they argued that children exposed to televised narratives would be better at forming story schemas. This, they suggest, leads to competency at retaining and interpreting the narrative content which, in turn, makes children better at retelling the story. Not only would they be better at retelling the story but they would need less cognitive effort to do so. They could then deploy their cognitive resources to difficult elements of the narrative such as inferring the characters' feelings and motives. Linebarger and Piotrowski conclude that programmes containing traditional narratives improve story knowledge skills while embedded narratives help in the retelling of stories.

This study demonstrates the usefulness of televised educational programmes in the development of children's literacy skills.

While televised educational programmes can be of benefit to children's cognitive development, it can also be problematic for specific aspects of social development. Researchers have primarily focused on three main areas that influence the social behaviour of children and adolescents:

1. impact of adult advertising of products such as alcohol;
2. impact of fashion and cosmetics advertising;
3. impact of televised violence and popularisation of antisocial models.

Impact of adult advertising (alcohol)

Television offers the consumer industry an opportunity to advertise their wares. Drinking portrayals and alcohol product placement is unfortunately often advertised using attractive people. These are often of high socioeconomic status and are presented in a 'cool' or glamourous way. Such stereotyping might appeal to older children and adolescents (Mathios et al. 1998; Wallack et al. 1990). This advertising format for alcohol often attracts adolescents into the lifestyle encapsulated by the stereotype presented. Teenagers attracted to the stereotype will want to capture the essence of the lifestyle and, in so doing, will accommodate their social behaviour to the image they see televised (Dring and Hope 2001). Dring and Hope (2001) found that most teenagers like to have fun and enjoy themselves by engaging in social activities like partying. Therefore alcohol-related advertisements depicting party scenes appealed most. As adolescence is a challenging time for most teenagers, drinking alcohol can be seen as a social lubricator by providing a sense of confidence when engaging in social interaction with others – a kind of 'Dutch courage'.

Correlational studies generally show a small significant relationship between the amount of television viewing and alcohol-related beliefs and behaviours. For example, Tucker (1985) found that adolescent boys who were considered to be heavy television viewers consumed more alcohol than those who watched television occasionally. Moreover, Neuendorf (1985) showed a relationship between the amount of television viewed and beliefs about drinking alcohol in 10–14-year-old teenagers. Those who were considered to be heavy viewers thought that people who drink alcohol are happier than those who did not and that drinking was necessary to have fun. Robinson et al. (1998) demonstrated that television viewing was linked with initiation of drinking behaviours. They calculated that for every 60-minute increase in television viewing the risk of being initiated to drinking alcohol rose by 9 per cent.

Plate 13.3 Teenagers drinking together unsupervised. (Shutterstock 41711074.)

A study in 2003 by Saffer and Dave considered the effect of advertising alcohol on the consumption of alcohol by adolescents. They used the datasets from the Monitoring the Future (MTF) and the National Longitudinal Survey of Youth 1997 (NLSY97). Their results showed that females are influenced by pricing and advertising more than males. Their findings based on the NLSY97 suggest that adolescent monthly consumption of alcohol could be reduced four per cent if there was a ban on local advertising of alcohol. Furthermore, in the case of binge drinking, this could be reduced by five per cent. The problem with this is that banning local advertising will have little effect as long as alcohol advertising is televised. Rebecca Smith, Medical Editor for the *Telegraph* in 2009, reported that the British Medical Association believe changes should be made to how alcohol is advertised. In Smith's report, Professor Gerard Hastings from the University of Sterling said that,

> *Children were 'groomed' in their attitude to drink, and research had shown that 96 per cent of 13-year-olds were aware of alcohol advertising in some form or other. Half of children aged 11 to 16 have drunk alcohol and consumed on average 9.2 units.*

According to Smith (2009), television and other sources of promotion provide a 'pro-drinking stereotype'. Drinking alcohol is advertised in a way suggesting sociability and physical attractiveness coupled with positive outcomes like success and leisure time (Postman et al. 1988). Children and adolescents are attracted to different types of advertisements concerning alcohol. Advertisements that are celebrity endorsed or contain humour, music and animation appeal particularly to both children and adolescents (Chen and Grube 2001; Martin et al. 2002). Teenage boys tend to find alcohol advertising linked to sport appealing (Slater et al. 1997). According to Kelly et al. (2002), adolescents prefer advertisements depicting a lifestyle or image to a focus on the product quality. Kelly and Edwards (1998) found image advertising appealed to younger male adolescents. It is both lifestyle and image advertising, however, that promotes favourable attitudes towards alcohol (Kelly et al. 2002). Alcohol consumption is clearly perceived as a social facilitator by providing teenagers with the confidence to socialise with others and be part of the adolescent scene. Moreover, it provides them with an image and lifestyle that they aspire to, which ultimately helps to develop their self-concept (see Chapter 8). This influences their social behaviour as they try to 'live the dream' (Dring and Hope 2001).

Impact of fashion and cosmetics advertising

During adolescence boys and girls undergo bodily changes that they may feel positive or negative about. Having a positive body image helps to develop a well-rounded self-concept and high self-esteem. The problem arises when there is body dissatisfaction. This can have a negative impact on self-concept development causing ambiguity over how one would like to be considered. Body dissatisfaction can be a cause of low self-esteem leading to drastic measures to make changes to bodily appearance (Hogan and Strasburger 2008). It is unsurprising, therefore, that such teenagers are vulnerable to televised advertisements concerning the ideal body size and shape. Television has been used by the fashion industry to advertise their clothing. This advertising has been criticised for encouraging children and adolescents to adopt the '**skinny model look**', which is related to eating disorders such as anorexia and binge eating. Models used for advertising clothes and cosmetics on television appear flawless in both their body shape and skin condition. These daily images can have a major impact on impressionable or vulnerable teenagers. This can lead to 'low self-worth, negative body image and eating disorders' (Kirsten Haglund, Community Relations

Plate 13.4 A thin model advertising swimwear. (Shutterstock 130038425.)

Representative for Timberline Knolls Residential Treatment Center 2015). Although advertising is not entirely responsible for young girls becoming anorexic, it certainly provides impressionable teenagers with images of what is considered to be the **ideal body shape**. This became apparent when television was introduced for the first time to ethnic Fijian adolescent girls (see Box 13.3).

Box 13.3   The desire to be skinny like the televised images of models

Becker et al. (2002) reported on the effects of television introduced to media-naïve Fijian adolescent girls. In particular they were interested to see how prolonged exposure to television impacted on eating attitudes and behaviours. The indigenous Fijian adolescent girls were previously unaware of Western images of ideal body shape and size and therefore had no issue with eating disorders. With the introduction of television, however, the exposure to models depicting an ideal body stereotype that was considered attractive to men arguably encouraged a host of eating disorders. This naturalistic longitudinal experiment provided direct evidence for there being a link between televised ideal body imagery and disordered eating behaviours and attitudes. This was supported by these girls' high scores on the 26-item eating attitudes test (EAT-26; Garner et al. 1982) and self-induced vomiting as a means of losing weight.

This study provides a convincing link between viewing 'skinny' models on television, the desire to have the same body size and image as these models and behaviours that help achieve this look.

While the naturalistic study of ethnic Fijian adolescent girls providing a strong link between televised images of 'skinny models' and these teenagers developing anorexia is very convincing, there have been studies suggesting this link is too simplistic. Using experimental media exposure researchers are finding that only vulnerable participants who already had symptoms of an underlying eating problem or experienced dissatisfaction with their body image were at risk of being adversely affected by televised body imagery (Hamilton and Waller 1993). However, in contrast to other studies, Cusumano and Thompson (1997) found no clear evidence of disordered eating as a consequence of media exposure. Clearly television is not alone in its portrayal of undersized models. Other media forms such as glossy magazines are geared towards advertising fashion and cosmetic icons, which also send the message that being underweight to achieve the 'perfect body' is a sacrifice necessary in order to be body beautiful. Also, media coverage on the Internet provides these images, to which most children and adolescents have access in the digital age. Television, however, has been further criticised for exposing children and adolescents to violence (Dubow et al. 2007; Huesmann and Taylor 2006; Murray 2007).

Impact of televised violence and popularisation of antisocial models

In Chapter 11 we considered the influence of televised images of violence and aggressive behaviour on the social development of children and adolescents. Various studies showed a marginal but robust impact of televised violence on the level of aggressive behaviour in children and adolescents (Huesmann and Eron 1986; Friedrich-Cofer and Huston 1986; Wood et al. 1991). Huesmann and Eron, for example, found that children who spent many hours watching televised violence showed increased levels of aggressive behaviour during adolescence. They further showed that eight year olds who watched a large amount of violence on television were more likely to be arrested for committing criminal acts as adults. An interesting twist that Huesmann and Eron found was that behaving aggressively as a child failed to predict the extent of violence watched as a teenager. In order to improve our understanding of the relationship between television viewing and aggression Leyens et al. (1975) studied delinquent boys residing in a home in Belgium. The boys were divided into those who saw violent films every evening over five nights and those who saw non-violent films. Boys exposed to the violent films showed more aggressive behaviour towards their peers by kicking, slapping and hitting. They argued that as these boys were already aggressive they had obtained aggressive scripts, which the violent films had triggered into action.

The current majority view, however, is that televised violence can cause children and teenagers to behave aggressively and antisocially (Anderson and Bushman 2002; Comstock and Scharrer 2006; Dubow et al. 2007). Anderson and Bushman (2002) claim that a link between prolonged exposure to violent televised programmes during childhood and later aggressive behaviour is gaining support. In Johnson et al.'s (2002) longitudinal study they assessed 707 individuals over a 17-year period for the amount and type of television viewing and level of aggressive behaviour. Their findings demonstrated a significant association between the amount of television viewed in adolescence and aggressive behaviour in later years. This link was significant even once factors such as childhood neglect, psychiatric disorders and neighbourhood violence were controlled for. Televised violence, however, is not the only media source believed to encourage aggressive and antisocial behaviour – video game programmes with violence have also been found to impact on social behaviour (see Box 13.4). Research findings suggest that televised violence and violent video games impact on the social development of children and adolescents such that they are at risk of becoming aggressive and behaving antisocially through their engagement in criminal activity.

Box 13.4   Do violent video games make you aggressive?

Video games are televised on the television set, a computer screen, consoles such as Wii, Playstation and Xbox, or devices like Gameboys and smartphones. The main difference between televised violence and playing a violent video game is the level of engagement experienced. The video game player becomes an active rather than a passive viewer. Playing video games, it has been argued, alters the state of the player's consciousness. Roberts et al. (2004) state that 'rational thought is suspended and highly arousing aggressive scripts are increasingly likely to be learned' (p. 498). Anderson et al. (2010a) claimed that 'the evidence strongly suggests that exposure to violent video games is a causal risk factor for increased aggressive behavior, aggressive cognition, and aggressive affect and for decreased empathy and prosocial behavior' (p. 151).

Another difference is that points are won for behaving in a particular way such as shooting the enemy. This type of mentality is rewarded and quite often in these games the more violent the behaviour, the higher the score. Anderson et al. (2007) showed a significant link between long-term violent video game playing and the risk of behaving aggressively and engaging in later delinquency. Other studies have supported this finding (Anderson 2003; Carnagey et al. 2007). Interestingly, despite obtaining similar findings to Anderson et al., Ferguson (2011) contends that laboratory findings cannot be extrapolated meaningfully to the real world. Children already at risk are likely to be attracted to violent video games and it is these other risks that cause aggressive behaviour.

As is the case with watching televised violence, the link between playing violent video games and aggressive behaviour is not straightforward. Children and adolescents already at risk of aggression are likely to be drawn towards violent media.

Donnerstein (2002) warns us that aggression has no single cause but arises out of a multitude of factors. Gentile and Bushman (2012) also argue that being exposed to media violence is merely one of many factors contributing towards developing an aggressive persona. In the scheme of Bronfenbrenner's Ecological Model there are many socialising agents impacting on the social development of the child (see Chapter 1). At the centre of his model, however, he places the child who is born with a number of inherited factors. These inherited factors influence the way the child interacts with the environment – and this includes the mass media. Despite the contribution of inherent risk factors for aggressive and antisocial behaviour, many developmentalists agree that violent media, such as that televised or experienced by playing video games, is associated with behaving aggressively. Viewing violent programmes is believed to increase desensitisation to violence (Bartholow et al. 2006; Bushman and Anderson 2009) and the imitation of violent behaviour (Bandura et al. 1963; Huesmann 1997; Iacoboni et al. 1999). Watching violent films and playing violent video games have even been linked to school killings (see Box 13.5).

Box 13.5   Violent viewing and playing games creates killers?

Imitation of violent behaviour has been considered to play an important role in mass killing. This can be exacerbated by being actively involved in playing violent video games. This was the case for two teenage boys attending the Columbine High School in Colorado, US (see Box 11.12). In 1999 Eric Harris and Dylan Klebold murdered 12 of their school-mates before killing themselves. It was documented at the time that they lived in a fantasy world that involved playing violent video games. The FBI concluded that Harris was a psychopath and Klebold a depressive, but not everyone agreed. Some argued that a possible cause for their mass killing was down to being obsessed with violent images portrayed in the video games and films that captivated their attentions. This helped them to depersonalise their victims. In another case, Jeff Weise was 16 when he shot dead nine people with a .22 calibre pistol in 2005. He murdered his grandfather and then murdered seven more people (mostly teenagers) at the reservation high school known as Red Lake Senior High School in Minnesota. He was obsessed with violent animation (Fletcher 2015). Vossekuil et al. (2002) in their report confirmed that when 37 incidents of school shootings were analysed, more than 50 per cent of the perpetrators were obsessed with watching violent films and television programmes, playing violent video games and reading about violence in books.

Although many school killers have watched televised violence or played violent video games there are many teenagers who also play such video games or watch films containing violence but who do not go out to kill people. In many of these cases it is very likely that these adolescents had other problems such as serious mental health issues.

Television and video games are not the only media sources that influence social development and social behaviour – magazines have a big impact on the behaviour of children and teenagers.

Influence of magazines on social behaviour

There are many different types of magazines marketed for teenagers. In the UK there are glossy magazines aimed primarily at girls and women that contain information about the fashion world and advertisements for cosmetics and clothes. There are also magazines that are less glossy but contain images of various celebrities and information about their lifestyle and appearance – in particular their body shape. Often these types of magazines run a commentary about specific celebrities with weight and size issues. Images often showed celebrities fitting a size '0' and looking unwell. Such images of celebrities and teenage idols create a culture of '**wanna-be-lookalikes**' often achieved through unhealthy methods.

In glossy magazines the models are often airbrushed or computer-enhanced to create an unrealistic portrayal of the female form (usually females although male models can be treated in the same way). These unrealistic images of models, according to Richardson (2003), would be on the threshold of a person with a clinical diagnosis signifying an eating disorder. Arguably it is these unrealistic images that encourage unhealthy eating styles and can ultimately lead to anorexia in impressionable and vulnerable children and adolescents. Females tend to be more influenced by media images in magazines than their male counterparts.

Plate 13.5 Display of commonly read glossy magazines. (Shutterstock 299331323.)

This is probably a consequence of there being more body image advertising aimed at females. Such advertising has caused body image problems for some females and, in extreme cases, is considered responsible for causing eating disorders (Altabe and Thompson 1996; Fallon 1990; Heinberg and Thompson 1995). Heinberg and Thompson (1995) argued that being dissatisfied with one's body image can decrease the self-esteem of many females (see Chapter 8). Because the media link beauty with femininity, Striegel-Moore and Smolak (2000) argue that this creates the **attractiveness stereotype** of women. This attractiveness stereotype has little room for teenage girls who are overweight (Striegel-Moore and Smolak 2000). The attractiveness stereotype considers thinness as the ideal body form and to be beautiful teenage girls and females per se are expected to conform to it.

Body image, according to Banfield and McCabe (2002), is multidimensional in that it consists of:

- cognitions and emotions about the body – thoughts and feelings about one's body;
- level of body importance – those who focus more on their body shape will perform behaviours to make their body look better such as dieting;
- perceptual body image – involves how accurate individuals are when judging their body shape and size.

These three factors play an important role in the decision to make body image changes such as by dieting. How a person thinks and feels about their body interacts with the extent of emphasis placed on body importance. This in turn receives feedback from how the body image is perceived by the person. When these three facets are integrated, the resulting behavioural response depends on the level of bodily dissatisfaction and the need to change it.

Magazines contain images about the ideal body image and shape that becomes internalised by our socio-culture. This allows for societal pressures to encourage individuals to change their current body image according to the ideal portrayed by the media. It is this social pressure that can be a causal factor in the development of eating problems such as anorexia

Plate 13.6 Teenage girls looking at a fashion magazine together. (Shutterstock 402321730.)

and low self-esteem issues. Cusumano and Thompson (1997), however, found there was a poor relationship between the exposure to body size ideals and the level of body satisfaction, eating problems and self-esteem. What was more influential was the level of internalised social norms regarding body image. However, the media is responsible for disseminating the social norms of the ideal body so, in a way, it is reinforcing the social norms. This was supported in a study by Turner et al. (1997) where one group of college female students viewed fashion magazines while the other group looked at news magazines. All females were asked to complete a body image survey once they had completed looking through the magazines. Those who viewed the fashion magazines indicated a lower self-esteem than the other group of females. All females were of similar height and weight hence exposure to the fashion magazines prompted body dissatisfaction and a desire to conform to the social norm.

One question we might ask is why do humans have this propensity for body dissatisfaction in the first place? Evolutionary psychologists expanded on Festinger's (1954) **social comparison theory** for why the media have an impact on the way we perceive ourselves. Festinger (1954) claimed, 'People evaluate their opinions and abilities by comparison respectively with the opinion and abilities of others' (p. 119). Evolutionary psychologists have developed this concept further to help explain why we might be more prone to depression in our current environment. They refer to this as the **social competition hypothesis** (see Box 13.6).

Box 13.6 Social competition hypothesis

The social competition hypothesis was introduced by Price in 1967 to account for a depressed mood observed in individuals who perceive themselves as low ranking when compared with their apparent peers. So how can the social competition hypothesis explain the impact of magazines on our self-perceptions? The answer is rather simple. In our evolutionary past when we

(continued)

(continued)

lived in small forager groups, individuals knew one another and would make social comparisons with one another. Within such relatively small groups, a female, for example, might compare herself with other females for the amount of male attention they received. When making such a comparison she might feel that she is not necessarily the most attractive in the group but, given attractiveness is based on a large number of characteristics, she may also consider that she has some features that were more attractive than many in the group. Hence, our self-image during our evolutionary past was constructed out of comparison with a limited range of competitors (note that this was also true for males). Today, however, we have other ways of gaining information that can be used to make social comparisons with others – for example reading magazines. Teenagers looking at magazines full of very skinny models receive a social message regarding body image. They make social comparisons with these unrealistic models and adjust their behaviour accordingly, such as eating less as a means to losing weight (Nesse and Williams 1995).

The social competition hypothesis explains why magazines can be a trigger to change the way we behave. We see the models and compare our own body image with their body size and want to be like that. We want to be like that because they are successful and have a positive status.

Using advertisements to address a young audience is an effective way of selling product brands. According to Goodman (1999), adolescents view approximately 3,000 adverts a day when the different media sources are collapsed (television, billboards, magazines and the Internet). Strasburger (2001) argues that children have no way to buffer themselves from the continuous bombardment of advertising inherent in our society. The target age for advertising

Plate 13.7 Does the camera prefer me or her I wonder? (Shutterstock 439030096.)

is increasingly being geared towards younger children with the aim of hooking them onto specific brand labels as early as possible (McNeal 1992). In the US children of 12 or less spend $25 billion a year whereas teenagers exceed this at $155 billion (Goodman 1999). According to the Consumer's Union in America (2005) there are more than 160 magazines aimed at children. Furthermore, Rumbelow (2002) noted that teenagers see 45 per cent more advertisements focused on beer and 27 per cent more focused on other types of alcohol in their magazines than adults view in magazines marketed for the adult populace. In the UK, advertising alcohol to people under the age of 18 years is not allowed. In 2005 the Advertising Standards Authority (ASA) tightened the rules regarding advertising alcohol to teenagers such that the UK has the most stringent rulings compared with other countries. Nevertheless, there are many magazines marketed today for a younger audience. Magazines are still purchased and read by adolescents but it is the influence of the Internet that has made the largest impact on the way we source the vast amount of information available to us.

Influence of the digital world on social behaviour

Electronic computers were developed in the 1950s but it was not until 1977 that personal computers were marketed to the masses. Prophetically, in 1962, John W. Mauchly wrote 'There is no reason to suppose the average boy or girl cannot be master of a personal computer' (*New York Times* 1962). This was an insightful statement as the usage of personal computers has escalated at an exponential rate ever since they became affordable to the masses. The use of personal computers has become even more popular since the introduction of the Internet. Initially the Internet was developed out of the idea of 'packet networking' where several computers could be linked and therefore communicate with one another from a distance. One of the earliest computer networking systems was ARPANET, which was used to send a message from Professor Leonard Kleinrock based at the University of California, Los Angeles, to a networked node at the Stanford Research Institute. Welsh computer scientist Donald Davies designed a network at the UK National Physics Laboratory in 1965 that enabled multiple simultaneous communication sessions. These early developments eventually gave rise to the Internet as we know it today. The use of personal computers and the Internet are so closely interwoven that it is difficult to ascertain how many people in the world have a computer without referencing Internet usage. Internet usage was estimated at 2,405,518,376 people in 2012 (InternetWorldStats.com). Interestingly, if we compare 2017 figures obtained from the Internet Live Statistics daily survey, it now stands at 3,551,448,000 and is constantly rising (go to this website to see the figures rise before your very eyes www. internetlivestats.com/internet-users). Note that, given the world population is 7.5 billion, this comprises half of everybody on the planet (see Figure 13.3).

The term 'Internet' is an acronym for 'International Network' describing a global computer network. This describes a digital connection across a network of networks. The Internet contains a variety of information that can, for example, be formatted as text, images, video streaming, broadcasts and podcasts. The Internet also enables people to communicate from all over the world using email, Internet telephony, instant messaging, Internet forums, blogs, Facebook and social networking. The Internet is popular because of the sheer amount of information that can be tapped into via a receptive electronic device (such as a computer) connecting to optical networking technologies (such as an Internet Service Provider (ISP)). Once an ISP is connected it is possible to 'surf' the Internet. There are different **Internet portals** such as 'Yahoo' (which is an acronym for 'Yet Another Hierarchical Officious Oracle') or 'Internet Explorer' that provide a **search engine**. A search engine contains a set of programmes that work in tandem and enable us to find the information we seek. For adolescents

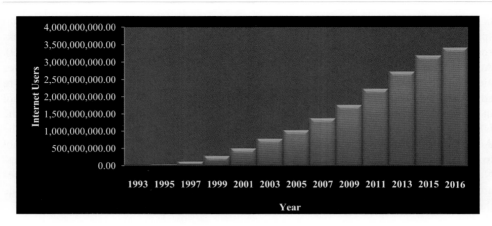

Figure 13.3 The increasing number of Internet users over the last 23 years.

in particular, the Internet has completely changed their social lives over the last 20 years. For example, in the US (arguably the most technologically advanced country in the world) in 2016 Internet access was close to 100 per cent for teenagers and young adults. In the UK, 89 per cent of the population is Internet active (Think Digital First 2017). Table 13.1 shows the statistical breakdown for the different types of Internet use.

As pointed out by numerous researchers, society still requires basic non-technologically driven skills, such as the ability to communicate well, solve problems and think in creative and logical ways. What has changed, however, is the way in which these skills are mediated in a digital world (Bitter and Legacy 2006; Wood and Smith 2006). This transition from traditional methods of communication (e.g., letter writing and landline telephone use) to digital

Table 13.1 UK active users for different types of Internet use (such as social media).

Various sources of Internet use	2016 active users
Facebook (social sharing network site)	32 million 2.5 million are 13–17 year olds
Twitter (microblogging)	15 million 4.65 million are 15–24 year olds
Instagram (video and photo social network sharing)	14 million 5.46 million are 16–24 year olds
LinkedIn (professional networking)	15 million 3.75 million are under 35 years
YouTube (video uploading and viewing)	19 million 1.9 million are 13–17 year olds
Google+ (social networking)	3.9 million 1.5 million are 18–24 year olds
Snapchat (send videos and images)	10 million 3 million are under 18 years

forms (e.g., mobile and smartphones, email and texting) is a skill that the young generation requires (Saettler 2005). While the ability to navigate the Internet and operate digital technology is a positive skill to have, there are drawbacks. Donnerstein (2002) found that 10 per cent of 1,000 websites visited on the Internet by teenagers were adult sex sites. Moreover, 44 per cent of adolescents had visited adult sites, 25 per cent had visited 'hate group' promotion sites and 12 per cent had visited sites providing information about gun purchase. Wolak et al. (2007) reported that 42 per cent of 10 to 17 year olds living in the US viewed pornography, of which 66 per cent was unintentional. This latter point is disturbing as it highlights the automaticity of 'pop-up' information. The online social world presents itself with other problematic issues – namely the self-disclosure of information to potential strangers (see Box 13.7).

Box 13.7   Problems of online self-disclosure

Children and adolescents are exposed to a variety of online communication sites such as instant messaging, blogs, **chatrooms**, email, Facebook and MySpace. While instant messaging is commonly used to communicate with friends (Gross 2004), chatroom communication is a public virtual space enabling simultaneous conversations with a multitude of people, most of whom will be strangers. Subrahmanyam et al. (2006), for example, found that 50 per cent of 583 chatroom participants self-disclosed personal details about themselves. Those aged 10–13 years provided more personal details than those aged between 18 and 24. Moreover, conversations included sex (occurring 5 per cent) and bad language (occurring 3 per cent). Unsurprisingly, older adolescents spoke in more depth about sex and males more overtly. MySpace was introduced in 2004 and Facebook was also brought online in 2004; they are a means of communicating with like-minded individuals. In both cases, users create a profile containing their interests, personal information and contact details. The problem with Facebook and MySpace is that the information can be exploited as profile content can be accessed by anyone. It is easy for **social media trolls** to cause emotional discombobulation by posting messages on Twitter or Facebook that are controversial and hostile. Robson and Warren (2012) reported a 16-year-old teenager from the US called Jessica Laney who committed suicide after receiving vile online messages from social media trolls (i.e., cyberbullies). There has been a spate of similar teenage suicides instigated by cyberbullies and individuals who generally incite self-harming.

Self-disclosing personal information is risky behaviour. Sites such as MySpace and Facebook have no privacy button to stop profiles from being open to public inspection. What type of person will look and respond to one's profile is a lottery – some will have good intentions and others will not.

Chatroom **grooming** has been given criminal status. In the UK in 2003 Section 15 of the Sexual Offences Act outlawed 'the meeting of children (online) with the intention of committing a sex offence' (Maher 2003/2004, p. 10). An offender of this law could receive a maximum penalty of a 10-year custodial sentence. Paedophile rings make use of the computer and the Internet as it is possible to lift and store images of children in a hidden file. These images can be passed on to other paedophiles via email attachments. Digital cameras have meant that paedophiles can take photos of children that can be downloaded onto their computers, sent via email attachments or burnt onto a CD/DVD and exchanged with other paedophiles. There are different types of paedophile but what they have in common is that they are not only attracted to children but they are also predators. With the advent of the Internet they can now be online predators and access chatrooms for the purpose of grooming their potential victims. The allure of the chatroom is that anyone can be anyone they want to be.

Plate 13.8 Online predator pretending to be someone else. (Shutterstock 48806890.)

It is possible to use instant messaging to communicate with many people or to block other users from listening in on a private conversation with a targeted user. There are also settings allowing users to 'leave the room' with a targeted user. Hence, this feature makes it possible for paedophiles to target their child victim and to chat together more privately and, in this way, groom the child to develop an emotional attachment. Paedophiles are more likely to initiate sexually explicit conversation, they will try to obtain personal information, show illicit imagery of child abuse and arrange to meet offline (Maher 2003/2004). Rachel O'Connell from the Home Office outlined a consistent pattern of behaviour shown by paedophiles (reported by David Batty 2003; see Box 13.8).

Box 13.8   Typical pattern of grooming behaviour shown by paedophiles

In a report for *The Guardian*, Rachel O'Connell claimed there are five typical phases to grooming. In the first phase, the paedophile tries to form a friendship with the child using flattering language. The child is encouraged to communicate in a private chatroom, which effectively isolates the child from other chatroom users. The paedophile will ask the child to send a non-sexual picture. In the second phase, strides are made by the paedophile to create the illusion of being a good friend to whom you can talk and disclose personal problems confidentially. The paedophile enquires about the child's computer location and other computer users in the third phase. This is to establish if their conversation can be kept secret from others. The fourth phase is about constructing affectionate and trusting bonds such that anything can be discussed. The fifth phase involves the exploitation of the child's trust. Here, the paedophile requests sexually explicit images of the child and engages in discussion and asking questions of a sexual nature. Questions might include:

- Have you ever been kissed?
- Do you have a boyfriend?
- Do you know what to do with your boyfriend?

They may also divulge that they would like to be the boyfriend and suggest meeting up somewhere.

These five phases typify the *modus operandi* of most paedophiles. They befriend their child targets in chatrooms and progressively isolate them. They try to create a level of emotional dependency in their potential victims and in this way manage to groom their child targets.

With the increasing risk of children being groomed by paedophiles while online, 'EU Kids Online' was formed as a counter measure. This is a multinational research network developed as a means of increasing knowledge about online opportunities, safety and inherent risks for European children using the Internet. There are at least 33 European countries participating in this project and other affiliated countries such as Australia and Brazil. EU Kids Online uses a variety of means to obtain information about the Internet experiences of children and their parents. They found that, when compared with other age groups, 11 to 16 year olds were more likely to be exposed to hate messages, pro-anorexia sites, self-harm sites and to cyberbullying. In 2014, EU Kids Online showed that 9 to 16 year olds were more likely to have seen something online that upset them compared with 2010 (up from 13 per cent to 17 per cent). EU Kids Online reported that increasingly younger children are going online and the Internet is used in more places on a daily basis. Now that

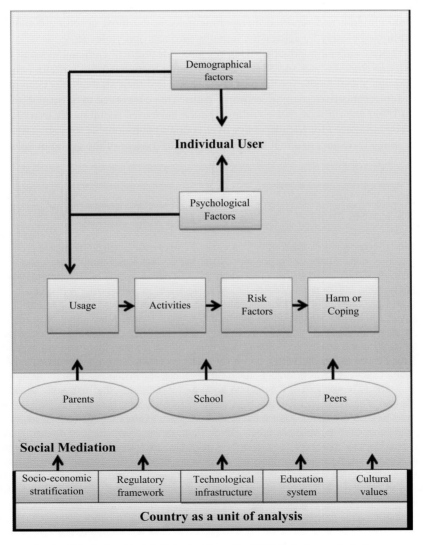

Figure 13.4 The EU Kids Online Model. (Adapted from the EU Kids Online website.)

many children have their own mobile devices, they can access the Internet without parental guidance, which increases their risk of being exposed to dangerous websites and users. The EU Kids Online Model (see Figure 13.4) is an interesting one as the individual user is placed within the context of social media and society. Their model resembles that proposed by Bronfenbrenner (Ecological Model; see Chapter 1). Like Bronfenbrenner, the EU Kids Online Model includes characteristics of the user such as psychological factors that interact with social mediation such as parents and peers. Parents and peers act as informal socialising agents in Bronfenbrenner's model. These, in turn, are influenced by society and the cultural values espoused. In effect, the EU Kids Online Model supports the view that how children interact with and respond to the Internet is part and parcel of their own psychological makeup and their social environment. This can explain why not all risk results in harm. Becoming upset or harmed by specific encounters online, for example, depends on the child's gender, age and ability to cope with these experiences. Hence, children will have different levels of resilience courtesy of their psychological development. EU Kids Online gathered responses from 10,000 children and reported that pornography is the most upsetting content on the Internet, followed closely by aggression, cruelty, goriness and violence.

The Internet is also a good advertising resource for political campaigners and terrorists such as Islamic State in Iraq and Syria (ISIS). Islamic State has been targeting children as recruits through social media for the past few years – and their strategy has been quite successful as adolescents from many European countries have travelled to Syria and joined ISIS (see Box 13.9). Other groups such as religious cults have used social media as a recruitment exercise. The influence group leaders have over young impressionable teenagers is profound. They encourage teenagers to adopt the belief and value system of the group in question and therefore change their social behaviour.

Box 13.9   ISIS crisis

The terrorist organisation known as ISIS operates an influential propaganda machine on social media (Jethro Mullen, CNN Correspondent 2015). Mullen has noted that children and adolescents feature in their video streams placed on the Internet as agents of recruitment. Boys are depicted wearing ISIS bandanas, dressed in camouflage and showing postures of combat. These boys even have a title, 'Cubs of the Caliphate'. Focus has turned towards luring female teenagers to Syria and Iraq to become brides for the ISIS fighters. Islamic State attempts at recruiting youngsters are successful and this is mainly down to how they use social media to disseminate their cause and beliefs. A US State Department official claimed that there are as many as 90,000 tweets (messages on Twitter) on a daily basis concerning ISIS propaganda (Mullen 2015). When Robert Hannigan was a senior Foreign Office official and in charge of the UK Government Communications Headquarters (GCHQ), he argued that ISIS and other extremist groups are using Twitter, Facebook and WhatsApp as ways to target young people who are potentially vulnerable to such propaganda. Such individuals are likely to embrace the beliefs, values, attitudes and behaviours espoused by these groups. Hannigan also says that one method ISIS uses is to exploit popular **hashtags** to spread their message. Because hashtags contain a word or phrase preceded by a hash sign (#) it is easier for users to find messages with specific content or themes. Therefore it is a good tactic for spreading the word. Once in Syria, the new recruits are used to communicate with other potential new recruits using social media. When David Cameron was British Prime Minister he made a broadcast in response to the disappearance of three British teenage girls who left for Syria via Turkey. He said, 'It needs every school, every university, every college, every community to recognise they have a role to play, we all have a role to play in stopping people from having their minds poisoned by this appalling death cult' (BBC News 21 February 2015). At the time of writing, ISIS is in retreat in the Middle East and have shifted strategies to terrorist attacks in the West (also instigated by social media).

As we are living in a digital world, young people are engaging with it. They use the Internet and communicate using social media so it is difficult to avoid the negative aspects of information sharing. Unfortunately, extremist groups such as ISIS have also engaged with the digital world and use social media for purposes of propaganda.

Social networks such as **Instagram**, Snapchat and Twitter enable children and adolescents to interact and exchange information through photo imagery, messaging and engaging in discussion groups. Teenagers aged 15–17 years tend to use Facebook, Snapchat and Twitter more than 13–14 year olds who favour Instagram (US Teen Rehab Center website 2016). Instagram is a social network enabling users to see and share photos. As with all social media, this can be accessed using mobile phones and smartphones. All types of photos can be posted, from images depicting the ISIS lifestyle to teenagers smoking marijuana or simply pictures of unusual diets. The use of Instagram by ISIS is more informal compared with Twitter. Supporters of ISIS often post pro-ISIS images such as home-cooked meals or attractive views all with hashtags or symbols indicating loyalty and support for ISIS (Carman 2015).

Away from terrorism, one current craze is the '**Wellness blogger**' who uses Instagram to post pictures of foods that he or she believes help to achieve a slim body. These images often create unrealistic expectations of what their followers should eat or avoid. Instagram enables wellness bloggers to share snapshots of their life including recipes and healthy eating suggestions. One example is an attractive young woman posting pictures of her kale juice (Freeman 2015).

Plate 13.9 Instagram of some healthy vegetable juices. (Shutterstock 268762826.)

Often these wellness bloggers are unqualified to provide advice on healthy eating and lifestyle (Nianias 2015). This can lead to misinformation and cause dangerous eating habits, especially when specific food categories are excluded such as dairy and grains. According to Nianias (2015), such wellness bloggers publish cookbooks that are supported by online publishing. In 2015 a wellness blogger called Ella Woodward (cited by Freeman 2015) published a cookbook called *Deliciously Ella* that became popular. Instagram is a gateway to sharing recipes and dietary habits despite not being a site dedicated to food-related issues. **Orthorexia nervosa** was introduced as a condition in 1996 and is considered to be the well-balanced sister of bulimia nervosa (Lisle 2016). Orthorexia is a condition where the sufferer shows unhealthy obsessive behaviour with eating healthy food. Lisle (2016) argues that as more people become obsessed with clean eating, such as excluding processed, fattening and sugary foods, they are at risk of 'pushing their bodies and minds to the limit' (p. 890). This obsession leads to extreme self-control over their approach to eating. Whereas anorexia can feasibly be conceived as the pursuit of thinness, orthorexia is the pursuit of gaining a toned physic. Even so, orthorexia resembles an eating disorder with a positive spin supported by social media. Is posting an Instagram of broccoli and cauliflower as the meal of the day healthy advice to give developing children and teenagers?

A relatively new problem associated with Instagram is **sexting**. This involves the transmission of nude or sexually explicit images using an electronic device such as a smartphone. The National Center for Missing and Exploited Children considers that sexting also includes the transmission of sexually explicit text messaging. Although Rice et al. (2012) explored the influence of sexually explicit messages and photos on sexual behaviour, they considered the two things as one activity. This makes it difficult to separate the effects of texting and sexting on sexual behaviour, as sexually explicit messages may impact differently on sexual behaviour than do images (Houck et al. 2014). Mitchell et al. (2012) found 1–2.5 per cent of 10 to 17 year olds reported that they appeared in or created a sexually explicit photograph. Sending sexually explicit images is common in high school teenagers, occurring between 18–28 per cent (Strassberg et al. 2013; Temple et al. 2012). Rice et al. (2012) found a strong relationship

Plate 13.10 Is this a healthy balanced meal for developing children and teenagers? (Shutterstock 266753045.)

between adolescents who sexted and being sexually active. In fact they found that teenagers who sexted were seven times more likely to be sexually active than those who were non-sexting and twice as likely to have unprotected sex. Temple et al. (2012) found teenage girls who sent naked images of themselves were likely to experience risky sex with multiple partners after using substances. In Houck et al.'s (2014) study, findings suggested that those teenagers who sexted received approval for their sexual behaviour from a variety of sources including parents and peers as well as the media. Interestingly, these teenagers also experienced lower emotional awareness and emotional self-esteem (see Chapters 8 and 12). They also found that teenagers who sent images were more likely to engage in all types of sexual activity than those who only sent text messages. Houck et al. concluded that teenagers who sexted scored higher on risk-related cognition questionnaires and lower on measures of emotional competency. This implies that they have reduced understanding and self-management of their emotions. Sexting for these teenagers might be a form of self-expression and a way of counteracting potentially emotionally difficult interactions with others.

When considering the impact on social behaviour that the mass media and social media in particular have on children and adolescents, it becomes apparent that individuals react

Plate 13.11 A happy response to an ambiguous text message. (Shutterstock 14472517.)

differently. This suggests that individual differences, in terms of personality and temperament (see Chapter 12), are contributing to the way children and adolescents engage and interact with the media. This is an important point that needs further discussion.

DO INDIVIDUAL DIFFERENCES INFLUENCE OUR RESPONSES TO THE MEDIA?

It is widely regarded that the media has a negative impact on young people's lives. As we have seen, children and adolescents spend an ever-increasing amount of time on social media. Many consider that these forms of media are likely to affect factors such as self-esteem in negative ways. But does such an assumption stand up to scrutiny? Interestingly, how social media affects young people may depend in part on temperament and personality (see Chapter 12).

Plate 13.12   A confused response to an ambiguous text message. (Shutterstock 133227056.)

Plate 13.13 Showing differences of temperament from an early age. (Shutterstock 196178363.)

As discussed previously in Chapter 12, personality psychologists consider there are five dimensions: openness; conscientiousness; extraversion; agreeableness and neuroticism (OCEAN as an acronym). Where individuals lie on each dimension will vary, hence offering a unique personality profile of traits, and we can see such differences from an early age.

An adolescent, for example, who is extremely extravert and neurotic might find that use of social media is another outlet for expression and sociability. If, however, he or she is highly neurotic, then receiving negative comments on Facebook and Twitter might cause anxiety and fearfulness at receiving further upsetting feedback. In contrast, a teenager who is high on extraversion but low in neuroticism is less likely to be upset by receiving negative comments due to feeling self-satisfied and secure in their 'own skin'. As we have seen earlier, teenage girls who send sexually explicit images of themselves tend to be risk takers (Temple et al. 2012). This trait suggests that they are careless and impulsive, which are listed in the lower end of the conscientiousness dimension of the 'Big 5'. Houck et al. (2014) also found those teenagers who sexted tended to score high on risk-related cognition, again suggesting a low score on the conscientiousness dimension. Houck et al. (2014) also alluded to teenagers sexting as a means of self-expression because they had problems engaging emotionally with others. This suggests that these teenagers are reserved and insecure (low scoring on the extraversion but high on the neuroticism dimensions respectively). These are only assumptions of course. To make the link between the Big 5 and how people behave and react to social media we will refer to findings from studies in the area.

The Big 5 and social media

There have been numerous studies designed to investigate the influence of personality (i.e., the Big 5) and the way we behave when using the Internet (see Box 13.10). Marshall et al. (2015) reported differences in how people use Facebook to update their posts about thoughts, feelings and activities. In their study they required 555 Facebook users to complete a variety of measures that included the Big 5, self-esteem, **narcissism**, reasons why they use Facebook and the nature of their post updating (see Table 13.2).

Box 13.10   The Big 5 and Internet behaviour

Findings connecting the Big 5 with specific Internet activity have provided insight into why people vary in their use of the latter. As we have seen in Chapter 12, an individual scoring high on the neuroticism dimension is very likely to experience feelings of distress, anxiety, anger and depression. Those who score low on neuroticism are described as emotionally stable. Various studies have demonstrated a link between scoring high on neuroticism and frequently using social media such as Facebook and blogs (Correa et al. 2010; Guadagno et al. 2008; Ross et al. 2009). Despite these findings, there are mixed conclusions. For example, Blumer and Renneberg (2010) showed how online communication can be useful for individuals who experience social exclusion for reasons of disability, mental health issues or sexual orientation. For emotionally unstable individuals, however, the Internet can become a source of addiction (Hardie and Tee 2007; Mehroof and Griffiths 2010). When considering introversion/extraversion the findings are distinctly mixed. Some researchers report that introverted individuals use the Internet more frequently than those considered as extraverts (Landers and Lounsbury 2006). Alternatively, Correa et al. (2010) found social media users to be extraverts. Social media has its plus points for those who are introverted. The anonymity involved in online communication can help boost outgoing behaviour by overriding social inhibitions (Amichai-Hamburger et al. 2002). In the case of the openness dimension, Tuten and Bosnjak (2001) found high scorers use the various Internet services to search for information and obtain new angles on different issues. Low scorers are likely to be overwhelmed by such new ideas. Correa et al. (2010) found that social media and blogs attract those who express openness to new information and experience. Agreeableness is an interesting one. Scoring high on this indicates cooperative behaviour whereas low scoring suggests unkind and disagreeable behaviour. However, while Mikami et al. (2010) found online and offline social behaviour of adolescents to be consistent, Swickert et al. (2002) showed that online altruistic behaviour can increase or decrease. This suggests that altruistic behaviour is not only influenced by agreeableness. Colquitt et al. (2002) reported that individuals scoring high on conscientiousness are likely to be organised and have skills enabling them to search for information, unlike low scorers who can become lost in cyberspace. Blumer and Doering (2012) asked the question of whether we behave the same online as we are offline – in other words, is our social behaviour, as reflected in how we score on the Big 5, also seen online? They studied a sample of 122 adolescent students who were familiar with media and Internet use. They found that, for personality expression on the Internet, openness, conscientiousness, extraversion and agreeableness scores tended to shift towards the midpoint. This suggests weaker personality expression when online. In the case of neuroticism, however, participants reported a shift towards higher emotional stability. This implies that computer- and Internet-based communication has a positive influence on users who tend to be highly neurotic. Interestingly, Gosling et al. (2011) found that extraverts engaged in higher levels of Facebook activity than introverts. They suggest that individuals using Online Social Networking sites (OSNs) extend their offline personalities into OSNs.

Research findings of online activity suggest that there is a link with personality as measured using the Big 5. Although there are differences in the extent and type of personality traits influencing specific types of online activity, the findings show a relationship between online and offline personality.

Results regarding networking behaviour suggest that extraversion and openness are key influential personality factors, unlike conscientiousness and emotional stability that have a negative relationship with the pursuit of linking to others (Wolff and Kim 2011). Wolff and Kim found that agreeableness was important for internal rather than external networking, which makes perfect sense given their cooperative nature and wanting to work within a team. The general conclusion is that there is a link between the use of social media and personality.

Table 13.2 How the Big 5, self-esteem and narcissism impacted on Facebook updating.

Measures	Descriptions of Facebook postings
Big 5	Extraverts frequently updated information about their social activities, which was prompted by using Facebook for communicating with others. High scorers on openness updated content on Facebook relating to intellectual topics. This reflected the way they use Facebook as an information-sharing facility. High scorers on conscientiousness used Facebook to update information about their children.
Self-esteem	Low self-esteem scorers used Facebook to update information about their romantic partners.
Narcissism	Those who scored high on narcissism used Facebook to update information about their accomplishments, exercise and diet schedules. Facebook was a tool for attention-seeking and validation of their worth.

An interesting question arising out of the research on the personality and social media connection is why do teenagers commit suicide after being abused by Internet trolls? It is difficult to comprehend why teenagers would commit suicide because of what a stranger says to them on social media (see Box 13.11).

Box 13.11 Why take your life for the sake of a troll?

There are teenagers who commit suicide because of the nasty comments they receive on social media. Some comments from trolls tell them to commit suicide. But why would you listen to trolls you do not even know? Cognitive neuropsychologist Nicholas Almond (2013) argues that social media use by 10–15 year olds has increased and yet the percentage of teenage suicides has decreased according to records from the Samaritans. He points out that these two figures do not necessarily explain what is happening but provides us with some indicator of there being a problem other than troll comments. Almond argues that, as children develop into adolescents, they are faced with numerous challenges regarding their personality, sexuality and image, which can affect their mental health. In recent years these challenges have been exacerbated by developments in social media. In the case of Hannah Smith, who took her life because of social media trolls, it was eventually discovered that many of the abusive messages received were sent from her own computer – her own IP address (suggesting she sent these herself). A teenage boy living in Miami, US, committed suicide live on the Internet in 2008 (Thompson 2008). According to Wolk-Wasserman (1986), suicide is a consequence of internal psychological conflict but external events also play a role. Harris et al. (2009) provided evidence of suicide-risk individuals scoring high on all suicide-risk measures including a history of psychiatric problems. In a Swedish study, Westerlund et al. (2015) found that 74 per cent of participants responded to an Internet posting of an individual who talked about committing suicide, and who eventually did, as being a consequence of a mental illness or feeling bad. Blaming society or social factors was considered to be the cause by 16 per cent of participants and 'stupidity' was cast as a causal factor by 10 per cent. Ozawa-De Silva (2008,

(continued)

(continued)

2010) discusses how people on the Internet who share their suicide with others do so as an attempt to break the social isolation and loneliness they feel.

While these researchers have been unable to fully explain why teenagers commit suicide following negative comments from trolls, they do make the point that frequently there is an underlying psychological problem. Psychological problems can be exacerbated by external stimuli such as abusive comments and general cyberbullying.

This is clearly a sensitive issue and will not be resolved without research investigating the triadic relationship between cyberbullying, the victim's and the perpetrator's personalities.

Summary

- Mass media (or 'the media') refers to the different ways of communicating information to large audiences. With the advent of the Digital Era, the communication of information is more quickly accessed through computer and Internet technology. There is a distinction between mass media and social media. Mass media provides limited information shared with large numbers of people. Social media has unlimited information that can be copied, adapted and shared with others.
- The mass media includes the following: broadcast media; print media; outdoor visual media and digital media. Before the influx of digital devices, children and adolescents would spend between three and four hours watching television daily. Some television programmes contain educational content and are beneficial to cognitive development. But developmentalists argue that face-to-face social interactions are more conducive for learning than television viewing.
- Three main areas where television has influenced social behaviour are: adult advertising of alcohol, fashion/cosmetic advertising and television violence. Drinking portrayals and alcohol product placement provide attractive stereotyping. The fashion industry promotes the 'skinny' model look and tends to use attractive people to advertise cosmetics. Daily viewing of these images can influence the eating habits of teenagers who want to look like the ideal body image being promoted. Studies have found that children who watched televised violence had increased levels of aggressive behaviour. Developmentalists consider televised violence as influencing the social behaviour of children and adolescents by encouraging them to be aggressive and antisocial. Playing video games depicting violence are considered to be a causal risk factor for increased aggressive behaviour, aggressive thinking and aggressive emotion, and decreased empathy and prosocial behaviour.
- Many magazines are aimed at young people and contain images of celebrities and other idols that teenagers strive to emulate. Some of these body images have been airbrushed to fit the ideal and present teenagers with unrealistic expectations of how they should look – often leading to eating disorders. The social comparison theory advocates that we evaluate our own appearance and abilities by comparing

with others. Magazines have largely replaced how we evaluate what is the ideal by presenting images of successful females with an ideal body image.

- Digital technology has brought the electronic world to life. The Internet is an encyclopaedia full of information that can be retrieved easily. It enables people to communicate from all over the world using email, Internet telephony, instant messaging, Internet forums, blogs, Facebook and social networking. There are many sources of Internet use such as Twitter, Instagram, LinkedIn, YouTube, Google+ and Snapchat to name just a few.
- Social media is a good way of communicating with many people but there are drawbacks. Profile information on Facebook and MySpace can be exploited due to accessibility by anyone. Hence, social media trolls can post hostile messages on Twitter or Facebook – such cyberbullying has led to teenage suicides. Chatrooms have been used by paedophiles for targeting children and adolescents. The allure of the chatroom is that anyone can be anyone they want to be – it's anonymous. Paedophiles can easily isolate their young victims and lull them into forming an emotional attachment. Social media has been used by political campaigners and terrorists. ISIS recruits children and adolescents using social media such as Twitter, Facebook and WhatsApp by posting propaganda. Young people have been influenced by such postings and have left their homeland for Syria.
- Instagram enables people to exchange information through photo imagery. ISIS has used this form of social media to send positive images of the ISIS lifestyle. Instagram has also been used by Wellness bloggers to show pictures of what foods are good to eat. Often unqualified, they can promote misinformation and dangerous eating habits such as orthorexia. Sexting of sexually explicit photographs is the latest craze. Teenage girls who sexted tended to experience risky sex with many partners.
- Individuals use and respond differently to social media. Using the Big 5, research findings suggest there are personality traits influencing online behaviour. For example, those who score highly on neuroticism make frequent use of Facebook and blogs, whereas those who score highly on agreeableness make use of the Internet for altruistic reasons.

Questions for discussion

1. What do different types of mass media have in common? Do you think that certain forms of mass media have more of a negative impact on social behaviour than others?
2. The Internet stores a huge amount of information. Discuss two aspects of the Internet that have been used in ways to cause problems for children or adolescents.
3. We are living in the digital world. Consider two ways in which social media has had a positive effect on your life and two ways in which it has had a negative effect.

(continued)

(continued)

4. Critically discuss the evolutionary approach to understanding how magazines for teenagers influence their social behaviour.
5. Critically explore the view that the Internet is an encyclopaedia rather than a means of communication.
6. Is there a relationship between scoring highly on specific personality traits and the way that individuals make use of the Internet, and especially of social media? Critically examine the methodology of research that suggests there is such a relationship.

Further reading

If you are interested in a comprehensive account of the influence that the Internet has on our lives, including such topics as gaming, shopping, pornography, self-diagnosis, cyberstalking and organised crime, look at:

- Aiken, M. (2016). *The Cyber Effect: A Pioneering Cyber-Psychologist Explains How Human Behaviour Changes Online.* London: Hodder and Stoughton General Division.

If you are interested in the question of whether there is any scientific evidence (using research and theory) for violent video games and media violence contributing towards child and adolescent aggressive and violent behaviour, look at:

- Anderson, C.A., Gentile, D.A. and Buckley, K.E. (2007). *Violent Video Game Effects on Children and Adolescents: Theory, Research, and Public Policy.* New York, NY: Oxford University Press.

If you are interested in a comprehensive account of how social media affects the quality of teenagers' lives and how it interacts with culture and technology (such as how paternalism and protectionism disrupt the process of becoming informed and engaged citizens), look at:

- Boyd, D. (2014). *It's Complicated: The Social Lives of Networked Teens.* New Haven and London: Yale University Press.

If you are interested in a textbook that addresses the ethical decision-making underlying the many aspects of the media (e.g., in entertainment and the arts, photography and video journalism), look at:

- Patterson, P. and Wilkins, L. (2008). *Media Ethics: Issues and Cases.* NY: McGraw Hill.

Contents

Introduction   449

Technology and understanding
social development   450

Epigenetics – biological and
environmental interactions on
social behaviour   457

Impact of DSM-5 for the classification
of mental disordered behaviour   462

How variation across cultures can
be used to explain differences
in social behaviour   465

Summary   471

The future for our understanding of social development

14

What this chapter will teach you

- How scanning techniques such as fMRI and PET are helping neuroscientists and developmentalists to understand the development of internal states in children.
- The importance of epigenetics in understanding the bi-directional relationship between genes and environment in development.
- How living in an individualistic or a collectivist culture can impact on social development.
- How cultural norms are now considered under DSM-5 when assessing mental health issues.
- The relationship between cultural differences and the transition from adolescence and adulthood.

INTRODUCTION

Social development has become an important topic in its own right within developmental psychology. The understanding of what causes us to behave socially in different ways from one another has been explored using different research methods (see Chapter 2). With the development of new technologies, it has become possible to explore what new-borns are capable of understanding and the extent to which they come equipped with competencies allowing them to engage in the social environment. These new sophisticated measures of infant competency help us to understand the relationship between environmental input and social development. It is interesting to note that various genes that babies are born with are not necessarily activated from birth. This latency effect of our genes on behaviour has been captured in the work of Annette Karmiloff-Smith, who sadly died recently. Her work has shown the importance of understanding the intricate interaction between biological and environmental factors and the longevity of these interactive effects (i.e., the contribution of epigenetics to our understanding of social development). Epigenetics is important in the understanding of how we develop individual differences, even when siblings experience a similar nurturing environment (see Chapters 1, 6, 7 and 12). The contribution of evolutionary psychology and behavioural genetics to our understanding of individual differences in social development has meant that developmentalists can now study this interaction between genes and environment more easily. How we interpret other people's social behaviour is influenced by our definitions of what is considered to be 'normal' and socially accepted behaviour. The differentiation between 'normal socially acceptable behaviour' from 'abnormal socially unacceptable behaviour' has been described in the *Diagnostic and Statistical Manual (DSM) of Mental Disorders*, the latest version being DSM-5 (American Psychiatric Association 2013). The DSM-5 is considered to be one of the major resources used in the categorisation of problematic behaviour in childhood and the ramifications for how social behaviour throughout the lifespan is then perceived and considered. There will, of course, be cultural variations in social behaviour, not only cross-culturally, but within countries as there will be pockets of cultural differences. Fortunately, DSM-5 has made improvements in the way culture is considered as a means of understanding individual differences in the development of mental health issues. This is important given that Western countries such as the UK, US, Australia and Canada have progressively become multi-cultural societies. This means people of different ethnic backgrounds have helped to diversify attitudes and values, and introduced a variety of cultural practices. This is especially important given the recent rise in terrorism and the resultant movement of people from one culture to another. Moreover, with the development of social media, adolescents can now access potentially dangerous political material and sources designed to alter attitudes in a hostile way.

In this chapter, we will therefore consider four themes.

1. How technological advances have helped developmentalists to uncover gene–environmental interactions in social development.
2. Epigenetics – contribution of biological and environmental interactions on social behaviour.
3. The impact of DSM-5 for the classification of mental-disordered behaviour.
4. How variation across cultures can be used to explain differences in social behaviour.

TECHNOLOGY AND UNDERSTANDING SOCIAL DEVELOPMENT

Technological advances in the 20th century have helped psychologists and neuroscientists to improve their understanding of human behaviour. Technologies such as different scanning techniques have enabled scientists to obtain computerised images of the human brain.

Scanning techniques

Scanning techniques have been available since the 1970s. In recent years, however, they have been refined in ways that allow developmentalists to study the structure and function of the human brain with great clarity. Essentially there are two types of information obtained depending on the type of scan used. It is possible to attain images of the structure of the brain by using **Computed Tomography (CT)** and structural Magnetic Resonance Imaging (MRI) scans, or information on how the brain functions by adopting functional MRI (fMRI) and Positron Emission Tomography (PET) scanning technology. Electroencephalography (EEG) is not a new technology but in recent years it has become increasingly available to developmental psychologists, allowing for detailed recording of electrical brain waves in infants and children. The range of commonly used techniques for measuring brain activity and structural mapping of the brain is outlined in Table 14.1.

These scanning techniques use computer technology to record the images created, which can then be reviewed at a later time. The EEG measurements have been used in many developmental psychological experiments. In Chapter 2 we considered how it can be used with infants as a means of ascertaining their brain activity when viewing faces. The necessary electrodes can be incorporated into a geodesic sensor net resembling a shower-cap. Johnson (2000) showed that babies are training areas of their brain to learn about faces by taking EEG measurements of the new-born's cerebral cortex while viewing faces. Johnson and de Haan (2001) further showed that there is widespread brain activity in infants when viewing facial stimuli. Brain activity in response to seeing faces, however, becomes more localised with increasing experience of looking at them, such that, by 12 months, a baby's brain pattern of activity is similar to an adult's. The EEG can be used as a means of detecting Event-Related Potential (ERP; see Chapter 2). Developmentalists have used ERPs to understand the processing of speech sounds in infants and children. Molfese and Molfese (1979) demonstrated that, like adults, infants respond faster to speech sounds in the left rather than the right hemisphere. This technique has also been used to investigate problems with differentiating the sounds of phonemes in children with dyslexia. Kraus et al. (1996) found that these children

Table 14.1 A selection of typically available scanning technologies.

Name	Description
Single-Photon Emission Computed Tomography (SPECT)	Used to construct both a two- and three-dimensional image of different active regions of the brain.
Diffusion Tensor MRI (DTMRI)	Used to gauge the thickness and density of areas connecting different neural networks in the brain.
High-Density Diffuse Optical Tomography (HD-DOT)	Has been compared with fMRI as it provides images of the connectivity between different regions of the brain when at rest.
Near Infrared Spectroscopy (NIRS)	Provides researchers with an indirect measure of brain activity.
Magnetoencephalography (MEG)	Used to understand how different parts of the brain function and the neurofeedback involved.
Event-Related Optical Signal (EROS)	Used to understand how neurons in the brain behave thereby providing a direct measure of brain cellular activity.
Cranial ultrasound	Mainly used in babies where an ultrasound image of the brain can be attained via the fontanelles.

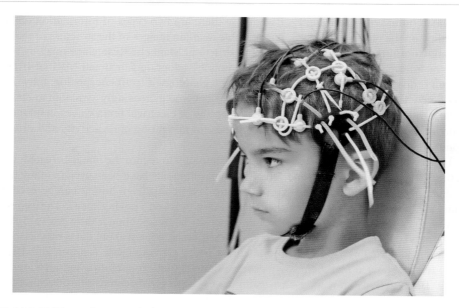

Plate 14.1 Child wearing a geodesic sensor net. (Shutterstock 445265269.)

were not able to process the difference between two separate sounds. Hence, the use of EEG has proved to be a successful way of understanding how the brain processes cognitive stimuli such as faces and language, and to increase our understanding of processing errors.

The fMRI scans are often used in psychological research, especially in cognitive tasking. Baron-Cohen et al. (1994) used fMRI to ascertain which parts of the brain are primarily involved in social cognition, such as interpreting and reasoning about the mental states of others. This was taken further by Morrison et al. (2004) who showed that a similar pattern of neural activity occurred in the anterior cingulate cortex (ACC) and anterior insula when we actually experience pain and when we observe it in others. Morrison et al., however, did find that there were qualitative differences of ACC activation, helping us to separate our own pains from the pains of others. The findings from this research using fMRI has furthered developmentalists' understanding of how our social cognition develops and the role played by different parts of the brain. It is only with the development of scanning technologies such as fMRI that developmentalists have discovered the important role played by mirror neurons in social cognition, and social cognition is important in understanding and interpreting the behaviours of others, which ultimately influences how we respond socially towards them. It is also possible, by using fMRI, to identify conditions where mirror neurons are dysfunctional and the consequences this has on social behaviour of the individuals concerned. This is the case for autism spectrum disorders (Nishitani et al. 2004; Oberman et al. 2005; Theoret et al. 2005).

The fMRI and PET scans have also contributed to our understanding of what happens in the brain when we hear sad stories and have to make moral decisions. The PET scan imagery shows activation of neural structures in the brain such as the amygdala on hearing a sad yarn (Decety and Chaminade 2003). Different brain activity has been observed using fMRI scanning under conditions of moral-personal and moral-impersonal decision-making (Greene et al. 2001). The areas of the brain more active in moral-personal decision-making indicated there was greater arousal here (see Chapter 10). You might recall that the moral-personal scenario presented in Chapter 10 involved physically pushing an individual onto a train line whereas the moral-impersonal decision involved pushing a lever to divert a train towards someone. Without scanning technology it would be difficult to observe differences in brain activation during different types of decision-making. It should be noted that, while scanning techniques inform developmentalists of brain activity occurring during cognitive tasking, it is not a precise tool. Therefore the use of scans should not be considered in a deterministic way (e.g., when a specific area of the brain appears active the person must be experiencing happiness).

Physiological measures

There are many different types of physiological measures used in psychological research. In Chapter 2 we considered vagal tone. Vagal tone cannot be measured directly but only indirectly through the effects the vagus nerve has on heart rate. The vagus nerve can send signals to relax the heart, which ultimately slows the heart beat down and calms the person. Heart-rate variations are indicative of the situation an individual encounters and the emotional effects this has. It is therefore a broad measure of the emotional state of a young infant who has difficulty communicating his or her feelings verbally. It is important for new-borns to be able to self-regulate their emotional state under stressful situations. Porges et al. (1994) found a high vagal tone to be associated with both positive emotional adjustment and irritability in infants between five and six months of age. Electrodermal reactivity (EDR) is one way of measuring changes in the electrical conductance of the skin. During a stressful situation it is normal for the skin to sweat, which is a sign of anxiety. The EDR can be used as one measure in polygraph readings (often utilised as 'lie detectors').

The EDR has been used as a measure of how skin conductance relates to empathy and sympathy in children averaging nine years and five months. In one study boys with higher levels of skin conductance on viewing negative slides were able to regulate their emotions successfully and were generally emotionally balanced in comparison with their counterparts

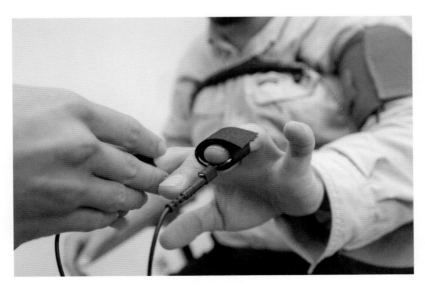

Plate 14.2 Showing the placement of electrodes on the fingers in order to obtain readings of EDR. (Shutterstock 319713404.)

who showed low skin conductance (Liew et al 2003). This supports previous findings by Fabes et al. (1994) where negative emotions in kindergarten and children in the second grade were associated with high skin conductance responses to film excerpts depicting children in pain. This, and facial expressions of distress, demonstrated a prosocial stance. Studies using vagal tone and EDR have provided developmentalists with valuable information concerning physiological processes underlying the emotions and behavioural responses shown by infants and children. Other physiological measures have been used to understand the changes seen in adolescence (e.g., studies of the endocrine system).

As we discussed in Chapter 1, changes occurring in the endocrine system lead to the development of secondary sexual characteristics seen in teenagers. These changes are associated with the transition from being a child to becoming an adolescent. The endocrine system produces the sex hormones making these changes possible. Developmentalists who are interested in the influence these sex hormones have on behaviour have studied the effects of testosterone on aggressive behaviour in males. Archer (2006) provides evidence of a small but robust positive correlation between levels of circulating testosterone and aggressive behaviour in male teenagers. Therefore, ascertaining levels of circulating hormones can provide important insights into the physiological factors underlying behaviour. Behaviours can be controlled experimentally by using film footage or creating situations that activate emotional responses. It then becomes possible to take salivary samples to test for the presence and levels of hormones such as testosterone, but also of other hormones associated with stress such as cortisol.

These physiological measurements are important, not just in studies looking at adolescent behaviour but in cases of abnormal development such as ODD (see Chapter 11). van Goozen et al. (2004) found cortisol levels to be lower in children with ODD. Other physiological measures in these children, such as low skin conductance and heart rate, have led developmentalists to conclude that ODD children are fearless and this explains why they are more likely to instigate fights. In another study, ODD boys were presented with experimental conditions designed to increase their frustration (van Goozen et al. 1998). As the frustration increased so did the boys' anger, heart rate and blood pressure. Cortisol levels decreased

Plate 14.3 Developmental differences between children and teenage siblings. (Shutterstock 75322075.)

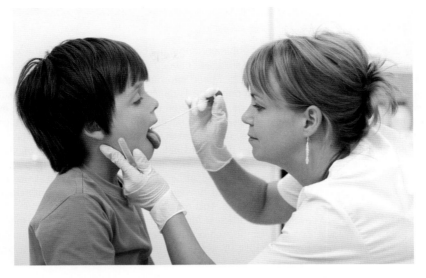

Plate 14.4 Researcher taking a sample of saliva for analysis. (Shutterstock 119876230.)

for the boys classified as highly aggressive and disruptive without being anxious. For those boys who, in addition to being classified as aggressive and disruptive, also experienced anxiety, cortisol levels increased. van Goozen et al. (1998) argued that this finding highlights the developmental progression from children with ODD to adults experiencing antisocial tendencies. Technological developments in how physiological measures are taken have provided developmentalists with new ways of studying infants, children and adolescents.

Behavioural genetics

The field of behavioural genetics has made strides in understanding the relative contribution our genes make towards our social behavioural responses (see Chapter 1). Much of this work has progressed as a consequence of new technologies in the way genetic material is analysed. Very much laboratory based, the science of molecular genetics considers **linkage analysis** (see Box 14.1) as a method of establishing linkage between genes. This is often used to map genes within families by establishing genetic relationships. Molecular biologists, for example, use electrophoresis equipment and automated DNA sequencing machines to enable them to make molecules and to intervene by altering the structure of DNA in animals. They then observe the consequences of these changes – of course this is not undertaken on human DNA.

Box 14.1   Linkage analysis in human research

Human DNA is subject to the methodology of linkage analysis. This involves the use of **molecular markers** to help identify what specific genes do. A molecular (or gene) marker is a gene or sequence of DNA whose position on a chromosome is known. These molecular markers can be used to diagnose specific genetically related disorders such as cystic fibrosis

(continued)

(continued)

(Bradley et al. 1998). Molecular markers are important in the process of identifying the location on a chromosome as well as looking for linkages between genes on the same chromosome. It is a rather complicated procedure but has been informative. Understanding which genes play a role in the development of social behaviour is difficult and complicated. The linkages between genes on the same chromosome, let alone on other chromosomes, makes it even more complicated. One gene, DRD4, involved in the development of temperament, has been identified (see Chapters 1, 3 and 12). The contribution of variant structural forms of this gene (i.e., 7-repeat allele; see Chapter 3) has been linked to variations in the temperament of infants. The 7-repeat allele form has been linked to babies with difficult behaviour such as problems in settling into sleep, feeding regimes and forming attachments with caregivers (Lakatos et al. 2000; Gervai et al. 2005). It has to be noted here, however, that such a temperamental disposition is probabilistic rather than deterministic. This means that having certain specific alleles increases the chances of developing a particular temperament rather than ensuring that this occurs (this will be addressed later on). Based on these earlier developments in molecular genetics, the Human Genome Project (HGP) sequenced the entire human genome in 2005. (Note this includes all of the genes that code for proteins and the 'non-coding' regions of DNA). A gene is therefore coded for by a large number of base pairs (see Plate 14.5).

Linkage analysis is often used by behavioural geneticists to find degrees of genetic relatedness between family members. This is why developmentalists find familial, twin and adoptive studies important to our understanding of behaviour.

Behavioural genetics has not only shown the contribution of our genes to behaviour but has highlighted the fact that genes and environment are not independent of each other. As we have seen in Chapter 1, our genes influence our social environment in three ways:

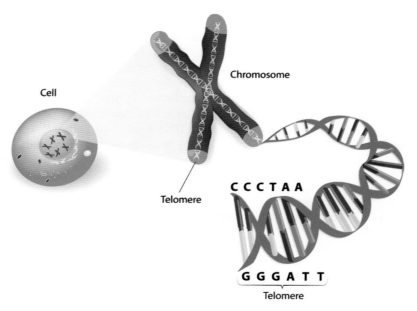

Plate 14.5 Shows the chromosome housing the genes that are sequenced according to base pairings (i.e., A, C, G and T). (Shutterstock 172842560.)

passive effects, active effects and evocative effects. As you may recall, a child 'inherits' the environment provided by the parents (i.e., passive effect) – such as, for example, having many instruments to play in the house. Active effects create niche picking such that the child will actively look for environments compatible with the genotype. For example, the child looks for instruments to play as she has an interest in music. Evocative effects refer to the child possessing a trait that is reinforced by the environment – a smiley baby is likely to evoke friendly responses from others, which reinforce further smiling.

Technological advances, not just in psychology but other subject areas such as neuroscience and biology, have clearly helped us to understand how social behaviour develops. It has also helped towards unravelling the intricate relationship between our genes and the environment, and provided information to fuel the study of epigenetics.

EPIGENETICS – BIOLOGICAL AND ENVIRONMENTAL INTERACTIONS ON SOCIAL BEHAVIOUR

The epigenetic stance emphasises a bi-directional interaction between genetic inheritance (i.e., nature) and the environment (i.e., nurture). This implies that the environment impacts on our complement of genes just as genes impact on an individual's environment. Epigenetics, as discussed in Chapter 1, is associated with the notion of an epigenetic landscape, which was first introduced by Conrad Waddington in 1957. For an innovative symbolic configuration of how our genes and the immediate environment interact to determine the structure and function of brain cells see Figure 1.6, Chapter 1. Waddington's model implies that, even if early developmental experiences are harsh, the effects of this on development are constrained by parameters of the epigenetic topography present at the time. Waddington was unaware at the time, however, that we have genes that can be switched 'on' or 'off' at different points in development. Hence, it is far more complex than originally understood during Waddington's research window. Our current understanding of this area is that environmental factors can alter the epigenetic landscape. This, and the understanding of how specific genes can be latently switched 'on' or 'off', has been exemplified in the work of Annette Karmiloff-Smith. In 1998, Karmiloff-Smith set up her own Neurocognitive Development Unit at the Institute of Child Health in London. She was interested in child development and believed that in order to address this effectively it was important to consider many approaches such as cognition, brain imaging, genes, behaviour and environmental factors. Karmiloff-Smith realised the importance of using brain imaging, behavioural genetics and computational modelling as a means to obtain detailed information about infant, child, adolescent and adult development. Developmental disorders were just as important to her research as was 'normal' development.

The basis of Karmiloff-Smith's work has highlighted the important bi-directional interaction between genes and environment and has influenced the way we consider the complex impact that 'nature has on nurture' and 'nurture on nature' (see Figure 14.1).

Throughout this text we have seen examples of this intricate relationship between nature and nurture, and how this impacts on our social development. When considering temperament, in particular during infancy, the effect of having the 7-repeat allele structure of the DRD4 gene can cause disruption to the attachment process between caregiver and baby and a host of other disorganised behaviours (see Chapters 3, 6 and 12). Despite having such a gene configuration, it is possible, with the right nurturing, to overcome this trajectory of development. Caregivers who are attentive, persistent and calm can override the effects of the 7-repeat allele format (see Chapter 3). Once again this highlights the importance of a bi-directional interaction between nature and nurture.

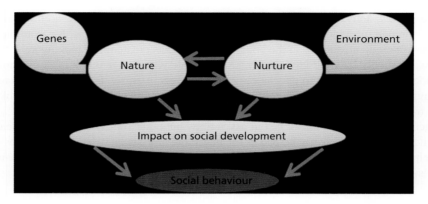

Figure 14.1 The bi-directional interaction between nature and nurture.

Research on resilience has shown how the effects of having a disruptive childhood can be largely reversed once the environmental circumstances have been changed to a loving home setting. Bowlby's research suggests long-term separation from caregiver input is an important factor in the development of problematic children, such as that seen in what Bowlby calls affectionless psychopathy (see Chapter 3). As we saw in Chapter 3, many developmentalists disagree with Bowlby's conclusion that being totally deprived of maternal input results in permanent and irreversible damage (Rutter et al. 1998; Skuse 1984).

Clearly, a change of environmental conditions can influence the development and behaviour of the child. As we have seen, nature can be modified by nurture. This is illustrated by Thomas and Karmiloff-Smith (2002) who introduced the concept of 'residual normality'. In their words this is the assumption that 'in the face of a selective developmental deficit, the rest of the system can nevertheless develop normally and independently of the deficit' (p. 729). Donnai and Karmiloff-Smith (2000) claimed that, despite a genetic defect defining a disorder, individuals will vary considerably in the way the symptoms are expressed. This implies that individuals will also respond differentially to environmental input. The symptoms might be attenuated, for example, as a consequence of environmental input aimed at counteracting the detrimental behaviours exhibited.

There are many examples of environmental input that can help individuals control their symptomatic behaviour. **Tourette's syndrome** has been considered a problem of specific executive dysfunctions that underlie many of the inappropriate behavioural (in particular involuntary movements) and verbal outbursts (Bornstein 1990; Ozonoff and Jensen 1999). Ozonoff and Jensen (1999) claim that as different disorders can be distinguished on the basis of their executive function profiles, these 'executive "fingerprints" may be useful aids in identification of the conditions, as well as in designing best practices for their remediation' (p. 175). In Box 14.2 we describe Tourette's syndrome and how specific executive dysfunctions separate it from other conditions. British-born psychologist John Morton demonstrates, using a model approach, how this might be represented diagrammatically (see Figure 14.2).

The environment can be influential in changing the influence of some genes. This means positive environmental influences may override our genes. In other words, can nurture, in part, alter the effects of nature? This will be explored next by looking at the effects of genes becoming 'switched on' or 'switched off' at different points in development.

Plate 14.6 Young girl adopted into a happy family. (Shutterstock 10704268.)

Box 14.2   Tourette's syndrome

The symptoms of Tourette's syndrome are often misconstrued as children behaving badly. As their symptoms typically involve saying inappropriate utterances out loud (often including profanities), people frown upon them. Their uncontrollable ticks (involuntary movements and verbal outbursts) are often considered either comic or disruptive. Ozonoff and Jensen (1999) hypothesise that 'specific types of executive impairment may be associated with specific neurodevelopmental disorders' (p. 171). Individuals with Tourette's syndrome tend to perform as well as controls on the Stroop Test and the Wisconsin Card Sorting Test (WCST). These tests

(continued)

(continued)

require focused attention. In the case of Stroop, this involves reading the names of colours written in a different ink colour to the named colour. In the case of WCST, this involves sorting the cards according to a rule that changes regularly. Performance on these executive function tests varies depending on which syndrome the child has. Morton argued in 2004 that 'genes are promiscuous' (p. 260). For example, he claims that the 7-repeat allele of the DRD4 gene can be associated with more than one condition (i.e., Tourette's syndrome, attention deficit disorder, attention deficit hyperactivity disorder and dyslexia). He says it is important to be clear that the 7-repeat allele of DRD4 is not the cause of these conditions but rather is responsible for a dopamine-related problem. (Note that dopamine is a chemical released by neurons as a mechanism for sending signals to other neurons. In the brain there are several dopamine pathways, one of which plays an important role in reward-motivated behaviour.) The point raised by Ozonoff and Jensen is that, once these symptoms can be identified, specific environmental factors can be used to attenuate the symptomology. For example, **Comprehensive Behavioural Intervention for Tics (CBiT)** includes various techniques. One such technique used is habit reversal therapy (HRT). In the first stage of this, the person learns to identify and understand what tics involve, where they occur in the body and which muscles are active at the time. When the individual is aware of when a tic is about to occur – the feeling that the tic is about to happen is called a premonitory urge – then the next stage can be implemented. In the next stage it is important for the individual to find a competing response. By doing so it is then possible to perform an intentional movement to suppress the tic. This can be done by harnessing the premonitory urge and placing a hand on their leg instead of flinging it out and possibly hitting someone. According to Conelea and Woods (2008), attentional processes are used to suppress tics. A different type of intervention is **deep brain stimulation** where neurostimulators in the form of electrodes are implanted into the brain to deliver electrical signals (specifically in areas such as the thalamus which relays signals relating to motor control). Deep brain stimulation is successful in cases of severe Tourette's syndrome (Huys et al. 2014).

It is possible for Tourette sufferers to self-control many of their tics using psychological interventions. Moreover, there are biological interventions that can be adopted in more severe cases.

Effects of genes 'switching on' and 'switching off' during development

People often conceive of the genome as a genetic blueprint that determines development. The reality is far more complex. Although genes 'code for' traits, which genes are activated often depends on environmental input. Change the input and frequently the output is also altered. In relation to epigenetics, this implies that environmental and lifestyle factors can influence how our genes behave without altering the 'genetic blueprint'. In other words, genes can be **'switched on'** (i.e., activated) or **'switched off'** (i.e., deactivated) as a consequence of environmental input or by lifestyle factors. This gene regulation is complex and involves the process of gene transcription. Gene transcription consists of all the stages involved with reading the genetic code to the formation of proteins (some of which will become neurotransmitters affecting internal states and behavioural responses). Interesting research by Kaminsky et al. (2008) have provided insight into how identical twins can have differences in personality traits (see Box 14.3).

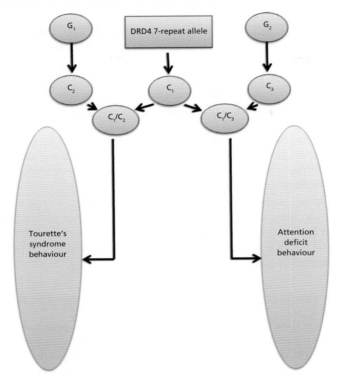

Figure 14.2 Model showing two possible conditions resulting from DRD4 7-repeat allele splitting at the cognitive level: G indicates factors separating the two conditions (genetic variations, environmental factors or both) and C represents the cognitive deficits. (Adapted from Morton 2004.)

Box 14.3   The impact of nurture on nature – insights from behavioural epigenetics

An approach that has been developed over the last 20 years seeks to understand how nurture can shape nature. Behavioural epigenetics is the field that examines how various environmental factors influence the expression of specific genes (i.e., how active a gene is). Such environmental factors vary from the food that we eat to early social experiences. Given that no two people experience identical environments, this means that even identical twins can exhibit subtle differences in personality traits (Kaminskye et al. 2008). These differences are related to changes in DNA **methylation**. Methylation is a chemical process responsible for turning off a gene and, in so doing, this affects neuronal development in the brain. This means that when, for example, one of a pair of identical twins experiences an early negative social encounter they are more likely to become more risk-avoidant later in life when compared with their sibling. The underlying difference between the two twins can therefore be traced back to certain specific genes being activated less during development.

Clearly epigenetics helps us to understand why we need both the nature and the nurture parts of the equation if we are to fully understand the development of social behaviour.

Recently, neuroscientists have used a chemical tracer that binds to an enzyme (a chemical substance that initiates natural bodily processes) called HDAC. Patients who were given this chemical tracer were subjected to a PET scan that allowed researchers to see how HDAC altered the activity of the gene expression. Areas of the brain that showed the highest density of this enzyme gave an indication of gene activity being most affected. This technique allows neuroscientists to look at gene expression of patients with Alzheimer's disease or schizophrenia. Moreover, as it scans in real-time, it is possible to see the impact of the environment and lifestyle of these patients. According to Wey et al. (2016), this technique can allow researchers to investigate and answer questions regarding why some people who have a genetic predisposition to a specific disease are protected from it and others are not. Also, answers might be forthcoming as to why some events during infancy and childhood can have lasting effects on brain function in adolescence.

The 'switching on' and 'switching off' of genes has made an impact on our current understanding of the intricate bi-directional interaction between nature and nurture. The importance of this bi-directional interaction has influenced the way in which different mental disorders are considered in the *Diagnostic Statistical Manual*, 5th Edition (DSM-5; American Psychiatric Association 2013).

IMPACT OF DSM-5 FOR THE CLASSIFICATION OF MENTAL DISORDERED BEHAVIOUR

The DSM-5 has been largely revised according to organisation and diagnostic criteria from previous versions (see Box 14.4). The different DSM publications have been influenced by the psychiatric, medical, psychological and sociological philosophies of the day. With rigorous research into different conditions and a better understanding of the underlying neurological, physiological, psychological and sociological factors causing symptoms of mental disorder, DSM-5 is hopefully a sharper instrument of clinical diagnosis. There is the argument, however, that with the collapse of different subtypes and subcategories, DSM-5 can potentially be a blunted tool of any diagnostic value.

Box 14.4   History of DSM revisions

The first *Diagnostic Statistical Manual of Mental Disorders* (DSM-I) was published in 1952 by the American Psychiatric Association. In the original format there were 130 pages listing 106 mental disorders (Grob 1991). One of the categories was 'personality disturbance', which was separated from 'neurosis' (nervousness; Oldham 2005). Homosexuality was considered as a sociopathic personality disturbance and remained in DSM until 1974 (Mayes et al. 2009). The DSM-II was published in 1968 and listed 182 disorders, but was nevertheless similar to DSM-I. Mayes and Horwitz (2005) describe DSM-II as reflecting a predominantly psychodynamic psychiatry, also known as dynamic psychology (an approach emphasising the psychological forces underlying behaviour and emotions; see Chapter 1). Biological perspectives were also addressed, including German-born psychiatrist Emil Kraepelin's system of classification based on biological and genetic malfunction. On the sixth printing of DSM-II, homosexuality was excluded as a category of disorder and instead became incorporated under the banner of 'ego-dystonic homosexuality' (i.e., having an attraction at odds with one's idealised self-image). In 1980 DSM-III was published consisting of 265 diagnostic categories. Robert Spitzer was behind making DSM classifications consistent with those used by the International Statistical Classification of Diseases and Related Health Problems (ICD) published by the World Health Organisation of the United Nations.

The result of this was that DSM became more research-based and founded on a regulatory or legislative model. In DSM-III a system using categories called axials was adopted and the manual was very much based on statistical census information instead of diagnosis alone. The DSM stated that 'Each of the mental disorders is conceptualized as a clinically significant behavioural or psychological syndrome' (cited by Mayes and Horwitz 2005). In the case of personality disorders they were classified in axis II with mental retardation (Oldham 2005). Spitzer criticised his work claiming that DSM-III medicalises 20–30 per cent of the population who have no serious mental problem. In 1987 DSM-III became DSM-III-R. Spitzer was dissatisfied with the naming and organisation of some of the categories. Six of the categories were deleted and others added. Homosexuality was now subsumed in the category of 'sexual disorder not otherwise specified'. There were now 292 diagnoses. The DSM-IV was published in 1994 and listed 297 disorders. The DSM now included a clinical clause for approximately 50 per cent of the categories. This meant that the symptoms had to cause 'clinically significant distress or impairment in social, occupational, or other important areas of functioning'. In 2000, DSM-IV had a text revision and was known as DSM-IV-TR. Categories and diagnoses remained unchanged (American Psychiatric Association 2000). The DSM was now organised according to a five-axial system, two of which were clinical disorders, and personality disorders and intellectual disabilities. In 2013 DSM-5 was published. There have been many changes to diagnoses and diagnostic definitions (Jayson 2013). The main changes include:

- discarding the five axial system for mental disorders (Kress 2014);
- deletion of subtypes of schizophrenia;
- deletion of subsets of autistic spectrum disorder (including Rett's syndrome; classic autism; Asperger's syndrome; childhood disintegrative disorder and pervasive developmental disorder not otherwise specified).

There have been many revisions over the years to the DSM format. The DSM-5, however, has been radically changed.

The DSM-5 is fundamentally different from previous versions. There is, for example, expanded inclusion of new information about the aetiology of different mental disorders. This, in part, arises out of research addressing how both genes and environmental factors impact on the developing brain and interact to influence behaviour. While this is important and is driven by developments in neuroscience, other changes to DSM-5 derived from psychiatric and psychological clinicians. Taking the example of autism spectrum disorder, we see that in DSM-IV-TR there were five subtypes, the symptoms of which overlapped. How these overlapping symptoms were considered and given a diagnosis by different clinicians depended largely on the clinical approach taken as there were, for instance, no definitive guideline standards of what differentiates childhood disintegrative disorder from Rett's syndrome. In many respects, by dissolving these different subtypes and subsuming the collection of symptoms using one umbrella term of autism spectrum disorder (ASD), clinicians have an easier task of gauging the level of impairment incurred to areas of cognitive, social and communicative function. With regard to social development, the ASD continuum ranges from more to less impaired. In DSM-5 it is stated that the symptoms associated with ASD must appear from early childhood even if these were not identified until much later. This may be a positive development because it not only encourages an earlier diagnosis but also allows for people who have slipped through the net (i.e., ASD symptoms are detected later) to receive a diagnosis. This may then allow for interventions to be put in place so that the social demands on those with late-diagnosed ASD symptoms do not exceed their capacity to cope.

There has been much research into ASD over the years that has initiated changes to the way clinicians understand individuals who have impairments typical of the disorder. This has generated the necessary changes to DSM in order to keep up with the findings from different sources of research into the area. This has also spurred on new ways of considering the diagnostic criteria (see Tables 14.2, 14.3 and 14.4).

Table 14.2 Diagnostic criteria used in ASD.

Persistent deficits in social communication and social interaction
Deficits in socioemotional reciprocity – this can be manifested in different ways such as an inability to approach a social situation; to engage in and follow rules of conversation; to share emotions and interests; to initiate or respond appropriately to social interactions.
Deficits in nonverbal communication used in social interactions – this ranges from poor verbal and nonverbal communication; poor use of eye contact and body language; poor use of gestures; lack of facial expressions.
Deficits in developing, maintaining and understanding relationships – this can range from difficulties in sharing imaginative play with other children; in making friends; behaving in ways to suit the social context; showing interest in peers.

Table 14.3 Diagnostic criteria used in ASD.

Restricted and repetitive patterns of behaviour
Repetitive motor movements (body movements) and in how objects and speech are used – this can be simple repetitions of hand wringing; lining up toys in a specific way or switching lights on and off; echolalia (which consists of repeating back words or phrases).
The insistence of following inflexible routines or ritualised verbal and nonverbal behaviour – extreme distress arises out of changes to routines such is the rigidity of thinking patterns; the need to follow set greeting behaviours; same dietary requirements.
Extreme and restricted fixations – this can be shown through abnormal intensity of focus with unusual objects.
Hyper or hypo-reactivity to sensory input or aspects of environment – this can be seen in responses of indifference to pain or temperature; excessive touching of objects; adverse response to specific sounds; visual intrigue with lights.

Table 14.4 Diagnostic criteria used in ASD.

Severity based on level of social communication impairments and extent of repetitive patterns of behaviour
Symptoms must be present during early development even if not fully shown until later – when social demands exceed restricted capacity to cope; or learned strategies mask symptoms.
Symptoms cause clinical impairment to daily life – can be to social and occupational events.
Resulting disturbances from symptoms cannot be explained by other means – such as intellectual disability or a general developmental delay.

Assessment leads to individuals being allocated to one of three levels of impairment severity.

- Level 3 means very substantial support is required for both social communication and restricted/repetitive behaviour.
- Level 2 means substantial support is required for both social communication and restricted/repetitive behaviour.
- Level 1 means support is required for both social communication and restricted/repetitive behaviour.

As we move up the scale from Level 1 to Level 3, the extent of intervention required increases.

Arguably, ASD is one example of how DSM-5 has improved diagnosis – thereby sharpening the tool. According to Reiger et al. (2013), 'Changes to the DSM were largely informed by advancements in neuroscience, clinical and public health need, and identified problems with the classification system and criteria put forth in the DSM-IV' (p. 92). This implies that DSM-5 was devised to integrate current scientific and clinical evidence to ensure that the information covered for mental disorders is empirically sound. This is one of the reasons why cultural influences have been included in the assessment of:

- anxiety and depression;
- psychotic disorders (Western and non-Western countries);
- socio-cultural factors inherent in somatic syndrome disorders (SSD – a mental illness causing one or more bodily symptoms such as pain or neurological problems).

Previous versions of DSM paid little attention to the impact that cultural factors have on the identification and assessment of mental health issues. Culture, age and gender are important factors in how our social environment is experienced. This, in turn, is linked to mechanisms involved in the epigenetic model. References to culture, age and gender in the discussion of risk, prevalence, diagnosis and how symptoms are expressed are included for many of the disorders considered in DSM-5, but not all (Reiger et al. 2013). Research on culture-related diagnosis of depressive disorders suggests there are substantial differences in how it is expressed cross-culturally. Very often it goes unnoticed and is misdiagnosed as a somatic symptom. In the case of schizophrenia spectrum disorder, cultural factors can influence how visual or auditory hallucinations are interpreted – for some countries hallucinations of a religious nature can be taken to mean that the individual has special qualities enabling communications with a supernatural being. Also, culture should be considered to assess disorganised speech as it can account for differences in the narrative format expressed. Moreover, nonverbal communication and levels of eye contact during social interactions can also vary cross-culturally.

It remains to be seen whether DSM-5 will make a big impact on the way mental health issues are perceived and assessed. Moreover, whether the inclusion of cultural factors will expand our way of understanding social behaviours that we might have once considered as odd. In our next section the influence of living in a multi-cultural Western world on social development will be addressed more generally.

HOW VARIATION ACROSS CULTURES CAN BE USED TO EXPLAIN DIFFERENCES IN SOCIAL BEHAVIOUR

Developmentalists can approach social development from an individualistic vantage point or from a cultural one. As we have discussed in Chapter 1, developmentalists such as Bronfenbrenner place the child in the centre of a multi-layer series of socialising agents. The child brings to the world his or her own genetic blueprint that is influenced by the environment (as discussed earlier in this chapter in the section on epigenetics). Bronfenbrenner's Ecosystem Model prises out these multi-layers from a close contact interactive interface (i.e., the microsystem) to increasingly indirect contact interfaces (i.e., exosystem and macrosystem; see Figure 1.5, Chapter 1). It is the macrosystem that is relevant to our discussion here, for it is the macrosystem that ultimately influences the socialisation of the child. The macrosystem is the cultural context the child experiences. It is not easily defined but the attitudes, values, mores, beliefs and acceptable behaviours are passed down through the various informal and formal socialising agents (e.g., caregivers and educational system respectively). Different cultures will vary in these attitudes, values, mores, beliefs and acceptable behaviours – but it should be noted here that there are more similarities than there are differences. Despite these similarities, Markus and Kitayama (1991) consider there are two broad forms of culture: individualistic and collectivistic (see Box 14.5).

Differences between individualistic and collectivistic cultures have a bearing on the social development of individuals (see Chapter 5). Cultural differences and how they impact on social development is currently a topical issue, especially in a multi-cultural Britain. In the UK there is a diversity of ethnic minorities who have kept their cultural traditions and, in so doing, have extended our knowledge of other countries in a variety of ways.

Box 14.5   Differences between individualistic and collectivistic cultures

In 1991 Markus and Kitayama considered the differences between individualistic and collectivistic cultures and how these can impact on the way citizens behave. Since these terms were introduced, many researchers have used them to explain differences in the behaviours of people from other cultures by applying this cross-cultural framework. For individualistic cultures (primarily Western countries) the focus is on developing an independent individual who is personally responsible for his or her destiny. In the case of collectivistic cultures (e.g., China, Japan and Korea) the focus is diverted from the individual to the formation of close ties in expanded social groups. This heightens the importance of being interdependent on one another – what we would probably conceive of as having a community spirit. So how does this influence our social behaviour? Darwish and Huber (2003) argue that conformity is more frequent in collectivistic cultures as a consequence of having socially defined norms prescribing how citizens should conduct themselves. For those individuals who exhibit deviant behaviours in conflict with these norms, there are clear sanctions in place. In the case of individualistic cultures, people are more likely to belong to more than one in-group, which moderates their behaviours according to the norms of each in-group – hence there are goals that apply to one group but not the other (see Chapters 7, 9, 10 and 11). According to Triandis et al. (1988), individuals affiliated to in-groups in collectivistic cultures will remain loyal regardless of the costly demands made. Furthermore, in collectivistic cultures such as East Asian and Middle Eastern countries, the collective self is emphasised more than is true of individualistic cultures. In contrast, however, in North American and European countries, the private self is encouraged – in other words the person's true feelings and notions of self-worth are shown publically. This fits in with the individualistic cultural ideology of self-expression of one's inner thoughts and feelings (Nisbett 2007). According to Darwish and Huber (2003), the message encapsulated within individualistic cultures is to promote the 'individual's and his/her immediate family's self-interest . . . personal autonomy, privacy, self-realization, individual initiative, independence, individual decision making, an understanding of personal identity . . . and less concern about the needs and interests of others' (p. 48). This is very different from collectivistic cultures where the emphasis is on group integration by showing 'loyalty . . . emotional dependence . . . interdependence, an understanding of personal identity as knowing one's place within the group . . . concern about the needs . . . of others' (Darwish and Huber 2003, p. 49). In relation to social behaviour, Sinha (1988) showed that people from individualistic cultures tend to have developed successful social skills when integrating into novel social groups. They appear to make acquaintances more readily. In the case of those from collectivistic cultures, they might not be as good at making new acquaintances, but those that they do associate with are more likely to become intimate friends lasting a lifetime.

Individualistic and collectivistic cultures differ in many respects regarding how individuals are expected to behave. While self-expression is frowned upon in collectivistic cultures, it is encouraged in individualistic cultures. These expectations will influence how people are socialised to behave, which, in turn, impacts on the social development of the young.

Many immigrants, refugees and ethnic minority groups now living in the UK and the US have expressed a desire to maintain their cultural customs rather than losing their identity to a homogenous population. In the context of social development, Britain's multi-cultural population has contributed to how we, as an individualistic culture, perceive ourselves. This extends to how we have developed levels of tolerance and understanding towards people we perceive as being different from ourselves. This tolerance is expressed in the way people integrate and learn about each other. In schools, for example, children are taught about other cultures and different religions and customs. Teaching 'British values' without making children from other cultural backgrounds feel uncomfortable is a tricky balancing act. Only recently, a report in the *Daily Mail* claimed that teachers want to stop promoting 'British values' as it makes children from other cultures feel inferior (Harding 2016). Hence, educational curriculums need to strike a balance between learning British values and those of other cultures. This will require an ongoing dialogue between parents, teachers and educational authorities. There is no doubt, however, that promoting an understanding of other cultures improves the way we socially interact with each other (Berry 2007). There are cultural differences that impact on how we understand different aspects of development, such as how we perceive intelligence and acquire social cognition.

Descriptions of intelligence vary between Western (i.e., individualistic) and Eastern (i.e., collectivistic) cultures (Matsumoto and Juang 2008). Whereas reasoning and thinking skills are advocated as important factors of intelligence in the West, being able to successfully navigate social roles within a community setting is paramount to Eastern countries (Nisbett 2003). Yang and Sternberg (1997), for example, highlighted the importance of being able to understand and relate to others among Taiwanese and Chinese individuals (which Gardner (2006) refers to as interpersonal intelligence). They further showed that knowing when to express intelligence and when not to is a cultural etiquette. There are differences in how parents from different cultures perceive academic achievement and how this is acquired (see Box 14.6).

Box 14.6 Parental cultural differences towards mathematical ability

It was discovered in a study by Stevenson (1995, 2000) that out of Chinese, Taiwanese, Japanese and American students, those of Asian origin out-performed US children quite significantly for mathematical skills. This was explained away by a number of factors. First, a quarter of classroom time in Japan was spent on learning mathematical skills whereas this was only one-tenth

(continued)

(continued)

in American schools. Second, 240 days per year were spent at school by Asian students as opposed to 178 days by their American counterparts. Interestingly, parents from these Asian countries believe that effort and training will help improve their children's mathematical skills. Also they are more likely to help their children complete their homework. American parents are of the view that mathematical achievement is based on an innate ability and therefore view helping out with homework as ineffective (Chen and Stevenson 1989). Stevenson et al. (1986) compared Japanese, Taiwanese and American mothers' attitudes towards their children's mathematical abilities. Mothers were asked to rank natural ability, effort, luck or chance and the level of difficulty involved in schoolwork in the order they believed contributed to the success of their children. They were then asked to score each of the 4 factors out of a total of 10 (10 being the highest value).

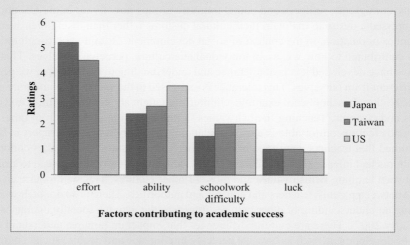

Figure 14.3 Japanese, Taiwanese and US mothers' beliefs concerning academic success. (Adapted from Stevenson et al. 1986.)

Attitudes to the degree to which mathematical achievement is innate clearly differ between Asian and American mothers. This, in turn, is likely to influence how children strive to make the grades. Other factors are also involved such as the amount of time mathematics is taught at school.

The time-line of different aspects of social cognition also appears to be influenced by cultural variations reflecting the individualistic and collectivistic divide. As we have seen in Chapter 5, there are differences in the acquisition order of learning different facets of theory of mind (ToM; an important aspect of social cognition) between individualistic and collectivistic cultures. Given that children in countries of the West are socialised to be independent thinkers and to express their feelings and thoughts openly, their *modus operandi* is to challenge existing ideas and shape their own beliefs (Nisbett 2007). According to Johnston and Wong (2002), children brought up in collectivistic cultures are taught to value the years of experience and wisdom that their elders hold. The infrastructure of collectivistic cultures rests on its citizens conforming to the mores, rules, beliefs, values and traditions of their culture. Children are encouraged to follow such norms. In Shahaeian et al.'s study in 2011, these underlying differences were found to influence the way Iranian and Australian children acquired different facets of ToM (see Chapter 5). Children in the study, regardless of culture, acquired all the facets of ToM, but it was the order in which they were learned that differed. This was explained by differences in how children in Iran acquire 'knowledge' and children in Australia obtain an understanding of 'diverse beliefs'. In the case of collectivistic cultures such as Iran, knowledge from elders would be respected and valued but they would have less experience of obtaining diverse beliefs. In contrast, the Australian children, living in an individualistic culture where there is less of a conformist mentality, would have been exposed to a variety of beliefs.

There are differences in the acquisition of false-belief understanding, not only across individualistic and collectivistic cultures but within different countries supporting either an individualistic or collectivistic infrastructure. Developmentalists have found that the age of acquiring false-belief understanding can vary by two years. You may recall that differences between Italy and Britain, and Japan and Korea were found. We have to be careful, however, when making such comparisons using only one aspect of ToM as a benchmark of ToM acquisition (Astington 2001). As we have discussed in Chapter 5, ToM per se is an important factor of social cognition and plays a major role in social development. Also important to social development is the way we acquire social knowledge. Developmentalists have considered three domains of social knowledge: moral, conventional and personal. The consensus is that moral understanding is universal and culture-free while conventional and personal understandings are culture-dependent.

Differences of culture also influence the nature of peer group formation and the importance of having friends outside of the extended family. Kovacs et al. (1996), for example, found a difference between African American and European American children in terms of friendship number and gender. They found that African American children exceeded the number of friends and friends of the opposite sex that their European American counterparts had. Other differences found can be related to the individualistic/collectivistic divide (see Box 14.7).

Box 14.7   Cultural differences in children's friendships

Peers can have an influential role in social development (see Chapter 7) but cultural background can modify the extent of this influence. Rothbaum et al. (2000) found a difference in the time spent with peers between American and Japanese adolescents. Whereas American youth prefer to spend time with their peers, Japanese adolescents are content to be at home. This finding can be explained by the underlying cultural differences between the US and Japan. The US is an example of an individualistic culture whereas Japan typifies a collectivistic ideology. Hence, in Japan, the value system adopted by adolescents comes more from the parents than peers. Similar findings occur in Latino cultures (DeRosier and Kupersmidt 1991). Ladd (2005) and Schneider (2000) showed how peer interaction was frowned upon by parents who played a key role in maintaining a family-based orientation. The individualistic and collectivistic divide modulates the formation and maintenance of peer relationships. This is, in part, a consequence of the socialisation process of children (see Chapters 6 and 7). In collectivistic cultures the impact of peer socialisation is attenuated. Parents and family in this type of culture play a dominant role in the socialisation of their children, which reflects how their own relationships were

(continued)

(continued)

shaped by collectivistic ideals. In a study by Orlick et al. (1990) Chinese and Canadian children showed differences in their level of prosocial behaviour and willingness to cooperate and share with peers. Here there are differences in levels of negative behavioural engagement such as fighting and behaving aggressively. Chinese children are more cooperative and willing to share than their Canadian counterparts. Canadian children, however, are more likely to be involved in conflict than the Chinese children. Orlick et al. concluded that this was a consequence of cultural differences. Other differences between Chinese and Canadian children pertained to the way they reacted to temperament. Sensitive children who were shy tended to be rejected by Canadian seven to nine year olds but in China these traits were embraced (Chen et al. 1992). With changes towards an assertive and self-initiative-based China, due to developing a market economy, ten-year-old children who are shy now tend to be rejected (Chen et al. 2005). Another major difference in how peers are perceived relates to the importance placed on education by Chinese parents. Udvari et al. (1995) uncovered among Chinese Canadian children a peer dislike of those who succeeded in physical activities such as sport. In the case of academic achievement, the competitive trait necessary to succeed received approval. Canadian children who were successful in sport activities were popular with their peers, whereas academic achievement showed no relatedness with peer acceptance.

Research findings suggest that the differences between individualistic and collectivistic cultures filter down to peer interactions and friendships. What are considered to be positive traits also influence how success is perceived in areas of physical or academic achievement.

There are also cross-cultural differences marking adolescent entry into adulthood. There is ambiguity in Western countries such as the UK and US as to when an adolescent is an adult. This, in part, is because there are no rites of passage or ceremonies to celebrate the transition from being a boy and becoming a man or being a girl and becoming a woman. Many collectivistic cultures commemorate this transition with a ritualised event. In Jewish culture, for example, this ritualised event is known as bat mitzvah for girls and bar mitzvah for boys. Gilbert Herdt (1994a) described how males of the Sambia living in the Papua New Guinea highlands must experience a long ritual process of initiation into adulthood (see Box 14.8).

Box 14.8   The initiation process by the Sambia

The Sambia value the notion of *jerungdu*, which refers to a state of being physically strong. *Jerungdu* is equivalent to our notions of showing prowess in battle, but in everyday use it refers to a strong man and masculine competence expressed through hunting, sex and ritual. During the ritual process, boys are separated from their mothers and younger siblings and live next to the cult house where the male adults stay during the initiation ceremony. As the belief of this culture is that semen is not produced internally and so has to be replaced, it is important that they are separated from the Sambian women. The initiation ritual is a way of leaving their feminised boyhood behind in favour of achieving masculinity. The ritual begins with the act of nose-bleeding – boys' noses are bled. After this the stinging-nettles ritual begins where fresh nettles are applied over the boy's entire body to open the skin. This is followed by the flute ceremony, where the boys are prepared by being dressed in a ceremonious grass-skirt and are enticed by the adult males to perform fellatio. In the meantime, flute players present the flute to the boys to be 'sucked'. This is in preparation for living in the cult house and performing fellatio and other homoerotic sexual acts on the adult bachelor men residing there until the five-day initiation is over. Herdt (1994b) states that, 'This is ritual custom: it is what men must do to be men, even if they must be dragged into manhood screaming all the way' (p. 253).

As we can see, here is a culture that believes it is important to be strong and masculine from a young age. In order to achieve this, young boys have to undergo a harsh and painful ritual that also involves homoerotic sexual activity. It is interesting that this activity, which is culturally valued by the Sambian, would be considered a serious crime in industrialised countries.

In individualistic cultures, given the ambiguity concerning the age of entry to adulthood, different milestones are reached at different ages. An adolescent can drive at a different age to when he or she can vote or have sex. In some US states it is illegal to drink alcohol below the age of 21 years even though young people can enlist in the armed forces at an earlier age. Activities normally associated with adults such as working, drinking, voting, driving a car or having sex, are legally permitted at different ages – which leave many teenagers confused as to when they have entered adulthood. Teenagers from collectivistic cultures have a structured and defined point of entry to adulthood and are therefore less confused concerning their adult status.

Summary

- The future for our understanding of social development can be considered using four themes: technological advances; epigenetics; DSM-5; and the impact of culture.
- One main technological advancement has been the development of scanning techniques. Different scanning techniques have helped neuroscientists to attain structural (e.g., CT) and functional (e.g., fMRI) images of the brain. Wearing a geodesic sensor net, EEG has shown developmentalists that new-borns are training their brain to learn about faces. The fMRI scans have provided information about how we interpret the mental states of others. Such scanning has identified the role of mirror neurons in understanding the behaviour of others. Both fMRI and PET scans have demonstrated the importance of the amygdala during emotional events such as hearing sad stories or having to make moral-personal decisions.
- Physiological measures such as vagal tone help developmentalists to understand how infants self-regulate their emotional state in times of stress. EDR, as a measure of skin conductivity, is used to detect anxiety. Boys who have higher levels of skin conductance are better at regulating their emotions than those with low skin conductivity. The endocrine system is responsible for producing sex hormones such as testosterone in males. Aggressive male teenagers tend to have higher levels of circulating testosterone than non-aggressive males. Low cortisol levels are found in aggressive children with oppositional defiant disorder (ODD).
- Behavioural genetics has helped to uncover the relationship between our genes and social behaviour using linkage analysis. Linkage analysis involves using molecular markers to identify what specific genes do. Variant structural forms of the DRD4 gene are implicated in babies with difficult temperaments and problems in attachment. Linkage analysis is useful in looking at genetic relatedness between family members.

(continued)

(continued)

- Epigenetics considers the bi-directional interaction between genetic inheritance and the environment. Waddington introduced the notion of the epigenetic landscape and believed that different pathways in development eventually converge to being back on track. He was unaware of the fact that genes can be 'switched on' and 'switched off'. This means that the environment can have more of an impact on the epigenetic landscape as genes can be latently switched on or off. Karmiloff-Smith realised the importance of this and has highlighted the bi-directional interaction between genes and environment and the complexities of how these impact on our social development. Hence, the effects of the 7-repeat allele of the DRD4 gene can be overridden if an appropriate environment is provided during infancy.

- The DSM-5 is the most recent version published in 2013. There have been many changes to the organisation and diagnostic criteria of mental disorders. The five axial system of classification was excluded; subtypes of schizophrenia deleted and the subsets of autistic spectrum disorder were also deleted. The DSM-5 changes were driven by developments in neuroscience and contributions from clinicians in psychiatric and psychological practice. By dissolving different subtypes of the autism spectrum, clinicians can standardise the way it is diagnosed and can diagnose individuals earlier (and at a later stage in the lifespan). There is a new section on how culture influences the way people behave under situations of stress and how this can cause mental disorders and influence social behaviour.

- Culture per se influences how we behave socially. Bronfenbrenner noted this in his Ecosystem Model. There are two types of culture: individualistic (representing Western countries) and collectivistic (representing Eastern countries). Individualistic cultures such as Britain are focused on developing an independent and self-expressive individual. This contrasts with collectivistic cultures where the emphasis is on the formation of close ties with social groups. There is more affiliation to life-long in-group membership and friendships. The collective self, relating to one's role within the group, is exhibited whereas the private self is discouraged. Immigrants, refugees and ethnic minority groups living in Western countries like to hold on to their cultural customs rather than losing their identity to the populace.

- Culture can influence when different aspects of ToM develop in children. There are also differences in how academic achievement is perceived. Mothers from collectivistic cultures believe mathematical achievement is down to effort and training, unlike those from individualistic cultures who view it as an innate ability. Cross-cultural differences in the transition from adolescence to adulthood occur. Rites of passage and ceremonies mark this transition and help individuals from collectivistic cultures with their self-identity. In individualistic cultures there are ambiguities concerning the transition from adolescence to adulthood – being able to do adult activities occurs at different ages. Friendship formation and maintenance varies cross-culturally. American youth prefer to be with their peers whereas Japanese adolescents prefer to spend their time with the extended family. These differences are linked to the individualistic and collectivistic divide, which, in turn, influences the socialisation process. Children from collectivistic cultures are more willing to share, cooperate and be prosocial than their individualistic counterparts.

Questions for discussion

1. Scanning techniques today allow us to 'look inside' the working brain. Such techniques have both strengths and limitations. Make a list of both strengths and limitations of scanning techniques with regard to social development.
2. How has the notion of an epigenetic landscape helped developmentalists understand the link between our genes and the environment? What are the limitations of this concept?
3. The development of theory of mind is influenced by the culture in which a child is reared. Discuss.
4. Behavioural geneticists consider there is a bi-directional interaction between genes and the environment in social development. Critically discuss this notion.
5. Critically evaluate how the major changes in DSM-5 have helped to inform developmentalists about mental disorders in children.
6. There are differences in social development across cultures. Critically discuss the extent to which these differences can be accounted for by the individualistic–collectivistic divide. Which culture would you rather belong to?

Further reading

If you are interested in neuroscience depictions of brain structure and function (including infant brains, telepathy and brain disorders) using scanning technologies, look at:

- Carter, R., Aldridge, S., Page, M. and Parker, S. (2014). *The Human Brain Book.* London: DK Publishing.

If you are interested in the impact our lifestyle choices have on our genetic code (including our 'biological scars' that we inherit and pass on down the generations), look at:

- Francis, R.C. (2012). *Epigenetics: How Environment Shapes our Genes.* New York: W.W. Norton and Company.

If you are interested in the different ways that cultural variation impacts on our social cognitive development, such as on our theory of mind, look at:

- Wassmann, J., Träuble, B. and Funke, J. (2013). *Theory of Mind in the Pacific: Reasoning Across Cultures.* Heidelberg, Germany: Universitätsverlag Winter.

If you are interested in an evaluation of the conceptual and pragmatic strengths and weaknesses of DSM-5 and the debate concerning psychiatric classification, look at:

- Paris, J. and Phillips, J. (2013). *Making the DSM-5: Concepts and Controversies.* New York: Springer-Verlag.

References

Abbott, L.C. and Winzer-Serhan, U.H. (2012). Smoking during pregnancy: lessons learned from epidemiological studies and experimental studies using animal models. *Critical Reviews in Toxicology*, 42(4), 279–303.

Abraham, M.R. and Renner, J.W. (1986). The sequence of learning cycle activities in high school chemistry. *Journal of Research in Science Teaching*, 23(2), 121–43.

Achenbach, T.M. (1991). *Manual for the Child Behaviour Checklist and 1991 Profile*. Burlington, VT: University of Vermont, Department of Psychiatry.

Achenbach, T.M. (1997). What is normal? What is abnormal? Developmental perspectives on behavioral and emotional problems. In S.S. Luthar, J. Burack, D. Cicchetti and J. Weisz (eds). *Developmental Psychopathology: Perspectives on Risk and Disorder* (pp. 93–114). New York: Cambridge University Press.

Ackerman, R. (1978). *The Economics of Corruption: A Study in Political Economy*. New York: Academic Press.

Adamson, I.B. (1995). *Communication Development During Infancy*. Madison, WI: Brown and Benchmark.

Adolphs, R., Tranel, D., Damasio, H. and Damasio, A.R. (1995). Fear and the human amygdala. *Journal of Neuroscience*, 15(9), 5879–91.

Advertising Standards Agency (2015). *Alcohol Advertising (2015)*. www.asa.org.uk/News-resources/Hot-Topics/Alcohol.aspx#.WIJgYlOLSM8.

Aiken, M. (2016). *The Cyber Effect: A Pioneering Cyber-Psychologist Explains How Human Behaviour Changes Online*. London: Hodder and Stoughton General Division.

Ainsworth, M.D. (1963). The development of infant–mother interactions among the Ganda. In D.M. Foss (ed.). *Determinants of Infant Behaviour* (Vol. 2, pp. 67–104). New York: Wiley.

Ainsworth, M.D. (1967). *Infancy in Uganda*. Baltimore, MD: Johns Hopkins University Press.

Ainsworth, M.D. (1973). The development of infant–mother attachment. In B.M. Caldwell and H.N. Ricciuti (eds). *Review of Child Development Research*, (Vol. 3, pp.1–94). Chicago: University of Chicago Press.

Ainsworth, M.D. (1979). Infant–mother attachment. *American Psychologist*, 34, 932–7.

Ainsworth, M.D., Bell, S.M. and Stayton, D.J. (1971). Individual differences in strange-situation behavior of one-year-olds. In H.R. Schaffer (ed.). *The Origins of Human Social Relations* (pp. 17–58). London and New York: Academic Press.

Ainsworth, M.D. and Bowlby, J. (1991). An ethological approach to personality development. *American Psychologist*, 46, 333–41.

Aldrich, N.J., Tenenbaum, H.R., Brooks, P.J., Harrison, K. and Sines, J. (2011). Perspective taking in children's narratives about jealousy. *British Journal of Developmental Psychology*, 29, 86–109.

Allan, N.P. and Lonigan, C.J. (2014). Exploring dimensionality of effortful control using hot and cool tasks in a sample of preschool children. *Journal of Experimental Child Psychology*, 122, 33–47.

Allen, J.P., McElhaney, K.B., Land, D.J., Kumpermin, G.P., Moore, C.W., O'Beirne-Kelly, H. et al. (2003). A secure base in adolescence: Markers of attachment security in the mother–adolescent relationship. *Child Development*, 74, 292–307.

Almond, N. (2013). *Are Trolls Really Responsible for Teenage Suicide and What Can the Websites Do About Them?* www.huffingtonpost.co.uk/dr-nicholas-m-almond/internet-trolls_b_3747964.html.

Alsaker, F.D. (1989). Perceived social competence, global self-esteem, social interactions, and peer dependence in early adolescence. In B.Y. Schneider, G. Attili, J. Nadel and R.P. Weissberg (eds). *Social Competence in Developmental Perspective* (pp. 390–2). Boston: Kluwer.

Altabe, M. and Thompson, J.K. (1996). Body image: A cognitive self-schema construct? *Cognitive Therapy and Research*, 20(2), 171–93.

American Psychiatric Association (2000). *Diagnostic and Statistical Manual of Mental Disorders (DSM-lV-TR)* (4th Edn, text rev.). Washington, DC: American Psychiatric Association.

American Psychiatric Association (2013). *Diagnostic and Statistical Manual of Mental Disorders* (5th Edn). Arlington, VA: American Psychiatric Publishing.

American Psychological Association (1992). Ethical principles of psychologists: code of conduct. *American Psychologist*, 44, 1597–611.

Amichai-Hamburger, Y., Wainapel, G. and Fox, S. (2002). "On the Internet no one knows I'm an introvert": Extroversion, neuroticism, and Internet interaction. *CyberPsychology and Behavior*, 5, 125–8.

Amsterdam, B.K. (1968). Mirror behaviour in children under two years of age. Unpublished doctoral dissertation. University of North Carolina, Chapel Hill.

Anderson, C.A. (2003). Video games and aggressive behaviour. In D. Ravitch and J.P. Viteritti (eds). *Kids Stuff: Marketing Sex and Violence to America's Children*. Baltimore, MD: John Hopkins University Press.

Anderson, C.A. and Bushman, B.J. (2002). The effects of media violence on society. *Science*, 295(5564), 2377–9.

Anderson, C.A., Gentile, D.A. and Buckley, K.E. (2007). *Violent Video Game Effects on Children and Adolescents: Theory, Research, and Public Policy*. New York: Oxford University Press.

Anderson, C.A., Ihori, N., Bushman, B.J., Rothstein, H.R., Shibuya, A., Swing, E.L., Sakamoto, A. and Saleem, M. (2010a). Violent video game effects on aggression, empathy, and prosocial behaviour in Eastern and Western countries: a meta-analytic review. *Psychological Bulletin*, 126(2), 151.

Anderson, C.A., Shibuya, A., Ihori, N., Swing, E.L., Bushman, B.J., Sakamoto, A., Rothstein, H.R., Saleem, M. and Barlett, C.P. (2010b). Violent video game effects on aggression, empathy, and prosocial behavior in Eastern and Western countries: A meta-analytic review. *Psychological Bulletin*, 136(2), 151–173.

Anderson, D.R. and Pempek, T. (2005). Television and very young children. *American Behavioral Scientist*, 48, 505–22.

Anderson, G. (2007). *Biological Influences on Criminal Behavior*. New York: Simon Fraser University Publications, CRC Press.

Anderson, L.T. and Ernst, M. (1994). Self-injury in Lesch-Nyhan disease. *Journal of Autism and Developmental Disorders*, 24, 67–81.

Andreau, E. (2004). Bully/victim problems and their association with Machiavellianism and self-efficacy in Greek primary school children. *British Journal of Educational Psychology*, 74, 297–309.

Ang, R.P. and Goh, D.H. (2010). Cyberbullying among adolescents: the role of affective and cognitive empathy, and gender. *Child Psychiatry and Human Development*, 41(4), 387–97.

Apperly, I. (2012). *Mindreaders: The Cognitive Basis of 'Theory of Mind'*. Hove, UK: Psychology Press.

Archer, J. (1991). The influence of testosterone on human aggression. *British Journal of Psychology*, 82(1), 1–28.

Archer, J. (2006). Testosterone and human aggression: an evaluation of the challenge hypothesis. *Neuroscience: Biobehavioural Review*, 30, 319–45.

Archer, J. (2009). Does sexual selection explain human sex differences in aggression? *Behavioral and Brain Sciences*, 32, 249–311.

Aristotle (1936). *On the Soul* (trans. W.S. Hett). London: William Heinemann.

Arnett, J.J. (1999). Adolescent storm and stress, reconsidered. *American Psychologist*, 54, 317–26.

Arsenio, W.F., Gold, J. and Adams, E. (2006). Children's conceptions and displays for moral emotions. In M. Killen and J.G. Smetana (eds). *Handbook of Moral Development* (pp. 581–609). Mahwah, NJ: Erlbaum.

Asher, S.R., Hymel, S. and Renshaw, P.D. (1984). Loneliness in children. *Child Development*, 55, 1456–64.

Aslin, R.N., Jusczyk, P.W. and Pisoni, D.B. (1998). Speech and auditory processing during infancy: constraints on and precursors to language. In W. Damon, D. Kuhn and R.S. Siegler (eds). *Handbook of Child Psychology: Vol. 2, Cognition, Perception, and Language* (5th Edn, pp.147–98). New York: Wiley.

Astington, J.W. (2001). The future of theory-of-mind research: understanding motivational states, the role of language, and real-world consequences. *Child Development*, 72(3), 685–7.

Astington, J.W. and Gopnik, A. (1991). Theoretical explanations of children's understanding of the mind. *British Journal of Developmental Psychology*, 9, 7–31.

Atkinson, J. (2000). *The Developing Visual Brain*. Oxford: Oxford University Press.

Axia, G. and Baroni, M.R. (1985). Linguistic politeness at different age levels. *Child Development*, 54, 918–27.

Axia, G., Bonichini, S. and Benini, F. (1999). Attention and reaction to distress in infancy: a longitudinal study. *Developmental Psychology*, 35(2), 500–4.

Babb, P. (2005). *A Summary of Focus on Social Inequalities,* Office for National Statistics, www.statistics.gov.uk/focuson/socialinequalities.

Baddeley, A.D. and Hitch, G. (1974). Working memory. In G.H. Bower (ed.). *The Psychology of Learning and Motivation: Advances in Research and Theory* (Vol. 8, pp. 47–89). New York: Academic Press.

Bagwell, C.L. (2004). Friendships, peer networks and antisocial behaviour. In J.B. Kupersmidt and K.A. Dodge (eds). *Children's Peer Relations* (pp. 37–57). Washington, DC: American Psychological Association.

Bagwell, C.L., Newcomb, A.F. and Bukowski, W.M. (2000). Preadolescent friendship and peer rejection as predictors of adult adjustment. *Child Development*, 69(1), 140–53.

Bai, M., Glick, D., Keene-Osborn, S., Gegax, T.T., Clemetson, L., Gordon, D. and Klaidman, D. (1999). Anatomy of a massacre. *Newsweek*, 133(18), 44.

Baillargeon, R. (1987). Object permanence in 3½ and 4 ½ month old infants. *Developmental Psychology*, 23, 655–64.

Baillargeon, R. and Graber, M. (1987). Where is the rabbit? 5.5-month-old infants' representation of the height of a hidden object. *Cognitive Development*, 2, 375–92.

Bakeman, R. and Gottman, J. (1997). *Observing Behaviour* (2nd Edn). New York: Cambridge University Press.

Baker, E., Baibazarova, E., Ktistaki, G., Shelton, K.H. and van Goozen, S.H. (2012). Development of fear and guilt in young children: stability over time and relations with psychopathology. *Developmental Psychopathology*, 24(3), 833–45.

Bakermans-Kranenburg, M.J. and van Ijzendoorn, H. (2004). No association of the dopamine receptor (DRD4) and -521 C/T promoter polymorphisms with infant attachment disorganisation. *Attachment and Human Development*, 6, 211–18.

Bakermans-Kranenburg, M.J. and van Ijzendoorn, H. (2006). Gene-environment interaction of the dopamine D4 receptor (DRD4) and observed maternal insensitivity predicting externalizing behavior in preschoolers. *Developmental Psychobiology*, 48(5), 406–9.

Bakermans-Kranenburg, M.J., van Ijzendoorn, H., Caspers, K. and Philibert, R. (2011). DRD4 genotype moderates the impact of parental problems on unresolved loss or trauma. *Attachment and Human Development*, 13(3), 253–69.

Baldwin, D.A. (1995). Understanding the link between joint attention and language. In C. Moore and P.J. Dunham (eds). *Joint Attention: Its Origin and Role in Development* (pp. 131–58). Hillsdale, NJ: Erlbaum.

Ball, H.A., Arsenault, L., Taylor, A., Maughan, B., Caspi, A. and Moffitt, T.E. (2008). Genetic influences on victims, bullies, and bully-victims in childhood. *The Journal of Child Psychology and Psychiatry*, 49, 104–12.

Baltes, P.B. (1987). Theoretical propositions of life-span developmental psychology: on the dynamics between growth and decline. *Developmental Psychology*, 23, 611–26.

Bandura, A. (1965). Influence of models' reinforcement contingencies on the acquisition of imitative response. *Journal of Personality and Social Psychology*, 1, 589–95.

Bandura, A. (1977). *Social Learning Theory*. New York: General Learning Press.

Bandura, A. (1986). *Social Foundations of Thought and Action: A Social Cognitive Theory*. Englewood Cliffs, NJ: Prentice Hall.

Bandura, A. (1991). Social cognitive theory of moral thought and action. In W.M. Kurtines and J.L. Gewirtz (eds). *Handbook of Moral Behavior and Development* (Vol. 1: Theory, pp. 45–104). New Jersey: Lawrence Erlbaum Associates.

Bandura, A. (2001). Social cognitive theory: an agentic perspective. *Annual Review of Psychology*, 52, 1–26.

Bandura, A. (2002). Selective moral disengagement in the exercise of moral agency. *Journal of Moral Education*, 31, 101–19.

Bandura, A. (2004). The role of selective moral disengagement in terrorism and counterterrorism. In F.M. Mogahaddam and A.J. Marsella (eds). *Understanding Terrorism: Psychological Roots, Consequences and Interventions* (pp. 121–150). Washington DC: American Psychological Association Press.

Bandura, A. (2007). Social cognitive theory. In W. Donsbach (ed.). *International Encyclopedia of Communication*. Thousand Oaks, CA: Sage.

Bandura, A. (2008). The reconstrual of 'free will' from the agentic perspective of social cognitive theory. In J. Baer, J.C. Kaufman and R.F. Baumeister (eds). *Are We Free? Psychology and Free Will* (pp. 86–127). Oxford: Oxford University Press.

Bandura, A. (2016). *Moral Disengagement: How People Do Harm and Live with Themselves*. New York: W.H. Freeman and Co Ltd.

Bandura, A., Ross, D. and Ross, S.A. (1963). Imitation of film-mediated aggressive model. *Journal of Abnormal and Social Psychology*, 66, 3–11.

Bandura, A. and Walters, R. (1963). *Social Learning and Personality Development*. NY: Holt, Rinehart and Winston.

Banerjee, R. and Yuill, N. (1999). Children's understanding of self-presentational display rules: associations with mental-state understanding. *British Journal of Developmental Psychology*, 17, 111–24.

Banerjee, R. and Watling, D. (2005). Children's understanding of faux-pas: associations with peer relations. *Hellenic Journal of Psychology*, 2(1), 27–45.

Banerjee, T.D., Middleton, F. and Faraon, S.V. (2007). Environmental risk factors for attention-deficit hyperactivity disorder. *Acta Paediatrica*, 96(9), 1269–74.

Banfield, S.S. and McCabe, M.P. (2002). An evaluation of the construct of body image. *Adolescence*, 37(146), 373–93.

Banks, J.A. (2008). *Introduction to Multicultural Education* (4th Edn). Boston: Allyn and Bacon.

Barchia, K. and Bussey, K. (2007). The role of moral disengagement in bullying and intervention: the development of a moral disengagement scale for bullying. Paper presented at the biennial meeting of the Society for Research in Child Development, Boston, MA.

Barkley, R.A. (1990). *Attention Deficit Hyperactivity Disorder: A Handbook for Diagnosis and Treatment*. New York: Guilford.

Barkley, R.A. (1998). *Attention-Deficit Hyperactivity Disorder: A Handbook for Diagnosis and Treatment* (2nd Edn). Guilford, New York.

Barkley, R.A. (2006). *Attention-Deficit Hyperactivity Disorder: A Handbook for Diagnosis and Treatment* (3rd Edn). New York: Guilford Press.

Barkow, J.H., Cosmides, L. and Tooby, J. (1992). *The Adapted Mind: Evolutionary Psychology and the Generation of Culture*. New York: Oxford University Press.

Baron-Cohen, S. (1987). Autism and symbolic play. *British Journal of Developmental Psychology*, 5(2), 139–48.

Baron-Cohen, S. (1995). *Mindblindness: An Essay on Autism and Theory of Mind*. Cambridge, MA: MIT Press.

Baron-Cohen, S. (2001). Theory of mind in normal development and autism. *Prisme*, 34, 174–83.

Baron-Cohen, S. (2003). *The Essential Difference: Male and Female Brains and the Truth about Autism*. New York: Basic Books.

Baron-Cohen, S., Jolliffe, T., Mortimore, C. and Robertson, M. (1997). Another advanced test of theory of mind: evidences from very high functioning adults with autism or Asperger syndrome. *Journal of Child Psychology and Psychiatry*, 38, 813–22.

Baron-Cohen, S., Ring, H., Moriarty, J., Shmitz, P., Costa, D. and Ell, P. (1994). Recognition of mental state terms: a clinical study of autism, and a functional neuroimaging study of normal adults. *British Journal of Psychiatry*, 165, 640–9.

Baron-Cohen, S., Wheelwright, S., Hill, J., Raste, Y. and Plumb, I. (2001). The 'reading the mind in the eyes' test revised version: a study with normal adults, and adults with Asperger syndrome or high-functioning autism. *Journal of Child Psychological Psychiatry*, 42(2), 241–51.

Barry, C.M and Wentzel, K.R. (2006). Friend influence on prosocial behaviour: the role of motivational factors and friendship characteristics. *Developmental Psychology*, 42(1), 153–63.

Barry, H., Child, I. and Bacon, M. (1959). Relation of child training to subsistence economy. *American Anthropologist*, 61(1), 51–63.

Barth, J.M. and Boles, D.B. (1999). *Positive Relations Between Emotion Recognition Skills and Right Hemisphere Processing.* Paper presented at the 11th Annual Convention of the American Psychological Society, http://membersaol.com/DBBoles/barth1999.html.

Barth, J.M. and Parke, R.D. (1993). Parent–child relationship influences on children's transition to school. *Merrill-Palmer Quarterly Journal of Developmental Psychology*, 39, 173–95.

Bartholow, B.D., Bushman, B.J. and Sestir, M.A. (2006). Chronic violent video game exposure and desensitization to violence: behavioural and event-related brain potential data. *Journal of Experimental Social Psychology*, 42, 532–9.

Barlett, C. and Coyne, S.M. (2014). A meta-analysis of sex differences in cyberbullying behaviour: the moderating role of age. *Aggressive Behavior*, 40(5), 474–88.

Basow, S.A. (1992). *Gender Stereotypes and Roles.* Pacific Grove, CA: Brooks/Cole.

Bates, E. and Goodman, J. (1999). On the emergence of grammar from the lexicon. In B. MacWhinney (ed.). *The Emergence of Language* (pp. 29–80). Mahwah, NJ: Erlbaum.

Bates, E., Thal, D., Whitsell, K., Fenson, L. and Oakes, I. (1989). Integrating language and gesture in infancy. *Developmental Psychology*, 25, 1004–19.

Batty, D. (2003). Paedophiles 'use children's websites to find victims'. *The Guardian.* Guardian News and Media Limited, www.theguardian.com/society/2003/jul/17/childrensservices.technology.

Bauman, S., Underwood, M.K. and Card, N.A. (2013). Definitions: another perspective and a proposal for beginning with cyberaggression. In S. Bauman, J. Walker and D. Cross (eds). *Principles of Cyberbullying Research: Definition, Methods, and Measures* (pp. 41–45). New York: Routledge.

Baumeister, R.F., Campbell, J.D., Krueger, J.I. and Vohs, K.D. (2003). Does high self-esteem cause better performance, interpersonal success, happiness, or healthier lifestyles? *Psychological Science in the Public Interest*, 4(1), 1–44.

Baumeister, R.F., Campbell, J.D., Krueger, J.I. and Vohs, K.D. (2005). Exploding the self-esteem myth. *Scientific American*, 292(1), 70–7.

Baumeister, R.F., Smart, L. and Boden, J.M. (1996). Relation of threatened egotism to violence and aggression: the dark side of high self-esteem. *Psychological Review*, 103, 5–33.

Bauminger, N., Chomsky-Smolkin, L., Orbach-Caspi, E., Zachor, D. and Levy-Shiff, R. (2008). Jealousy and emotional responsiveness in young children with ASD. *Cognition and Emotion,* 22(4), 595–619.

Baumrind, D. (1972). An exploratory study of socialisation effects on black children: some black–white comparisons. *Child Development*, 43, 261–7.

Baydar, N. (1988). Effects of parental separation and reentry into union on the emotional well-being of children. *Journal of Marriage and the Family*, 50(4), 967–81.

BBC News (2004). *Gay couples to get joint rights.*

BBC News (2015). *Syria-bound London girls: PM 'deeply concerned'* (21 February), www.bbc.co.uk/news/uk-31564014.

Becker, A.E., Burwell, R.A., Herzog, D.B., Hamburg, P. and Gilman, S.E. (2002). Eating behaviours and attitudes following prolonged exposure to television among ethnic Fijian adolescent girls. *The British Journal of Psychiatry*, 180(6), 509–14.

Bednar, R.L., Wells, M.G. and Peterson, S.R. (1995). *Self-Esteem* (2nd Edn). Washington, DC: American Psychological Association.

Bekoff, M. and Allen, C. (1998). Intentional communication and social play: how and why animals negotiate and agree to play. In M. Bekoff and J.A. Byers (eds). *Animal Play: Evolutionary, Comparative and Ecological Perspectives* (pp. 221–42). Cambridge: Cambridge University Press.

Bell, M.A. and Deater-Deckard, K. (2007). Biological systems and the development of self-regulation: integrating behavior, genetics, and psychophysiology. *Journal of Developmental and Behavioral Pediatrics*, 28(5), 409–20.

Bell-Gredler, M.E. (1986). *Learning and Instruction: Theory into Practice*. NY: Macmillan.

Belsky, J. (1997). Variation in susceptibility to rearing influence: an evolutionary argument. *Psychological Inquiry*, 8, 182–6.

Belsky, J. (1999). Interactional and contextual determinants of attachment security. In J. Cassidy and P. Shaver (eds). *Handbook of Attachment* (pp. 249–64). NY: Guilford Press.

Belsky, J. (2001). Developmental risks (still) associated with early child care. *Journal of Child Psychology and Psychiatry*. 42, 845–59.

Belsky, J. (2005). Differential susceptibility to rearing influence: an evolutionary hypothesis and some evidence. In B. Ellis and D. Bjorklund (eds). *Origins of the Social Mind: Evolutionary Psychology and Child Development* (pp. 139–63). New York: Guilford.

Belsky, J., Bakermans-Kranenburg, M.J. and van Ijzendoorn, M.H. (2007). For better and for worse: differential susceptibility to environmental influences. *Current Directions in Psychological Science*, 16(6), 300–4.

Belsky, J. and Domitrovich, C. (1997). Temperament and parenting antecedents of individual difference in three-year-old boys' pride and shame reactions. *Child Development*, 68, 456–66.

Belsky, J. and Pluess, M. (2012). Genetic moderation of early child care effects on social functioning across childhood: a developmental analysis. *Child Development*, 84(4), 1209–25.

Belsky, J., Spritz, B. and Crnic, K. (1996). Infant attachment security and affective cognitive information processing at age 3. *Psychological Science*, 7, 111–4.

Berk, L.E., Mann, T.D. and Ogan, A.T. (2006). Make-believe play: wellspring for development of self-regulation. In D.G. Singer, R.M. Golinkoff and K. Hirsh-Pasek (eds). *Play=Learning: How Play Motivates and Enhances Children's Cognitive and Social-Emotional Growth* (pp. 74–100). Oxford: Oxford University Press.

Berlin, L.J., Ispa, J.M., Fine, M.A., Malone, P.S., Brooks-Gunn, J., Brady-Smith, C. and

Bai, Y. (2009). Correlates and consequences of spanking and verbal punishment for low-income white, African American, and Mexican American toddlers. *Child Development*, 80(5), 1403–20.

Berman, G. (2011). Knife crime statistics. Standard Note: SN/SG/4304 for Members of Parliament. *Social and General Statistics*, 2 February 2011.

Berndt, T. (2002). Friendship quality and social development. *Current Directions in Psychological Science*, 11(1), 7–10.

Bernier, A., Carlson, S.M. and Whipple, N. (2010). From external regulation to self-regulation: Early parenting precursors of young children's executive functioning. *Child Development*, 81(1), 326–39.

Berry, J.W. (2007). Acculturation. In J.E. Grusec and P.D. Hastings (eds). *Handbook of Socialisation*. New York: Guilford.

Besag, V.E. (2006). *Understanding Girls' Friendships, Fights and Feuds: A Practical Approach to Girls' Bullying*. Maidenhead: Open University Press.

Besel, L.D.S. and Yuille, J.C. (2010). Individual differences in empathy: the role of facial expression in recognition. *Personality and Individual Differences*, 49(2), 107–12.

Best, D.L., Williams, J.E., Cloud, J.M., Davis, S.W., Robertson, L.S., Edwards, J.R., Giles, H. and Fowles, J. (1977). Development of sex-trait stereotypes among young children in the United States, England and Ireland. *Child Development*, 48, 1375–84.

Best, J.W. and Kahn, J.V. (2006). *Research in Education* (10th Edn). Boston: Allyn and Bacon.

Bettelheim, B. (1973). Bringing up children. *Ladies Home Journal*, 90, 28.

Betts, J., Gullone, E. and Allen, J.S. (2009). An examination of emotion regulation, temperament and parenting as potential predictors of adolescent depression risk status. *British Journal of Developmental Psychology*, 27, 473–85.

Biben, M. (1998). Squirrel monkey playfighting: making the case for cognitive training function for play. In M. Bekoff and J.A. Byers (eds). *Animal Play: Evolutionary, Comparative and Ecological Perspectives* (pp. 221–42). Cambridge: Cambridge University Press.

Bibou-Nakou, I., Tsiantis, J., Assimopoulos, H. and Chatzilambou, P. (2012). Bullying/victimisation from a family perspective: a qualitative study of secondary school student views. *European Journal of Psychology of Education*, 28, 53–71.

Bierman, K.L. (2004). *Peer Rejection: Developmental Processes and Intervention Strategies*. New York, NY: Guilford.

Bishop, J. and Inderbitzen-Nolan, H.M. (1995). Peer acceptance and friendship: an investigation of their relation to self-esteem. *Journal of Early Adolescence*, 15, 476–89.

Bitter, G.G. and Legacy, J.M. (2006). *Using Technology in the Classroom* (Brief version). Boston: Allyn and Bacon.

Björkqvist, K., Lagerspetz, K.M.J. and Kaukiainen, A. (1992). Do girls manipulate and boys fight? Developmental trends regarding direct and indirect aggression. *Aggressive Behavior*, 18, 117–27.

Black, B. and Hazen, N. (1990). Social status and patterns of communication in acquainted and unacquainted preschool children. *Developmental Psychology*, 26, 379–87.

Blair, C. and Razza, R.P. (2007). Relating effortful control, executive function, and false belief understanding to emerging math and literacy ability in kindergarten. *Child Development*, 78(2), 647–63.

Blair, R.J.R. (1997). Moral reasoning and the child with psychopathic tendencies. *Personality and Individual Differences*, 22, 731–9.

Blair, R.J.R., Monson, J. and Frederickson, N. (2001). Moral reasoning and conduct problems in children with emotional and behavioural difficulties. *Personality and Individual Differences*, 31, 799–811.

Blakemore, S-J. and Choudhury, S. (2006). Development of the adolescent brain: implications for executive function and social cognition. *Journal of Child Psychology and Psychiatry*, 47(3), 296–312.

Blakemore, S-J. and Frith, C. (2003). Self-awareness and action. *Current Opinion Neurobiology*, 13(2), 219–24.

Bloom, L. (1998). Language acquisition in its developmental context. In W. Damon, R.S. Siegler and D. Kuhn (eds). *Handbook of Child Psychology: Vol. 2, Cognition, Perception, and Language* (5th Edn, pp. 309–70). New York: Wiley.

Bloom, L. and Tinker, E. (2001). The intentionality model and language acquisition. *Monographs of the Society for Research in Child Development*, 66 (4, Serial No. 267).

Bloomfield, K.A., Robinson, E.J. and Robinson, W.P. (2002). Children's understanding about white lies. *British Journal of Developmental Psychology*, 20, 47–65.

Blumer, T. and Doering, N. (2012). Are we the same online? The expression of the five factor personality traits on the computer and the Internet. *Cyberpsychology: Journal of Psychosocial Research on Cyberspace*, 6(3), article 1.

Blumer, T. and Renneberg, B. (2010). Easy living in a virtual world? Borderline-specific cognitions and Internet usage. *Zeitschrift fur Psychiatrie, Psychologie und Psychotherapie*, 58, 55–62.

Blurton-Jones, N. (1972). *Ethological Studies of Child Behaviour*. Cambridge, UK: Cambridge University Press.

Boivin, M., Brendgen, M., Vitaro, F., Dionne, G., Girard, A., Pérusse, D. and Tremblay, R.E. (2013a). Strong genetic contribution to peer relationship difficulties at school entry: findings from a longitudinal twin study. *Child Development*, 84(3), 1098–114.

Boivin, M., Brendgen, M., Vitaro, F., Forget-Dubois, N., Feng, B., Tremblay, R.E. and Dionne, G. (2013b). Evidence of gene-environment correlation for peer difficulties: disruptive behaviors predict early peer relation difficulties in school through genetic effects. *Development and Psychopathology*, 25(1), 79–92.

Bornstein, M.H. (2002). *Handbook of Parenting: Practical Issues in Parenting* (2nd Ed., Vol. 5). Mahwah, NJ: Lawrence Erlbaum Associates, Inc.

Bornstein, M.H. (2007). On the significance of social relationships in the development of children's earliest symbolic play: an ecological perspective. In A. Göncü and S. Gaskins (eds). *Play and Development: Evolutionary, Sociocultural and Functional Perspectives*. New York: Lawrence Erlbaum Associates.

Bornstein, M.H., Cote, L.R., Haynes, O.M., Suwalsky, J.T. and Bakeman, R. (2012). Modalities of infant–mother interaction in Japanese, Japanese American immigrant, and European American dyads. *Child Development*, 83(6), 2073–88.

Bornstein, R.A. (1990). Neuropsychological performance in children with Tourette's syndrome. *Psychiatry Research*, 33, 73–81.

Boucher, J. (1999). Pretend play as improvisation: conversation in the preschool classroom. *British Journal of Developmental Psychology*, 17, 164–5.

Boulton, M.J. (2013). The effects of victim of bullying reputation on adolescents' choice of friends: mediation by fear of becoming a victim of bullying, moderation by victim status, and implications for befriending interventions. *Journal of Experimental Child Psychology*, 114, 146–60.

Bowes, L., Arsenault, L., Maughan, B., Taylor, A., Caspi, A. and Moffitt, T.E. (2009). School, neighbourhood, and family factors are associated with children's bullying involvement: a nationally representative longitudinal study. *Journal of the American Academy of Child and Adolescent Psychiatry*, 48, 545–53.

Bowes, L., Maughan, B., Caspi, A., Moffitt, T.E. and Arseneault, L. (2010). Families promote educational and behavioural resilience to bullying: evidence of an environmental effect. *Journal of Child Psychology and Psychiatry*, 51, 809–17.

Bowker, J.C.W., Rubin, K.H., Burgess, K.H., Booth-LaForce, C. and Rose-Klasnor, I. (2006). Behavioral characteristics associated with stable and fluid best friendship patterns in childhood. *Merrill-Palmer Quarterly*, 52, 671–93.

Bowlby, J. (1944). Forty-four juvenile thieves. *International Journal of Psychoanalysis*, 25, 1–57.

Bowlby, J. (1958). The nature of the child's tie to his mother. *International Journal of Psychoanalysis*, 39, 350–73.

Bowlby, J. (1969). *Attachment and Loss: Attachment* (Vol. 1). New York: Basic Books.

Bowlby, J. (1982). Attachment and loss: retrospect and prospect. *The American Journal of Orthopsychiatry*, 52(4), 664–78.

Bowlby, J. (1988). *A Secure Base: Parent–Child Attachment and Healthy Human Development*. New York: Basic Books.

Bowlby, J. (1989). *Secure and Insecure Attachment*. New York: Basic Books.

Boyd, D. (2014). *It's Complicated: The Social Lives of Networked Teens*. New Haven and London: Yale University Press.

Boyum, L. and Parke, R.D. (1995). Family emotional expressiveness and children's social competence. *Journal of Marriage and the Family*, 57, 593–608.

Bradley, L.A., Johnson, D.A., Chaparro, C.A., Robertson, N.H. and Ferrie, R.M. (1998). A Multiplex ARMS Test for 10 Cystic Fibrosis (CF) mutations: evaluation in a prenatal CF screening program. *Genetic Testing*, 2(4), 337–41.

Bradley, R.H. (1993). Children's home environments, health, behavior, and intervention efforts: a review using the HOME inventory as a marker measure. *Genetic, Social and General Psychology Monographs*, 119, 437–90.

Brennan, K.A., Shaver, P.R. and Tobey, A.E. (1991). Attachment styles, gender, and parental problem drinking. *Journal of Social and Personal Relationships*, 8, 451–66.

Bretherton, I. (1985). Attachment theory: retrospect and prospect. In I. Bretherton and E. Waters (eds). *Growing Points of Attachment Theory and Research* (Vol. 50, pp. 3–35). Chicago: Monographs of the Society for Research in Child Development, Nos. 1–2, Serial No. 209.

Bretherton, I. (2005). In pursuit of the working model construct and its relevance to attachment relationships. In K.E. Grossmann, K. Grossmann and E. Waters (eds). *Attachment from Infancy to Adulthood* (pp. 13–47). NY: Guilford Press.

Bretherton, I. and Munholland, K.A. (1999). Internal models in attachment relationships: a construct revisited. In J. Cassidy and P. Shaver (eds). *Handbook of Attachment* (pp. 89–114). NY: Guilford Press.

Bronfenbrenner, U. (1977). Toward an experimental ecology of human development. *American Psychologist*, 32(7), 513–31.

Bronfenbrenner, U. (1979). *The Ecology of Human Development*. Cambridge, MA: Harvard University Press.

Bronfenbrenner, U. (2005). *Making Human Beings Human*. Thousand Oaks, CA: Sage Publications.

Bronfenbrenner, U. and Morris, P.A. (2006). The ecology of developmental processes. In

W. Damon and R. Lerner (eds). *Handbook of Child Psychology* (6th Edn). New York: Wiley.

Brown, B.B. (2011). Popularity in peer group perspective: the role of status in adolescent peer systems. In A.H.N. Cillessen, D. Schwartz and L. Mayeux (eds). *Popularity in the Peer System* (pp. 165–92). New York: Guilford Press.

Browne, K. (2013). Working at the cutting edge. *The Psychologist*, 26(6), 424–6.

Brownell, C. and Carriger, M. (1990). Changes in cooperation and self-other differentiation during the second year. *Child Development*, 61, 1164–74.

Bruner, J.S. (1957). *Going Beyond the Information Given.* New York: Norton.

Bruner, J.S. (1960). *The Process of Education.* Cambridge, MA: Harvard University Press.

Bruner, J.S. (1961). The act of discovery. *Harvard Educational Review*, 31, 21–32.

Bruner, J.S. (1966). *Toward a Theory of Instruction.* Cambridge, MA: Belkapp Press.

Bruner, J.S. (1972). Nature and uses of immaturity. *American Psychologist*, 27(8), 687–708.

Bruner, J.S. (1973). *The Relevance of Education.* New York: Norton.

Bruner, J.S. (1978). The role of dialogue in language acquisition. In A. Sinclair, R.J. Jarvelle, and W.J.M. Levelt (eds). *The Child's Concept of Language.* New York: Springer-Verlag.

Bruner, J.S. (1983). *Children's Talk.* NY: Norton.

Bruner, J.S., Cole, M. and Lloyd, B. (1977). *The Developing Child.* London: Fontana/ Open Books.

Brunner, H.G., Nelen, M., Breakefield, X.O., Ropers, H.H. and van Oost, B.A. (1993). Abnormal behaviour associated with a point mutation in the structural gene for monoamine oxidase A. *Science*, 262(5133), 578–80.

Bryk, A.S. and Schneider, B. (2002). *Trust in Schools: A Core Resource for Improvement.* New York: Russell Sage Foundation.

Buhrmester, D. (2001). *Romantic Development: Does Age at Which Romantic Involvements Start Matter?* Paper presented at the meeting of the Society for Research in Child Development, Minneapolis.

Buhrmester, D., Furman, W., Wittenberg, M.T. and Reis, H.T. (1988). Five domains of interpersonal competence in peer relationships. *Journal of Personality and Social Psychology*, 55(6), 991–1008.

Bukatko, D. and Daehler, M.W. (2004). *Child Development: A Thematic Approach* (5th Edn). Boston: Houghton Mifflin.

Bukowski, W.M., Brendgen, M. and Vitaro, F. (2007). Peers and socialisation: effects on externalising and internalising problems. In J. Grusec and P.D. Hastings (eds). *Handbook of Socialisation: Theory and Research* (pp. 355–81). New York: Guilford Press.

Bull, R., Espy, K.A. and Wiebe, S.A. (2008). Short-term memory, working memory, and executive functioning in preschoolers: longitudinal predictors of mathematical achievement at age 7 years. *Developmental Neuropsychology*, 33, 205–28.

Bullock, M. and Lutkenhaus, P. (1990). Who am I? Self-understanding in toddlers. *Merrill-Palmer Quarterly*, 36, 217–38.

Burchinal, M.R. and Cryer, D. (2003). Diversity, child care quality, and developmental outcomes. *Early Childhood Research Quarterly*, 18, 401–26.

Burger, P.H., Goecke, T.W., Fasching, P.A., Moll, G., Heinrich, H., Beckmann, M.W. and Kornhuber, J. (2011). How does maternal alcohol consumption during pregnancy affect the development of attention deficit/ hyperactivity syndrome in the child. *Fortschritte Neurologie-Psychiatrie*, 79(9), 500–6.

Burt, S.A. (2009). Rethinking environmental contributions to child and adolescent psychopathology: a meta-analysis of shared environmental influences. *Psychology Bulletin*, 135 (4), 608–37.

Burton, R.V. (1963). Generality of honesty reconsidered. *Psychological Review*, 70(6), 481–99.

Bushman B.J. and Anderson C.A. (2001). Is it time to pull the plug on the hostile versus instrumental aggression dichotomy? *Psychological Review*, 108, 273–9.

Bushman B.J. and Anderson C.A. (2009). Comfortably numb: desensitizing effects of violent media on helping others. *Psychological Sciences*, 20(3), 273–7.

Bushnell, I.W.R., Sai, F. and Mullin, J.T. (1989). Neonatal recognition of the mother's face. *British Journal of Developmental Psychology*, 7, 3–15.

Buss, D.M. and Hawley, P. (2011). *The Evolution of Personality and Individual.* Oxford: Oxford University Press.

Bussey, K. (1992). Lying and truthfulness: children's definitions, standards and evaluative reactions. *Child Development*, 63(1), 129–37.

Bussey, K. and Bandura, A. (1999). Social cognitive theory of gender development and differentiation. *Psychological Review*, 106, 676–713.

Byrne, R. and Whiten, A. (1991). Computation and mindreading in primate tactical deception. In Whiten (ed.). *Natural Theories of Mind: Evolution, Development and Simulation of Everyday Mindreading* (pp. 127–41). Cambridge: Basil Blackwell.

Byrne, R. and Workman, L. (2014). Out of Africa. *The Psychologist*, 26, 2–4.

Byrnes, J.P., Miller, D.C. and Schafer, W.D. (1999). Gender differences in risk taking. *Psychological Bulletin*, 125(33), 367–83.

Callaghan, T., Rochat, P., Lillard, A., Claux, M.L., Odden, H., Itakura, S. et al. (2005). Synchrony in the onset of mental-state reasoning: evidence from five cultures. *Psychological Science*, 16, 378–84.

Calvert, S.L., Rideout, V., Woolard, J., Barr, R. and Strouse, G. (2005). Age, ethnicity, and socioeconomic patterns in early computer use: a national survey. *American Behavioral Scientist*, 48, 590–607.

Calvete, E., Orue, I., Estévez, A., Villardón, L. and Padilla, P. (2010). Cyberbullying in adolescents: modalities and aggressors' profile. *Computers in Human Behavior*, 26, 1128–35.

CAMH (2001). *Ontario Student Drug Use Survey 2001*. World Health Organization Collaborating Centre: University of Toronto.

Campbell, A. (in press). Survival, selection, and sex differences in fear. In L. Workman, W. Reader and J. Barkow (eds). *Cambridge Handbook of Evolutionary Perspectives on Human Behavior*. Cambridge, UK: Cambridge University Press.

Campos, J.J. (2005). Prelude to a theme on emotion and gratitude. *Journal of Personality*, 74(1), 3–8.

Campos, J.J., Hiatt, D., Ramsay, D., Henderson, C. and Svejda, M. (1978). The emergence of fear on the visual cliff. In M. Lewis and L. Rosenblum (eds) *The Development of Affect* (pp. 149–82). New York: Plenum.

Camras, L.A. (1992). Expressive development and basic emotions. *Cognition and Emotion*, 6, 269–84.

Camras, L., Malatesta, C. and Izard, C. (1991). The development of facial expressions in infancy. In R. Feldman and B. Rime (eds). *Fundamentals of Nonverbal Behaviour* (pp. 73–105). New York: Cambridge University Press.

Caprara, G., Barbanelli, C., Pastorelli, C., Bandura, A. and Zimbardo, P. (2000). Prosocial foundations of children's academic achievement. *Psychological Science*, 11, 302–6.

Caravita, S.C.S., Di Blasio, P. and Salmivalli, C. (2009). Unique and interactive effects of empathy and social status on involvement in bullying. *Social Development*, 18, 140–63.

Carman, A. (2015). Filtered extremism: how ISIS supporters use Instagram. *The Verge*, www.theverge.com/2015/12/9/9879308/isis-instagram-islamic-state-social-media.

Carnagey, N.L., Anderson, C.A. and Bushman, B.J. (2007). The effect of video game violence on physiological desensitization to real-life violence. *Journal of Experimental Social Psychology*, 43, 489–96.

Carney, A.G. and Merrell, K.W. (2001). Bullying in schools: perspectives on understanding and preventing an international problem. *School Psychology International*, 22(3), 364–82.

Carpendale, J.L. and Chandler, M.J. (1996). On the distinction between false belief understanding and subscribing to an interpretive theory of mind. *Child Development*, 67, 1686–706.

Carpendale, J.I.M. and Lewis, C. (2004). Constructing an understanding of mind: the development of children's social understanding within social interaction. *Behavioral and Brain Sciences*, 27, 79–151.

Carpenter, J., Nagell, K. and Tomasello, M. (1998). Social cognition, joint attention, and communicative competence from 9 to 15 months of age. *Monographs of the Society for Research in Child Development*, 70 (1, Serial No. 279).

Carter, R., Aldridge, S., Page, M. and Parker, S. (2014). *The Human Brain Book*. London: DK Publishing.

Carver, C.S. and White, T. (1994). Behavioral inhibition, behavioural activation, and affective responses to impending reward and punishment: the BIS/BAS scales. *Journal of Personality and Social Psychology*, 67, 319–33.

Carver, K., Joyner, K. and Udry, J.R. (2003). National estimates of adolescent romantic relationships. In P. Florsheim (ed.). *Adolescent Romantic Relations and Sexual Behavior: Theory, Research, and Practical Implications* (pp. 23–56). Mahwah, NJ: Erlbaum.

Carruthers, E. and Worthington, M. (2006). *Children's Mathematics*. London: Sage.

Case, R. (1998). The development of conceptual structures. In W. Damon, D. Kuhn and R.S. Siegler (eds). *Handbook of Child Psychology: Vol. 2, Cognition, Perception, and Language* (5th Edn, pp.745–800). New York: Wiley.

Case, R., Hayward, S., Lewis, M. and Hurst, P. (1988). Toward a neo-Piagetian theory of cognitive and emotional development. *Developmental Review*, 8, 1–51.

Case, R., Kurland, D.M. and Goldberg, J. (1982). Operational efficiency and the growth of short-term memory span. *Journal of Experimental Child Psychology*, 33, 386–404.

Casler, K. and Kelemen, D. (2005). Young children's rapid learning about artifacts. *Developmental Science*, 8(6), 472–80.

Caspi, A. and Moffitt, T. (2006). Gene–environment interactions in psychiatry: joining forces with neuroscience. *Nature Reviews Neuroscience*, 7, 583–90.

Cassen, R. and Kingdon, G. (2007). *Tackling Low Educational Achievement*. York, UK: Joseph Rowntree Foundation.

Chakraborti, N., Garland, J. and Hardy, S-J. (2014). *The Leicester Hate Crime Project*. Leicester: University of Leicester, www2. le.ac.uk/departments/criminology/hate/documents/fc-full-report.

Chamorro-Premuzic, T. (2015). *Personality and Individual Differences* (3rd Edn). Chichester, UK: British Psychological Society and John Wiley and Sons.

Chandler, D.J., Waterhouse, B.D. and Gao, W.J. (2014). New perspectives on catecholaminergic regulation of executive circuits: evidence for independent modulation of prefrontal functions by midbrain dopaminergic and noradrenergic neurons. *Frontal, Neural Circuits*, 8, 53.

Chandler, M.J., Greenspan, S. and Barenboim, C. (1973). Judgements of intentionality in response to videotaped and verbally presented moral dilemmas: the medium is the message. *Child Development*, 44(2), 315–20.

Chandler, M.J. and Sokol, B.W. (1999). Representation once removed: children's developing conceptions of representational life. In I. Sigel (ed.). *Development of Mental Representation: Theories and Applications* (pp. 201–30). Mahwah, NJ: Erlbaum.

Chapman, R.S. and Hesketh, L.J. (2000). Behavioural phenotype of individuals with Down syndrome. *Mental Retardation and Developmental Disability Research Reviews*, 6, 84–95.

Charman, T., Swettenham, J., Baron-Cohen, S., Cox, A., Baird, G. and Drew, A. (1997). Infants with autism: an investigation of empathy, pretend play, joint attention, and imitation. *Developmental Psychology*, 33(5), 781–9.

Chasdi, E.H. (1994). *Culture and Human Development: The Selected Papers of John Whiting*. New York: Cambridge University Press.

Chen, C. and Stevenson, H.W. (1989). Homework: a cross-cultural examination. *Child Development*, 60, 551–61.

Chen, M.J. and Grube, J.W. (2001). *TV Beer and Soft Drink Advertising: What Young People Like and What Effects*. Paper presented at the annual meeting of the Research Society on Alcoholism: Montreal, Quebec, Canada.

Chen, X., Rubin, K.H. and Sun, Y. (1992). Social reputation and peer relationships in Chinese and Canadian children: a cross-cultural study. *Child Development*, 63, 1336–43.

Chen, X., Cen, G., Li, D. and He, Y. (2005). Social functioning and adjustment in Chinese children: the imprint of historical time. *Child Development,* 76, 182–95.

Cherry, K. (2017). How psychologists tested babies' depth perception, www.verywell.com/what-is-a-visual-cliff-2796010.

Chi, M.T.H. (1978). Knowledge structures and memory development. In R.S. Siegler (ed.). *Children's Thinking: What Develops?* (pp. 73–96). Hillsdale, NJ: Erlbaum.

Chisholm, J.S. (1980). Development and adaptation in infancy. *New Directions for Child Development,* 8, 15–30.

Chisholm, J.S. (1999). Steps to an evolutionary ecology of the mind. In A.L. Hinton (ed.). *Biocultural Approaches to the Emotions* (pp. 117–49). Cambridge, UK: Cambridge University Press.

Chobhthaigh, S.N. and Wilson, C. (2015). Children's understanding of embarrassment: integrating mental time travel and mental state information. *British Journal of Developmental Psychology*, 33, 324–39.

Choi, J. and Silverman, I. (2003). Processes underlying sex differences in route-learning strategies in children and adolescents. *Personality and Individual Differences*, 34, 1153–66.

Chomsky, N. (1957). *Syntactic Structures*. The Hague: Mouton.

Christie, J.F. and Roskos, K.A. (2006). Standards, science, and the role of play in early literacy education. In D.G. Singer, R.M. Golinkoff and K. Hirsh-Pasek (eds). *Play = Learning*. Oxford: Oxford University Press.

Cicchetti, D. and Sroufe, L. (1976). The relationship between affective and cognitive development in Down's syndrome infants. *Child Development*, 47, 920–9.

Cicchetti, D. and Toth, S.L. (2006). Developmental psychopathology and preventive intervention. In W. Damon, R.M. Lerner, K.A. Renninger and I.E. Sigel (eds). *Handbook of Child Psychiatry: Vol. 4. Child Psychology and Practice* (6th Edn, pp. 497–547). New York: Wiley.

Cillessen, A.H. and Mayeux, L. (2004). From censure to reinforcement: developmental changes in the association between aggression and social status. *Child Development*, 75, 147–63.

Cillessen, A.H.N. and Rose, A.J. (2005). Understanding popularity in the peer system. *Current Directions in Psychological Science*, 14, 102–5.

Civil Partnership Act of 2004, www.legislation.gov.uk/ukpga/2004/33/contents.

Clarke-Stewart, K.A. and Hevey, C.M. (1981). Longitudinal relations in repeated observations of mother–child interaction from 1 to 2 1/2 years. *Developmental Psychology*, 17, 127–45.

Closson, L.M. (2009). Aggressive and prosocial behaviours within early adolescent friendship cliques: what's status got to do with it? *Merrill-Palmer Quarterly*, 55(4), 406–35.

Code of Ethics and Conduct: Guidance (2009). Published by the Ethics Committee of the British Psychological Society.

Cohen, D. and Strayer, J. (1996). Empathy in conduct-disordered and comparison youth. *Developmental Psychology*, 32, 988–98.

Cohen, P. and Flory, M. (1998). Issues in the disruptive behaviour disorders: attention deficit disorder without hyperactivity and the differential validity of oppositional defiant and conduct disorders. In T. Widiger (ed.). *DSM-lV Sourcebook* (Vol. 4, pp. 455–63). Washington, DC: American Psychiatric Press.

Coie, J.D. (2004). The impact of negative social experiences on the development of antisocial behaviour. In J.B. Kupersmidt and K.A. Dodge (eds). *Children's Peer Relations: From Development to Intervention*. Washington, DC: American Psychological Association.

Coie, J.D. and Dodge, K A. (1997). Aggression and antisocial behaviour. In W. Damon and N. Eisenberg (eds). *Handbook of Child Psychology (Vol.3): Social, Emotional and Personality Development* (pp. 779–862). New York: Wiley.

Colby, A. and Kohlberg, L. (1987). *The Measurement of Moral Judgment. Vol 1: Theoretical Foundations and Research Validation*. New York: Cambridge University Press.

Colby, A., Kohlberg, L., Gibbs, J.C. and Lieberman, M. (1983). A longitudinal study of moral judgment. *Monographs of the Society for Research in Child Development*, 48, 1–94.

Cole, K. and Mitchell, P. (2000). Siblings in development of executive control and a theory of mind. *British Journal of Developmental Psychology*, 18, 279–95.

Cole, M. (2006). Culture and cognitive development in phylogenetic, historical, and ontogenetic perspective. In W. Damon and R. Lerner (eds). *Handbook of Child Psychology* (6th Edn). New York: Wiley.

Cole, P.M., Bruschi, C.J. and Tamang, B.L. (2002). Cultural differences in children's emotional reactions to difficult situations. *Child Development*, 73(3), 983–96.

Cole, P.M., Martin, S.E. and Dennis, T.A. (2004). Emotional regulation as a scientific construct: methodological challenges and directions for child developmental research. *Child Development*, 75(2), 317–33.

Collins, W.A. and Van Dulmen, M. (2006). The course of true love(s): origins and pathways in the development of romantic relationships. In A.C. Crouter and A. Booth (eds). *Romance* and Sex in Adolescence and Emerging Adulthood: Risks and Opportunities (pp. 63–86). Mahwah, NJ: Erlbaum.

Colonnesi, C., Engelhard, I.M. and Bögels, S.M. (2010). Development in children's attribution of embarrassment and the relationship with theory of mind and shyness. Cognition and Emotion, 24, 514–21.

Colquitt, J.A., Hollenbeck, J.R., Ilgen, D.R., LePine, J.A. and Sheppard, L. (2002). Computer-assisted communication and team decision-making performance: the moderating effect of openness to experience. Journal of Applied Psychology, 87, 402–10.

Comstock, G. and Scharrer, E. (2006). Media and popular culture: child psychology in practice. In K.A. Renninger, I.E. Sigel, W. Damon and R.M. Lerner (eds). Handbook of Child Psychology: Vol. 4 – Child Psychology in Practice (6th Edn, pp. 817–63). Hoboken, NJ: John Wiley and Sons.

Conelea, C.A. and Woods, D.W. (2008). Examining the impact of distraction on tic suppression in children and adolescents with Tourette syndrome. Behaviour Research and Therapy, 46(11), 1193–1200.

Connolly, J., Craig, W., Goldberg, A. and Pepler, D. (2004). Mixed-gender groups, dating, and romantic relationships in early adolescence. Journal of Research on Adolescence, 14, 185–207.

Connor, D.F. (2002). Aggression and Antisocial Behavior in Children and Adolescents: Research and Treatment. New York: The Guilford Press.

Consumers Union. Selling America's Kids: Commercial Pressures on Kids of the 90's, www.consumersunion.org/other/sellingkids/index.htm.

Cook, C.R., Williams, K.R., Guerra, N.G., Kim, T.E. and Sadek, S. (2010). Predictors of bullying and victimization in childhood and adolescence: a meta-analytic investigation. School Psychology Quarterly, 25, 65–83.

Cook, T.D., Murphy, R.F. and Hunt, H.D. (2000). Comer's school development program in Chicago: a theory-based evaluation. American Educational Research Journal, 37(2), 535–97.

Cooper, H.M., Lindsay, J.J., Nye, B.A. and Greathouse, S. (1998). Relationships among attitudes about homework assigned and completed and student achievement. Journal of Educational Psychology, 90, 70–83.

Cooper, M.L., Shaver, P.R. and Collins, N.L. (1998). Attachment styles, emotional regulation, and adjustment in adolescence. Journal of Personality and Social Psychology, 74, 1380–97.

Cornell, D.G. (1996). Coding Guide for Violent Incidents: Instrumental versus Hostile/Reactive Aggression. Virginia: University of Virginia.

Cornew, L., Dobkins, K.R., Akshoomoff, N., McCleery, J.P. and Carver, L.J. (2012). Atypical social referencing in infant siblings of children with autism spectrum disorders. Journal of Autism Developmental Disorders, 42(12), 2611–21.

Correa, T., Hinsley, A.W. and de Zuñiga, H.G. (2010). Who interacts on the web? The intersection of users' personality and social media use. Computers in Human Behavior, 26, 247–53.

Corsaro, W.A. (1981). Friendship in the nursery school: social organisation in a peer environment. In S.R. Asher and J.M. Gottman (eds). The Development of Children's Friendships (pp. 207–41). New York: Cambridge University Press.

Costa, P.T., Terracciano, A. and McCrae, R.R. (2001). Gender differences in personality traits across cultures: robust and surprising findings. Journal of Personality and Social Psychology, 81(2), 322–31.

Cote, S.M., Boivin, M., Nagin, D.S., Japel, C., Xu, Q., Zoccolillo, M. et al. (2007). The role of maternal education and nonmaternal care services in the prevention of children's physical aggression problems. Archives of General Psychiatry, 64, 1305–12.

Cote, S.M., Borge, A.I., Geoffroy, M., Rutter, M. and Tremblay, R.E. (2008). Nonmaternal care in infancy and emotional/behavioural difficulties at 4 years old: moderation by family risk characteristics. Developmental Psychology, 44, 155–68.

Courage, M.L., Edison, S.C., Howe, M.L and Howe, M. (2004). Variability in the early development of visual self-recognition. Infant Behavior and Development, 27(4), 509–32.

Cowie, H. and Myers, C.A. (2015). Bullying Among University Students: Cross-national Perspectives. New York: Routledge.

Crain, S. and Nakayama M. (1986). Structure dependence in children's language. *Language*, 62, 522–43.

Crane, D.A. and Tisak, M.S. (1995). Mixed-domain events: the influence of moral and conventional components on the development of social reasoning. *Early Education and Development*, 6, 169–80.

Crick, N. and Dodge, K.A. (1994). A review and reformulation of social information processing in children's social adjustment. *Psychological Bulletin*, 115, 74–101.

Crick, N.R. and Dodge, K.A. (1996). Social information-processing mechanisms in reactive and proactive aggression. *Child Development*, 67, 993–1002.

Crick, N.R. and Grotpeter, J.K. (1995). Relational aggression, gender, and social-psychological adjustment. *Child Development*, 66, 710–22.

Crick, N.R. and Rose, A.J. (2000). Toward a gender-balanced approach to the study of social-emotional development: a look at relational aggression. In M. Cole, S.R. Cole and C. Lightfoot (eds). *The Development of Children* (p. 554). New York: Worth Publishers.

Crowell, J.A. and Feldman, S.S. (1991). Mothers' working models of attachment relationships and mother and child behaviour during separation and reunion. *Developmental Psychology*, 27, 597–605.

Crowell, J.A., Treboux, D., Gao, Y., Fyffe, C., Pan, H. and Waters, E. (2002). Assessing secure base behaviour in adulthood: development of a measure, links to adult attachment representations and relations to couples' communication and reports of relationships. *Developmental Psychology*, 38, 679–93.

Crowley, J.A., Callahan, M.A., Tennenbaum, H.R. and Allen, E. (2001). Parents explain more often to boys than to girls during shared scientific thinking. *Psychological Science*, 12, 258–61.

Cummings, E.M. and Davies, P.T. (2002). Effects of marital conflict on children: recent advances and emerging themes in process-oriented research. *Journal of Child Psychology and Psychiatry*, 43, 31–63.

Cummings, E.M., Davies, P. and Campbell, S. (2000). *Developmental Psychopathology and Family Process*. New York: Guilford Press.

Cushman, F., Sheketoff, R., Wharton, S. and Carey, S. (2013). The development of intent-based moral judgment. *Cognition*, 127, 6–21.

Cushman, F., Young, L. and Hauser, M. (2006). The role of conscious reasoning and intuition in moral judgment: testing three principles of harm. *Psychological Science*, 17, 1082–9.

Cusumano, D.L. and Thompson, J.K. (1997). Body image and body shape ideals in magazines: exposure, awareness, and internalisation. *Sex Roles*, 37(9–10), 701–21.

Cutting, A. and Dunn, J. (1999). Theory of mind, emotion understanding, language, and family background: individual differences and interrelations. *Child Development*, 70, 853–65.

Damon, W. and Hart, D. (1988). *Self-Understanding in Childhood and Adolescence*. New York: Cambridge University Press.

Darvill, D. and Cheyne, J.A. (1981). *Sequential Analysis of Response to Aggression: Age and Sex Effects*. Paper presented at the biennial meeting of the Society for Research in Child Development, Boston.

Darwin, C. (1859). *On the Origin of the Species*. London: John Murray.

Darwin, C. (1871). *The Descent of Man, and Selection in Relation to Sex*. London: John Murray.

Darwin, C. (1872). *The Expression of the Emotions in Man and Animals*. London: John Murray.

Darwish, A.E. and Huber, G.L. (2003). Individualism vs collectivism in different cultures: a cross-cultural study. *Intercultural Education*, 14, 47–56.

Davidson, D. (1967). Truth and Meaning. *Synthese*, 17(3), 304–23.

Davidson, P., Turiel, E. and Black, A. (1983). The effect of stimulus familiarity on the use of criteria and justifications in children's social reasoning. *British Journal of Developmental Psychology*, 1(1), 49–65.

Davies, P.T. and Windle, M. (2000). Middle adolescents' dating pathways and psychosocial adjustment. *Merrill-Palmer Quarterly*, 46, 90–118.

Davis, M.H. (1994). *Empathy*. Madison, WI: Brown and Benchmark.

Davis, M.H. (1996). *Empathy: A Social Psychological Approach*. Boulder, CO: Westview Press.

Davis, M.H., Luce, C. and Kraus, S.J. (1994). The heritability of characteristics associated with dispositional empathy. *Journal of Personality*, 62(3), 369–91.

Davis, M.H. and Stone, T. (2003). Synthesis: psychological understanding and social skills. In B. Repacholi and V. Slaugher (eds). *Individual Differences in Theory of Mind: Implications for Typical and Atypical Development* (pp. 306–52). New York: Psychology Press.

Dawkins, R. (1989). *The Selfish Gene*. New York: Oxford University Press.

Deater-Deckard, K., Pike, A., Petrill, S.A., Cutting, A.L., Hughes, C. and O'Connor, T.G. (2001). Nonshared environmental processes in social–emotional development: an observational study of identical twin differences in the preschool period. *Developmental Science*, 4, F1–F6.

Decety, J. and Chaminade, T. (2003). Neural correlates of feeling sympathy. *Neuropsychologia*, 41, 127–38.

Decety, J. and Ingvar, D.H. (1990). Brain structures participating in mental simulation of motor behaviour: a neuropsychological interpretation. *Acta Psychologica*, 73(1), 13–34.

Decety, J. and Jackson, P.L. (2004). The functional architecture of human empathy. *Behavioural and Cognitive Neuroscience Reviews*, 3, 71–100.

de Haan, M. (2001). The neuropsychology of face processing during infancy and childhood. In C. A. Nelson and M. Luciana (eds). *Handbook of Developmental Cognitive Neuroscience* (pp. 381–98). Cambridge, MA: MIT Press.

de Haan, M., Humphreys, K. and Johnson, M.H. (2002). Developing a brain specialised for face perception: a converging methods approach. *Developmental Psychobiology*, 40, 200–12.

Deloache, J.S., Simcock, G. and Macari, S. (2007). Planes, trains, automobiles – and tea sets: extremely intense interests in very young children. *Developmental Psychology*, 43, 1579–86.

Demaray, M.K. and Malecki, C.K. (2002). The relationship between perceived social support and maladjustment for students at risk. *Psychology in the Schools*, 39(3), 305–16.

Demetriou, A. (1993). In quest of the functional architecture of the developing mind: the Aristotelian project. *Educational Psychology Review*, 5(3), 275–92.

Demetriou, A. and Kazi, S. (2013). *Unity and Modularity in the Mind and the Self: Studies on the Relationships Between Self-awareness, Personality, and Intellectual Development from Childhood to Adolescence*. London: Routledge, Taylor and Francis Group.

Demie, F. and Lewis, K. (2010a). White working achievement: an ethnographic study of barriers to learning in schools. *Educational Studies*, 37(3), 215–31.

Demie, F. and Lewis, K. (2010b). *Raising Achievement of White Working Class Pupils: Barriers to Learning*. London Borough of Lambeth: Research and Statistics Unit.

Demie, F. and Lewis, K. (2010c). *Raising Achievement of White Working Class Pupils: School Strategies*. London Borough of Lambeth: Research and Statistics Unit.

Demie, F. and Lewis, K. (2014). *Raising the Achievement of White Working Class Pupils: Barriers and School Strategies*. London: Lambeth Research and Statistics Unit; Education, Learning and Skills.

Denham, S.A. (1986). Social cognition, prosocial behaviour, and emotion in preschoolers: contextual validation. *Child Development*, 57, 194–201.

Denham, S.A. (1998). *Emotional Development in Young Children*. New York: Guilford Press.

Denham, S.A., Bassett, H. and Wyatt, T. (2007). The socialisation of emotional competence. In J. Grusec and P. Hastings (eds). *Handbook of Socialisation: Theory and Research* (pp. 614–37). New York: Guilford Press.

Dennett, D.C. (1996). Facing backwards on the problem of consciousness. *Journal of Consciousness Studies*, 3(1), 4–6.

Dennis, M., Agostino, A., Taylor, H.G., Bigler, E.D., Rubin, K., Vannatta, K., et al. (2013a). Emotional expression and socially modulated emotive communication in children with traumatic brain injury. *Journal of the International Neuropsychological Society*, 19(1), 34–43.

Dennis, M., Purvis, K., Barnes, M.A., Wilkinson, M. and Winner, E. (2001). Understanding of literal truth, ironic criticism, and deceptive praise after childhood head injury. *Brain and Language*, 78, 1–16.

Dennis, M., Simic, N., Bigler, E., Abildskov, T., Agostino, A., Taylor, H.G., Rubin, K., Vannatta, K., Gerhardt, C.A., Stancin, T. and Yeates, K.O. (2013b). Cognitive, affective, and conative theory of mind (ToM) in children with traumatic brain injury. *Developmental Cognitive Neuroscience*, 5, 25–39.

Dennis, M., Simic, N., Taylor, H.G., Bigler, E.D., Rubin, K.R., Vannatta, K., Gerhardt, C.A., Stancin, T., Roncadin, C. and Yeates, K.O. (2012). Theory of mind in children with traumatic brain injury. *Journal of the International Neuropsychological Society*, 18(5), 908–16.

Deocampo, J.A. and Hudson, J.A. (2005). When seeing is not believing: two-year-olds' use of video representations to find a hidden toy. *Journal of Cognition and Development*, 6, 229–58.

Depue, R.A. and Collins, P.F. (1999). Neurobiology of the structure of personality: dopamine, facilitation of incentive motivation, and extraversion. *Behavioral and Brain Sciences*, 22, 491–569.

DeRosier, M. and Kupersmidt, J.B. (1991). Costa Rican children's perceptions of their social networks. *Developmental Psychology*, 27, 656–62.

Deutsch, W. and Pechmann, T. (1982). Social interaction and the development of definite descriptions. *Cognition*, 11, 159–84.

DeVries, R. (2006). Games with rules. In D.P. Fromberg and D. Bergen (eds). *Play from Birth to Twelve* (2nd Edn.). Abingdon, UK: Routledge.

DeVries, R. and Zan, B.S. (2012). *Moral Classrooms, Moral Children: Creating a Constructivist Atmosphere in Early Childhood*. New York: Teachers' College Press.

Dewey, J. (1910). *How We Think*. London: D.C. Heath.

Dewey, J. (1916). *Democracy and Education* (p. 230). New York: Macmillan.

Diamond, A. (2013). Executive functions. *Annual Review of Psychology*, 64, 135–68.

Diamond, A., Barnett, W.S., Thomas, J. and Munro, S. (2007). Preschool program improves cognitive control. *Science*, 318, 1387–8.

Dickson, K.L., Fogel, A. and Messinger, D. (1998). The development of emotion from a social process view. In M.F. Mascolo and S. Griffin (eds). *What Develops in Emotional Development?* (pp. 253–71). New York: Plenum.

Diener, E. and Diener, M. (1995). Cross-cultural correlates of life satisfaction and self-esteem. *Journal of Personality and Social Psychology*, 68, 653–63.

Diener, E., Wolsic, B. and Fujita, F. (1995). Physical attractiveness and subjective well-being. *Journal of Personality and Social Psychology*, 69, 120–9.

Dijkstra, J.K., Cillessen, A.H.N. and Borch, C. (2012). Popularity and adolescent friendship networks: selection and influence dynamics. *Developmental Psychology*, 49(7), 1242–52.

Dijkstra, J.K., Lindenberg, S., Verhulst, F.C., Ormel, J. and Veenstra, R. (2009). The relation between popularity and aggressive, destructive, and norm-breaking behaviours: moderating effects of athletic abilities, physical attractiveness, and prosociality. *Journal of Research on Adolescence*, 19(3), 401–13.

Dingemanse, N.J., Both, C., Drent, P.J. and Tinbergen, J.M. (2004). Fitness consequences of avian personalities in a fluctuating environment. *Proceedings of the Royal Society of London, Series B: Biological Sciences*, 271(1541), 847–52.

Dion, K., Berscheid, E. and Walster, E. (1972). What is beautiful is good. *Journal of Personality and Social Psychology*, 24, 285–90.

Dishion, T.J., Nelson, S.E. and Yasui, M. (2005). Predicting early adolescent gang involvement from middle school adaptation. *Journal of Clinical Child and Adolescence Psychology*, 34(1), 62–73.

Dishion, T.J., Spracklen, K.M., Andrews, D.W. and Patterson, G.R. (1996). Deviancy training in male adolescent friendships. *Behavior Therapy*, 27, 373–90.

Ditch the Label (2016). *Bullying Statistics in the UK: The Annual Bullying Survey 2016*, www.ditchthelabel.org/annual-bullying-survey-2016/.

Dodd, H., Porter, M., Peters, G. and Rapee, R. (2010). Social approach in pre-school children with Williams syndrome: the role of the face. *Journal of Intellectual Disability Research*, 54(3), 194–203.

Dodge, K.A. (2006). Translational science in action: hostile attributional style and the development of aggressive behavior problems. *Development and Psychopathology*, 18, 791–814.

Dodge, K.A., Coie, J.D. and Lynam, D.R. (2006). Aggression and antisocial behavior in youth. In N. Eisenberg, D. William and R.M. Lerner (eds). *Handbook of Child Psychology: Vol. 3. Social, Emotional, and Personality Development* (6th Ed., pp. 719–88). Hoboken, NJ: Wiley.

Dodge, K.A. and Frame, C.L. (1982). Social cognitive biases and deficits in aggressive boys. *Child Development*, 53, 629–35.

Dodge, K.A., Pettit, G.S., McClaskey, C.L. and Brown, M.M. (1987). Social competence in children. *Monographs of the Society for Research in Child Development*, 51 (2, Serial No. 213).

Dodge, K.A. and Rutter, M. (2011). *Gene: Environment Interactions in Developmental Psychopathology*. New York: Guildford Press.

Dodge, K.A., Schlundt, D., Schocken, I. and Delugach, J. (1983). Social competence and children's sociometric status: the role of peer group entry strategies. *Merrill-Palmer Quarterly*, 29, 309–36.

Donnai, D. and Karmiloff-Smith, A. (2000). Williams syndrome: from genotype through to the cognitive phenotype. *American Journal of Medical Genetics*, 97, 164–71.

Donnerstein, E. (2002). The Internet. In B.J. Wilson and V.C. Strasburger (eds). *Children, Adolescents, and the Media*. Thousand Oaks, CA: Sage.

Dring, C. and Hope, A. (2001). *The Impact of Alcohol on Advertising on Teenagers in Ireland*. Galway: Health Promotion Unit, Department of Health and Children.

Driscoll, M.P. (1994). *Psychology of Learning for Instruction*. Needham Heights, MA: Allyn and Bacon.

Driscoll, M.P. (2000). *Psychology for Learning for Instruction* (2nd Edn). Needham Heights, MA: Allyn and Bacon.

Dubow, E.F., Huesmann, L. and Greenwood, D. (2007). Media and youth socialisation. In J.E. Grusec and P.D. Hastings (eds). *Handbook of Socialisation*. New York: Guilford.

Duchenne, B. (1862 [1990]). *Mechanisme de la physionomie humaine ou analyse electrophysiologique de l'expression des passions*. Paris: Bailliere: Duchenne, B. The mechanism of human facial expression or an electro-physiological analysis of the expression of the emotions (trans. A. Cuthbertson). New York: Cambridge University Press.

Dugdale, R.L. (1877). *The Jukes: A Study in Crime, Pauperism, and Heredity*. New York: Putnam.

Dunham, P. and Dunham, F. (1992). Lexical development during middle infancy: a mutually driven infant-caregiver process. *Developmental Psychology*, 28, 414–20.

Dunkel, C. and Kerpelman, J. (2004). *Possible Selves: Theory, Research, and Application*. Huntington, NY: Nova.

Dunn J. (1983). Sibling relationships in early childhood. *Child Development*, 54, 787–811.

Dunn, J. (1999). Siblings, friends, and the development of social understanding. *Relationships As Developmental Contexts*, 30, 263–79.

Dunn, J. (2004). *Children's Friendships: The Beginnings of Intimacy*. Oxford: Blackwell.

Dunn, J., Brown, J., Slomkowski, C., Tesla, C. and Youngblade, L. (1991). Young children's understanding of other people's feelings and beliefs: individual differences and their antecedents. *Child Development*, 62, 1352–66.

Dunn, J. and Hughes, C. (1998). Young children's understanding of emotions within close relationships. *Cognition and Emotion*, 12, 171–90.

Dunn, J. and Hughes, C. (2001). "I got some swords and you're dead!": violent fantasy, antisocial behaviour, friendship, and moral sensibility in young children. *Child Development*, 72(2), 491–505.

Dunn, J. and Kendrick, C. (1982). *Siblings: Love, Envy, and Understanding*. Cambridge, MA: Harvard University Press.

Dunn, J.F. and Plomin, R. (1990). *Separate Lives: Why Siblings Are So Different*. New York: Basic Books.

Dunn, J., Slomkowski, C., Beardsall, L. and Rende, R. (1994). Adjustment in middle childhood and early adolescence: links with earlier and contemporary sibling relationships. *Journal of Child Psychology and Psychiatry*, 35, 491–504.

Durlak, J.A., Weissberg, R.P., Dymnicki, A., Taylor, R. and Schellinger, K.B. (2011). The impact of enhancing students' social and emotional learning: a meta-analysis of school-based universal interventions. *Child Development*, 82(1), 405–32.

Durston, S., Davidson, M.C., Tottenham, N.T., Galvan, A., Spicer, J., Fossella, J.A. and Casey, B.J. (2006). A shift from diffuse to focal cortical activity with development. *Developmental Science*, 9(1), 1–8.

Dusek, J.B. and McIntyre, J.G. (2003). Self-concept and self-esteem development. In G. Adams and M. Berzonsky (eds). *Blackwell Handbook of Adolescence*. Malden, MA: Blackwell.

Dvash, J. and Shamay-Tsoory, S.G. (2014). Theory of mind and empathy as multidimensional constructs: neurological foundations. *Top Lang Disorders*, 34(4), 282–95.

Dwyer, S. (1999). Moral competence. In K. Murasugi and R. Strainton (eds). *Philosophy and Linguistics*, (pp. 169–90). Boulder, CO: Westview Press.

Dwyer, S. (2006). How good is the linguistic analogy? In P. Carruthers, S. Laurence and S. Stich (eds). *The Innate Mind*, (Vol. 2). New York: Oxford University Press.

Eagly, A.H. (1995). The science and politics of comparing women and men. *American Psychologist*, 50, 145–58.

Eagly, A.H. and Wood, W. (1999). The origins of sex differences in human behavior: evolved dispositions versus social roles. *American Psychologist*, 54, 408–23.

Eagly, A.H. and Wood, W. (2011). Feminism and the evolution of sex differences and similarities. *Sex Roles*, 64, 758–67.

Eagly, A.H. and Wood, W. (2012). Social role theory. In P. van Lange, A. Kruglanski and E. T. Higgins (eds). *Handbook of Theories in Social Psychology* (pp. 458–76) Thousand Oaks, CA: Sage Publications.

Eagly, A.H. and Wood, W. (2013). The nature–nurture debates: 25 years of challenges in understanding the psychology of gender. *Perspectives on Psychological Science*, 8, 340–57.

Eagly, A.H. and Workman, L. (2008) Men, women and leadership with Alice Eagly. *The Psychologist*, 21, 216–7.

Egley, A. Jr. (2002). *National Youth Gang Survey Trends from 1996 to 2000: Fact Sheet #2002–03*. Washington, DC: US Department of Justice, Office of Juvenile Justice and Delinquency Prevention.

East, P.L. (1991). The parent–child relationships of withdrawn, aggressive, and sociable children: child and parent perspectives. *Merrill-Palmer Quarterly*, 37, 425–43.

Eckerman, C.O. and Peterman, K. (2001). Peers and infant social /communicative development. In G. Bremner and A. Fogel (eds). *Blackwell Handbook of Infant Development* (pp. 326–350). Malden, MA: Blackwell Publishers.

Eder, D. (1985). The cycle of popularity: interpersonal relations among female adolescents. *Sociology of Education*, 58, 154–65.

Eder, D. (1987). *The Role of Teasing in Adolescent Peer Group Culture*. Paper presented at the Conference on Ethnographic Approaches to Children's Worlds and Peer Culture, Tronheim, Norway.

Eder, D. and Kinney, D.A. (1995). The effect of middle school extracurricular activities on adolescents' popularity and peer status. *Youth and Society*, 26, 298–324.

Eder, R.A. (1989). The emergent personologist: the structure and content of 3½-, 5½-, and 7 ½-year-olds' concepts of themselves and other persons. *Child Development*, 60, 1218–28.

Eder, R.A. (1990). Uncovering young children's psychological selves: individual and developmental differences. *Child Development*, 61(3), 849–63.

Edgeworth, M. and Edgeworth, R.L. (1798/1997). *Practical Education*. Brookfield, VT: Pickering and Chatto.

Eibl-Eibesfeldt, I. (1967). Concepts of ethology and their significance in the study of human behaviour. In W.W. Stevenson and H. Rheingold (eds). *Early Behaviour: Comparative and Developmental Approaches*. New York: Wiley.

Eisenberg, N. (1986). *Altruistic Emotion, Cognition, and Behavior*. Hillsdale, NJ: Erlbaum.

Eisenberg, N. (2000). Empathy and sympathy. In M. Lewis and J.M. Haviland-Jones (eds). *Handbook of Emotions* (2nd Edn, pp. 677–91). New York: Guilford Press.

Eisenberg, N., Cumberland, A., Spinrad, T.L., Fabes, R.A., Shepard, S.A., Reiser, M. et al. (2001). The relations of regulation and emotionality to children's externalizing and internalizing problem behaviour. *Child Development*, 2, 1112–34.

Eisenberg, N. and Fabes, R.A. (1998). Prosocial development. In N. Eisenberg (ed). *Handbook of Child Psychology* (5th Ed, Vol. 3). NY: Wiley.

Eisenberg, N., Fabes, R.A., Guthrie, I.K. and Reiser, M. (2002). The role of emotionality and regulation in children's social competence and adjustment. In L. Pulkkinen and A. Caspi (eds). *Paths to Successful Development: Personality in the Life Course* (pp. 46–70). New York: Cambridge University Press.

Eisenberg, N., Fabes, R.A., Nyman, M., Bernzweig, J. and Pinuelas, A. (1994). The relations of emotionality and regulation to children's anger-related reactions. *Child Development*, 65, 109–28.

Eisenberg, N., Fabes, R.A., Shepard, S.A., Murphy, B.C., Jones, J. and Guthrie, I.K. (1998). Contemporaneous and longitudinal prediction of children's sympathy from dispositional regulation and emotionality. *Developmental Psychology*, 34, 910–24.

Eisenberg, N., Fabes, R.A. and Spinrad, T.L. (2006). Prosocial behavior. In N. Eisenberg, W. Damon and R.M. Lerner (eds). *Handbook of Child Psychology: Vol. 3. Social, Emotional, and Personality Development* (6th Edn, pp. 646–718). New York: Wiley.

Eisenberg, N. and McNally, S. (1993). Socialisation and mothers' and adolescents' empathy-related characteristics. *Journal of Research on Adolescence*, 3, 171–91.

Ekman, P. (2003). *Emotions Revealed*. New York: Times Books.

Ekman, P. and Friesen, W.V. (1971). Constants across cultures in the face and emotion. *Journal of Personality and Social Psychology*, 17(2), 124–9.

Ekman, P. and Friesen, W.V. (1975). *Unmasking the Face*. Englewood Cliffs, NJ: Prentice-Hall.

Elias, M.J., Zins, J.E., Weissberg, R.P., Frey, K.S., Greenberg, M.T., Haynes, N.M. et al. (1997). *Promoting Social and Emotional Learning: Guidelines for Educators*. Alexandria, VA: Association of Supervision and Curriculum Development.

Elliott, B.J. and Richards, M.P.M. (1991). Children and divorce: educational performance and behaviour before and after parental separation. *International Journal of Law and the Family*, 5, 258–76.

Ellis, B.J., del Giudice, M., Dishion, T.J., Figueredo, A.J., Gray, P., Griskevicius, V., Hawley, P.H., Jacobs, W.J., James, J., Volk, A.A. and Wilson, D.S. (2012). The evolutionary basis of risky adolescent behavior: implications for science, policy, and practice. *Developmental Psychology*, 48, 598–623.

Ellis, S., Rogoff, B. and Cromer, C. (1981). Age segregation in children's social interactions. *Developmental Psychology*, 17, 399–407.

Ellsworth, C.P., Muir, D.W. and Hains, S.M.J. (1993). Social competence and person–object differentiation: an analysis of the still-face effect. *Developmental Psychology*, 29, 63–73.

Elsabbagh, M. and Johnson, M.H. (2007). Infancy and autism: progress, prospects, and challenges. *Progress in Brain Research. Progress in Brain Research*, 164, 355–83.

Embry, L. and Dawson, G. (2002). Disruptions in parenting related to maternal depression: Influences on children's behavioral and psychobiological development. In J.G. Borkowski, S. Ramey and M. Bristol-Power (eds). *Parenting and the Child's World* (pp. 203–13). Mahwah, NJ: Erlbaum.

Eme, R (2012). ADHD: an integration with pediatric traumatic brain injury. *Expert Review Neurotherapy*, 12(4), 475–83.

Emler, N. and Reicher, S. (1995). *Adolescence and Delinquency: The Collective Management of Reputation*. Oxford: Blackwell.

Engen, H.G. and Singer, T. (2013). Empathy circuits. *Current Opinion in Neurobiology*, 23, 275–82.

Erikson, E.H. (1950). *Childhood and Society*. New York: W.W. Norton.

Eshleman, J.R. and Bulcroft, R.A. (2010). *The Family* (12th Edn). Boston, MA: Allyn and Bacon.

Eslea, M. and Rees, J. (2001). At what age are children most likely to be bullied at school? *Aggressive Behavior*, 27, 419–29.

Eslinger, P.J. (1998). Neurological and neuropsychological bases of empathy. *European Neurology*, 39, 193–9.

Estabrook, A. (1916). *The Jukes in 1915*. Paper no. 25 of the Station for Experimental Evolution at Cold Spring Harbor, New York. Washington, DC: The Carnegie Institution of Washington Publication No. 240.

Estrada, P., Arsenio, W.F., Hess, R.D. and Holloway, S.D. (1987). Affective quality of the mother–child relationship: longitudinal consequences for children's school-relevant cognitive functioning. *Developmental Psychology*, 23, 210–15.

Eubig, P.A., Aguiar, A. and Schantz, S.L. (2010). Lead and PCBs as risk factors for attention deficit/hyperactivity disorder. *Environmental Health Perspectives*, 118(12), 1654–67.

EU Kids Online (2014), http://eprints.lse.ac.uk/60512/1/EU%20Kids%20onlinie%20III%20.pdf.

Evans, G. (2006). *Educational Failure and Working Class White Children in Britain.* Basingstoke, UK: Palgrave MacMillan.

Ewing, K. and Pratt, M.W. (1995). *The Role of Romantic Adult Attachment in Marital Communication and Parenting Stress.* Poster presented at the Society for Research Child Development Meetings, Indianapolis, March.

Eysenck, H.J. and Eysenck, S.B.G. (1975). *Manual of the Eysenck Personality Questionnaire (Adult and Junior).* London: Hodder & Stoughton.

Fabes, R.A., Eisenberg, N., Karbon, M., Bernzweig, J., Speer, A.L. and Carlo, G. (1994). Socialisation of children's vicarious emotional responding and prosocial behaviour: relations with mothers' perceptions of children's emotional reactivity. *Developmental Psychology*, 30, 44–55.

Fabes, R.A., Hanish, L.D., Martin, C.L., Moss, A. and Reesing, A. (2012). The effects of young children's affiliations with prosocial peers on subsequent emotionality in peer interactions. *British Journal of Developmental Psychology*, 30(4), 569–85.

Fabes, R.A., Martin, C.L. and Hanish, L.D. (2003). Young children's play qualities in same-, other-, and mixed-sex peer groups. *Child Development*, 74, 921–32.

Fagan, J. and Tyler, T.R. (2005). Legal socialisation of children and adolescents. *Social Justice Research*, 18(3), 217–41.

Fagot, B.I. (1974). Sex differences in toddlers' behaviour and parental reaction. *Developmental Psychology*, 4, 554–8.

Fagot, B.I. and Gauvain, M. (1997). Mother–child problem solving: continuity through the early childhood years. *Developmental Psychology*, 33, 480–8.

Fagot, B.I. and Leinbach, M.D. (1989). The young child's gender schema: environmental input, internal organization. *Child Development*, 60, 663–72.

Fallon, A. (1990). Culture in the mirror: sociocultural determinants of body image. In T.F. Cash and T. Pruzinsky (eds). *Body Images: Development, Deviance, and Change* (pp. 80–109). New York: The Guilford Press.

Fantz, R.L. (1961). The origin of form perception. *Scientific American*, 204(5), 66–72.

Fantz, R. and Miranda, S. (1975). Newborn infant attention to form of contour. *Child Development*, 46, 224–8.

Faraone, S.V. and Doyle, A.E. (2001). The nature and heritability of attention-deficit/hyperactivity disorder. *Child and Adolescent Psychiatric Clinics of North America*, 10(2), 299–316.

Farhadian, M., Gazanizad, N. and Shakerian, A. (2011). Theory of mind and siblings among preschool children. *Asian Social Science*, 7(3), 224–31.

Farr, R.H. and Patterson, C.J. (2009). Transracial adoption by lesbian, gay, and heterosexual couples: who completes transracial adoptions and with what results? *Adoption Quarterly*, 12(3–4), 187–204.

Farrington, D.P. (1983). Offending from 10 to 25 years of age. In K. Van Dusen and S.A. Mednick (eds). *Prospective Studies of Crime and Delinquency* (pp. 17–38). Boston: Kluwer-Nijhoff.

Farrington, D.P., Jolliffe, D., Loeber, R., Stouthamer-Loeber, M. and Kalb, L.M. (2001). The concentration of offenders in families, and family criminality in the prediction of boys' delinquency. *Journal of Adolescence,* 24, 579–96.

Farver, J.A., Xu, Y., Eppe, S., Fernandez, A. and Schwartz, D. (2005). Community violence, family conflict, and preschoolers' socioemotional functioning. *Developmental Psychology*, 41(1), 160–70.

Fasig, L. (2000). Toddlers' understanding of ownership: implications for self-concept development. *Social Development*, 9, 370–82.

Federal Bureau of Investigations (2016). *Statistic Brain: Gang Member Statistics.* Statistic Brain Research Institute, www.statisticbrain.com/gang-statistics/.

Fedewa, A.L. and Clark, T.P. (2009). Parent practices and home-school partnerships: a differential effect for children with same-sex coupled parents? *Journal of GLBT Family Studies*, 5(4), 312–39.

Feeney, J.A. and Noller, P. (1992). Attachment style and romantic love: relationship dissolution. *Australian Journal of Psychology*, 44(2), 69–74.

Feiring, C. and Lewis, M. (1987). The ecology of some middle class families at dinner. *International Journal of Behavioral Development*, 10, 377–90.

Fenson, L., Dale, P.S., Reznick, J.S., Bates, E., Thal, D.J. and Pethick, S.J. (1994). Variability in early communicative development. *Monographs of the Society for Research in Child Development*, 59 (Serial No. 242).

Ferchmin, P.A. and Eterovic, V.A. (1982). Play stimulated by environmental complexity alters the brain and improves learning abilities in rodents, primates and possibly humans. *Behavioral and Brain Sciences*, 5, 164–5.

Feresin, E. (2009) Lighter sentence for murderer with 'bad genes'. *Nature News*. doi:10.1038/news.2009.1050.

Ferguson, C.J. (2011). Video games and youth violence: a prospective analysis in adolescents. *Journal of Youth and Adolescence*, 40(4), 377–91.

Ferguson, T. (1952). *The Young Delinquent in His Social Setting*. London: Oxford University Press.

Ferguson, T.J. and Rule, B.G. (1980). Children's evaluations of retaliatory aggression. *Child Development*, 59(4), 961–8.

Festinger, L.A. (1954). A theory of social comparison processes (p. 119). *Human Relations*, 7, 117–40.

Field, A. and Workman, L. (2008). The man who frightens small children: Lance Workman talks to Andy Field about his work on childhood anxiety. *The Psychologist*, 21, 760–1.

Field, T., Gewirtz, J., Cohen, D., Garcia, R., Greenberg, R. and Collins, K. (1984). Leave-takings and reunions of infants, toddlers, preschoolers, and their parents. *Child Development*, 55, 628–35.

Fiese, B.H. (2006). *Family Routines and Rituals*. New Haven, CT: Yale University Press.

Fine, M.A., Voydanoff, P. and Donnelly, B.W. (1993). Relations between parental control and warmth and child well-being in stepfamilies. *Journal of Family Psychology*, 7(2): 222–32.

Finn, R. (1991). Different minds. *Discover*, 55–8.

Fiske, S.T. and Taylor, S.E. (2008). *Social Cognition: From Brains to Culture*. New York: McGraw-Hill.

Flavell, J.H. (1970). Developmental studies of mediated memory. In H.W. Reese and L.P. Lipsitt (eds). *Advances in Child Development and Behavior (Vol. 5)*. New York: Academic Press.

Flavell J.H. (1981). Cognitive monitoring. In P. Dickson (ed.). *Children's Oral Communication Skills* (pp. 35–9). New York: Academic Press.

Flavell, J.H., Flavell, E. and Green, F.L. (1983). Development of the appearance-reality distinction. *Cognitive Development*, 15, 95–120.

Fletcher, L. (2015). Mass murders linked to violent video games. *CharismaNews*, www.charismanews.com/culture/52651-14-mass-murders-linked-to-violent-video-games.

Flint, J., Greenspan, R.J. and Kendler, K.S. (2010). *How Genes Influence Behaviour*. Oxford: Oxford University Press.

Florsheim, P., Moore, D. and Edgington, C. (2003). Romantic relationships among pregnant and parenting adolescents. In P. Florsheim (ed.). *Adolescent Romantic Relations and Sexual Behaviour*. Mahwah, NJ: Erlbaum.

Forsyth, D. (2010). *Group Dynamics* (5th Edn). Belmont, CA: Wadsworth, Cengage Learning.

Fox, C.L. and Boulton, M.J. (2006). Friendship as a moderator of the relationship between social skills problems and peer victimisation. *Aggressive Behavior*, 32, 110–21.

Fox, N. and Calkins, S.D. (2003). The development of self-control of emotion: intrinsic and extrinsic influences. *Motivation and Emotion*, 27, 7–26.

Fox, N.A. and Davidson, R.J. (1988). Patterns of brain electrical activity during facial times of emotion in 10-month-old infants. *Developmental Psychology*, 24, 230–6.

Fox, N.A. and Field, T.M. (1989). Individual differences in preschool entry behavior. *Journal of Applied Developmental Psychology*, 10, 527–40.

Francis, R.C. (2012). *Epigenetics: How Environment Shapes our Genes.* New York: W.W. Norton and Company.

Frazier, T.W., Thompson, L., Youngstrom, E.A., Law, P., Hardan, A.Y., Eng, C. and Morris, N. (2014). A twin study of heritable and shared environmental contributions to autism. *Journal of Autism Developmental Disorder*, 44(8), 2013–25.

Frede, E.C. (1995). The role of program quality in producing early childhood program benefits. *The Future of Children*, 5(3), 115–32.

Freeman, B.J., Guthrie, D., Ritvo, E., Schroth, P., Glass, R. and Frankel, F. (1979). Behavior Observation Scale: preliminary analysis of the similarities and differences between autistic and mentally retarded children. *Psychological Reports*, 44(2), 519–24.

Freeman, H. (2015). Green is the new black: the unstoppable rise of the healthy-eating guru. *The Guardian*, Guardian News and Media Limited, www.theguardian.com/lifeandstyle/2015/jun/27/new-wellness-bloggers-food-drink-hadley-freeman.

Freud, A. and Dann, S (1951). An experiment in group upbringing. *Psychoanalytic Study of the Child* 6, 127–168. Reprinted in A. Freud (1969) *Indications for Child Analysis, and Other Papers, 1945–1956* (Chapter 8, pp. 163–229). London: Hogarth Press.

Freud, S. (1905). *Three Essays on the Theory of Sexuality.* Se, 7. Leipzig and Vienna: Franz Deuticke

Freud, S. (1920). *A General Introduction to Psychoanalysis.* New York: Basic Books.

Freud, S. (1920/1975). *Beyond the Pleasure Principle.* New York: W.W. Norton.

Frick, J.E., Colombo, J. and Saxon, T.F. (1999). Individual and developmental differences in disengagement of fixation in early infancy. *Child Development*, 70, 537–48.

Frick, P.J. (1993). Childhood conduct problems in family context. *School Psychology Review*, 22, 376–85.

Frick, P.J. and Silverthorn, P. (2001). Psychopathology in children. In H.E. Adams and P.B. Sutker (eds). *Comprehensive Handbook of Psychopathology* (3rd Ed., pp. 881–920). New York: Kluwer-Plenum.

Friedrich-Cofer, L. and Huston, A.C. (1986). Television violence and aggression: the debate continues. *Psychological Bulletin*, 100(3), 364–78.

Fröbel, F. (1887/1906). *Education of Man* (p. 55), (trans. W.N. Hailmann). New York: Appleton.

Fröbel, F. (1888/1910). *Mother's Songs, Games and Stories*, (trans. F. Lord and E. Lord). London: William Rice.

Fu, G. and Lee, K. (2007). Social grooming in the kindergarten: the emergence of flattery behavior. *Developmental Science*, 10(2), 255–65.

Furman, W. and Buhrmester, D. (1992). Age and sex in perceptions of networks of personal relationships. *Child Development*, 63, 103–15.

Furnham, A. and Kanazawa, S. (in press). The evolution of personality. In L. Workman, W. Reader and J. Barkow (eds). *Cambridge Handbook of Evolutionary Perspectives on Human Behavior*. Cambridge: Cambridge University Press.

Gagné, R.M. (1977). *The Conditions for Learning.* New York: Holt, Rinehart and Winston.

Gagné, R.M., Briggs, L.J. and Wager, W.W. (1988). *Principles of Instructional Design* (3rd Edn). New York: Holt, Rinehart and Winston.

Gallagher, S. (2004). Understanding interpersonal problems in autism: interaction theory as an alternative to theory of mind. *Philosophy, Psychiatry, and Psychology*, 11(3), 199–217.

Gallup, A.C., O'Brien, D.T. and Wilson, D.S. (2011). Intrasexual peer aggression and dating behavior during adolescence: an evolutionary perspective. *Aggressive Behavior*, 37, 258–67.

Gander, K. (2014). Facebook and Twitter have become 'command and control network of choice' for ISIS, GCHQ chief warns. *Independent* Online, www.independent.co.uk/news/uk/home-news/gchq-head-demands-internet-firms-open-up-to-intelligence-services-claiming-privacy-is-not-an-9837169.html.

Garandeau, C.F., Lee, I.A. and Salmivalli, C. (2013). Inequality matters: classroom status hierarchy and adolescents' bullying. *Journal of Youth Adolescence*, 43(7), 1123–33.

Garbarino, J. (2001). An ecological perspective on the effects of violence on children. *Journal of Community Psychology*, 29(3), 361–78.

Garcia, M.M., Shaw, D.S., Winslow, E.B. and Yaggi, K.E. (2000). Destructive sibling conflict and the development of conduct problems in young boys. *Developmental Psychology*, 36, 44–53.

Gardner, H.W. (1983). *Frames of Mind: The Theory of Multiple Intelligences*. New York: Basic Books.

Gardner, H.W. (2006). *Multiple Intelligences: New Horizons*. New York: Basic Books.

Gardner, H.W. (2010). A debate on 'multiple intelligences'. In J. Traub (ed.). *Cerebrum: Forging Ideas in Brain Science* (pp. 34–61). Washington: Dana Press.

Garner, D.M., Olmsted, M.P., Bohr, Y. and Garfinkel, P.E. (1982). The Eating Attitudes Test: psychometric features and clinical correlates. *Psychological Medicine*, 12, 871–8.

Garrison, M. and Christakis, D.A. (2005). *A Teacher in the Living Room: Educational Media for Babies, Toddlers, and Preschoolers*. Menlo Park, CA: The Henry J. Kaiser Family Foundation.

Gartrell, N. and Bos, H. (2010). US National Longitudinal Lesbian Family Study: psychological adjustment of 17-year-old adolescents. *Pediatrics*, 126(1), 28–36.

Garvey, C. (1990). *Play*. Cambridge, MA: Harvard University Press.

Gass, K., Jenkins, J. and Dunn , J. (2007). Are sibling relationships protective? A longitudinal study. *Journal of Child Psychology and Psychiatry*, 48, 167–75.

Gasser, L. and Keller, M. (2010). Are the competent the morally good? Perspective taking and moral motivation of children involved in bullying. *Social Development*, 18(4), 798–816.

Geake, J. (2008). Neuromythologies in education. *Educational Research*, 50 (2): 123–33.

Geary, D.C. and Bjorklund, D.F. (2000). Evolutionary developmental psychology. *Child Development*, 71, 57–65.

Gelfand, D.M., Jensen, W.R. and Drew, C.J. (1997). *Understanding Child Behaviour Disorders* (3rd Edn). Fort Worth, TX: Harcourt Brace.

Genta, M.L., Brighi, A. and Guarini, A. (2008). *Cyberbullying Among Italian Students: An Explorative Study of Bullying Through New Technologies and Its Psychological Impact*. Paper presented at the 4th World Conference on Violence in School and Public Policies, Lisbon (Portugal).

Genta, M.L., Brighi, A. and Guarini, A. (2009). European project on bullying and cyberbullying granted by Daphne II programme. *Journal of Psychology*, 217(4), 233.

Gentile, D.A. and Bushman, B.J. (2012). Reassessing media violence effects using a risk and resilience approach to understanding aggression. *Psychology of Popular Media Culture*, 1(3), 1–14.

Gershoff, E.T. (2002). Corporal punishment by parents and associated child behaviors and experiences: a meta-analysis and theoretical review. *Psychological Bulletin*, 128, 539–79.

Gervai, J., Nemoda, Z., Lakatos, K., Ronai, Z., Toth, I., Ney, K. and Sasvari-Szekely, M. (2005). Transmission disequilibrium tests confirm the link between DRD4 gene polymorphism and infant attachment. *American Journal of Medical Genetics Part B Neuropsychiatric Genetics*, 132B(1), 126–30.

Gery, I., Miljkovitch, R., Berthoz, S. and Soussignan, R. (2009). Empathy and recognition of facial expressions of emotion in sex offenders, non-sex offenders and normal controls. *Psychiatry Res*, 165(3), 252–62.

Gibbs, J.C. (1993). Moral-cognitive interventions. In A.P. Goldstein and C.R. Huff (eds). *The Gang Intervention Handbook* (pp. 159–85). Champaign, IL: Research Press.

Gibson, E.J. and Walk, R.D. (1960). The 'visual cliff'. *Scientific American*, 202, 64–71.

Gilligan, C. (1982). *In a Different Voice: Psychological Theory and Women's Development*. Cambridge, MA: Harvard University Press.

Gilligan, C. (1996). The centrality of relationship in human development: a puzzle, some evidence, and a theory. In K. Fischer and G. Noam (eds). *Development and Vulnerability in Close Relationships*. Hillsdale, NJ: Lawrence Erlbaum.

Gilliom, M., Shaw, D.S., Beck, J.E., Schonberg, M.A. and Lukon, J.L. (2002). Anger regulation in disadvantaged preschool boys: strategies, antecedents, and the development of self-control. *Developmental Psychology*, 38, 222–35.

Gill-Spector, K. and Malach, R. (2001). fMR-adaptations: a tool for studying the functional properties of human cortical neurons. *Acta Psychologica*, 107, 293–321.

Gini, G. (2006). Social cognition and moral cognition in bullying: what's wrong? *Aggressive Behavior*, 32, 528–39.

Ginsburg, K.R., Durbin, D.R., Garcia-España, J.F., Kalicka, E.A. and Winston, F.K. (2009). Associations between parenting styles and teen driving, safety-related behaviors and attitudes. *Pediatrics*, 124(4), 1040–51.

Gizer, I.R., Ficks, C. and Waldman, I.D. (2009). Candidate gene studies of ADHD: a meta-analytic review. *Human Genetics*, 126 (1), 51–90.

Gleik, J. (2000). *Faster: The Acceleration of Just About Everything*. New York: Vintage.

Gleitman, L. (1990). The structural sources of verb meanings. *Language Acquisition*, 1, 3–55.

Gnepp, J. and Hess, D.L. (1986). Children's understanding of verbal and facial display rules. *Developmental Psychology*, 22(1), 103–8.

Goldbaum, S., Craig, W.M., Pepler, D. and Connolly, J. (2003). Developmental trajectories of victimisation: identifying risk and protective factors. *Journal of Applied School Psychology*, 19, 59–68.

Goldberg, A.D., Allis, C.D. and Bernstein, E. (2007). Epigenetics: a landscape takes shape. *Cell*, 128, 635–8.

Golding, J., Pembrey, M.S., Jones, R. and The ALSPAC Study Team (2001). ALSPAC – The Avon Longitudinal Study of Parents and Children. *Paediatric and Perinatal Epidemiology*, 15(1), 74–87.

Goldin-Meadow, S. (2006). Nonverbal communication: the hand's role in talking and thinking. In W. Damon, R.M. Lerner, D. Kuhn and R. Siegler (eds). *Handbook of Child Psychology, Vol 2* (6th Edn, pp. 336–71). New York: Wiley.

Goldin-Meadow, S. and Butcher, C. (2003). Pointing toward two-word speech in young children. In S. Kita (ed.). *Pointing: Where Language, Culture, and Cognition Meet* (pp. 85–107). Hillsdale, NJ: Erlbaum Associates.

Goldstein, S., Naglieri, J.A., Princoptta, D. and Otero, T.M. (2014). Introduction: a history of executive functioning as a theoretical and clinical construct. In S. Goldstein and J.A. Naglieri (eds). *Handbook of Executive Functioning* (pp. 3–13). New York: Springer.

Golinkoff, R.M. and Hirsh-Pasek, K. (1999). *How Babies Talk*. New York: Penguin Group.

Goodman, E. (1999). Ads pollute most everything in sight. *Albuquerque Journal*, 27, C3.

Goos, L.M., Erratian, P. and Schachar, R. (2007). Parent-of-origin effects in attention-deficit hyperactivity disorder. *Psychiatry Research*, 149, 1–9.

Gopnik, A. (2016). *The Gardener and the Carpenter: What the New Science of Child Development Tells Us about the Relationship Between Parents and Children*. New York: Farrar, Straus and Giroux.

Gopnik, A., Meltzoff, A. and Kuhl, P. (1999). *The Scientist in the Crib: What Early Learning Tells Us About the Mind*. New York: HarperCollins Publishers.

Gosling, S.D., Augustine, A.A., Vazire, S., Holtzman, N. and Gaddis, S. (2011). Manifestations of personality in online social networks: self-reported Facebook-related behaviours and observable profile information. *Cyberpsychology, Behavior and Social Networking*, 14, 483–8.

Gottlieb, B. (1993). *The Family in the Western World from the Black Death to the Industrial Age*. New York: Oxford University Press.

Gottlieb, G. and Lickliter, R. (2007). Probabilistic epigenesis. *Developmental Science*, 10(1), 1–11.

Gottlib, I.H., Joormann, J., Minor, K.L. and Cooney, R.E. (2006). Cognitive and biological functioning in children at risk for depression. In T. Canli (ed.). *Biology of Personality and Individual Differences*. New York: Guilford Press.

Gottman, J.M. and Parker, J.G. (1986). *The Conversations of Friends*. New York: Cambridge University Press.

Gould, P. (2005). Life of crime (part 1). *BBC News*, http://news.bbc.co.uk/hi/english/static/in_depth/uk/2001/life_of_crime/yob_culture.stm.

Graham, S. (2005). Commentary in *USA TODAY*, p. 2D.

Graham, S., Doubleday, C. and Guarino, P.A. (1984). The development of relations between perceived controllability and the emotions of pity, anger, and guilt. *Child Development*, 55, 561–5.

Grammarist (2009–2014). http://grammarist.com/usage/ethnicity-race/.

Gray, J.A. (1982). *The Neuropsychology of Anxiety*. New York: Oxford University Press.

Graziano, A.M. and Raulin, M.L. (2007). *Research Methods* (6th Edn). Boston: Allyn and Bacon.

Greenberg, M., Weissberg, R., O'Brien, M., Zins, J., Fredricks, L., Resnick, H. and Elias, M. (2003). Enhancing school-based prevention and youth development through coordinated social, emotional and academic learning. *American Psychologist*, 58 (6/7), 466–74.

Greene, J.D., Sommerville, R.B., Nystrom, L.E., Darley, J.M. and Cohen, J.D. (2001). An fMRI investigation of emotional engagement in moral judgment. *Science*, 293(5537), 2105–8.

Greenfield, P.M., Keller, H., Fulingni, A. and Maynard, A. (2003). Cultural pathways through universal development. *Annual Review of Psychology*, 54, 461–90.

Gray, J. (1992). *Men are from Mars, Women are from Venus*. London and New York: HarperCollins.

Griffin, A.S., Pemberton, J.M., Brotherton, P.N.M., McIlrath, G.M., Gaynor, D., Kansky, R. and Clutton-Brock, T.H. (2003). A genetic analysis of breeding success in the cooperative meerkat (*Suricata suricatta*). *Behavioral Ecology*, 14, 472–80.

Grob, G.N. (1991). Origins of DSM-I: a study in appearance and reality. *American Journal of Psychiatry*, 148(4), 421–31.

Groman, C.M. and Barzman, D.H. (2014). The impact of ADHD on morality development. *Attention Deficit Hyperactivity Disorder*, 6(2), 67–71.

Groos, K. (1898). *Die Spiele der Tiere*, (trans. by E.L. Baldwin as *The Play of Animals*). New York: Appleton.

Groos, K. (1901). *Die Spiele der Menschen*, (trans. by E.L. Baldwin as *The Play of Man*). New York: Appleton.

Gross, F.F. (2004). Adolescent Internet use: what we expect, what teens report. *Journal of Applied Developmental Psychology*, 24, 633–49.

Grossmann, K., Grossmann K.E. and Kindler, H. (2005). Early care and the roots of attachment and partnership representations: The Bielefeld and Regensburg longitudinal studies. In K.E. Grossmann, K. Grossmann and E. Waters (eds). *Attachment from Infancy to Adulthood* (pp. 98–136). New York: Guilford Press.

Grusec, J.E. (2006). The development of moral behaviour and conscience from a socialisation perspective. In M. Killen and J.G. Smetana (eds). *Handbook of Moral Development*

(pp. 243–65). Mahwah, NJ: Lawrence Erlbaum Associates Publishers.

Guadagno, R., Okdie, B. and Eno, C. (2008). Who blogs? Personality predictors of blogging. *Computers in Human Behavior*, 24, 1993–2004.

Guarini, A., Passini, S., Melotti, G. and Brighi, A. (2012). Risk and protective factors on perpetration of bullying and cyberbullying. *Studia Edukacyjne*, 23, 33–55.

Guerra, N.G., Williamson, A.A. and Lucas-Molina, B. (2012). Normal development: infancy, childhood, and adolescence. In J.M. Rey (ed.). *International Handbook of Child and Adolescent Mental Health (e-Textbook)*. Geneva, Switzerland: International Association for Child and Adolescent Psychiatry and Applied Professions.

Gummerum, M., Keller, M., Takezawa, M. and Mata, J. (2008). To give or not to give: children's and adolescents' sharing and moral negotiations in economic decision situations. *Child Development*, 79(3), 562–76.

Gutenberg, J. (1452/1996). *The Gutenberg Bible*, (trans. M. Davies). London: The British Library.

Haglund, K. (2015). The modeling industry and body image. Eating disorder. *HOPE*, www.eatingdisorderhope.com/blog/the-modeling-industry-and-body-image.

Halberstadt, A.G., Denham, S.A. and Dunsmore, J.C. (2001). Affective social competence. *Social Development*, 10(1), 79–119.

Halpern, D.F. (2000). *Sex Differences in Cognitive Ability* (3rd Edn). Mahwah, NJ: Erlbaum.

Halpern, D.F. (2004). A cognitive process taxonomy for sex differences in cognitive abilities. *Current Directions in Psychological Science*, 13, 135–9.

Halverson, C.F. and Deal, J.E. (2001) Temperamental change, parenting, and the family context. In T.D. Wachs and G.A. Kohnstamm (eds). *Temperament in Context* (pp. 61–79). Mahwah, NJ: Lawrence Erlbaum Associates Publishers.

Halverson, H.M. (1933). The acquisition of skill in infancy. *Journal of Genetic Psychology*, 43, 3–48.

Hamilton, K. and Waller, G. (1993). Media influences on body size estimation in anorexia and bulimia: an experimental study. *British Journal of Psychiatry*, 162, 837–40.

Hamilton, W.D. (1964 a and b). The genetical evolution of social behaviour (Vols I and II). *Journal of Theoretical Biology*, 7, 1–52.

Hamlin J.K. (2013). Failed attempts to help and harm: intention versus outcome in preverbal infants' social evaluations. *Cognition*, 128(3), 451–74.

Hardie, E. and Tee, M.Y. (2007). Excessive Internet use: the role of personality, loneliness and social support networks in Internet addiction. *Society*, 5, 34–47.

Harding, E. (2016). Militant teachers demand schools stop promoting 'British values' as it makes children from other cultures feel inferior. *Daily Mail*, www.dailymail.co.uk/news/article-3512619/Teachers-want-stop-promoting-British-values-cultural-supremacy-fears.html.

Hargreaves, D.H. (1980). Classrooms, schools, and juvenile delinquency. *Educational Analysis*, 2, 75–87.

Harlow, H.F. (1962). Development of affection in primates. In E.L. Bliss (ed.). *Roots of Behaviour* (pp. 157–66). New York: Harper.

Harlow, H.F. and Zimmerman, R.R. (1959). Affectional responses in the infant monkey. *Science*, 130, 421–32.

Harris, J.R. (1995). Where is the child's environment? A group-socialisation theory of development. *Psychological Review*, 102(3), 458–89.

Harris, J.R. (1998). *The Nurture Assumption: Why Children Turn Out the Way They Do* (p. 147). New York: Simon and Schuster.

Harris, J.R. (2009). *The Nurture Assumption: Why Children Turn Out the Way They Do* (2nd Edn). New York, NY: Free Press.

Harris, J.R. and Workman, L. (2016). 'When life hands you a lemon, just bite in'. *The Psychologist*, 29(9), 696–7.

Harris, K.M., McLean, J.P. and Sheffield, J. (2009). Examining suicide-risk individuals who go online for suicide-related purposes. *Archives of Suicide Research*, 13, 264–76.

Harris, P.L., Johnson, C., Hutton, D., Andrews, G. and Cooke, T. (1989). Young children's theory of mind and emotion. *Cognition and Emotion*, 3, 379–400.

Harrison, L.J. and Ungerer, J.A. (2002). Maternal employment and infant-mother attachment security at 12 months postpartum. *Developmental Psychology*, 38, 758–73.

Hart, B. and Risley, T.R. (1995). *Meaningful Differences in the Everyday Experience of American Children*. Baltimore: Brookes.

Hart, D. and Karmel, M.P. (1996). Self-awareness and self-knowledge in humans, great apes, and monkeys. In A. Russon, K. Bard and S. Parker (eds). *Reaching into Thought*. New York: Cambridge University Press.

Hart, S. and Carrington, H. (2002). Jealousy in 6-month-old infants. *Infancy*, 3(3), 395–402.

Harter, S. (1990). Processes underlying adolescent self-concept formation. In R. Montemayor, G.R. Adams and T.P. Gullotta (eds). *From Childhood to Adolescence: A Transitional Period?* Newbury Park, CA: Sage.

Harter, S. (2006). The self. In W. Damon, R.M. Lerner and N. Eisenberg (eds). *Handbook of Child Psychology* (6th Edn, Vol. 3, pp. 505–70). New York: Wiley.

Hartshorne, H., May, M.A. and Shuttleworth, F.K. (1930). *Studies in the Organization of Character*. Oxford: Macmillan.

Hartup, W.W. (1975). The origins of friendship. In M. Lewis and L.A. Rosenblum (eds). *The Origins of Behaviour: ETS Symposium on Friendship and Peer Relations* (pp. 11–27). New York: Wiley.

Hartup, W.W. (1978). Children and their friends. In H. McGurk (ed.). *Issues in Childhood Social Development*. London: Methuen and Co. Ltd.

Haslam, N., Smillie, L. and Song, J. (2017) *An Introduction to Personality, Individual Differences and Intelligence* (2nd Edn). Thousand Oaks, CA: Sage.

Hastings, P.D., Rubin, K.H. and DeRose, L. (2005). Links among gender, inhibition, and parental socialization in the development of prosocial behavior. *Merrill-Palmer Quarterly*, 51(4), 467–93.

Hauser, M.D. (2006). *Moral Minds*. New York: Harper Collins.

Hauser, M.D., Young, L. and Cushman, F.A. (2008). Reviving Rawl's linguistic analogy. In W. Sinnott-Armstrong (ed.). *Moral Psychology and Biology*. New York: Oxford University Press.

Hawkins, J.D., Catalano, R.F., Kosterman, R., Abbott, R. and Hill, K.G. (1999). Preventing adolescent health-risk behaviors by strengthening protection during childhood.

Archives of Pediatrics and Adolescent Medicine, 153(3), 226–34.

Hawley, P.H. (1999). The ontogenesis of social dominance: a strategy based evolutionary perspective. *Developmental Review*, 19, 97–132.

Hawley, P.H. (2002). Social dominance and prosocial and coercive strategies of resource control in preschoolers. *International Journal of Behavioral Development*, 26, 167–76.

Hawley, P.H. (2003). Strategies of control, aggression and morality in preschoolers: an evolutionary perspective. *Journal of Experimental Child Psychology*, 85, 213–35.

Hawley, P.H. (2007). Social dominance in childhood and adolescence. In P.H. Hawly, T.D. Little and P. Rodkin (eds). *Aggression and Adaptation: The Bright Side to Bad Behaviour*. Mahwah, NJ: Erlbaum.

Hawley, P.H. and Little, T.D. (1999). On winning some and losing some: a social relations approach to social dominance in toddlers. *Merrill-Palmer Quarterly*, 45, 188–214.

Hawley, P., Little, T.D. and Rodkin, P. (2007). *Aggression and Adaptation*. Mahwah, NJ: Lawrence Erlbaum.

Hay, D.F. (2006). Yours and mine: toddlers' talk about possessions with familiar peers. *British Journal of Developmental Psychology*, Special Issue: the role of conversations in children's social, emotional and cognitive development, 24(1), 39–52.

Hay, D.F., Castle, J. and Davies, L. (2000). Toddlers' use of force against familiar peers: a precursor of serious aggression? *Child Development*, 71, 457–67.

Hay, D.F. and Cook, K.V. (2007). The transformation of prosocial behaviour from infancy to childhood. In C. Brownell and C.B. Kopp (eds). *Socioemotional Development in the Toddler Years* (pp. 100–31). New York: Guilford Press.

Hay, D.F., Pederson, J. and Nash, A. (1982). Dyadic interaction in the first year of life. In K.H. Rubin and H.S. Ross (eds). *Peer Relationships and Social Skills in Childhood* (pp. 11–40). New York: Springer-Verlag.

Hazan, C. and Shaver, P.R. (1987). Romantic love conceptualized as an attachment process. *Journal of Personality and Social Psychology*, 52, 511–24.

Hazler, R.J. (1996). *Breaking the Cycle of Violence: Interventions for Bullying and Victimization*. Washington, DC: Accelerated Development.

Hein, G. and Singer, T. (2008). I feel how you feel but not always: the empathic brain and its modulation. *Current Opinion in Neurobiology*, 18, 153–8.

Heinberg, L.J. and Thompson, J.K. (1995). Body image and televised images of thinness and attractiveness: a controlled laboratory investigation. *Journal of Social and Clinical Psychology*, 14(4), 325–38.

Helwig, C.C. (2008). The moral judgment of the child re-evaluated. In C. Wainryb, J.G. Smetana and E. Turiel (eds). *Social Development, Social Inequalities, and Social Justice* (pp. 27–52). New York: Erlbaum.

Helwig, C.C., Zelazo, P.D. and Wilson, M. (2001). Children's judgments of psychological harm in normal and noncanonical situations. *Child Development*, 72, 66–81.

Henrich, J., McElreath, R., Barr, A., Ensimger, J., Barrett, C., Bolyanatz, A., Cardenas, J.C., Gurven, M., Gwako, E., Henrich, N., Lesorgol, C., Marlowe, F., Tracer, D. and Ziker, J. (2006). Costly punishment across human societies. *Science*, 312(5781), 1767–70.

Herba, C. and Philips, M. (2004). Annotation: development of facial expression recognition from childhood to adolescence: behavioral and neurological perspectives. *Journal of Child Psychology and Psychiatry*, 45, 1185–98.

Herbert-Myers, H., Guttentag, C., Swank, P., Smith, K. and Landry, S. (2006). The importance of language, social, and behavioral skills across early and later childhood as predictors of social competence with peers. *Applied Developmental Science*, 10(4), 174–87.

Herdt, G.H. (1994a). *Guardians of the Flute: Idioms of Masculinity*, Vol. 1 (Rev. Edn). Chicago: University of Chicago Press.

Herdt, G.H. (1994b). *The Sambia: Ritual, Sexuality, and Change in Papua New Guinea* (2nd Edn, p. 253). UK: Thomson, Wadsworth.

Hesslow, G. (2002). Conscious thought as simulation of behaviour and perception. *Trends in Cognitive Sciences*, 6(6), 242–7.

Hetherington, E.M. (1991). Family, lies and video tapes. *Journal of Adolescent Research*, 1(4), 323–48.

Heyman, G.D., Sweet, M.A. and Lee, K. (2009). Children's reasoning about lie-telling and truth-telling in politeness contexts. *Social Development*, 18(3), 728–46.

Hill, M., Laybourn, A. and Borland, M. (1996). Engaging with primary-aged children about their emotions and well-being: methodological considerations. *Children and Society*, 10, 129–44.

Hill, P. and McCune-Nicolich, L. (1981). Pretend play and patterns of cognition in Down's syndrome children. *Child Development*, 52, 611–7.

Hinde, R.A., Titmus, G., Easton, D. and Tamplin, A. (1985). Incidence of 'friendship' and behavior toward strong associates versus nonassociates in preschoolers. *Child Development*, 56, 234–45.

Hindelang, M.J. (1973). Causes of delinquency: a partial replication and extension. *Social Problems*, 20, 471–87.

Hinduja, S. and Patchin, J.W. (2008). Cyberbullying: an exploratory analysis of factors related to offending and victimization. *Deviant Behavior*, 29(2), 129–56.

Hirschi, T. (1969). *Causes of Delinquency*. California: University of California Press.

Hirsh-Pasek, K. and Golinkoff, R.M. (1991). Language comprehension: a new look at some old themes. In N. Krasnegor, D.M. Rumbaugh, R.L. Schiefelbusch and M. Studdert-Kennedy (eds). *Biological and Behavioral Determinants of Language Development*. Hillsdale, NJ: Erlbaum.

Hobbs, G., Vignoles, A. and the ALSPAC Study Team Centre for the Economics of Education (2007). *Is Free School Meal Status a Valid Proxy for Socio-Economic Status (in Schools Research)?* Brief no.CEE03-07, May. London: DfES.

Hobson, C., Scott, S. and Rubia, K. (2011). Investigation of cool and hot executive function deficits in ODD/CD independently of ADHD. *Journal of Child Psychology and Psychiatry*, 52, 1035–43.

Hobson, J.A., Hobson, R.P., Malik, S., Bargiota, K. and Caló, S. (2013). The relation between social engagement and pretend play in autism. *British Journal of Developmental Psychology*, 31(1), 114–27.

Hoff, E. (2005). *Language Development* (3rd Edn). Belmont, CA: Wadsworth/Thomson.

Hoffman, M.L. (1970). Moral development. In P.H. Mussen (ed.). *Carmichael's Manual of Child Psychology* (Vol. 2, pp. 457–557). New York: Wiley.

Hoffman, M.L. (1977). Moral internalisation: current theory and research. In L. Berekowitz (ed.). *Advances in Experimental Social Psychology* (Vol. 10). New York: Academic Press.

Hoffman, M.L. (2000). *Empathy and Moral Development: Implications for Caring and Justice*. New York: Cambridge University Press.

Hoffman, M.L. and Saltzstein, H.D. (1967). Parent discipline and the child's moral development. *Journal of Personality and Social Psychology*, 5, 45–57.

Hogan, M.L. and Strasburger, V.C. (2008). Body image, eating disorders, and the media. *Adolescent Medicine*, 19, 521–46.

Hollos, M., Leis, P. and Turiel, E. (1986). Social reasoning in Ijo children and adolescents in Nigerian communities. *Journal of Cross-Cultural Psychology*, 17, 352–76.

Home Office (2014). *Anti-Social Behaviour, Crime and Policing Act 2014: Reform of Anti-Social Behaviour Powers. Statutory Guidance for Frontline Professionals*. London: Home Office, Crown Copyright, www.gov.uk/government/uploads/system/uploads/attachment_data/file/352562/ASB_Guidance_v8_July2014_final__2_.pdf.

Houck, C.D., Barker, D., Rizzo, C., Hancock, E., Norton, A. and Brown, L.K. (2014). Sexting and sexual behaviour in at-risk adolescents. *Pediatrics*, 133(2), 276–82.

Howes, C. (1996). The earliest friendships. In W.M. Bukowski, A.F. Newcomb and W.W. Hartup (eds). *The Company They Keep: Friendship in Childhood and Adolescence* (pp. 66–86). Cambridge, MA: Cambridge University Press.

Howes, C. (2000). Social-emotional classroom climate in childcare, child–teacher relationships and children's second grade peer relations. *Social Development*, 9, 191–204.

Howes, C. and Phillipsen, L. (1998). Continuity in children's relationships with peers. *Social Development*, 7, 340–9.

Hubbard, J.A., McAuliffe, M.D., Morrow, M.T. and Romano, L.J. (2010). Reactive and proactive aggression in childhood and adolescence: precursors, outcomes, processes, experiences, and measurement. *Journal of Personality*, 78(1), 95–118.

Huebner, A. and Garrod, A. (1993). Moral reasoning among Tibetan monks: a study of Buddhist adolescents and young adults in Nepal. *Journal of Cross-Cultural Psychology*, 24, 167–85.

Huesmann, L.R. (1997). Observational learning of violent behaviour: social and biosocial processes. In A. Raine, D. Farrington, P.O. Brennen and S.A. Mednick (eds). *The Biosocial Basis of Violence* (pp. 69–88). New York: Plenum Press.

Huesmann, L.R. and Eron, L.D. (1986). *Television and the Aggressive Child: A Cross-national Comparison*. Hillsdale, NJ: Erlbaum.

Huesmann, L.R., Eron, L.D., Lefkowitz, M.M. and Walder, L.O. (1984). Stability of aggression over time and generations. *Developmental Psychology*, 20, 1120–34.

Huesmann, L.R, and Guerra, N.G. (1997). Normative beliefs and the development of aggressive behavior. *Journal of Personality and Social Psychology*, 72, 1–12.

Huesmann, L.R. and Taylor, L.D. (2006). Media effects in middle childhood. In A.C. Huston and M.N. Ripke (eds). *Developmental Contexts in Middle Childhood*. New York: Cambridge University Press.

Hughes, B. (2002). *A Playworker's Taxonomy of Play Types* (2nd Edn). London: PlayLink.

Hughes, C. and Cutting, A. (1999). Nature, nurture and individual differences in early understanding of mind. *Psychological Science*, 10, 429–32.

Hughes, C. and Ensor, R. (2005). Executive function and theory of mind in 2 year olds: a family affair? *Developmental Neuropsychology*, 28(2), 645–68.

Hughes, F.P. (2010). *Children, Play, and Development*. Thousand Oaks, CA: Sage.

Hughes, M. (1975). Egocentrism in preschool children. Unpublished doctoral dissertation. Edinburgh University.

Hughes, T. (1857). *Tom Brown's Schooldays*. Cambridge: Macmillan and Co.

Huis in't Veld, E.M.J., Vingerhoets, A.J.J.M. and Denollet, J. (2011). Attachment style and self-esteem: the mediating role of Type D personality. *Personality and Individual Differences*, 50, 1099–103.

Humphrey, N. (1976). The social function of intellect. In P.P.G. Bateson and R.A. Hinde, (eds). *Growing Points in Ethology* (pp. 303–17). Cambridge: Cambridge University Press.

Hunter, P. (2010). The psycho gene. *Science and Society Feature*, 11(9), 667–9.

Huttenlocher, J. and Lui, F. (1979). The semantic organisation of some simple nouns and verbs. *Journal of Verbal Learning and Verbal Behavior*, 18, 141–62.

Huttenlocher, J. and Smiley, P. (1987). Early word meanings: the case for object names. *Cognitive Psychology*, 19, 63–89.

Huttenlocher, J., Smiley, P. and Charney, R. (1987). Emergence of action categories in the child: evidence from verb meanings. *Psychological Review*, 90, 72–93.

Huys, D., Bartsch, C., Koester, P., Lenartz, D., Maarouf, M., Daumann, J., Mai, J.K., et al. (2014). Motor improvement and emotional stabilisation in patients with Tourette Syndrome after deep brain stimulation of the ventral anterior and ventrolateral motor part of the thalamus. *Biological Psychiatry*, 79(5), 392–401.

Hyde, J.S. (2005). The gender similarities hypothesis. *American Psychologist*, 60, 581–92.

Hyde, J.S. (2007). New directions in the study of gender similarities and differences. *Current Directions in Psychological Science*, 16(5), 259–63.

Hymel, S., Rocke Henderson, N. and Bonanno, R.A. (2005). Moral disengagement: a framework for understanding bullying among adolescents. *Journal of Social Sciences*, 8, 1–11.

Iacoboni, M., Woods, R.P., Brass, M., Bekkering, H., Mazziotta, J.C. and Rizzolatti, G. (1999). Cortical mechanisms of human imitation. *Science*, 286(5449), 2526–8.

InternetWorldStats.com, www.internetlivestats.com/internet-users/.

Irwin, D.M. and Moore, S.G. (1971). The young child's understanding of justice. *Developmental Psychology*, 5, 406–10.

Isabella, R.A., Belsky, J. and von Eye, A. (1989). The origins of infant–mother attachment: an examination of interactional synchrony during the infant's first year. *Developmental Psychology*, 25, 12–21.

Ishikawa, F. and Hay, D.F. (2006). Triadic interaction among newly acquainted 2-year-olds. *Social Development*, 15(1), 145–68.

Ishikawa, S. and Raine A. (2003). Prefrontal deficits and antisocial behaviour: a causal model. In B. Lahey, T.E. Moffitt and A. Caspi (eds). *Causes of Conduct Disorder and Delinquency* (pp. 277–304). New York: Guilford Press.

Izard, C.E. (1994). Innate and universal facial expressions: evidence from developmental and cross-cultural research. *Psychological Bulletin*, 115, 288–99.

Izard, C.E., Fantauzzo, C.A., Castle, J.M., Haynes, O.M. and Slomine, B.S. (1995). The morphological stability and social validity of infants' facial expressions. Unpublished manuscript, University of Delaware.

Izard, C.E., Fine, S.E., Schultz, D., Mostow, A.J., Ackerman, B.P. and Youngstrom, E.A. (2008). Emotion knowledge as a predictor of social behaviour and academic competence in children at risk. *Psychological Science*, 12, 18–23.

Izard, C., Hembree, E.A. and Heubner, R.B. (1987). Infants' emotion expressions to acute pain: developmental change and stability of individual differences. *Developmental Psychology*, 23, 105–13.

Jackson, P., Meltzoff, A. and Decety, J. (2005). How do we perceive the pain of others? A window into the neural processes involved in empathy. *Neuroimage*, 24, 771–9.

Jackson, S.I. (2006). Research methods and statistics: a critical thinking approach (2nd Edn). Belmont, CA: Wadsworth.

Jaffe, S. and Hyde, J.S. (2000). Gender differences in moral orientation: a meta-analysis. *Psychological Bulletin*, 126(5), 703–26.

Jaffee, S.R., Moffitt, T.E., Caspi, A. and Taylor, A. (2003). Life with (or without) father: the benefits of living with two biological parents depend on the father's antisocial behavior. *Child Development*, 74, 109–26.

James, A. (2013). *Socialising Children*. Basingstoke, UK: Palgrave Macmillan.

James, W. (1890/1981). *The Principles of Psychology*, Cambridge, MA: Harvard University Press.

Jarrett, O. and Maxwell, D. (1999). Physical education and recess: are both necessary? *American Association of Child's Rights to Play*, 55, 3–20.

Jayson, S. (2013). Books blast new version of psychiatry's bible, the DSM. *USA Today*, www.usatoday.com/story/news/nation/2013/05/12/dsm-psychiatry-mental-disorders/2150819/.

Jenkins, J.M. and Astington, J.W. (1996). Cognitive factors and family structure associated with theory of mind development in young children. *Developmental Psychology*, 32, 70–8.

Johnson, J.G., Cohen, P., Smailes, E.M., Kasen, S. and Brook, J.S. (2002). Television viewing and aggressive behaviour during adolescence and adulthood. *Science*, 295(5564), 2468–71.

Johnson, J.H. and Jason, L.A. (1994). The development of a parent-tutor assessment scale. *Urban Education*, 29(1), 22–33.

Johnson, M.H. (2000). Functional brain development in infants: effects of an interactive specialization network. *Child Development*, 71, 75–81.

Johnson, M.H. and de Haan, M. (2001). Developing cortical specialisation for visual–cognitive function: the case of face recognition. In J.L. McClelland, and R.S. Seigler (eds). *Mechanisms of Cognitive Development: Behavioral and Neural Perspectives* (pp. 253–270). Mahwah, NJ: Lawrence Erlbaum Associates.

Johnson, M.H., Dziurawiec, S., Ellis, H.D. and Morton, J. (1991). Newborns' preferential tracking of face-like stimuli and its subsequent decline. *Cognition*, 40, 1–19.

Johnson, M.H. and Morton J. (1991). *Biology and Cognitive Development: The Case of Face Recognition*. Oxford: Blackwells.

Johnson, S.P. and Aslin, R.N. (1996). Perception of object unity in young infants: the roles of motion, depth, and orientation. *Cognitive Development*, 11, 161–80.

Johnson, W., Emde, R.N., Pannabecker, B., Sternberg, C. and Davis, M. (1982). Maternal perception of infant emotion from birth through 18 months. *Infant Behavior and Development*, 5, 313–22.

Johnston, J.R. and Wong, M-Y.A. (2002). Cultural differences in beliefs and practices concerning talk to children. *Journal of Speech, Language, and Hearing Research*, 45, 916–26.

Jolliffe, D. and Farrington, D.P. (2011). Is low empathy related to bullying after controlling for individual and social background variables? *Journal of Adolescence*, 34, 59–71.

Jones, W., Bellugi, U., Lai, Z., Chiles, M., Reilly, J., Lincoln, A. and Adolphs, R. (2000). II: hypersociability in Williams syndrome. *Journal of Cognitive Neuroscience*, 12, 30–46.

Juvonen, J., Graham, S. and Schuster, M.A. (2003). Bullying among young adolescents: the strong, the weak, and the troubled. *Pediatrics*, 112(6), 1231–7.

Kagan, J. (2010). Temperamental contributions to the development of psychological profiles. In S.G. Hofman and P.M. DiBartolo (eds). *Social Anxiety: Clinical, Developmental, and Social Perspectives* (2nd Edn, pp. 323–45). London: Elsevier Academic Press.

Kagan, J., Kearsley, R.B. and Zelazo, P.R. (1978). *Infancy: Its Place in Human Development*. Cambridge, MA: Harvard University Press.

Kail, R.V. and Cavanaugh, J.C. (2004). *Human Development: A Life-Span View* (3rd Edn). Belmont, CA: Thomson Wadsworth.

Kaminsky, Z., Petronis, A., Wang, S.C., Levine, B., Ghaffar, O., Floden, D. and Feinstein, A. (2008). Epigenetics of personality traits: an illustrative study of identical twins discordant for risk-taking behaviour. *Twin Research and Human Genetics*, 11(1), 1–11.

Kanner, L. (1943). Autistic disturbances of affective contact. *The Nervous Child: Journal of Psychopathology, Psychotherapy, Mental Hygiene, and Guidance of the Child*, 2, 217–50.

Kaplan, A. (2012). Violence in the media: what effects on behaviour? *Child Adolescent Psychiatry, Addiction, Antisocial Personality Disorder, Psychiatric Emergencies, Psychotic Affective Disorders, Trauma and Violence*, www.psychiatrictimes.com/child-adolescent-psychiatry/violence-media-what-effects-behavior.

Karmiloff-Smith, A. (1996). *Beyond Modularity: A Developmental Perspective on Cognitive Science*. Cambridge, MA: MIT Press.

Karmiloff-Smith A. (1998). Development itself is the key to understanding developmental disorders. *Trends in Cognitive Sciences*, 2(10), 389–8.

Karmiloff-Smith, A. (2002). *Beyond Modularity: A Developmental Perspective on Cognitive Science*. London: MIT Press.

Karmiloff-Smith, A. (2007). Williams syndrome. *Current Biology*, 17(24), R1035–R1036.

Keenan, K. and Shaw, D.S. (2003). Starting at the beginning: exploring the etiology of antisocial behaviour in the first years of life. In B. Lahey, T.E. Moffitt and A. Caspi, (eds). *Causes of Conduct Disorder and Delinquency* (pp. 153–81). New York: Guilford Press.

Keller, A., Ford, L. and Meacham, J. (1978). Dimensions of self-concept in preschool children. *Developmental Psychology*, 14, 483–9.

Kelly, K.J. and Edwards, R.W. (1998). Image advertisements for alcohol products: is their appeal associated with adolescents' intention to consume alcohol? *Adolescence*, 33(129), 47–59.

Kelly, K.J., Slater, M.D. and Karan D. (2002). Image advertisements' influence on adolescents' perceptions of the desirability of beer and cigarettes. *Journal of Public Policy and Marketing*, 21(2), 295–304.

Keltner, D. and Haidt, J. (1999). Social functions of emotions at four levels of analysis. *Cognition and Emotion*, 13, 505–21.

Kendeou, P., Bohn-Gettler, C., White, M. and van den Broek, P. (2008). Children's inference generation across different media. *Journal of Research in Reading*, 31, 259–72.

Kenney, M.E. and Barton, C.E. (2003). Attachment theory and research. In J. Demick and C. Andreoletti (eds). *Handbook of Adult Development*. New York: Kluwer.

Kerig, P.K. (2008). Boundary dissolution in the family context: the search for the ties that bind marriage, parenting, and child development. In M. Schultz, M.K. Pruett, P. Kerig and R.D. Parke (eds). *Feathering the Nest: Couples' Relationships, Couples' Interventions, and Children's Development*. Washington, DC: American Psychological Association.

Kertzer, D.I. and Barbagli, M. (2002). *The History of the European Family: Family Life in the Long Nineteenth Century (1789–1913)*. New Haven and London: Yale University Press.

Killen, M. (1990). Children's evaluations of morality in the context of peer, teacher–child, and familial relations. *Journal of Genetic Psychology*, 151, 395–411.

Killen, M., Mulvey, K.L., Richardson, C., Jampol, N. and Woodward, A. (2011). The accidental transgressor: morally-relevant theory of mind. *Cognition*, 119, 197–215.

Killen, M. and Smetana, J.G. (1999). Social interactions in preschool classrooms and the development of young children's conceptions of the personal. *Child Development*, 70(2), 486–501.

Killen, M. and Smetana, J.G. (2014). *Handbook of Moral Development* (2nd Edn). New York: Psychology Press/Taylor and Francis Group.

Kim, S., Nordling, J. K., Yoon, J. E., Boldt, L. J. and Kochanska, G. (2013). Effortful control in "hot" and "cool" tasks differentially predicts children's behavior problems and academic performance. *Journal of Abnormal Child Psychology*, 41(1), 43–56.

Kim-Cohen, J., Caspi, A., Taylor, A., Williams, B., Newcombe, R., Craig, I.W., et al. (2006). MAOA, maltreatment, and gene–environment interaction predicting children's mental health: new evidence and a meta-analysis. *Molecular Psychiatry*, 11, 903–13.

Kindermann, T.A., McCollam, T.L. and Gibson, E. Jr. (1995). Peer networks and students' classroom engagement during childhood and adolescence. In K. Wentzel and J. Juvonen (eds). *Social Motivation: Understanding Children's School Adjustment* (pp. 279–312). New York: Cambridge University Press.

Kirkpatrick, L.A. and Hazan, C. (1994). Attachment styles and close relationships: a four-year prospective study. *Personal Relationships*, 1, 123–42.

Kirschner, S. and Tomasello, M. (2010). Joint music making promotes prosocial behavior in 4-year-old children. *Evolution and Human Behavior*, 31(5), 354–64.

Klahr, D. and MacWhinney, B. (1998). Information processing. In W. Damon, D. Kuhn and R.S. Siegler (eds). *Handbook of Child Psychology: Vol. 2, Cognition, Perception, and Language* (5th Edn, pp. 631–78). New York: Wiley.

Klimes-Dougan, B. and Kistner, J. (1990). Physically abused preschoolers' responses to peers' distress. *Developmental Psychology*, 26(4), 599–602.

Knebelmann, B., Boussin, L., Guerrier, D., Legeai, I., Kahn, A., Josso, N. and Picard, J.Y. (1991). Anti-Mullerian hormone Bruxelles: a nonsense mutation associated with the persistent Mullerian duct syndrome. *Proceedings of the National Academy of Sciences USA*, 88, 3767–71.

Kochanska, G. (1992). Children's interpersonal influence with mothers and peers. *Developmental Psychology*, 28, 491–9.

Kochanska, G. (2002). Mutually-responsive orientation between mothers and their children: a context for the early development of conscience. *Current Directions in Psychological Science*, 11, 191–5.

Kochanska, G. and Aksan, N. (1995). Mother-child mutually positive affect, the quality of child compliance to requests and prohibitions, and maternal control as correlates of early internalisation. *Child Development*, 66(1), 236–54.

Kochanska, G., Aksan, N., Prisco, T.R. and Adams, E.E. (2008). Mother–child and father–child mutually responsive orientation in the first 2 years and children's outcomes at preschool age: mechanisms of influence. *Child Development*, 79(1), 30–44.

Kochanska, G., Gross, J.N., Lin, M-H. and Nichols, K.E. (2002). Guilt in young children: development, determinants, and relations with a broader system of standards. *Child Development*, 73, 461–82.

Kohlberg, L. (1966). A cognitive-developmental analysis of children's sex-role concepts and attitudes. In E.E. Maccoby (ed.). *The Development of Sex Differences* (pp. 82–173). Stanford, CA: Stanford University Press.

Kohlberg, L. (1969). Stage and sequence: the cognitive-developmental approach to socialization. In D. Goslin (ed.). *Handbook of Socialization Theory and Research* (pp. 347–480). Chicago, IL: Rand McNally.

Kohlberg, L. (1985). The just community approach to moral education in theory and practice. In M. Berkowitz and F. Oser (eds). *Moral Education: Theory and Application* (pp. 27–87). Hillsdale, NJ: Lawrence Erlbaum.

Koluchová, J. (1976). The further development of twins after severe and prolonged deprivation: a second report. *Journal of Child Psychological Psychiatry*, 17(3), 181–8.

Komarovsky, M. (1964). *Blue-collar Marriage*. New York: Random House.

Kopp, C.B. (1987). The growth of self-regulation: caregivers and children. In N. Eisenberg (ed.). *Contemporary Topics in Developmental Psychology*. New York: Wiley.

Kopp, C.B. (2002). Commentary: the codevelopments of attention and emotion regulation. *Infancy*, 3(2), 199–208.

Kovacs, D.M., Parker, J.G. and Hoffman, L.W. (1996). Behavioural, affective and social correlates of involvement in cross-sex friendship in elementary school. *Child Development*, 67, 2269–86.

Kraepelin, E. (1915). *Psychiatrie: Ein Lehrbuch* (8th Edn, Vol. 4). Leipzig: Barth.

Krain, A.L. and Castellanos, F.X. (2006). Brain development and ADHD. *Clinical Psychology Review*, 26(4), 433–44.

Kraus, N., McGee, T.J., Carrell, T.D., Zecker, S.G., Nicol, T.G., Koch, D.B. (1996). Auditory neurophysiologic responses and discrimination deficits in children with learning problems. *Science*, 273, 971–73.

Krebs, D.L. (1998). The evolution of moral behaviour. In C. Crawford and D.L. Krebs (eds). *Handbook of Evolutionary Psychology: Ideas, Issues, and Applications* (pp. 337–68). Hillsdale, NJ: Erlbaum.

Krebs, D.L. (in press). Can evolutionary processes explain the origins of morality? In L. Workman, W. Reader and J. Barkow (eds). *Cambridge Handbook of Evolutionary Perspectives on Human Behavior*. Cambridge: Cambridge University Press.

Kress, V. (2014). The removal of the Multiaxial System in the DSM-5: implications and practice suggestions for counsellors. *The Professional Counsellor Journal*, 4(3), 191–201.

Kring, A.M., Johnson, S.L., Davison, G.C. and Neale, J.M. (2012). *Abnormal Psychology* (12th Edn). Chichester: Wiley.

Kristen, S., Thoermer, C., Hofer, T., Aschersleben, G. and Sodian, B. (2006). Scaling of theory of mind tasks. *Zeitschrift für Entwick-ungspsychologie und Pädagogische Psychologie*, 38, 186–95.

Krznaric, R. (2015). *Empathy: Why It Matters, and How To Get It*. London: Rider.

Kuczynski, L., Marshall, S. and Schell, K. (1997). Value socialization in a bidirectional relational context. In J. Grusec and L. Kuczynski (eds). *Parenting and Children's Internalization of Values: A Handbook of Contemporary Theory* (pp. 23–50). New York: Wiley.

Kuhn, D., Nash, S.C. and Brucken, L. (1978). Sex role concepts of two- and three-year-old children. *Child Development*, 49, 445–51.

Kunce, L.J. and Shaver, P.R. (1994). An attachment-theoretical approach to caregiving in romantic relationships (pp. 205–37). In K. Bartholomew and D. Perlman (eds). *Advances in Personal Relationships* (Vol. 5). London: Jessica Kingsley.

Kupersmidt, J. and Dodge, K.A. (2004). *Children's Peer Relations: From Development to Intervention*. Washington, DC: American Psychological Association.

Kwon, K. and Lease, A.M. (2007). Clique membership and social adjustment in children's same-gender cliques: the contribution of the type of clique to children's self-reported adjustment. *Merrill-Palmer Quarterly*, 53(2), 216–42.

Ladd, G.W. (2005). *Peer Relationships and Social Competence of Children and Youth*. New Haven, CT: Yale University Press.

Ladd, G.W. and Pettit, G.S. (2002). Parenting and the development of children's peer relationships. In M.H. Bornstein (ed.). *Handbook of Parenting: Vol. 5. Practical Issues in Parenting* (2nd Edn, pp. 269–309). Mahwah, NJ: Erlbaum.

Laërtius, Diogenes (3rd century). *The Lives and Opinions of Eminent Philosophers, Book 5: The Peripatetics*, 9. Translated by C.D. Yonge (1853). London: H.G. Bohn.

LaFontana, K.M. and Cillessen, A.H.N. (2002). Children's perceptions of popular and unpopular peers: a multimethod assessment. *Developmental Psychology*, 38(5), 635–47.

La Freniere, P.J. (2000). *Emotional Development: A Biosocial Perspective*. Belmont, CA: Wadsworth Press.

Lagattuta, K.H., Wellman, H.M. and Flavell, J.H. (1997). Preschoolers' understanding of the link between thinking and feeling: cognitive cuing and emotional change. *Child Development*, 68, 1081–104.

LaGrange, R.L. and Raskin, H.W. (1985). Age differences in delinquency: a test of theory. *Criminology*, 23, 19–46.

La Greca, A.M. and Harrison, H.M. (2005). Adolescent peer relations, friendships, and romantic relationships: do they predict social anxiety and depression? *Journal of Clinical Child Adolescent Psychology*, 34(1), 49–61.

Lahey, B.B., Moffitt, T.E. and Caspi, A. (2003). *Causes of Conduct Disorder and Juvenile Delinquency*. London: The Guilford Press.

Laible, D.J. and Thompson, R.A. (2007). Early socialisation: a relationship perspective. In J.E. Grusec and P.D. Hastings (eds). *Handbook of Socialisation*. New York: Guilford.

Lakatos, K., Nemoda, Z., Birkas, E., Ronai, Z., Kovacs, E., Ney, K., Toth, I., Sasvari-Szekely, M. and Gervai, J. (2003). Association of D4 dopamine receptor gene and serotonin transporter promoter polymorphisms with infants' response to novelty. *Molecular Psychiatry*, 8, 90–7.

Lakatos, K., Toth, I., Nemoda, Z., Ney, K., Sasvari-Szekely, M. and Gervai, J. (2000). Dopamine D4 receptor (DRD4) gene polymorphism is associated with attachment disorganization in infants. *Molecular Psychiatry*, 5(6), 633–7.

Lamb, M.E. and Ahnert, L. (2006). Nonparental child care: context, concepts, correlates, and consequences. In W. Damon, R.M. Lerner, K.A. Renninger and I.E. Sigel (eds). *Handbook of Child Psychology: Vol. 4. Child Psychology in Practice* (6th Edn, pp. 950–1016). Hoboken, NJ: Wiley.

Lamb, M.E. and Nash, A. (1989). Infant–mother attachment, sociability, and peer competence (p. 240). In T.J. Berndt and G.W. Ladd (eds). *Peer Relationships in Child Development* (pp. 219–46). New York: Wiley.

Lamb, M.E., Suomi, S.J. and Stephenson, G.R. (1979). *Social Interaction Analysis: Methodological Issues*. Madison: University of Wisconsin Press.

Lamm, C. and Majdandžić, J. (2015). The role of shared neural activations, mirror neurons, and morality in empathy: a critical comment. *Neuroscience Research*, 90, 15–24.

Lamm, C., Silani, G. and Singer, T. (2015). Distinct neural networks underlying empathy for pleasant and unpleasant touch. *Cortex*, 70, 79–89.

Landers, R.N. and Lounsbury, J.W. (2006). An investigation of Big Five and narrow personality traits in relation to Internet usage. *Computers in Human Behavior*, 22, 283–93.

Landry, S.H., Smith, K.E. and Swank, P.R. (2006). Responsive parenting: establishing early foundations for social, communication, and independent problem-solving skills. *Developmental Psychology*, 42, 627–42.

Landry, S.H., Smith, K.E., Swank, P.R. and Miller-Loncar, C.L. (2000). Early maternal and child influences on children's later independent cognitive and social functioning. *Child Development*, 71, 358–75.

Lange, J.S. (1931). *Crime and Destiny*. London: Allen and Unwin.

Langlois, J.H. (1986). From the eye of the beholder to behavioural reality: the development of social behaviours and social relations as a function of physical attractiveness, In C.P. Herman, M.P. Zanna and E.T. Higgins (eds). *Physical Appearance, Stigma, and Social Behaviour. The Ontario Symposium* (pp. 23–51). Hillsdale, NJ: Erlbaum.

Langlois, J.H. and Downs, C.A. (1980). Mothers, fathers and peers as socialization agents of sex-typed play behaviors in young children. *Child Development*, 51, 1237–47.

Langlois, J.H., Kahakanis, L., Rubenstein, A.J., Larson, A., Hallam, N. and Smoot, M. (2000). Maxims or myths of beauty: a meta-analytic and theoretical review. *Psychological Bulletin*, 126, 390–423.

Larson, R. (1997). The emergence of solitude as a constrictive domain of experience in early adolescence. *Child Development*, 68, 80–93.

Larzelere, R.E. and Baumrind, D. (2010). Are spanking injunctions scientifically supported? *Law and Contemporary Problems*, 73(2), 57–87.

Larzelere, R.E. and Kuhn, B.R. (2005). Comparing child outcomes of physical punishment and alternative disciplinary tactics: a meta-analysis. *Clinical Child Family Psychology Review*, 8(1), 1–37.

Lauber, M.O., Marshall, M.L. and Meyers, J. (2005). Gangs. In S.W. Lee (ed.). *Encyclopedia of School Psychology*. Thousand Oaks, CA: Sage.

Lawson, D. and Mace, R. (2008). Sibling configuration and childhood growth in contemporary British families. *International Journal of Epidemiology*, 37, 1408–21.

Layton, T., Chuang, M.-C. and Hao, G. (2014). Play behaviors in Chinese toddlers with Down syndrome. *Journal of Psychological Abnormalities in Children*, 3(4), 131–5.

Leaper, C. and Friedman, C.K. (2007). The socialization of gender. In J. Grusec and P. Hastings (eds). *Handbook of Socialization* (pp. 561–87). New York: Guilford Press.

Leaper, C., Tenenbaum, H.R. and Shaffer, T.G. (1999). Communication patterns of African American girls and boys from low-income, urban background. *Child Development*, 70, 1485–503.

Leapman, B. (2008). Violent youth crime up a third. *The Telegraph*, www.telegraph.co.uk/news/uknews/1576076/Violent-youth-crime-up-a-third.html.

Lease, A.M., Kennedy, C.A. and Axelrod, J.L. (2002). Children's social constructions of popularity. *Social Development*, 11(1), 87–109.

Lease, A.M., Musgrove, K.T. and Axelrod, J.L. (2002). Dimensions of social status in preadolescent peer groups: likability, perceived popularity, and social dominance. *Social Development*, 11(4), 508–33.

Lecce, S. and Hughes, C. (2010). The Italian job? Comparing theory of mind performance in British and Italian children. *British Journal of Developmental Psychology*, 28, 747–66.

Leekum, S. (1993). Children's understanding of mind. In M. Bennett (ed.). *The Development of Social Cognition: The Child as Psychologist* (pp. 26–61). New York: Guilford Press.

Lemert, E. (1967). *Human Deviance, Social Problems, and Social Control* (2nd Edn). Englewood Cliffs, NJ: Prentice-Hall.

Lemish, D. (2007). *Children and Television: A Global Perspective*. Oxford: Blackwell.

Lempers, J.D. and Clark-Lempers, D.S. (1993). A functional comparison of same-sex and opposite sex friendships during adolescence. *Journal of Adolescent Research*, 8, 89–108.

Lengua, L.J. and Kovacs, E.A. (2005). Bidirectional associations between temperament and parenting and the prediction of adjustment problems in middle childhood. *Journal of Applied Developmental Psychology*, 26, 21–38.

Lenneberg, E. (1967). *Biological Foundations of Language*. New York: Wiley.

Leslie, A. (1994). ToMM, ToBY and Agency: core architecture and domain specificity. In L. Hirschfeld and S. Gelman (eds). *Mapping the Mind: Domain Specificity in Cognition and Culture* (pp. 119–48). Cambridge: Cambridge University Press.

Levenson, R.W. and Ruef, A.M. (1992). Empathy: a physiological substrate. *Journal of Personality and Social Psychology*, 63(2), 234–46.

Levine, S.C. and Levy, J. (1986). Perceptual asymmetry for chimeric faces across the life span. *Brain and Cognition*, 5, 291–306.

Levy, J., Heller, W., Banich, M. and Burton, L. (1983). Asymmetry of perception in free viewing of chimeric faces. *Brain and Cognition*, 2, 404–19.

Lewis M. (2003). The development of self-consciousness. In J. Roessler and N. Eilan (eds). *Agency and Self-awareness* (pp. 275–295). Oxford: Clarendon.

Lewis, M. (2005). Selfhood. In B. Hopkins (ed.). *The Cambridge Encyclopedia of Child Development* (p. 363). Cambridge, UK: Cambridge University Press.

Lewis, M. (2010). Self-conscious emotions: embarrassment, price, shame, and guilt. In L. Michael, J.M. Haviland-Jones and L.F. Barrett (eds). *Handbook of Emotions* (pp. 742–56). New York: Guilford.

Lewis, M., Alessandri, S. and Sullivan, M.W. (1992). Differences in shame and pride as a function of children's gender and task difficulty. *Child Development*, 63, 630–8.

Lewis, M. and Brooks, J. (1974). Self, other, and fear: infants' reactions to people. In M. Lewis and I. Rosenblum (eds). *The Origins of Fear* (pp. 195–227). New York: Wiley.

Lewis, M. and Brooks-Gunn, J. (1979). *Social Cognition and the Acquisition of Self*. New York: Plenum Press.

Lewis, R. (2007). *Human Genetics* (7th Edn). New York: McGraw-Hill.

Leyens, J-P., Camino, L., Parke, R. and Berkowitz, L. (1975). Effects of movie violence on aggression in the field setting as a function of group dominance and cohesion. *Journal of Personality and Social Psychology*, 32(2), 346–60.

Liben, L.S. (1991). Adults' performance on horizontality tasks: conflicting frames of reference. *Developmental Psychology*, 27, 285–94.

Lieberman, M., Doyle, A. and Markiewicz, D. (1999). Developmental patterns in security of attachment to mother and father in late childhood and early adolescence: association with peer relations. *Child Development*, 70, 202–13.

Liew, J., Eisenberg, N., Losoya, S.H., Fabes, R.A., Guthrie, I.K. and Murphy, B.C. (2003). Children's physiological indices of empathy and their socioemotional adjustment: does caregivers' expressivity matter? *Journal of Family Psychology*, 17, 584–97.

Lindenberg, S. (1996). Continuities in the theory of social production functions. *Verklarende Sociologie: Opstellen Voor Reinhard Wippler* (pp. 169–184). Amsterdam: Thesis Publishers.

Linebarger, D.L. (2006). *Teaching Language and Literacy on Television: A Ready to Learn Report.* Philadelphia, PA: Annenberg School for Communication, University of Pennsylvania.

Linebarger, D.L. and Piotrowski, J. (2009). TV as storyteller: how exposure to television narratives impacts at-risk preschoolers' story knowledge and narrative skills. *British Journal of Developmental Psychology,* 27, 47–69.

Lisle, R. (2016). Orthorexia: slipping through the net? *The Psychologist,* 29(12), 890.

Little, T.D., Miyashita, T., Karasawa, M., Mashima, M., Oettingen, G., Azuma, H. and Baltes, P.B. (2003). The links among action-control beliefs, intellective skill, and school performance in Japanese, US, and German school children. *International Journal of Behavioral Development,* 27, 41–8.

Little, T.D., Oettingen, G., Stretsenko, A. and Baltes, P.B. (1995). Children's action-control beliefs and school performance: how do American children compare with German and Russian children? *Journal of Personality and Social Psychology,* 69, 686–700.

Locke, J. (1693/1989). *Some Thoughts Concerning Education.* London: A. and J. Churchill.

Loeber, R. (1982). The stability of antisocial and delinquent child behavior: a review. *Child Development,* 53, 1431–46.

Loeber, R. and Stouthamer-Loeber, M. (1998). Development of juvenile aggression and violence: some common misconceptions and controversies. *American Psychologist,* 53, 242–59.

Loehlin, J.C. (1992). *Genes and Environment in Personality Development.* Newbury Park, CA: Sage.

Logothetis, N.K. (2008). What we can do and what we cannot do with fMRI. *Nature,* 453, 869–78.

Lorenz, K.Z. (1965). *Evolution and the Modification of Behaviour.* Chicago: University of Chicago Press.

Low, J. and Durkin, K. (1998). Structure and causal connections in children's on-line television narratives: what develops? *Cognitive Development,* 13, 201–25.

Luck, S. J. (2005). *An Introduction to the Event-Related Potential Technique.* The MIT Press: The University of Michigan.

Lynam, D.R. and Henry, W. (2001). The role of neuropsychological deficits in conduct disorders. In J. Hill and B. Maughan (eds). *Conduct Disorders in Childhood and Adolescence.* Cambridge: Cambridge University Press.

Lynch, J. (2014). *Resurfacing Specters in the House of Media: The Ghosts of Columbine in American Horror Story: Murder House.* Muncie, IN: Ball State University, http://bsu.edu/dlr/past/issue1_lynch.pdf.

Lystra, K. (1989). *Searching the Heart: Women, Men, and Romantic Love in Nineteenth-Century America.* New York: Oxford University Press.

Maccoby, E.E. (1990). Gender and relationships: a developmental account. *American Psychologist,* 45, 513–20.

Maccoby, E.E. (1992). The role of parents in the socialisation of children: an historical overview. *Developmental Psychology,* 28(6), 1006–17.

Maccoby, E.E. (1998). *The Two Sexes: Growing up Apart, Coming Together.* Cambridge, MA: Harvard University Press.

Maccoby, E.E. (2007). Historical overview of socialization research and theory. In J.E. Grusec and P.D. Hastings (eds). *Handbook of Socialization.* New York: Guilford.

Maccoby, E.E. and Martin, J.A. (1983). Socialisation in the context of the family: parent–child interaction. In E.M. Hetherington (ed.). *Handbook of Child Psychology,* Vol. 4. New York: Wiley.

Magforum (2012). *Teen magazines,* www.magforum.com/glossies/teen.htm.

Magnuson, K.A., Ruhm, C. and Waldfogel, J. (2007). Does prekindergarten improve school preparation and performance? *Economics of Education Review,* 26, 33–51.

Maher, M.R. (2003/2004). Protecting children from the dangers of chat rooms. *Computing with Management,* 1–61.

Main, M. (1985). Attachment: a move to the level of representation. Symposium presented at the meeting of the Society for Research in Child Development, Toronto, Canada.

Malatestsa, C.Z., Culver, C., Tesman, J.R. and Shepard, B. (1989). The development of emotion expression during the first two years of life. *Monographs of the Society for Research in Child Development*, 54(1–2), 1–104; 105–36.

Malecki, C.K., Demaray, M.K. and Elliott, S.N. (2000). *The Child and Adolescent Social Support Scale*. DeKalb, IL: Northern Illinois University.

Malecki, C.K. and Elliot, S.N. (2002). Children's social behaviors as predictors of academic achievement: a longitudinal analysis. *School Psychology Quarterly*, 17(1), 1–23.

Malenka, R.C., Nestler, E.J. and Hyman, S.E. (2009). Chapter 10: Neural and neuroendocrine control of the internal milieu. In A. Sydor and R.Y. Brown (eds). *Molecular Neuropharmacology: A Foundation for Clinical Neuroscience* (2nd Edn, pp. 249–66). New York: McGraw-Hill Medical.

Malenka, R.C., Nestler, E.J. and Hyman, S.E. (2009). Chapter 13: Higher cognitive function and behavioral control. In A. Sydor and R.Y. Brown (eds). *Molecular Neuropharmacology: A Foundation for Clinical Neuroscience* (2nd Edn, pp. 313–21). New York: McGraw-Hill Medical.

Malti, T., Gasser, L. and Buchmann, M. (2009a). Aggressive and prosocial children's emotion attributions and moral reasoning. *Aggressive Behaviour*, 35(1), 90–102.

Malti, T., Gasser, L. and Gutzwiller-Helfenfinger, E. (2010). Children's interpretive understanding, moral judgments, and emotion attributions: relations to social behaviour. *British Journal of Developmental Psychology*, 28, 275–92.

Malti, T., Gummerum, M., Keller, M. and Buchmann, M. (2009b). Children's moral motivation, sympathy, and prosocial behaviour. *Child Development*, 80(2), 442–60.

Mangelsdorf, S.C., Shapiro, J.R. and Marzolf, D. (1995). Developmental and temperamental differences in emotional regulation in infancy. *Child Development*, 66, 1817–28.

Mangelsdorf, S., Watkins, S. and Lehn, L. (1991). The role of control in the infant's appraisal of strangers. Paper presented at the biennial meeting of the Society for Research in Child Development, Seattle, Washington.

Manning, W.D., Fettro, M.N. and Lamidi, E. (2015). Child well-being in same-sex parent families: review of research prepared for American Sociological Association Amicus Brief. *Population Research and Policy Review*, 33(4), 485–502.

Mares, M.L. and Woodard, E.H. (2007). Positive effects of television on children's social interaction. In P.R. Press, B.M. Gayle, N. Burrell, M. Allen and J. Bryant (eds). *Mass Media Effects Research*. Mahwah, NJ: Erlbaum.

Markman, E.M. (1990). Constraints children place on word meanings. *Cognitive Science*, 14, 154–73.

Markman, E.M. (1992). Constraints on word learning: speculations about their nature, origins, and domain specificity. In M.R. Gunnar and M. Maratsos (eds). *Modularity and Constraints in Language and Cognition* (Vol. 25, pp. 59–101). Hillsdale, NJ: LEA.

Markman, E.M. and Hutchinson, J.E. (1984). Children's sensitivity to constraints on word meaning: taxonomic vs thematic relations. *Cognitive Psychology*, 16, 1–27.

Markman, E.M. and Wachtel, G.F. (1988). Children's use of mutual exclusivity to constrain the meanings of words. *Cognitive Psychology*, 20, 121–57.

Markman, E.M., Wasow, J.L. and Hansen, M.B. (2003). Use of the mutual exclusivity assumption by young word learners. *Cognitive Psychology*, 47, 241–75.

Markus, H.R. and Kitayama, S. (1991). Culture and self: implications for cognition, emotion and motivation. *Psychological Review*, 98, 224–53.

Marsh, H.W. (1990). A multidimensional, hierarchical model of self-concept: theoretical and empirical justification. *Educational Psychology Review*, 2, 77–172.

Marshall, T.C., Lefringhausen, K. and Ferenczi, N. (2015). The Big Five, self-esteem, and narcissism as predictors of the topics people write about in Facebook status updates. *Personality and Individual Differences*, 85, 35–40.

Martin, C.L. and Halverson, C.F. (1983). The effects of sex-typing schemas on young children's memory. *Child Development*, 54, 563–74.

Martin, S.E., Snyder, L., Hamilton, M., Fleming-Milici, F., Slater, M., Stacy, A., Chen, M.J.

and Grube, J.W. (2002). Alcohol advertising and youth. *Alcoholism: Clinical and Experimental Research*, 26, 900–6.

Mascolo, M.F. and Fischer, K. (2007). The co-development of self and socio-moral emotions during the toddler years. In C.A. Brownell and C.B. Kopp (eds). *Transitions in Early Development*. New York: Guilford.

Masten, A.S. (2001). Ordinary magic: resilience processes in development. *American Psychologist*, 56, 227–38.

Masten, A.S. (2004). Regulatory processes, risk and resilience in adolescent development. *Annals of the New York Academy of Sciences*, 1021, 310–19.

Masten, A.S. (2006). Developmental psychopathology: pathways to the future. *International Journal of Behavioral Development*, 31, 46–53.

Masten, A.S., Burt, K. and Coatsworth, J.D. (2006). Competence and psychopathology in development. In D. Cicchetti and D. Cohen (eds). *Developmental Psychopathology* (2nd Edn). New York: Wiley.

Masten, A.S. and Obradovic, J. (2007). Competence and resilience in development. In B.M. Lester, A. Masten and B. McEwen (eds). *Resilience in Children.* Malden, MA: Blackwell.

Mathieson, K. and Banerjee, R. (2011). Peer play, emotion understanding, and socio-moral explanation: the role of gender. *British Journal of Developmental Psychology*, 29(2), 188–96.

Mathios, A., Avery, R., Bisogni, C. and Shanahan, J. (1998). Alcohol portrayal on primetime television: manifest and latent messages. *Journal of Studies on Alcohol*, 59, 305–10.

Matsumoto, D. and Juang, L. (2008). *Culture and Psychology* (4th Edn). Belmont, CA: Wadsworth.

Matthews, J. (2011). *Starting from Scratch: The Origin and Development of Expression, Representation and Symbolism in Human and Non-Human Primates*. Hove, UK: Psychology Press.

Matza, D. (1969). *Becoming Deviant*. New Jersey: Prentice Hall.

Mayes, R., Bagwell, C. and Erkulwater, J.L. (2009). *Medicating Children: ADHD and Pediatric Mental Health*. Cambridge, MA: Harvard University Press.

Mayes, R. and Horwitz, A.V. (2005). DSM-III and the revolution in the classification of mental illness. *Journal of the History of the Behavioral Sciences*, 41(3), 249–67.

McBurnett, K. (1992). Psychobiological theories of personality and their application to child psychopathology. In B.B. Lahey and A. Kazdin (eds). *Advances in Child Clinical Psychology* (pp. 107–64). New York: Plenum Press.

McBurney, D.H. and White, T.L. (2007). *Research Methods* (7th Edn). Belmont, CA: Wadsworth.

McClure, E. (2000). A meta-analytic review of sex differences in facial expression processing and their development in infants, children, and adolescents. *Psychological Bulletin*, 126, 242–453.

McCrae, R.R., and Costa Jr, P.T. (1987). Validation of the Five-Factor Model of personality across instruments and observers. *Journal of Personality and Social Psychology*, 52, 81–90.

McCrae, R.R., Costa Jr, P.T., Terracciano, A., Parker, W.D., Mills, C.J., De Fruyt, F. and Mervielde, I. (2002). Personality trait development from 12 to 18: longitudinal, cross-sectional, and cross-cultural analyses. *Journal of Personality and Social Psychology*, 83, 1456–68.

McHale, J.P. (2008). The construct of co-parenting: evolution of a key family paradigm. In M Schultz, M.K. Pruett, P. Kerig and R.D. Parke (eds). *Feathering the Nest: Couples' Relationships, Couples' Interventions, and Children's Development*. Washington, DC: American Psychological Association.

McHale, S.M., Shanahan, L., Updegraff, K.A., Crouter, A.C. and Booth, A. (2004). Developmental and individual differences in girls' sex-typed activities in middle childhood and adolescence. *Child Development*, 75, 1575–93.

McHale, S.M., Updegraff, K.A., Helms-Erikson, H. and Crouter, A.C. (2001). Sibling influences on gender development in middle childhood and early adolescence: a longitudinal study. *Developmental Psychology*, 37, 115–25.

McHale, S.M., Whiteman, S.D., Kim, J-Y. and Crouter, A.C. (2007). Characteristics and correlates of sibling relationships in two-parent African American families. *Journal of Family Psychology*, 21, 227–35.

McKee, L., Roland, E., Coffelt, N., Olson, A.L., Forehand, R., Massari, C. and Zens, M.S. (2007). Harsh discipline and child problem behaviors: the roles of positive parenting and gender. *Journal of Family Violence*, 22(4), 187–96.

McMillan, J.H. (2007). *Educational Research* (5th Edn). Boston: Allyn and Bacon.

McNeal, J. (1992). *Kids as Customers: A Handbook of Marketing to Children*. Lexington, MA: Lexington Books.

McPherson, M., Smith-Lovin, L. and Cook, J.M. (2001). Birds of a feather: homophily in social networks. *Annual Review of Sociology*, 27, 415–44.

McQuade, J.D., Murray-Close, D., Shoulberg, E.K. and Hoza, B. (2013). Working memory and social functioning in children. *Journal of Experimental Child Psychology*, 115, 422–35.

McQuigge, M. (2013). Victims' genes play role in school bullying: Quebec study. *Toronto Star*. Toronto: Toronto Star Newspapers Ltd, www.thestar.com/news/canada/2013/01/16/victims_genes_play_role_in_school_bullying_quebec_study.html.

Meadows, S. (1986). *Understanding Child Development: Psychological Perspectives in an Interdisciplinary Field of Inquiry*. New York: Routledge.

Meadows, S. (2010). *The Child as Social Person*. London: Routledge, Taylor and Francis Group.

Meaney, M.J., Mitchell, J.B., Aitken, D.H. and Bhatnagar, S. (1991). The effects of neonatal handling on the development of the adrenocortical response to stress: implications for neuropathology and cognitive deficits in later life. *Psychoneuroendocrinology*, 16, 85–103.

Mehroof, M. and Griffiths M.D. (2010). Online gaming addiction: the role of sensation seeking, self-control, neuroticism, aggression, state anxiety, and trait anxiety. *Cyberpsychology, Behavior, and Social Networking*, 13, 313–6.

Meins, E., Fernyhough, C., Johnson, F. and Lidstone, J. (2006). Mind-mindedness in children: individual differences in internal-state talk in middle childhood. *British Journal of Developmental Psychology*, 24, 181–96.

Meins, E., Fernyhough, C., Wainwright, R., Gupta, M.D., Fradley, E. and Tuckey, M. (2002). Maternal mind-mindedness and attachment security as predictors of theory of mind understanding. *Child Development*, 73, 1715–26.

Melotti, G., Biolcati, R. and Passini, S. (2009). A psychosocial reading of cyberbullying. In M.L. Genta, A. Brighi and A. Guarini (eds). *Cyberbullying* (pp. 78–103). Rome: Carocci.

Menesini, E. and Camodeca, M. (2008). Shame and guilt as behaviour regulators: relationships with bullying, victimisation and prosocial behaviour. *British Journal of Developmental Psychology*, 26, 183–96.

Menzel, E. (1974). A group of young chimpanzees in a one acre field. In Schrier and Stolnitz (eds). *Behaviour of Non-Human Primates* (pp. 5, 83–153). New York: Academic Press.

Messenger, D.S., Fogel, A. and Dickenson, K.L. (1999). What's in a smile? *Developmental Psychology*, 35, 701–98.

Messenger, D.S., Fogel, A. and Dickenson, K.L. (2001). All smiles are positive, but some smiles are more positive than others. *Developmental Psychology*, 37, 642–53.

Messer, D. (1981). Non-linguistic information which could assist the young child's interpretation of adults' speech. In W. P. Robinson (ed.). *Communication in Development* (pp. 39–62). London: Academic Press.

Messer, D. (1994). *The Development of Communication: From Social Interaction to Language*. West Sussex, UK: Wiley.

Mikami, A.Y., Szwedo, D.E., Allen, J.P., Evans, M.A. and Hare, A.L. (2010). Adolescent peer relationships and behaviour problems predict young adults' communication on social networking websites. *Developmental Psychology*, 46, 46–56.

Miller, E.K., Freedman, D.J. and Wallis, J.D. (2002). The prefrontal cortex: categories, concepts and cognition. *Philosophical Transactions of the Royal Society of London. Series B, Biological Sciences*, 357 (1424), 1123–36.

Miller, J.G. (2006). Insights into moral development from cultural psychology. In M. Killen and J.G. Smetana (eds). *Handbook of Moral Development* (pp. 375–98). Mahwah, NJ: Erlbaum.

Miller, J.G. (2007). Cultural psychology of moral development. In S. Kitayama and D. Cohen (eds). *Handbook of Cultural Psychology* (pp. 477–99). New York: Guilford.

Miller, J.L. and Eimas, P.D. (1994). Observations on speech perception, its development, and the search for a mechanism. In J.C. Goodman and H.C. Nusbaum (eds). *The Development of Speech Perception: The Transition from Speech Sounds to Spoken Words* (pp. 37–56). Cambridge, MA: MIT Press.

Miller, P.A., Eisenberg, N., Fabes, R.A. and Shell, R. (1996). Relations of moral reasoning and vicarious emotion to young children's prosocial behaviour toward peers and adults. *Developmental Psychology*, 32, 210–9.

Miller, P.T. (2016). *Theories of Developmental Psychology* (6th Edn). New York: Worth Publishers.

Miller, S.A. (2013). *Developmental Research Methods* (4th Edn). Los Angeles: Sage Publications, Inc.

Millichap, J.G. (2008). Etiologic classification of attention-deficit/hyperactivity disorder. *Pediatrics*, 121(2), e358–65.

Millichap, J.G. and Yee, M.M. (2012). The diet factor in attention-deficit/hyperactivity disorder. *Pediatrics*, 129(2), 330–7.

Minuchin, P. (2002). Looking toward the horizon: present and future in the study of family systems. In J. McHale and W. Grolnick (eds). *Retrospect and Prospect in the Psychological Study of Families* (pp. 259–78). Mahwah, NJ: Erlbaum.

Mischel, W. (1968). *Personality and Assessment*. New York: Wiley.

Mischel, W., Ebbesen, E.B. and Raskoff Zeiss, A. (1972). Cognitive and attentional mechanisms in delay of gratification. *Journal of Personality and Social Psychology*, 21(2), 204–18.

Mischel, W. and Patterson, C.J. (1976). Substantive and structural elements of effective plans for self-control. *Journal of Personality and Social Psychology*, 34, 942–50.

Mitchell, K.A. and Elias, M.J. (2003). Before the crisis starts: social competence and social support in third grade, minority, low-income, urban school children. Presentation at the annual meeting of the Easter Psychological Association, Baltimore, MD.

Mitchell, K.J., Finkelhor, D., Jones, L.M. and Wolak, J. (2012). Prevalence and characteristics of youth sexting: a national study. *Pediatrics*, 129(1), 13–20.

Mitchell, P. and Ziegler, F. (2007). *Fundamentals of Development: The Psychology of Childhood*. Hove, UK: Psychology Press.

Miyake, A. and Friedman, N.P. (2012). The nature and organization of individual differences in executive functions: four general conclusions. *Current Directions in Psychological Science*, 21, 8–14.

Moffitt, A.R. (1971). Consonant cue perception by twenty-to-twenty-four-week-old infants. *Child Development*, 42, 717–32.

Moffitt, T.E. (1993). Adolescence-limited and life-course-persistent antisocial behaviour: a developmental taxonomy. *Psychological Review*, 100, 674–701.

Moffitt, T.E. (2005). Genetic and environmental influences on antisocial behaviors: evidence from behavioral-genetic research. *Advances in Genetics*, 55, 41–104.

Molcho, M., Craig, W., Due, P., Pickett, W., Harel-fisch, Y., Overpeck, M. and HBSC Bullying Writing Group (2009). Cross-national time trends in bullying behaviour 1994–2006: findings from Europe and North America. *International Journal of Public Health*, 54 (S2), 225–34.

Molfese, D.L. and Molfese, V.J. (1979). Hemisphere and stimulus differences as reflected in the cortical responses of newborn infants to speech stimuli. *Developmental Psychology*, 15, 505–11.

Mongon, D. (2014). *Underachievement in Education by White Working Class Children. Addressing the Problem*. Education Committee, Parliamentary Business, www.publications.parliament.uk/pa/cm201415/cmselect/cmeduc/142/14207.htm#note123.

Monks, C.P., Ortega, R. and Torrado, E. (2002). Unjustified aggression in a Spanish pre-school. *Aggressive Behavior*, 28, 458–76.

Montessori, M. (1912). *The Montessori Method* (trans. A.E. George). New York: Frederick A. Stokes Company.

Montie, J.E., Xiang, Z. and Schweinhart, L.J. (2006). Preschool experience in 10 countries: cognitive and language performance at age 7. *Early Childhood Research Quarterly*, 21, 313–31.

Montroy J.J., Bowles R.P., Skibbe L.E. and Foster T.D. (2014). Social skills and problem behaviors as mediators of the relationship between behavioral self-regulation and academic achievement. *Early Childhood Research Quarterly*, 29, 298–309.

Moody, J., Brynildsen, W.D., Osgood, D.W., Feinberg, M.E. and Gest, S. (2011). Popularity trajectories and substance use in early adolescence. *Social Networks*, 33(2), 101–12.

Moore, A., Clark, B. and Kane, M. (2008). Who shall not kill? Individual differences in working memory capacity, executive control, and moral judgment. *Psychological Science*, 19, 549–57.

Moore, C. and Macgillivray, S. (2004). Altruism, prudence, and theory of mind in preschoolers. *New Directions for Child and Adolescent Development*, (103), 51–62.

Morelen, D., Zeman, J. and Perry-Parrish, C. (2012). Children's emotional regulation across and within nations: a comparison of Ghanaian, Kenyan, and American youth. *British Journal of Developmental Psychology*, 30, 415–31.

Morelli, S.A., Rameson, L.T. and Lieberman, M.D. (2014). The neural components of empathy: predicting daily prosocial behaviour. *Social Cognitive and Affective Neuroscience*, 9, 39–47.

Morgan, B.L. (1998). A three-generational study of tomboy behaviour. *Sex Roles*, 39, 787–858.

Morrison, I., Lloyd, D., di Pellegrino, G. and Roberts, N. (2004). Vicarious responses to pain in anterior cingulate cortex: is empathy a multisensory issue? *Cognitive, Affective, and Behavioral Neuroscience*, 4, 270–8.

Morton, J. (2004). *Understanding Developmental Disorders: A Causal Modelling Approach* (p. 260). Oxford: Blackwell Publishing.

Motti, F., Cicchetti, D. and Sroufe, L. (1983). From infant affect expression to symbolic play: the coherence of development in Down syndrome children. *Child Development*, 54, 1168–250.

Moyles, J. (1989). *Just Playing: The Role and Status of Play in Early Childhood Education*. Maidenhead: Open University Press.

Mroczek, D.K., Stawski, R.S., Turiano, N.A., Chan, W., Almeida, D.M., Neupert, S.D. and Spiro, A., III (2013). Emotional reactivity and mortality: longitudinal findings from the VA normative aging study. *Journals of Gerontology, Series B: Psychological Sciences and Social Sciences*, 70(3), 398–406.

Mullen, J., CNN (2015). What is ISIS' appeal for young people? *CNN* International Edition (25 February). Cable News Network, http://edition.cnn.com/2015/02/25/middleeast/isis-kids-propaganda/.

Mulvey, K.L. (2016). Evaluations of moral and conventional intergroup transgressions. *British Journal of Developmental Psychology*, 34(4), 489–501.

Mundy, P., Sigman, M., Ungerer, J. and Sherman, T. (1987). Play and nonverbal communication correlates of language development in autistic children. *Journal of Autism and Developmental Disorders*, 17, 349–63.

Muñoz, L.C., Qualter, P. and Padgett, G. (2011). Empathy and bullying: exploring the influence of callous-unemotional traits. *Child Psychiatry and Human Development*, 42, 183–96.

Murdock, G.P. and White, D.R. (1969). Standard cross-cultural sample. *Ethnology*, 8, 329–69.

Muris, P., Meesters, C., de Kanter, E. and Timmerman, P.E. (2005). Behavioural inhibition and behavioural activation system scales for children: relationships with Eysenck's personality traits and psychopathological symptoms. *Personality and Individual Differences*, 38, 831–41.

Murray, J.P. (2007). TV violence: research and controversy. In N. Pecora, J.P. Murry and E. A. Wartella (eds). *Children and Television*. Mahwah, NJ: Erlbaum.

Murray, L., Hipwell, A., Hooper, R., Stein, A. and Cooper, P.J. (1996). The cognitive development of five year old children of postnatally depressed mothers. *Journal of Child Psychology and Psychiatry*, 37, 927–35.

Nabuzoka, D. and Smith, P.K. (1993). Sociometric status and social behaviour of children with and without learning difficulties. *Journal of Child Psychology and Psychiatry*, 34, 1435–48.

Nangle, D.W., Erdley, C.A., Newman, J.E., Mason, C.A. and Carpenter, E. (2003). Popularity, friendship quantity, and friendship quality: interactive influences on children's loneliness and depression. *Journal of Clinical Child and Adolescent Psychology*, 32(4), 546–55.

Nasby, W., Hayden, B. and DePaulo, B.M. (1979). Attributional bias among aggressive boys to interpret ambiguous social stimuli as displays of hostility. *Journal of Abnormal Psychology*, 89, 459–68.

Nash, A.S., Pine, K.J. and Messer, D. (2009). Television alcohol advertising: do children really mean what they say? *British Journal of Developmental Psychology*, 27, 85–104.

National Center for Missing and Exploited Children. *Policy Statement on Sexting*, http://esd113.org/cms/lib3/WA01001093/Centricity/Domain/22/policystatementonsexting-ncmec.pdf.

National Longitudinal Survey of Youth (NLSY) (1979). Bureau of Labor Statistics, National Longitudinal Surveys, www.bls.gov/nls/.

Neale, B.M., Medland, S.E., Ripke, S. Asherson, P., Franke, B., Lesch, K.P., Faraone, S.V., Nquyen, T.T., et al. (2010). Meta-analysis of genome-wide association studies of attention-deficit/hyperactivity disorder. *Journal of the American Academy of Child and Adolescent Psychiatry*, 49(9), 884–97.

Neff, K.D. and Helwig, C.C. (2002). A constructivist approach to understanding the development of reasoning about rights and authority within cultural contexts. *Cognitive Development*, 17, 1429–50.

Neill, S.R.St.J. (2005). Knives and other weapons in London schools. *The International Journal on School Disaffection*, 3(2), 27–32.

Nelson, J.R., Smith, D.J. and Dodd, J. (1990). The moral reasoning of juvenile delinquents: a meta-analysis. *Journal of Abnormal Child Psychology*, 18, 231–9.

Nelson, K. (1973). Structure and strategy in learning to talk. *Monographs of the Society for Research in Child Development*, 38 (Serial No. 149).

Nelson, N.L., Hudspeth, K. and Russell, J.A. (2013). A story superiority effect for disgust, fear, embarrassment, and pride. *British Journal of Developmental Psychology*, 31, 334–48.

Nelson S.A. (1980). Factors influencing young children's use of motives and outcomes as moral criteria. *Child Development*, 51, 823–9.

Nesse, R.M. and Williams, G.C. (1995). *Evolution and Healing: The New Science of Darwinian Medicine*. London: Weidenfeld and Nicolson.

Neuendorf, K.A. (1985). Alcohol advertising and media portrayals. *Journal of the Institute of Socioeconomic Studies*, 10, 67–78.

Neville, H. (1995). Developmental specificity in neurocognitive development in humans. In M. Gazzaniga (ed.). *The Cognitive Neurosciences* (pp. 219–31). Cambridge, MA: Bradford.

Newcombe, N. and Huttenlocher, J. (1992). Children's early ability to solve perspective-taking problems. *Developmental Psychology*, 28(4), 635–43.

Newman, J.P., Wallace, J.F., Schmitt, W.A. and Arnett, P.A. (1997). Behavioral inhibition system functioning in anxious, impulsive and psychopathic individuals. *Personality and Individual Differences*, 23, 583–92.

The New York Times (1962). Pocket computer may replace shopping list. 3 November.

Neyer, F.J., Wrzus, C., Wagner, J. and Lang, F.R. (2011). Principles of relationship differentiation. *European Psychologist*, 16, 267–77.

New England Historic Genealogical Society. AmericanAncestors.org. Retrieved 27/03/2017.

Nianias, H. (2015). 'Eat clean'? The smug Instagram lifestyle might not be so healthy after all. *Vice*, www.vice.com/en_uk/read/why-your-eat-clean-lifestyle-might-not-be-so-healthy-after-all-252.

NICHD Early Child-Care Research Network (2000). The relation of child care to cognitive and language development. *Child Development*, 71, 960–80.

Nichols, S. (2004). *Sentimental Rules: On the Natural Foundations of Moral Judgment*. Oxford: Oxford University Press.

Nikolaidis, A. and Gray, J.R. (2010). ADHA and the DRD4 exon III 7-repeat polymorphism: an international meta-analysis. *Social Cognitive and Affective Neuroscience*, 5(2–3): 188–93.

Nisan, M. (1987). Moral norms and social conventions: a cross-cultural comparison. *Developmental Psychology*, 23, 719–25.

Nisbett, N. (2007). Friendship, consumption, morality: practising identity, negotiating hierarchy in middle-class Bangalore. *Journal of the Royal Anthropological Institute*, 13(4), 935–50.

Nisbett, R. (2003). *The Geography of Thought*. New York: Free Press.

Nishitani, N., Avikainen, S. and Hari, R. (2004). Abnormal imitation-related cortical activation sequences in Asperger's syndrome. *Annals of Neurology*, 55, 558–62.

Noble, K.G., Norman, M.F. and Farah, M.J. (2005). Neurocognitive correlates of socioeconomic status in kindergarten children. *Developmental Science*, 8(1), 74–87.

Nolen-Hoeksema, S. (2013). *Abnormal Psychology* (6th Edn). New York: McGraw-Hill Education.

Nolen-Hoeksema, S., Wolfson, A., Mumme, D. and Guskin, K. (1995). Helplessness in children of depressed and nondepressed mothers. *Developmental Psychology*, 31(3), 377–87.

Nomaguchi, K.M. (2006). Maternal employment, nonparental care, mother-child interactions, and child outcomes during preschool years. *Journal of Marriage and the Family*, 68, 1341–69.

Nucci, L.P. (1981). Conceptions of personal issues: a domain distinct from moral or societal concepts. *Child Development*, 52, 114–21.

Nucci, L.P. (2001). *Education in the Moral Domain*. Cambridge: Cambridge University Press.

Nucci, L.P. (2010). *Nice Is Not Enough: Facilitating Moral Development*. Upper Saddle River, NJ: Pearson.

Nucci, L.P., Killen, M. and Smetana, J.G. (1996). Autonomy and the personal: negotiation and social reciprocity in adult-child exchanges. In M. Killen (ed.). *Children's Autonomy, Social Competence, and Interactions with Adults and Other Children: Exploring Connections and Consequences (New Directions for Child Development)* (pp. 7–24). San Francisco: Jossey-Bass.

Nucci, L.P. and Nucci, M. (1982). Children's social interactions in the context of moral and conventional transgressions. *Child Development*, 53, 403–12.

Nucci, L.P. and Turiel, E. (1978). Social interactions and the development of social concepts in preschool children. *Child Development*, 49, 400–7.

Nucci, L.P. and Turiel, E. (1993). God's word, religious rules, and their relation to Christian and Jewish children's concepts of morality. *Child Development*, 64, 1475–91.

Nucci, L.P., Turiel, E. and Encarnacion-Gawrych, G. (1983). Children's social interactions and social concepts: analysis of morality and convention in the Virgin Islands. *Journal of Cross-Cultural Psychology*, 14, 469–87.

Nucci, L.P. and Weber, E.K. (1995). Social interactions in the home and the development of young children's conceptions of the personal. *Child Development*, 66, 1438–52.

Nunner-Winkler, G. (2007). Development of moral motivation from childhood to early adulthood. *Journal of Moral Education*, 36, 399–414.

Oberman, L.M., Hubbard, E.M., McCleery, J.P., Altschuler, E.L., Ramachandran, V.S. and Pineda, J.A. (2005). EEG evidence for mirror neuron dysfunction in autism spectrum disorders. *Brain Research: Cognitive Brain Research*, 24, 190–8.

Obler, L.K. (1993). Neurolinguistic aspects of second language development and attrition. In K. Hylstenstam and A.Viberg (eds). *Progression and Regression in Language* (pp. 178–95). Cambridge: Cambridge University Press.

Obradović, J., Pardini, D.A., Long, J.D. and Loeber, R. (2007). Measuring interpersonal callousness in boys from childhood to adolescence: an examination of longitudinal invariance and temporal stability. *Journal of Clinical Child and Adolescence Psychology*, 36(3), 276–92.

Odgers, C.L., Milne, B., Caspi, A., Crump, R., Poulton, R.P. and Moffitt, T.E. (2007). Predicting prognosis for the conduct-problem boy: can family history help? *Journal of the American Academy of Child and Adolescent Psychiatry*, 46, 1240–9.

Offer, D., Ostrov, E., Howard, K.I. and Atkinson, R. (1988). *The Teenage World: Adolescents' Self-image in Ten Countries*. New York: Plenum Press.

Office for National Statistics (2013). *Statistical Bulletin: Divorces in England and Wales 2013*, www.ons.gov.uk/peoplepopulationandcommunity/birthsdeathsandmarriages/divorce/bulletins/divorcesinenglandandwales/2013.

Office for National Statistics (2014). *Stepfamilies in 2011*. Crown Copyright.

Office for National Statistics (2015).The Marriage Act (2013). *Statistical Bulletin:*

Families and Households. Crown Copyright.

Office for National Statistics (2015). Trends in living arrangements including families (with and without dependent children), people living alone and people in shared accommodation, broken down by size and type of household. *Statistical Bulletin: Families and Households*. Crown Copyright.

Oh, S. and Lewis, C. (2008). Korean preschoolers' advanced inhibitory control and its relation to other executive skills and mental state understanding. *Child Development*, 79(1), 80–99.

Oldham, J.M. (2005). Personality disorders. *FOCUS*, 3, 372–82.

Olweus, D. (1973). *Aggression in Schools: Bullies and Whipping Boys*. Washington, DC: Hemisphere.

Olweus, D. (1978). *Aggression in Schools: Bullies and Whipping Boys*. Washington, DC: Hemisphere.

Olweus, D. (1986). Aggression and hormones: behavioral relationship with testosterone and adrenaline. In D. Olweus, J. Block and M. Radke-Yarrow (eds). *Development of Antisocial and Prosocial behaviour* (pp. 51–72). New York: Academic Press.

Olweus, D. (1999). Sweden. In P.K. Smith, Y. Morita, J. Junger-Tas, D. Olweus, R. Catalano and P. Slee (eds). *The Nature of School Bullying: A Cross-national Perspective* (pp. 7–27). London and New York: Routledge.

Ontai, L.L. and Thompson, R.A. (2002). Patterns of attachment and maternal discourse effects on children's emotion understanding from 3 to 5 years of age. *Social Development*, 12, 657–75.

Orlick, T., Zhou, Q. and Partington, J. (1990). Co-operation and conflict within Chinese and Canadian kindergarten settings. *Canadian Journal and Behavioral Science*, 22, 20–5.

Osborne, L.R. (2006). The molecular basis of a multisystem disorder. In C.A. Morris, H.M. Lenhoff and P.P. Wang (eds). *Williams-Beuren Syndrome: Research, Evaluation, and Treatment* (pp. 18–58). Baltimore, MD: Johns Hopkins University Press.

Ostrov, J.M. and Crick, N.R. (2006). How recent developments in the study of relational aggression and close relationships in early childhood advance the field. *Journal of Applied Developmental Psychology*, 27, 189–92.

Ostrov, J.M. and Crick, N.R. (2007). Forms and functions of aggression during early childhood: a short-term longitudinal study. *School Psychology Review*, 36, 22–43.

Ozawa-De Silva, C. (2008). Too lonely to die alone: internet suicide pacts and existential suffering in Japan. *Culture, Medicine, and Psychiatry*, 32, 516–51.

Ozawa-De Silva, C. (2010). Shared death: self, sociality and internet group suicide in Japan. *Transcultural Psychiatry*, 47, 392–419.

Ozonoff, S. and Jensen, J. (1999). Brief report: specific executive function profiles in three neurodevelopmental disorders (p. 171). *Journal of Autism and Developmental Disorders*, 29, 171–7.

Paikoff, R.L. and Savin-Williams, R.C. (1983). An exploratory study of dominance interactions among adolescent females at summer camp. *Journal of Youth and Adolescence*, 12, 419–33.

Palmer, B. (2011). Double inanity: twin studies are pretty much useless. *State Magazine*, www.slate.com/id/2301906/.

Palmer, E.J. and Hollin, C.R. (1997). The influence of perceptions of own parenting on sociomoral reasoning, attributions for criminal behaviour, and self-reported delinquency. *Personality and Individual Differences*, 23, 193–7.

Palmer, E.J. and Hollin, C.R. (2000). The inter-relations of sociomoral reasoning perceptions of own parenting, and attribution of intent with self-reported delinquency. *Legal and Criminological Psychology*, 5, 201–18.

Palmer, S.B., Rutland, A. and Cameron, L. (2015). The development of bystander intentions and social-moral reasoning about intergroup verbal aggression. *British Journal of Developmental Psychology*, 33(4), 419–33.

Panksepp J. (2010). The evolutionary sources of jealousy: cross-species approaches to fundamental issues. In S.L. Hart and M. Legerstee (eds). *Handbook of Jealousy: Theory, Research, and Multidisciplinary Approaches* (pp. 101–20). Malden, MA: Wiley-Blackwell.

Pardini, D.A. and Fite, P.J. (2010). Symptoms of conduct disorder, oppositional defiant disorder, attention-deficit/hyperactivity disorder, and callous-unemotional traits as unique predictors of psychosocial maladjustment in boys: advancing an evidence base for DSM-V. *Journal of American Academy of Child and Adolescent Psychiatry*, 49(11), 1134–44.

Paris, J. and Phillips, J. (2013). *Making the DSM-5: Concepts and Controversies*. New York: Springer-Verlag.

Parke, R.D. (1988). Families in life-span perspective: a multi-level developmental approach. In E.M. Hetherington, R.M. Lerner and M. Perlmutter (eds). *Child Development in Life-span Perspective* (pp. 159–90). Hillsdale, NJ: Erlbaum.

Parke, R.D. (2002). *Fatherhood*. Cambridge, MA: Harvard University Press.

Parke, R. and Gauvain, M. (2009). *Child Psychology: A Contemporary Viewpoint* (7th Edn). New York: McGraw-Hill.

Parker, J.G. and Asher, S.R. (1993). Friendship and friendship quality in middle childhood: links with peer group acceptance and feelings of loneliness and social dissatisfaction. *Developmental Psychology*, 29(4), 611–21.

Parker, J.G. and Gottman, J.M. (1989). Social and emotional development in a relational context: friendship interaction from early childhood to adolescence. In T.J. Berndt and G.W. Ladd (eds). *Peer Relations in Child Development* (pp. 95–131). New York: Wiley.

Parker, J.G., Low, C.M., Walker, A.R. and Gamm, B.K. (2005). Friendship jealousy in young adolescents: individual differences and links to sex, self-esteem, aggression, and social adjustment. *Developmental Psychology*, 41(1), 235–50.

Parker, J.G. and Seal, J. (1996). Forming, losing, renewing, and replacing friendships: applying temporal parameters to the assessment of children's friendship experiences. *Child Development*, 67, 2248–68.

Parkhurst, J.T. and Hopmeyer, A. (1998). Sociometric popularity and peer-perceived popularity: two distinct dimensions of peer status. *Journal of Early Adolescence*, 18(2), 125–44.

Parten, M. (1932). Social participation among preschool children. *Journal of Abnormal and Social Psychology*, 27, 243–69.

Pascalis, O., de Haan, M., Nelson, C.A. and de Schonen, S. (1998). Long-term recognition memory for faces assessed by visual paired comparison in 3- and 6-month-old infants. *Journal of Experimental Psychology: Learning, Memory, and Cognition*, 24, 249–60.

Pascalis, O., de Schonen, S., Morton, J., Deruelle, C. and Fabre-Grenet, M. (1995). Mother's face recognition in neonates: a replication and an extension. *Infant Behavior and Development*, 17, 79–85.

Pascual-Leone, J. (1970). A mathematical model for the transition rule in Piaget's developmental stages. *Acta Psychologica*, 32, 301–45.

Patchin, J.W. and Hinduja, S. (2010). Cyberbullying and self-esteem. *Journal of School Health*, 80(12), 614–21.

Patterson, C. (2004). Gay fathers. In M.E. Lamb (ed.). *The Role of the Father in Child Development* (pp. 397–416). New York: Wiley.

Patterson, G.R. (1982). *Coercive Family Process*. Eugene, OR: Castalia.

Patterson, G.R. (1986). Performance models for antisocial boys. *American Psychologist*, 41, 432–44.

Patterson, G.R. (1996). Some characteristics of a developmental theory for early-onset delinquency. In M.F. Lenzenweger and J.J. Haugaard (eds). *Frontiers of Developmental Psychopathology* (pp. 81–124). New York: Oxford University Press.

Patterson, G.R. (2002). The early development of coercive family processes. In J.B. Reid, G.R. Patterson and J. Snyder (eds). *Antisocial Behaviour in Children and Adolescents* (pp. 25–44). Washington, DC: American Psychological Association.

Patterson, G.R., DeBaryshe, B. and Ramsey, R. (1989). A developmental perspective on antisocial behaviour. *American Psychologist*, 44(2), 329–35.

Patterson, P. and Wilkins, L. (2008). *Media Ethics: Issues and Cases*. New York: McGraw Hill.

Pattiselanno, K., Dijkstra, J.K., Steglich, C., Vollebergh, W. and Veenstra, R. (2015). Structure matters: the role of clique hierarchy in the relationship between adolescent social status and aggression and prosociality. *Journal of Youth Adolescence*, 44(12), 2257–74.

Pavlov, I.P. (1927). *Conditioned Reflexes*. London: Oxford University Press.

Peeters, M., Cillessen, A.H.N. and Scholte, R.H.J. (2010). Clueless or powerful? Identifying subtypes of bullies in adolescence. *Journal of Youth and Adolescence*, 39, 1041–52.

Pelaez, M., Virues-Ortega, H. and Gewirtz, J. (2012). The acquisition of social referencing via discrimination training in infants. *Journal of Applied Behavior Analysis*, 45(1), 23–35.

Pellegrini, A.D. and Smith, P.K. (1998). Physical activity play: the nature and function of a neglected aspect of playing. *Child Development*, 69(3), 577–98.

Pellis S. and Pellis V. (2009). *The Playful Brain: Ventures to the Limits of Neuroscience*. Oxford: Oneworld Press.

Penton-Voak, I.S., Allen, T., Morrison, E., Gralewski, L. and Campbell, N. (2007). Performance on a face perception task is associated with empathy quotient scores, but not systemizing scores or participant sex. *Personality and Individual Differences*, 43, 2229–36.

Pepler, D., McKenney, K.S., Craig, W. and Connolly, J. (2006). *Bullying: The Risks for Ethnic Minority Youth*. Symposium presented at the Society for Research on Adolescence Conference, San Francisco.

Pergadia, M.L., Madden, P.A., Lessov, C.N., Todorov, A.A., Bucholz, K.K., Martin, N.G., et al. (2006). Genetic and environmental influences on extreme personality dispositions in adolescent twins. *Journal of Child Psychology and Psychiatry*, 47, 902–9.

Perner, J., Brandl, J.L. and Garnham, A. (2003). What is a perspective problem? Developmental issues in belief ascription and dual identity. *Facta Philosophica*, 5, 355–78.

Perner, J., Frith, U., Leslie, A.M. and Leekam, S.R. (1989). Exploration of the autistic child's theory of mind: knowledge, belief, and communication. *Child Development*, 60(3), 688–700.

Perner, J., Kain, W. and Barchfeld, P. (2002). Executive control and higher-order theory of mind in children at risk of ADHD. *Infant Child Development*, 11, 141–58.

Perner, J., Leekam, S.R. and Wimmer, H. (1987). Three year olds difficulty with false belief: the case for a conceptual deficit. *British Journal of Developmental of Psychology*, 5, 125–37.

Perner, J., Ruffman, T. and Leekam, S.R. (1994). Theory of mind is contagious: you catch it from your sibs. *Child Development*, 65, 1228–38.

Perry, D., Hendler, T. and Shamay-Tsoory, S.G. (2012). Can we share the joy of others? Empathic neural responses to distress vs joy. *Social Cognitive and Affective Neuroscience*, 7, 909–16.

Perry, D.G., Hodges, E.V. and Egan, S. (2001). Determinants of chronic victimisation by peers: a review and new model of family influence. In J. Juvonen and S. Graham (eds). *Peer Harassment in School: The Plight of the Vulnerable and Victimised* (pp. 73–104). New York: Guilford Press.

Peru, A., Moro, V., Tellini, P. and Tassinari, G. (2006). Suggestive evidence for an involvement of the right hemisphere in the recovery of childhood aphasia: a 3-year follow-up case. *Neurocase*, 12, 179–90.

Peterson, C. (2000). Kindred spirits: influences of siblings' perspectives on theory of mind. *Cognitive Development*, 15(4), 435–55.

Peterson, C.C. and McAlister, A. (2006). Metal playmate: siblings, executive functioning and theory of mind. *Journal of British Psychological Society*, 24, 733–51.

Peterson, C.C. and Wellman, H.M. (2009). From fancy to reason: scaling deaf children's theory of mind and pretence. *British Journal of Developmental Psychology*, 27, 297–310.

Pettit, G.S., Bakshi, A., Dodge, K.A. and Cole, J.D. (1990). The emergence of social dominance in young boys' play groups: developmental differences and behavioural correlates. *Developmental Psychology*, 26, 1017–25.

Piaget, J. (1932). *The Moral Judgement of the Child*. London: Routledge and Kegan Paul.

Piaget, J. (1952). *The Origins of Intelligence in Children* (trans. M. Cook). New York: International Universities Press.

Piaget, J. (1954). *The Construction of Reality in the Child*. New York: Basic Books.

Piaget, J. (1960). *The Psychology of Intelligence*. Totowa, NJ: Littlefield Adams & Co.

Piaget, J. (1962). *Play, Dreams, and Imitation in Childhood*. New York: W.W. Norton & Co.

Piaget, J. (1965). *The Moral Judgment of the Child*. New York: The Free Press.

Piaget, J. and Inhelder, B. (1956). *The Child's Conception of Space*. London: Routledge and Kegan Paul.

Pikas, A. (1989). A pure concept of mobbing gives the best results for treatment. *School Psychology International*, 10, 95–104.

Pinker, S. (1997). *How the Mind Works*. New York, NY: W.W. Norton and Company.

Pinker, S. (2002). *The Blank Slate: The Modern Denial of Human Nature*. London: Allen Lane.

Plato (348 BCE/1970). *The Laws* (trans. T.J. Saunders). Harmondsworth, UK: Penguin.

Plimoth Plantation, www.plimoth.org/.

Plomin, R. (2011). Commentary: why are children in the same family so different? Non-shared environment three decades later. *International Journal of Epidemiology*, 40(3), 582–92.

Plomin, R., Chipuer, H.M. and Neiderhiser, J.M. (1994). Behavioral genetic evidence for the importance of nonshared environment. In E.M. Hetherington, D. Reiss and R. Plomin (eds). *Separate Social Worlds of Siblings: Importance of Nonshared Environment on Development* (pp. 1–31). Hillsdale, NJ: Erlbaum.

Plomin, R. and Daniels, D. (1987). Why are children in the same family so different from one another? *The Behavioral and Brain Sciences*, 10, 1–16.

Plomin, R., DeFries, J.C. and Fulker, D.W. (2007). *Nature and Nurture During Infancy and Childhood*. Mahwah, NJ: Erlbaum.

Plomin, R., DeFries, J.C., Knopik, V.S. and Neiderhiser, J.M. (2012). *Behavioral Genetics* (6th Edn). New York: Worth Publishers.

Plomin, R., DeFries, J.C., McClearn, G.E. and McGuffin, P. (2001). *Behavioral Genetics* (4th Edn). New York: Worth Publishers.

Plomin, R., DeFries, J.C., McClearn, G.E. and McGuffin, P. (2008). *Behavioral Genetics* (5th Edn). New York: Worth Publishers.

Plutchik, R. (1987). Evolutionary bases of empathy. In N. Eisenberg and J. Strayer (eds). *Empathy and its Development* (pp. 38–46). Cambridge: Cambridge University Press.

Poland, S.E., Monks, C.P. and Tsermentseli, S. (2016). Cool and hot executive function as predictors of aggression in early childhood: differentiating between the function and form of aggression. *British Journal of Developmental Psychology*, 34(2), 181–97.

Porges, S.W., Doussard-Roosevelt, J.A. and Maiti, A.K. (1994). Vagal tone and the physiological regulation of emotion. In N.A. Fox (ed.). Emotional regulation: behavioral and biological considerations. *Monographs of the Society for Research in Child Development*, 59(240), 167–96.

Posner M.I. and Rothbart, M.K. (2000). Developing mechanisms of self-regulation. *Development and Psychopathology*, 12(3), 427–41.

Posner, M.I., Rothbart, M.K. and Sheese, B.E. (2010). Genetic variation influences how the social brain shapes temperament and behavior. In P.A. Reuter-Lorenz, K. Baynes, G.R. Mangun and E.A. Phelps (eds). *The Cognitive Neuroscience of Mind. A Tribute to Michael S. Gazzaniga* (pp.125–38). Cambridge, MA: MIT Press.

Postman, N., Nystrom, C., Strate, L. and Weingartner, C. (1988). *Myths, Men and Beer: An Analysis of Beer Commercials on Broadcast Television, 1987*. Falls Church, VA: AAA Foundation for Traffic Safety.

Potegal, M. and Einon, D. (1989). Aggressive behaviors in adult rats deprived of playfighting experience as juveniles. *Developmental Psychobiology*, 22, 159–72.

Pottebaum, S.M., Keith, T.Z. and Ehly, S.W. (1986). Is there a causal relation between self-concept and academic achievement? *Journal of Educational Research*, 79, 140–4.

Poulin, F., Dishion, T. and Haas, E. (1999). The peer influences paradox: friendship quality and deviancy training within male adolescents. *Merrill-Palmer Quarterly*, 45, 42–61.

Powell, J. (2013). *Introducing Family Psychology: A Practical Guide*. London: Icon Books Ltd.

Powers, S.I., Hauser, S.T. and Kilner, L.A. (1989). Adolescent mental health. *American Psychologist*, 44, 200–8.

Premack, D. and Woodruff, G. (1978). Does the chimpanzee have a 'theory of mind'? *Behavioral and Brain Sciences*, 4, 515–26.

Price, J.S. (1967). The dominance hierarchy and the evolution of mental illness. *Lancet*, 2, 243–6.

Prior, J. and Van Herwegen, J. (2016). *Practical Research with Children Research Methods in Developmental Psychology – A Handbook Series*. Abingdon: Routledge.

Pryor, J. and Rodgers, B. (2001). *Children in Changing Families: Life After Parental Separation*. Oxford: Blackwell Publishers.

Psychogiou, L., Daley, D., Thompson, M.J. and Sonuga-Barke, E.J.S. (2008). Parenting empathy: associations with dimensions of parent and child psychopathology. *British Journal of Developmental Psychology*, 26, 221–32.

Putallaz, M., Grimes, C.L., Foster, K.J., Kupersmidt, J.B., Coie, J.D. and Dearing, K. (2007). Overt and relational aggression and victimization: multiple perspectives within the school setting. *Journal of School Psychology*, 45, 523–47.

Pyżalski, J. (2012). From cyberbullying to electronic aggression: typology of the phenomenon. *Emotional and Behavioural Difficulties*, 17(3–4), 305–17.

Quale, G.R. (1992). *Families in Context: A World History of Population*. New York: Greenwood Press.

Quay, H.C. (1988). Attention deficit disorder and the behavioural inhibition system: the relevance of the neuropsychological theory of Jeffrey A. Gray. In L.M. Bloomingdale and J.A. Sergeant (eds). *Attention Deficit Disorder: Criteria: Cognition, Intervention*. (pp. 117–26). Oxford: Pergamon Press.

Quay, H.C. (1993). The psychobiology of undersocialised aggressive conduct disorder: a theoretical perspective. *Development and Psychopathology*, 5, 165–80.

Quay, H.C. (1997). Inhibition and attention deficit hyperactivity disorder. *Journal of Abnormal Child Psychology*, 25, 7–13.

Rabiner, D.L. and Gordon, L.V. (1992). The coordination of conflicting social goals: differences between rejected and nonrejected boys. *Child Development*, 63, 1344–50.

Racine, T.P. (2004). Wittgenstein's internalistic logic and children's theories of mind. In J.I.M. Carpendale and U. Müller (eds). *Social Interaction and the Development of Knowledge*. New Jersey: Erlbaum.

Racine, T.P. and Carpendale, J.I.M. (2007a). The role of shared practice in joint attention. *British Journal of Developmental Psychology*, 25, 3–25.

Racine, T.P. and Carpendale, J.I.M. (2007b). Shared practices, understanding, language and joint attention. *British Journal of Developmental Psychology*, 25, 45–54.

Radke-Yarrow, M. and Zahn-Waxler, C. (1986). The role of familial factors in the development of prosocial behaviour: research findings and questions. In D. Olweus, J. Block and M. Radke-Yarrow (eds).

Development of Antisocial and Prosocial Behaviour: Research, Theories and Issues (pp. 207–33). New York: Academic Press.

Radziszewska, B. and Rogoff, B. (1988). Influence of adult and peer collaborators on the development of children's planning skills. *Developmental Psychology*, 24, 840–8.

Raine, A. (1993). *The Psychopathology of Crime: Criminal Behavior as a Clinical Disorder*. San Diego: Academic Press.

Rakoczy, H. (2008). Taking fiction seriously: young children understand the normative structure of joint pretend games. *Developmental Psychology*, 44(4), 1195–201.

Rakoczy, H., Warneken, F. and Tomasello, M. (2008). The sources of normativity: young children's awareness of the normative structure of games. *Developmental Psychology*, 44(3), 875–81.

Randall, P.E. (1997). *Adult Bullying: Perpetrators and Victims* (p. 94). London: Routledge.

Reddy, L.A. (2011). *Group Play Interventions for Children: Strategies for Teaching Prosocial Skills*. Washington, DC: American Psychological Association.

Reiger, D.A., Kuhl, E.A. and Kupfer, D.J. (2013). The DSM-5: classification and criteria changes. *World Psychiatry*, 12(2), 92–8.

Reiss, D., Neiderhiser, J.M., Hetherington, E.M. and Plomin, R. (2000). *The Relationship Code: Deciphering Genetic and Social Influences on Adolescent Development*. Cambridge, MA: Harvard University Press.

Renfrew, C. (2009). *Prehistory: The Making of the Human Mind*. New York: The Random House Publishing Group.

Repacholi, B.M. and Gopnik, A. (1997). Early reasoning about desires: evidence from 14- and 18-month-olds. *Developmental Psychology*, 33(1), 12–21.

Repacholi, B.M., Slaughter, V., Pritchard, M. and Gibbs, V. (2003). Theory of mind, Machiavellianism, and social functioning in childhood. In B.M. Repacholi and V. Slaughter (eds). *Individual Differences in Theory of Mind* (pp. 99–120). New York, NY: Psychology Press.

Rest, J.R. (1979). *Development in Judging Moral Issues*. Minneapolis: University of Minnesota Press.

Rest, J.R. (1986). Moral research methodology. In S. Modgil and C. Modgil (eds). *Lawrence*

Kohlberg. Consensus and Controversy (pp. 455–69). Philadelphia: Falmer Press.

Rest, J.R., Narvaez, D., Bebeau, M.J. and Thoma, S.J. (1999). *Postconventional Moral Thinking: A Neo-Kohlbergian Approach*. New Jersey: Lawrence Erlbaum Associates.

Reynolds, P.C. (1976). Play, language and human evolution. In J.S. Bruner, A. Jolly and K. Sylva (eds). *Play: Its Role in Development and Evolution* (pp. 621–35). New York: Basic Books.

Rheingold, H.L. and Cook, K. (1975). The contents of boys' and girls' rooms as an index of parents' behaviour. *Child Development*, 46(2), 459–63.

Rhode, G., Jenson, W.R. and Reavis, H.K. (1993). *The Tough Kid Book: Practical Classroom Management Strategies*. Longmont, CO: Sopris West.

Rice, E., Rhoades, H., Winetrobe, H., Sanchez, M., Montoya, J., Plant, A. and Kordic, T. (2012). Sexually explicit cell phone messaging associated with sexual risk among adolescents. *Pediatrics*, 130(4), 667–73.

Richardson, S. (2003). The media and eating disorders: overcoming the messages that make our kids sick. Presentation at the Benjamin Franklin Institute, Adolescent Conference, Baltimore.

Richman, A.L., Miller, P.M. and LeVine, R.A. (1992). Cultural and educational variations in maternal responsiveness. *Developmental Psychology*, 28(4), 614–21.

Richman, A.L., Miller, P.M. and LeVine, R.A. (2010). Cultural and educational variations in maternal responsiveness (Chapter 13). In R. LeVine (ed.). *Psychological Anthropology: A Reader on Self in Culture*. West Sussex, UK: Wiley-Blackwell.

Ridley, M. (1996). *The Origins of Virtue*. London: Penguin Group.

Rivers, I. and Noret, N. (2010). 'I h 8 u': findings from a five-year study of text and email bullying. *British Educational Research Journal*, 36(4), 643–71.

Rivers, I. and Smith, P.K. (1994). Types of bullying behaviour and their correlates. *Aggressive Behavior*, 20, 359–68.

Rizzolatti, G., Fadiga, L., Gallese, V. and Fogassi, L. (1996). Premotor cortex and the recognition of motor actions. *Brain Research: Cognitive Brain Research*, 3, 131–41.

Roberts, B.W., Walton, K.E. and Viechtbauer, W. (2006). Patterns of mean-level change in personality traits across the life course: a meta-analysis of longitudinal studies. *Psychological Bulletin*, 132, 1–25.

Roberts, D.F. and Foehr, U. (2008). Trends in media use. *Children and Electronic Media*, 18(1), 11–37.

Roberts, D.F., Foehr, V.G. and Rideout, V.J (2005). *Generation M: Media in the Lives of 8- to 18-year-olds*. Menlo Park, CA: Kaiser Family Foundation.

Roberts, D.F., Henrikson, L. and Foehr, V.G. (2004). Adolescents and the media. In R. Lerner and I. Sternberg (eds). *Handbook of Adolescent Psychology* (p. 498). New York: Wiley.

Roberts, M.W. and Powers, S.W. (1990). Adjusting chair timeout enforcement procedures for oppositional children. *Behavior Therapy*, 21, 257–71.

Robertson, J. (1956). A mother's observations on the tonsillectomy of her four-year-old daughter. *The Psychoanalytic Study of the Child*, 11, 410–33.

Robertson, J. (1958a). Children in hospital. Letter to the editor. *The Lancet*, November 8, 1958.

Robertson, J. (1958b). Children in hospital. Letter to the editor. *The Lancet*, November 29, 1958.

Robertson, J. (1958c). *Going to Hospital with Mother* [Film]. London: Tavistock Child Development Research Unit.

Robertson, L. and Monsen, J.J. (2001). Issues in the development of a homosexual identity: practice implications for educational psychologists. In J.J. Monsen (ed.). Gay and lesbian identities: working with young people, their families and school. *Educational and Child Psychology (Special Issue)*, 18(1), 13–32.

Robins, R.W., Trzesniewski, K.H., Tracy, J., Gosling, S.D. and Potter, J. (2002). Global self-esteem across the life span. *Psychology and Aging*, 17, 423–34.

Robinson, G., Fernald, R. and Clayton, D. (2008). Genes and social behavior. *Science*. 322(5903), 896–900.

Robinson, T.N., Chen, H.L. and Killen, J.D. (1998). Television and music video exposure and risk of adolescent alcohol use. *Pediatrics*, 102(5), 54–9.

Robson, S. and Warren, L. (2012). 'Can you kill yourself already?' The vile online messages from internet trolls 'that led girl, 16, to hang herself'. *The Mail Online*, www.dailymail.co.uk/news/article-2246896/Jessica-Laney-16-committed-suicide-internet-trolls-taunted-told-kill-herself.html.

Roisman, G.I., Aguilar, B. and Egeland, B. (2004). Antisocial behaviour in the transition to adulthood: the independent and interactive roles of developmental history and emerging developmental tasks. *Developmental Psychopathology*, 16(4), 857–71.

Rosch, E. (1975). Cognitive representations of semantic categories. *Journal of Experimental Psychology: General*, 104, 192–233.

Rosenberg, M. (1985). Self-concept and psychological well-being in adolescence. In R.L. Leaky (ed.). *The Development of the Self* (pp. 205–46). New York: Academic Press.

Rosenfeld, M.J. (2010). Nontraditional families and childhood progress through school. *Demography*, 47(3), 755–75.

Rosler, M., Retz, W., Retz-Junginger, P., Hengesch, G., Schneider, M., Supprian, T., et al. (2004). Prevalence of attention deficit-/hyperactivity disorder (ADHD) and comorbid disorders in young male prison inmates. *European Archives of Psychiatry and Clinical Neuroscience*, 254, 365–71.

Ross, C., Orr, E.S., Sisic, M., Arseneault, J.M., Simmering, M.G. and Orr, R. (2009). Personality and motivations associated with Facebook use. *Computers in Human Behavior*, 25, 578–86.

Ross, H.S., Conant, C., Cheyne, J.A. and Alevizos, E. (1992). Relationships and alliances in the social interactions of kibbutz toddlers. *Social Development*, 1, 1–17.

Rothbart, M.K. (2011) *Becoming Who We Are: Temperament and Personality in Development*. New York: Guilford Press.

Rothbart, M.K. and Bates, J. (2006). Temperament. In N. Eisenberg, W. Damon and L.M. Richard (eds). *Handbook of Child Psychology: Vol. 3, Social, Emotional, and Personality Development* (6th Edn, pp. 99–166). Hoboken, NJ: John Wiley and Sons Inc.

Rothbart, M.K., Derryberry, D. and Hershey, K. (2000). Stability of temperament in childhood: laboratory infant assessment to parent report at seven years. In V.I. Molfese

and D.L. Molfese (eds). *Temperament and Personality Development across the Life Span* (pp. 85–119). Mahwah, NJ: Lawrence Erlbaum Associates.

Rothbaum, F., Pott, M., Azuma, H., Miyake, K. and Weisz, J. (2000). The development of close relationships in Japan and the United States: paths of symbiotic harmony and generative tension. *Child Development*, 71, 1121–42.

Rothbaum, F. and Trommsdorff, G. (2007). Do roots and wings complement or oppose one another? The socialization of relatedness and autonomy in cultural context. In J. Grusec and P. Hastings (eds). *Handbook of Socialization*. New York: Guilford.

Rottman, J. and Young, L. (2015). Mechanisms of moral development. In J. Decety and T. Wheatly (eds). *The Moral Brain: A Multidisciplinary Perspective* (pp. 123–42). Cambridge, MA: MIT Press.

Rousseau, J-J. (1762/1921). *Émile* (trans. B. Foxley). London: J.M. Dent and Sons Ltd.

Rubin, K.H., Bukowski, W.M. and Parker, J.G. (2006). Peer interactions, relationships, and groups. In W. Damon, R.M. Lerner and Eisenberg, N. *Handbook of Child Psychology: Vol. 3. Social, Emotional, and Personality Development* (6th Edn, pp. 571–645). New York: Wiley.

Rubin, L.B. (1976). *Worlds of Pain: Life in the Working-class Family*. New York: Basic Books.

Rubin, Z. (1980). *Children's Friendships* (p. 11). Cambridge, MA: Harvard University Press.

Ruble, D., Martin, C. and Berenbaum, S. (2006). Gender development. In W. Damon, R.M. Lerner and N. Eisenberg (eds). *Handbook of Child Psychology: Vol. 3. Social, Emotional, and Personality Development* (6th Edn, pp. 858–932). New York: Wiley.

Ruble, T.L. (1983). Sex stereotypes: issues of change in the 1970s. *Sex Roles*, 9(3), 397–402.

Ruffman, T., Perner, J., Naito, M., Parkin, L. and Clements, W. (1998). Older but not younger siblings facilitate false belief understanding. *Developmental Psychology*, 34, 161–74.

Ruma, E.H. and Mosher, D.L. (1967). Relationship between moral judgment and guilt in delinquent boys. *Journal of Abnormal Psychology*, 72, 122–7.

Rumbelow, H. (2002). Study: alcohol ads often reach teens. *Washington Post*, September 24, A03.

Ruse, M. and Wilson, E. (1985). The evolution of morality. *New Scientist*, 1478, 108–28.

Rushton, J.P., Brainerd, C.J. and Pressley, M. (1983). Behavioral development and construct validity: the principle of aggregation. *Psychological Bulletin*, 94(1), 18–38.

Russell, A., Russell, G. and Midwinter, D. (1991). Observer effects on mothers and fathers: self-reported influence during a home observation. *Merrill-Palmer Quarterly*, 38, 263–83.

Rust, J., Golombok, S., Hines, M., Johnston, K., Golding, J. and the ALSPAC Study Team (2000). The role of brothers and sisters in the gender development of preschool children. *Journal of Experimental Child Psychology*, 77, 292–303.

Rutland, A., Killen, M. and Abrams, D. (2010). A new social-cognitive developmental perspective on prejudice: the interplay between morality and group identity. *Perspectives on Psychological Science*, 5, 279–91.

Rutter, M. (1976). *Helping Troubled Children*. New York: Plenum.

Rutter, M. (1981). *Maternal Deprivation Reassessed* (2nd Edn). Harmondsworth: Penguin.

Rutter, M. and the English and Romanian Adoptees (ERA) Study Team (1998). Developmental catch-up, and deficit, following adoption after severe early privation. *Journal of Child Psychology and Psychiatry*, 39, 465–76.

Rutter, M. and Giller, H. (1983). *Juvenile Delinquency: Trends and Perspective*. Harmondsworth: Penguin.

Rutter, M., Kreppner, J., O'Connor, T. and the English and Romanian Adoptees (ERA) Study Team (2001). Risk and resilience following profound early global privation. *British Journal of Psychiatry*, 179, 97–103.

Rutter, M., Maughan, B., Mortimore, P. and Ouston, J. (1979). *Fifteen Thousand Hours: Secondary Schools and Their Effects on Children*. London: Open Books.

Ryan, R.M. and Claessens, A. (2012). Associations between family structure changes and children's behavior problems: the moderating effects of timing and marital birth. *Developmental Psychology*, 49(7):1219–31.

Ryan, S. (2007). Parent-child interaction styles between gay and lesbian parents and their adopted children. *Journal of GLBT Family Studies*, 3(2–3), 105–32.

Saarni, C. (1999). *The Development of Emotional Competence*. New York: Guilford Press.

Saarni, C., Campos, J.J. and Camras, L. (2006). Emotional development. In W. Damon, R.M. Lerner and N. Eisenberg (eds). *Handbook of Child Psychology: Vol 3. Social, Emotional, and Personality Development* (6th Edn, pp. 226–99). New York: Wiley.

Saarni, C., Mumme, D. and Campos, J. (1998). Emotional development: action, communication, and understanding. In N. Eisenberg (Vol. ed.). *Social, Emotional, and Personality Development* (pp. 237–311): Vol. 3 of W. Damon (Series ed.), *Handbook of Child Psychology*. New York: John Wiley.

Saettler, P. (2005). *The Evolution of American Educational Technology* (3rd Edn). Mahwah, NJ: Erlbaum.

Saffer, H. and Dave, D. (2002). Alcohol consumption and alcohol advertising bans. *Applied Economics*, 34(11), 1325–34.

Şahin M. (2012). The relationship between the cyberbullying/cybervictimization and loneliness among adolescents. *Children and Youth Services Review*, 34, 834–7.

Sala, M.N., Pons, F. and Molina, P. (2014). Emotion regulation strategies in preschool children. *British Journal of Developmental Psychology*, 32, 440–53.

Salkind, N.J. (2008). *Encyclopedia of Educational Psychology*. London: Sage.

Salmivalli, C. (2010). Bullying and the peer group: a review. *Aggression and Violent Behavior*, 15, 112–20.

Salmivalli, C., Kaukiainen, A. and Lagerspetz, K. (2000). Aggression and sociometric status among peers: do gender and type of aggression matter? *Scandinavian Journal of Psychology*, 41(1), 17–24.

Salmivalli, C., Lagerspetz, K., Björkqvist, K.,Österman, K. and Kaukiainen, A. (1996). Bullying as a group process: participant roles and their relations to social status within the group. *Aggressive Behavior*, 22, 1–15.

Sammons, P., Sylva, K., Melhuish, E., Siraj-Blatchford, I., Taggart, B. and Elliot, K. (2002). *Measuring the Impact of Pre-school on*

Children's Cognitive Progress over the Pre-school Period (EPPE Tech. Paper 8a). London: DfES/Institute of Education.

Sampson, G. (1997). *Educating Eve*. London: Cassell.

Sanghani, S. (2016). The shocking reality of racist bullying in British schools. *The Telegraph*, www.telegraph.co.uk/women/life/the-shocking-reality-of-racist-bullying-in-british-schools/.

Santrock, J.W. (1999). *Life-span Development*. New York: McGraw-Hill Education.

Santrock, J.W. (2005). *Life-span Development* (9th Edn). New York: McGraw-Hill Education.

Santrock, J.W. (2008). *A Topical Approach to Life-span Development* (4th Edn). New York: McGraw-Hill.

Saudino, K.J. (1997). Moving beyond the heritability question: new directions in behavioral genetic studies of personality. *Current Directions in Psychological Science*, 6, 86–90.

Saunders, I., Sayer, M. and Goodale, A. (1999). The relationship between playfulness and coping in preschool children: a pilot study. *American Journal of Occupational Therapy*, 53, 221–6.

Sauter, D.A., Panattoni, C. and Happé, F. (2013). Children's recognition of emotions from vocal cues. *British Journal of Developmental Psychology*, 31, 97–113.

Savin-Williams, R. (1987). *Adolescence: An Ethological Perspective*. New York: Springer-Verlag.

Savolainen, J., Hughes, L.A., Mason, W., Hurtig, T.M., Taanila, A.M., Ebeling, H. and Kivivuori, J. (2012). Antisocial propensity, adolescent school outcomes, and the risk of criminal conviction. *Journal of Research on Adolescence*, 22(1), 54–64.

Savolainen, J., Hurtig, T., Ebeling, H., Moilanen, I., Hughes, L.A. and Taanila, A. (2010). Attention deficit hyperactivity disorder and criminal behavior: the role of adolescent marginalization. *European Journal of Criminology*, 7, 442–59.

Saxe, R. and Wexler, A. (2005). Making sense of another mind: the role of the right temporo-parietal junction. *Neuropsychologia*, 43, 1391–9.

Scaramella, L. and Conger, R.D. (2003). Intergenerational continuity of hostile parenting and its consequences: the moderating influence of children's negative emotional reactivity. *Social Development*, 12, 420–39.

Scarr, S. (1996). How people make their own environments: implications for parents and policy makers. *Psychology, Public Policy and Law*, 2, 204–28.

Scarr, S. and McCartney, K. (1983). How people make their own environments: a theory of genotype greater than environment effects. *Child Development*, 54(2), 424–35.

Schaffer, H.R. (1996). *Social Development*. Cambridge, MA: Blackwell.

Schiller, F. (1794/1992). *On the Aesthetic Education of Man, in a Series of Letters*. Edited and translated by E.M. Wilkinson and L.A. Willoughby. Oxford: Clarendon Press; Oxford University Press.

Schmitt, D.P., Realo, A., Voracek, M., and Allik, J. (2008). Why can't a man be more like a woman? Sex differences in Big Five personality traits across 55 cultures. *Journal of Personality and Social Psychology*, 94, 168–82.

Schneider, B.H. (2000). *Friends and Enemies: Peer Relations in Childhood*. London: Arnold.

Schulenberg, J.E. and Zarrett, N.R. (2006). Mental health during emerging adulthood: continuity and discontinuity in courses, causes, and functions. In J.J. Arnett and J.L. Tanner (eds). *Emerging Adults in America: Coming of Age in the 21st Century* (pp. 135–72). Washington, DC: APA Books.

Schunk, D.H. and Zimmerman, B.J. (2006). Competence and control beliefs: distinguishing means and ends. In P.A. Alexander and P.H. Winne (eds). *Handbook of Educational Psychology* (2nd Edn). Mahwah, NJ: Erlbaum.

Scott, S., Briskman, J., Woolgar, M., Humayun, S. and O'Connor, T.G. (2011). Attachment in adolescence: overlap with parenting and unique prediction of behavioural adjustment. *The Journal of Child Psychology and Psychiatry*, 52(10), 1052–62.

Segal, N.L. (2013). Personality similarity in unrelated look-alike pairs: addressing a twin study challenge. *Personality and Individual Differences*, 54, 23–8.

Selman, R.L. (1971a). The relation of role taking to the development of moral judgement in children. *Child Development*, 42, 79–91.

Selman, R.L. (1971b). Taking another's perspective: role-taking development in early childhood. *Child Development*. 42, 1721–34.

Semrud-Clikeman, M., Walkowiak, J., Wilkinson, A. and Butcher, B. (2010). Executive functioning in children with Asperger syndrome, ADHD-combined type, ADHD-predominately inattentive type, and controls. *Journal of Autism Developmental Disorder*, 40, 1017–27.

Serbin, L.A., Poulin-Dubois, K.A., Colburne, K.A., Sen, M.G. and Eichstedt, J.A. (2001). Gender stereotyping in infancy: visual preferences for and knowledge of gender-stereotyped toys in the second year. *International Journal of Behavioral Development*, 25, 7–15.

Sexual Offence Act (2003). Section 15. Home Office, www.legislation.hmso.gov.uk/acts/acts2003/30042--b.htm.

Shackelford, T.K., Voracek, M., Schmitt, D.P., Buss, D.M., Weekes-Shackelford, V.A. and Michalski, R.L. (2004). Romantic jealousy in early adulthood and in later life. *Human Nature*, 15, 283–300.

Shaffer, D.R. (2000). *Social and Personality Development* (4th Edn). Belmont, CA: Wadsworth.

Shahaeian, A., Nielsen, M., Peterson, C.C., Aboutalebi and Slaughter, V. (2014a). Knowledge and belief understanding among Iranian and Australian preschool children. *Journal of Cross-cultural Psychology*, 45(10), 1643–54.

Shahaeian, A., Nielsen, M., Peterson, C.C. and Slaughter, V. (2014b). Cultural and family influences on children's theory of mind development: a comparison of Australian and Iranian school-age children. *Journal of Cross-cultural Psychology*, 45(4), 555–68.

Shahaeian, A., Peterson, C.C., Slaughter, V. and Wellman, H.M. (2011). Culture and the sequence of steps in theory of mind development. *Developmental Psychology*, 47(5), 1239–47.

Shamay-Tsoory, S.G. and Aharon-Peretz, J. (2007). Dissociable prefrontal networks for cognitive and affective theory of mind: a lesion study. *Neuropsychologia*, 45 (13), 3054–67.

Shamay-Tsoory, S.G., Tomer, R., Goldsher, D., Berger, B.D. and Aharon-Peretz, J. (2004). Impairment in cognitive and affective empathy in patients with brain lesions: anatomical and cognitive correlates. *Journal of Clinical and Experimental Neuropsychology*, 26(8), 1113–27.

Shanahan, L., Kim, J-Y., McHale, S.M. and Crouter, A.C. (2007). Sibling similarities and differences in time use: a pattern-analytic, within-family approach. *Review of Social Development*, 16(4), 662–81.

Shantz, M. (1983). Communication. In P.H. Mussen (ed.). *Handbook of Child Psychology* (Vol. 3, pp. 841–89). New York: Wiley.

Sharpe, L.L. (2005a). Play fighting does not affect subsequent fighting success in wild meerkats. *Animal Behaviour*, 69, 1023–9.

Sharpe, L.L. (2005b). Play does not enhance social cohesion in a cooperative mammal. *Animal Behaviour*, 70, 551–8.

Sharpe, L.L. (2005c). Frequency of social play does not affect dispersal partnerships in wild meerkats. *Animal Behaviour*, 70, 559–69.

Sharpe, L.L. and Cherry, M.I. (2003). Social play does not reduce aggression in wild meerkats. *Animal Behaviour*, 66, 989–97.

Sharp, S. and Cowie. H. (1994). Empowering students to take positive action against bullying (pp. 108–31). In P.K. Smith and S. Sharp (eds). *School Bullying: Insights and Perspectives*. London: Routledge.

Sheffield, E.G. and Hudson, J.A. (2006). You must remember this: effects of video and photograph reminders on 18-month-olds' event memory. *Journal of Cognition and Development*, 7, 73–93.

Sherif, M. (1954). *Experimental Study of Positive and Negative Intergroup Attitudes Between Experimentally Produced Groups: Robbers Cave Study*. Oklahoma: Norman.

Shiner, R.L., Buss, K.A., McClowry, S.G., Putnam, S.P., Saudino, K.J. and Zentner, M. (2012). What is temperament *now*? Assessing progress in temperament research on the twenty-fifth anniversary of Goldsmith et al. (1987). *Child Development Perspectives*, 6, 436–44.

Shoemaker, D. (2009). Responsibility and disability (p. 448). *Metaphilosophy*, 40(3–4), 438–61.

Siegler, R.S. (1994). Cognitive variability: a key to understanding cognitive development. *Current Directions in Psychological Science*, 3, 1–5.

Siegler, R.S. (1998). *Children's Thinking* (3rd Edn). Upper Saddle River, NJ: Prentice Hall.

Siegler, R.S. (2006). Microgenetic analysis of learning. In W. Damon and R. Lerner (eds). *Handbook of Child Psychology* (6th Edn). New York: Wiley.

Siegler, R.S. and Alibali, M.W. (2005). *Children's Thinking* (4th Edn). Upper Saddle River, NJ: Prentice Hall.

Sigman, M. and Ruskin, E. (1999). Continuity and change in the social competence of children with autism, Down Syndrome, and developmental delays. *Monographs of the Society for Research in Child Development*, 64, 1–114.

Simion, F., Valenza, E., Umilta, C. and Dalla Barba, B. (1998). Preferential orientation to faces in newborns: a temporal-nasal asymmetry. *Journal of Experimental Psychology: Human Perception and Performance*, 24, 1399–405.

Sinha, D. (1988). The family scenario in a developing country and its implications for mental health: the case of India. In P.R. Dasen, J.W. Berry and N. Sartorius (eds). *Health and Cross-cultural Psychology: Toward Applications* (pp. 48–70). Newbury Park, CA: Sage.

Siviy, S.M. (1998). Neurobiological substrates of play behavior: glimpses into the structure and function of mammalian playfulness. In M. Bekoff and J.A. Byers (eds). *Animal Play: Evolutionary, Comparative and Ecological Perspectives* (pp. 221–42). Cambridge: Cambridge University Press.

Skeels, H.M. (1936). Mental development of children in foster homes, *Journal of Genetic Psychology*, 49, 91–106.

Skinner, B.F. (1938). *The Behavior of Organisms: An Experimental Analysis*. New York: Appleton-Century-Crofts.

Skinner, B.F. (1953). *Science and Human Behavior*. New York: Macmillan.

Skinner, B.F. (1957). *Verbal Behavior*. New York: Appleton-Century-Crofts.

Skuse, D. (1984). Extreme deprivation in early childhood. II. Theoretical issues and a comparative review. *Journal of Child Psychology and Psychiatry*, 25, 543–72.

Slaby, R.G. and Frey, K.S. (1975). Development of gender constancy and selective attention to same-sex models. *Child Development*, 46, 849–56.

Slack, B. (2014). Immigration and diversity: Britain must integrate to accumulate. *The Guardian*, Tuesday 30 September, 20.31 BST, www.theguardian.com/uk-news/2014/sep/30/uk-capitalise-on-immigration-integration-diversity.

Slater, A., Johnson, S.P., Brown and Badenoch, E.M. (1996). Newborn infant's perception of partly occluded objects. *Infant Behavior and Development*, 19, 145–8.

Slater, M., Rouner, D., Domenech-Rodriquez, M., Beauvais, F., Murphy, K. and Van Leuven, J.K. (1997). Adolescent responses to TV beer ads and sports content/context: gender and ethnic differences. *Journalism and Mass Communication Quarterly*, 74, 108–22.

Slomkowski, C., Rende, R., Conger, K.J., Simons, R.L. and Conger, R.D. (2001). Sisters, brothers, and delinquency: evaluating social influence during early and middle adolescence. *Child Development*, 72, 271–83.

Smetana, J.G. (1981). Preschool children's conceptions of moral and social rules. *Child Development*, 52(4), 1333–6.

Smetana, J.G. (1983). Social-cognitive development: domain distinctions and coordinations. *Developmental Review*, 3, 131–47.

Smetana, J.G. (1985). Preschool children's conceptions of transgressions: the effects of varying moral and conventional domain-related attributes. *Developmental Psychology*, 21, 18–29.

Smetana, J.G. (1989). Adolescents' and parents' reasoning about actual family conflict. *Child Development*, 60, 1052–67.

Smetana, J.G. (1990). Morality and conduct disorders. In M. Lewis and S.M. Miller (eds). *Handbook of Developmental Psychopathology*. New York: Plenum Press.

Smetana, J.G. (1993). Understanding of social rules. In Bennett, M. (ed.). *The Development of Social Cognition: The Child as Psychologist*. New York: Guilford Press.

Smetana, J.G. (2006). Social domain theory: consistencies and variations in children's moral and social judgments. In M. Killen and J.G. Smetana (eds). *Handbook of Moral Development* (pp. 119–54). Mahwah, NJ: Erlbaum.

Smetana, J.G. (2013). Moral development: the social domain theory view. In P. Zelazo (ed.). *Oxford Handbook of Developmental*

Psychology (Vol. 1, pp. 832–66). New York: Oxford University Press.

Smetana, J.G. and Bitz, B. (1996). Adolescents' conceptions of teachers' authority and their relations to rule violations in school. *Child Development*, 67, 1153–72.

Smetana, J.G. and Braeges, J.L. (1990). The development of toddlers' moral and conventional judgments. *Merrill-Palmer Quarterly*, 36, 329–46.

Smetana, J.G., Toth, S., Cicchetti, D., Bruce, J., Kane, P. and Daddis, C. (1999). Maltreated and nonmaltreated preschoolers' conceptions of hypothetical and actual moral transgressions. *Developmental Psychology*, 35, 269–81.

Smith, A. (2006). Cognitive empathy and emotional empathy in human behaviour and evolution. *The Psychological Record*, 56, 3–21.

Smith, L. (2000). Learning how to learn words: an associative crane. In R.M. Golinkoff, K. Hirsh-Pasek, L. Bloom, L. Smith, A. Woodward, N. Akhtar, et al. (eds). *Becoming a Word Learner: A Debate on Lexical Acquisition* (pp. 51–80). New York: Oxford University Press.

Smith, P.B. and Pederson, D.R. (1988). Maternal sensitivity and patterns of infant-mother attachment. *Child Development*, 59, 1097–101.

Smith, P.K. (2010). *Children and Play*. Oxford: Wiley-Blackwell.

Smith, P.K. (2014). *Understanding School Bullying: Its Nature and Prevention Strategies*. London: Sage.

Smith, P.K. (2016). Bullying: definition, types, causes, consequences and intervention. *Social and Personality Psychology Compass*, 10(9), 519–32.

Smith, P.K., Kwak, K. and Toda, Y. (2016). *School Bullying in Different Cultures: Eastern and Western Perspectives*. Cambridge: Cambridge University Press.

Smith, P.K. and Sharp, S. (1994). The problem of school bullying. In P.K. Smith and S. Sharp (eds). *School Bullying: Insights and Perspectives*. London: Routledge.

Smith, R. (2009). Ban all alcohol advertising and sponsorship, says BMA. *The Telegraph*, Health News. Telegraph Media Group Limited, www.telegraph.co.uk/news/health/news/6155375/Ban-all-alcohol-advertising-and-sponsorship-says-BMA.html.

Smith, R.H., Kim, S.H. and Parrott, W.G. (1988). Envy and jealousy: semantic problems and experiential distinctions. *Personality and Social Psychology Bulletin*, 14, 401–9.

Smollar, J. and Youniss, J. (1982). Social development through friendship. In K.H. Rubin and H.S. Ross (eds). *Peer Relationships and Social Skills in Childhood* (pp. 279–98). New York: Springer-Verlag.

Snarey, J. (1987). A question of morality. *Psychology Today*, June, 6–8.

Sodian, B., Taylor, C., Harris, P.L. and Perner, J. (1991). Early deception and the child's theory of mind: false trails and genuine markers. *Child Development*, 62(3), 468–83.

Solomon, D., Battisch, V., Watson, M., Schaps, E. and Lewis, C. (2000). A six-district study of educational change: direct and mediated effects of the child development project. *Social Psychology of Education*, 4(1), 3–51.

Solomon, E.P., Berg, L.R. and Martin, D.W. (2002). *Biology* (6th Edn). Boston, MA: Brooks/Cole.

Soloman, J. and George, C. (1999). The measurement of attachment security in infancy and childhood. In J. Cassidy and P. Shaver (eds). *Handbook of Attachment* (pp. 287–318). New York: Guilford Press.

Soto, C.J., John, O.P., Gosling, S.D. and Potter, J. (2011). Age differences in personality traits from 10 to 65: Big Five domains and facets in a large cross-sectional sample. *Journal of Personality and Social Psychology*, 100, 330–48.

Souweidane, V.S. (2012). An initial test of an intervention designed to help youth question negative ethnic stereotypes. PhD thesis, http://deepblue.lib.umich.edu/bitstream/handle/2027.42/91482/visaad_1.pdf?sequence=1&isAllowed=y.

Speicher, B. (1994). Family patterns of moral judgment during adolescence and early adulthood. *Developmental Psychology*, 30, 624–32.

Spence, S.H., Barrett, P.M. and Turner, C.M. (2003). Psychometric properties of the Spence Children's Anxiety Scale with young adolescents. *Journal of Anxiety Disorders*, 17(6), 605–25.

Spencer, H. (1855/1977). *The Principles of Psychology*. Boston: Longwood Press.

Spencer, H. (1861/1963). *Education: Intellectual, Moral, and Physical*. Paterson, NJ: Littlefield Adams.

Spergel, I.A., Curry, G.D., Ross, R. and Chance, R. (1989). *Survey: National Youth Gang Suppression and Intervention Project*. Chicago: University of Chicago.

Spitz, R.A. (1945). Hospitalism. An inquiry into the genesis of psychiatric conditions in early childhood. *Psychoanalytic Study of the Child*, Vol 1. New York; International: Universities Press.

Spitzer, R. (1987). Promoting policy theory: revising the arenas of power. *Policy Studies Journal*, 15(4), 675–89.

Sroufe, L.A. (1983). Infant-caregiver attachment and patterns of adaptation in preschool: the roots of maladaptation and competence. In M. Perlmutter (ed.). *Minnesota Symposium in Child Psychology*, 16, 41–91. Hillsdale, NJ: Erlbaum.

Sroufe, L.A. (1996). *Emotional Development: The Organization of Emotional Life in the Early Years*. New York: Cambridge University Press.

Sroufe, L.A., Egeland, B., Carlson, E.A. and Collins, W.A. (2005). *The Development of the Person: The Minnesota Study of Risk and Adaptation from Birth to Adulthood*. New York: Guilford Press.

Sroufe, L.A. and Waters, E. (1976). The ontogenesis of smiling and laughter: a perspective on the organization of development in infancy. *Psychological Review*, 83, 173–89.

Sroufe, L.A. and Wunsch, J.P. (1972). The development of laughter in the first year of life. *Child Development*, 43, 1326–44.

Stannage, E. and Taylor, S. (2012). Gender differences and correlation links in empathy, systemizing and emotion recognition. *BPS: Book of Abstracts*, Annual Conference 2012, p.71–2.

State Assemblyman, John Vasconcellos (1986). Now, the California task force to promote self-esteem. *New York Times*, www.nytimes.com/1986/10/11/us/now-the-california-task-force-to-promote-self-esteem.html.

Stenberg, C.R. and Campos, J. (1990). The development of anger expressions in infancy. In N. Stein, B. Leventhal and T. Trabasso (eds). *Psychological and Bio-logical Approaches to Emotion* (pp. 247–82). Hillsdale, NJ: Erlbaum.

Stenberg, C.R., Campos, J. and Emde, R. (1983). The facial expression of anger in seven-month-old infants. *Child Development*, 54, 178–84.

Stern, H.H. (1983). *Fundamental Concepts of Language Teaching*. Oxford: Oxford University Press.

Sternberg, R.J. (1991). Death, taxes, and bad intelligence tests. *Intelligence*, 15(3), 257–70.

Sterzer, P., Stadler, C., Krebs, A., Kleinschmidt, A. and Poustka, F. (2005). Abnormal neural responses to emotional visual stimuli in adolescents with conduct disorder. *Biological Psychiatry*, 57, 7–15.

Stevens, R. (2008). *Sigmund Freud: Examining the Essence of his Contribution*. Basingstoke, UK: Palgrave MacMillan.

Stevenson, H.W. (1995). Mathematics achievement of American students: first in the world by the year 2000? In C.A. Nelson (ed.). *Basic and Applied Perspectives on Learning, Cognition, and Development*. Minneapolis: University of Minnesota Press.

Stevenson, H.W. (2000). Middle childhood: education and schooling. In A. Kazdin (ed.). *Encyclopedia of Psychology*. Washington, DC, and New York: American Psychological Association and Oxford University Press.

Stevenson, H.W., Lee, S-Y. and Stigler, J.W. (1986). Mathematics achievement of Chinese, Japanese, and American children. *Science*, 231(4739), 693–9.

Stocker, C.M., Burwell, R.A. and Briggs, M.L. (2002). Sibling conflict in middle childhood predicts children's adjustment in early adolescence. *Journal of Family Psychology*, 16, 50–7.

Stoel-Gammon, C. and Otorno, K. (1986). Babbling development of hearing-impaired and normally hearing subjects. *Journal of Speech Hearing Disorder*, 51(1), 33–41.

Stoneman, Z., Brody, G. and MacKinnon, C.E. (1986). Same sex and cross-sex siblings: activity choices, roles, behaviour, and gender stereotypes. *Sex Roles*, 15, 495–511.

Stout, J.T. and Caskey, C.T. (1989). HPRT: gene structure, expression, and mutation. *Annual Review of Genetics*, 19, 127–48.

Strand, S. (2014). Ethnicity, gender, social class and achievement gaps at Age 16: intersectionality and 'getting it' for the white working class. *Research Papers in Education*, 29(2), 131–71.

Strasburger, V.C. (2001). Children and TV advertising: nowhere to run, nowhere to hide. *Journal of Development and Behavioural Pediatrics*, 22, 185–7.

Strassberg, D.S., McKinnon, R.K., Sustaíta, M.A. and Rullo, J. (2013). Sexting by high school students: an exploratory and descriptive study. *Archives of Sexual Behavior*, 42(1), 15–21.

Strassberg, Z., Dodge, K.A., Pettit, G.S. and Bates, J.E. (1994). Spanking in the home and children's subsequent aggression towards kindergarten peers. *Development and Psychopathology*, 6, 445–61.

Strayer, J. (1987). Affective and cognitive perspectives on empathy. In N. Eisenberg and J. Strayer (eds). *Empathy and Its Development* (pp. 218–244). Cambridge: Cambridge University Press.

Striano, T. (2016). *Doing Developmental Research: A Practical Guide*. New York: The Guilford Press.

Striegel-Moore, R. and Smolak, L. (2000). The influence of ethnicity on eating disorders in women. In R. Eisler and M. Hersen (eds). *Handbook of Gender, Culture, and Health* (pp. 227–53). Mahwah, NJ: Lawrence Erlbaum Associates, Inc.

Subrahmanyam, K., Smahel, D. and Greenfield, P. (2006). Connecting developmental constructions on the Internet: identity presentation and sexual exploration in online chat rooms. *Developmental Psychology*, 42, 395–406.

Suddendorf, T. and Busby, J. (2005). Making decisions with the future in mind: developmental and comparative identification of mental time travel. *Learning and Motivation*, 36, 110–25.

Suddendorf, T., Simcock, G. and Nielsen, M. (2007). Visual self-recognition in mirrors and live videos: evidence for a developmental asynchrony. *Cognitive Development*, 22, 185–96.

Sullivan, H.S. (1953). *The Interpersonal Theory of Psychiatry*. New York: Norton.

Sullivan, M.W. and Lewis, M. (2003). Contextual determinants of anger and other negative expressions in young infants. *Developmental Psychology*, 39(4), 693–705.

Sullivan, M.W., Lewis, M. and Alessandri, M. (1992). Cross-age stability in emotional expressions during learning and extinction. *Developmental Psychology*, 28, 58–63.

Sulloway, F.J. (1996). *Born to Rebel: Birth Order, Family Dynamics, and Creative Lives*. New York: Pantheon.

Sulloway, F.J. (in press). Birth order and evolutionary psychology. In L. Workman, W. Reader and J. Barkow (eds). *Cambridge Handbook of Evolutionary Perspectives on Human Behavior*. Cambridge: Cambridge University Press.

Sutherland, E.H. (1939). *Principles of Criminology*. Philadelphia: J. Lippincott.

Sutton, J. and Keogh, E. (2000). Social competition in school: relationships with bullying, Machiavellianism and personality. *British Journal of Educational Psychology*, 70, 443–56.

Sutton, J., Smith, P.K. and Swettenham, J. (1999). Bullying and theory of mind: a critique of the social skills deficit view of anti-social behaviour. *Social Development*, 8, 117–27.

Sutton-Smith, B. (1994). Does play prepare the future? In J. Goldstein (ed.). *Toys, Play and Child Development*. New York: Cambridge University Press.

Swickert, R.J., Hittner, J.B., Harris, J.L. and Herring, J.A. (2002). Relationships among Internet use, personality, and social support. *Computers in Human Behavior*, 18, 437–51.

Sylva, K., Melhuish, E., Sammons, P., Siraj-Blatchford, I. and Taggart, B. (2004). *The Effective Provision of Pre-School Education (EPPE) Project: Final Report*. A longitudinal study funded by the DfES 1997–2004. London: DfES/Institute of Education.

Sylva, K., Stein, A., Leach, P. Barnes, J., Malmberg, L-E. and the FCCC-team (2011). Effects of early child-care on cognition, language, and task-related behaviours at 18 months: an English study. *British Journal of Developmental Psychology*, 29(1), 18–45.

Szabó, M.K. (2014). Patterns of play activities in autism and typical development: a case study. *Procedia – Social and Behavioral Sciences*, 140, 630–7.

Tajfel, H. (1963). Stereotypes. *Race*, 5, 3–14.

Talwar, V. and Lee, K. (2002a). Development of lying to conceal a transgression: children's control of expressive behavior during verbal deception. *International Journal of Behavioral Development*, 26, 436–44.

Talwar, V. and Lee, K. (2002b). Emergence of white lie-telling in children between 3 and 7 years of age. *Merrill-Palmer Quarterly*, 48, 160–81.

Talwar, V., Murphy, S. and Lee, K. (2007). White lie-telling in children for politeness purposes. *International Journal of Behavioral Development*, 31, 1–11.

Tamis-LeMonda, C.S., Bornstein, M.H. and Baumwell, L. (2001). Maternal responsiveness and children's achievement of language milestones. *Child Development*, 72, 748–67.

Tan, T.X. and Baggerly, J. (2009). Behavioral adjustment of adopted Chinese girls in single-mother, lesbian-couple, and heterosexual-couple households. *Adoption Quarterly*, 12, 171–86.

Tapscott, J.L., Hancock, M. and Hoaken, P. (2012). Severity and frequency of reactive and instrumental violent offending: divergent validity of subtypes of violence in an adult forensic sample. *Criminal Justice and Behavior*, 39(2), 202–19.

Tardy, C. (1985). Social support measurement. *America Journal of Community Psychology*, 13(2), 187–202.

Taylor, D.C. and Ounsted, C. (1972). The nature of gender differences explored through ontogentic analysis of sex ratios in disease. In C. Ounsted and D.C. Taylor (eds). *Gender Differences: Their Ontogeny and Significance* (pp. 215–40). London: Churchill Livingstone.

Taylor, S. (2015). *Forensic Psychology: The Basics*. London and New York: Routledge, Taylor and Francis.

Taylor, S. (2016). *Crime and Criminality: A Multidisciplinary Approach*. London and New York: Routledge; Taylor and Francis.

Tawile, M. (2016). *Why social media will never be like mass media*, http://visionarymarketing. com/en/blog/2016/02/social-media-will-never-like-mass-media-social-marketing-social-selling/.

Teen Rehab Center (2016). *How Social Media Impacts Teens*, www.teenrehabcenter.org/resources/social-media-impact/.

Temple, J.R., Paul, J.A., van den Berg, P., Le, V.D., McElhany, A. and Temple, B.W.

(2012). Teen sexting and its association with sexual behaviours. *Archives of Pediatrics and Adolescent Medicine*, 166(9), 828–33.

Ten Dam, G. and Volman, M. (2007). Educating for adulthood or for citizenship: social competence as an educational goal. *European Journal of Education*, 42(2), 281–98.

Thelen, E., Corbetta, D. and Spencer, J.P. (1996). The development of reaching during the first year: the role of movement speed. *Journal of Experimental Psychology: Human Perception and Performance*, 22, 1059–76.

Thelen, E. and Smith, L.B. (1994). *A Dynamic Systems Approach to the Development of Cognition and Action*. Cambridge, MA: MIT Press.

Theoret, H., Halligan, E., Kobayashi, M., Fregni, F., Tager-Flusberg, H. and Pascual-Leone, A. (2005). Impaired motor facilitation during action observation in individuals with autism spectrum disorder. *Current Biology*, 15, R84–R85.

Think Digital First (2017). *The Demographics of Social Media Users in 2017*. @ 2017 Warren Knight, www.thinkdigitalfirst. com/2016/01/04/the-demographics-of-social-media-users-in-2016/.

Thomas, A. and Chess, S. (1986). The New York longitudinal study: from infancy to early adult life. In R. Plomin and J. Dunn (eds). *The Study of Temperament: Changes, Continuities and Challenges* (pp. 39–52). Hillsdale, NJ: Erlbaum.

Thomas, M.S. and Karmiloff-Smith, A. (2002). Are developmental disorders like cases of adult brain damage? Implications from connectionist modelling. *Behavioural Brain Sciences*, 25, 727–50.

Thompson, C., Barresi, J. and Moore, C. (1997). The development of future-oriented prudence and altruism in preschoolers. *Cognitive Development*, 12, 199–212.

Thompson, P. (2008). Teenager commits suicide live online while 1,500 people watch video stream. *The Daily Mail*, 21 November, www.dailymail.co.uk/news/article-1088173/Teenager-commits-suicide-live-online-1-500-people-watch-video-stream. html:ixzz3QuFja9dk.

Thompson, R.A. (2006a). The development of the person: social understanding, relationships, conscience, self. In N. Eisenberg and W. Damon (eds). *Handbook of*

Child Psychology: Vol 3. Social, Emotional, and Personality Development (6th Edn, pp. 24–98). New York: Wiley.

Thompson, R.A. (2006b). Emotional regulation in children. In J. Gross (ed.). *Handbook of Emotional Regulation* (pp. 249–68). New York: Guilford Press.

Thornberg, R. (2008a). A categorisation of school rules. *Educational Studies*, 34, 25–33.

Thornberg, R. (2008b). Values education as the daily fostering of school rules. *Research in Education*, 80(1), 52.

Thornberg, R. (2010). A study of children's conceptions of school rules by investigating their judgements of transgressions in the absence of rules. *Educational Psychology*, 30(5), 583–603.

Thornberg, R. and Jungert, T. (2013). School bullying and the mechanisms of moral disengagement. *Aggressive Behavior*, 40(2), 99–108.

Thornberry, T.P., Freeman-Gallant, A., Lizotte, A.J., Krohn, M.D. and Smith, C.A. (2003). Linked lives: the intergenerational transmission of antisocial behaviour. *Journal of Abnormal Child Psychology*, 31(2), 171–84.

Thornton, S. (1999). Creating the conditions for cognitive change: the interaction between task structures and specific strategies. *Developmental Psychology*, 70, 588–603.

Thornton, S. (2002). *Growing Minds: An Introduction to Cognitive Development*. Basingstoke, UK: Palgrave Macmillan.

Tisak, M.S. (1993). Preschool children's judgments of moral and personal events involving physical harm and property damage. *Merrill-Palmer Quarterly*, 39, 375–90.

Tizard, B. and Hodges, J. (1978). The effect of early institutional rearing on the development of eight-year-old children. *Child Development*, 43, 337–58.

Toates. F. (2011). *Biological Psychology: An Integrative Approach* (3rd Edn). Harlow: Pearson Education.

Tokunaga, R.S. (2010). Following you home from school: a critical review and synthesis of research on cyberbullying victimization. *Computers in Human Behavior*, 26, 277–87.

Tolan, P.H., Gorman-Smith, D. and Henry, D.B. (2003). The developmental ecology of urban males' youth violence. *Developmental Psychology*, 39(2), 274–91.

Tomasello, M. (1998). *The New Psychology of Language: Cognitive and Functional Approaches to Language Structure*. Mahwah, NJ: Erlbaum.

Tomasello, M. (1999). The cultural ecology of young children's interactions with objects and artefacts. In E. Winograd, R. Fivush and W. Hirst (eds). *Ecological Approaches to Cognition: Essays in Honour of Ulric Neisser*. New Jersey: Erlbaum.

Tomasello, M. (2003). *Constructing a Language: A Usage-based Theory of Language Acquisition*. Cambridge, MA: Harvard University Press.

Tomasello, M. (2006). Acquiring metalinguistic constructions. In W. Damon, R.M. Lerner, D. Kuhn and R. Siegler (eds). *Handbook of Child Psychology, Vol 2* (6th Edn, pp. 255–98). New York: Wiley.

Tomasello, M. and Akhtar, N. (1995). Two-year-olds use pragmatic cues to differentiate reference to objects and actions. *Cognitive Development*, 10, 201–24.

Tomasello, M., Carpenter, M., Call, J., Behne, T. and Moll, H. (2005). Understanding and sharing intentions: the origins of cultural cognition. *Behavioral and Brain Sciences*, 28, 675–735.

Tomasello, M., Carpenter, M. and Liszkowski, U. (2007). A new look at infant pointing. *Child Development*, 78, 705–22.

Tomasello, M. and Farrar, J. (1986). Joint attention and early language. *Child Development*, 57, 1454–63.

Topping, A. (2011). Knife crime and gang violence on the rise as councils reduce youth services. *The Guardian*, www.guardian.co.uk/uk/2011/jul/29/gang-violence-rises-as-councils-cut-youth-services.

Tremblay, R.E. (2000). The development of aggressive behaviour during childhood: what have we learned in the past century? *International Journal of Behavioral Development*, 24, 129–41.

Triandis, C.H., Bontempo, R., Villareal, M.J., Asai, M. and Lucca, N. (1988). Individualism and collectivism: cross-cultural perspectives on self-ingroup relationships. *Journal of Personality and Social Psychology*, 54(2), 323–38.

Trivers, R.L. (1972). Parental investment and sexual selection. In B. Campbell (ed.). *Sexual*

Selection and the Descent of Man (pp.139–79). Chicago: Aldine.

Trivers, R.L. (1985). *Social Evolution*. Menlo Park, CA: Benjamin/Cummings.

Tronick, E.Z., Morelli, G.A. and Ivey, P.K. (1992). The Efe forager infant and toddler's pattern of social relationships: multiple and simultaneous. *Developmental Psychology*, 28, 568–77.

Troseth, G.L. (2003). TV guide: two-year-old children learn to use video as a source of information. *Developmental Psychology*, 39, 140–50.

Trueman, C.N. (2016). *Gangs and Crime*. The Learning History Site, www.historylearningsite.co.uk/sociology/crime-and-deviance/gangs-and-crime/.

Ttofi, M.M. and Farrington, D.P. (2011). Effectiveness of school-based programs to reduce bullying: a systematic and meta-analytic review. *Journal of Experimental Criminology*, 7, 27–56.

Tucker, C.J., Updegraff, K.A., McHale, S.M. and Crouter, A.C. (1999). Older siblings as socializers of younger siblings' empathy. *Journal of Early Adolescence*, 19, 176–98.

Tucker, D.M., Watson, R.T. and Heilman, K.M. (1977). Affective discrimination and evocation in patients with right parietal disease. *Neurology*, 27, 947–50.

Tucker, L.A. (1985). Television's role regarding alcohol use among teenagers. *Adolescence*, 20, 593–8.

Turiel, E. (1979). Distinct conceptual and developmental domains: social convention and morality. In H. Howe and C. Keasey (eds). *Nebraska Symposium on Motivation, 1977: Social Cognitive Development* (pp. 77–116). Lincoln, NE: University of Nebraska Press.

Turiel, E. (1983). *The Development of Social Knowledge: Morality and Convention*. Cambridge: Cambridge University Press.

Turiel, E. (2002). *The Culture of Morality: Social Development, Context, and Conflict*. Cambridge: Cambridge University Press.

Turiel, E. (2006). The development of morality. In N. Eisenberg (ed.). *Handbook of Child Psychology, 6th Edn, Volume 3: Social, Emotional, and Personality Development* (William Damon, series ed., pp. 789–857). New York: Wiley.

Turiel, E. (2008). Thought about actions in social domains: morality, social conventions, and social interactions. *Cognitive Development*, 23, 136–54.

Turiel, E. (2015). *The Culture of Morality: Social Development, Context, and Conflict*. Cambridge: Cambridge University Press.

Turkheimer, E. (2000). Three laws of behaviour genetics and what they mean. *Current Directives in Psychological Science*, 9, 160–4.

Turkheimer E. (2006). In D. Kirp. After the bell curve. *New York Times*, 23 July, www.nytimes.com/2006/07/23/magazine/23wwln_idealab.html.

Turkheimer, E., Haley, A.P., Waldron, M. and Gottesman, I.I. (2003). Socioeconomic status modifies heritability of IQ in young children. *Psychological Science*, 14(6), 623–8.

Turner, S.L., Hamilton, H., Jacobs, M., Angood, L.M. and Dwyer, D.H. (1997). The influence of fashion magazines on the body image satisfaction of college women: an exploratory analysis. *Adolescence*, 32(127), 603–14.

Tuten, T.L. and Bosnjak, M. (2001). Understanding differences in web usage: the role of need for cognition and the five factor model of personality. *Social Behavior and Personality: An International Journal*, 29, 391–8.

Udvari, S., Schneider, B.H., Labovitz, G. and Tassi, F. (1995). A multidimensional view of competition in relation to children's peer relations. Paper presented at the meeting of the American Psychological Association, New York.

Uekermann, J., Kraemer, M., Abdel-Hamid, M., Schimmelmann, B.G., Hebebrand, J., Daum, I., Wiltfang, J. and Kis, B. (2010). Social cognition in attention-deficit hyperactivity disorder (ADHD). *Neuroscience and Biobehavioral Reviews*, 34,734–43.

UN International Children's Fund (UNICEF) (2015). *Committing to Child Survival: A Promise Renewed*. Progress Report. UNICEF: Division of Data, Research, and Policy.

United Nations, Department of Economic and Social Affairs, Population Division (2015). *World Population Prospects: The 2015 Revision*. Copyright @ United Nations.

Urberg, K.A., Degirmencioglu, S.M. and Pilgrim, C. (1997). Close friend and group influence on adolescent cigarette smoking and alcohol use. *Developmental Psychology*, 33, 834–44.

URMC (2017). *Williams Syndrome*, www.
urmc.rochester.edu/childrens-hospital/
developmental-disabilities/conditions/
williams-syndrome.aspx.

Vaish, A., Missana, M. and Tomasello, M.
(2011). Three-year-old children intervene
in third-party moral transgressions. *British
Journal of Developmental Psychology*, 29,
124–30.

Valenza, E., Simion, F., Macchi Cassia, V.
and Umilta, C. (1996). Face preference at
birth. *Journal of Experimental Psychology:
Human Perception and Performance*, 22,
892–903.

Van Bavel, J.J., Packer, D.J., Haas, I.J. and
Cunningham, W.A. (2012). The importance
of moral construal: moral versus non-moral
construal elicits faster, more extreme,
universal evaluations of the same actions.
PLoS ONE, 7(11), e48693.

Van Berckelaer-Onnes, I.A. (2003). Promoting
early play. *Autism*, 7(4), 415–23.

Vandenbrouke, L., Verschueren, K.,
Ceulemans, E., De Smedt, B., De Roover,
K. and Baeyens, D. (2016). Family
demographic profiles and their relationship
with the quality of executive functioning
subcomponents in kindergarten. *British
Journal of Developmental Psychology*, 34,
226–44.

Van Evra, J. (2004). *Television and Child
Development* (3rd Edn). Mahwah, NJ:
Lawrence Erlbaum Associates.

van Goozen, S.H.M., Matthys, W., Cohen-
Kettenis, P.T., Gispen-de Wied, C., Wiegant,
V.M. and van Engeland, H. (1998). Salivary
cortisol and cardiovascular activity during
stress in oppositional defiant disorder boys
and normal controls. *Biological Psychiatry*,
43, 531–9.

van Goozen, S.H.M., Snoek, H., Matthys, W.,
van Rossum, I. and van Engeland, H. (2004).
Evidence of fearlessness in behaviourally
disordered children: a study on startle reflex
modulation. *Journal of Child Psychology and
Psychiatry*, 45(4), 884–92.

van Krevelen-Wing, L. (1991). The relationship
between Asperger's syndrome and Kanner's
autism. In U. Frith (ed.). *Autism and Asperger
Syndrome*. Cambridge: Cambridge University
Press.

Van Roekel, E., Scholte, R.H.J. and Didden, R.
(2009). Bullying among adolescents with

autism spectrum disorders: prevalence
and perception. *Journal of Autism and
Developmental Disorders*, 40, 63–73.

Vaughn, B.E., Kopp, C.B. and Krakow, J.B.
(1984). The emergence and consolidation of
self-control from eighteen to thirty months
of age: normative trends and individual
differences. *Child Development*, 55(3),
990–1004.

Veenstra, R., Lindenberg, S., Zijlstra, De Winter,
A.F. Verhulst, F.C. and Ormel, J. (2007). The
dyadic nature of bullying and victimisation:
testing a dual-perspective theory. *Child
Development*, 78, 1843–54.

Vitanova, N.A. (1976). *Play as a Social System*.
Sofia.

Vitaro, F. and Brendgen, M. (2005). Proactive
and reactive aggression: a developmental
perspective. In R.E. Tremblay, W.W. Hartup
and J. Archer (eds). *Developmental Origins
of Aggression* (pp. 178–201). New York:
Guilford Press.

Vitaro, F., Brendgen, M., Girard, A., Dionne,
G., Tremblay, R.E. and Boivin, M. (2016).
Links between friends' physical aggression
and adolescents' physical aggression: what
happens if gene-environment correlations
are controlled? *International Journal of
Behavioral Development*, 40(3), 234–42.

Vlachou, M., Andreou, E., Botsoglou, K. and
Didaskalou, E. (2011). Bully/victim problems
among preschool children: a review of current
research evidence. *Educational Psychology
Review*, 23, 329–58.

Volk, A., Camilleri, J.A., Dane, A. and
Marini, Z. (2012). Is adolescent bullying
an evolutionary adaptation? *Aggressive
Behavior*, 38, 222–38.

Volling, B.L., McElwain, N.L. and Miller, A.L.
(2002). Emotion regulation in context: the
jealousy complex between young siblings
and its relations with child and family
characteristics. *Child Development*, 73,
581–600.

Völlink, T., Dehue, F. and Mc Guckin, C.
(2016). *Cyberbullying: From Theory to
Intervention*. Abingdon, Oxford: Taylor &
Francis Group.

von Hofsten, C. (1991). Structuring of early
reaching movements: a longitudinal study.
Journal of Motor Behavior, 23, 280–92.

Vossekuil, B., Fein, R., Reddy, M., Borum, R.
and Modzeleski, W. (2002). *The Final Report*

and Findings of the Safe School Initiative: Implications for the Prevention of School Attacks in the United States. Washington, DC: US Department of Education, Office of Elementary and Secondary Education, Safe and Drug-Free Schools Program and US Secret Service, National Threat Assessment Center.

Votruba-Drzal, E., Coley, R.L. and Chase-Lansdale, P.L. (2004). Child care and low-income children's development: direct and moderated effects. *Child Development*, 75 (1), 296–312.

Voyer, D., Voyer, S. and Bryden, M.P. (1995). Magnitude of sex differences in spatial abilities: a meta-analysis and consideration of critical variables. *Psychological Bulletin*, 117, 250–70.

Vurpillot, E. (1968). The development of scanning strategies and their relation to visual differentiation. *Journal of Experimental Child Psychology*, 6, 632–50.

Vygotsky, L.S. (1930). *Mind and Society.* Cambridge, MA: Harvard University Press.

Vygotsky, L.S. (1934). *Thought and Language.* Cambridge, MA: MIT Press.

Vygotsky, L.S. (1967). Play and its role in the mental development of the child. *Soviet Psychology*, 5, 6–18.

Vygotsky, L.S. (1978). *Mind in Society: The Development of Higher Psychological Functions.* Cambridge, MA: Harvard University Press.

Vygotsky, L.S. (1978). The Role of Play in Development. In M. Cole (trans. ed.). *Mind in Society* (pp. 92–104). Cambridge, MA: Harvard University Press.

Waddington, C. (1957). *The Strategy of the Genes.* London: Allen and Unwin.

Waddington, C. (1977). *Tools for Thought.* New York: Basic Books.

Wainright, J.L. and Patterson, C.J. (2008). Peer relations among adolescents with female same-sex parents. *Developmental Psychology*, 44(1), 117–26.

Wainright, J.L., Russell, S.T. and Patterson, C.J. (2004). Psychosocial adjustment, school outcomes, and romantic relationships of adolescents with same-sex parents. *Child Development*, 75(6), 1886–98.

Wainryb, C. (2006). Moral development in culture: diversity, tolerance, and justice. In M.

Killen and J.G. Smetana (eds). *Handbook of Moral Development* (pp. 211–40). Mahwah, NJ: Erlbaum.

Waldman, I. (1988). Relationships between non-social information processing, social perceptual deficits and biases, and social status in 7- to 12-year-old boys. Unpublished Dissertation, Waterloo, Ontario, Canada: University of Waterloo.

Waldman, M.R. and Dieterich, J.H. (2007). Throwing a bomb on a person versus throwing a person on a bomb: intervention myopia in moral intuitions. *Psychological Science*, 18, 247–53.

Walker, L.J. (2004). Gus in the gap: bridging the judgment–action gap in moral functioning. In D.K. Lapsley and D. Narvaez (eds). *Moral Development, Self, and Identity* (pp. 1–20). Mahwah, NJ: Erlbaum.

Walker, L.J. (2006). Gender and morality. In M. Killen and J.G. Smetana (eds). *Handbook of Moral Development* (pp. 93–115). Mahwah, NJ: Erlbaum.

Walker, L.J. and Taylor, J.H. (1991). Family interactions and the development of moral reasoning. *Child Development*, 62, 264–93.

Wallack, L., Grube, J.W., Madden, P.A. and Breed, W. (1990). Portrayals of alcohol on prime-time television. *Journal of Studies on Alcohol*, 51, 428–37.

Walsh, D. (1988). Critical thinking to reduce prejudice. *Social Education*, 52, 4.

Want, S.C. and Harris, P.L. (2001). Learning from other people's mistakes: causal understanding in learning to use a tool. *Child Development*, 72, 431–43.

Warneken, F. and Tomasello, M. (2006). Altruistic helping in human infants and young chimpanzees. *Science*, 311, 1301–3.

Warneken, F. and Tomasello, M. (2007). Helping and cooperation at 14 months of age. *Infancy*, 11, 271–94.

Wassmann, J., Träuble, B. and Funke, J. (2013). *Theory of Mind in the Pacific: Reasoning Across Cultures.* Heidelberg, Germany: Universitätsverlag Winter.

Waterhouse, L. (2006). Multiple intelligences, the Mozart effect, and emotional intelligence: a critical review. *Educational Psychologist*, 41(4), 207–25.

Waters, E., Hamilton, C.E. and Weinfield, N.S. (2000a). The stability of attachment security from infancy to adolescence and early adulthood: general introduction. *Child Development*, 71, 678–83.

Waters, E., Merrick, S., Treboux, D., Crowell, J. and Albersheim, L. (2000b). Attachment security in infancy and early childhood: a twenty-year longitudinal study. *Child Development*, 71, 684–9.

Watson, J.B. (1913). Psychology as the behaviorist views it. *Psychological Review*, 20, 158–78.

Watson, J.B. (1930). *Behaviorism* (Rev. Edn). Chicago: University of Chicago Press.

Watson, J.B. and Rayner, R. (1920). Conditioned emotional reactions. *Journal of Experimental Psychology*, 3(1), 1–14.

Watson-Jones, R.E. and Legare, C.H. (2016). The social functions of group rituals. *Current Directions in Psychological Science*, 25(1), 42–6.

Watson-Jones, R.E., Whitehouse, H. and Legare, C. (2015). In-group ostracism increases high-fidelity imitation in early childhood. *Psychological Science*, 27(1), 34–42.

Weiss, B., Dodge, K.A., Bates, J.E. and Pettit, G.S. (1992). Some consequences of early harsh discipline: child aggression and a maladaptive social information processing system. *Child Development*, 63, 1321–35.

Weiss, G. and Hechtman, L. (1993). *Hyperactive Children Grown Up* (2nd Edn). New York: Guilford.

Weiss, R. (1974). The provisions of social relationships. In Z. Rubin (ed.). *Doing Unto Others* (pp.17–26). Englewood Cliffs, NJ: Prentice Hall.

Weissberg, R.P. and Greenberg, M.T. (1998). School and community competence-enhancement and prevention programs. In I.E. Siegel and K.A. Renninger (eds). *Handbook of Child Psychology: Vol. 4. Child Psychology in Practice* (5th Edn, pp. 877–954). New York: Wiley.

Weizman, Z.O. and Snow, C.E. (2001). Lexical output as it relates to children's vocabulary acquisition: effects of sophisticated exposure as a support for meaning. *Developmental Psychology*, 37, 265–79.

Welch, K.J. (2010). *Family Life Now* (2nd Edn). Upper Saddle River, NJ: Prentice Hall.

Wellman, H.M. (1990). *Children's Theories of Mind*. Cambridge, MA: MIT Press.

Wellman, H.M. (2012). Theory of mind: better methods, clearer findings, more development. *European Journal of Developmental Psychology*, 9(3), 313–30.

Wellman, H.M., Cross, D. and Watson, J. (2001). Meta-analysis of theory of mind development: the truth about false belief. *Child Development*, 72, 655–84.

Wellman, H.M., Fang, F., Liu, D., Zhu, L. and Liu, G. (2006). Scaling of theory of mind understanding in Chinese children. *Psychological Sciences*, 17, 1075–81.

Wellman, H.M. and Liu, D. (2004). Scaling of theory-of-mind tasks. *Child Development*, 75(2), 523–41.

Wentzel, K.R., Barry, C.M. and Caldwell, K.A. (2004). Friendships in middle school: Influences on motivation and school adjustment. *Journal of Educational Psychology*, 96, 195–203.

West, D.J. and Farrington, D.P. (1973). *Who Becomes Delinquent?* London: Heinemann.

Westerlund, M., Hadlaczky, G. and Wasserman, D. (2015). Case study of posts before and after a suicide on a Swedish internet forum. *The British Journal of Psychiatry*, 207(6) 476–82.

Weston, D. and Turiel, E. (1980). Act-rule relations: children's concepts of social rules. *Developmental Psychology*, 16, 417–24.

Wey, H.Y., Gilbert, T.M., Zürcher, N.R., She, A., Bhanot, A., Taillon, B.D., Schroeder, F.A., Wang, C., Haggarty, S.J. and Hooker, J.M. (2016). Insights into neuroepigenetics through human histone deacetylase PET imaging. *Science Translational Medicine*, 8(351), 351ra106.

Whitebread, D. and Jameson, H. (2010). Play beyond the Foundation Stage: story-telling, creative writing and self-regulation in able 6-7 year olds. In J. Moyles (ed.). *The Excellence of Play* (pp. 95–107). Maidenhead: Open University Press.

Whitehurst, G.J. and Vasta, R. (1975). Is language acquired through imitation? *Journal of Psycholinguistic Research*, 4(1), 37–59.

Whiteman, S., McHale, S. and Crouter, A. (2007). Competing processes of sibling influence: observational learning and sibling deidentification. *Social Development*, 16, 642–61.

Whiten, A. (1993). Evolving a theory of mind: the nature of non-verbal mentalism in other primates. In S. Baron-Cohen, H.

Tager-Flusberg and D.J. Cohen (eds). *Understanding Other Minds: Perspectives from Autism* (pp. 367–96). New York: Oxford University Press.

Whiten, A. and Byrne, R. (1988). The manipulation of attention in primate tactical deception. In R. Byrne and A. Whiten (eds). *Machiavellian Intelligence: Social Expertise and the Evolution of Intellect in Monkeys, Apes and Humans.* Oxford: Clarendon Press.

Williams, E. (2003). A comparative review of early forms of object-directed play and parent-infant play in typical infants and young children with autism. *Autism*, 7(4), 361–77.

Williams, E., Reddy, V. and Costall, A. (2001). Taking a closer look at functional play in children with autism. *Journal of Autism and Developmental Disorders*, 31(1), 67–77.

Williams, J.E. and Bennett, S.M. (1975). The definition of sex stereotypes via the adjective check list. In J. Archer and B. Lloyd (eds). *Sex and Gender* (pp. 38–41). Cambridge: Cambridge University Press.

Wimmer, H. and Perner, J. (1983). Beliefs about beliefs: representation and constraining function of wrong beliefs in young children's understanding of deception. *Cognition*, 13, 103–28.

Wing, L. (1991). The relationship between Asperger's syndrome and Kanner's autism. In U. Frith (ed.). *Autism and Asperger Syndrome* (pp. 93–121). Cambridge: Cambridge University Press.

Winner, E. (1988). *The Point of Words.* Cambridge, MA: Harvard University Press.

Witherell, C.S. and Edwards, C.P. (1991). Moral versus social-conventional reasoning: a narrative and cultural critique. *Journal of Moral Education*, 20(3), 1–21.

Witherington, D.C., Campos, J.J., Harriger, J.A., Bryan, C. and Margett, T.E. (2010). Emotion and its development in infancy. In G. Bremner and T.D. Wachs (eds). *The Wiley-Blackwell Handbook of Infant Development, Vol. 1, Basic Research* (2nd Edn, pp. 568–91). Cambridge: Blackwell.

Wittgenstein, L. (1958). *Philosophical Investigations* (trans. G. E. M. Anscombe). Oxford: Basil Blackwell.

Wolak, J., Mitchell, K. and Finkelhor, D. (2007). Unwanted and wanted exposure to online pornography in a national sample of youth Internet users. *Pediatrics*, 119, 247–57.

Wolfberg, P.J. (2003). *Peer Play and the Autism Spectrum. The Art of Guiding Children's Socialization and Imagination.* Shawnee Mission, KS: Autism Asperger Publishing.

Wolff, H-G. and Kim, S. (2011). The relationship between networking behaviours and the Big Five personality dimensions. *Career Development International*, 17(1), 43–66.

Wolff, W. (1933). The experimental study of forms of expression. *Character and Personality*, 2, 168–76.

Wolk-Wasserman, D. (1986). Suicidal communication of persons attempting suicide and responses of significant others. *Acta Psychiatrica Scandinavica*, 73, 481–99.

Wood, A.F. and Smith, M.J. (2006). *Online Communication.* Mahwah, NJ: Erlbaum.

Wood, D., Bruner, J.S. and Ross, G. (1976). The role of tutoring in problem solving. *Journal of Child Psychology and Psychiatry*, 17(2), 89–100.

Wood, W. and Eagly, A.H. (2012). Biosocial construction of sex differences and similarities in behaviour. In J.M. Olson and M.P. Zanna (eds). *Advances in Experimental Social Psychology* (Vol. 46, pp. 55–123). London: Elsevier.

Wood, W., Wong, F.Y. and Chachere, J.G. (1991). Effects of media violence on viewers' aggression in unconstrained social interaction. *Psychological Bulletin*, 109(3), 371–83.

Workman, L., Chilvers, L., Yeomans, H. and Taylor, S. (2006). Development of cerebral lateralisation for recognition of emotions in chimeric faces in children aged 5 to 11. *Laterality: Asymmetries of Body, Brain and Cognition*, 11(6), 493–507.

Workman. L. and Mischel, W. (2014). The master of self-control: Walter Mischel speaks to Lance Workman about his famous 'Marshmallow Test' and more. *The Psychologist*, 27, 942–4.

Workman, L., Peters, S. and Taylor, S. (2000). Laterality of perception processing of pro- and antisocial emotion displayed in chimeric faces. *Laterality*, 5, 237–49.

Workman, L. and Reader, W. (2014). *Evolutionary Psychology* (3rd Edn). Cambridge: Cambridge University Press.

Workman, L. and Reader, W. (2015). *Evolution and Behavior*. London: Routledge.

World Health Organization (WHO) (2015). *Under-five Mortality Rate*. World Health Statistics, http://apps.who.int/gho/data/node.sdg.3-2-viz?lang=en.

Wright, I., Lewis, V. and Collis, G.M. (2006). Imitation and representational development in young children with Down syndrome. *British Journal of Developmental Psychology*, 24(2), 429–50.

Wright, J.C. and Huston, A.C. (1995). *Effects of Educational TV Viewing of Lower Income Preschoolers on Academic Skills, School Readiness, and School Adjustment One to Three Years Later*. Report to Children's Television Workshop, Center for Research on the Influences of Television on Children. Lawrence: University of Kansas.

Wyman, E., Rakoczy, H. and Tomasello, M. (2009). Normativity and context in young children's pretend play. *Cognitive Development*, 24, 146–55.

Xie, H., Cairns, B.D. and Cairns, R.B. (2004). The development of aggressive behaviors among girls: measurement issues, social functions, and differential trajectories. In D.J. Pepler, K. Madsen, C. Webster and K. Levene (eds). *Development and Treatment of Girlhood Aggression* (pp. 103–34). Mahwah, NJ: Lawrence Erlbaum Associates.

Yale, M.E., Messinger, D.S., Cobo-Lewis, A.B. and Delgado, C.F. (2003). The temporal coordination of early infant communication. *Developmental Psychology*, 39, 815–24.

Yang, S. and Sternberg, R.J. (1997). Taiwanese Chinese people's conceptions of intelligence. *Intelligence*, 25, 21–36.

Yang, Y. and Raine, A. (2009). Prefrontal structural and functional brain imaging findings in antisocial, violent, and psychopathic individuals: a meta-analysis. *Psychiatry Research – Neuroimaging*, 174 (2), 81–8.

Yau, J. and Smetana, J.G. (2003). Conceptions of moral, social-conventional, and personal events among Chinese preschoolers in Hong Kong. *Child Development*, 74, 647–58.

Yochelson, S. and Samenow, S. (1976). *The Criminal Personality, Volume I: A Profile for Change*. New York: Jason Aronson.

Young, S. (2007). Forensic aspects of ADHD. In M. Fitzgerald, M. Bellgrove and M. Gill (eds). *Handbook of Attention Deficit Hyperactive Disorder*. Chichester: John Wiley and Sons.

Young, S.K., Fox, N.A. and Zahn-Waxler, C. (1999). The relations between temperament and empathy in 2-year-olds. *Developmental Psychology*, 35:1189–97.

Youniss, J. (1980). *Parents and Peers in Social Development: A Sullivan-Piaget Perspective*. Chicago: University of Chicago Press.

Youth Justice Board (2009). *Youth Survey 2009*. Research study conducted for the Youth Justice Board for England and Wales.

Zack, E., Barr, R., Gerhardstein, P., Dickerson, K. and Meltzoff, A.N. (2009). Infant imitation from television using novel touch-screen technology. *British Journal of Developmental Psychology*, 27(1), 13–26.

Zahn-Waxler, C. (2000). The development of empathy, guilt, and internalization of distress: implications for gender differences in internalising and externalising problems. In R. Davidson (ed.). *Wisconsin Symposium on Emotion: Vol. 1. Anxiety, Depression, and Emotion* (pp. 222–65). Oxford: Oxford University Press.

Zahn-Waxler, C., Klimes-Dougan, B. and Kendziora, K.T. (1998). The study of emotion socialization: conceptual, methodological, and developmental considerations. *Psychological Inquiry*, 9, 313–6.

Zametkin, A.J., Nordahl, T.E., Gross, M., King, A.C., Semple, W.E., Rumsey, J., Hamburger, S. and Cohen, R.M. (1990). Cerebral glucose metabolism in adults with hyperactivity of childhood onset. *The New England Journal of Medicine*, 323, 1361–6.

Zarbatany, L., McDougall, P. and Hymel, S. (2000). Gender-differentiated experience in the peer culture: links to intimacy in preadolescence. *Social Development*, 9, 62–79.

Zelazo, P.D. and Carlson, S.M. (2012). Hot and cool executive function in childhood and adolescence: development and plasticity. *Child Development Perspectives*, 6, 354–60.

Zelazo, P.D., Qu, L. and Müller, U. (2005). Hot and cool aspects of executive function: relations in early development. In W. Schneider, R. Schumann-Hengsteler and B. Sodian (eds). *Young Children's Cognitive Development: Interrelationships Among Executive Functioning, Working Memory, Verbal Ability, and Theory of Mind* (pp. 71–93). Mahwah, NJ: Erlbaum.

Zeskind, P.S., Klein, L. and Marshall, T.R. (1992). Adults' perceptions of experimental modifications of durations and expiratory sounds in infant crying. *Developmental Psychology*, 28, 1153–62.

Zimmerman, F.J., Christakis, D.A. and Meltzoff, A.N. (2007). Television and DVD/video viewing by children 2 years and younger. *Archives of Pediatric and Adolescent Medicine*, 161, 437–79.

Zych, I., Ortega-Ruiz, R. and Del Rey, R. (2015). Scientific research on bullying and cyberbullying: where have we been and where are we going. *Aggression and Violent Behavior*, 24, 188–98.

Glossary

ABAB designs: can be used to provide scientific validity to the findings from case studies. This design begins with taking a baseline level of a child's usual behaviour, in a classroom for instance, followed by a teacher's new response to the behaviour (for which the child's behaviour is recorded), and what happens when the teacher reverts back to the original response, and finally the reinstatement of the new response if this changes the child's behaviour for the better.

Accommodation: is one of three interacting mechanisms enabling new information to be incorporated into mental structures that have been modified.

Activational effects: in biology, the concept that some hormones activate areas of the brain or other parts of the body at various points in the life cycle. Such target areas may previously have been organised by the same or other hormones. An example is male hormones that, during adolescence, develop a mature male musculature and 'typical male' type behavioural responses. In other species this concept is not problematic, but in our own species there are debates as to the extent to which hormones have a causal activational role in behaviour.

Active effects: or 'active gene-environment correlation' refers to the fact that a child's genotype leads them to seek out an environment which then has an effect on their development (e.g., an 'extravert' child is likely to seek out more thrilling aspects of the environment which, in turn, has an effect on their personality development).

Adaptation: a trait that has been selected over evolutionary time due to its positive effects on survival or reproduction.

Adaptionist account: is used by evolutionists to provide an account of the connection between adult reproductive strategy styles and early infant attachment. Secure attachments in infancy tend to lead to higher relationship security in adulthood.

Adolescence-limited: is one of two typologies of antisocial behaviour in adolescence. In this case antisocial behaviour occurs during the teen years and stops by adulthood.

Adult–Child speech (A–C): (see also **motherese**) is a type of speech communication between a caregiver (also other adults) and the child.

Adverse factors: can actively harm an individual's development such as experiencing parental rejection and neglect.

Affectional bond: refers to a tie with an individual that is not only relatively long enduring but is unique to that person.

Affectionless psychopathy: describes individuals who find the expression of care and affection for others challenging. This is because they were deprived of being cared for as infants.

Affective (or emotional) empathy: is considered one aspect of empathy (the other being cognitive empathy). It involves the sharing of apparent emotion.

Agentic perspective: a view that people are not simply reactive organisms (reacting to environmental input) but rather self-organising and proactive. Particularly associated with Albert Bandura.

Aggression: generally refers to angry or violent feelings or behaviour that can result in violent behaviour or hostility.

Agreeableness: the extent to which a person is helpful and good company, in a word how 'nice' they are.

Allele: (allelomorph) different forms of a gene that can occur at each locus (position) on a chromosome.

Altruistic acts: are behaviours that help another individual without expectation of concrete rewards.

Amygdala: is an area of the brain involved in the perception of our emotions, particularly fear.

Androgens: are sex hormones particularly associated with males.

Angular gyrus: is located in the parietal lobe of the brain. It plays an important role in a number of functions including social cognition.

Anterior cingulate cortex (ACC): is a part of the brain found in the frontal lobe. It plays an important role in emotional functions, in particular the regulation of emotions.

Anterior insula: is a part of the brain found between the temporal and parietal lobe. It plays an important role in the experience of emotions and the anticipation of negative stimuli such as receiving a pain from a sharp probe.

Antisocial behaviour: is the antithesis of being prosocial. Antisocial behaviours are inappropriate, negative and against the consensus of what is acceptable behaviour.

Antisocial Personality Disorder (APD): describes an individual who continuously manipulates and exploits others often resulting in the violation of other peoples' rights.

Assimilation: is one of three interacting mechanisms enabling new information to be incorporated into existing mental structures.

Attachment figure: (see also **caregiver**) is an individual to whom there is a strong bond of affection that cannot be replaced by another person.

Attachment: is an example of a relationship that offers security and contains caregiving properties.

Attention Deficit Hyperactivity Disorder (ADHD): is a condition affecting an individual's ability to concentrate and be still for any length of time.

Attitudes: are considered to be organised cognitions, emotions and behavioural inclinations directed towards a socially important event.

Attractiveness stereotype: presents an image of how women should look. The media present this stereotype by associating femininity with being beautiful.

Authoritarian: a parenting style of discipline that is equivalent to power assertion where extreme rejection and inappropriate demands are made.

Authoritative: a parenting style of discipline that is equivalent to induction where a balance is made between acceptance and making appropriate demands.

Autism spectrum disorder (ASD): is a dimension used to describe individuals with problems of social communication and interaction, and restricted and repetitive behavioural patterns. The dimension is a continuum ranging from low to high levels of ability.

Autonomous morality: is based on the behaviours children consider to be right or wrong.

Autosomal chromosomes: all chromosomes bar the sex chromosomes. Also known simply as autosomes.

Babbling: is the sound infants make when stringing together a repetitive consonant–vowel combination such as 'mamama'.

Behavioural activation system (BAS): is responsible for regulating positive emotion and approach behaviour towards a pleasant stimulus.

Behavioural deficits: are appropriate behaviours that occur infrequently or not at all, such as morally driven behaviours of remorse or concern for others.

Behavioural excesses: are inappropriate behaviours that occur frequently, such as violent and aggressive outbursts and non-compliance.

Behavioural genetics: a discipline that considers the relative effect of genetics and the environment on individual differences such as personality factors.

Behavioural inhibition system (BIS): is responsible for regulating aversive emotion and avoidance behaviour from an unpleasant stimulus.

Big 5: refers to five personality traits that, when assessed, are considered by many psychologists to provide a comprehensive account of a person's personality. Also known as the five factor model (FFM).

Biological organisation: refers to the hierarchy of biological systems.

Biopsychosocial interactionism: a view of the development of person that takes into account the interacting factors of biology, psychology and social factors.

Biosocial interaction: the view that behaviour and internal states are the outcome of an interaction between biological and social factors.

Bipolar depression: is a mental illness characterised by periods of deep lethargic depression and periods of manic elation.

Bistrategic controllers: one of four types of strategies individuals use to acquire resources, utilising coercive and prosocial tactics.

Blended or reconstituted family: describes new families formed from two pre-existing family structures such that the children from the different families become step-brothers and step-sisters.

Blooming: is a term used to describe the proliferation of neural synaptic connections.

Bobo doll: is an inflatable child-sized doll which bobs back when a child strikes it. Used by Albert Bandura and co-workers in experiments to examine aggressive responses in children by Albert Bandura and co-workers.

Bullying: describes intentional and repetitive physical or verbal abuse towards an individual. Typically there is a power imbalance between the perpetrator and victim concerned.

Callous-unemotional: is a trait measure used to identify individuals who exhibit cruel and insensitive disregard for others and fail to show any positive emotion.

Caregiver: (see also **Attachment figure**) is an individual (normally the mother) onto whom an infant depends on for survival (fulfilling all needs such as thirst, hunger and care).

Case study: can be used to obtain in-depth information about a specific individual. This information cannot be extended to other individuals but may provide a platform for further exploring aspects of the information obtained further using one of many different methods.

Categorical speech perception: refers to a baby's ability to differentiate between discrete sound-bites such as 'bah' and 'gah'.

Categories of play: vary in the number of play types depending on the researcher. The first recognised categories of play consisted of six: unoccupied, solitary, onlooker, parallel, associative and cooperative play.

Cause and effect: is the purpose of conducting experiments. By introducing individuals to the **IV**, it is possible to ascertain the effect it has on behaviour.

Central executive: manages how information is allocated for processing.

Chatroom: represents a public virtual space where users can engage in simultaneous conversations with many other users.

Child leader: can be of three types as established using a sociometric approach: organisational, informative and communicative. The organiser coordinates aspects of play; the informant supplies useful knowledge the group can use while the communicative leaders uses prosocial skills to maintain group cohesiveness.

Chimeric face: is divided longitudinally into two sides where one side displays a neutral expression while the other shows one of the primary emotions.

Chromosomes: a string of genes found in the nucleus of a cell.

Classical conditioning: is an automatic form of learning in which a stimulus gains the capacity to evoke a response that was previously evoked by a different stimulus.

Clinical interviews: allow researchers and practitioners to obtain in-depth information about an individual concerning how they think, feel and behave.

Cliques: comprise small groups of young adolescents based on friendship.

Co-dominance: a genetic trait whereby both alleles for a gene are equally strong, leading to both being expressed simultaneously.

Coercive controllers: one of four types of strategies individuals use to acquire resources, utilising coercive tactics.

Cognitive-behavioural therapy (CBT): is a type of **Psychotherapy** designed to alter or modify negative patterns of thought that lead to inappropriate and unwanted behaviours.

Cognitive development: is a field of study that focuses on a child's development of information processing, conceptual learning, perceptual skills and language.

Cognitive distortions: refer to biased ways of thinking that convince us of something that is not the case.

Cognitive empathy: refers to making inferences about the emotional state of another person thereby implying that we can cognitively recognise emotional states.

Cognitive Social Learning Theory: is used in developmental psychology to describe how an individual's knowledge is acquired by observing others. In observing others we also see the consequences of their actions, which thereby reinforces the learning. Also known as social cognitive learning theory.

Cold cognition: is a term used to describe bullies who are good at judging how a potential victim might feel when bullied. This makes it easier for them to devise effective ways of hurting their victim.

Collectivistic cultures: describe countries that subscribe to the socialisation of conformity to rules, mores and traditions, and to respect older members of society.

Communication: refers to the disclosure of all types of information, which can be of a verbal or nonverbal nature.

Comorbidity likeness: refers to the likelihood of related family members having the same behavioural problems.

Competence: as an ethical principle referring to the researcher's awareness

of ethics and conducting research competently.

Comprehensive Behavioural Intervention for Tics (CBiT): contains various techniques designed to help sufferers of Tourette's syndrome to control some of their symptoms.

Computed Tomography (CT): is a scanning technique used in research to explore brain structure that can be viewed on a computer as layered images.

Concrete operational: is the third out of four stages of cognitive development outlined by Piaget. The mental structure has become modified further as the child encounters new information.

Conditioned response: is a learned response to a previously neutral stimulus in **classical conditioning**.

Conditioned stimulus: is a previously neutral stimulus which, following becoming associated with an unconditioned stimulus, then triggers a conditioned response.

Conduct Disorders (CDs): describes a clustering of antisocial behaviours exhibited in children and adolescents.

Conlearn: guided by **conspec**, based on experience of looking at faces, conlern fleshes out the primitive facial representation to form a realistic representation of what a face looks like.

Conscientiousness: the extent to which a person is reliable and demonstrates self-discipline.

Conspec: innately specified set of principles responsible for

guiding attention of a new born towards stimuli that resemble a primitive human face.

Contextual perspective: considers that we can only fully understand an organism (and in particular humans) through a knowledge of historical and current situational variables.

Control group: refers to the individuals who have not been subjected to the **IV** in an experiment. This is so that researchers can determine whether the **IV** is causing the effect found.

Conventional behaviour: describes consensus behaviour derived from shared standardised rules dictating how we should conduct ourselves.

Conventional domain: is concerned with consensus behaviour defined by society. The main judgement base concerns the mantra of following social standards during social interactions.

Conventional morality: is the second of three levels depicting the nature of moral development achieved. Moral standards are based on adult role models and moral reasoning on group norms.

Conventional transgression: describes behaviours which break the social conventions dictating how we should conduct ourselves, such as listening to a teacher.

Cooing: is the sound infants make when stringing together a repetitive combination of discrete vowels such as 'oooo'.

Cool executive function: (see also **Hot executive function**) operates on the basis of working memory and other cognitive processes enabling effective decision-making.

Correlational designs: provide information about how one variable (e.g., dancing) and another variable (e.g., weight loss) correspond to each other. Does weight loss increase as the amount of dancing increases for instance? A strong association or correlation between these two variables allow researchers to make predictions about how these relate to one another but fail to provide any causal link.

Criminogenic environment: describes a setting conducive for creating criminally inclined individuals and providing opportunities for criminal activity.

Cross-cultural studies: examine behaviour by considering differences and similarities between different cultures.

Cross-domain interactions: refers to the fact that, although modules are designated specific functions, under some circumstances they may be able to work together to solve a specific task.

Cross-sectional method: is an easy way of comparing individuals varying in age using the same timeframe. This saves time by allowing researchers to study the here-and-now as opposed to waiting for five year olds to become seven year olds for instance.

Culture-specific: something that pertains to a specific culture.

Cupboard love: is an expression used to describe an infant's fulfilment of drives such as hunger and thirst.

Cyberbullying: describes bullying behaviour using electronic communication enabling threatening messages to be sent to an online victim.

Cybercrime: refers to aggressive and criminal behaviour committed through the medium of computers or the Internet that cause psychological harm.

Declarative statement: (see **Protodeclarative**) provides another person with information about an object that can be of interest. In the caregiver–child relationship, pointing at an object is an action used to share object interest.

Deep brain stimulation: is an intervention designed to help sufferers experiencing severe symptoms of Tourette's syndrome. Electrodes are implanted into the brain delivering electrical signals to areas such as the thalamus to control motor movements.

Delinquents: is the label given to children and adolescents who commit petty criminal acts known as delinquency.

Dependent variable (DV): refers to an individual's response to a controlled or manipulated variable. In response to hearing elevated levels of noise, a child, for example, might find it difficult to concentrate and solve a simple numerical task.

Descriptive research designs: describe information attained through other forms of investigation such as from naturalistic observation. This method can only provide a commentary of what is found and not why.

Design stance: enables us to make predictions about the workings of designed things, such as the switch that turns a computer on, or, as in nature, that pierced skin will bleed.

Deviant: describes behaviours, thoughts and feelings that lie outside of what is considered to be the norm and expressed by the majority of people.

Deviant behaviour: consists of responses that do not adhere to societal or cultural norms.

Diagnostic Statistical Manual of Mental Disorders (DSM): is a manual describing and enabling clinicians to diagnose a variety of psychological conditions.

Diathesis-stress theory: explains behaviour as an outcome of predispositional vulnerabilities and stressful environmental factors.

Digital Era: refers to a period stemming from the mid-to-late 20th century when printing increased the way in which information was disseminated. This would develop further with computer and Internet development such that printing transformed into a new digital form.

Disorganised/disoriented: is an insecure attachment style added as a consequence of studying the connection between caregiver childhood experiences and the type of attachments they have with their offspring. Caregivers who had a traumatic attachment tend to have disorganised/disoriented infants.

Disruptive Behaviour Disorders (DBDs): describe a series of disorders where children and adolescents exhibit a clustering of negative and socially undesirable behaviours that continue to last throughout development.

Dizygotic twins: are derived from two different fertilised ovum and sperm (who thereby share 50 per cent of their genes through common descent) but develop in the uterus at the same time. They are also called fraternal twins.

DNA (deoxyribonucleic acid): a giant double helix molecule; the chemical of which genes are composed.

Domain-relevant: is a concept used to take account of how our brain develops processing biases for specific types of stimuli over others. This approach suggests modules are not hard-wired but the outcome of an interaction between inherited factors and environmental experiences during development.

Domain-specificity: is the notion that different cognitive skills operate independently in a modular fashion. Modules have their own specialised area of function and respond to specific forms of stimuli.

Doppelgängers: are unrelated individuals who happen to look identical.

Down syndrome (DS): is a condition caused by a chromosomal anomaly where there are three instead of two chromosomes for Chromosome 21. This causes many physical problems but also specific mental issues for the individual.

DRD4 gene: plays an important role in the attachment styles of infants. This gene can take on different structures, such as a 7-repeat allele that features strongly among infants who are classified as difficult and show a disorganised pattern of attachment.

Dyadic peer relationships: consist of two individuals who are considered as equals and provide the same level of affection for one another.

Dynamic systems theory: is the study of processes that unfold over time in, and react to, perturbations.

Ecological niche: the place, role and function of an organism within its ecosystem and that affects its ability to survive and reproduce.

Ecological Theory: is an approach to child development, developed by Urie Bronfenbrenner, that provides a framework to study how children interact with a series of environmental systems with which they interact.

Ecological validity: provides researchers with an indication of how accurate and representative their findings are of real-life occurrences.

Ecosystem model: considers development of the child

in the context of the environmental systems with which he or she interacts. Associated with Urie Bronfenbrenner.

Ego: is a part of the mind, which, according to Freud, has a controlling influence on the **id** in that it guides the latter towards more reasonable responses.

Egocentric thinking: defining Piaget's preoperational stage, this signifies the difficulty children have in disengaging their own mental states when trying to understand those of others.

Egoistic personal distress: is different from **empathy** as it relates to the negative feelings we are personally experiencing.

Electrodermal reactivity (EDR): is a physiological measurement detecting changes in electrical skin conductance.

Electroencephalogram (EEG): is a measurement used for the recording of electrical activity in the brain.

Embedded narrative: is a story within a story that parallels the main storyline.

Emotional display rules: help individuals to show socially acceptable emotional expression under different situations and circumstances. These are also influenced by the enveloping culture.

Empathic/caring model: applies principles of empathy and care when making moral judgements about people instead of a moral reasoning based on notions of justice.

Empathisers: use the processing style of understanding the emotions and thoughts underlying the behaviours of the systems studied.

Empathy: is an example of a second higher-order emotion enabling us to understand, imagine and to some extent feel what another person is experiencing.

Empty praise: signifies praise given to an individual even though the performance is non-deserving of it. This can lead to notions of being better at something than is actually the case.

Endocrine: relating to a system of glands that release hormones into the body such as the adrenal glands in situ above each kidney.

Endogamy: refers to spouses having a similar demography such as social class.

Epigenetic landscape: refers to a model of development (originally applied to cell development) by Conrad Waddington. In the model development is likened to a marble rolling down a hill that contains many different paths. As the marble rolls down the hill, paths become increasingly restricted by the landscape.

Epigenetic rules: are influenced by our genes and reinforced by our environment. An example of this would be inbreeding as an inappropriate reproductive strategy as problems of offspring viability decreases as genetic mutation increases. Incestuous relationships are socially frowned upon and are illegal. Hence environment supporting epigenetic rules.

Epigenetic view: since epigenetics is the developmental process that leads from genotype to phenotype within a given environment, the epigenetic view is the notion that, depending on the environment encountered, some genes are expressed and others are not.

Epistemic mental states: represent the full range of different mental states possible such as knowing, thinking or dreaming.

Equilibration: is one of three interacting mechanisms enabling mental structures to be updated as new information is experienced and incorporated.

Ethical research: is the aim of researchers. In psychology this is ensured through the professional body representing psychologists. In Britain it is the British Psychological Society which issues a code of practice to follow.

Ethological perspective: the study of animal behaviour that focuses on the responses developed under natural circumstances and sees them as adaptations produced by natural (and sexual) selection. See also **human ethology**.

EU Kids Online: is a website developed as a counter measure to the risk of online grooming that children might experience. In addition to providing helpful information, research findings concerning children and online activity increase the awareness of the potential risks many children face when they are Internet-active.

Event-Related Potential (ERP): is the brain's response to a stimulus. It appears as a waveform with spikes as detected by EEG.

Event sampling: refers to the recording of all behaviour occurring in response to particular events. This is decided before the observational study begins.

Evocative effects: or 'evocative gene–environment correlation' refers to the fact that a child's genotype can evoke a response from the environment (including the social environment). This then affects the development of the child (e.g., a 'moody' child might lead to a negative response from parents while growing up).

Evolutionary psychology: is a theoretical framework for understanding human behaviour, postulating that the mind has been shaped by evolutionary pressures to aid survival and reproduction in the ancestral past.

Executive attention system: manages which information is held in working memory and how well a person focuses on such information. Involves frontal lobe activity.

Executive functions (EF): are collectively considered to be high-ordered cognitive processes such as attention and memory.

Exogamy: refers to spouses having a different demography such as crossing the barriers of social class status.

Exosystem: refers to social settings that do not have an immediate link to the child, but can affect the child indirectly. Examples might include the fact that a child's experiences at home might be affected by the parents' experiences in a work environment.

Experimental dialogue: is used to explain how the extent and type of play is dependent on the degree to which animals are flexible in their behaviour. Species driven by instinct are bound by a rigid script defining behaviour whereas animals less bound by instinct will show play behaviour that is influenced by their environment.

Experiments: enable researchers to draw conclusions about the effects of variables (e.g. loud noise on concentration) on behaviour (e.g. performing badly) within a controlled environment.

Extended family: is also known as the joint family system and arose out of young brides co-residing with the husband's family. This increased the family size and varied the ages of family members.

Externalised behaviour: refers to inappropriate and problematic behaviours directed at the external environment such as aggression and destruction.

Extra-familial factors: experiences that occur outside of the family setting.

Extraversion: the extent to which a person is outgoing and sensation-seeking.

Facebook: is a website used for social networking. It enables users to create profiles and to add visual material as well as sending messages to people.

False-belief tasks: belong to a research paradigm used to test an individual's understanding of another person's current state of mind by asking two fundamental belief questions.

Feminine roles: derived as a consequence of division of labour within the nuclear family. Females managed the home and looked after the children.

Feminine traits: refer to characteristics commonly seen in females. These characteristics can, for instance, relate to personality, temperament and emotion.

Fictive kin: is a term used to describe close friends of the family who are regarded as family members cemented by their label as an aunt or uncle.

Focus groups: are considered to be an in-depth interview but conducted within a group context. A topic for consideration is provided and members of the group contribute by discussing their thoughts about aspects relating to the subject in question.

Formal operational: is the fourth out of four stages of cognitive development outlined by Piaget. The mental structure has become modified further still as the child encounters new information.

Free-riders: are individuals in our evolutionary past who cheated by exploiting the moral codes of sharing and cooperating with others in their group.

Frequency dependent selection: is an evolutionary concept that suggests that the success of a given strategy (e.g., behavioural responses) may depend on the strategies others adopt. An example of this is that, when everybody else is cooperating, it might pay an individual to free-ride ('pay' in evolutionary terms that is).

Frontal-limbic system: describes the collective functions of both the frontal and limbic areas of the brain. The limbic system provides information about the state of the body in terms of emotion and arousal that is shared with the frontal lobes via intersecting nerve pathways. This information is then interpreted by the frontal lobe where decisions of appropriate action are made.

Fronto-parietal area: is a portion of the cortex of the brain where the frontal and parietal lobes meet.

Functional magnetic resonance imaging (fMRI): is a scanning technique used in research to explore brain activity via images of activation.

Galvanic skin response (GSR): is a physiological measurement detecting changes in electrical skin conductance.

Games with rules: describes regimented play where there are set ways of doing things such as counting to 20 in a game of hide-and-seek before searching for the players.

Gangs: consist of a group of individuals who share the

same attitudes, values, beliefs and mores that define how members of the group should behave. Gangs can have a positive or negative ethos that can conform to or conflict with mainstream cultural views.

Gender: male and female categories that are associated with cultural norms.

Gender consistency: refers to retaining a boy or girl gender despite dressing in the style of the opposite sex.

Gender Consistency Theory: refers to the establishment of gender identity through the imitation of how others of the same-sex behave.

Gender identity: refers to the self-labelling as a boy or girl.

Gender paradox: is a concept used to account for why females show more extreme symptoms than males for conditions and disorders that normally have a high preponderance of males.

Gender-role stereotypes: are gender-based beliefs of what are considered to be appropriate male and female roles. These gender-roles are influenced by concepts of masculinity and femininity.

Gender Schema Theory: refers to the acceptance of rules and schemas of how males or females should conduct themselves.

Gender stability: refers to the understanding of continuously being a boy or a girl.

Gender stereotypes: are gender-based beliefs of how males and females should conduct themselves. These beliefs develop from observing male and female role models.

General self-esteem: reflects an overall subjective emotional evaluation of self-worth. It is an umbrella term used to describe different areas where self-esteem can be assessed such as the academic, social and physical.

Genetic karyotype: the number and appearance of chromosomes in the nucleus of a cell.

Genetic predisposition: a propensity to develop a **trait** due to inherited factors.

Genotype: refers to the genetic constitution of an individual encoded in the nucleus of each cell.

Global evaluations: provide an overall assessment or evaluation of the self as opposed to focusing on the feedback of specific qualities such as social performance.

Grooming: is a method used to convince an unsuspecting individual (such as a child) that the person they are conversing with online is a good friend and understands how he or she is feeling. In reality the person is unalike that to which he or she presents as online.

Group play: involves children playing in groups, each member with his or her own role.

Group Socialisation Theory (GST): challenges the nurture assumption by considering peers as having the most impact on the behaviour of the developing child.

Gutenberg Bible: is the first book to be printed using the printing press invented by Gutenberg, hence the name.

Habituation–dishabituation: is an experimental design used to find out what stimuli sustains an infant's interest. This is often referred to as the looking paradigm as researchers observe what infants are looking at and for how long. After a period of time the infant will stop looking at the stimulus, which is referred to as habituation. When the stimulus is altered in some way, the infant will show interest in the stimulus once again because a difference has been detected. This is referred to as dishabituation.

Halo effect: refers to the phenomenon that physically attractive individuals must also have positive traits in all spheres such as personality, ability and behaviour.

Happy slapping: is a recent trend where youngsters use their mobile phones to take photographs of their victims being slapped to the head.

Hashtags: follow a word or phrase used on social media websites to highlight messages concerning specific topics.

Heteronomous morality: is based on external rules that children follow.

Heterosexual: refer to couples in a relationship who are of the opposite sex.

Homeostasis: is the tendency of a system to maintain a stable internal state due to the coordinated response of its parts to changes.

Hominins: are species regarded as human, related

to humans or have a direct ancestral link to humans.

Homozygous: having identical **alleles** at the same **locus** on each of a pair of **chromosomes**.

Hostile attributional bias: is the name given to a hostile interpretation of another person's intentions.

Hostile versus instrumental aggression dichotomy: refers to the desire to hurt someone in the case of hostile aggression, which is also referred to as reactive aggression; or to plan harmful behaviour towards another individual for goal attainment as is the case in instrumental aggression. The hostile versus instrumental aggression dichotomy refers to the independent and interdependent interplay between the two forms of aggression.

Hot executive function: (see also **Cold executive function**) operates on the basis of active emotional and motivational factors that increase the need for immediate gratification.

Hot spots: refers to the evolutionary argument that children have particular periods in development when they are susceptible to fears of specific stimuli (because these held specific dangers at different ages during our evolutionary history).

Human ethology: is the scientific study of human behaviour under naturalistic circumstances and in which evolutionary origins of responses are emphasised.

Human moral code: houses behaviours considered universally as appropriate ways of behaving. Behaviours contravening these codes are considered to be heinous acts such as rape and murder.

Hypercognitive system: is a complex hierarchical model describing how different facets of the self can be conceptualised. Information pertaining to self-concept and self-esteem are processed and organised separately but interact interdependently.

Id: is a part of the mind, which, according to Freud, consists of a set of instinctive drives.

Ideal body shape: is presented as the ideal size and body shape to which teenagers should aspire. Unfortunately, the advertised body shape is often an unhealthy one.

Independent variable (IV): refers to a variable (e.g., loud noise) that can be controlled and manipulated by the researcher.

Individualistic cultures: describe countries that subscribe to the socialisation of independent thinkers who openly express their thoughts and feelings.

Induction: is a form of discipline using reasoning to make children understand the connection between behaviour and consequences.

Indulgent: a parenting style of discipline that consists of over-acceptance and failure to make appropriate demands.

Information processing: is the change or processing of information that is detectable.

Information processing approach: perceives the goal of understanding human thinking in terms of how we process information, taking the lead from a knowledge of computer systems.

Informed consent: is required from individuals participating in research. This is to ensure that they understand what will happen and that their results will be confidential.

In-group mentality: represents a common way of thinking, feeling and acting amongst members of the same group.

Inner speech: is a form of conversation children have with themselves but is spoken out loud during play sessions to provide guidance on how actions should be performed.

Insecure avoidant: also referred to as the A-dyad, is one of the insecure attachments observed in the Strange Situation. Infants are indifferent to their caregiver when she is present in the room, leaves and then returns.

Insecure resistant: also referred to as the C-dyad, is one of the insecure attachments observed in the Strange Situation. Infants are wary of the caregiver when she is present in the room, show distress when she leaves but will seek her attention when she returns only to rebuff her.

Instagram: is a photo-sharing service enabling users to share their pictures and videos using a mobile phone device and using social networking platforms such as Facebook.

Instrumental aggression: describes planned and harmful behaviour towards another individual in order to achieve a desired outcome.

Integrity: is an ethical principle referring to the researcher's honesty, accuracy, fairness and clarity in any interactions with their participants.

Intentional stance: enables us to make predictions about other people's intentions based on what they do.

Interactionist: refers to the perspective that behaviour and internal states are the outcome of the interface between social, cultural, psychological and biological factors.

Intergenerational effect of attachment type: describes how the nature of attachment formed as an infant continues throughout the lifespan and becomes the attachment form used with his or her own future offspring.

Intergenerational transmission: refers to traits occurring in families from one generation to the next.

Interhemispheric transfer: is the transfer of information between the **cerebral hemispheres**.

Internal state language: is synonymous with the verbalisation of feelings and the causality of feelings expressed by the caregiver.

Internal working models: are memories formed by an infant's series of appraisals of the caregiver's responses to his or her needs.

Internalised values: refer to the integration of values into one's own sense of self or identity.

Internet: is an acronym for International Network because it contains many interconnected networks that use standardised communication protocols. It can be used to search for a variety of information and as a portal for communication.

Internet portals: are specially designed websites that bring information together from many different sources. This information is presented on a page or a portal. An example of an Internet portal is Yahoo.

Interviews: are commonly conducted face-to-face but, with modern technology, can occur using video links. There are different types of interview but they all involve asking questions to which the interviewee can respond.

Intraorganismic organisation: refers to an infant's innate predisposition to form an attachment to a caregiver. This operates on a biological readiness to bond with and attach to the caregiver.

Intra-sexual selection: the Darwinian process that leads to evolutionary change due to competition between members of one sex for access to members of the other sex.

Kindergarten: is a German concept meaning child garden or nursery. The philosophy behind this is to enable children to learn through play.

Labelling theory: describes a process of how an individual comes to believe a label assigned to them and consequently behaves in a manner befitting that label.

Laboratory settings: are linked with the observation of individuals within a contrived environment, which can be in a university observation room or a clinic. Unlike a naturalistic setting, the location is unfamiliar to the individual and the room is set up with specialised equipment for studying the person's response to study criteria. An example of this could be how long it takes before a child decides to eat a marshmallow when left waiting alone in a room.

Language acquisition device (LAD): is an innate device housing rules that are applicable to all languages.

Language acquisition support system (LASS): is a supportive environment enabling young children to acquire language. A caregiver's linguistic response to the developing child helps to accelerate language learning.

Lateralisation: (see also **Lateralised**) refers to how different aspects of brain function can become predominantly processed by the left or the right hemisphere of the brain.

Lateralised: the differential functioning of the left and right cerebral hemispheres (see also **lateralisation**).

Lax or permissive: a parenting style of discipline that is equivalent to indulgent approaches. Misbehaving children go undisciplined and have no rules to abide by.

Legal socialisation: refers to the process of socialising children and adolescents into accepting prosocial values and behaving in accordance with these values.

Libido: describes the energy created by survival and sexual instincts. The libido is a sexual energy or force that drives the **id** and sometimes causes conflict with conventional behaviour.

Life-course-persistent: is one of two typologies of antisocial behaviour in adolescence. In this case antisocial behaviour has an early onset of around 10 years of age but continues throughout the lifespan.

Life history theory: a theory that considers the way organisms allocate time and resources to different activities throughout the life span.

Lifespan perspective: is the idea that development continues throughout life and that humans continue to demonstrate plasticity.

Linkage analysis: is a method used by molecular geneticists to establish linkage between genes as a means of finding genetic relationships.

Locus: the position of a gene on a **chromosome**.

Longitudinal method: allows researchers to study individuals over an extensive length of time. This provides in-depth information covering the different aspects of an individual's life.

Long-term hypercognition: is a component of the hypercognitive system responsible for analysing the products of working hypercognition by following

rules and knowledge previously learned.

Love withdrawal: is a form of discipline using the deprivation of affection as a means of non-physical disapproval.

Machiavellian intelligence: is used to describe the ability of individuals to manipulate others using deceit.

Macrosystem: refers to the culture in which children develop, such as whether they grow up in a pre- or post-industrial environment.

Majority-rules rule: refers to the consensus group norms and behaviours that all group members must adopt. Any newcomers to the group who express variant behaviours have to either adopt those of the group, as the majority-rules rule applies, or join a different group.

Mala in se **crimes**: are criminal acts that contravene a sense of humanity rather than the laws of the land. These acts defy morality and are considered to be heinous crimes such as rape or murder.

Masculine roles: derived as a consequence of division of labour within the nuclear family. Males worked and earned money to look after the family.

Masculine traits: refer to characteristics commonly seen in males. These characteristics can, for instance, relate to personality, temperament and emotion.

Mass media: is a term used to describe various forms of communication used to spread information across a large audience of people.

Maternal deprivation: occurs when an individual is deprived of having caring input from a caregiver during the early years of life.

Maternal Deprivation Hypothesis: stipulates that an individual's social interpretation of the world stems from early caregiver interaction. If there is lost or damaged caregiver input then a negative social understanding of the world will occur.

Maternal mind-mindedness: describes caregivers who are good at verbalising their feelings and providing reasons for their feelings.

Medial frontal gyrus: is located in the frontal lobe of the brain, comprising approximately one-third of its surface space, and playing an important role in theory of mind where the mental state of others can be interpreted and used to predict their behaviour. A gyrus is a prominent ridge on the brain's surface area.

Meiosis: consists of the process of producing cells that have half the number of **chromosomes** of the mother cell (that is, such cells are **haploid**). Meiosis leads to the formation of **gametes**.

Mendelian genetics: a theory of inheritance developed by Gregor Mendel in the 1860s.

Mental space (M space): refers to short-term memory capacity that determines the upper limits of problem-solving ability. As M space increases so does problem-solving ability.

Mental structures: are also referred to as mental blueprints and are responsible for what we understand of the world around us and enable cognitive development.

Mental switches: also referred to as parameters, become activated in accordance with the linguistic environment experienced.

Mesosystem: refers to the interconnections between groups and institutions within the **microsystem**.

Meta-analysis: is used for comparing study findings from a host of studies that have the same research criteria. This enables researchers to compare like-with-like in a very large sample.

Methylation: is a chemical process that plays a role in the deactivation of a gene by repressing gene transcription (that prevents a particular segment of DNA from being copied).

Microsystem: refers to the groups and institutions that immediately surround and impact on a child's development.

Mindblindness: is a term used to describe individuals who find it difficult to understand that other people have different perspectives to their own. They find it challenging to realise differences between their own and other people's thoughts and feelings.

Mind-mapping theory: provides an architectural explanation of how our minds work. It describes different levels, systems and principles involved in the processing of information.

Mindreading: refers to the ability to ascertain the covert beliefs from the minds of others.

Mirror neurons: (see also **Sensorimotor neurons**) in addition to becoming activated when we perform actions or copy the actions of others, mirror neurons will also become active when viewing a simulation of another person's internal state (e.g., when they experience pain).

Mirror test: is a method used to examine an infant's ability to recognise its image in a mirror. The test is to see if an infant can see a difference in its image in the mirror after rouge has been added to its face.

Mismatch hypothesis: is used to account for maladaptive ways of behaving arising out of a mismatch between current and ancestral environments.

Mitosis: consists of the process of producing cells that have the same number of **chromosomes** as the mother cell (that is, such cells are **diploid**). Mitosis is the normal process of forming new body cells.

Modelling: consists of learning that follows observation, imitation and modelling the behaviour of others.

Modified nuclear family: has retained some extended family characteristics, such as close proximity to extended family members, but at the same time has retained nuclear family status.

Modularity: is the concept that the mind is composed of discrete modules each of which encapsulates a specific cognitive or emotional skill.

Modulating: our emotional arousal state involves the performance of behaviours that help reduce the emotional intensity experienced to a safe and comfortable level. An example would be an infant turning away from a source of discomfort.

Modus operandi (MO): refers to a method of operating.

Molecular markers: are fragments of DNA associated with a specific location within the genome. These help to identify a specific sequence of DNA within a pool of unfamiliar DNA.

Monoamine oxidase A (MAOA): is an enzyme coded for by the monoamine oxidase A gene. Low levels of this enzyme are associated with aggressive criminal behaviour.

Monogamy: refers to a relationship between one man and one woman normally tied through marriage.

Monozygotic twins: are derived from one fertilised egg (who thereby share all of their genes and are therefore identical).

Moral behaviour: describes behaviours arising as a consequence of a social interaction with another person. Moral behaviour is not arbitrary or rule-bound but rather is culture-free and follows a code of what is the right way to behave when engaging with another person.

Moral competence: refers to the ability to perform moral behaviours.

Moral/conventional paradigm: is a method used by social constructivists to study children's understanding of differences between a moral and conventional transgression.

Moral dilemmas: are stories presented to children that contain content depicting characters who behave in ways that can be perceived as wrong at one level but right at another. This creates ambiguity over what is the correct way of behaving.

Moral domain: is concerned with welfare, justice and human rights, all of which influence how we behave in our social relationships. The main judgement base concerns the mantra that it is wrong to harm another person.

Moral-impersonal decision-making: involves a decision that has an effect on potential victims who are far removed from personal contact with the protagonist.

Moral performance: refers to the performance of moral behaviours in different situations and under varying circumstances.

Moral-personal decision-making: involves a decision that has an effect on potential victims who are in close personal contact with the protagonist.

Moral reasoning: refers to the thinking process used to ascertain whether behaving in a certain way is right or wrong in a given situation.

Moral stories: is a method used to explore children's understanding and reasoning about morally-laden events.

Moral transgression: describes behaviours, such as murder, that are considered to be inherently wrong and that contravene the human moral code.

Motherese: (see also **Adult–Child speech**) was initially used to describe the speech communication between the caregiver and child. This has become largely replaced with A–C speech.

Multiple intelligences: refers to the concept that, in addition to the abilities that are normally measured in intelligence tests, such as mathematical and linguistic skills, humans have a range of other forms of intelligence such as bodily-kinaesthetic and interpersonal.

Mutual exclusivity assumption: refers to the naming of discrete objects such that each object has one label only.

Naming explosion: refers to the period when infants acquire many words at a fast rate.

Narcissism: refers to an extreme and unhealthy interest and admiration of one's appearance. This also extends to having a personality that maintains grandiose self-views and a craving for admiration.

Natural experiments: occur in the real world without the need for researchers to manipulate variables (e.g., the effects of stress on a foetus during an aversive event).

Natural selection: Darwin's term for what might today be defined as differential gene replication. The prime mechanism of evolutionary change.

Naturalistic settings: are linked with the observation of individuals within their natural environment, which can be the home or in a playground depending on the characteristics of what the researcher is studying.

Nature–nurture: the interaction between biological and social factors (note: can also refer to the nature–nurture debate, that is, the extent to which traits are the outcome of biological or social factors).

Neglecting: a parenting style of discipline that consists of rejection and failure to make appropriate demands.

Neolocality: occurred as a consequence of late marriages where separate households were established.

Neurodevelopmental disorders: are considered to be mental disorders whereby there is impairment of growth and development of the brain leading to problems involving emotion, memory, self-control and learning ability.

Neuroticism: the extent to which a person is likely to be in a negative emotional state such as anxious or the degree to which they are stable.

Neurotransmitter: a chemical released by a neuron to relay information to one or more other neurons.

Niche picking: is a psychological theory that individuals choose the type of environment that suits their inherited traits. An extravert may, for example, choose to associate with and engage in activities with other extraverts.

Non-controllers: one of four types of strategies individuals use to acquire resources, utilising neither coercive nor prosocial tactics.

Non-shared environment: refers to aspects of the environment that individuals living together do not share (e.g., siblings having different peer group experiences).

Normative: refers to assumed 'norms', that is, what is regarded as standard or correct.

Nuclear family: has a simple structure consisting of husband, wife and children. This originally arose through late marriages.

Nurture assumption: conceptualises the family, as an informal socialising agent, to have the most impact on the behaviour of the developing child.

Object substitution: is used in symbolic play where the true function of an object is substituted with an alternative one such as a banana for a telephone.

Observational methods: are commonly used by developmentalists to study the behaviour of individuals. The researcher observes the behaviours of others and records what happens either using a camera or written notes.

OCEAN: a mnemonic used to recall the **Big 5** personality traits: **Openness, Conscientiousness, Extraversion, Agreeableness** and **Neuroticism**.

Oestrogens: are sex hormones particularly associated with females.

Openness: the extent to which a person is open to new experiences.

Operant conditioning: is a form of learning that comes about through reward or punishment of a response. This means that an association is formed between a behavioural response and the consequences of that response.

Oppositional Defiant Disorder (ODD): is an example of a DBD that is typified by angry, defiant and vindictive behaviour.

Organisational effects: in biology, the concept that some hormones (in particular sex steroid hormones) alter early development of the brain and other areas so that specific areas can be activated later on in life. An example includes male embryos having areas of the brain masculinised, which later leads to mature masculine behaviour.

Organism: any individual life form. Includes viruses, bacteria, fungi, plants and animals.

Orthorexia nervosa: is a condition where the sufferer is obsessed with eating healthy food to such an extreme that, by excluding fats and sugary foods, they are pushing their bodies to the limit in order to attain a toned body.

Ostensive communication: involves the ability to turn-take and attending to what the other person is communicating. This

is supported by cognitive mechanisms such as comprehension of which aspect of an object pointed at is being named.

Out-group mentality: represents a common way of thinking, feeling and acting amongst members of a different group to one's own.

Overlapping waves theory: describes how the most successful problem-solving tactic becomes the preferred and predominant one.

Passive effects: or 'passive gene-environment correlation' refers to the effects of the rearing environment, which is a reflection of the parental genes. It is argued that this environment is genetically suitable for the child.

Patriarchal system: refers to men wielding power and influence within society. This extends to the family where men have authority over how the family is run.

Patrilocality: refers to the wife's co-residency with the husband's family in the area where that family is located.

PDD model: is an acronym describing the behaviours of protest, despair and detachment exhibited during separation.

Personal domain: is concerned with behavioural choice and self-preference behaviours. These can be of a prudential (cause harm to the self) or non-prudential nature. The main judgement base concerns the mantra of following personal choice and preference.

Personal transgressions: are wrongdoings based on individual choice and preference behaviours.

Such transgressions are judged less harshly than conventional transgressions. Personal transgressions of a prudential nature, however, are perceived just as negatively as moral transgressions. Non-prudential personal transgressions tend to be down-played.

Personality: relatively enduring ways of responding that can be encapsulated by a number of dimensions (such as extraversion and openness to experience).

Personality factors: the subdivisions that a personality can be broken down into such as **Extraversion** and **Agreeableness**.

Person-situation debate: a debate that considers to what extent people have enduring personality traits (specific sub-divisions of personality) and the extent to which responses are driven by a specific situation.

Perspective-taking: enables us to adopt the point of view of another person. Some argue it is one aspect of attaining cognitive empathy.

PET scan: is a type of brain scanning technique; PET is an abbreviation of positron emission tomography. A special dye containing radioactive tracers is injected and the scanner highlights areas where the dye has been absorbed thereby highlighting the function of organs such as the brain. This provides an image of how well the organs are functioning in real time.

Phenotype: the characteristics of an individual that result from environmental interaction of an organism's **genotype**.

Phonemes: are units of sound that are distinct and are the building blocks for forming words such as the 'c' in the word 'cat' or the 'm' in the word 'mat'.

Physical play: describes motor activity such as rough-and-tumble play or more subtle motor activity such as sewing or toy construction.

Physical stance: enables us to make predictions about actions observed using physical laws. For example, an apple falls from a tree due to gravity.

Plasticity principle: in personality psychology this is the view that personality traits are relatively plastic and open to change through environmental influence throughout the lifespan.

Pleasure principle: was introduced by Freud when describing an instinctual need to avoid pain by seeking pleasure. This is the driving force of the **id**.

Polyandry: refers to a woman having more than one husband.

Polygyny: refers to a man having more than one wife.

Postconventional morality: is the third of three levels depicting the nature of moral development achieved. Moral reasoning is based on individuals' rights and justice and is governed by a sense of what is right and wrong rather than reasoning based on rules and the consequences for breaking them.

Posterior cingulate gyrus: is an area of the cortex located in either brain hemisphere but tucked below the rest of the cortex. It plays an important role in emotional processing.

Posterior parietal cortex: located at the back of the parietal lobe of the brain, the posterior parietal cortex is responsible for the operation of planned movements, attention and spatial reasoning.

Power assertion: is a form of discipline using physical punishment for controlling behaviour.

Pragmatics: refers to the context in which language is spoken and its appropriateness across different situations.

Precocial: born or hatched in an advanced stage.

Pre-conventional morality: is the first of three levels depicting the nature of moral development achieved. The moral standards at this level are rule-bound and based on what the consequences are for breaking the rules.

Preferential looking technique: has been used to study the processing of faces in infants. This technique has shown that infants prefer complex patterns, which the human face is, and habituate very quickly to simple patterns.

Prefrontal cortex: located at the front of the frontal lobe of the brain, the prefrontal cortex is responsible for the regulation of higher cognitive, emotional and behavioural functioning.

Preoperational: is the second of four stages of cognitive development outlined by Piaget. The mental structure has become modified as the infant encounters new information.

Pretence/socio-dramatic play: describes games of pretence such as pretending to be a nurse or doctor. This type of play is said to enhance social, cognitive and academic performance as it helps to self-regulate behaviour.

Primary emotions: occur early in development and are considered to be expressed in the same way cross-culturally. These include: happiness, fear, anger, sadness, disgust and surprise.

Privation: is when an individual fails to form an emotional bond with a caregiver rather than that bond being lost or damaged as is the case with deprivation.

Prosocial: refers to behaviour that is positive and helpful to others.

Prosocial controllers: one of four types of strategies individuals use to acquire resources, utilising prosocial tactics.

Prosodic characteristics: are the sound patterns inherent within A–C speech to which infants are particularly attuned.

Protective factor: describes attributes in an individual that helps promote coping with stressful events.

Protodeclarative: (see **Declarative statement**) is the label given to a declarative statement.

Protoimperative: provides another person with information about intention. In the caregiver–child relationship, pointing at an object is used for requesting an action.

Provocative victims: is a label given to individuals who behave in ways that others find annoying and that provokes a negative response such as being bullied. In this way they become victims as a consequence of how they behave.

Pruning: is a term used to describe disconnection of unused neural synaptic connections.

Psychosexual stages: were introduced by Freud to account for the different zones of the body harvesting sexual energy. There are five of these stages varying in the zones of the body that harvest sexual energy: oral, anal, phallic, latent and genitalia.

Psychotherapy: is psychological intervention for the treatment of mental disorder.

Questionnaires: are considered as part of the survey approach for collecting data. These take the form of questions, normally presented in writing, but can be read to participants, requiring a tick response to set answers (e.g., yes or no).

Reactive aggression: describes an impulsive and spontaneous reaction in response to feelings of anger or fear, but usually to the need for retaliation.

Reactive heritability: allows for individuals to alter their behaviour depending on how others treat them within the context of the genes they inherit.

Reactive–instrumental dichotomy: refers to the independent and interdependent interplay between the two forms of aggression.

Reality principle: was introduced by Freud to describe how pleasure-seeking is replaced by the need to assess the external world using reason. This is the driving force of the **ego**.

Reciprocal altruism (RA): refers to behaviours that can reduce an individual's fitness in the short-term while helping to increase another individual's fitness with the expectation of reciprocation in the long-term.

Referential opacity: is our ability to suspend normal truths embedded within propositions.

Relational aggression: describes the harm caused by damaging an individual's reputation, relationships or social status. It is often considered to be a form of hidden or covert bullying behaviour.

Reliability: is the extent to which a measurement will be the same either when measured twice by the same measuring tool or the extent to which two different tools provide the same result.

Repetition compulsion: describes the need for children to repeat their play actions in an attempt to re-experience, resolve and control a challenging situation.

Reports by others: provide information about an individual based on observations made. This is particularly useful for preverbal children who are unable to convey their thoughts using language. Although a useful method, it can be inaccurate as a consequence of memory fallibility.

Representative sample: is a smaller sample of individuals who reflect the same qualities of individuals from the larger population.

Reputation-Enhancement Theory (RET): highlights the importance of maintaining and enhancing one's self-image, often by focusing on the reputation acquired.

Resilience: is an individual's ability to adapt to tasks or disadvantages in life and to recover rapidly from negative stressful experiences.

Resource control theory: is the notion that animals (including humans) have evolved strategies to enable them to manage resources such as assets or food stores.

Respect: is an ethical principle referring to the dignity shown to all research participants regardless of, for example, age, gender, ethnicity and disability. This also means that the research conducted should avoid prejudice and unfairness.

Responsibility: is an ethical principle referring to the researcher's professional conduct at all times. This means that they are responsible for their participants' safety and must ensure no harm comes to them.

Right inferior parietal cortex: is one of four lobes of the brain. The right inferior parietal cortex plays an important role in knowing the difference between our own feelings and those of another person.

Risky teenage behaviours: are considered to be maladaptive behaviours such as using drugs or aggression to cope with different situations and contexts. Such ways of behaving originate from poor socialisation often interacting with a biological predisposition.

Robbers Cave: is the name given to an experiment where boys were divided into two groups and developed their own group norms and identity such that they became competitive and would do whatever it took to be the victors.

Same-sex family: refers to a family consisting of a same-sex couple who have taken a civil partnership or have married as is legally allowed in England and Wales.

Scaffolding: refers to the support given when learning tasks are tailored to the specific needs of the learner.

Schemas: refer to the current understanding of the world that an individual has. These schemas can be modified through mechanisms of assimilation, accommodation and equilibration. In so doing schemas ultimately cause changes to mental structures in a progressive way. It is the changes to schemas

and the mental structures that we progress through in the four stages outlined by Piaget.

Schizophrenia: is a serious mental disorder characterised by positive symptoms such as hallucinations and delusions and by negative symptoms such as social withdrawal.

Search engine: is provided by an Internet portal such as Yahoo or Internet Explorer. It contains many programmes enabling us to find the information we want.

Second higher-order emotions: are referred to as self-conscious emotions because they provide information that can either cause injury to or enhancement of our self-worth. We can feel pride for an achievement or guilt for doing something wrong.

Secondary emotions: are emotional responses that are reactions to primary emotions and arise out of them. An example might be the shame that follows showing public sadness.

Securely attached: also referred to as the B-dyad, is a secure attachment observed in the Strange Situation. Infants engage with the caregiver, are distressed when she leaves the room and seek contact on her return.

Self-control: is a cognitive process important in the regulation of behaviour. It can inhibit specific behaviours from being performed in the light of temptation and impulse and promote behaviours that help to achieve specified goals.

Self-esteem: is the subjective emotional evaluation an individual makes about his or her worth.

Self-fulfilling prophesy: is used to explain how individuals' behaviour can be shaped by receiving a label. A label can be positive or negative and it sets up a process of believing the label and behaving in ways that fulfil the label thereby conforming to the original prophesy made.

Self-identity: refers to the personality, beliefs, appearance and other qualities that define a person.

Self-image: refers to the conception or idea we have of ourselves.

Self-organisation: refers to the ability of a system to spontaneously arrange itself in a purposeful way.

Self-regulatory processes: allow us to guide our thoughts, emotions and behaviours in the direction of reaching specified goals.

Self-reporting: allows the individual to provide information about themselves through a series of set questions. This only works effectively if the individual can communicate using language.

Self-understanding: also referred to as self-awareness, is where we attain insight of, for instance, what motivates us, our attitudes and our weaknesses and strengths.

Semi-structured interviews: contain features of both the clinical and structured interview format. There is more flexibility such that questions can be asked in a non-sequential order and the responses given can be explored further to encourage elaboration.

Sensitive periods: refer to timeframes when individuals are optimally receptive to learning specific forms of information.

Sensorimotor: is the first of four stages of cognitive development outlined by Piaget. It is the simplest mental structure, allowing the infant to perform limited and repetitive actions. These modify as new information is experienced and incorporated.

Sensorimotor neurons: (see also **Mirror neurons**) are situated in the premotor cortex of the brain known as F5. These neurons become activated when we perform actions or copy the actions of others.

Separation protest: is another form of fear expressed by infants. In addition to fear the infant often experiences other negative emotions such as sadness and a sense of loss. Crying, screaming and calling out are behaviours occurring during separation protest.

Septo-hippocampal structure: is involved in resolving conflicting motivational states such as avoidance or approach. The BIS and BAS systems are part of the septo-hippocampal structure.

Sequential method: is a combination of both cross-sectional and longitudinal approaches. Researchers begin by adopting a cross-sectional approach and select a specific theme for further and later examination using the longitudinal method.

Sex-linked: inheritance of a trait means that a characteristic is determined (or influenced) by a gene that is found on one of the sex chromosomes.

Sexting: uses Instagram for posting sexually explicit images using an electronic device.

Sexual dimorphism: the degree to which the males and females of a species differ in terms of physical and behavioural traits.

Sexual selection: Darwin's second mechanism of evolutionary change whereby physical and psychological traits evolve because they are favoured by members of the opposite sex or through competition with members of the same sex.

Shaping behaviour: consists of producing new responses by reinforcement and conditioning. A form of operant conditioning that, in theory, allows an experimenter to create any new form of behaviour.

Shared environment: refers to environmental influences that might make individuals similar (in addition to shared genes). These include the home, personal and school environments.

Skinny model look: refers to models that appear under-nourished and underweight.

Sleeper effect: is a psychological phenomenon that describes how a message may have a stronger persuasive influence following a delay since the message was received.

Smartphones: are mobile phones but can be used as a touchscreen interface for access to the Internet and other systems installed on computers.

Social agents: refer to individuals and organisations that are responsible for the socialisation of children. Informal social agents include the parents and formal socialising agents can be the legal system.

Social and Emotional Learning (SEL): has been introduced to schools and communities as a means of instilling coordinated social, emotional and academic learning, as well as a supportive infrastructure to help youngsters develop useful life skills.

Social Bond Theory: consists of four facets – that of attachment, commitment, involvement in activities and a common value system. These four facets explain how individuals conform to group or societal values and norms.

Social-cognitive domain theory: accounts for how children construct their social knowledge into three separate domains: moral, conventional and personal.

Social Comparison Theory: describes how we evaluate our opinions and abilities by comparing them with those of others.

Social Competition Hypothesis: describes how in our evolutionary past we would compare ourselves to other members of our small group. We identified those we were in direct competition with and aspired to be better. For example, a young woman who commanded male attention would be considered as competition.

Social development: refers to the development of social and emotional skills over the lifespan, with particular emphasis on childhood and adolescence.

Social dominance hierarchy: is established through judgements of status made by members about other members of a group.

Social media: refers to the websites and applications enabling users to create and share information and spread this across their social network.

Social media sites: are social networking sites such as Facebook. These allow users to share information.

Social media trolls: are social media users who post controversial and hostile messages on social media sites such as Facebook and MySpace.

Social networking: describes the number of friends a teenager has.

Social play: describes children of the same age interacting with each other and engaging together in a common play activity.

Social play with language: involves playing with words by spontaneous rhyming or making up words. This form of play is only understood by children who are verbal.

Social referencing: is the process whereby infants monitor their caregiver's emotional facial expressions to guide how they should respond towards a stranger.

Socialisation: refers to a continual process whereby we learn to acquire identity and social skills and norms from our society.

Socially facilitating behaviours: behaviour such as smiling, elicits a positive response from others. This is important in the formation of an emotional bond between infant and caregiver.

Sociocultural contexts: refers to intersections of cultural and social events in a given time that impact on development and behaviour.

Socioemotional: refers to the development of a child's increasing ability to manage emotions and expressions and to create and maintain relationships.

Sociometric approach: refers to a method of ascertaining the social dynamics among a group of individuals. It is used as a means of establishing those considered as popular or unpopular amongst their peers.

Spanking: is a form of physical discipline used to punish misbehaviour.

Specimen record: refers to the recording of all behaviour an individual does within a set timeframe. This is decided before the observational study begins.

Spiral curriculum: describes a system of teaching children complex concepts simply in a way that the child can understand. Once the child understands, the level of difficulty can be incremented and then incremented further as understanding increases.

Standardised age-related behaviours: are behaviours expected to be exhibited by the majority of children and adolescents of the same age. These behaviours can be positive or negative.

Status hierarchy divide: occurs when there is disagreement concerning status amongst group members. In such groups, bullying is more likely to occur.

Story grammar: refers to an understanding of a story's structuring.

Strange situation: is an observational study method based in a laboratory setting. Infant and caregiver behaviours are observed under controlled conditions as a means of exploring the type of attachment patterns between them.

Stranger distress: occurs when an infant experiences negative arousal such as that felt when fearful. This tends to occur when the infant encounters an unfamiliar person.

Structuralism: refers to an approach to studying the mind by describing its most primitive elements. This includes a focus on individual elements of consciousness, and, in particular, how they are organised to allow for conscious experience.

Structural–organismic approach: is one that considers psychological

development as involving qualitative stage-like changes.

Structured interviews: enable researchers to obtain much information but this is likely to be of less depth than that obtained in the clinical interview. Structured interviews have a list of questions that are asked in a sequential order thereby not allowing the individual to elaborate on responses made. Questions are normally geared towards ascertaining individuals' self-reported attitudes.

Subscales: are commonly presented in questionnaires where a number of specific subtopics are explored. An example of this would be a subscale to measure extraversion (one of five personality factors).

Superego: is a part of the mind that, according to Freud, reflects internalised cultural norms, mainly developed from parental influence. The superego attempts for perfection and is generally considered to be the antithesis of the **id**.

Surveys: as used in psychological research, refer to a method of collecting data. Surveys are generally used to obtain factual information about individuals or the opinions they hold (e.g., self-report data).

Switched off genes: are genes that have been deactivated by some environmental input.

Switched on genes: are genes that have been activated by some environmental input.

Symbolic play: describes a form of play where the child transforms the true function of objects to a symbolic form fitting their creative play scenarios.

Systemisers: use the processing style of analysing how things work and the principles underlying behaviours of the systems studied.

Taxonomic assumption: refers to the naming of separate objects belonging to the same category such as the name of one's cat as opposed to next-door's cat.

Telegraphic speech: normally consists of combinations of two-word utterances minus small words such as the definitive article and prepositions.

Temperament: refers to a person's specific personal characteristics (such as mental, physical and emotional traits). Mental traits are considered to have a biological foundation.

Temperamental dispositions: attentional, affective and motor responses to various situations.

Terminal end: the end of an axon where neurotransmitter substances are released in order to communicate with other axons.

Testosterone: is a specific male sex hormone related to the development of both primary and secondary male sex characteristics.

Theory of Mind (ToM): describes the ability to infer the different mental states of others from their actions.

Theory of Mind Mechanism (ToMM): drives our ability to make inferences about other people's behaviour thereby supporting **ToM**.

Time sampling: refers to the recording of all behaviour of interacting individuals (such as siblings) within an observational timeframe of 180 minutes divided into 10-minute sections. During each 10-minute section the researcher observes and records behaviour for one minute. This amounts to one minute in every 10 minutes.

Tourette's syndrome: is a condition affecting the normal workings of the executive function resulting in uncontrollable involuntary movements and verbal outbursts.

Traditional narratives: refer to programmes and stories which have dialogue and characters that develop in a linear fashion.

Trait: an individual characteristic, either physical or behavioural, that is considered to be a fundamental unit of the **phenotype**.

Translocated: in genetics, translocation means an abnormality due to a rearrangement of part or parts of a chromosome.

Trial and error: learning involves attempting a range of methods to solve a problem until one is successful.

Tripartite model of ToM: refers to the three aspects of **ToM**: cognitive, affective and conative (or behaviour).

Unconditioned response: is an unlearned response that follows an unconditioned stimulus in **classical conditioning**.

Unconditioned stimulus: is one that naturally triggers a response in **classical conditioning**.

Uniquely primed moral computations: are analogous to algorithms enabling us to fast track the processing of morally related information.

Universal ethical principles: are considered in the **postconventional** level and are moral reasoning based on following laws grounded in justice and disobeying unjust laws. Just laws are based on ethical principles that occur throughout humanity.

Universal Grammar (UG): is a language organ containing the grammar of all languages throughout the world.

Unresolved: a parenting style of discipline that is equivalent to neglecting approaches. Misbehaving children go undisciplined, receive little emotional support and have no rules to abide by.

Vagal tone: is a physiological measurement used to examine the influence of the vagus nerve on heart rate.

Validity: is the extent to which a measurement really measures the phenomenon it is designed to measure.

Video deficit effect: refers to the ineptness of infants to transfer their learning from television to real-life events.

Violence: generally refers to behaviours containing physical force aimed at hurting another individual or causing damage to that individual's property.

Visual self-recognition: (see also **Mirror test**) is an infant's ability to see and know that the image seen in a mirror is its own reflection. This is assessed by the number of attempts an infant makes to wipe the rouge off its nose.

Wanna-be-lookalikes: is a section of the teenage population who aspire to the look of their idols and emulate how they dress and behave – this includes eating habits.

Wellness blogger: is an individual who posts photos using Instagram of the type of food they like to eat and what they believe to be healthy and slimming.

White lies: are false statements aimed at deception but for good reasons.

Whole object assumption: refers to the naming of the whole object and not its parts.

Wiring diagram: is a term used to describe the neural synaptic brain landscape after modifications via blooming and pruning.

Working hypercognition: is a component of the hypercognitive system enabling us to monitor our thoughts and modify them according to our current goals.

Working memory: conceptualises a system of short-term storage for information waiting on further processing for transference to long-term memory. Verbal information is processed by the phonological loop and visual information by the visuo-spatial sketchpad, which are both controlled by the **Central executive**.

Xenophobia: is a term used to describe a dislike or prejudice expressed towards specific groups of people, cultures or countries.

Yob culture: is a term used to describe drunken youths misbehaving in the streets, often by picking fights with each other and with innocent bystanders.

Zone of proximal development: refers to the differences between what a learner can do with and without help.

Zygote: a fertilised egg, that is, a cell formed from the fusion of two **gametes**.

Index

ABAB designs 63–5, 69
Abraham, M.R. 111
abuse 4, 64, 88, 93, 98;
    Conduct Disorder 354;
    disorganised attachment
    100; hostile attributional
    bias 207; intergenerational
    transmission 195; online
    grooming 416, 418, 433–5;
    Oppositional Defiant
    Disorder 349
academic achievement 136,
    139, 140, 233; bullies 371;
    children from same-sex
    families 184–5; Conduct
    Disorder 352; cultural
    differences 467–8, 470,
    472; delinquency 372,
    373; disruptive behaviour
    disorders 379; gangs 383,
    385; peer rejection 235,
    241; pretend play 280; self-
    esteem 251, 252, 254, 255;
    self-regulation 256; social
    class differences 374; social
    skills 133
ACC see anterior cingulate
    cortex
accommodation 111–12, 122
Achenbach, T.M. 349, 350
achievement, aiming for high
    201; see also academic
    achievement
activational effects 410
active effects 13, 456–7
adaptation 19, 55
adaptationist model of
    attachment 98, 99
addiction 442
ADHD see Attention Deficit
    Hyperactivity Disorder
adolescence: advertising
    targeted at young people
    430–1; aggression 363;
    alcohol advertising 422–3,
    431; antisocial behaviour
    346; attachment 103–4,
    106; bullying 369, 371,
    378; bystander intentions
    337; Conduct Disorder
    350; conscientiousness
    406; cultural differences
    469, 470–1, 472; endocrine

system 454; friends
    216, 217, 221, 240, 290;
    hormones 12–13; Internet
    use 431–2, 433; ISIS
    436; jealousy 94; mental
    health problems 82; moral
    development 308, 338;
    normative behaviour 3;
    peers 227–8, 232, 234, 335;
    personality development
    403–4, 412; pragmatic
    skills 126; prosocial
    behaviour 317; risky teenage
    behaviours 380–1; romantic
    relationships 232–3; self-
    concept 246; self-esteem
    253–4, 264; self-regulation
    257; self-understanding 249,
    251; sexting 438–9; social
    cognition 159–60; social
    comparison 415–16; social
    dominance 234, 293; social
    media 437, 443, 450; social
    networks 270, 290–1, 295;
    status hierarchies 293–4;
    teenage suicides 433,
    443–4, 445
Adolphs, R. 166
Adult Attachment Interview
    99–100
Adult–Child (A–C) speech
    130–1, 132, 140
advertising 430–1; alcohol 55,
    422–3, 431, 444; fashion and
    cosmetics 423–5, 427–8, 444
affectional bonds 95
affectionless psychopathy 102,
    103, 458
affective empathy 150–1
agentic perspective 22
aggregation 317
aggression 82, 137, 328,
    343–4, 345, 384; affective
    empathy 150; antisocial
    behaviour 346–7, 360;
    Bobo doll experiment 52;
    bullying 365; bystander
    intentions 337; cliques
    293–4; Conduct Disorder
    350, 352, 403; cortisol
    levels 454–5; cultural
    differences 470; evolutionary
    psychology 379–80, 381;

executive function 136,
    140; fearlessness theory
    of antisocial behaviour
    349; gender differences
    263, 265, 359, 363–4, 410;
    hostile attributional bias
    194; information processing
    theory 24; media influence
    375; moral disengagement
    369; moral transgressions
    48; negative affectivity
    392; observational methods
    50; parental support 199;
    parenting style 189–90; peer
    interactions 335, 378; peer
    rejection 229, 234, 235, 236;
    privation 103; self-esteem
    256; serotonin 205; sibling
    rivalry 215; Social Learning
    Theory 22; television
    violence 425–7, 444;
    testosterone 13, 454, 471;
    theory of mind 165; types of
    361–3; see also violence
agoraphobia 45, 251–2
agreeableness 380, 389, 395,
    411; adolescence 404, 412;
    changes across the lifespan
    405, 412; Conduct Disorder
    403; gender differences 263,
    265, 406, 407, 409–10, 412;
    genetic influences 396, 402;
    reactive heritability 397;
    social media 441, 442, 445
Ainsworth, Mary 100, 133,
    134, 399; categories of
    attachment 53, 98–9, 102,
    106, 144; 'strange situation'
    5, 51, 52–3, 90, 98, 99;
    stranger distress 89
Aksan, N. 196
alcohol advertising 55,
    422–3, 431, 444
alcohol use 358
alcoholism 203
Allan, N.P. 136
Allen, C. 293
Almond, Nicholas 443
Alsaker, F.D. 233
altruism 315–16, 317;
    reciprocal 329–30, 339;
    social media use 442, 445;
    see also prosocial behaviour

Alzheimer's disease 462
ambivalent/resistant attachment 53, 98–100, 104, 106, 399
American Psychiatric Association 462
American Psychological Association (APA) 66
amygdala 166–7, 174, 333, 349, 471
Anderson, C.A. 362, 425–6
Anderson, D.R. 420
Andreau, E. 370
androgens 12–13
Ang, R.P. 377
anger 84, 90–1, 93, 106; abused children 93; aggression 363; Conduct Disorder 354; cultural differences in expression of 83; facial expressions 86; infants 81, 82; jealousy 94; negative affectivity 392; negative emotional environments 83; Oppositional Defiant Disorder 347, 349; sadness blended with 91–2; social media 442
animal behaviour 31, 145–6; personality 396; play 270, 277–8, 291–2, 293, 295
anorexia 424, 425, 427, 428–9, 435
anterior cingulate cortex (ACC) 168, 174, 452
antisocial behaviour 2, 3, 330–1, 342–86; definitions of 344–5; disruptive behaviour disorders 346–54, 359, 360–1, 384; evolutionary psychology 379–81, 385; gangs 383, 385; hostile attributional bias 195; insecure attachment 106; intergenerational transmission 204–5, 206, 207; media influence 375–7; mother-infant relationship 102; parental punishment 190, 191; peer rejection 236; play 278; privation 103; progression of 192; schools 371–4; stress 105; television violence 426, 444; see also bullying; delinquency; deviant behaviour
antisocial personality disorder (APD) 361
anxiety: bullies 256; DSM-5 465; empathy 169;

evolutionary psychology 32; gender differences 263, 265, 408; infants 81, 82; modulation 90; Oppositional Defiant Disorder 348; ostracised children 289; peer rejection 229, 235; physiological measures 471; separation 45, 95, 96; social 104, 369; social media 441, 442; Spence Children's Anxiety Scale 45; teenage 185
anxious/insecure ambivalent/resistant attachment 53, 98–100, 104, 106, 399
anxious/insecure avoidant attachment 53, 98–100, 102, 104, 106, 399
APA see American Psychological Association
APD see antisocial personality disorder
approach-avoidance 32, 75, 80–1, 84, 88, 95, 100, 105–6
AQS see Attachment Q Sort
Archer, J. 454
Aristotle 74–5, 216
Arnett, P.A. 404
arranged marriages 197–8
Arsenio, W.F. 335
ASD see autism spectrum disorder
Asher, S.R. 232
assimilation 111–12, 122
Astington, J.W. 161, 163
attachment 2, 5, 73, 95–105, 106; attachment figures 95; categories of 53, 98–9, 144; Conduct Disorder 354; criticism of 104–5; cultural differences 102; DRD4 gene 13–15, 100–1; ethological perspective 32, 36; facial processing 80; intergenerational transmission 99–100, 102, 106; laboratory settings 51; orphans 222; personality development 399; play 276; relationships 213, 221; separation protest 90; Social Bond Theory 236, 237; socioemotional development 102–4, 133
Attachment Q Sort (AQS) 99
attention 118–19, 121, 135; information-processing

approach 116; joint 41, 123, 126–7, 140, 172, 285; shifting 81
Attention Deficit Hyperactivity Disorder (ADHD) 34, 185, 346, 348, 354–60, 384; academic achievement 379; bullies 368; DRD4 gene 460, 461; empathy 93; executive functions 136; moral and conventional transgressions 323; spanking 191; victims of bullying 369, 370
attitudes: cultural 466; ethnic groups 238; interviews 47; moral behaviour 301, 316; multi-cultural societies 450; peer groups 212, 236, 283–4; prejudicial 238, 239–40, 241; schools 371; socialisation 325; societal 178, 314
attractiveness 232, 233, 251, 252, 255
attractiveness stereotype 428
authoritarian parenting style 188–9, 190, 207, 354
authoritative parenting style 188, 190, 207, 332
authority, deference to 332, 338, 339
autism spectrum disorder (ASD) 4, 34, 115, 139, 169–72, 174, 206; DSM-5 170, 463–5, 472; executive functions 136; mirror neurons 452; play 284–5, 295; systemisers 156; theory of mind 145
autonomous morality 303, 304–5, 306, 338
autosomal chromosomes 9–10
avoidant attachment 53, 98–100, 102, 104, 106, 399
Avon Longitudinal Study of Parents and Children 42, 43, 66
Axia, G. 81

Babb, P. 374
babbling 124
Bacon, M. 200
Baddeley, A.D. 115
Bagwell, C.L. 232, 235
Bai, M. 383
Baillargeon, Rene 40
Bakeman, R. 50

Baker, E. 312
Bakermans-Kranenburg, M.J. 101
Ball, H.A. 378
Baltes, P.B. 27
Bandura, Albert 52, 190, 197; Cognitive Social Learning Theory 21, 22–3, 207, 318; interactionist approach 300; moral behaviour 310; moral development 318–19, 339; moral disengagement 369; social and cognitive development 137–9
Banerjee, R. 165, 282
Banfield, S.S. 428
Barchia, K. 369
Barenboim, C. 305
Barkley, R.A. 350, 355
Barkow, Jerome 33
Barlett, C.P. 368
Baron-Cohen, Simon: autism spectrum disorder 171, 284; fMRI scans 58, 452; gender differences 262; theory of mind 144, 147–8, 154–6, 157, 173
Barry, C.M. 335
Barry, H. 200
Barth, J.M. 86, 199–200
Barzman, D.H. 359–60
BAS see behavioural activation system
Basow, S.A. 260
Bates, E. 132
Baumeister, R.F. 254, 255, 256
Baumrind, D. 191, 200
Baydar, N. 183
Becker, A.E. 424–5
Bednar, R.L. 254
behavioural activation system (BAS) 352–3
behavioural change 65–6, 69
behavioural deficits 350–1
behavioural disorders 344
behavioural epigenetics 461
behavioural excesses 350–1
behavioural genetics 7, 13–17, 35, 450, 471; bullying 378; family influences 202, 203; personality 393, 399, 400–3, 411; reactive heritability 397; technological developments 455–7; see also genetics
behavioural inhibition system (BIS) 352–3

behaviourism 20–1, 22, 95, 132
Bekoff, M. 293
Bell-Gredler, Margaret 110
Belsky, Jay 98, 99, 104, 106, 135, 226, 240
Bennett, S.M. 258–9
Berk, L.E. 280
Berlin, L.J. 190
Besel, L.D.S. 157
Best, D.L. 261
Best, J.W. 48
Bettelheim, B. 358
Betts, J. 82
Biben, M. 293
Bibou-Nakou, I. 370–1
'Big 5' personality factors 358–9, 394–5, 398, 411; gender differences 406–9; heritability 396, 397; social media 441–3, 445
biological factors 1, 4–5, 34; biopsychosocial interactionism 397–8; empathy 332; family 201–6; gender differences in personality 410, 412; Oppositional Defiant Disorder 349; personality 399; physiological measures 55–9, 68, 453–5, 471; sociocultural theory 27; temperament 392; theory of mind 166–9, 174; see also genetics
biological genetics 6, 7–13; see also genetics
biological organisation 29, 36
biopsychosocial interactionism 397–8
biosocial interaction 9, 203, 410, 412
bipolar depression 202
birth order 215, 397
BIS see behavioural inhibition system
Bishop, J. 256
bistrategic controllers 379, 380
Bjorklund, David 33
Björkqvist, K. 366
Black, B. 228
Blair, C. 135
Blakemore, S-J. 159–60
blended families 181, 182–3
'blends' 91–2
blogs 431, 433, 437–8, 442, 445
Bloom, L. 125, 131

Bloomfield, K.A. 166
'blooming' 116–17
Blumer, T. 442
Blurton-Jones, Nicholas 52
Bobo doll experiment 22, 52, 190
body image and body dissatisfaction 423–5, 427–31, 444–5
Boivin, M. 378
Boles, D.B. 86
bonding 52–3, 73–4, 77, 80, 87–8, 95–6, 105–6, 150–1, 177; see also attachment
bootstrapping 131, 132, 140
Bornstein, M.H. 195
Bos, H. 185
Bosnjak, M. 442
Boucher, J. 284
Boulton, M.J. 371
boundaries 320
Bowes, L. 371, 378
Bowlby, John 5, 51, 95–6, 99, 133, 458; criticism of 104–5; internal working models 98, 102; maternal deprivation 102, 103; primary caregivers 134; stability of attachment over time 106
Boyum, L. 49
BPS see British Psychological Society
Braeges, J.L. 325
brain 10–12, 35; ADHD 357–8; 'blooming' and 'pruning' 116–17; cognitive and socioemotional development 246; deep brain stimulation 460; domain-relevant approach 115; emotional expressions 85, 86–7; face recognition 76, 77; genetic influences 411; hypercognitive system 257; maturation 9, 111, 139, 306; moral development 333–4; prefrontal cortex 257, 357; scanning techniques 56–8, 68, 450–3, 471; septo-hippocampal structure 353; social cognition 159–60, 166–9, 174; testosterone influence 410
Brendgen, M. 362
Bretherton, I. 98
Brighi, A. 376
British Psychological Society (BPS) 66–7

Bronfenbrenner, Urie 6, 24–5, 26, 35, 436; culture 373, 472; exosystem 375; family 177–8, 186, 187, 211–12; genetic predispositions 201, 207; schools 137, 371; socialisation 246, 300, 328, 426, 465–6
Brooks-Gunn, J. 248, 249
Brooks, J. 90
Browne, K. 104
Brownell, C. 246
Bruner, Jerome 27, 113, 132, 278, 282–3
Brunner, H.G. 205
Buhrmester, D. 215, 255–6
Bukowski, W.M. 231–2
Bulger, James 235
bulimia nervosa 438
bullying 6, 82, 165, 234–5, 365–71, 384–5; anti-bullying programmes 374; behavioural disorders 344; Columbine High School massacre 383; Conduct Disorder 350; evolutionary perspective 379, 380, 381, 385; gender differences 368, 369, 378; genetics 378; moral disengagement 319; school processes 371, 373; self-esteem of bullies 256; self-image of bullies 377; status hierarchy divide 293; types of 344, 366, 368, 385; *see also* cyberbullying
Burger, P.H. 358
Burton, R.V. 317
Bushman, B.J. 362, 425–6
Bushnell, I.W.R. 80
Bussey, K. 369
Byrne, R. 144–5
bystander intentions 337

Calkins, S.D. 82
callous-unemotional (CU) trait 359, 370
Calvert, S.L. 420
Calvete, E. 377
Cambridge Study 104
Cameron, David 436–7
Camodeca, M. 94
Campos, J. 80, 90
Camras, Linda 63, 90, 92
Caravita, S.C.S. 369, 371
care perspective 309–10
caregiver bonding 52–3, 73–4, 77, 80, 87–8, 95–6,

105–6, 150–1, 177; *see also* attachment
caregiver verbalisation 160, 173
Carlson, S.M. 136
Carney, A.G. 370
Carpendale, J.I.M. 127
Carpendale, J.L. 152
Carpenter, J. 281
Carriger, M. 246
Carver, K. 232–3
Case, Robbie 114, 139
case study research design 63–5, 69
Casler, K. 281
categorical speech perception 123–4
cause and effect 62
Cavanaugh, J.C. 90
CBiT *see* Comprehensive Behavioural Intervention for Tics
CBT *see* cognitive-behavioural therapy
CD *see* Conduct Disorder
celebrities 417, 423, 427, 444
central executive 115–16, 135
Chaminade, T. 333
Chandler, D.J. 358
Chandler, M.J. 152, 305
Charman, T. 285
chatrooms 433, 445
Chess, S. 353
Chi, M.T.H. 114
Child and Adolescent Social Support Scale 291
Child, I. 200
child leaders 293, 295–6
childcare 133–5
chimeric face test 85, 86
chimpanzees 145–6
Chisholm, James 98, 106
Chobhthaigh, S.N. 93
Choudhury, S. 159–60
Christakis, D.A. 419–20
Christie, J.F. 279
chromosomes 8–10, 455–6
chronosystem 25
Cicchetti, D. 186, 285
Cillessen, A.H. 229
Claessens, A. 183
Clark, T.P. 185
classical conditioning 20–1, 35
clinical interviews 53, 68
cliques 290, 293–4, 295, 296
Closson, L.M. 293

co-dominance 8–9
coaching 83, 84
coding 49, 50, 51
coercive controllers 379, 380
cognition 2, 109–23, 139–40; cognitive-social connection 110, 122–3, 133–9, 140; epigenetic landscape 121–2; gender differences 262–3, 265; information processing 115–21; neo-Piagetians 113–15; Piaget 110–12; self-control 318; Vygotsky 112–13; word learning 125; *see also* cognitive development; social cognition
cognitive ability: play 294–5; shared environment 203, 204; twin studies 17; zone of proximal development 27; *see also* intelligence
cognitive-behavioural therapy (CBT) 348
cognitive development 4, 121; feral children 64; neo-Piagetians 113–15; neural maturity 246; perspective-taking 158, 173; Piaget 5–6, 19–20, 35, 40, 110–12, 306; play 294; social development and 137, 139, 140; social information processing 230; social learning 121–3; television impact on 60; Vygotsky 112–13, 135; *see also* cognition
cognitive distortions 360
cognitive empathy 150–1, 194
cognitive psychology 21, 278
cognitive self-image 257–8
Cognitive Social Learning Theory 21, 22–3, 197, 207, 318, 339
Cohen, P. 348
Coie, J.D. 263
Colby, A. 310
'cold cognition' 366
'cold' executive function 136
Cole, K. 161–2
Cole, M. 25
Cole, P.M. 83
collectivist cultures 25, 164, 466–71, 472
Colquitt, J.A. 442
Columbine High School massacre 383, 427

commitment 212, 236, 240
communication 2, 123–33, 140;
autism spectrum disorder
295, 464, 465; digital 431,
432–3; friendship 219;
mass media 417; play 277,
278, 280, 294; sociocultural
theory 27; *see also* language;
nonverbal communication;
verbal communication
comorbidity likeness 202
competence 67
Comprehensive Behavioural
Intervention for Tics
(CBiT) 460
Computed Tomography
(CT) 451, 471
Comstock, G. 418
concrete operational stage 19,
20, 111, 117, 193
conditioned response 21
conditioned stimulus 21
conditioning 20–1, 35, 126
Conduct Disorder (CD) 346,
349–54, 384, 403; bullying
368; compared with ADHD
359; cyberbullying 377;
moral and conventional
transgressions 323;
progression from ODD to
348; spanking 191
Conelea, C.A. 460
confidence 28, 188, 254, 392
conformity 466, 469
Conger, R.D. 190
conlern 32, 77, 78–80, 105
Connor, D.F. 348
conscience 309, 313, 314–15,
320, 338, 350, 352
conscientiousness 389, 395,
411; adolescence 404,
412; changes across the
lifespan 405, 412; Conduct
Disorder 403; evolutionary
psychology 396; gender
differences 406, 409–10,
412; genetic influences
402; insecure-avoidant
attachment 399; life
expectancy linked to 405;
social media 441, 442, 443
conspec 32, 77, 78–80, 105
constructivism 300, 321–8, 339
context 4, 6, 35
contextual perspective
24–8, 35
continuity 4, 5–6, 35
control groups 62

conventional domain 325–6,
339, 469
conventional morality 308,
310, 338
conventional transgressions
321–8, 337, 338, 339
conventions 299–300,
322, 338
cooing 124
Cooper, H.M. 138
cooperation: cultural
differences 470, 472;
evolutionary psychology
330; joint music-making
280; play 277, 278, 279,
294; sensitive periods 274
Cornell, D.G. 361
Correa, T. 442
correlational research designs
59, 60, 68–9, 223–4, 251,
320, 400
Corsaro, W.A. 221
cortisol 63, 349, 454–5, 471
cosmetics advertising
423–5, 444
Cosmides, Leda 33
Costa, P.T. 406
Cote, S.M. 133
Courage, M.L. 248–9
Cowie, H. 370
Coyne, S.M. 368
creativity 278, 280
Crick, N.R. 229–30, 231, 361
criminality 189, 235–6, 345;
ADHD 359; antisocial
behaviour 344, 361;
attachment influence 104;
callous-unemotional trait
359; Conduct Disorder 350,
352; disruptive behaviour
disorders 360–1; family
influences 204, 205–6, 207;
parental 371; self-esteem
254, 255; television and
video game violence 426;
see also delinquency
criminogenic environment 346
cross-cultural studies 25, 44;
cyberbullying 376; self-
esteem 252, 254; separation
protest 90; stranger distress
89; *see also* culture/cultural
differences
Cross, D. 159
cross-domain interactions 115
cross-referencing 245–6
cross-sectional method 66,
69, 310

crowds 290
Crowell, J. 99
Crowley, J.A. 49
crying 32, 90, 95–6, 106
CT *see* Computed Tomography
culture/cultural differences 450,
465–71, 472; attachment
102; DSM-5
assessment 465, 472;
Ecological Theory 6, 25;
emotional expression 83;
gender stereotypes 260;
moral development 310–11,
339; play 277, 290, 294;
prejudice reduction 241;
research ethics 67; self-
esteem 254; sociocultural
contexts 25, 35; stranger
distress 89; surveys 44;
theory of mind 162–4;
Vygotsky 112; word learning
125; *see also* cross-cultural
studies
Cummings, E.M. 45–6, 354
'cupboard love' 96
customs 299
Cusumano, D.L. 425, 429
Cutting, A. 160–1
cyberbullying 365, 366–7,
376–7, 385, 386n2, 418;
demography of bullies 368;
EU Kids Online 435; teenage
suicides 433, 443–4, 445

Damon, W. 246, 247
Daniels, D. 17, 203
Dann, Sophie 105, 221–2
Darwin, Charles 30–1, 32,
33, 34
Darwish, A.E. 466–7
data collection 44–59;
interviews 44, 47–8, 53–5,
68; observational methods
48–53, 68; physiological
measurements 55–9, 68;
surveys 44–8, 68
Dave, D. 423
Davidson, D. 283
Davidson, P. 48
Davidson, R.J. 87
Davies, Donald 431
Davies, P.T. 233, 354
Davis, M.H. 150, 151, 332
Dawkins, R. 379
DBDs *see* disruptive behaviour
disorders
de Haan, M. 57–8, 76, 451
de Waal, Anastasia 369

Deater-Deckard, K. 332
deception 144–6, 148, 153, 165, 172, 173, 350, 352
Decety, J. 167, 168, 333
decision-making 135, 136; moral 332, 334, 452–3, 471; social information processing 230
declarative statements 123
deep brain stimulation 460
deference to authority 332, 338, 339
Defining Issues Test (DIT) 310
delayed gratification 61–2, 135, 257, 320, 392
delinquency 4, 5, 191–3, 345; academic failure 373; aggression 363; Conduct Disorder 350; developmental pathways to 352, 353; gangs 381–4; insecure attachment 104, 106; mother-infant relationship 102; parental discipline 189–90; parental rejection 195, 207; school processes 371, 372, 373; Social Bond Theory 237; *see also* antisocial behaviour; criminality; deviant behaviour
Deloache, J.S. 262
Demetriou, A. 251, 257, 264–5
Demie, F. 374
Denham, Suzanne 82–3, 84, 282, 295
Dennett, Daniel 145–7, 171, 172
Dennis, M. 152–4, 173
dependent variable (DV) 62, 69
depression 206, 348; bipolar 202; DSM-5 465; emotional suppression 82; gender differences 408; parental 101, 202; peer rejection 235; postnatal 138; self-esteem 254; social media 442; teenage 185
depth perception 80
descriptive research designs 59, 68
design stance 145, 171, 172
deviant behaviour 2–3, 4, 5, 345; collectivist cultures 466; peer rejection 235–6; Social Bond Theory 237, 383; *see also* antisocial behaviour; delinquency; transgressive behaviours

devotion 332, 339
Dewey, John 273–4
Diagnostic and Statistical Manual of Mental Disorders (DSM) 169–70, 450, 462–5, 472; ADHD 346, 354; Conduct Disorder 349, 350–1; Oppositional Defiant Disorder 347
Diamond, A. 135
diathesis-stress theory 358
Dickson, K.L. 87
Diener, E. 255
diets 437–8
Digital Era 417, 444
digital media 417–18, 431–9, 444, 445; *see also* Internet; social media
Dijkstra, J.K. 293
Dion, K. 232
disability 368, 369, 370, 442
discipline 187–93, 207, 310, 332, 354
discontinuity 4, 5–6, 35
discrimination 238
disgust 84, 86, 90, 93, 106
Dishion, T. 335, 383
disorganised attachment 13–15, 53, 100–1, 104, 399
disruptive behaviour disorders (DBDs) 346–54, 359, 360–1, 379, 384
DIT *see* Defining Issues Test
divorce 182, 183
dizygotic twins 15, 332
DNA (deoxyribonucleic acid) 8, 455–6, 461
Dodd, H. 286
Dodge, K.A. 5, 24, 137, 229–30, 231, 263, 353, 361–2
Doering, N. 442
domain relevance 115, 139
domain specificity 114, 139; hypercognitive system 257, 258, 265; self-esteem 247, 251
dominance *see* social dominance
Donnai, D. 458
Donnerstein, E. 426, 433
dopamine 11, 353, 358, 460
doppelgängers 402
Down syndrome (DS) 10, 284, 285–6, 295
Downs, C.A. 198–9
DRD4 gene 13–15, 203, 206, 403; ADHD 358; attachment 100–1; Conduct Disorder

353; epigenetic processes 457, 460, 461, 472; linkage analysis 456; temperament 393, 471
Dring, C. 422
Driscoll, M.P. 113
drug abuse 5, 349
DS *see* Down syndrome
DSM *see* Diagnostic and Statistical Manual of Mental Disorders
Duchenne smile 87
Dugdale, Richard 204–5, 207
Dunn, J. 160, 161, 213, 214, 216, 218
Durkin, K. 421
Durlak, J.A. 137
Durston, S. 257
Dusek, J.B. 247
DV *see* dependent variable
Dvash, J. 150
dyadic peer relationships 227, 235–6
dynamic systems perspectives 28–30, 36
dyslexia 58, 451, 460

Eagly, Alice 262, 265, 410, 412
East, P.L. 199
eating disorders 423–5, 427–9, 438, 444, 445
ecological niches 397
Ecological (Ecosystem) Theory 6, 24–5, 26, 35, 436, 472; family 177–8, 186, 211–12; genetic predispositions 201, 207; schools 371; socialisation 246, 300, 328, 426, 466
ecological validity 62
Eder, R.A. 246
Edgeworth, Maria 271
Edgeworth, Richard Lovell 271
Edison, S.C. 248–9
EDR *see* electrodermal reactivity
education 270–1; attitudes towards 374; 'British values' 467; prejudice reduction 239, 241; television 419–21, 444; *see also* schools
Edwards, R.W. 423
Edward's syndrome 9
EEG *see* electroencephalogram
effortful control 392, 411
egalitarianism 193, 294, 295, 307

Egley, A. Jr. 382
ego 18, 35, 312–15, 338
egocentric speech 135
egocentric thinking 158–9, 173, 193
egoistic personal distress 93
Eibl-Eibesfeldt, Irenaus 277, 294
Eisenberg, Nancy 83, 300, 315–16, 338
Ekman, P. 32, 63, 85, 86, 87
Electra complex 314
electrodermal reactivity (EDR) 59, 453–4, 471
electroencephalogram (EEG) 52, 56–8, 68, 76, 451–2, 471
Elias, M.J. 133
Elliot, S.N. 139
Elliott, J.B. 183
Ellis, B.J. 380, 381
Ellis, S. 217–18
Ellsworth, C.P. 85
email 431, 433
embarrassment 82, 92, 93, 106, 317
embryo development 7–8
Eme, R. 357
Emler, N. 377
emotional development 2, 72–107; approach-avoidance 80–1; face recognition 74–80; modulation of emotions 81–4; primary emotions 84–92; secondary emotions 84, 92–5; see also attachment; emotions; socioemotional development
emotional stability 405, 442; see also neuroticism
emotional support: Child and Adolescent Social Support Scale 291; family 194, 196–201; friends 219, 240; improving self-esteem 254
emotional understanding 282, 295
emotions: affective empathy 150–1; emotional display rules 83; expression of 75–6, 81–2, 83; Freud 35; moral development 312, 335, 337; perception and 148–9; physiological measures 453–4, 471; primary 84–92, 106; regulation of 81–4, 106, 257, 264, 277, 294, 318, 354, 453–4, 471; secondary 84,

92–5, 106; self-understanding 249; skin conductance studies 59; universal 32, 33, 63; see also emotional development
empathic/caring model 309–10
empathy 82, 92, 93–4, 106, 149–50, 173; ADHD 359, 360; biological measures 332; cognitive and affective 150–1, 315; Conduct Disorder 350; cyberbullying 377, 385; disruptive behaviour disorders 361; effortful control 392; gender differences 171; impact of video games 426, 444; mirror neurons 168–9; moral development 334–5, 337–8; parental 194; prosocial behaviour 317; reciprocal altruism 330; skin conductance 59, 453–4; systemisers and empathisers 154–7, 262; temperament 391
empiricism 74–5
'empty praise' 253–4, 264
Encarnacion-Gawrych, G. 324
endocrine system 10, 12–13, 454, 471
endogamy 181
Engen, H.G. 169
Ensor, R. 282
environmental factors 1, 4–5, 34, 206; attachment 101; behavioural genetics 456–7; biopsychosocial interactionism 397–8; biosocial interaction 203; Cognitive Social Learning Theory 22, 23; criticism of correlational studies 400; Ecological Theory 35; epigenetic landscape 30, 139–40; epigenetic processes 63, 457–62, 472; gender differences in personality 410, 412; intelligence 15–16; Oppositional Defiant Disorder 349; peers 221; personality and individual differences 399–400, 402, 403, 411; sociocultural theory 27; temperament 392–3; twin studies 15; see also nature versus nurture; non-shared environment; shared environment

Environmental Risk (E-Risk) Study 378
epigenetic landscape 29, 30, 36, 457, 472; neo-Piagetians 114–15; social development and cognitive development 110, 121–2, 139–40; zone of proximal development 113
epigenetic rules 331–2
epigenetics 9, 63, 450, 457–62, 472
epistemic mental states 147–8, 173
equilibration 111–12, 122
equity 193
Erikson, Erik 17, 18–19, 35, 275, 289, 294
Eron, L.D. 375, 425
ERPs see Event-Related Potentials
Eslea, M. 368
Estabrook, Arthur 205
Estrada, P. 138
ethics: research 42, 66–7; universal 309; see also moral development
ethnicity: bullying 368–9, 370; multi-cultural societies 450; peers 227; prejudice 238–9, 241; research ethics 67; sociocultural contexts 25–6, 35
ethological perspective 31–2, 36; attachment 95, 96; play 277, 291, 294, 295
EU Kids Online 416, 435–6
Eubig, P.A. 358
eugenics 205
Evans, G. 374
Event-Related Potentials (ERPs) 57, 58, 68, 76, 451
event sampling 50, 68
evocative effects 13, 456–7
evolutionary psychology 32–4, 36, 450; aggression 13; antisocial behaviour and bullying 379–81, 385; attachment 95, 96; individual differences 396–7, 399, 411; moral behaviour 300–1, 339; play 270, 273; prosocial behaviour 328–35; social competition hypothesis 429–30; theory of mind 172
evolutionary theory 30–1
executive attention system 392

executive functions (EF) 135–6, 140, 349, 353–4, 357, 458
exogamy 181
exosystem 24–5, 26, 177–8, 328, 375, 466
expectations 260, 372, 410, 412
experimental research designs 59, 60–3, 68–9
expiatory punishment 303
extended family 178, 179–80, 185, 206, 300–1, 472
externalising behaviours 82, 101, 355, 392
extra-familial factors 28
extraversion 389, 391–2, 394, 395, 411; changes across the lifespan 404–5; evolutionary psychology 396; gender differences 408, 412; genetic influences 396, 400–2; reactive heritability 397; social media 441, 442, 443; temperament 411
Eyes Test 154–7, 173

Fabes, R.A. 335, 336, 454
face recognition 32, 36, 57–8, 75–80, 105–6, 451
Facebook 416, 431–2, 433, 436–7, 441–3, 445
facial expressions 81, 84–5, 92, 159, 454; autism spectrum disorder 464; brain lateralisation 86–7; cognitive empathy 150; communication 123; social referencing 89–90; theory of mind 153
Fagan, J. 331
Fagot, B.I. 198, 262
fairness 303, 325
false-belief tasks 151–4, 160, 162–3, 172, 173, 174, 469
family 2, 5, 176–208; biological factors 201–6; bullying 370–1; changes over time 178–86; Conduct Disorder 354; cultural differences 469, 472; Ecological Theory 6, 25; emotional support 194, 196–201; jealousy 94–5; moral reasoning 193–6, 207; parental discipline 187–93, 207; relationships 213; resilience 28; self-reporting 45–6; social functions 186–7, 206–7; socialisation

82–4, 206–7; strategic specialisation within the 397, 411; see also parents; siblings
family therapy 348
Fantz, R.L. 76–7, 143
Farhadian, M. 162
Farrar, J. 132
Farrington, David 104, 206, 207, 370, 374
fashion advertising 423–5, 427–8, 444
fear 84, 88–90, 91, 106; abused children 93; behavioural inhibition system 353; evolutionary psychology 32–3; facial expressions 86; guilt proneness 311–12; infants 82; physical injury 45; social media 441; temperament 391, 392
fearlessness theory of antisocial behaviour 349, 454
Fedewa, A.L. 185
feedback 121
Feiring, C. 49
feminine roles 179
feminine traits 198, 199, 258–61
Fenson, L. 124, 125
feral children 63, 64
Ferguson, C.J. 426
Ferguson, T. 205–6
Ferguson, T.J. 362
Festinger, L.A. 429
Fettro, M.N. 184–5
fictive kin 186, 300–1
Field, T.M. 59, 90
Fiese, B.H. 186
Fine, M.A. 183
Finn, R. 286
Fischer, K. 248
Fite, P.J. 359
Flavell, J.H. 119, 159
flexibility 278, 294
floccinaucinihilipilification 255
Flory, M. 348
fMRI see functional magnetic resonance imaging
focus groups 48
Fogel, A. 87
formal operational stage 19, 20, 111, 117, 193
Forsyth, D. 289
Foucault, Michel 17
Fox, N.A. 59, 82, 87
Frame, C.L. 362
Frazier, T.W. 171

Frede, E.C. 112
free-riders 331, 332, 397
Freedman, D.J. 357
frequency dependent selection 396–7, 411
Freud, Anna 105, 221–2
Freud, Sigmund 17–18, 35, 221–2; moral development 300, 312–15, 338; play 270, 274–5, 294
Frey, K.S. 198
Frick, P.J. 354
Friedrich-Cofer, L. 375
friends 2, 213, 216–20, 221, 240; cliques 290, 293–4, 295, 296; Conduct Disorder 352; cross-gender friendships 232; cultural differences 469–70, 472; Ecological Theory 6; peer rejection 235; play 276; self-esteem 254; self-understanding 250; see also peers
Friesen, W.V. 32, 63, 85, 86
Fröbel, Friedrich 272, 294
frontal-limbic system 358
frustration 392, 454–5
Fu, G. 165
functional magnetic resonance imaging (fMRI) 58, 68, 451–2, 471; emotional arousal 334; mirror neurons 168, 169; social cognition 167; theory of mind 174
Furman, W. 215

Gagné, Robert 120–1, 123
Gallagher, S. 127
galvanic skin response (GSR) 59
games with rules 276, 280, 294, 302–3, 306
gametes 8
gangs 237, 344, 379, 381–4, 385
Garandeau, C.F. 293
Garbarino, J. 383
Gardner, Howard 390, 411, 467
Garrison, M. 419–20
Gartrell, N. 185
Gass, K. 214
Gasser, L. 165
Gauvain, Mary 28–9, 31, 89, 190, 229, 362
Geary, David 33
Gelfand, D.M. 346

gender: aggression 363–4; autism spectrum disorder 171; bullying 368, 369, 370, 378; Cognitive Social Learning Theory 207; criticisms of attachment theory 104; cyberbullying 377; DSM-5 assessment 465; emotional reading ability 154–7; family role divisions 179, 180; friendship preferences 217; Gender Consistency Theory 198; gender paradox 358; Gender Schema Theory 198; gender typing 258, 265; girls' body image and body dissatisfaction 423–5, 427–30; guilt 311; media influence 415; moral reasoning 309–10; patriarchal system 178; peer networks 227; peer status 232–3; personality differences 358–9, 406–10, 412; play 277, 294; psychosexual stages 314; research ethics 67; socialisation 198–9, 258–9, 261; sociocultural contexts 25, 26, 35
gender identity 198, 212, 258–63, 265
general self-esteem 251, 252
generalised anxiety 45
genes 8–9, 13–14, 35, 202–3, 206; ADHD 358; attachment 100–1; biosocial interaction 203; epigenetic landscape 30, 139–40, 457; epigenetic processes 63, 472; epigenetic rules 331; gene transcription 460; individual differences 17, 396; influence on behaviour 402–3, 411; latency effect 450; linkage analysis 455–6, 471; peer interactions 378; personality traits 224; 'switching on' and 'switching off' 457, 458, 460–2, 472; see also DRD4 gene; heritability
genetic karyotype 4
genetic predispositions 4, 13, 201, 206, 207, 226
genetics: antisocial behaviour 204–5; attachment 100–1; autism spectrum disorder

171; behavioural 7, 13–17, 35; biological 6, 7–13; bullying 378, 379; Conduct Disorder 353; criticism of correlational studies 400; Group Socialisation Theory 400; Oppositional Defiant Disorder 348–9; personality and individual differences 396, 400–3, 411; technological developments 455–7; temperament 392, 393; see also behavioural genetics; biological factors; epigenetics; nature versus nurture
genotype 8, 34, 457
Genta, M.L. 376
Gentile, D.A. 426
geodesic sensor net 57, 76, 451, 471
George, C. 100
Gery, I. 150
Gibbs, J.C. 310
Gibson, E.J. 80
Giller, H. 189–90, 371
Gilligan, Carol 300, 309–10
Gilliom, M. 82
Ginsburg, K.R. 190
Gizer, I.R. 358
Gleitman, L. 131, 140
global evaluations 247, 250, 251, 264
Gnepp, J. 166
Goh, D.H. 377
Goldin-Meadow, S. 123
Goldstein, S. 136
Golinkoff, R.M. 129
Goodman, E. 132, 430
Google+ 432
Goos, L.M. 358
Gopnik, A. 117
Gordon, L.V. 234
Gosling, S.D. 442
Gottlieb, G. 179
Gottman, J.M. 50, 219
Gould, Peter 345
Graham, S. 94, 253
grammar 124, 125, 129–30, 140
Gray, J.R. 358
Graziano, A.M. 48
Greenberg, M.T. 137
Greene, J.D. 334
Greenspan, R.J. 305
Grey, John 406
Groman, C.M. 359–60
grooming 416, 418, 433–5

Groos, Karl 270, 272–3
group play 283–4, 287–94, 295
Group Socialisation Theory (GST) 84, 203–4, 212, 220, 222–6, 240, 283, 328, 400
'group-think' 289, 295
Grusec, J.E. 318
GSR see galvanic skin response
GST see Group Socialisation Theory
Guarini, A. 376, 377
guilt 82, 84, 92, 94, 106, 193–4; Conduct Disorder 350; effortful control 392; moral development 311–12, 317, 319, 335, 337–8; temperament 391
Gummerum, M. 165, 335
Gutenberg, Johannes 417

habit reversal therapy (HRT) 460
habituation–dishabituation paradigm 40–1, 76
Haglund, Kirsten 423–4
Halberstadt, A.G. 83
hallucinations 465
'halo effect' 232, 255
Halpern, D.F. 265
Halverson, C.F. 198
Halverson, H.M. 29
Hamilton, W.D. 329–30
Hamlin J.K. 305
Hannigan, Robert 436
happiness 84, 85–8, 95, 106; empathy 169; facial expressions 86; play 282–3; positive emotional environments 83; self-esteem 251, 252–3, 254
'happy slapping' 345
Hargreaves, D.H. 373
Harlow, Harry 96, 102, 103
Harris, Eric 383, 427
Harris, Judith Rich: criticism of correlational studies 400; Group Socialisation Theory 84, 203–4, 212, 220, 221–6, 240, 283, 328, 400; parenting 399; strategic specialisation 397
Harris, K.M. 443
Harris, P.L. 139, 152
Harrison, H.M. 104
Hart, B. 131
Hart, D. 246, 247, 248
Harter, S. 225, 250, 251, 253, 254

Hartshorne, H. 316–17
hashtags 436
Hastings, Gerard 423
Hastings, P.D. 332
hate groups 433, 435
Hauser, S.T. 254
Hawley, P.H. 293, 379, 380
Hay, Dale 49–50
Hazen, N. 228
HDAC 462
heart rate 58, 68, 312, 349, 453
Hechtman, L. 358
hedonistic reasoning 315, 316, 338
Heinberg, L.J. 428
Helwig, C.C. 306, 325
Herba, C. 159
Herbert-Myers, H. 139
Herdt, Gilbert 470–1
heritability 204–5, 222–3; ADHD 358; IQ 15; personality and individual differences 17, 396, 402; reactive heritability 397, 411; temperament 393; see also genes; genetics
Hess, D.L. 166
Hesslow, G. 167
heteronomous morality 303, 304–5, 306, 338
heterozygous genes 8–9
HGP see Human Genome Project
Hill, M. 48
Hill, P. 285
Hinde, R.A. 227
Hindelang, M.J. 237
Hinduja, S. 376–7
Hirschi, T. 236, 237, 241, 373
Hirsh-Pasek, K. 129
Hitch, G. 115
Hitler, Adolf 319
Hobbs, G. 373
Hobson, J.A. 285
Hodges, J. 105
Hoffman, M.L. 165, 188, 310, 332
Hollin, C.R. 195
homework 138
homosexuality 462, 463
homozygous genes 8
honesty 317
Hope, A. 422
Hopmeyer, A. 234
hormones 12–13, 35, 404; aggression 363; measurement of 55; stress

405; testosterone 13, 55, 409, 410, 412, 454, 471
Horwitz, A.V. 462
hostile attributional bias 194, 195, 207, 231, 361, 362
hostile versus instrumental aggression dichotomy 362
'hot' executive function 136
hot spots 33
Houck, C.D. 439, 441
Howe, M.L 248–9
Howes, C. 216
HRT see habit reversal therapy
Hubbard, J.A. 362–3
Huber, G.L. 466–7
Huesmann, L.R. 362, 363, 375, 425
Hughes, Bobby 280–1, 294
Hughes, C. 160–1, 282
Hughes, F.P. 285
Hughes, Thomas 365
Human Genome Project (HGP) 456
human moral code 331
humour 282–3
Humphrey, Nick 145
Huston, A.C. 60, 375
Hutchinson, J.E. 128
Huttenlocher, J. 125, 128, 159
Hyde, J.S. 309–10
Hymel, S. 369
hyperactivity 355–7, 359, 378
hypercognitive system 251, 257–8, 264–5

id 18, 35, 312–15, 338
ideal body shape 424
ideal self 250, 251
identity 195, 222, 246, 377; see also gender identity; self-concept; self-identity
imitation: Down syndrome 285; language acquisition 133; learning from television 420, 421; observational learning 22, 52; ostracised children 289, 295; play 278, 281; violence 427
immigrants 467, 472
imprinting 31–2, 36, 75, 76, 105
impulse control 135
impulsivity 355–7, 359, 370, 378, 392, 405, 441
in-group mentality 212, 236–8, 241, 289; bullying 369; bystander intentions 337; media influence 415; peer preferences 217

incest 331
independence 201
independent variable (IV) 62, 69
Inderbitzen-Nolan, H.M. 256
individual differences 17, 388–413; epigenetics 450; evolutionary psychology 396–7; media and 416, 440–4, 445; see also personality; temperament
individual factors 4, 6, 35
individualistic cultures 25, 164, 466–71, 472
induction 188, 207, 310
indulgent parenting style 188, 207
infant mortality 180
information processing 22–3, 35, 110, 115–21, 139; epigenetic landscape 122–3; neo-Piagetians 114; sensation and perception 109; social 229–31
informed consent 67
Ingvar, D.H. 167
Inhelder, B. 158–9
inhibition 136
initiation rituals 470–1
inner speech 276
insecure ambivalent/resistant attachment 53, 98–100, 104, 106, 399
insecure avoidant attachment 53, 98–100, 102, 104, 106, 399
Instagram 432, 437, 438, 445
instant messaging 431, 433, 434
institutional care 104, 105
instrumental aggression 344, 361–2, 363, 384
integrity 67
intelligence 15–16, 390, 411, 467; intelligence tests 390; moral reasoning 193; offending behaviour 104; Piaget 110, 112; see also cognitive ability
intentional stance 145, 146–7, 171–2
inter-rater reliability 50
interactionism 4, 131–2, 300, 397–8, 410
intergenerational transmission: antisocial behaviour 204–5, 206, 207; attachment 99–100, 102, 106; hostile and

ineffective parenting 190;
    hostile attributional bias 195;
    rejecting behaviour 201;
    societal values 178
interhemispheric transfer 12
internal-state language 160, 173
internal working models 97–8,
    99, 102, 106, 144, 221–2
internalised values 315, 316,
    317, 338
internalising problems 392
Internet 376, 377, 416, 417,
    431–8, 441–4, 445; see also
    social media
interviews 44, 47–8, 53–5, 68
intimacy 212, 213, 221,
    240, 276
intra-sexual selection 13
intraorganismic
    organisation 96
introversion 399, 442
IQ 15, 104; see also
    intelligence
irritability 58–9, 81, 347, 353
Irwin, D.M. 306
Islamic State in Iraq and Syria
    (ISIS) 436–7, 445
IV see independent variable
Izard, C.E. 85, 90

Jackson, P.L. 168
Jackson, S.I. 60
Jaffe, S. 309–10
Jaffee, S.R. 353, 354
James, William 74, 75
Jameson, H. 280
Jarrett, O. 289
jealousy 84, 92, 94–5, 275
Jenkins, J.M. 161, 214
Jensen, J. 458, 459–60
Johnson, J.G. 426
Johnson, Mark 57–8,
    77–80, 451
Johnson, W. 84
Johnston, J.R. 468
joint attention 41, 123, 126–7,
    140, 172, 285
Jolliffe, D. 370
joy 84–5, 169; see also
    happiness
Juke family 204–5, 207
Jungert, T. 319

Kagan, J. 84
Kahn, J.V. 48
Kail, R.V. 90
Kaminsky, Z. 460
Kanner, Leo 170

Kant, Immanuel 75
Karmel, M.P. 248
Karmiloff-Smith, Annette
    114–15, 139, 450, 457,
    458, 472
Keenan, K. 353
Kelemen, D. 281
Keller, M. 165
Kelly, K.J. 423
Kendeou, P. 420
Kendrick, C. 214
Keogh, E. 370
Kilner, L.A. 254
Kim, S. 136, 442
kin selection 329–30
kindergartens 272, 294
Kindermann, T.A. 290
Kirschner, S. 280
Kitayama, S. 25, 466
Klahr, D. 22, 115
Klebold, Dylan 383, 427
Kleinrock, Leonard 431
Klinefelter's syndrome 10
Kochanska, G. 196, 200,
    311–12, 320
Kohlberg, Lawrence 198, 300,
    306–11, 338
Koluchová, J. 105
Komarovsky, M. 196
Kopp, C.B. 257, 319–20
Kovacs, D.M. 469
Kraepelin, Emil 462
Kraus, N. 58, 451–2
Krebs, Dennis 331–2, 339
Kuczynski, L. 320
Kuhl, E.A. 465
Kuhn, B.R. 191
Kuhn, D. 260
Kupersmidt, J.B. 24
Kupfer, D.J. 465
Kwon, K. 294

La Freniere, P.J. 81–2, 89
La Greca, A.M. 104
labelling theory 192, 193
laboratory settings 48–9, 50–2,
    59, 62, 68
LAD see language acquisition
    device
Ladd, G.W. 192–3, 229, 469
Lagerspetz, Kirsti 366
LaGrange, R.L. 237
Laible, D.J. 257
Lakatos, K. 100–1
Lamidi, E. 184–5
Lamm, C. 168–9
Laney, Jessica 433
Lange, Johannes 203

Langlois, J.H. 198–9, 232
language 20, 110, 123–33, 140;
    autism spectrum disorder
    295; case studies 63; EEG
    measures 58; feral children
    64; gender differences 262–3;
    information-processing
    approach 116; internal-state
    160, 173; play 276, 278, 279,
    283, 294; self-reports 45; self-
    understanding 249; sensitive
    periods 274; theory of mind
    172; Vygotsky 27, 113; see
    also communication
language acquisition device
    (LAD) 129
language acquisition support
    system (LASS) 132
Larson, R. 217
Larzelere, R.E. 191
LASS see language acquisition
    support system
lateralisation 11–12, 85, 86–7
Lauber, M.O. 382–3
laughter 82, 85, 87–8,
    282–3, 391
law and order morality 308
Lawson, D. 214–15
lax parenting style 189,
    190, 191
Layton, T. 285–6
Leaper, C. 260
learning 20–4, 35; attachment
    stages 96–7; Bobo doll
    experiment 52; epigenetic
    landscape 30; information
    processing 110, 120–1,
    123; observational 22, 52;
    sensitive periods 274; from
    television 419–21, 444; see
    also social learning
Lease, A.M. 294
Lee, K. 165
Leekum, S. 172
legal socialisation 331
Legare, C.H. 289
Leinbach, M.D. 198, 262
Lemert, E. 192, 193
Lenneberg, Erik 64
Lesch-Nyhan disorder 9
Leslie, A. 147
Levenson, R.W. 168
Levine, S.C. 86
Levy, J. 86
Lewis, K. 374
Lewis, M. 49, 84, 90, 91–2, 93,
    248, 249
Lewis, R. 4

Leyens, J-P. 425
LHT *see* life history theory
libido 313, 314
Liew, J. 59
life-course-persistent antisocial behaviour 346
life expectancy 180, 405
life history theory (LHT) 32
lifespan perspective 27–8, 36, 65–6, 398
Lindenberg, S. 293–4
Linebarger, D.L. 420, 421
linkage analysis 455–6, 471
LinkedIn 432
Lisle, R. 438
literacy 420–1
Little, T.D. 293
Liu, D. 163
Locke, John 74, 270–1
Loeber, R. 358
Loehlin, John 400–2
Logothetis, N.K. 169
loneliness 231–2, 234–5, 377, 443–4
long-term hypercognition 257, 265
longitudinal method 66, 69
Lonigan, C.J. 136
Lorenz, Konrad 31
love 197
love withdrawal 188, 207
Low, J. 421

M space 113–14, 122, 139
Maccoby, E.E. 188, 190, 207, 363
Mace, R. 214–15
Macgillivray, S. 164
Machiavellian attitudes 370
Machiavellian intelligence 144–5, 146, 172
macrosystem 24–5, 26, 35, 177–8, 328, 373, 466
MacWhinney, B. 22, 115
magazines 415–16, 425, 427–31, 444–5
Main, M. 99–100, 104
Majdandžić, J. 168–9
majority-rules rule 224–5
mala in se crimes 331
Malatestsa, C.Z. 81
Malaya, Oxana 64
Malecki, C.K. 139, 291
Malenka, R.C. 357
Malti, T. 165, 282, 335
Manning, W.D. 184–5
MAOA *see* monoamine oxidase A

marbles 302–3
Markman, Ellen 127–8, 140
Markus, H.R. 25, 466
marriage 181, 182, 197–8
Marsh, H.W. 251, 264
Marshall, T.C. 441
'marshmallow test' 61–2, 257, 320
Martin, C.L. 198
Martin, J.A. 188, 190, 207
Mascolo, M.F. 248
masculine roles 179
masculine traits 198, 199, 258–61
mass media 415, 416–19, 444; *see also* magazines; media; television
Masten, A.S. 28
maternal deprivation 102–3, 104–5, 188, 458
maternal instinct 96
maternal mind-mindedness 160, 173
mathematical ability 60, 467–8, 472
Mathieson, K. 282
Matthews, J. 280
Mauchly, John W. 431
Maximally Discriminative Facial Movement (MAX) coding system 85
Maxwell, D. 289
Mayes, R. 462
Mayeux, L. 229
McAlister, A. 162
McBurnett, K. 353
McCabe, M.P. 428
McCartney, K. 194
McCune-Nicolich, L. 285
McHale, S. 199
McIntyre, J.G. 247
McKee, L. 190
McMillan, J.H. 60
McPherson, M. 226–7
McQuade, J.D. 135, 136
Meaney, M.J. 292
media 414–46; antisocial behaviour 375–7, 385; digital 417–18, 431–9, 444, 445; individual differences in responses to 440–4, 445; influence of magazines 427–31, 444–5; influence of television 419–27, 444; *see also* social media; television
medication 348, 357
meerkats 292

Meins, E. 160
meiosis 8, 9, 10
Melotti, G. 377
memory 10, 110, 135; gender differences 263; hypercognitive system 265; improvement with age 119; information-processing approach 115–16, 120–1; mental space 113–14, 122; working 115–16, 121, 135, 136, 392
Mendellian genetics 8
Menesini, E. 94
mental space (M space) 113–14, 122, 139
mental switches 130
mentors 95, 135, 213
Menzel, E. 145
Merrell, K.W. 370
mesosystem 24–5, 177–8, 328
Messer, D. 131
Messinger, D.S. 87
meta-analysis 44, 68, 159
methylation 461
microsystem 24–5, 26, 177–8, 187, 328, 466
Mikami, A.Y. 442
Miller, E.K. 357
Miller, P.A. 335
Millichap, J.G. 358
mind-mapping theory 257
mindblindness 171
Miranda, S. 76
mirror neurons 167–9, 171, 174, 452, 471
'mirror test' 246, 248–9, 264
mirroring 81
Mischel, Walter 61–2, 257, 318, 320, 394, 411
mismatch hypothesis 381, 385
Mitchel, P. 161–2
Mitchell, K.J. 438
mitosis 9
mobile devices 435–6, 437
modelling: Conduct Disorder 354; emotional expression 83, 84; group play 290; observational learning 22, 52; parents 223, 224; siblings 199, 206; *see also* role models
modified nuclear family 185, 206
modularity 114, 139
modulation 81–4, 90, 106

Moffitt, A.R. 123–4
Moffitt, T.E. 346, 353
molecular markers
    455–6, 471
Molfese, D.L. 58, 451
Molfese, V.J. 58, 451
Mongon, Denis 374
Monks, C.P. 368
monoamine oxidase A
    (MAOA) 205, 353
monogamy 181, 206
monozygotic (MZ) twins 15,
    332, 401, 402
Montessori, Maria 274
Moore, C. 164
Moore, S.G. 306
moral behaviour 2, 300, 310,
    316; Bandura 318–19;
    Conduct Disorder 352;
    parental influence on
    moral reasoning 193–6,
    207; prosocial behaviour
    165; self-control 320;
    socialisation 24–5; see also
    prosocial behaviour
moral competence 318, 339
moral decision-making 332,
    334, 452–3, 471
moral development 298–340;
    ADHD 360; affective
    empathy 150; authoritarian
    parenting style 188–9;
    bullies 370; cognitive social
    learning 318–20, 339;
    evolutionary psychology
    328–35, 339; social
    constructivism 321–8,
    339; stage theorists 300,
    301–17, 338
moral disengagement
    319, 369
moral domain 325–6,
    339, 469
moral performance 318, 339
moral realism 193, 303
moral reasoning 301, 303, 305,
    335, 337; Eisenberg 315–16,
    338; Kohlberg 306–11, 338;
    prosocial behaviour 360
moral relativism 303
moral stories 304–6
moral transgressions 48, 321–8,
    332, 335–7, 338, 339, 345
Morelli, S.A. 169
Morris, P.A. 25
Morrison, I. 168, 452
Morton, John 77, 458, 460
motherese 130–1, 140

motor skills 29, 81, 274
Moyles, J. 279–80, 294
Mroczek, D.K. 405
Mullen, Jethro 436
multi-cultural societies 450,
    466, 467
multiple intelligences 390, 411
multiple models 98
Mulvey, K.L. 337
Mundy, P. 284–5
Muñoz, L.C. 370
Murdock, G.P. 178
Murray, L. 138
music-making 280
mutual exclusivity assumption
    127–8, 140
MySpace 433, 445

naming explosion 124
narcissism 441, 443
Nash, A.S. 55
National Institute of Child
    Health and Human
    Development Early Child-
    Care Research Network
    (NICHD ECCRN) 133
National Longitudinal Survey
    of Youth (NLSY) 42, 423
nativism 75
natural experiments 62–3
natural selection 30–1, 32, 34,
    36, 397, 403
naturalistic settings 49–50,
    62, 68
nature versus nurture 1, 5, 34,
    74–5, 204, 207; behavioural
    epigenetics 461; birth
    order 397; criminality 206;
    epigenetic view 9, 457–8;
    gender differences 263;
    identity and personality
    development 222; moral
    development 334–5; see
    also biological factors;
    environmental factors;
    genetics
Neff, K.D. 325
negative affectivity 392, 411
neglect 88, 96, 100, 104, 195,
    207, 349
neglecting parenting style 188,
    189, 207
Neill, S.R.St.J. 373
Nelson, J.R. 194
Nelson, N.L. 93
Nelson, S.A. 306

neo-Piagetians 113–15,
    122, 139
neolocality 178–9
Neuendorf, K.A. 422
neurodevelopmental disorders
    346, 354–60, 384, 459
neurons 10–11, 57, 460; mirror
    neurons 167–9, 171, 174,
    452, 471
neuroticism 395, 411;
    adolescence 404; attachment
    399; gender differences 406,
    407–8, 409–10, 412; genetic
    influences 400–2; life
    expectancy linked to 405;
    social media 441, 442, 445
neurotransmitters 10–11, 35,
    349, 353, 358
new-borns 73, 74–84, 95, 105,
    177, 206; attention 118–19;
    brain processes 57–8;
    emotional expressions 84–5,
    90; emotional states 32;
    empathy 338; new measures
    of competencies 449–50,
    471; perception 110; self-
    regulation 453; temperament
    58–9, 74, 135
Newcombe, N. 159
Nianias, H. 438
NICHD ECCRN see National
    Institute of Child Health
    and Human Development
    Early Child-Care Research
    Network
niche picking 13
Nikolaidis, A. 358
Nishitani, N. 171
NLSY see National
    Longitudinal Survey of
    Youth
Noble, K.G. 135
Nolen-Hoeksema, S. 138, 358
non-controllers 379, 380
non-shared environment 17, 35,
    203–4, 393, 400,
    402, 411
nonverbal communication
    123, 132, 140, 217; autism
    spectrum disorder 464;
    cultural differences 465;
    executive function 135;
    gender differences
    263, 265
Noret, N. 366–7
normative behaviour 2–3
norms: body image 429;
    bullying 369; collectivist

cultures 466, 468–9;
embarrassment 93;
emotional display rules 83;
ethnic groups 238; gangs
384; moral reasoning 308;
peer groups 236, 241, 283–4,
287, 290, 294, 337; play 277,
290, 294; sensitive periods
274; Social Bond Theory
237, 383; social contract
309; socialisation 325;
societal 314, 344
Nucci, L.P. 300, 324, 325
nuclear family 178, 179–80,
181, 185, 206
Nunner-Winkler, G. 335
nursery care 133–4
nurturance 200
nurture assumption 212, 220,
223, 240, 400

obedience 200
Oberman, L.M. 171
objects: habituation–
dishabituation paradigm
40; language acquisition
126, 127–9, 140; object
substitution 285; play
279, 281, 284, 285, 294;
sensitive periods 274;
symbolic play 276
observational learning 22, 52
observational methods 39–40,
46, 48–53, 59, 68
obsessive compulsive
anxiety 45
OCEAN 395, 441; see also
'Big 5' personality factors
O'Connell, Rachel 434
ODD see Oppositional Defiant
Disorder
Odgers, C.L. 403
Oedipus complex 314
oestrogens 12–13, 410
Offer, D. 254
Olweus, Dan 256, 366, 371
Ontario Student Drug Use
Survey 378
openness 395, 411; changes
across the lifespan 404–5;
gender differences 408, 409,
412; genetic influences 402;
social media 441, 442, 443
operant conditioning 21,
35, 126
opportunistic sampling 42
Oppositional Defiant Disorder
(ODD) 346, 347–9, 384;

bullying 368; compared with
ADHD 359; cortisol levels
454–5, 471; spanking 191
organisational effects 410
Orlick, T. 470
orphans 221–2
orthorexia nervosa 438, 445
ostensive communication
127, 140
ostracism 288, 289, 295, 364,
369, 383, 384
Otorno, K. 124
Ounsted, C. 358
out-group mentality 212,
236–8, 241, 289; bullying
369; bystander intentions
337; media influence 415;
peer preferences 217
'overlapping waves'
theory 119
Ozawa-De Silva, C. 443–4
Ozonoff, S. 458, 459–60

paedophiles 416, 418,
433–5, 445
Paikoff, R.L. 234
pain 168, 169, 174, 452
Palmer, E.J. 195
Palmer, S.B. 337
panic 45
Panksepp, J. 92
Pardini, D.A. 359
parents: abusive 4; attitudes
to education 374; Avon
Longitudinal Study of
Parents and Children 43;
cultural differences 469;
declining influence of 222;
discipline 187–93, 207;
Ecological Theory 24–5;
emotional expression 83–4;
emotional support 194,
196–201; empathy 93;
ethological perspective
32; EU Kids Online 436;
Freud's psychosexual stages
313–14; gangs 382, 383;
homework support 138;
infant preferences for 216–
17; influence on personality
399, 403; influence on social
development 223, 226, 240;
influence on temperament
393; modelling 223, 224;
moral reasoning 193–6;
parent management training
348; resilience 28; self-
reporting 45–6; socialisation

178, 186, 206–7, 338; see
also attachment; family
Parke, Ross 28–9, 31, 49, 89,
190, 199–200, 229, 362
Parker, J.G. 219, 220
Parkhurst, J.T. 234
Parten, Mildred 279, 294
Pascalis, O. 80, 119
Pascual-Leone, Juan 113–14,
122, 139
passive effects 13, 456–7
Patau's syndrome 9
Patchin, J.W. 376–7
patriarchal system 178
patrilocality 178
pattern recognition 29, 121
patterned speech 124
Patterson, C.J. 185, 318
Patterson, G.R. 46, 189,
190, 193
Pattiselanno, K. 294
Pavlov, I.P. 20–1
PDD model 98
Pederson, D.R. 100
peers 2, 5, 212, 213, 216–20,
240; antisocial behaviour
192; bullying 371; cultural
differences 469–70, 472;
Ecological Theory 25;
emotional regulation 84; EU
Kids Online 436; genetic
influences 378; possessive
conflicts 49–50; prosocial
behaviour 335–6; self-esteem
254, 264; self-understanding
250; socialisation by 204,
212, 221–6, 240, 283, 335,
338, 400; sociometrics
226–34, 241, 282, 336;
status differentiation 293–4;
unpopularity 234–6, 241;
see also friends
Peeters, M. 366
Pellegrini, A.D. 284
Pempek, T. 420
Penton-Voak, I.S. 157
Pepler, D. 368
perception 109–10; emotions
and 148–9; information-
processing approach 115,
116; interpersonal 212, 240
permissive parenting style
190, 191
Perner, J. 152, 161, 172, 173,
282, 295, 359
Perry, D. 169
person-situation debate
394, 411

personal domain 325–6, 339, 469
personality 2, 389–90, 411–12; bullies 369; changes across the lifespan 404–5, 412; evolutionary psychology 396–7, 411; gender differences 263, 358–9, 406–10, 412; genetic influences 224, 400–3, 411; influence on friendships 220, 240; measurement of 398, 411; media influence 416; nature-nurture interaction 204, 222; peer influence 224; resilience 28; responses to the media 440–4, 445; self-understanding 249; social development 397–403; stability of 398, 403–5; structure of 394–5; temperament relationship 393–4; twin studies 17, 460, 461
personality disorders 203, 348, 403, 462–3
perspective-taking 150, 157–9, 173
PET see Positron Emission Tomography
Peterson, C.C. 162
Pettit, G.S. 293
phenotype 8
Phillips, J. 159
Phillipsen, L. 216
phobias 21, 22
phonemes 124
phonological loop 115–16, 135
physical attractiveness 232, 233, 251, 252, 255
physical injury fears 45
physical play 279, 280, 282, 294
physical punishment 190–1, 207
physical stance 145, 171, 172
physiological measurements 55–9, 68, 453–5, 471
Piaget, Jean 17, 19–20, 24, 35, 110–12, 139; case studies 65; clinical interviews 53; epigenetic landscape 122; evolved adaptation 4; moral development 300, 301–6,

338; moral reasoning 193; observation techniques 39–40, 48; perspective-taking 158–9, 173; play 270, 275–6, 279, 294; progression through stages 5–6
Pikas, A. 370
Pinker, Steven 379, 397
Piotrowski, J. 420, 421
plasticity principle 398, 404, 412
Plato 270, 271
play 2, 212, 268–97; atypical development 284–7; autism spectrum disorder 464; classifications of 279–81, 294; different understandings of 270–7; emotional regulation 84; facets of 278; functions of 277–8; group dynamics 287–94, 295; peer interactions 217; prosocial behaviour 216; reduced by television watching 416; self-reports 45; social skill development 281–4, 294; theory of mind development 162
play-fighting 291–2, 293, 295
pleasure principle 275
Plomin, R. 4, 17, 203–4, 223, 402, 410
Pluess, M. 135
Plutchik, R. 150–1
pointing 123, 126–7, 140
Poland, S.E. 136
polyandry 181, 206
polygyny 181, 206
popularity 228–32, 233–4, 241, 256, 287, 366, 384; see also sociometric approach
Porges, S.W. 58, 453
pornography 433, 436
positive emotionality 392, 393
Positron Emission Tomography (PET) 167, 174, 333, 358, 451–2, 462, 471
Post Traumatic Stress Disorder (PTSD) 62–3
postconventional morality 308, 309, 310, 338
posterior parietal cortex 357
Pottebaum, S.M. 255
power assertion 188, 207
Powers, S.I. 254
Powers, S.W. 191
pragmatics 126

pre-conventional morality 307, 308, 338
precociality 31
preferential looking technique 76
prefrontal cortex 257, 357
prejudice 212, 237–40, 241; bias-prejudiced bullying 344, 368, 386n1
Premack, D. 145
prenatal development 7–8, 9
preoperational stage 19, 20, 111, 158, 159, 173, 193
pretend play 270, 280, 281–2, 294, 295; autism spectrum disorder 284–5; Down syndrome 286; Freud's view 274–5; peer interactions 217; theory of mind development 162; see also symbolic play
Price, J.S. 429
pride 82, 84, 92–3, 106, 317
primary emotions 84–92
primates 145–6, 270, 292, 293
privation 103, 105
proactive aggression 362–3
problem-solving 5, 137; Conduct Disorder 352; executive function 135; information processing 24, 110, 115, 116, 117–19, 139; intelligence 390; play 278; pride and shame 93; sociocultural theory 27
progesterone 410
propaganda 436, 445
prosocial behaviour 2, 216, 315–16, 360; age demarcation for 317; bystander intentions 337; cultural differences 470, 472; empathy 93–4; evolutionary psychology 328–35, 339, 379; impact of video games 426, 444; joint music-making 280; moral behaviour 300, 322, 338; peer influence 335–6; play 278, 295; skin conductance 454; social cognitive development 282; theory of mind 164–5, 173; see also altruism; empathy; moral behaviour
prosocial controllers 379, 380
prosodic characteristics 131
protective factors 235
protodeclarative pointing 123, 127, 140

protoimperative pointing 123,
   127, 140
provocative victims 368, 369,
   370, 379, 385
'pruning' 116–17
Pryor, J. 183
psychoanalysis 17–18, 95, 96,
   274–5
psychodynamic approach
   17–18, 278, 462
psychometrics 398, 411
psychopathy 392, 396–7;
   affectionless 102, 103, 458;
   privation 103
psychosexual stages 18,
   313–14, 338
psychosocial stages
   18–19, 275
psychotherapy 348
PTSD see Post Traumatic
   Stress Disorder
puberty 64, 232, 253, 369,
   381, 410
punishment 21, 35, 306,
   320, 328; expiatory 303;
   immanent justice 304;
   parental discipline 188,
   189–90, 354; physical
   190–1, 207; pre-conventional
   morality 307; reciprocal 303;
   teachers 372
Pyżalski, J. 377

Quay, H.C. 353
Quebec Study of New-Born
   Twins (QSNT) 378
questionnaires 43, 44–5,
   68, 398

Rabiner, D.L. 234
race 25–6, 67; see also
   ethnicity
Racine, T.P. 127
Radke-Yarrow, M. 332
Radziszewska, B. 113
Rakoczy, H. 281–2
Randall, P.E. 369
random sampling 42
Raskin, H.W. 237
Raulin, M.L. 48
Razza, R.P. 135
reaching behaviour 29
reactions 83, 84
reactive aggression 344,
   361–3, 384
reactive heritability 397, 411
Reader, W. 329
reading 13

Reading the Mind in the Eyes
   Test (RMET) 154–7, 173
real self 250, 251
reciprocal altruism 329–30, 339
reciprocity 212, 214, 240,
   332, 464
Rees, J. 368
referential opacity 147–8,
   153, 173
Reicher, S. 377
Reiger, D.A. 465
reinforcement 132–3, 278, 358
rejection 93, 98, 104; bullies
   384; delinquency linked to
   189; gangs 383, 384, 385;
   hostile attributional bias
   194, 207; intergenerational
   transmission 195, 201;
   Oppositional Defiant Disorder
   349; peer 227–8, 229, 231–2,
   234–6, 241, 379, 383, 385;
   progression of antisocial
   behaviour 192, 193; school
   processes 373; victims of
   bullying 385
relational aggression
   363, 364
relationships 2, 210–42;
   adaptationist model of
   attachment 99; attachment
   95, 106, 399; autism
   spectrum disorder 464;
   dyadic peer 227, 235–6;
   insecure attachment 106;
   play 270; romantic 99,
   103–4, 106, 160, 197, 232–3,
   381; same-sex families 185;
   secure attachment 103; types
   of 212–15, 240; see also
   friends; peers
reliability 398, 411
religion 325, 331, 339
Renneberg, B. 442
Renner, J.W. 111
Repacholi, B.M. 165
repetition compulsion 274–5
repetitive behaviour 464, 465
representative sampling
   41–4, 68
Reputation-Enhancement
   Theory (RET) 377
research methods 38–70;
   change over a time span
   65–6, 69; data collection
   44–59, 68; ethical research
   66–7; representative
   sampling 41–4; research
   designs 59–65, 68–9

'residual normality' 458
resilience 6, 28, 35, 222,
   378, 457
resistant attachment 53,
   98–100, 102, 106, 399
resource control theory 379
respect 67
responsibility 67, 200, 280
Rest, J.R. 310
RET see Reputation-
   Enhancement Theory
reward 21, 35, 328
Rice, E. 438–9
Richards, M.P.M. 183
Rideout, V. 419
righteous indignation 146
risk resilience 6
risk-taking 359, 392, 404;
   gender differences 263,
   265, 406; life expectancy
   linked to 405; risky teenage
   behaviours 380–1; sexting
   439, 441
Risley, T.R. 131
rituals 186, 289, 470–1
Rivers, I. 366–7
Rizzolatti, G. 167
RMET see Reading the Mind
   in the Eyes Test
'Robber's Cave' study
   237–8, 241
Roberts, B.W. 404
Roberts, D.F. 426
Roberts, M.W. 191
Robertson, J. 105
Robins, R.W. 253
Robinson, T.N. 422
Robson, S. 433
Rodgers, B. 183
Rogoff, B. 113
Roisman, G.I. 346
role models 190, 240, 258, 328,
   415, 416; see also modelling
romantic relationships 99, 103–
   4, 106, 160, 197, 232–3, 381
Rose, A.J. 229
Rosenberg, M. 251
Rosenberg Self-Esteem
   Scale 66
Rosenfeld, M.J. 185
Roskos, K.A. 279
Rosler, M. 359
Ross, H.S. 218
Rothbaum, F. 469
Rousseau, Jean-Jacques 271
Rubin, K.H. 47, 229, 290
Rubin, L.B. 196
Rubin, Z. 219

Ruble, T.L. 259–60
Ruef, A.M. 168
Ruffman, T. 161, 162
Rule, B.G. 362
rules 281–2, 290, 295;
    Conduct Disorder 350,
    352; conventions 299–300;
    games with 276, 280, 294,
    302–3, 306; moral reasoning
    307, 308, 337, 338, 339;
    schools 326–8, 371;
    social constructivism 322;
    socialisation 325; theory of
    mind development 165
Rumbelow, H. 431
Ruse, M. 331
Rushton, J.P. 317
Russell, S.T. 185
Rust, J. 199
Rutland, A. 337
Rutter, Michael 6, 103, 105,
    189–90, 371, 372
Ryan, R.M. 183

Saarni, C. 81–2, 83, 89
sadness 84, 90, 91–2, 106,
    335; facial expressions
    86; jealousy 94; negative
    affectivity 392; negative
    emotional environments 83;
    separation protest 90
Saffer, H. 423
Şahin, M. 377
Sala, M.N. 83
Salmivalli, C. 366, 369
Saltzstein, H.D. 188
Sambia 470–1
same-sex families 181, 183–5
Samenow, Stanton 360
Sammons, P. 133
sampling 41–4, 68
Santrock, J.W. 60–1, 249
Saudino, Kimberly 226
Savin-Williams, R.C. 234
Saxe, R. 168
scaffolding 27, 113, 127,
    140; language acquisition
    130, 132; parental help
    with homework 138; social
    competence 136–7
scanning techniques 56–8,
    68, 450–3, 471; see also
    electroencephalogram;
    functional magnetic
    resonance imaging; Positron
    Emission Tomography
Scaramella, L. 190
Scarr, S. 13, 194

SCAS see Spence Children's
    Anxiety Scale
Schaffer, H.R. 97
Scharrer, E. 418
schemas 111, 112, 122,
    139, 421
Schiller, Friedrich von 272
schizophrenia 202, 206, 462,
    463, 465, 472
Schmitt, D.P. 406
Schneider, B.H. 469
Schneider, M. 216
schools 371–4; Avon
    Longitudinal Study of
    Parents and Children 43;
    bullying 6, 344, 365–6,
    368–9, 374; prejudice
    reduction 239; rules
    326–8; social and emotional
    learning 137; social skills
    133; teachers' perceptions of
    children 47; word acquisition
    41; see also education
Schunk, D.H. 247, 256
Scott, S. 354
SCT see Social Cognitive
    Theory
Seal, J. 220
secondary emotions 32, 84,
    92–5, 106
secure attachment 53,
    98–100, 106, 144, 195, 221;
    adaptationist model 99;
    cultural differences 102;
    influence on personality 399;
    separation protest 90; social
    competence 103
secure base 99
Segal, Nancy 402
SEL see social and emotional
    learning
self-awareness 92, 93, 95, 135,
    257, 265
self-concept 2, 244–66; alcohol
    advertising 423; body
    dissatisfaction 423; facets
    of self-development 247,
    264; gender identity 258–63;
    hypercognitive system 257–8,
    264–5; labelling theory
    192; media influence 415;
    peer relationships 212; self-
    fulfilling prophesies 373;
    social comparison 225
self-conscious emotions 82, 84,
    92–5; see also guilt; shame
self-control 62, 188, 200,
    318; moral development

319–20, 339; peer rejection
    229; prefrontal cortex
    activation 257; psychosexual
    development 314; self-
    concept 246, 247
self-disclosure 433
self-esteem 195, 246, 247,
    250–6, 264; adolescence
    404; authoritarian
    parenting style 188;
    body dissatisfaction 423,
    428–9; bullies 366, 371;
    cross-gender friendships
    232; cyberbullies 377;
    disorganised attachment
    399; friends 216; gender
    differences 263, 265,
    359; group play 290;
    hypercognitive system
    258; media influence
    440; Oppositional Defiant
    Disorder 348; ostracised
    children 289; peer rejection
    235; peer relationships 212;
    resilience 28; romantic
    relationships 233; Rosenberg
    Self-Esteem Scale 66;
    secure attachment 103;
    self-fulfilling prophesies
    373; social comparison 225;
    social media use 441, 443;
    teenage girls 185; victims of
    bullying 6, 369, 385
self-fulfilling prophesies
    373, 379
self-harm 9, 433
self-identity 198, 216, 217,
    264; adolescence 160;
    cultural differences 472;
    self-understanding 249;
    see also identity
self-image 247, 250–1, 253,
    257–8, 264, 377, 430
self-interest 307, 315, 379
self-organisation 29, 36
self-regulation 247, 256–7,
    264; effortful control 392;
    hypercognitive system
    257, 258, 264–5; moral
    development 318, 319–20;
    play 280; temperament 393;
    vagal tone 58, 453, 471;
    see also modulation
self-reliance 200
self-reporting 44, 45–6, 68
self-understanding 247,
    248–50, 251, 264
Selman, Robert 157–8, 173

semi-structured interviews
53–4, 55, 68
sensation 109, 115
sensitive periods 274
sensorimotor neurons *see*
mirror neurons
sensorimotor stage 19, 20,
111, 122
separation anxiety 45, 95, 96
separation protest 90
septo-hippocampal
structure 353
sequential method 66, 69
Serbin, L.A. 262
serotonin 205, 349, 353
SES *see* socioeconomic status
sex differences 262–3,
265; aggression 363–4;
autism spectrum disorder
171; bullying 368, 378;
cyberbullying 377; emotional
reading ability 154–7; guilt
311; personality 358–9,
406–10, 412; *see also* gender
sex-linked abnormalities 9, 10
sexting 438–9, 441, 445
sexual development 12–13
sexual dimorphism 34
sexual relationships 251
sexual reproduction 396, 411
sexual selection 13, 32, 34, 36
Shahaeian, A. 164, 469
Shamay-Tsoory, S.G. 150
shame 82, 84, 92–3, 94, 106;
effortful control 392; moral
development 311–12, 317,
337–8
shaping behaviour 21
shared environment 17, 35,
203–4, 393, 399, 402–3, 411
Sharp, S. 365, 370
Sharpe, Lynda 292
Shaw, D.S. 353
Sherif, Muzafer 237, 241
Shiner, R.L. 391
Shoemaker, D. 359
siblings: blended families
183; delinquency 190, 371;
gender socialisation 199;
individual differences 397;
jealousy 94–5; modelling
206; play 282; relationships
213–15, 216; shared and
non-shared environment
203, 204; theory of mind
development 160–2; *see also*
family; twins
Siegler, Robert 24, 116, 117–19

Singer, T. 169
Sinha, D. 467
situational context 394, 411
Siviy, S.M. 292
Skeels, H.M. 104
skin conductance 59, 68, 312,
349, 453–4, 471
Skinner, Burrhus Frederic 21,
126, 129, 132
'skinny model look' 423, 444
Skuse, D. 105
Slaby, R.G. 198
Slack, Becky 239
Slater, A. 118–19
sleeper effects 6
Smetana, J.G. 48, 310, 325
smiling 83, 85, 87–8, 95, 106,
123, 282–3, 391
Smith, A. 151
Smith, Hannah 443
Smith, L. 126
Smith, L.B. 29
Smith, P.B. 100
Smith, Peter K. 284, 292–3,
295, 344, 365, 366, 370, 385,
386n1
Smith, Rebecca 423
Smolak, L. 428
Snapchat 432, 437
social agents 186
social and emotional learning
(SEL) 137
social anxiety 104, 369
Social Bond Theory 236–7,
241, 383
social categories 226, 245, 247
social class 186, 187,
196–7, 373–4; *see also*
socioeconomic status
social cognition 2, 139, 143;
aggression 362; autism
115; biological factors
166–9, 174; brain processes
452; bullies 366, 370,
384; cultural differences
468; definition of 172;
development of 159–60;
emotional understanding
282; peer status 229; play
295; self-understanding 249;
see also social development;
theory of mind
social-cognitive domain theory
301, 325
social cognitive theory (SCT)
22, 198, 300; *see also*
Cognitive Social Learning
Theory

social comparison 224–5,
227–8, 250, 415–16; social
comparison theory 429,
444–5; social competition
hypothesis 429–30
social competence 139, 221,
231, 241; attachment
influence 103; effortful
control 392; group dynamics
287; play 280; scaffolding
136–7; self-regulation 257;
see also social skills
social competition hypothesis
429–30
social constructivism 300,
321–8, 339
social contract 309
social cues 33, 135, 230–1, 285
social development: cognition
and 110, 121–3, 133–9, 140;
cultural differences 465–71;
feral children 64; meaning
of 2–4; moral reasoning
337; multiple intelligences
390; nature versus nurture 1;
new technologies 449–50;
peer rejection 235, 236,
241; personality 397–403;
see also social cognition;
socioemotional development
social dominance 233, 234,
379; bullies 366, 369;
changes across the lifespan
404–5; play 293, 295–6
social functioning 234
social identity 195
social information processing
229–31
social interaction: autism
spectrum disorder 172, 174,
284, 295, 464; language
development 130; learning
from 420, 444; new-borns
74; play 279, 280, 290,
291, 295; reduced by
television watching 416;
scaffolding 140; shame
93; sociocultural theory
27; Vygotsky 112–13, 122;
Williams syndrome 286
social learning: cognitive
development 121–3;
emotional expression 83,
84; group play 290; moral
development 318–20, 339;
play 278
Social Learning Theory 21, 22,
383, 384

social media 376, 416, 431–2,
444, 445, 450; bullying
365; ISIS 436–7, 445;
personality and responses
to 440–3, 445; trolls 433,
443–4, 445
social monitoring 41–2
social networks 213, 287, 289,
294; adolescence 270,
290–1, 295; online 431, 437
social phobia 45
social play 280, 282, 291, 295;
with language 283
social prestige 233
social referencing 89–90, 92,
258, 264
social role modelling 415
social role theory 410
social skills 6, 111, 122, 133;
academic achievement
139; bistrategic controllers
380; friends 216; gender
differences 262; group
dynamics 287; groups and
cliques 296; individualistic
cultures 467; language 110,
132; moral competence
318; Oppositional Defiant
Disorder 347–8; parental
discipline 188; parental
influence 199–200; peer
popularity 228–9, 230–1;
peer rejection 235; play
276–7, 278, 280, 281–4,
289–90, 294, 295;
preschoolers 246; self-
concept 264; victims of
bullying 385; see also social
competence
social support 291
social vitality 404–5
socialisation 5, 178, 186,
206–7, 211, 246; ADHD
360; criminality 206;
cultural differences
164, 467, 469–70, 472;
Ecological Theory 24–5, 35;
emotional expression 82–4;
gender 198–9, 258–9, 261,
263; group play 290; legal
331; macrosystem 466;
media 416; moral behaviour
300, 319, 328, 335, 338;
mother-infant relationship
102; nuclear families 180;
peers 204, 212, 221–6,
240, 283, 335, 338, 400;
personality 402; self-control

320; social class 374; social
information processing 230;
social rules 325
socially facilitating behaviours
87, 95–6, 97, 106, 144
sociocultural contexts
25–6, 35
socioeconomic status (SES)
131, 135–6, 140, 185, 189,
371, 373; see also social
class
socioemotional development
4; attachment 102–4, 105,
106; gender differences 263;
neural maturity 246; play
294; sex differences 265; see
also emotional development;
social development
sociometric approach 212,
226–34, 241, 336, 380;
bullying 366, 384; child
leaders 293; peer conflict
resolution 282
Socrates 194
Sokol, B.W. 152
Soloman, J. 100
Solomon, E.P. 29
somatic syndrome disorders
(SSD) 465
Soto, C.J. 406
Souweidane, V.S. 239
spanking 190–1
specimen records 50, 68
Speicher, B. 194
Spence Children's Anxiety
Scale (SCAS) 45
Spencer, Herbert 270, 272
Spergel, I.A. 381
spiral curriculum 132
Spitz, R.A. 104
Spitzer, Robert 462–3
Sroufe, L.A. 87, 88, 89,
103, 285
SSD see somatic syndrome
disorders
standardised age-related
behaviours 346, 347
Stannage, E. 156–7, 262
status hierarchy divide
293, 295
Stenberg, C. 90
stepfamilies 182–3
stereotypes 35, 238, 241;
alcohol advertising 422, 423;
attractiveness 428; gender
179, 258–63, 370, 408, 415;
prejudice reduction 239, 240
Stern, H.H. 131

Sternberg, R.J. 467
Sterzer, P. 350
Stevenson, H.W. 467–8
Stocker, C.M. 214
Stoel-Gammon, C. 124
Stone, T. 150
story schemas 421
Stouthamer-Loeber, M. 358
'strange situation' 5, 51, 52–3,
90, 98, 99
stranger distress 88–90
Strasburger, V.C. 430
Strassberg, Z. 194
strategic specialisation
397, 411
stratified sampling 42
stress: adolescence 404;
animal play behaviour 292;
antisocial behaviour 105;
cortisol 454; diathesis-
stress theory 358; executive
functions 135–6; life
expectancy 405; maternal
62–3; skin conductance 59
Striano, T. 41–2
Striegel-Moore, R. 428
Stroop test 459–60
structural-organismic
perspective 17–20, 35, 306
structuralism 17, 37n1
structured interviews 53, 68
Subrahmanyam, K. 433
subscales 45
suicide 433, 443–4
Sullivan, Harry 276, 335
Sullivan, M.W. 91–2
Sulloway, Frank 397
superego 18, 35,
312–15, 338
surgency 392, 394, 411
surprise 84, 86, 90, 106
surveys 42, 43, 44–8, 68
Sutherland, E.H. 383
Sutton, J. 370
Sutton-Smith, B. 277
Swickert, R.J. 442
Sylva, K. 133, 134
symbolic play 275–6, 278,
279–80, 284–6, 294, 295;
see also pretend play
sympathy 59
synapses 116–17
systematic sampling 42
systemisers 154–7, 262
systems theory 28–30, 36, 186

Tajfel, Henri 238
Talwar, V. 165

tantrums 3, 171, 189, 190, 347, 353
Tapscott, J.L. 361–2
Tardy, C. 291
Tawile, Mia 416
taxonomic assumption 127–8, 140
Taylor, D.C. 358
Taylor, J.H. 194
Taylor, S. 156–7, 262, 345, 360, 383
TBI *see* traumatic brain injury
teachers 47, 372
technology 180, 449–57, 471; *see also* digital media
telegraphic speech 125
television 416, 419–27; alcohol advertising 55, 422–3, 444; fashion and cosmetics advertising 423–5, 444; impact on cognitive development 60; time spent watching 418, 419, 444; violence on 375, 385, 425–7, 444
temperament 2, 4, 31, 389–93, 411, 457; behavioural genetics 13, 456, 471; bullies 369; Conduct Disorder 353, 354; cultural differences 470; emotional socialisation 84; influence of childcare 135; media influence 416; new-borns 74; personality relationship 393–4; prosocial behaviour 334; responses to the media 440; shy 226; siblings 214; vagal tone 58–9
temperamental dispositions 391, 393–4, 456
Temple, J.R. 439
Ten Dam, G. 133
terrorism 319, 437, 445, 450
testosterone 13, 55, 409, 410, 412, 454, 471
Thelen, E. 29
Theoret, H. 171
theory of mind (ToM) 33–4, 36, 142–75, 359; autism 169–72, 174; biological factors 166–9, 174; bullies 366, 380; cognitive and emotional 149–54, 173; cultural differences 468–9, 472; definition of 144, 172; development of 159–66; perspective-taking 157–9, 173; prosocial behaviour

164–5; systemisers and empathisers 154–7
theory of mind mechanism (ToMM) 147–9, 173
thinking errors 360, 361
Thomas, A. 353
Thomas, M.S. 458
Thompson, C. 164–5
Thompson, J.K. 425, 428, 429
Thompson, R.A. 257, 264
Thompson, Robert 235–6
Thornberg, R. 319, 327–8
Thornberry, T.P. 381
Thornton, S. 23, 116
thought 110, 113, 116
thrill-seeking 352–3
time sampling 50, 68
Tinker, E. 131
Tisak, M.S. 326
Tizard, B. 105
ToM *see* theory of mind
Tom Brown's School Days 365
Tomasello, M. 126, 127, 132, 280
ToMM *see* theory of mind mechanism
Tooby, John 33
Toth, S. 186
Tourette's syndrome 458, 459–60, 461
toy preferences 262, 263
transgressive behaviours 48, 335; antisocial behaviour 345; conventional transgressions 321–8, 337, 338, 339; embarrassment 93; guilt and shame 94; harm against third parties 336–7; moral reasoning 306–7; moral transgressions 48, 321–8, 332, 335–7, 338, 339, 345; *see also* deviant behaviour
traumatic brain injury (TBI) 153, 154, 357
trial and error 23, 24, 116, 117, 129
Triandis, C.H. 466
tripartite model of ToM 152–4, 173
Trivers, R.L. 330, 331, 339
trolls 433, 443–4, 445
Ttofi, Marie 374
Tucker, L.A. 422
Turiel, Elliot 165, 300, 301, 306, 310, 322–4, 325, 335
Turkheimer, E. 15, 16, 17
Turner, S.L. 429

Turner syndrome 10
Tuten, T.L. 442
twins 15–17, 35, 202–3; ADHD 358; autism spectrum disorder 171; bullying 378; Conduct Disorder 353; empathy 332; personality and individual differences 399, 400–2, 411, 460, 461
Twitter 432, 436–7, 441, 445
Tyler, T.R. 331

Udvari, S. 470
Uekermann, J. 359
unconditioned response (UCR) 20–1
unconditioned stimulus (UCS) 20–1
uniquely primed moral computations 324–5
universal ethics 309
Universal Grammar (UG) 129–30, 140
unresolved discipline 190

vagal tone 58–9, 68, 453, 454, 471
Vaish, A. 336–7
validity 62, 398, 411
values: 'British' 467; cultural 450, 466, 468–9; ethnic groups 238; internalised 315, 316, 317, 338; parental discipline 187; peer groups 212, 224, 236, 241, 283–4, 290; schools 371; sensitive periods 274; Social Bond Theory 236, 237, 383; social class 186; social contract 309; socialisation 206, 325, 331; societal 178, 314, 319
Van Berckelaer-Onnes, I.A. 284
van Goozen, S.H.M. 349, 454–5
van Ijzendoorn, M.H. 101
van Krevelen-Wing, L. 171
Van Roekel, E. 368
Vandenbrouke, L. 135–6
Vasconcellos, John 255
Vasta, R. 126
Vaughn, B.E. 320
Veenstra, R. 366
Venables, Jon 235–6
verbal communication 123, 135, 140, 217; autism spectrum disorder 464; Conduct Disorder 353;

self-understanding 249; sex differences 265
video deficit effect 420
video games 419, 426, 427, 444
Vignoles, A. 373
vindictiveness 347
violence 345, 361, 384; Conduct Disorder 350, 354, 403; delinquency 352; gangs 381, 382, 385; MAOA gene 353; media influence 375, 385, 425–7, 444; moral disengagement 369; Oppositional Defiant Disorder 349; see also aggression
visual cliff 80
visual self-recognition 248–9, 264
visual tracking 77–80
visuo-spatial sketchpad 115–16, 135
Vitanova, N.A. 293, 295–6
Vitaro, F. 362, 378
Volk, A. 379
Volman, M. 133
von Hofsten, C. 29
Vossekuil, B. 427
Vurpillot, E. 119
Vygotsky, Lev 27, 112–13, 114, 136–7, 139; epigenetic landscape 122; play 270, 276–7, 294; social environment 110, 135, 140

Waddington, Conrad 30, 110, 457, 472
Wainright, J.L. 185
Waldman, M.R. 194
Walk, R.D. 80
Walker, L.J. 194, 310
Wallis, J.D. 357
Walsh, D. 239
'wanna-be-lookalikes' 427
Want, S.C. 139
Warren, L. 433

Watson, J. 159
Watson, John B. 20, 21
Watson-Jones, R.E. 289
WCST see Wisconsin Card Sorting Test
Weise, Jeff 427
Weiss, B. 188–9
Weiss, G. 358
Weiss, R. 95, 213, 240
Weissberg, R.P. 137
Welch, K.J. 190
Wellman, H.M. 148–9, 151–2, 159, 163–4, 173
Wellness bloggers 437–8, 445
Wentzel, K.R. 335
West, D.J. 104
Westerlund, M. 443
Weston, D. 306
Wexler, A. 168
Wey, H.Y. 462
WhatsApp 436, 445
White, D.R. 178
white lies 165, 173, 303
Whitebread, D. 280
Whitehurst, G.J. 126
Whiten, A. 144–5
whole object assumption 127–8, 140
Williams, E. 284, 285
Williams, J.E. 258–9
Williams syndrome (WS) 115, 139, 284, 286–7
Wilson, C. 93
Wilson, E. 331
Wimmer, H. 172, 173
Windle, M. 233
'wiring diagram' 116
Wisconsin Card Sorting Test (WCST) 459–60
Witherington, D.C. 88
Wolak, J. 433
Wolff, H-G. 442
Wolk-Wasserman, D. 443
women 26, 179, 180; see also gender
Wong, M-Y.A. 468

Wood, D. 27, 113
Wood, Wendy 262, 375, 410, 412
Woodruff, G. 145
Woods, D.W. 460
Woodward, Ella 438
word learning 41, 125–6, 127–9, 140
working hypercognition 257, 265
working memory 115–16, 121, 135, 136, 392
Workman, Lance 86, 224, 226, 329
Wright, I. 285
Wright, J.C. 60
WS see Williams syndrome
Wundt, Wilhem 37n1
Wunsch, J.P. 87
Wyman, E. 282

xenophobia 238, 241

Yang, S. 467
Yee, M.M. 358
Yehuda, Rachel 63
yob culture 345
Yochelson, Samuel 360
Young, S. 359
Young, S.K. 334
Youniss, J. 335
YouTube 432
Yuill, N. 165
Yuille, J.C. 157

Zack, E. 420
Zahn-Waxler, C. 332
Zametkin, A.J. 358
Zarbatany, L. 232
Zelazo, P.D. 136
Zimmerman, B.J. 247, 256
Zimmerman, F.J. 420
Zimmerman, R.R. 96
zone of proximal development 27, 112–13, 122, 135, 136–7, 138, 139–40
zygotes 7–8

Taylor & Francis eBooks

Helping you to choose the right eBooks for your Library

Add Routledge titles to your library's digital collection today. Taylor and Francis ebooks contains over 50,000 titles in the Humanities, Social Sciences, Behavioural Sciences, Built Environment and Law.

Choose from a range of subject packages or create your own!

Benefits for you

» Free MARC records
» COUNTER-compliant usage statistics
» Flexible purchase and pricing options
» All titles DRM-free.

Benefits for your user

» Off-site, anytime access via Athens or referring URL
» Print or copy pages or chapters
» Full content search
» Bookmark, highlight and annotate text
» Access to thousands of pages of quality research at the click of a button.

REQUEST YOUR FREE INSTITUTIONAL TRIAL TODAY

Free Trials Available
We offer free trials to qualifying academic, corporate and government customers.

eCollections – Choose from over 30 subject eCollections, including:

Archaeology	Language Learning
Architecture	Law
Asian Studies	Literature
Business & Management	Media & Communication
Classical Studies	Middle East Studies
Construction	Music
Creative & Media Arts	Philosophy
Criminology & Criminal Justice	Planning
Economics	Politics
Education	Psychology & Mental Health
Energy	Religion
Engineering	Security
English Language & Linguistics	Social Work
Environment & Sustainability	Sociology
Geography	Sport
Health Studies	Theatre & Performance
History	Tourism, Hospitality & Events

For more information, pricing enquiries or to order a free trial, please contact your local sales team:
www.tandfebooks.com/page/sales

 Routledge
Taylor & Francis Group

The home of
Routledge books

www.tandfebooks.com